Principles of Behavioral Neuroscience

Jon C. Horvitz
City College, City University of New York

Barry L. Jacobs
Princeton University

Rosa I. Caamaño Tubío
Scientific Art Director

CAMBRIDGE
UNIVERSITY PRESS

CAMBRIDGE
UNIVERSITY PRESS

University Printing House, Cambridge CB2 8BS, United Kingdom

One Liberty Plaza, 20th Floor, New York, NY 10006, USA

477 Williamstown Road, Port Melbourne, VIC 3207, Australia

314–321, 3rd Floor, Plot 3, Splendor Forum, Jasola District Centre, New Delhi – 110025, India

103 Penang Road, #05–06/07, Visioncrest Commercial, Singapore 238467

Cambridge University Press is part of the University of Cambridge.

It furthers the University's mission by disseminating knowledge in the pursuit of education, learning, and research at the highest international levels of excellence.

www.cambridge.org
Information on this title: www.cambridge.org/highereducation/isbn/9781108488525
DOI: 10.1017/9781108770774

First published 2023

Printed in the United Kingdom by TJ Books Limited, Padstow Cornwall

A catalogue record for this publication is available from the British Library.

ISBN 978-1-108-48852-5 Hardback
ISBN 978-1-108-72078-6 Paperback

Additional resources for this publication at www.cambridge.org/horvitz-jacobs.

Principles of Behavioral Neuroscience

How does brain activity give rise to sleep, dreams, learning, memory, and language? Do drugs like cocaine and heroin tap into the same neurochemical systems that evolved for life's natural rewards? What exactly are the powerful new tools of molecular biology that are revolutionizing neuroscience? This undergraduate textbook explores the relation between brain, mind, and behavior. It clears away the extraneous detail that so often impedes learning, and describes critical concepts step-by-step, in straightforward language. Rich illustrations and thought-provoking review questions further illuminate the relations between biological, behavioral, and mental phenomena.

With writing that is focused and engaging, even the more challenging topics of neurotransmission and neuroplasticity become enjoyable to learn. While this textbook filters out non-critical details, it includes all key information, allowing readers to remain focused and enjoy the feeling of mastery that comes from a grounded understanding of a topic, from its fundamentals to its implications.

Jon C. Horvitz grew up in Philadelphia, and graduated from Haverford College before receiving his PhD in Psychology at the University of California, Santa Barbara. After postdoctoral work in neuroscience at Princeton University, he was a professor of psychology at Columbia University, Boston College, and now City College of New York/CUNY. A passionate teacher who enjoys finding ways to excite his students, his brain–mind courses have won many accolades. His research examines brain circuits underlying natural and drug rewards, and he has been a grant reviewer for the National Institute on Drug Abuse. He loves to play jazz piano. He and his wife regularly travel to Spain to visit her family.

Barry L. Jacobs was a professor of psychology and neuroscience at Princeton University. He taught one of the university's most popular courses, "The Brain: A User's Guide," and was a leading researcher in the areas of serotonin, sleep, and depression. He grew up in Chicago, graduated from the University of Illinois-Chicago, and received his doctorate in psychology from the University of California, Los Angeles. He was a postdoctoral fellow in the psychiatry department at Stanford University Medical School before coming to Princeton. He has taken joy in being a mentor to many young neuroscientists throughout the world.

We held hands in the Alameda, and never let go – JH

For Suzie (Susyn), *my love through thick and thin – BLJ*

Brief Contents

Contents

Preface

The Conception

This book was conceived early one evening at an outdoor table at a restaurant near my home. Barry and I were talking about our introductory Brain–Mind courses, his at Princeton University, mine at City College of New York. He asked me which textbook I used. I told him I'd used several of the popular ones over the years. "They all have good qualities," I said. "But in my view, they all suffer from the same problem – too much extraneous detail." Barry felt the same way about the Biopsychology and Behavioral Neuroscience textbooks he'd used. "When chapters are loaded with so much detail, students can't see the forest for the trees," he said. We both agreed:

"Principles and key ideas first; details later."

Of course, the crucial details are important to include, and leaving these out can lead to cryptic textbook passages. The extraneous details were the real culprits in the textbooks we'd used. Students were spending too much time trying to figure out what was important in the chapters. I used to tell students to try to understand entire chapters – until I read the chapters myself. Barry and I wished we could find a more manageable textbook.

By the end of the conversation, we were convinced of three points: A behavioral neuroscience textbook should filter out the non-essential, describe the key points (and *crucial* details) in a clear, conversational manner, and complement the text with compelling illustrations. By the end of this long dinner, we'd tested the waiter's patience, and we'd decided to write a textbook.

What Could Be More Interesting?

People are naturally fascinated by the relation between brain, mind, and behavior. We're all drawn to the shocking fact that a 3-pound hunk of biological tissue inside the skull gives rise to thought, memories, and other intangible mental phenomena. Our students all come to the course with first-hand knowledge of emotional and cognitive *products* of brain activity. We're all experts on the subjective aspects of brain functioning.

However, readers new to the topic may be surprised to find that understanding mental processes requires some background in neurotransmission. To understand how the brain stores memories, one needs to know something about the neural plasticity that allows experiences to alter the strength of connections between neurons. No matter how much one introspects about one's own learning and memory, nothing about neural plasticity becomes apparent. There are events going on behind the scenes, outside of awareness, that influence the contents of mind and behavior.

Of course, what we learn about the brain mechanisms occurring "behind the scenes" sometimes *fits* with our inner experience in an intuitive and satisfying manner. For instance, we've all experienced dreams containing visual scenes and strong emotional content, but lacking a logical connection between the dream events. On the basis of our own introspection, we may not be surprised to learn that during REM sleep, when dreams occur, visual cortical areas associated with mental imagery are highly active; areas associated with emotional tone, such as the sympathetic nervous system, are often in high gear as well. Yet the frontal cortex, which normally tracks the sequence in which events occur, and notes violations in their logical order – this is one of the few cortical regions that goes "off-line" during REM. Here, the behind-the-scenes brain events are as one might expect on the basis of our *experience* of dreams.

A Note to Students

While most brain–mind topics have obvious relevance to the reader, some may feel intimidated when it comes to learning about neurotransmission. Learning how neurons communicate with one another requires familiarizing yourself with some concepts that are new and unfamiliar. Terms like "depolarization" and "excitatory postsynaptic potential" can be offputting at first. This is a brief word of advice to anyone who may say to themselves that technical material is "not for me": *Don't be so sure*. We all find some kinds of material difficult at first. I recently had the experience of reading online accounting columns that described the grant money I'd spent and the amount I had left for my lab. Faced with these confusing columns, I thought "Accounting is not my thing." (I think I literally said that to myself.) My initial solution was to simply cross my fingers and hope I don't run out of money.

Then I asked myself how much time I'd actually spent on those accounting columns. About 25 minutes total, compared to the thousands of hours I'd spent on what I considered "my kind of things," like reading about the brain, or playing the piano. So, I set the goal of spending just 20 minutes each day on those budget pages. Within a few days (a few hours at most), I'd discovered that they weren't difficult. My concern went away once I'd applied some time to the task. It was a good feeling.

There are some topics in this textbook that involve technical details: like neural communication or learning-related synaptic plasticity. If this doesn't seem like "your kind of thing," we hope you will put your doubts on hold. When it comes to the chapter on "How Neurons Work," relax and take the concepts one step at a time. Don't be surprised if you discover that this kind of material is *your thing* after all.

If you understand the basics of how neurons work, you will also have a deeper appreciation for the relations between brain, mind, and behavior discussed in the later chapters. We've worked hard to present the material in a clear, straightforward manner. But if you find passages that are not clear enough, please email us, and we'll see if we can make them clearer. You'll be doing a real service to other students.

What's in This Book?

Principles of Behavioral Neuroscience is for a first course in behavioral neuroscience for undergraduates. It examines key concepts and findings related to brain, mind, and behavior that motivate neuroscience researchers to dig deeper. How do we perceive, move our bodies, and carry out goals? What makes us hungry – that is, from the point of view of the brain? How does the activity of the sleeping brain change as we go from deep, "slow-wave" sleep, where the conscious mind finally quiets down, to the mentally intense stage of REM sleep, and then back again to slow-wave sleep? How does the brain give rise to learning, memory, and language?

We'll examine the effects of brain damage on language, memory, and emotion. For instance, we'll learn of the woman who lacked the amygdala (on both sides of her brain) and lost nearly all aspects of fear. To understand more precisely how brain activity contributes to cognition, motivation, and behavior, we will examine the activity of individual neurons as animals sleep, learn, attend, and seek out food and other rewards in the environment. Modern optogenetic techniques allow researchers to record the activity of specific *types* of neurons in particular brain areas, or to experimentally change the activity of these neurons while animal subjects are learning, behaving, or both. Recent work in epigenetics shows us what it means for our environment and genes to interact by revealing the ways in which certain life experiences alter the molecules surrounding our genes. Such studies pull back the curtain on the mental, emotional, and behavioral processes that make up our inner and outer worlds.

How to Use This Book

The first two chapters of this textbook concern the structure of the nervous system and neurotransmission. It is useful to begin with these chapters, or at least to present them early in the course, because the concepts introduced in these chapters appear in later chapters as well. While the subsequent chapters work well in their order within the textbook, they can be covered in the order the professor chooses. Some courses will cover all fourteen chapters; others will choose to spend more time on a smaller number of chapters.

Many professors will already have a set of topics they wish to cover, and a preferred order for covering them. We believe that readings for existing course syllabi are easily adapted to the chapters included here. Material within each chapter is broken into digestible subsections with numbered headings. This allows an instructor either to assign entire chapters or to assign subsections of chapters. Because we've worked hard to present material in a clear, conversational tone, and to avoid extraneous details, the instructor will be able to confidently assign chapters and test textbook material regardless of whether the material has been covered in class.

Pedagogical Features

In each chapter, students will find three tools that help consolidate what they've learned.

- Key Concepts are summarized at several points in each chapter. This list of concepts serves to reinforce the key points that the student has just read. In addition, because each concept is boiled down to just a sentence or two, the student can use the list to go back through the chapter section and outline the details relevant to each concept.
- Review Questions allow students to test themselves on the just-presented material. Some of the questions simply allow the student to check their retention of key information in the section. Others motivate the student to review and organize their knowledge of a topic.
- Creative Thinking questions at the end of each chapter are designed to stimulate creative thinking about the chapter material. Many of these questions will be useful for group discussions.

A Final Word to Our Fellow Instructors

While some of our students will pursue careers in science, those who do not will nevertheless have the opportunity to read about new findings on brain function long into the future. Some of our former students will have the joy of reading about discoveries that come to light many years after we instructors are gone. In this course, we give them the background that allows them to do so.

Online Resources

Instructor's Resources

This text is accompanied by teaching tools that can only be accessed by instructors. These tools are designed to support lectures and classroom activities, assessments, and course planning. All resources are freely available with registration. Instructors can register at: www.cambridge.org/highereducation.

Instructor resources include:

Chapter summaries

- Streamlined outline of each chapter containing the essential information and pointing to key figures, with:
  - highlighted "Useful Examples and Analogies" to illuminate key concepts
  - links to video clips and animations directly pertinent to the material at hand

Individual and group activities

- In-class activities designed for students to work creatively with chapter concepts, and to provide a sense of agency and ownership of the material

Annotated lecture slides

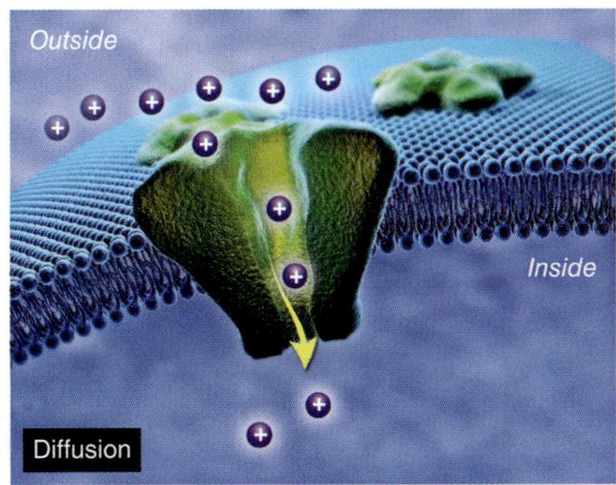

- Ready made lecture slides providing key concepts and select figures from each chapter
- Length is kept appropriate for coverage in one or two standard lecture periods

- In addition, a full set of figures in JPG and PDF format allows instructors to create their own sets of lecture slides, or to add to the annotated set provided by the authors

Testbanks

- Over 85 test questions for each chapter, allowing the instructor to use different sets of questions each semester
- Each question has been edited and approved for clarity by the textbook authors

Student Resources

The companion website hosts additional content that will help you to master the material from each chapter and spur further exploration of topics covered in the text.

Organized chapter-by-chapter, this material includes various study aids, video links, and readings. This is also where you can find answers to the Test Yourself questions interspersed throughout each chapter.

Student resources include:

- Flashcards with key terms from each chapter on one side and definitions on the other.
- Figures with select labels removed so that you can test your knowledge as you review key figures, rather than simply reviewing figures in a passive manner.

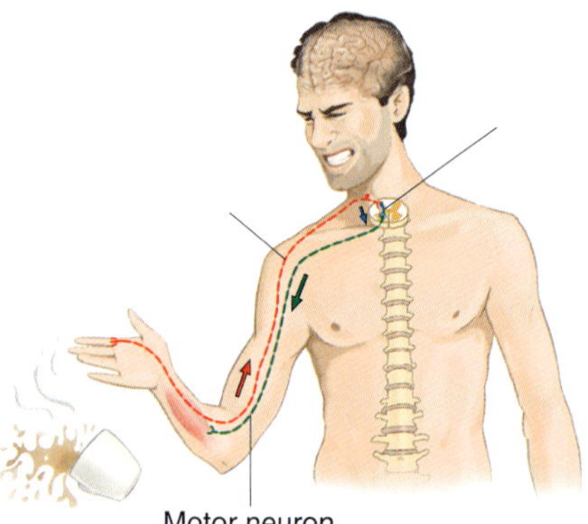

- Videos and animations relevant to specific chapter material
- Additional readings to probe deeper into select chapter topics
- Answers to chapter Test Yourself questions

Blog

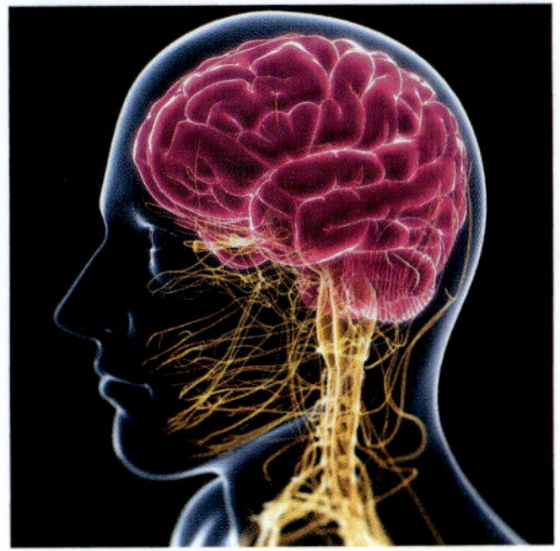

- Highlights the relevance of Behavioral Neuroscience course material in everyday life events, including brain underpinnings of addiction, conscious awareness, and other relevant topics.

Finally, the author would be happy to hear from you. Please send any comments, thoughts, corrections, or requests to: HorvitzNeuroscience@gmail.com.

1 Nervous Systems

Science Photo Library - SCIEPRO / BrandXPictures / Getty Images

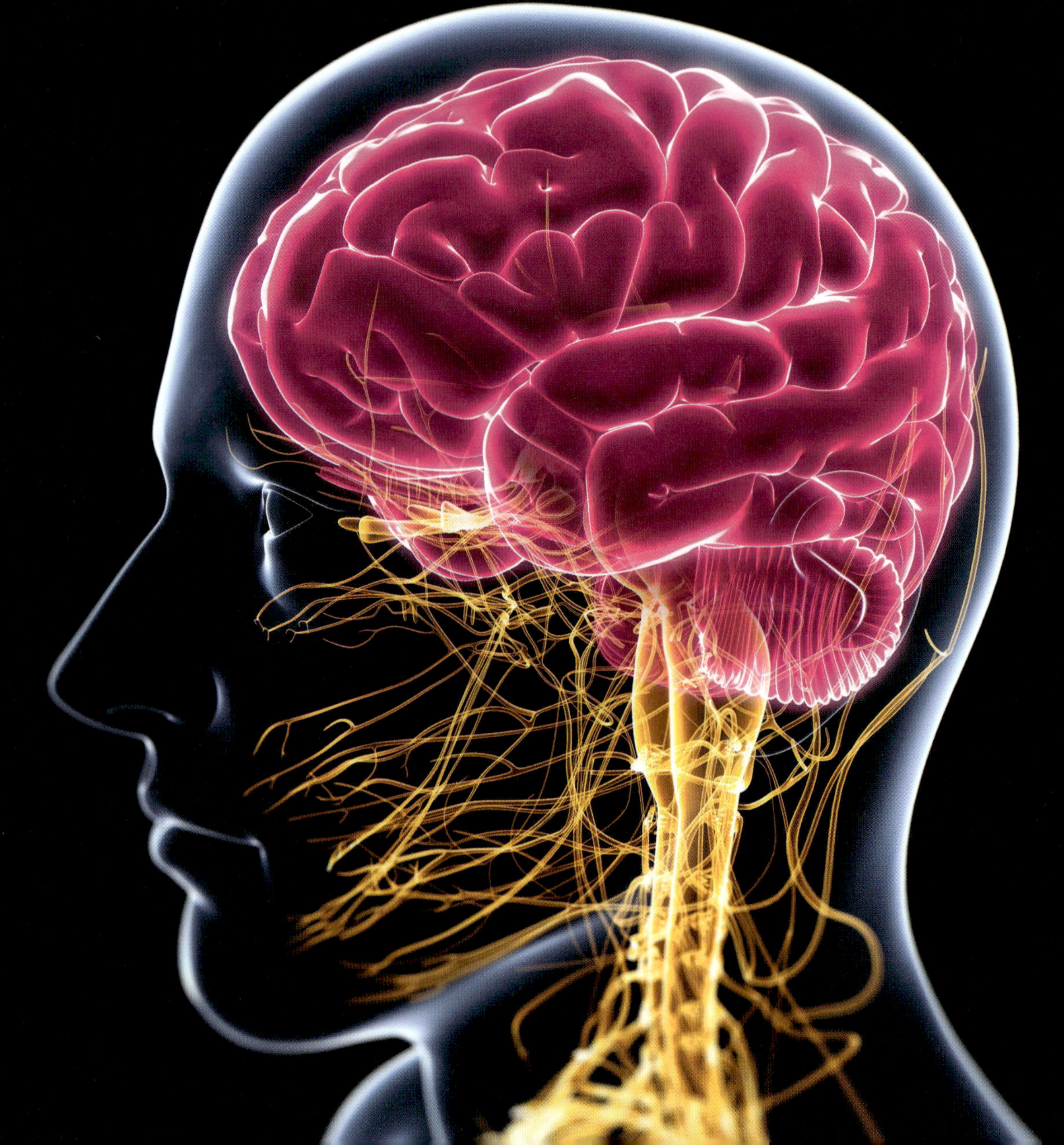

Consider This …

A 44-year-old man entered a neurology clinic in France complaining of mild leg weakness. His doctors were shocked when they examined images of his brain. Where they had expected to see brain tissue, they found mostly fluid and only a thin strip of brain surrounding the inside of his skull (Feuillet, Dufour, & Pelletier, 2007). The parts of the brain normally necessary for thought, speech, and memory were largely absent and replaced by a massive cavern in his head (Figure 1.1). Although his IQ of 75 was far below average, his social functioning was relatively normal. He was married with two children and had a job as a civil servant. How is it possible that he could speak, remember, carry out everyday tasks, and hold a job, with so much of his brain missing?

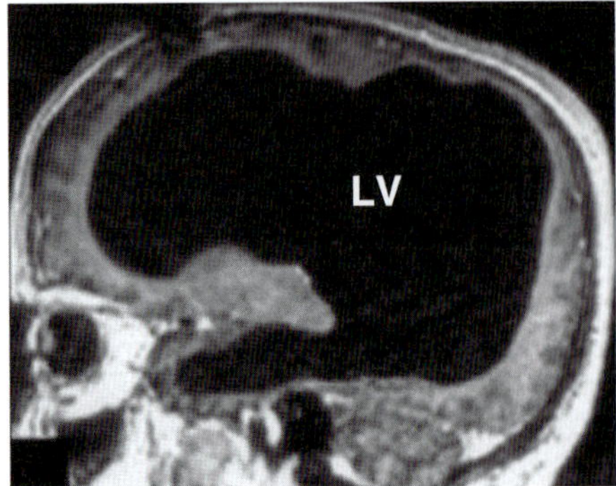

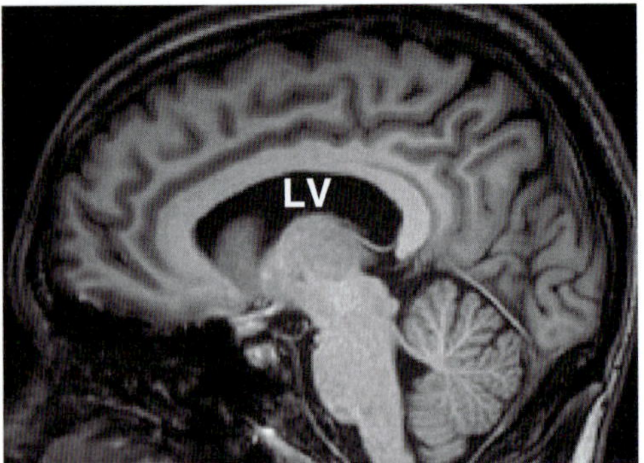

Figure 1.1 The man with a thin strip of brain. The image on the left reveals that areas in the center of the man's brain that would normally be filled with brain tissue were instead filled only with fluid. The image to the right shows a normal brain. LV = lateral ventricle, a fluid-filled compartment. (Left, from Feuillet, Dufour, & Pelletier, 2007, © 2007 Elsevier Ltd. All rights reserved; right, © Sherbrooke Connectivity Imaging Lab (SCIL)/Getty Images.)

The French philosopher René Descartes advocated for **dualism** during the early 1600s. The immaterial (non-physical) mind (Descartes referred to it as the soul) exists separately from the physical brain and body. But how do the two realms interact? Descartes believed that when you decide to lift your right arm, the *immaterial* decision in your mind sets your nerves and muscles in motion. When you listen to music, the *physical* sense organs in the ear cause melodies to arise in your (*immaterial*) mind. But *where* do the mind and the physical brain interact, asked Descartes? He believed the interaction occurred in the pineal gland, a small pine-cone-shaped structure near the center of the brain (Figure 1.2).

> [The] mechanism of our body is so constructed that simply by this [pineal] gland's being moved in any way by the soul ... it drives the surrounding spirits towards the pores of the brain, which direct them through the nerves to the muscles; and in this way the gland makes the spirits move the limbs. (Descartes, 1984)

From this point of view, the man in our opening anecdote lacking so much brain tissue might have required no brain at all to generate decisions! So long as the immaterial wishes of his soul could move the pineal gland, the rest of the brain would only need to set in motion physical processes to carry out his actions.

Even if one believed that Descartes had localized the site of mind–body interaction to the pineal gland, many thinkers noticed that a deeper problem remained: If a decision is *non-material*, how can it affect the pineal gland? How can a non-material cause have an effect on a *material* body? To get from the immaterial to the material seems like a bridge one cannot logically cross, and philosophers refer to this problem as the *Cartesian impasse*.

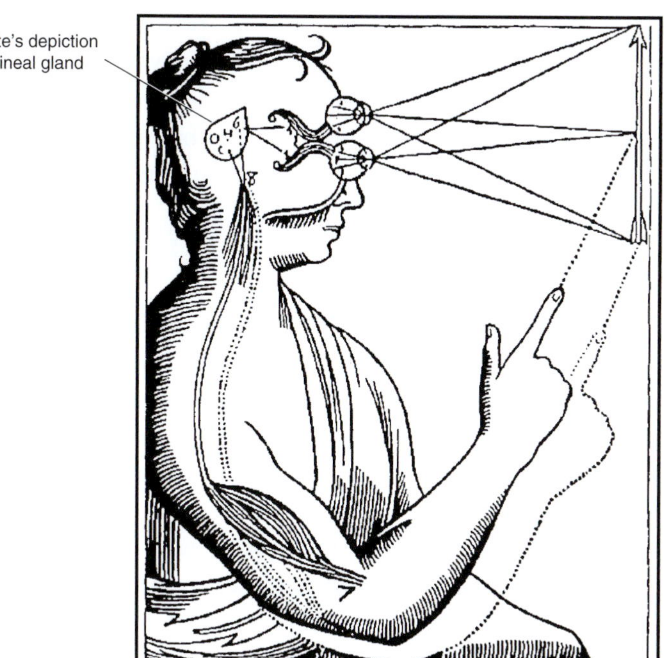

Figure 1.2 Descartes' view of the brain and mind. Descartes believed that visual input enters the eyes, and travels through nerves to cause movement of the teardrop-shaped pineal gland. The immaterial soul detects these movements of the gland, allowing the soul to see the world outside. When deciding to act, the soul moves the pineal gland, and drives wind-like "spirits" to move the limbs and other body parts. (Descartes,1972.)

Let's try a simple experiment right now: Lift your left arm. (Go ahead, play along.) You may not know much (yet) about the how the brain controls arm movements. However, you can imagine the basic idea that neurons send signals from the brain down the spinal cord, and that nerves from the spinal cord activate muscles in the shoulder. Contraction of the proper set of muscles causes the arm to lift. We'll fill in the details in Chapter 4, but you can see that there's nothing particularly puzzling or "spooky" about neurons in the brain controlling an arm movement.

But now let's try something slightly different: Lift one of your arms – you choose which one – but don't do it right away. Exert your free will and *decide upon* the moment when you want to lift it. (Take a moment to do this.) Is your decision material or immaterial? If, like Descartes, you believe it's "immaterial," how did your immaterial decision set in motion the neural activity that ultimately led to the arm movement? This is the Cartesian impasse. How can a non-material decision, located nowhere in particular, produce a physical effect on neurons? This dualist view is commonly held (at least among those who haven't studied neuroscience); but it is kind of spooky.

Dualism is not the view of neuroscience, or of most contemporary philosophy for that matter. The chapters that follow in this book will show that our ability to think, remember, decide, to have any mental experience at all, depends on the activity of the brain. As you'll see in Chapter 4, the very *decision* or *urge* to move a limb at a particular moment depends upon the activity of neurons located in an area of the frontal cortex near the midline of the brain, called the supplementary motor area.

This **monist** perspective rejects the idea of a duality between the mind and the brain. While there are many variants of monism, we're interested here in the monist view that mental phenomena like thoughts and desires arise as products of brain activity – the activation of neurons. How can a thought arise from the activity of neurons? The monist believes that neural activity has various properties. On one hand, neurons produce electrical signals allowing them to communicate with one another; the neuronal activity can be monitored with physical measuring devices. On the other hand, when the neurons are *your* neurons communicating with other neurons in *your* brain, you may experience the neural activity as a thought, desire, or some other mental event. By analogy, a cloud gives a particular impression when viewed from the ground looking up at it; but upon closer inspection, one discovers that the cloud contains various molecules interacting in ways that seem quite "un-cloudlike." From the monist perspective of neuroscience, your decision to move your arm was itself the result of *material* processes, that is, neuronal activity in some part of your brain. Those neurons then activate other neurons, eventually those in your spinal cord, and finally your muscles, causing your arm to lift. There is no logical impasse.

Similarly, from the monist view, the man in the opening scenario owes all his mental and behavioral functions to the small amount of brain tissue that he possesses. Even with much of his brain tissue lost, he retains many mental functions because the brain tissue was lost when he was very young. The human brain is highly **plastic**, that is to say, capable of structural and functional change, especially during our early years. It is likely that the neurons that remained in the man's brain took over some of the cognitive, sensory, and motor functions that were lost as a result of brain damage.

In this chapter, we give an overview of the amazing 3.3-pound mass of soft, gray tissue sitting snugly inside your skull. It is one of the most powerful instruments in the known universe. Its 100 billion or so neurons make an estimated 100 trillion connections among themselves. The human brain and its product, the mind, are responsible for all of our thoughts, emotions, memories, and actions. We'll begin by examining neurons and glia, the main cells of the nervous system, and then we'll step back to take a bird's eye view of the peripheral nervous system, the spinal cord, and the brain. We'll fill in the details in later chapters.

1.1 THE CELLS OF THE NERVOUS SYSTEM ARE THE NEURONS AND GLIA

Neurons are the fundamental units by which information moves through the nervous system. Sights, sounds, thoughts, memories – all depend upon communication between neurons. The nervous system's other major cell type is the glial cell, which contributes to neuronal function in important ways.

1.1.1 Neurons

Information processing is what sets the brain apart as a wondrous organ capable of generating thoughts, emotions, and behaviors. Neurons carry information through the brain. The four basic parts of the neuron are the dendrites, cell body, axon, and terminal (Figure 1.3A and B). **Dendrites** are branch-like extensions that receive input from other neurons. Some neurons have dendrites that branch wildly, with additional dendrites coming from each branch like branches of a tree (Figure 1.3C). Information travels along the dendrites toward the **cell body** (also called the soma), which can be thought of as the "factory" of the neuron. It has organelles, compartments that generate energy and package chemicals, as well as a nucleus containing the DNA. The DNA is the cell's instructions about the necessary materials (proteins) that the neuron will need to manufacture. Finally, a thread-like **axon** leaves the cell body and carries an electrical signal to the end or **terminal** of the axon. Neurons communicate with one another (or with muscles or organs) primarily by releasing chemicals called **neurotransmitters** (dopamine, serotonin, and others) from the axon terminal. The transmitters cross a **synaptic cleft** (a tiny gap) and bind to neurotransmitter **receptors** on other neurons, muscle fibers, or cells of internal organs (Figure 1.4).

Understanding how neurons send information from one part of the nervous system to another is fundamental to understanding how the brain generates emotions, thoughts, and behavior. In Chapter 2, we will ask how neurons communicate, or send signals, to one another. We will see in many chapters of this book that the strength of connections between neurons are plastic; they can change as a result of experience. We will ask how changes in the strength of synaptic connections between neurons give rise to memories and skills.

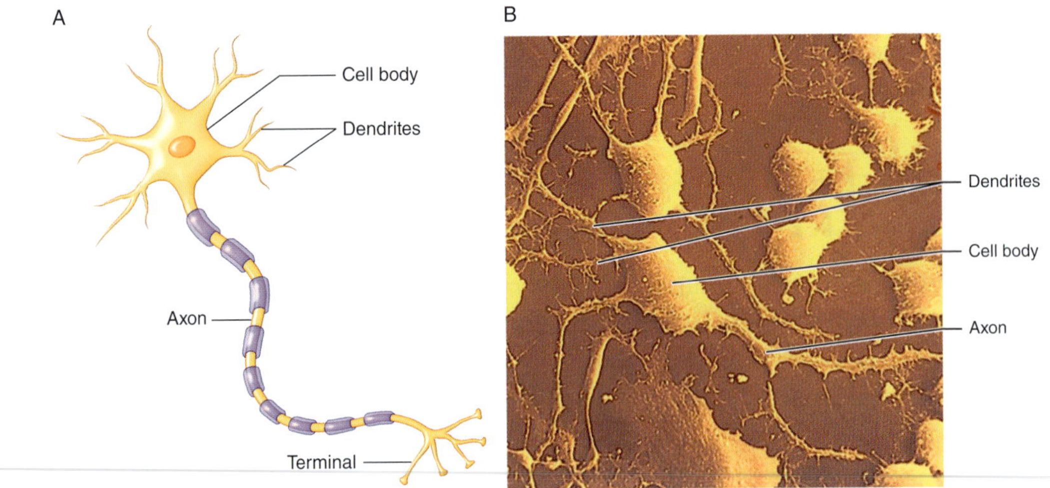

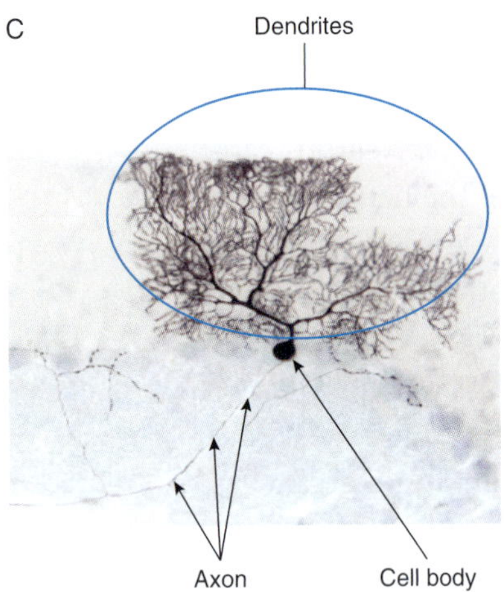

Figure 1.3 The four major components of a neuron. (A) Dendrites receive information, the cell body collects it, and the axon transmits an electrical signal to the terminal. The small circle within the cell body represents the nucleus of the cell. (B) This microscopic image shows that neurons can form dense connections with one another. (David M. Phillips/Visuals Unlimited.) (C) Neurons vary in their morphology (shape). For instance, the neuron in this microscopic image has a huge dendritic tree. (Adapted from Sugihara et al., 2009, fig. 12A, © 2009 Wiley-Liss, Inc.)

1.1.2 Glia

Glia carry out a large number of processes critical to the workings of the nervous system. Let's take a look at five major types of glial cells found in the nervous system: astrocytes, oligodendrocytes, Schwann cells, microglia, and radial glia.

Astrocytes look like stars (hence the name "astro"). They do many things, including bringing nutrients to neurons and storing biochemicals (such as glucose and neurotransmitters) that the neuron can use later. Astrocytes may also enter a brain site to provide assistance when neurons

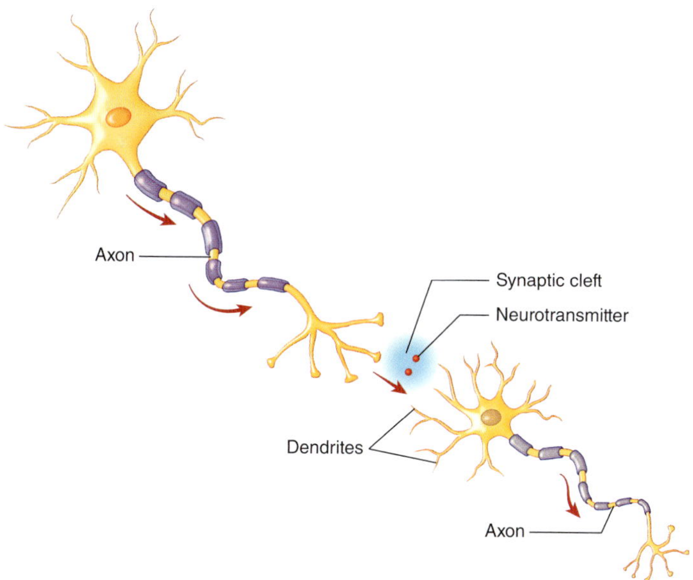

Figure 1.4 Neurons release neurotransmitters which cross a synapse to communicate with receiving neurons.

have been damaged. While these glial cells have traditionally been considered a kind of support staff for the health and activity of nearby neurons, research is leading to dramatic changes in how we view astrocytes. Recent evidence suggests that astrocytes may influence the activity of nearby neurons to affect a person's mood, and that abnormalities in astrocyte function may play a role in mood disorders (Zhou et al., 2019). Astrocytes also play a still-mysterious role in learning (see Box 1.1).

Oligodendrocytes form the whitish tissue (**myelin**) that surrounds and insulates axons in the brain and spinal cord to speed information transfer across the axon. Chapter 2 examines what it means for "information" or "signals" to move along an axon. For now, imagine that a bee lands on your shoulder and "information" about this event travels along axons of several neurons to reach brain areas that perceive tactile events. If the axons are myelinated (surrounded by myelin), the information travels along the axons more quickly, perhaps in time for you to move your body before the bee stings you. While oligodendrocytes produce myelin in the brain and spinal cord (the central nervous system), **Schwann cells** are the glial cells that produce myelin in the nerves that target peripheral body parts and organs (i.e., in the peripheral nervous system, discussed below).

Microglia are tiny compared to the other glia (hence the name "micro"). They are the brain's cleanup crew. When neurons die or suffer damage, microglia remove the debris left behind. Lastly, **radial glia** play a critical role in early brain development. They provide cellular scaffolding that guides newly born neurons to their final destination in the brain.

BOX 1.1 Glial Cells Do More than We Thought

Evidence for a role of glial cells in learning came, in part, from an experiment so strange that it seems like science fiction. Investigators at the University of Rochester in New York were studying immature cells that normally develop to become astrocytes (Goldman, Nedergaard, & Windrem, 2015). In their immature form, they are called **glial progenitor cells** or **GPCs**. The experimenters placed human GPCs into the brains of newborn mice (Figure 1.5A), taking steps to ensure that the mouse immune system wouldn't reject the human cells. Sure enough, the immature human cells migrated (traveled) throughout the mouse brain and increased in number. They soon developed into astrocytes, which competed with and replaced most of the mouse astrocytes. *Within about ten months, most of the astrocytes in the mouse brain were human in origin* (Figure 1.5B). Researchers sometimes refer to this procedure as "glial humanization," or more specifically, "astrocytic humanization" of the mouse brain. The mice are described as **chimeric**, for their brains are part mouse, part human. (Chimera were mythical hybrid creatures with body parts from more than one animal.)

The team of neuroscientists trained the mice on a learning task in which a tone came on a few seconds before a mild shock was delivered to the floor of the cage. A group of mice that were not transplanted with foreign astrocytes eventually learned the tone–shock association; they would often "freeze" (become briefly immobilized with fear) when the tone came on, reflecting their expectation of shock. Another group of mice were transplanted with astrocytes *from other mice*. These mice gradually learned the tone–shock association as well. However, the mice with human astrocytes (the "chimeric mice") were by far the fastest learners. After one day of training, they showed better learning than the other mice showed after four days' training (see Figure 1.5C). The long, thin extensions of astroctyes often wrap around synapses between neurons. Evidence suggests that astrocytes enhance synaptic plasticity, the ability of neuronal connections to strengthen, and thereby enhance learning (Han et al., 2013; Hussaini & Jang, 2018). Investigators do not yet understand the precise manner in which astrocytes strengthen synaptic connections and promote learning.

1.1.3 Gray versus White Matter

In many of the chapters to come, you will read about environmental and psychological conditions associated with changes in the brain's **gray matter** (Figure 1.6A). For instance, London cab drivers show increased gray matter in brain areas related to spatial memory (remembering locations), musicians show increased gray matter in auditory areas of the brain, major depression is associated with reduced gray matter in several brain regions, and antidepressant medications restore gray matter. Gray matter is mostly made up of cell bodies, dendrites, and unmyelinated axons of neurons.

As seen in Figure 1.6B, an increase in gray matter within a particular brain region may mean that:

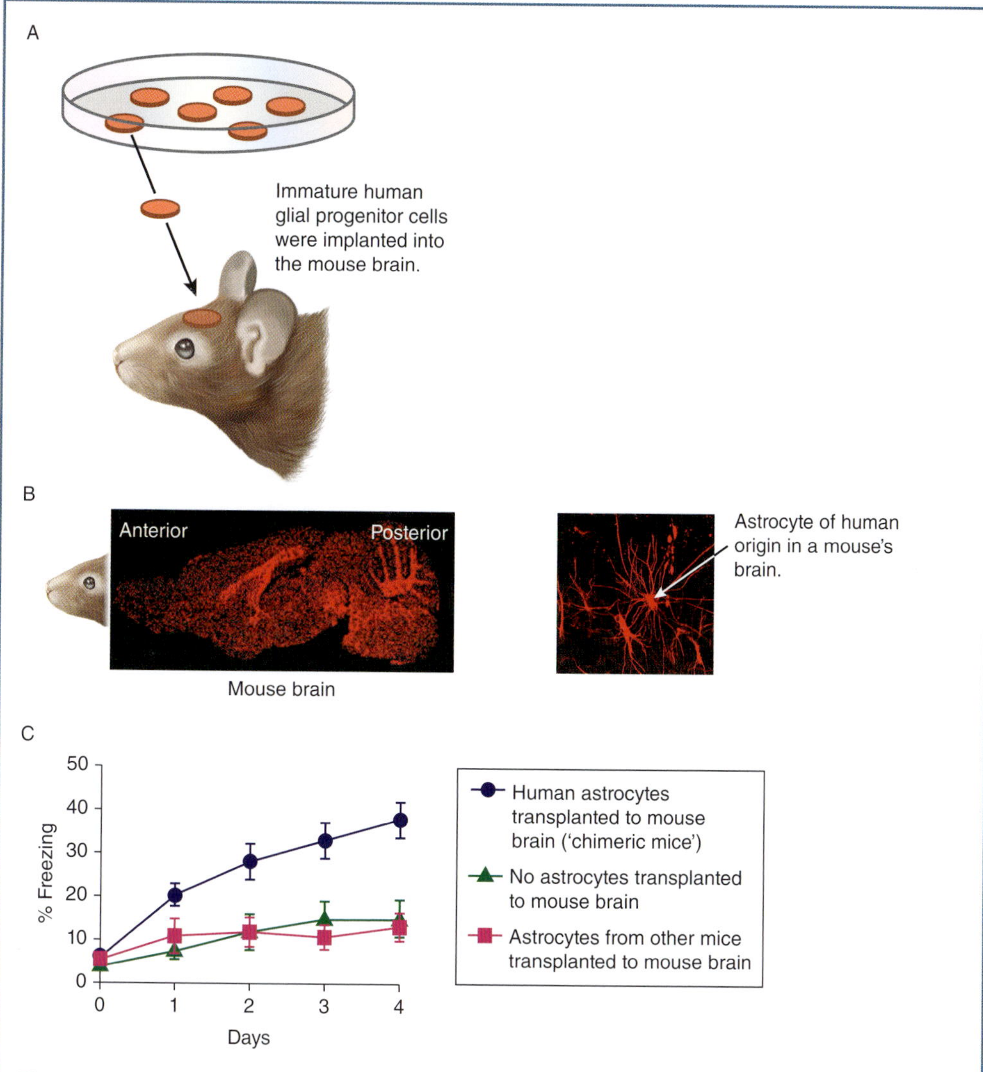

Figure 1.5 Human glial cells transplanted to the mouse brain. (A) Mice were transplanted with human glial progenitor cells (GPCs). (B) The human GPCs (stained red) quickly spread across the entire mouse brain, increased in number, and developed into astrocytes. The photograph of the mouse brain on the left is cut from the anterior to posterior end. (As described later in the chapter, this is called a "sagittal slice.") On the right, an arrow points to a human astrocyte in a mouse's brain. Notice the long, thin extensions radiating outward. Some of these extensions make contact with the much smaller mouse astrocytes. (Left, Goldman et al., 2015, fig. 1; right, Han et al., 2013, fig. 3A, © 2013 Elsevier Inc. All rights reserved.) (C) The *y*-axis shows the percentage of time mice spent freezing in fear during a tone that signaled shock. Mice with human astrocytes learned the tone–shock association quicker than control mice.
(Adapted from Han et al., 2013, fig. 6A, © 2013 Elsevier Inc. All rights reserved.)

- axons have sprouted new branches
- dendrites have grown new branches, and/or
- new neurons have been born (**neurogenesis**, discussed in Chapters 8 and 9).

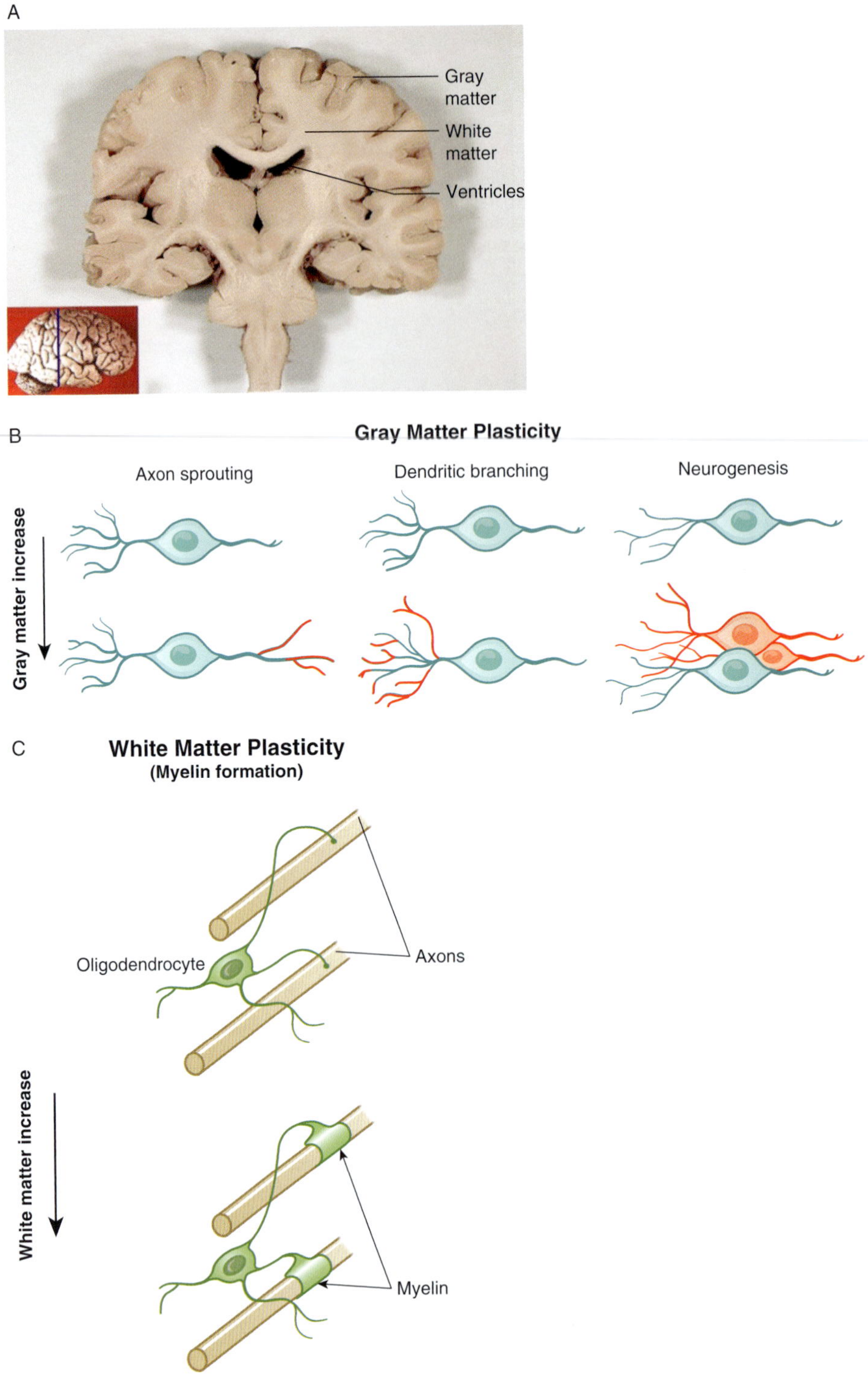

A

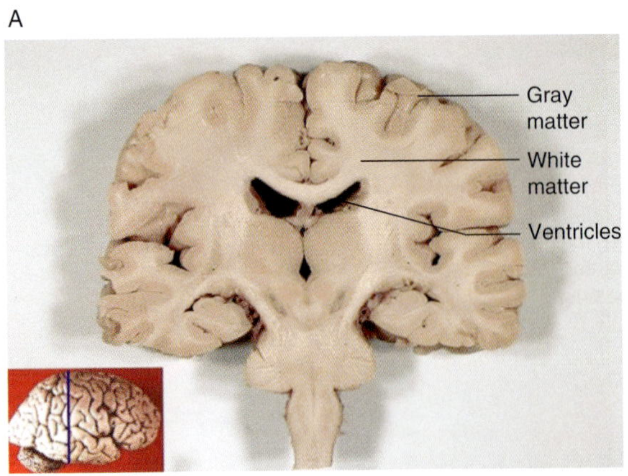

B

Gray Matter Plasticity

Axon sprouting

Dendritic branching

Neurogenesis

Gray matter increase

C

White Matter Plasticity
(Myelin formation)

Oligodendrocyte

Axons

White matter increase

Myelin

Figure 1.6 **Changes in gray versus white matter**. (A) Gray and white matter seen in a slice from a human brain. (John Beal, LSU Health Sciences Center.) (Ventricles are discussed later in this chapter.) (B) Increases in gray matter can result from increased branching of axons (left) or dendrites (middle), or from neurogenesis (right). (C) Increases in white matter result from increases in the axon myelination formed by nearby oligodendrocytes.
(B and C adapted from Zatorre, Fields, & Johansen-Berg, 2012, figs. 3A and 3B respectively.)

White matter is comprised of myelinated axons. (Myelin gives the white matter its color.) Changes in white matter can result from increases in axon myelination produced by nearby oligodendrocytes (Figure 1.6C).

We'll revisit gray and white matter later in this chapter. For now, it is useful to be aware of the fact that neurons, their dendrites and axons, and the myelin produced by glial cells, do not remain in a fixed state from birth. They undergo plasticity, adapting to environmental changes throughout our lives.

KEY CONCEPTS

- **Most neurons consist of dendrites, a cell body, an axon, and a terminal. Neurons transmit signals to one another, as well as to bodily organs and muscles.**
- **Glia provide various kinds of support for neurons, and some produce myelin, which speeds the conduction of signals along neuronal axons. Emerging research suggests additional glial functions, including the contribution of astrocytes to learning.**
- **Gray matter consists of neuronal cell bodies, dendrites, and unmyelinated axons. White matter is made up of myelinated axons.**

TEST YOURSELF

1. **What are the key roles for a neuron's (a) dendrites, (b) cell body, (c) axon, and (d) terminal?**
2. **When a ______ (chemical) is released from a neuron's axon terminal, it crosses a _______ (tiny gap) and binds to ____ located on other neurons, muscles, or organs.**
3. **List some of the major processes that glial cells perform (including a surprising role recently discovered for astrocytes).**
4. **How does gray matter differ from white matter?**

1.2 THE NERVOUS SYSTEM CONSISTS OF PERIPHERAL AND CENTRAL DIVISIONS

Every complex journey requires a map. Our journey begins with a map of the neurons that reside *outside* the brain and spinal cord, that is, in the **peripheral nervous system** (**PNS**). We will then move on to explore the brain and spinal cord, that is, the **central nervous system** (**CNS**) (see Figure 1.7).

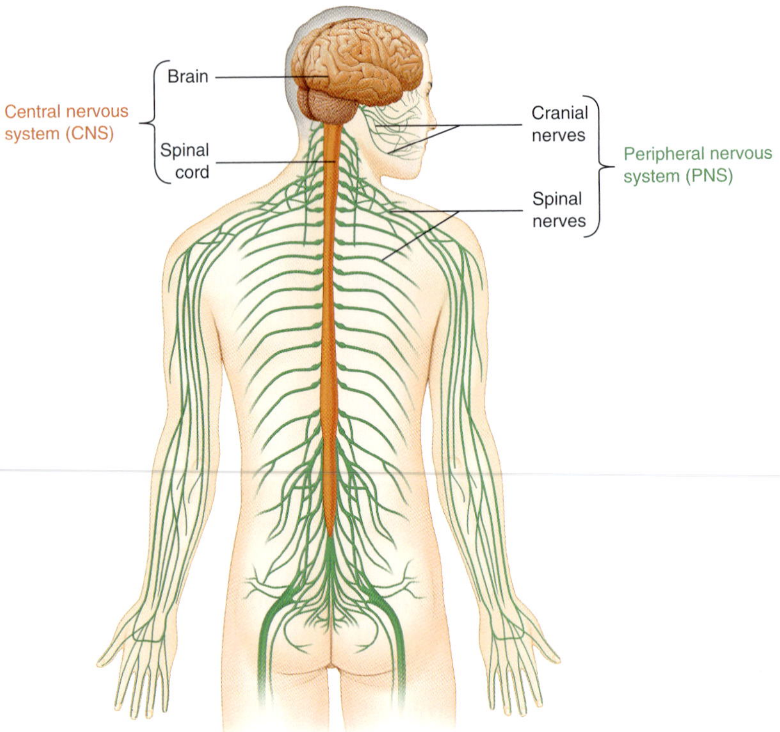

Figures 1.7 **The central and peripheral divisions of the nervous system.** Neurons in the CNS (orange) reside entirely within the brain and spinal cord. Nerves that extend from the CNS to the PNS (or vice versa) are part of the PNS (green).

1.2.1 Peripheral Nervous System (PNS)

Nerves are axons of neurons within the PNS that bundle together and carry information between the periphery of the body and the CNS. Some of these nerves carry sensory information from the outside world. For instance, touch-sensitive peripheral nerves carry information about the texture of objects to the CNS, letting you distinguish the feel of soft cotton from a sharp toothpick. Auditory nerves of the PNS allow you to distinguish the sound of a bird from the roar of a car engine. Olfactory neurons allow you to notice the pleasing and foul smells around you. As you can see, the CNS depends upon the nerves of the PNS to bring it information about the outside world. In addition, motor commands from the brain travel through the nerves of the PNS to reach the muscles that control the movement of the arms, legs, and other body parts. The **somatic division** of the PNS refers to both (1) the *sensory* nerves that carry information to the CNS, and (2) *motor* nerves that carry information from the CNS to the muscles.

The activity of the somatic nervous system is analogous to the work of a mail carrier. Your mail carrier brings you information about events in the outside world; so too, the somatic nervous system brings the CNS information about tactile events occurring in the hands, arms, and other body parts (the periphery of the body). However, you do not feel the touch sensation until the information reaches particular regions of the CNS, in this case **somatosensory** (bodily sensation) regions of the brain. When tactile nerves of the PNS are damaged, the brain no longer receives information about touch sensations; when auditory nerves are damaged, we lose auditory information. When mail service stops, we no longer receive letters from the outside world.

However, there are some ways in which the somatic nervous system differs from a mail carrier. When you listen to a guitar, the sound of the musical notes arrives to the brain via a large number of different auditory neurons, each with a piece of the auditory information traveling along its axon. Of the 40,000 or so axons that make up the auditory nerve, some carry high-frequency (high-pitched) sounds to the brain, others carry low frequencies, and still other carry intermediate frequencies. Your perception of even a single note depends upon the convergence of these various neural signals as they travel along auditory pathways toward the brain. The same is true for touch and other sensory modalities. Instead of a single mail carrier responsible for delivering a letter to you, imagine tens of thousands of mail carriers, each one dedicated to carrying a piece of your letter, with information being combined along the way to your door. (So, it turns out that carrying sensory information to the brain is more complex than carrying mail to your home. What did you expect?)

The mail carrier, or group of mail carriers, sometimes delivers information that requires a written response. So too, the somatic nervous system not only brings sensory information to the CNS, but also sends information from the CNS to the periphery. For instance, when the somatic nervous system sends information to the brain about a mosquito on your upper arm, your brain decides upon the appropriate motor response and sends a command to the spinal cord, which transmits a message via peripheral nerves to muscle fibers which move your body parts appropriately. In some cases, the motor response is more complex than merely swatting a mosquito. You may decide to move your fingers to play a melody on the guitar, or move your mouth, tongue, and other parts of the vocal apparatus to say the words of a sentence. These complex motor behaviors require activation of many motor neurons, each causing contractions of particular muscles in just the right pattern to produce the music, speech, or other behaviors you wish to carry out.

The somatic branch of the PNS, then, has both a sensory and a motor component. When referring to the nerves that carry these sensory inputs and motor outputs, two terms are key: Nerves that carry sensory information from the periphery to the central nervous system (e.g., a tactile sensation from the hand to the spinal cord) are called **afferent** nerves. Those that carry motor information from the central nervous system to the periphery (e.g., a command from the brain to move a body part) are **efferent** nerves. To remember the distinction, you might keep in mind the earlier example of the mosquito landing on the skin and generating activity in afferent nerves. The brain responded by sending signals via efferent nerves to muscles that allow the person to swat it away. Just as sensory input often precedes motor output, the first letter of the word afferent (A) comes before the first letter of efferent (E).

In addition to the somatic nervous system, the PNS contains a second major division. The **autonomic division** of the PNS monitors and controls the state of internal organs. The autonomic nervous system itself has two division.

1. The **sympathetic** nervous system prepares the body for emergency situations by accelerating heart rate and breathing, directing blood to the muscles, and producing other changes associated with a state of high arousal. These behavioral responses are sometimes referred to as "fight or flight" responses. However, in humans, with our highly developed cognitive faculties, the responses of the sympathetic nervous system are better described as "fight, flight, or worry." While the sympathetic nervous system evolved to cope with life or death events like escaping a ferocious lion, it is also activated when we fear failing an exam.
2. The **parasympathetic** nervous system has mostly opposite effects on the internal organs. It restores the resting state and stores energy by actions such as slowing the heart rate and increasing digestion ("rest and digest").

Let us return to the ferocious lion in order to examine in more detail the connections between the sympathetic and parasympathetic nerves and their target organs. As you can see in Figure 1.8, sympathetic nerves leave the spinal cord and activate a second group of nerves found in clusters (ganglia) just outside the spinal cord. Together, these clusters comprise the chain of **sympathetic ganglia**. Nerves leave the sympathetic ganglia to activate the heart, lungs, and other organs, preparing them for the threatening situation. After the lion has left, and assuming we are still alive, activity levels of the parasympathetic nerves increase. These nerves originate in the brainstem and the lower portion of the spinal cord, and communicate with an additional group of nerves clustered in ganglia close to the organs themselves (**parasympathetic ganglia**). Nerves of the parasympathetic ganglia communicate with the organs, allowing the body to return to a more relaxed state once danger has passed. When we discuss stress and anxiety in Chapter 12, we will examine the sympathetic nervous system in more detail.

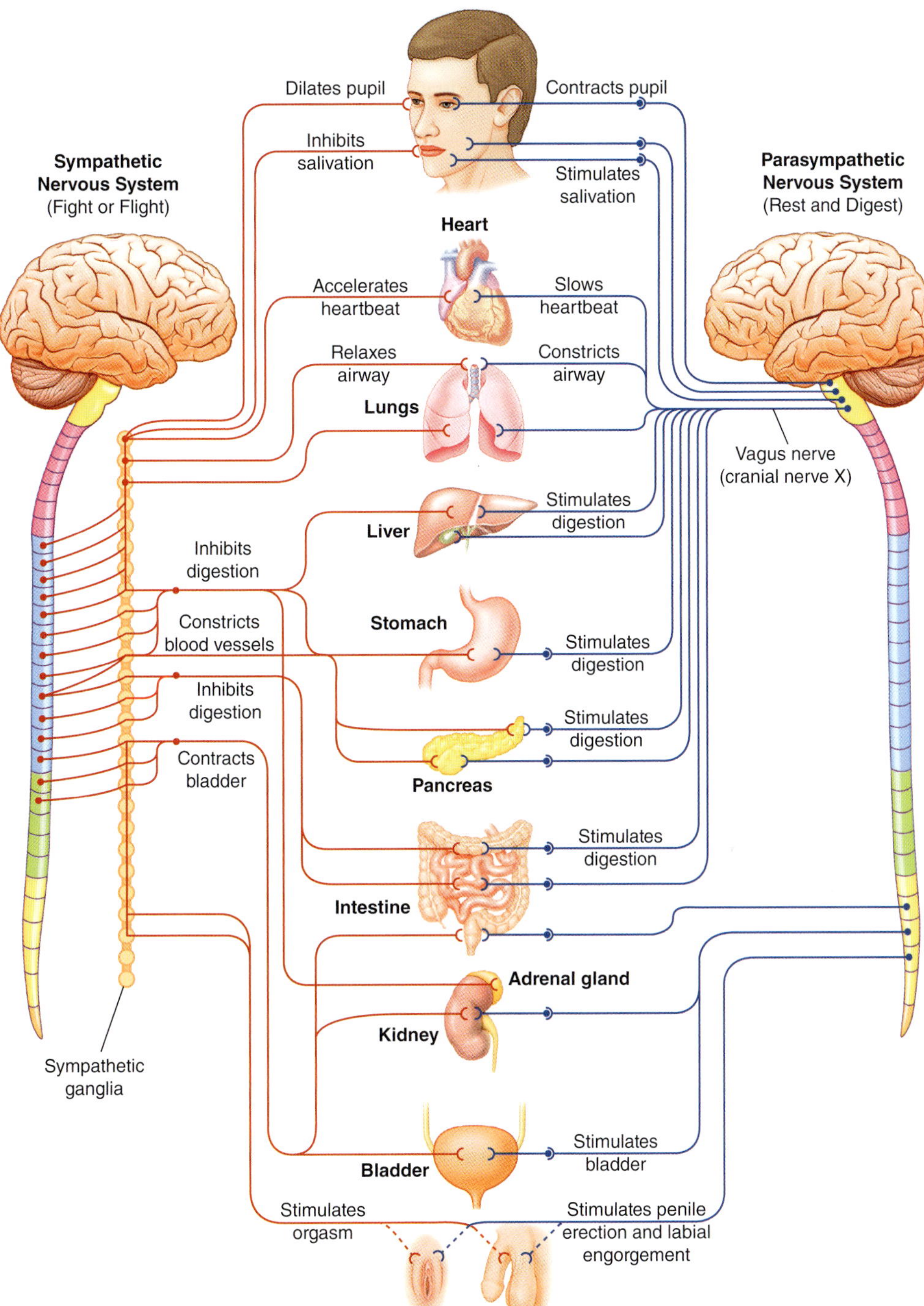

Figure 1.8 The autonomic nervous system. Sympathetic and parasympathetic branches of the autonomic nervous system influence the activity state of bodily organs.

So far, we've described the sympathetic and parasympathetic systems as if each is in an "on" or "off" state at a given moment. The truth is that sympathetic activation is usually balanced by at least some level of parasympathetic activation. If this were not the case, activation of sympathetic nerves would increase heart rate, cardiac muscle contractions, and constriction of blood vessels to dangerously high levels. In fact, the brain has specialized sensors that detect excessive sympathetic activity (for instance, high blood pressure) and that trigger reductions in sympathetic activity and increases in parasympathetic activity as a remedy. Without the restraining effects of parasympathetic activity, excessive sympathetic activation can cause cardiovascular disease and/or death.

In many cases, the brain communicates with the body via the spinal cord. (Recall that both the brain and the spinal cord comprise the CNS.) However, in other cases, the brain communicates directly with the body via **cranial nerves** (Figure 1.9), bypassing the spinal cord altogether. Cranial nerves, for instance, transmit information about odors, tastes, sounds, sights, and tactile sensations directly to the brain. The brain also sends motor commands, via cranial nerves, allowing us to turn the head, and move the eyes, tongue, face, and jaw. Even some autonomic nerves bypass the spinal cord and communicate with their target organs directly via cranial nerves (see Figures 1.8 and 1.9).

1.2.2 Central Nervous System

The brain is the command center sitting atop the rest of the nervous system. The most productive way to begin to understand the brain is to think of it as an elaboration of more basic components of the nervous systems of primitive organisms. For instance, simple **vertebrates** (animals with a vertebral column, or backbone), such as the fish that lived in the sea 500 million years ago, had little more than a spinal cord representing their central nervous systems. As we ascend to birds, mammals, and other vertebrates with complex behaviors, we find additional neural structures, like the brainstem, added on top of the spinal cord. The **cerebral cortex** – the crowning glory of the brain – makes its first appearance with the emergence of mammals.

A key feature of the CNS is its bilateral symmetry. Just as the left and right sides of the body are symmetrical, the left and right sides of the brain and spinal cord are nearly mirror images. When we speak about particular brain structures, keep in mind that a nearly identical structure is almost always located on the **contralateral** (opposite) half of the brain. Despite their similar appearances, the left and right hemispheres of the brain are not identical in function. For instance, for most people, language depends largely (although not exclusively) on the left hemisphere. The right has its own specialized functions. The two halves of the brain normally work together,

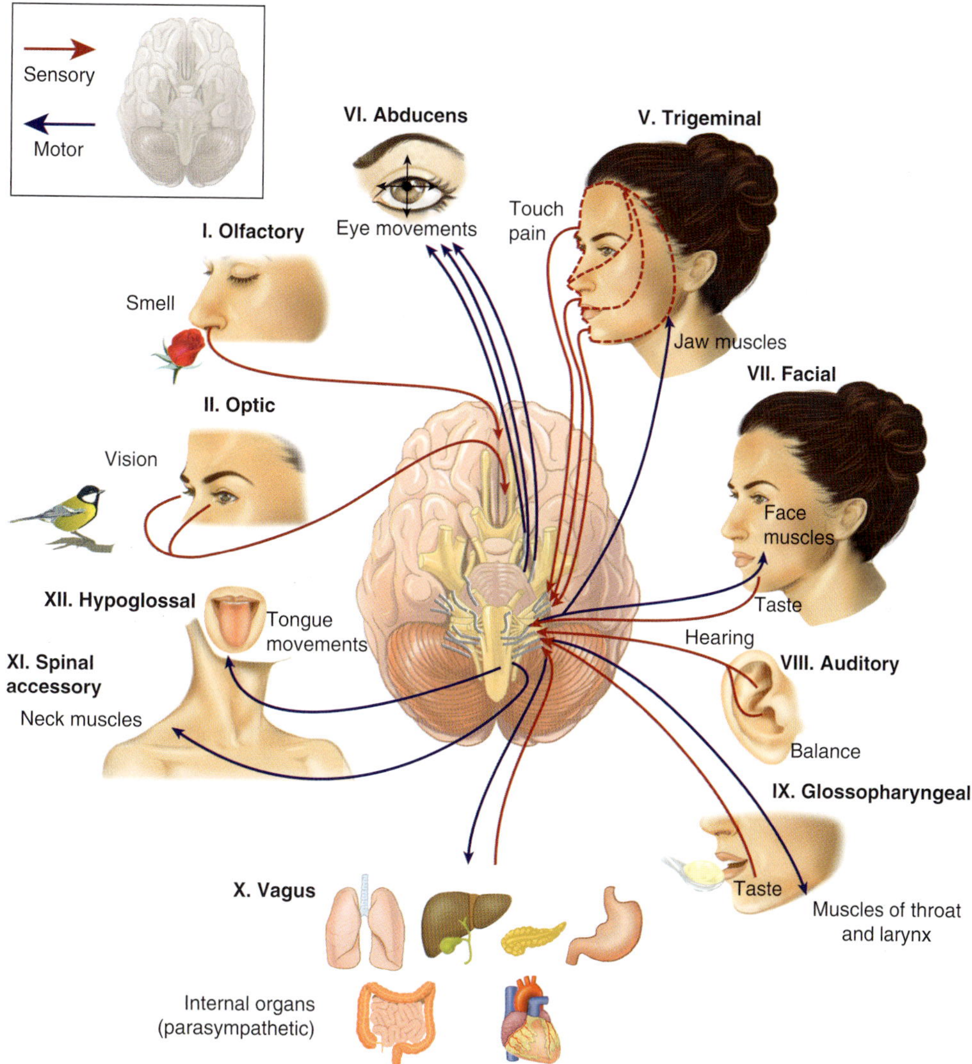

Figure 1.9 The cranial nerves. The twelve cranial nerves, as seen from below the brain, control the sensory and motor functions for the neck and the head and regulate activity of some of the organs.

communicating with one another via a bundle of neurons called the **corpus callosum**, which connects the two hemispheres. However, strange behaviors result when the corpus callosum is surgically severed and the two cerebral hemispheres are largely isolated from one another (Chapter 14).

In addition to "left" and "right," neuroscientists use other pairs of terms to locate structures within the brain and spinal cord (Figure 1.10). Comfort with these terms will help you picture locations of brain regions described throughout this book. The part of the brain closest to the nose is **anterior**, also called **rostral**, while the back of the brain is **posterior**, or **caudal**. For instance, in Figure 1.10A, area 1 is anterior to areas 2 and 3.

A

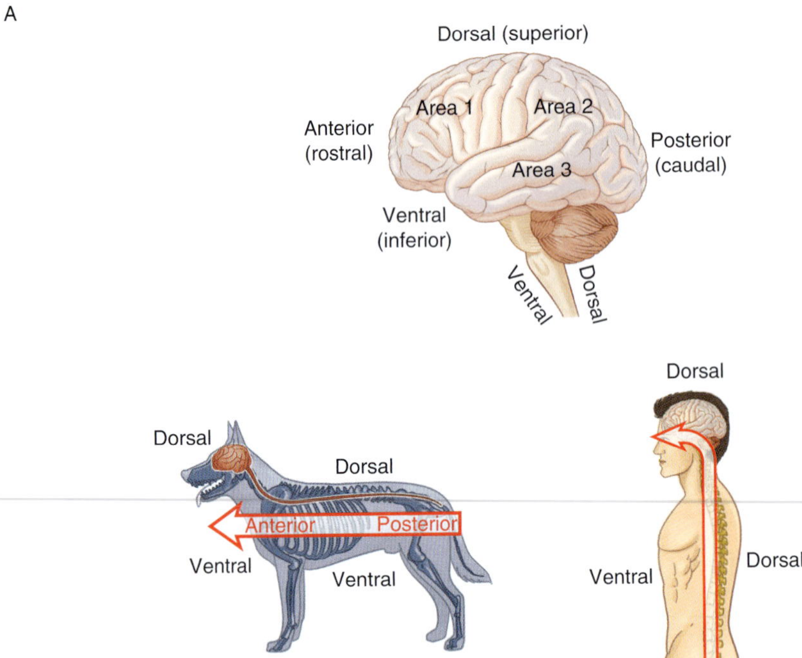

B

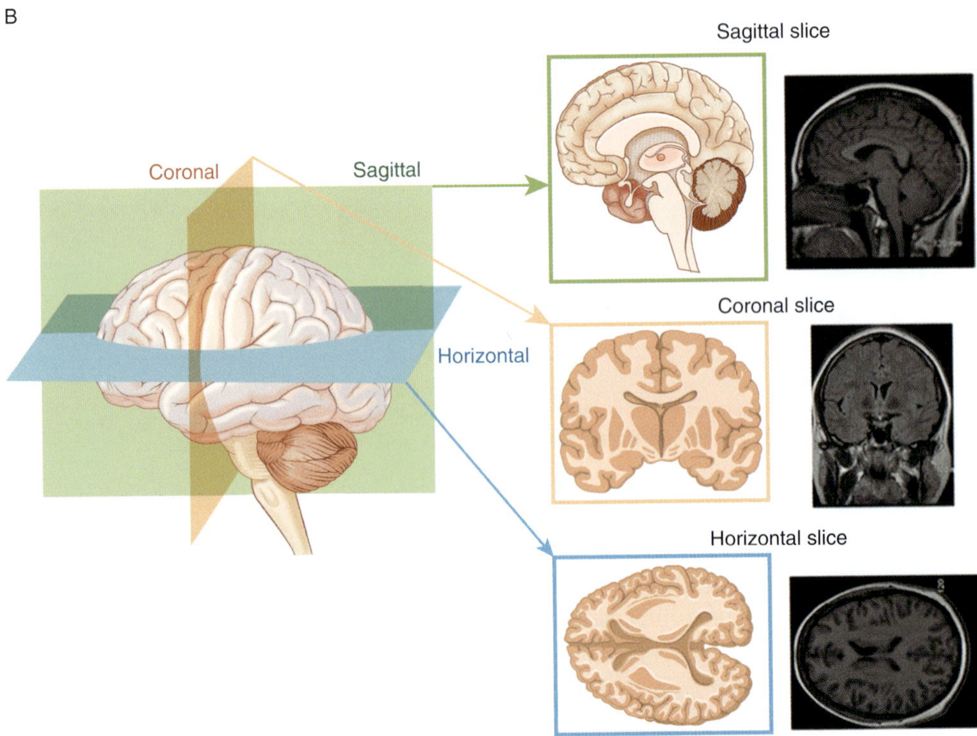

Figure 1.10 Neuroanatomical locations and planes. (A) Dorsal–ventral and anterior–posterior locations of the brain and spinal cord are shown for the human and the four-legged animal. Area 1 is anterior to areas 2 and 3. Area 3 is ventral to areas 1 and 2. (B) Brain imaging techniques, such as MRI shown here, display the brain in either the sagittal, the coronal, or the horizontal plane.
(MRI images from Kumar & Dharun, 2016, fig. 1.)

Dorsal and **ventral** refer to the top and bottom, respectively. (In Figure 1.10A, brain area 2 is dorsal to area 3.) Sometimes the terms **superior** and **inferior** are used for dorsal and ventral, respectively. When describing dorsal and ventral areas of the spinal cord, things get tricky. Imagine a four-legged animal: the dorsal part of the spinal cord (pointing upward) is the part closest to its back. The back is therefore dorsal to the stomach. In humans, we use this same convention – the part of the spinal cord closest to the back is dorsal, and the part closest to the stomach is ventral, as if we were walking on all fours (again, see Figure 1.10A).

Finally, **medial** is toward the midline of the brain. Imagine a string going from the nose to the back of the head, dividing the brain into two halves. The string runs along the midline of the brain. **Lateral** is away from the midline, that is, toward the ears.

Notice in Figure 1.10B that the brain can be viewed from different directions and angles, or two-dimensional planes. A **sagittal** slice shows the brain as if it were cut vertically to divide the left side from the right. A **coronal**, or **frontal**, slice divides the brain into front and back regions. A **horizontal** slice divides the brain into top and bottom regions. When looking at a horizontal slice of the brain using magnetic resonance imaging (MRI) or other imaging techniques, you can imagine looking down upon the brain from a position at the ceiling of the room.

Today, neuroscientists, neurologists, and neurosurgeons make great use of MRI and other imaging devices that show the precise location of tumors or other CNS abnormalities, revealing their anterior–posterior, dorsal–ventral, and medial–lateral positions in the brain. Some imaging techniques bring to light not only the location of brain structures, but also their levels of activity at particular moments in time (Box 1.2).

BOX 1.2 Looking into the Black Box of the Brain

Our story begins in the late nineteenth century, when a German physicist, Wilhelm Röntgen, used x-rays to visualize objects. In an early demonstration, Röntgen used x-rays to visualize the bones inside his wife's hands. The high-density bones selectively absorbed the rays, while the other parts of the hand allowed rays to pass through unobstructed. This produced an image with strong contrast between the bones and other hand tissue. However, x-rays passed through the brain failed to produce clear images; the brain lacks high-density structures (like bones) that absorb x-rays and produce high contrast images. With refinements to the procedure, x-rays eventually became useful for visualizing the brain's blood vessels and fluid-filled ventricles, but failed to reveal many other brain structures.

CT scans (computerized axial tomography; CAT scans) came about seventy years later. CT scans take thousands of x-ray measurements from different angles around the head of a subject who lies motionless inside a doughnut-shaped scanner (see Figure 1.11A). A sophisticated computer algorithm

BOX 1.2 (cont.)

is able to use these x-ray data to produce 3-D images of the brain in fine detail that is not otherwise possible with x-ray imaging (Figure 1.11B). CT scans are able to detect strokes, tumors, and other brain abnormalities, allowing doctors to identify their locations with high precision.

However, because CT scans use x-rays, which can damage healthy tissue, the search was on for a safer approach. The **PET** (positron-emission tomography) scan takes advantage of the fact that active brain areas use more glucose. Before a PET scan, the patient receives an intravenous injection of a short-acting radioactive material attached to a glucose molecule. This means that the brain areas that are most active, i.e., those that use the most glucose, emit the most radiation. Radiation sensors can collect information before, during, and after the subject experiences an emotion like fear or performs a mental task such as memory retrieval. By measuring the brain areas that use increased

A

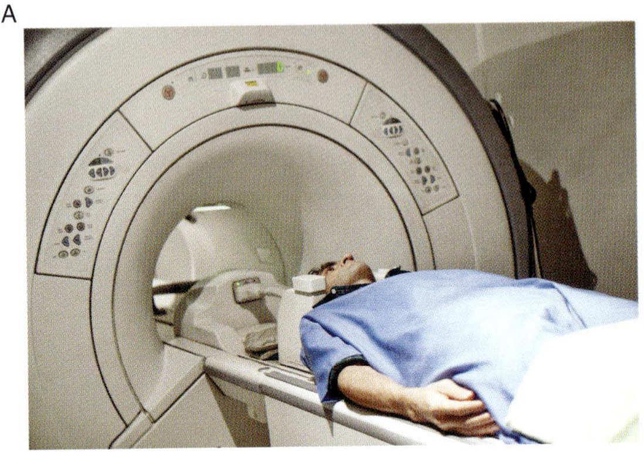

B

CT scans

Ventral section (Base of the brain)

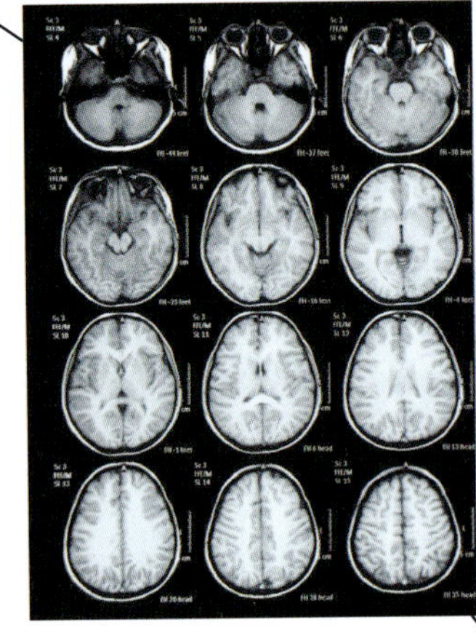

Dorsal section (Top of the brain)

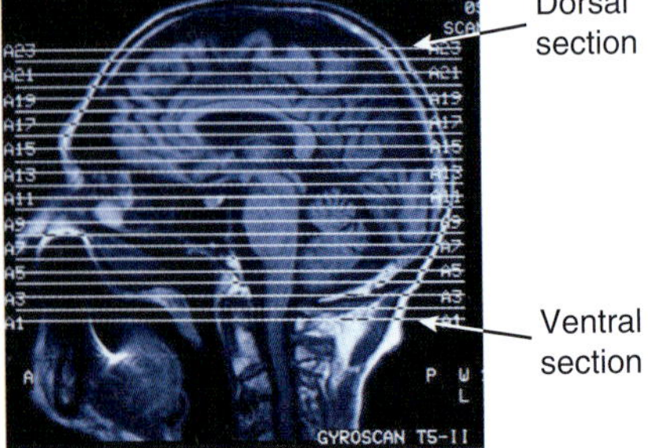

Dorsal section

Ventral section

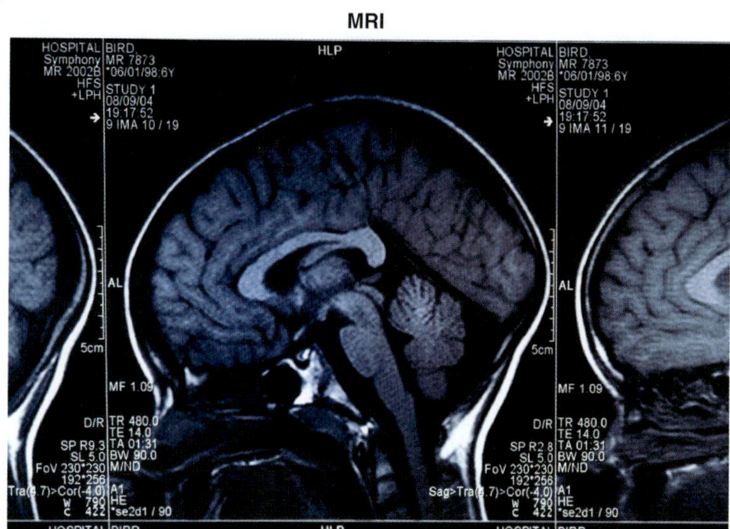

Figure 1.11 Imaging the brain. (A) Brain scans typically require the individual to place the head in a doughnut-shaped scanner while multiple brain images are collected. (© selimaksan /Getty Images.) (B) Computerized tomography (CT) scans at horizontal sections from the base (most ventral) to more superficial (dorsal) sections of the brain. (Left, © fmajor/Getty Images; right, © Steve Chenn/Getty Images.) (C) Magnetic resonance imaging (MRI) produces images that are more finely detailed than those generated by CT scans.
(© haydenbird/Getty Images.)

glucose during the task, we have moved from simply studying the structure of the brain to looking at what the brain is doing during mental activity.

MRI (magnetic resonance imaging) was introduced in the 1970s and 1980s. A real understanding of how it works requires details of physics outside the present scope. Here, we note simply that the head is exposed to a powerful magnetic field, which causes atoms within the various brain areas to face a particular direction (either toward or away from the magnetic field). The magnetic field is then briefly disrupted with a "pulse" of radiofrequency energy. A few atoms absorb the energy and flip to face the opposite direction. When the pulse is turned off, the atoms that had flipped return to their original direction, and in the process, they emit radiofrequency signals, which are detected by antennae circling the brain. A computer uses this information to construct brain images that are more detailed than the images produced by CT scans (Figure 1.11C).

fMRI (functional MRI) takes advantage of the fact that activated brain areas need an increase in oxygen (not just glucose). When a particular brain area becomes highly active, it receives blood that contains lots of oxygen. fMRI detects these high levels of oxygenated blood and produces what is called a blood oxygenation level-dependent, or **BOLD**, activation. The fMRI scanner detects BOLD activations (or reductions) in order to estimate the increases (or decreases) in activity within particular brain areas. Like the PET scan, fMRI examines the brain while the subject is engaged in mental activity. It has the additional advantage

BOX 1.2 (cont.)

of revealing changes in brain activity that occur in less than 1 second. PET can only reveal changes that occur over the course of minutes.

In the chapters to come, we'll look at brain imaging studies in individuals engaged in cognitive tasks. However, these human imaging techniques cannot reveal the activity of *individual neurons*, or examine changes in the brain *at very precise moments in time*. Other neuroscience techniques record the activity of individual neurons with millisecond precision (**single-neuron recording**), or allow experimenters to activate or inhibit specific neuronal pathways at precise moments in time (**optogenetics**). These techniques and many others use animal subjects to shed light on details of brain–mind and brain–behavior relationships.

1.3 AN INFORMATION HIGHWAY TO THE BRAIN: THE SPINAL CORD

Three meninges (membranes) surround and protect the spinal cord and the brain: the **pia mater**, **arachnoid mater**, and **dura mater**. The spinal cord and meninges lie inside a protective bony column of vertebrae. You can feel the top few vertebrae of the bony column as bumps in the back of your neck (Figure 1.12). The spinal cord runs from the lower back to the topmost vertebrae in the neck. It is the main highway for information traveling to and from the brain.

The spinal cord carries information in two directions, toward and away from the brain. Information traveling toward the brain (afferent information) includes input such as touch to the body surface, or information about the heart rate or expansion of the stomach when you're full. Sensory signals from the somatic nervous system and internal signals from the autonomic nervous system send afferent information, which ascends through the spinal cord to the brain. Information traveling away from the brain (efferent information) includes motor commands that leave the brain, descend the spinal cord, and exit toward muscles to control body movements.

In the central portion of the spinal cord lies a structure that resembles a gray butterfly (Figure 1.13). This butterfly-shaped gray matter contains the cell bodies of neurons that communicate with nearby body parts. For instance, the cell bodies of neurons that communicate with the arms reside in the spinal cord at approximately the level of the arms. Neurons at the top of the spinal cord communicate with the head; those at the bottom communicate with the legs and feet. In the area outside the spinal cord's butterfly-shaped gray matter lie large

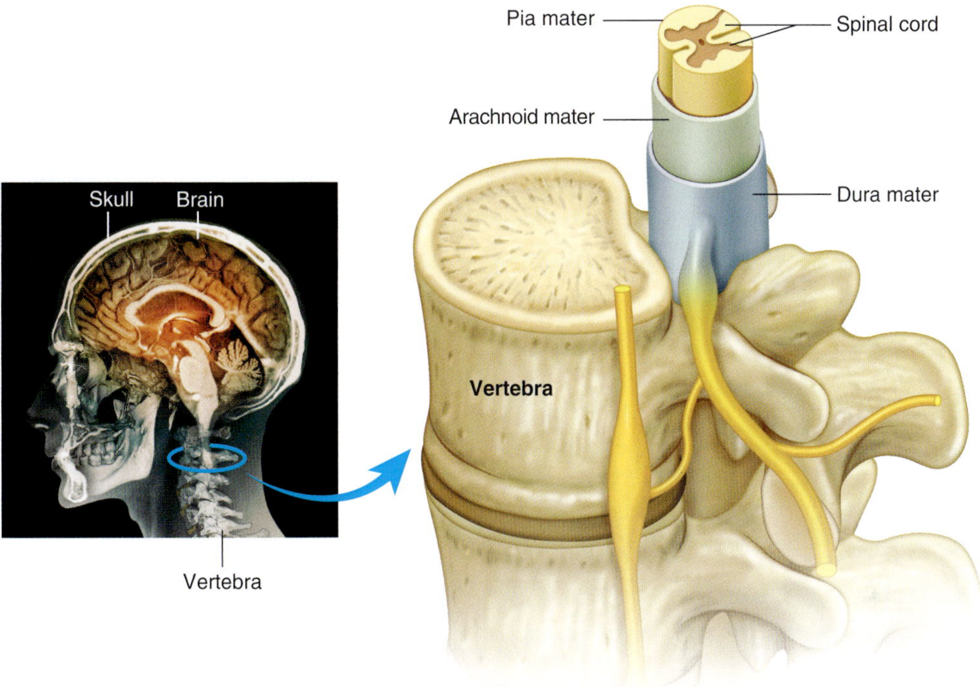

Figure 1.12 **Meninges, skull, and vertebrae protect the brain and spinal cord**. The spinal cord is surrounded by the three meninges (pia, arachnoid, and dura mater), which are protected by the vertebrae. The brain is surrounded by the same three meninges (not shown here) and protected by the skull.
(© ZEPHYR/SCIENCE PHOTO LIBRARY/Getty Images.)

columns of axon bundles covered in white myelin. These axon bundles ascend toward the brain (shown in red) or descend from the brain (shown in blue).

In the center of the butterfly, a small canal runs the length of the spinal cord and connects to the brain's fluid-filled chambers called **ventricles** (Figure 1.14). The ventricles and the spinal cord's canal (the **central canal**) contain cerebrospinal fluid, which helps keep the brain buoyant, acts as a cushion from mechanical damage, assists in maintaining chemical stability, and carries nutrients to the brain. There are four ventricles: the two **lateral ventricles** (one on the left and one on the right side of the brain); the **third ventricle**; and the **fourth ventricle**. The **cerebral aqueduct** is a fluid-filled channel that connects the third and fourth ventricles. The cerebrospinal fluid is produced in a group of cells located within each of the four ventricles called the **choroid plexus**.

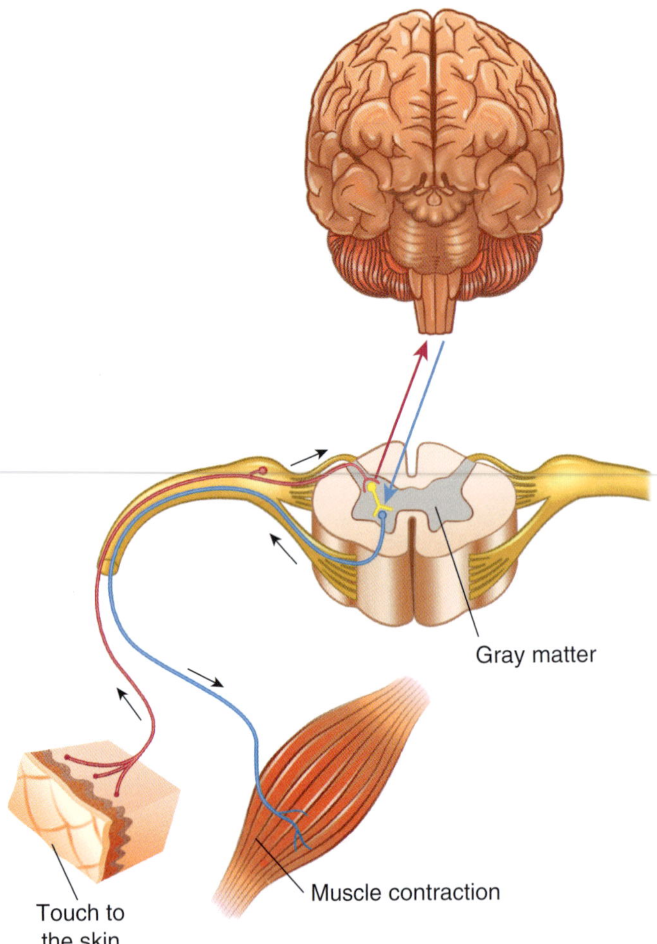

Figure 1.13 **Inputs and outputs to and from the spinal cord**. Tactile information (shown in red) reaches the butterfly-shaped gray matter of the spinal cord, which in turn sends this information to the brain. The brain sends motor commands to the spinal cord (blue), and neurons in the spinal cord communicate with muscles.

KEY CONCEPTS

- **The central nervous system (CNS) includes the brain and the spinal cord. The peripheral nervous system (PNS) includes nerves (bundles of axons) that allow the brain and spinal cord to communicate with the skin, muscles, and organs of the body.**
- **The PNS has a somatic and an autonomic division. The somatic division carries information between the CNS and the body parts. The autonomic division allows the CNS to communicate with the body organs.**
- **The spinal cord brings information about the environment to the brain, and carries signals from the brain out toward the muscles and organs of the body.**
- **Each level of the spinal cord receives and sends information from portions of the body located at approximately that same level. For**

example, the upper portions of the spinal cord communicate with the arms and fingers, whereas the lower portions communicate with the legs and feet.

TEST YOURSELF

1. Distinguish the functions of the somatic and autonomic nervous system.
2. What are the two divisions of the autonomic nervous system? Describe their functions.
3. How do cranial nerves differ from other PNS nerves?
4. What do we find inside the "gray butterfly" region of the spinal cord?

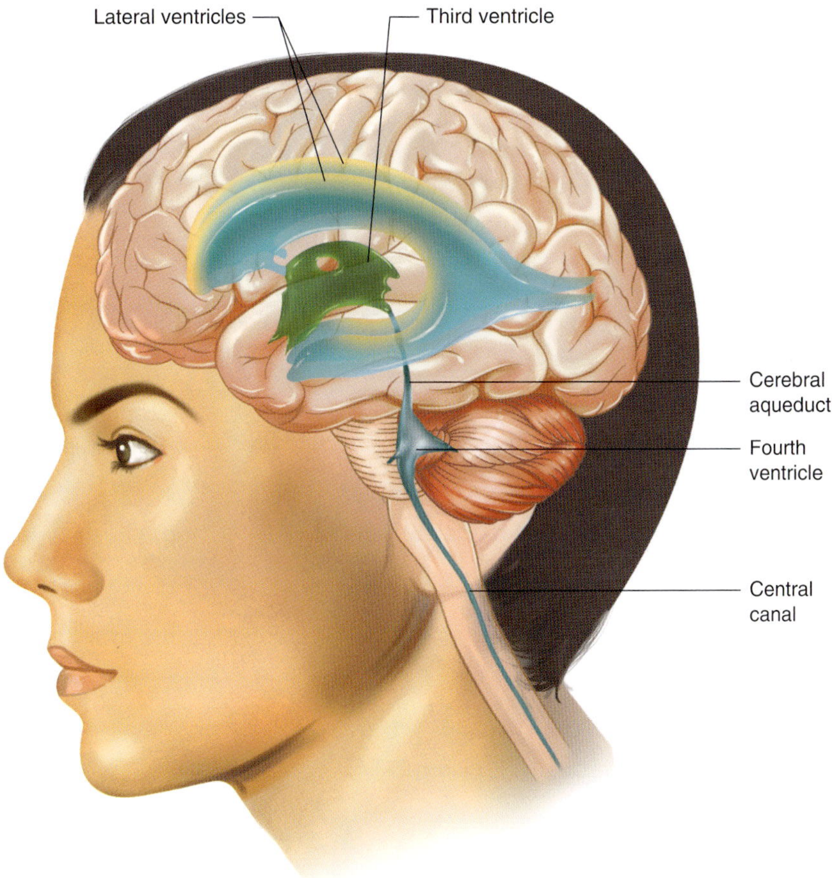

Figure 1.14 **The central canal of the spinal cord and the four ventricles of the brain**. Cerebrospinal fluid fills the ventricles, cerebral aqueduct, and central canal.

1.4 CRITICAL FUNCTIONS IN THE BASEMENT OF THE BRAIN: THE BRAINSTEM

As we emerge from the top of the spinal cord (within the neck) and enter the brain, we depart from the butterfly-shaped organization of the spinal cord, with its white columns of myelinated axon bundles. The first area of the brain that we reach is the **brainstem**, comprised of several key structures (Figure 1.15). These areas carry out critical functions, including some that are necessary for life. So long as the brainstem is functioning and connected to the rest of the body, an individual can often survive damage to other brain regions (with some outside assistance such as feeding). On the other hand, damage to the brainstem from trauma (e.g., car accident, gunshot) or from disease frequently results in death.

The brainstem also contains small clusters of neurons that regulate sleep and arousal (Chapter 5). Some of these brainstem neurons release

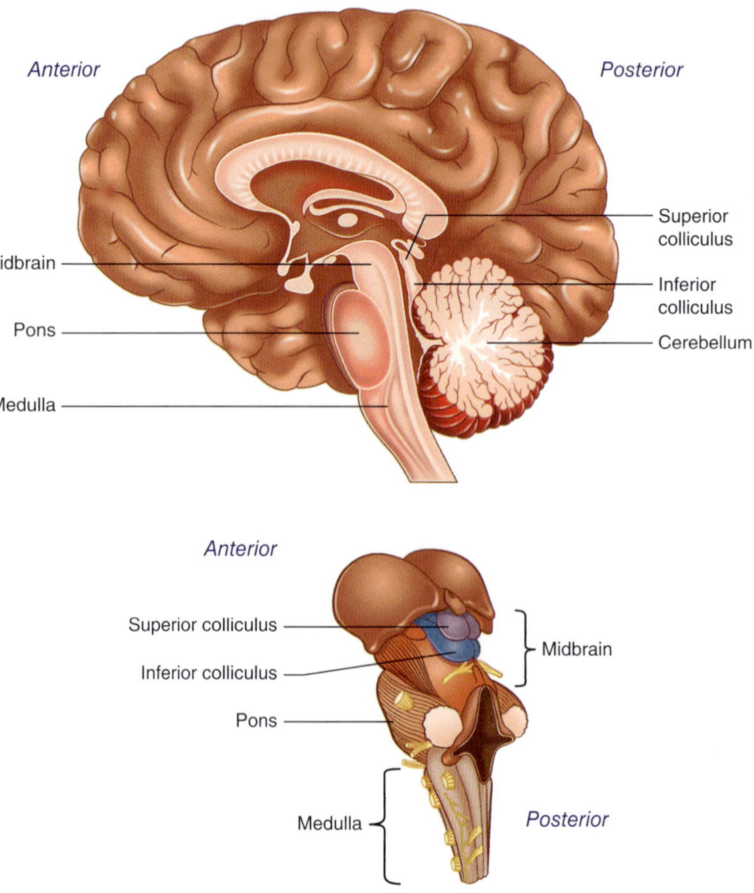

Figure 1.15 The brainstem. The four major brainstem structures – the medulla, pons, cerebellum, and midbrain – carry out a number of critical brain functions.

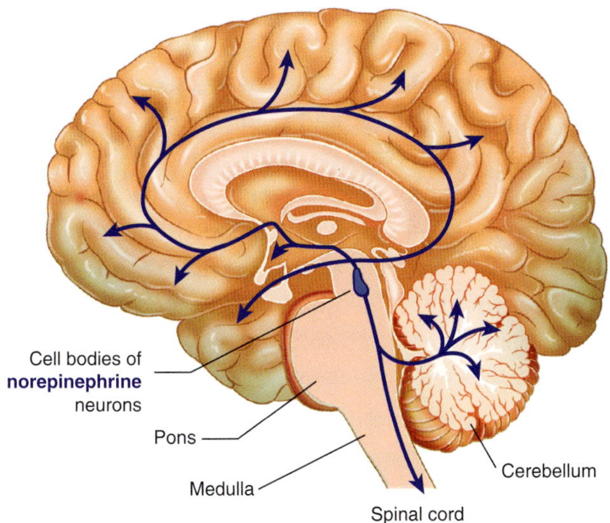

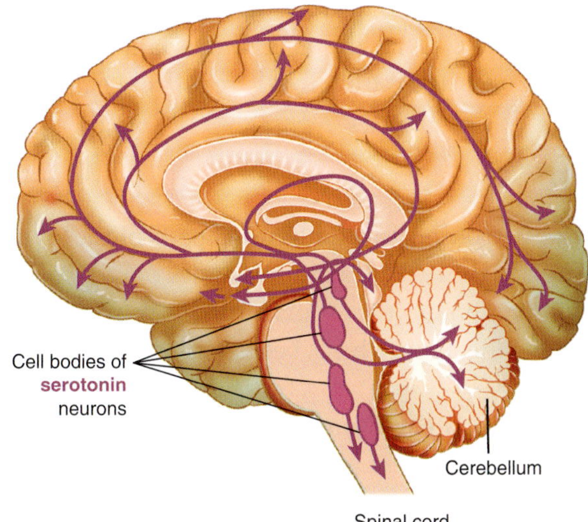

Figure 1.16 Brainstem nuclei regulating sleep and arousal. The brainstem contains clusters of norepinephrine and serotonin cell bodies that release their neurotransmitter widely throughout the brain and spinal cord.

the neurotransmitters norepinephrine or serotonin through axons that project widely throughout the brain (Figure 1.16).

Before we examine each major brainstem structure, it is worth noting that the slithering snake and eel rely largely upon the brainstem, which allows them to perform simple movements. More complex behavior came with the evolution of brain regions anterior (and dorsal) to the brainstem, that is, the **forebrain**. It is the forebrain, and especially the cortex, that allows us to reflect upon our life experiences, to communicate with one another, and to carry out other higher cognitive functions (Chapter 14). However, as the forebrain evolved, brainstem structures were maintained. Let's examine the four key structures of the brainstem: the medulla, pons, cerebellum, and midbrain (again, see Figure 1.15).

1.4.1 Medulla

Above the spinal cord is the **medulla**, which governs essential physiological processes such as respiration, sleep, and regulation of blood pressure and heart rate. The medulla also contains the cell bodies of most of the cranial nerves controlling sensation and movement of the head and neck. In addition, axons carrying motor commands pass through the medulla on their way to the spinal cord, and axons carrying sensory information from the periphery ascend the medulla on their way to sensory areas of the forebrain.

1.4.2 Pons

The **pons** appears as a swelling in the brainstem. This bulge is attributable to the huge number of axon bundles that provide the intimate connection between the pons and the cerebellum, a key structure for motor control described below. The pons also contains neurons that are important in sleep and waking states. Also, like the medulla, the pons is important in regulating the physiology of the body, such as controlling respiration and heart rate.

1.4.3 Cerebellum

The **cerebellum** remains one of the least understood parts of the brain. It lies behind the pons. Although the cerebellum occupies only 10 percent of the volume of the human brain, it is estimated to contain more neurons than the entire rest of the brain! This is because most of its neurons are small and tightly packed.

The cerebellum does not initiate movements, but it is vital for carrying them out accurately and smoothly. Damage to this area often leads to uncoordinated body movements. One symptom of cerebellar damage is difficulty in smoothly bringing the finger to touch the nose. With cerebellar damage, a person may jerk the finger rapidly toward the nose, move it too far to the left, then correct by moving to the right, and so on, until finally hitting the nose. Another sign of cerebellar damage is difficulty walking without losing one's balance.

In addition to its role in the coordination and accuracy of body movements, the cerebellum is important for motor learning, particularly in learning to predict the consequences of a movement (Ito, 2008). Imagine, for instance, that before you throw a ball your brain is preparing certain shoulder, arm, and hand movements that will allow you to toss the ball to a desired location. The cerebellum receives information about these prepared movements and calculates where the ball is likely to land. As you gain more experience throwing the ball and observing the consequences (where the ball landed), your cerebellum better anticipates the result of your intended bodily movements. If the cerebellum predicts that the ball will miss its target, it signals this prediction to other brain regions, which alter the movement plan (such as the amount of force to use in your forward arm movement) even before you have released the ball. Imagine the value of this for a basketball player. We will examine the role of the cerebellum in movement in Chapter 4, and its role in learning in Chapter 9.

1.4.4 Midbrain

The **midbrain**, or **mesencephalon**, lies above the pons (again, see Figure 1.15). Particularly important are the two clusters of neurons that release the neurotransmitter dopamine to wide areas of the forebrain. One of these clusters is the **substantia nigra**, which plays an important role in movement. The other cluster of midbrain dopamine neurons is in the **ventral tegmental area**, implicated in reinforcement and addiction. Midbrain dopamine neurons are activated by rewards such as food, sex, money, even a smile. The dopamine response is especially strong when the reward is unexpected. The neurons release dopamine to the basal ganglia and the frontal cortex (both described below). The distinction between the roles of the substantia nigra (motoric) and ventral tegmental area (reinforcement) is not black and white, for both structures contribute to aspects of movement and to reward processes. In later chapters, we'll examine dopamine's role in movement (Chapter 4), and in addiction (Chapter 11). We'll also ask how the death of dopamine neurons in Parkinson's disease disrupts aspects of normal movement (Chapter 13).

Another part of the midbrain is comprised of two pairs of small bumps – the **inferior colliculi** and **superior colliculi** (again, see Figure 1.15). (Colliculi is plural for colliculus; for instance, one may speak of the left inferior colliculus, or the left and right inferior colliculi.) The inferior and superior colliculi are important in orienting and attending to significant auditory and visual events, respectively. For instance, a loud and bright firecracker would activate the inferior and superior colliculi, rapidly causing you to turn your head in its direction, and sending signals to the cerebral cortex to inform it about the occurrence of the potentially important event.

KEY CONCEPTS

- **The brainstem consists of four major structures: the medulla, pons, cerebellum, and midbrain.**
- **The medulla and pons contribute to processes critical for maintaining life (respiration, cardiovascular control), sleep and arousal, and basic sensory and motor responses.**

- The cerebellum is critical for bodily balance, and for smooth and accurate limb movements.
- The midbrain contains dopamine neurons that play a role both in bodily movement and in brain responses to rewarding stimuli.

TEST YOURSELF

1. In what life-sustaining functions is the medulla involved?
2. Why might medulla damage produce problems in generating body movements and in body sensations?
3. Disruption of the ______ often produces serious problems with movement coordination.
4. The ______ contains neurons whose activity is implicated in addiction.

1.5 A GATEWAY TO THE CORTEX AND A CENTER FOR MOTIVATION: THE DIENCEPHALON

Just above the brainstem lies the **diencephalon**, composed of a number of structures (Figure 1.17). Of particular importance is the **thalamus**,

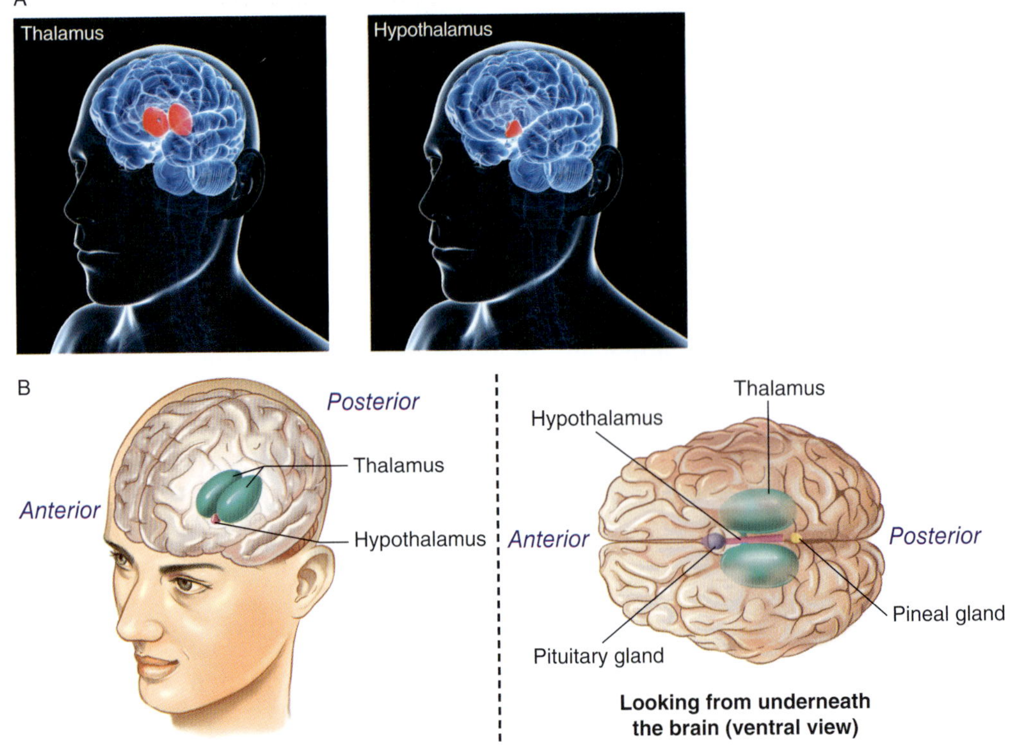

Figure 1.17 The diencephalon. The diencephalon includes two key structures, the thalamus and the hypothalamus, as well as the pituitary and pineal glands.
(© SCIEPRO/Getty Images.)

which transmits sensory information to the cortex. The **hypothalamus** (along with the associated **pituitary gland**) is important in motivation. In addition, the **pineal gland** plays a role in sleep regulation.

1.5.1 Thalamus

In humans, the thalamus is approximately the size of a walnut shell. It acts as a relay for visual, auditory, and all other kinds of sensory information (except for smell) on their way to the cerebral cortex. Damage to the thalamus isolates the cortex from much of the communication it normally receives from the outside world.

The thalamus is made up of about thirty bilaterally symmetrical clusters of neurons (nuclei) on both the left and right sides of the midline of the brain (Figure 1.18). Each of the nuclei transmits a distinct kind of information. For instance, one of the bilateral nuclei receives visual information, another receives auditory, and so on. The nuclei then send outputs directly to the appropriate sensory areas of the cortex.

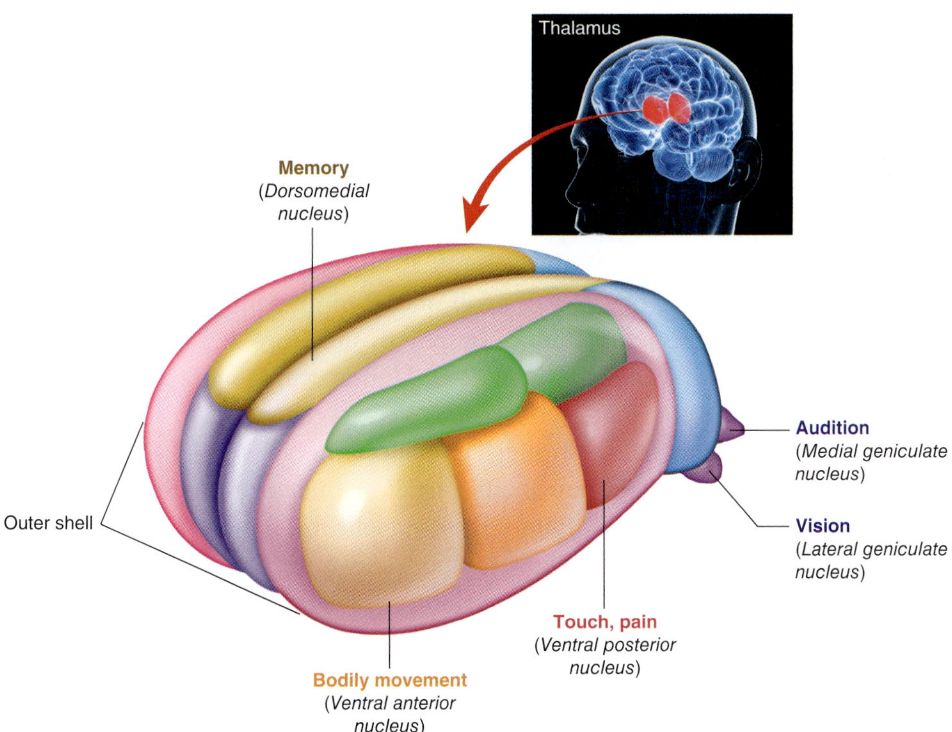

Figure 1.18 The thalamus. The thalamus is made of thirty nuclei, each of which transmits a specific kind of cognitive (e.g., memory-related), sensory, or motor information to the cortex. The illustration highlights the functions of a few of these nuclei. (Inset, © SCIEPRO/Getty Images.)

One can think of the thalamus as a kind of "attentional gatekeeper," permitting some sensory information to ascend to the cortex while filtering out other information. Later in this chapter, we'll see that the cerebral cortex contains six layers of cells. One of the six cortical layers specifically contains neurons that provide feedback to the thalamus. This allows sensory cortical areas, such as parts of the visual cortex, to instruct the thalamus to send either more or less of the information currently reaching the cortex. For instance, when you reach for an apple from the branch of a tree, the visual cortex is receiving information about the apple, and may send feedback to the visual nucleus of the thalamus, instructing it to send more information about that shiny, red object.

In addition to relaying sensory information to the cortex, the thalamus transmits information necessary for body movements to brain areas involved in motor planning. For example, as your brain is calculating how to move your arm to lift a cup, motor areas of the cortex send information about the motor plan to other movement-related brain areas, such as the cerebellum and basal ganglia (described below), which in turn send information to the thalamus. The thalamus finally sends this motor information back to motor areas of the cortex, allowing a refinement of the intended movement plan. Given its key role in transmitting sensory information, regulating attention, and processing movement commands, it may not be a surprise to learn that damage to the thalamus can lead to loss of awareness.

1.5.2 Hypothalamus

The hypothalamus lies just below and slightly anterior to the thalamus (Figure 1.19). Like the thalamus, it is bilaterally symmetrical and composed of dozens of separate small nuclei. In humans, the hypothalamus is only the size of an almond. Despite its small size, it plays a key role in motivated behaviors that include sex, eating, thirst, sleep, and body temperature maintenance.

The hypothalamus strongly influences the activity of the **pituitary gland** situated just below it, and therefore influences the release of pituitary hormones. The pituitary is only about the size of a pea in humans. Like other glands, it releases hormones into the bloodstream. However, the pituitary is considered the master gland because the hormones released by the pituitary reach and influence activity of many other glands of the body, including the ovaries and testes (important in sexual behavior) and the adrenal gland (important in stress responses).

For instance, during stressful situations, when the brain recognizes a threat, the hypothalamus signals the pituitary gland to release pituitary

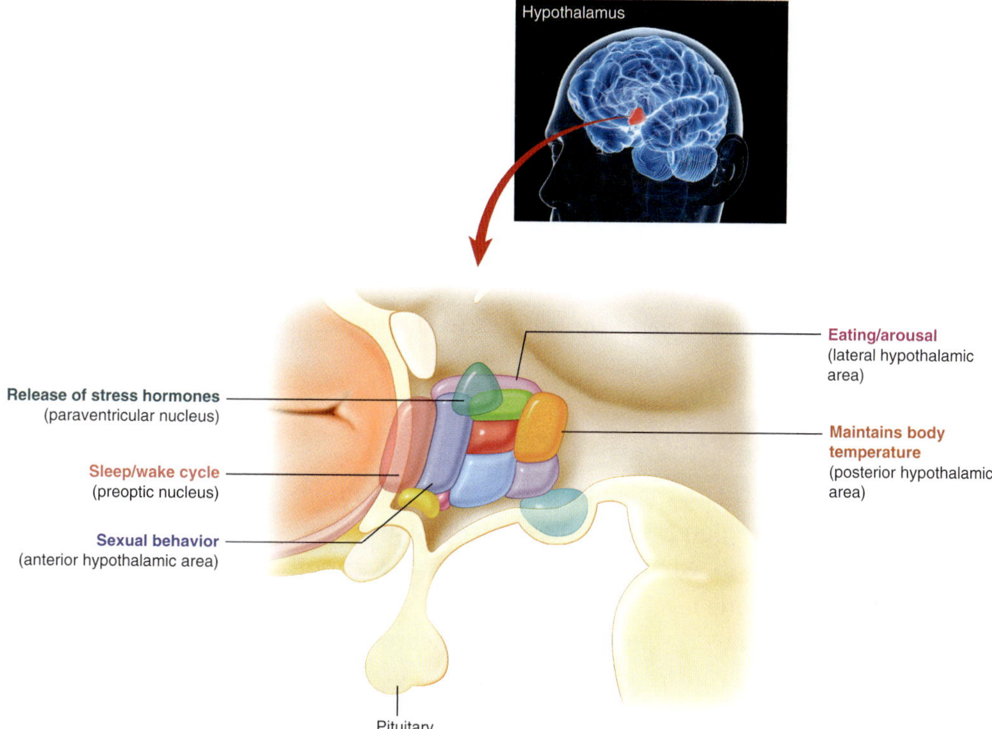

Figure 1.19 Nuclei of the hypothalamus. Specific nuclei of the hypothalamus contribute to distinct motivational states such as sleep, eating, and sex.
(Inset, © SCIEPRO/Getty Images.)

hormones, which travel through the bloodstream and cause the adrenal glands to release stress hormones. The adrenal hormones prepare both the brain and the periphery of the body to respond to the perceived threat. Later chapters will examine how the hypothalamus and pituitary hormone release contribute to eating, sex, and stress.

1.5.3 Pineal Gland

The tiny pineal gland is located near the center of the brain, tucked in a groove where the left and right thalamus come together (again, see Figure 1.17). In the introduction to this chapter, we spoke of Descartes' view that the pineal gland permitted communication between the immaterial mind and the physical brain. While there is no evidence to suggest such a role, the pineal gland is known to release melatonin, a hormone important in regulating sleep and wakefulness (Chapter 5).

KEY CONCEPTS

- **The thalamus coordinates information flowing to and from the cerebral cortex.**
- **The hypothalamus regulates sex, eating, thirst, sleep, and body temperature, as well as other motivated behaviors. In addition, the hypothalamus works closely with the pituitary, the master gland that controls many other glands throughout the body via release of hormones into the bloodstream.**
- **The pineal gland contributes to the regulation of sleep and wakefulness.**

TEST YOURSELF

1. **Why is the thalamus critical to consciousness of the external world? This region is sometimes described as a "gatekeeper." In what sense?**
2. **Through what mechanism does the hypothalamus influence stress hormone levels?**
3. **The tiny _____ gland releases a neurochemical called melatonin which plays a role in _____.**

1.6 VOLUNTARY MOVEMENT, EMOTION, AND MEMORY: THE BASAL GANGLIA AND THE LIMBIC SYSTEM

There are many nuclei and neural pathways in the area between the diencephalon and the cerebral cortex at the outer surface of the brain. Here, we limit our discussion to some of the major structures we will encounter later in this book. We divide them into two groups: the basal ganglia and portions of the limbic system.

1.6.1 Basal Ganglia

The **basal ganglia** are a group of interconnected forebrain structures critical for voluntary movements such as opening a door, reaching for a cup, and so on. Key regions within the basal ganglia are the striatum (caudate and putamen) and globus pallidus (Figure 1.20). Midbrain dopamine neurons within the substantia nigra release dopamine to the striatum, and the death of these **nigrostriatal** dopamine neurons leads to the movement problems associated with Parkinson's disease (Chapter 13).

The basal ganglia are also important for learning new behaviors, especially behaviors that are reinforced by rewards such as food, sex, money, and social approval (Chapter 11). Recall that dopamine neurons with cell

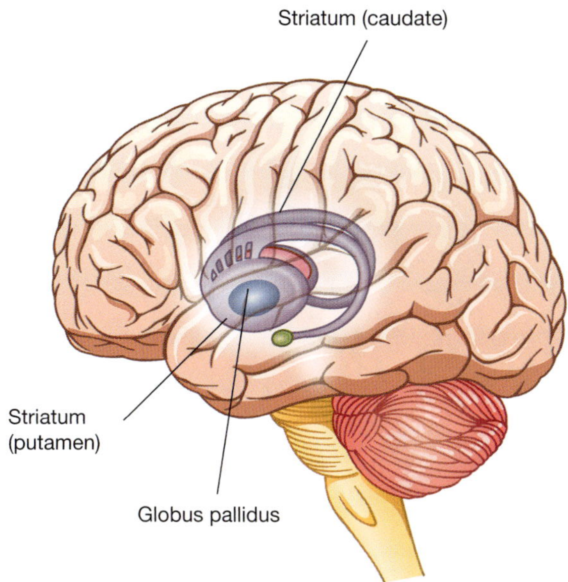

Figure 1.20 The basal ganglia. The basal ganglia are critical for voluntary movement and motor learning. Key basal ganglia structures are the striatum (comprised of the putamen and caudate) and the globus pallidus.

bodies in the midbrain play a role in drug addiction. This is due largely to their release of dopamine within the basal ganglia.

1.6.2 Limbic System

The **limbic system** is a collection of brain structures significantly involved in emotion and memory. Definitions vary as to precisely which brain structures form part of the limbic system. Here, we focus on two important limbic structures: the amygdala and hippocampus. The amygdala lies at the anterior tip of the hippocampus (Figure 1.21).

When you encounter a threatening bear, or walk through a deserted alley late at night, your amygdala will likely become activated. The **amygdala** recognizes the threatening situation and activates the sympathetic nervous system as well as brain areas that trigger defensive responses to danger (e.g., tensing of muscles, increased vigilance). A woman who suffered bilateral damage to the amygdala would eagerly pick up wild snakes slithering in the grass, and reported no fear from this or from other normally frightening events (Feinstein, Adolphs, Damasio, & Tranel, 2011). A key memory function of the amygdala is to form associations between painful or threatening stimuli (snakes, painful dental procedures) and the environmental stimuli that predict them (the slithering sound of the snake, the buzz of the dentist's drill).

The **hippocampus** is a key brain structure for storing and recalling episodic memories (memories of personal experiences). Individuals with bilateral damage to the hippocampus are often unable to remember someone they met only a few minutes ago. While some hippocampal regions play a

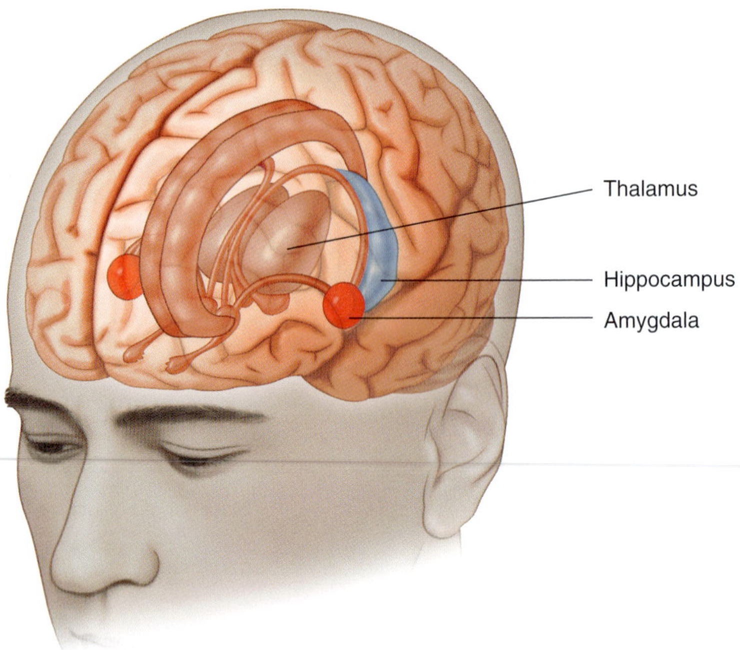

Figure 1.21 **The amygdala and the hippocampus are key structures in the limbic system**. The thalamus is shown here only as a point of reference.

key role in memory, other (anterior) parts of the hippocampus are implicated in emotional regulation. Anatomical changes in the anterior hippocampus are often seen in those suffering major depression (Chapter 13).

KEY CONCEPTS

- **The basal ganglia are important in a variety of motor functions, and diseases of the basal ganglia result in movement disorders.**
- **Dopamine release in the basal ganglia plays a role in natural reward processes, and the addictive properties of drugs of abuse.**
- **Two of the major subcortical limbic structures are the amygdala and hippocampus. Both of these structures play a role in aspects of memory and emotion.**

TEST YOURSELF

1. **Describe some ways your life would be altered if you had impairment of the basal ganglia.**
2. **Describe some ways your life would be altered if you had no amygdala.**
3. **Describe some ways your life would be altered if you had no hippocampus.**

1.7 SENSORY, MOTOR, AND HIGHER COGNITIVE PROCESSES: THE CEREBRAL CORTEX

Cortex loosely translates from the Latin, as cover or shell. Here, it refers to the thin cover overlying the rest of the forebrain (Figure 1.22). As we discussed earlier in the chapter, the cerebral cortex carries out complex cognitive processes that define the human species. The first evidence for the beginning of a cortex comes from birds and amphibians. All mammals have a cortex. The cortical surface is comprised of gray matter. It has a gray appearance because of the density of neuronal cell bodies there (again, see Figure 1.6A). The area underlying the cortex contains white matter. As we saw earlier, the whitish appearance is due to the myelin covering the bundles of axons traveling to and from the cortex.

The human cortex has a crumpled look with hills (**gyri**) and valleys/grooves (**sulci**) throughout (again, see Figure 1.22). (Gyri and sulci are the plural of **gyrus** and **sulcus**, respectively.) Flattened out, the cortex would cover the size of the front page of a daily newspaper. A human skull that could contain a flattened out form of the cortex would be so large that we would be unable to navigate about our environment without tipping over! Crumpling allows the cortex to fit snugly inside our heads. The cortex of more primitive animals, like mice and rats, is smooth with no sulci or gyri.

A deep canyon called the **longitudinal fissure** runs along the midline from the front to the back of the forebrain and separates the brain into two halves referred to as the left and right hemispheres (Figure 1.23). Each hemisphere mainly controls the opposite (contralateral) side of the body. For instance, the left hemisphere of the cortex controls movement of, and receives touch information from, the right side of the body. Each of the two hemispheres is further divided into four sections or lobes: occip-

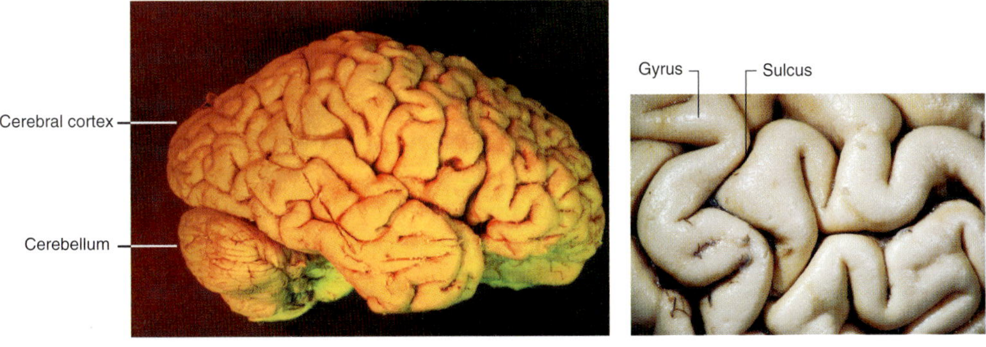

Figure 1.22 The cerebral cortex. The crumpled appearance of the cerebral cortex comes from its gyri (hills) and sulci (valleys).
(Left, @ Dr. Colin Chumbley/Getty Images; right, © Geoff Tompkinson/Getty Images.)

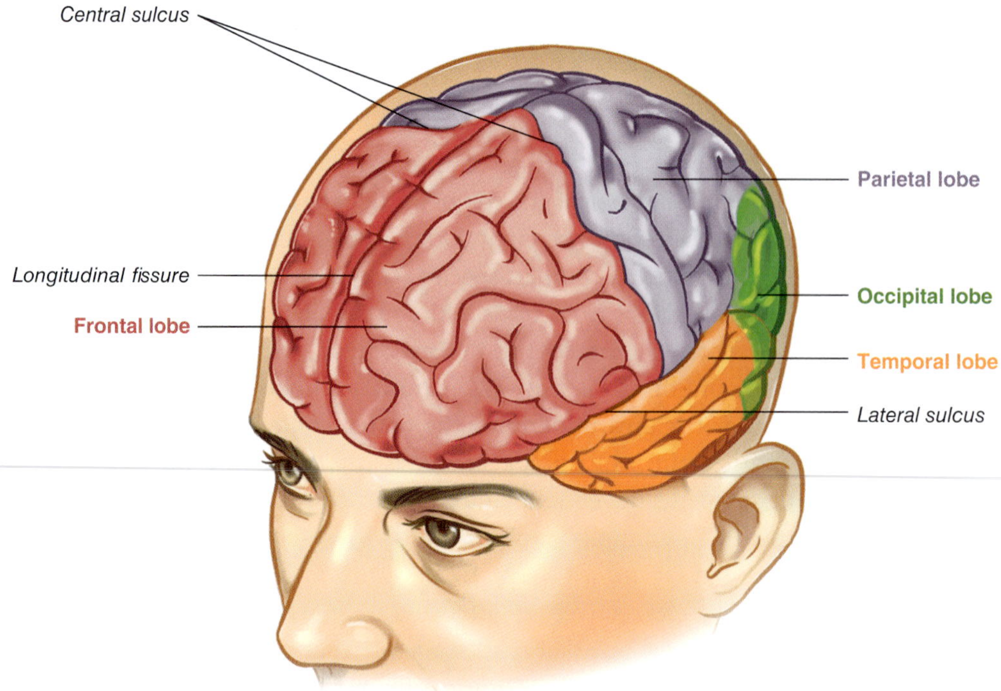

Figure 1.23 The four lobes of the brain. Notice that the central sulcus divides the frontal lobe from the parietal lobe. The longitudinal fissure separates the left and right cerebral hemispheres.

ital, parietal, temporal, and frontal. Take note of the **central sulcus** and **lateral sulcus** because they separate and define three of the lobes.

The human cortex is a mere 4 millimeters thick in most places (about the width of a pencil eraser) but it contains 20 billion neurons. The 4 millimeters are divided into six horizontal **cortical layers** of cells. Notice in Figure 1.24 that layer I contains almost no cell bodies, but mostly dendrites from neurons with cell bodies in lower layers. Also notice that the largest neurons are in layer V. We will consider the functions associated with some of these cortical layers when we examine the visual cortex in Chapter 3.

It may be an oversimplification to say that the cortex is the seat of complex cognition, for the cortex interacts with a number of subcortical areas (including the hippocampus, basal ganglia, and cerebellum) to think about past events and future plans, and to learn complex behaviors (playing the piano or chess, driving a motorcycle). However, without the cortex we would no longer have the capacity to reason logically, to express ourselves in words, to reflect upon our experiences. Our closest neighbor in the animal kingdom is the chimpanzee. With the chimp and human cortex removed, their brains would be very similar. It is our cortex that most strongly differentiates us from other animals (and makes humans better chess players than chimps).

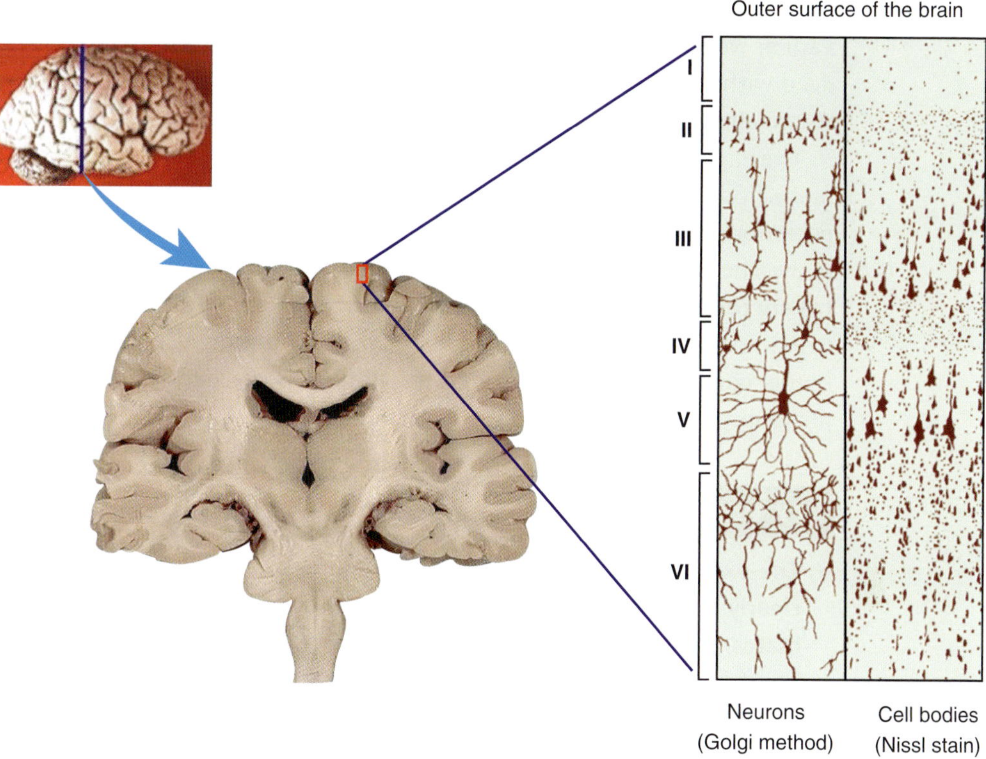

Figure 1.24 Six layers of the cerebral cortex. Neurons in layers I–VI are visualized with a technique that stains entire neurons (dendrites, cell body, and axon, Golgi method) and one that stains only cell bodies (Nissl stain). Notice that the largest neurons in the cortex are found in layer V.
(Left, John Beal, LSU Health Sciences Center.)

To provide a brief taste of what's to come in the remainder of the book, let's take a look at some basic functions of the four lobes (again, see Figure 1.23). The function of the **occipital lobe** is the simplest to describe because it is solely involved in vision. However, its anatomical boundary is the most difficult to specify since there is no clear delineation of where it ends and where the temporal and parietal lobes begin.

The **parietal lobe** is separated from the frontal lobe by the central sulcus. The area of the parietal lobe just posterior to the central sulcus is the primary site for the sensation of touch. The parietal lobe localizes objects in the environment, and assists in guiding movements of the body toward those points (Rizzolatti & Luppino, 2001). For instance, particular neurons in the parietal lobe are activated when you prepare the shape of your hand to grasp the handle of a coffee cup. Such neurons ensure that the position of your fingers is appropriate to the size and shape of the object you're about to handle, and that your arm moves along the proper path to grasp the object (Chapter 4).

The **temporal lobe** is separated from the frontal and parietal lobes by the lateral sulcus. Temporal lobe functions include hearing (audition), speech and language, emotion, memory, and complex aspects of vision. Earlier, we discussed the hippocampus and amygdala, both of which lie deep within **subcortical** areas of the temporal lobe, that is to say, below the cerebral cortex.

The expansion of the **frontal lobe** most strongly separates the human brain from those of other animals. The primary motor cortex and other posterior areas of the frontal cortex are dedicated to movement of the body. The most anterior parts of the frontal lobe, including the **prefrontal cortex**, are important in cognitive functions including attention and working memory (Chapter 10), behavioral inhibition (Chapter 4), and higher cognitive functions such as the ability to consider what other people might be thinking or feeling (Chapter 14).

KEY CONCEPTS

- **The explosive expansion of the frontal lobes in humans is what most clearly differentiates us from other animals, including non-human primates, our closest relatives in the animal kingdom.**
- **The human cortex contains many gyri and sulci that allow an enormous amount of brain tissue to fit within the skull.**
- **The cortex is separated into four *lobes* (occipital, parietal, temporal, and frontal), with distinct (but interacting) sensory, motor, and cognitive functions.**

TEST YOURSELF

1. **What advantages do the gyri and sulci of the cortex provide?**
2. **What is a major function of each of the four cortical lobes?**

1.8 The Big Picture

We began this chapter by considering the dualist perspective that mental life exists independently of the brain. This view runs into the following paradox: How can a non-physical mind exert effects on a physical brain and body? On the other hand, the monist view that mental life arises from brain activity raises conceptual challenges as well. For instance, how is it possible that neuronal activity gives rise to a perception, a thought, or a desire?

No matter how long you stare into a microscope and look at neurons taken from the occipital lobe, you will see nothing to suggest that their activities should give rise to visual experience. Contrast this with the heart. One could examine the movement of its muscles and the flow of blood through its chambers, and immediately perceive that blood circulation might arise from such a system. As we learn more about brain–behavior and brain–mind relations, neuroscientists continue to puzzle at the relation between the activity of the brain and the mental events that arise from it.

It seems clear however that our understanding of brain–mind relations requires an understanding of how brain areas communicate with one another. Interacting networks of neurons throughout the brain give rise to thought, memory, emotion, and behavior. The remainder of this book focuses on how mental and behavioral phenomena arise from the combined activity of neurons communicating with one another. The next chapter asks, "How do neurons communicate?"

1.9 Creative Thinking

1. What afferent information is traveling to your brain via the somatic nervous system at this moment? Which if any of this afferent information is traveling via cranial nerves?
2. What would your life be like if you had a functioning CNS but no PNS? Could you move, or perceive the external world? Could you think?
3. As our brains evolve, what features might you expect to find in a million years? Will brains give us abilities that we do not currently possess?
4. Might future college students have brain implants to enhance their intellectual performance? If it were possible, would you be in favor of it?
5. If you were developing a drug to enhance cognitive performance, what functions would you like to see enhanced?
6. If you sent neurons carrying visual input from the retina to areas of the auditory cortex, would you expect your experience to be visual or auditory? What might the experience be like?

Key Terms

afferent 14
amygdala 35
anterior 17
arachnoid mater 22
astrocyte 6
autonomic nervous system 14
axon 5
basal ganglia 34
BOLD activation, fMRI 21
brainstem 26
caudal 17
cell body 5
central canal 23
central nervous system (CNS) 11
central sulcus 38
cerebellum 28

References

Descartes, R. (1972). *Treatise of Man*, trans. T. S. Hall. Cambridge, MA: Harvard University Press.

(1984). *The Philosophical Writings of Descartes*, trans. J. Cottingham, R. Stoothoff, & D. Murdoch. 2 vols. Cambridge: Cambridge University Press, Vol. 1.

Feinstein, J. S., Adolphs, R., Damasio, A., & Tranel, D. (2011). The human amygdala and the induction and experience of fear. *Current Biology*, *21*(1), 34–38.

Feuillet, L., Dufour, H., & Pelletier, J. (2007). Brain of a white-collar worker. *Lancet*, *370*(9583), 262.

Goldman, S. A., Nedergaard, M., & Windrem, M. S. (2015). Modeling cognition and disease using human glial chimeric mice. *Glia*, *63*(8), 1483–1493.

Han, X., Chen, M., Wang, F., Windrem, M., Wang, S., Shanz, S., ... Nedergaard, M. (2013). Forebrain engraftment by human glial progenitor cells enhances synaptic plasticity and learning in adult mice. *Cell Stem Cell*, *12*(3), 342–353.

Hussaini, S. M. Q., & Jang, M. H. (2018). New roles for old glue: astrocyte function in synaptic plasticity and neurological disorders. *International Neurourology Journal*, *22*, S106–S114.

Ito, M. (2008). Control of mental activities by internal models in the cerebellum. *Nature Reviews Neuroscience*, *9*(4), 304–313.

Kumar, P. S., & Dharun, V. S. (2016). A study of MRI segmentation methods in automatic brain tumor detection. *International Journal of Engineering and Technology*, *8*, 609–614.

Rizzolatti, G., & Luppino, G. (2001). The cortical motor system. *Neuron*, *31*(6), 889–901.

Sugihara, I., Fujita, H., Na, J., Quy, P. N., Li, B. Y., & Ikeda, D. (2009). Projection of reconstructed single Purkinje cell axons in relation to the cortical and nuclear aldolase C compartments of the rat cerebellum. *Journal of Comparative Neurology*, *512*(2), 282–304.

Zatorre, R. J., Fields, R. D., & Johansen-Berg, H. (2012). Plasticity in gray and white: neuroimaging changes in brain structure during learning. *Nature Neuroscience*, *15*(4), 528–536.

Zhou, X. Y., Xiao, Q., Xie, L., Yang, F., Wang, L. P., & Tu, J. (2019). Astrocyte, a promising target for mood disorder interventions. *Frontiers in Molecular Neuroscience*, *12*.

2 How Neurons Work

ALFRED PASIEKA/SCIENCE PHOTO LIBRARY / Science Photo Library / Getty Images

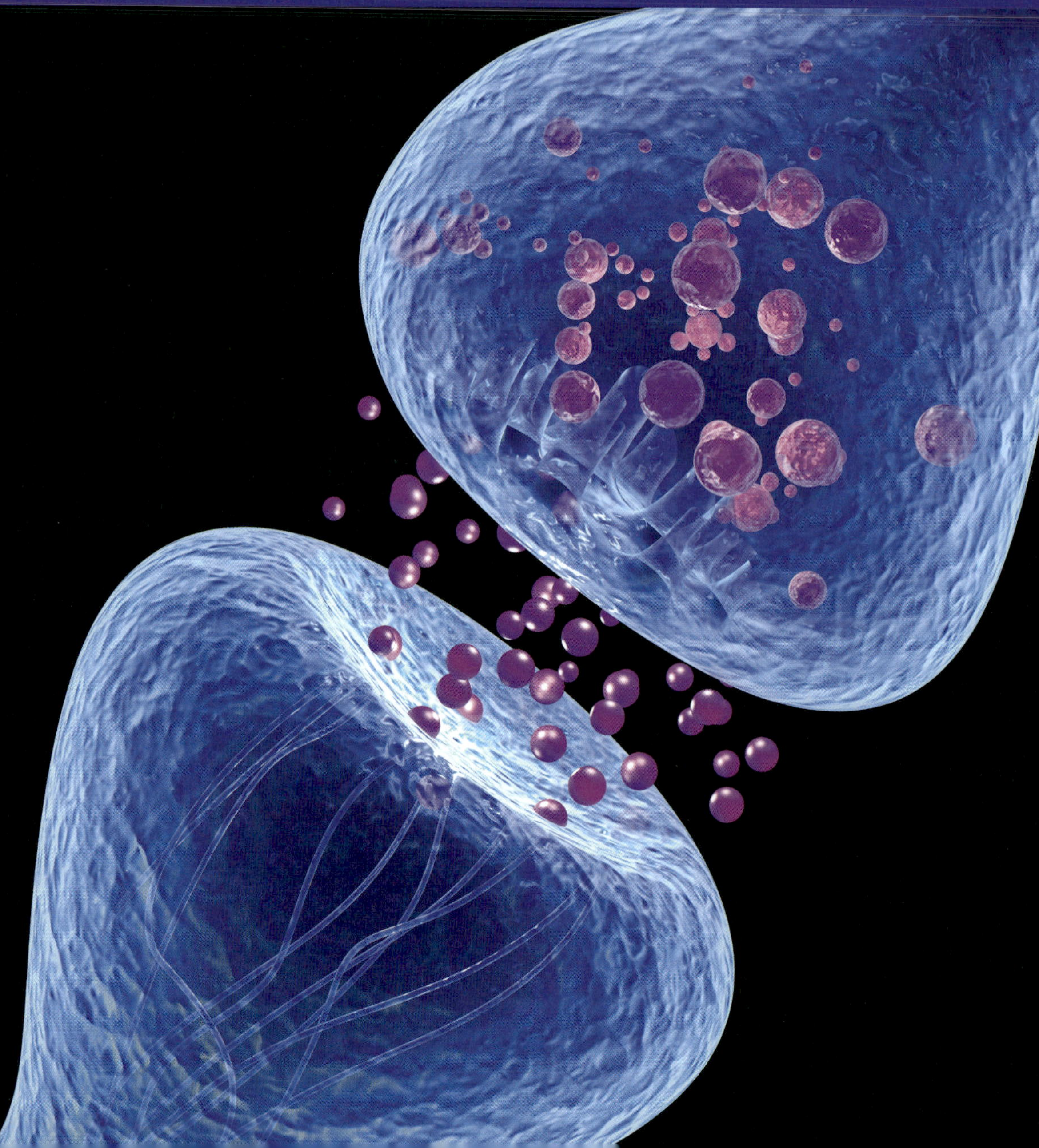

Consider This ...

Dr. Dresnin's patient, Sarah, enters the room, and the dentist administers an injection of lidocaine into her gum. He will need to do a lot of drilling, and the local anesthetic will prevent pain sensations. He makes sure to apply the anesthetic generously. Dentistry is difficult enough without a screaming patient first thing in the morning.

After a few minutes, he asks Sarah if the lidocaine's taken effect. She grinds her teeth together and says, "Yes, I think I'm numb now." As he prepares the drill, Sarah asks, "Doctor, why can't I feel my teeth? How does lidocaine work?"

Here was Dr. Dresnin's reply, verbatim: "*Lidocaine blocks sodium channels in the neurons that carry pain and other sensations from your teeth to the brain.*"

"Sodium who?" replied Sarah.

"*Sodium channels. In order for a neuron to become activated, sodium must pass from outside the neuron to the inside of the neuron. To do so, it passes through channels – little gates – within the wall of the neuron. If enough sodium enters, the neuron becomes sufficiently activated, or depolarized, to send a signal along its axon.*"

Sarah did her best to make sense of these many unfamiliar words.

"When the signal gets to the axon terminal, a neurotransmitter is released; the neurotransmitter crosses a synapse and excites a receiving neuron. That neuron sends a signal to other neurons, which, in turn, send signals to areas of the brain that produce pain sensations. By blocking sodium channels, lidocaine prevents the pain signal from arriving to your brain."

Sarah caught enough of the explanation to pose an incisive question: "In other words, the pain's not really in my teeth or gums – it really depends upon my brain."

"Exactly. No matter what I do to your teeth, you won't feel it if I use lidocaine to interrupt the neural signals that go to the pain areas of the brain."

Sarah wasn't crazy about the phrase "no matter *what I do* to your teeth," but she let it go, and focused instead upon what he'd said about lidocaine blocking sodium channels and interrupting neural signals. Not having studied neuroscience, she did not understand much of this. If she'd have read this chapter, all her questions would have been answered. Read on.

Communication between neurons allows you to perceive pleasure, pain, and other sensations; it allows you to move your body, to speak, and to carry out other behavioral and mental functions. But *how* do neurons communicate with one another? What does it mean for a "signal" to move along a neuron's axon? How does a neurotransmitter released by one neuron affect the activity of receiving neurons?

2.1 TO DROP A HOT CUP, OR NOT

For a perspective on how neurons send signals to one another, imagine this example:

> You pick up a coffee cup but suddenly drop it to the floor because it is too hot to hold. You did not consciously "decide" to drop it; neurons of the peripheral nervous system and spinal cord carried out an automatic **reflex** without brain involvement (Figure 2.1).

Let's look at these neurons in more detail. As seen in Figure 2.2A, most neurons possess dendrites that radiate outward from the **cell body**. The cell body contains the neuron's DNA enclosed within a nucleus, and cellular machinery necessary for the life of the neuron. Information typically enters a neuron at its dendrites, passes to the cell body, and, if the neuron becomes activated, an electrical signal travels along the **axon**, causing release of **neurotransmitter** from the axon terminal into a small gap between neurons called the **synaptic cleft**. When we consider dropping a hot cup, we begin with the activation of heat-sensing neurons in the skin. Like most other neurons, sensory neurons in the skin have dendrites at one end (in this case, the

A

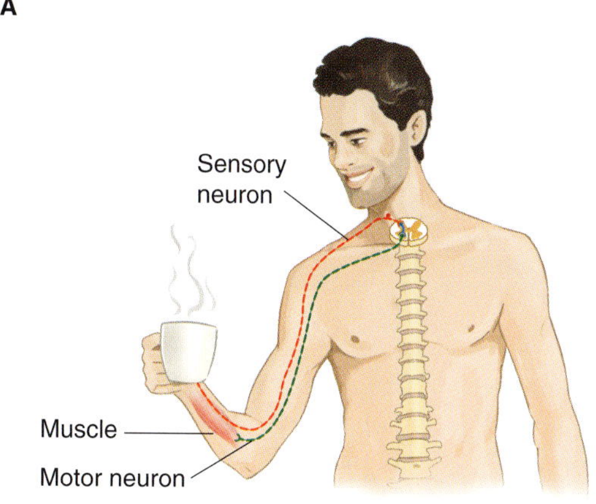

B

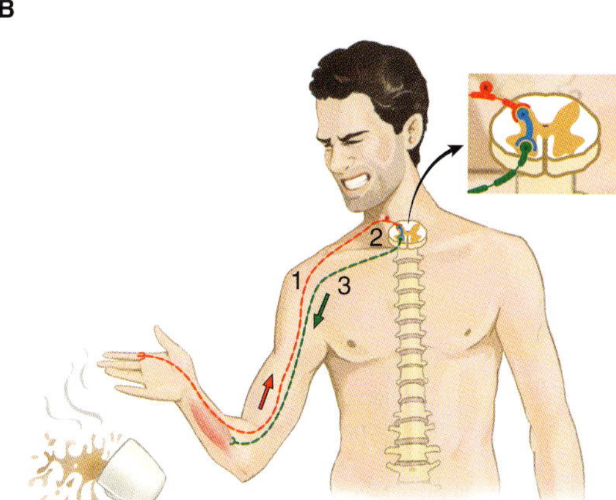

Figure 2.1 Dropping the cup. (A) Sensory neurons carry information from the skin to the spinal cord. Motor neurons carry information from the spinal cord to muscles. (B) A reflex circuit carries a heat signal from (1) the sensory neurons in the hand to (2) neurons in the spinal cord to (3) motor neurons that activate muscles to extend the palm and fingers, causing the cup to drop.

dendrites are embedded in the skin), and an axon terminal at the other end. Like other neurons, they also have a cell body. What makes these sensory neurons unusual is that information that enters along the dendrites (in this case from the heat of the cup) travels directly along the axon to the terminal, bypassing the cell body (Figure 2.2B).

As illustrated in Figure 2.3A, when you touched the hot cup, the heat-sensing neurons in your hand sent an electrical signal from the dendrites along the length of the axon to the terminal, where a neurotransmitter was released into the synaptic cleft. The neurotransmitter activated a small neuron inside the spinal cord. Because it is contained *entirely* within the spinal cord, we refer to it as a **local spinal cord neuron**. Once activated, the local spinal cord neuron released its own neurotransmitter, which activated a motor neuron. When the electrical signal moved to the end of the motor neuron's axon, the neuron released a neurotransmitter that crossed a synapse and activated a muscle, causing the hand to open. That is when the cup crashed to the floor.

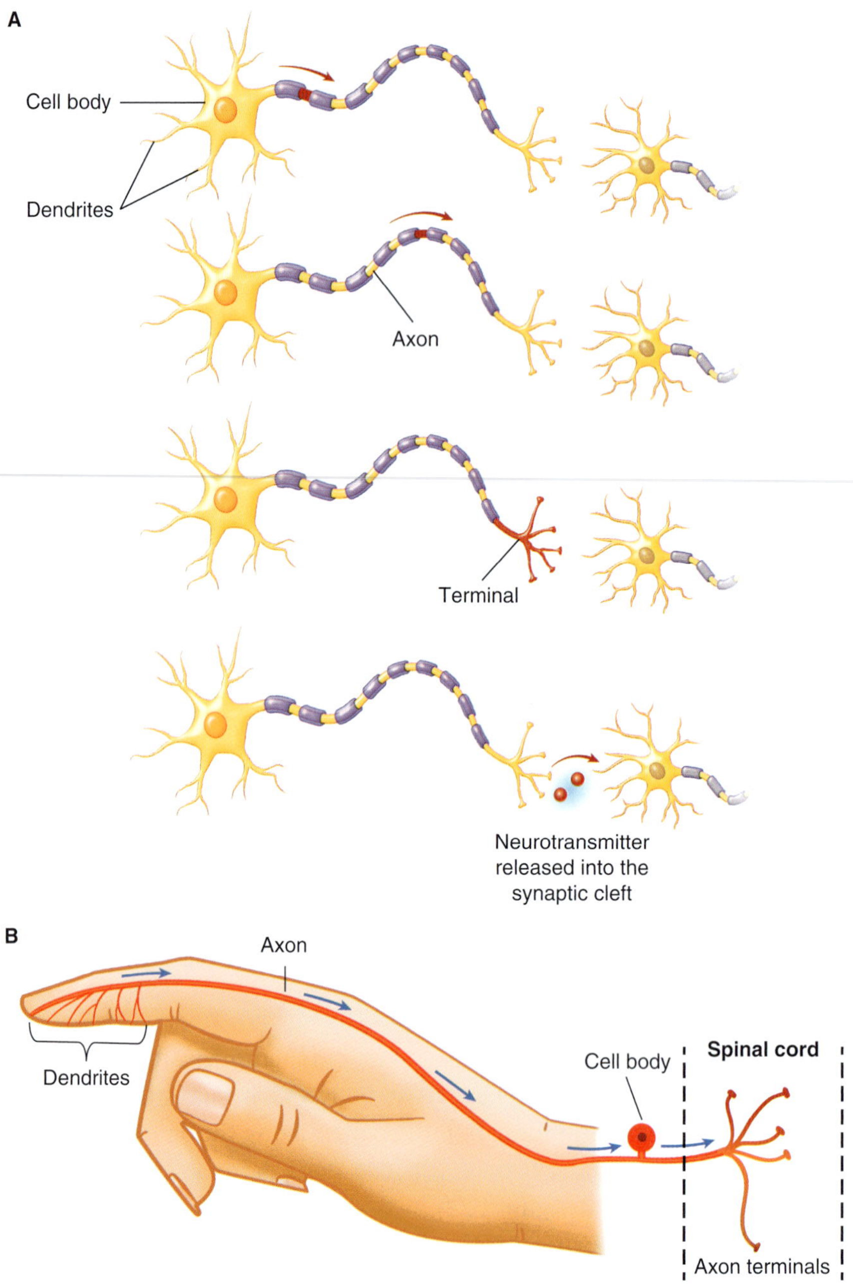

Figure 2.2 Review of the major parts of the neuron. (A) In a typical neuron, information passes from the dendrites to the cell body, travels along the axon, and reaches the axon terminal where it releases neurotransmitter into the synaptic cleft. (B) For sensory neurons in the skin, dendrites send information directly along the axon to axon terminals in the spinal cord, bypassing the cell body.

But what if the cup were very valuable, e.g., fancy china? Could you have inhibited the activity of the neuronal circuit just long enough to place the cup safely on a table? Yes. In this scenario, the brain recognizes that the cup is valuable. A signal from the brain travels down axons that terminate upon the local spinal cord neuron (Figure 2.3B), causing release of a neurotransmitter. In this case, the neurotransmitter *inhibits* the firing of the local spinal cord neuron. Notice that the same spinal cord neuron that receives *inhibition* from the brain receives *excitation* from the heat-sensing neuron in the hand (Figure 2.3C). If the local spinal cord neuron receives more excitation from the heat-sensing neuron than inhibition from the brain, it will activate the motor neuron, causing the hand to open, and the cup to drop.

This simple example reflects something fundamental about the way neurons interact. Neurons in the brain and spinal cord receive many different inputs to their dendrites and cell bodies. In some parts of the brain, a single neuron receives thousands of inputs from other neurons. Some

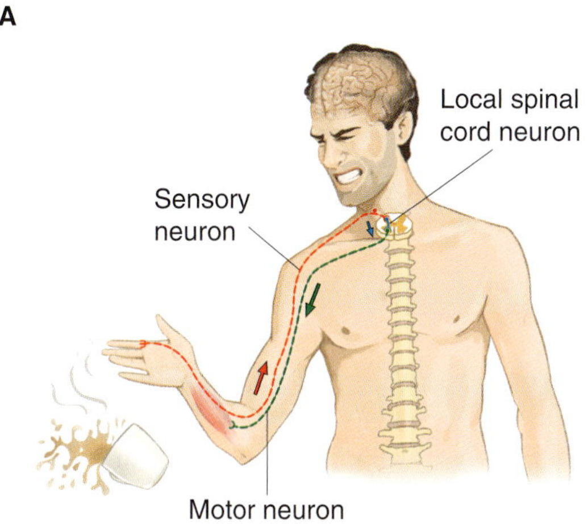

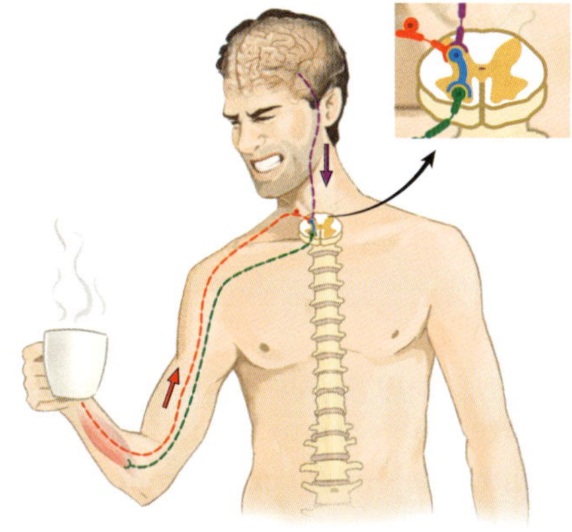

Figure 2.3 To drop the cup, or not – that is the question. (A) A reflex circuit responds to the heat of the cup and causes the hand to open, dropping the cup. (B) The brain recognizes that the cup is valuable and sends an inhibitory signal along its axon to the local spinal cord neuron. This inhibits the local spinal cord neuron, and consequently prevents activation of the motor neuron – perhaps long enough to place the cup safely on a table. (C) A closer look at how the brain may inhibit this reflex circuit.

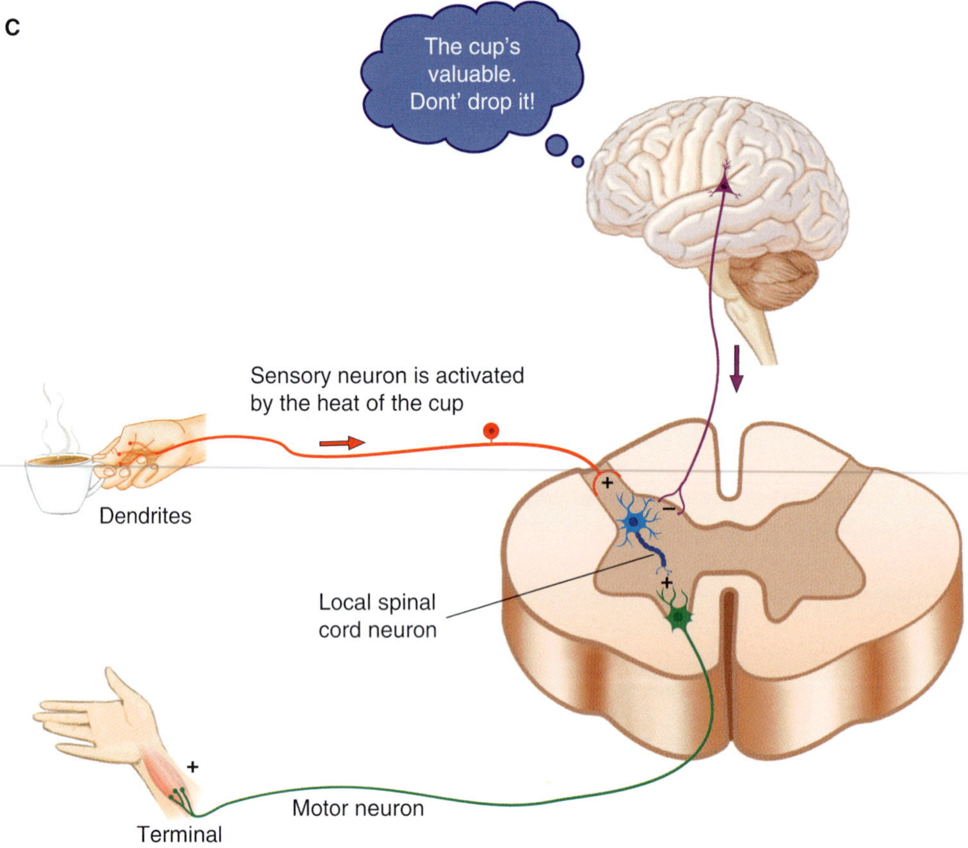

Figure 2.3 (cont.)

of these inputs are excitatory and others are inhibitory. The fundamental principle here is that a neuron becomes activated when it receives more excitatory than inhibitory input from other neurons. Some neurons have internal mechanisms that allow them to become "spontaneously active" even without input from other neurons. When these spontaneously active neurons do receive synaptic inputs from other neurons, and excitation exceeds inhibition, their activity level increases further; when they receive more inhibitory than excitatory input, their spontaneous activity diminishes or ceases altogether.

KEY CONCEPTS

- **When activated, a neuron may send an electrical signal along its axon and release a neurotransmitter to excite or inhibit a receiving neuron.**
- **A receiving neuron is activated when it receives more excitation than inhibition from other neurons.**

2.2 NEURONS ARE ACTIVATED BY THE ENTRY OF SODIUM IONS (NA^+)

In the preceding example, we took a bird's eye view of a neuron becoming activated, a signal moving along its axon, the release of neurotransmitter into a synaptic cleft, and the fact that combined excitatory and inhibitory inputs determine whether the receiving neuron will fire. Let's take this a step at a time. What does it mean for a neuron to become activated?

To understand neuronal activation, we need to become familiar with the **sodium ion**, abbreviated **Na^+**. An **ion** is an atom with a positive or negative charge. Consider table salt, sodium chloride (abbreviated NaCl), which is made of one sodium ion (Na^+) and one **chloride ion** (**Cl^-**). The + and – signs represent the fact that the Na^+ and Cl^- ions have a positive and negative charge, respectively. As you will see, the ability of Na^+ to enter a neuron plays a key role in neuronal activation.

2.2.1 Two Factors Cause Sodium to Pass through Ion Channels

A thin cell membrane separates the inside from the outside of a neuron. Like a wall, the membrane prevents substances inside the neuron from leaving and those outside the neuron from entering. As can be seen in Figure 2.4, the fluid inside the neuron (**intracellular fluid**) contains high concentrations of negatively charged proteins ($Prot^-$) as well as **potassium ions** (**K^+**). The fluid outside the membrane (**extracellular fluid**) contains high concentrations of Na^+ and Cl^-.

Many tiny openings called **sodium channels** are embedded within the membrane (Figure 2.5). When a neuron is not active, the sodium channels are closed, and Na^+ is unable to enter the neuron. However, as soon as the sodium channels open, Na^+ enters.

Why does Na^+ flow into the neuron after the channels open? The fact that a passageway allows you to enter a room does not mean you will enter. On the other hand, you might enter a room if it is less crowded than the room in which you are currently located. Similarly, Na^+ enters the neuron because the inside of the neuron is less concentrated with Na^+ than the outside (again, see Figure 2.4). The movement of a substance from an area of high concentration to a region of lesser concentration is called **diffusion**. Na^+ diffuses across the membrane toward the less concentrated interior of the neuron (Figure 2.6, *left*).

But Na^+ enters the neuron for a second reason as well. It has a positive charge. The *inside* of the neuron is negatively charged due to negatively charged proteins trapped inside. Opposite charges attract, so when given the opportunity, Na^+ enters the neuron. The attractive force of opposite

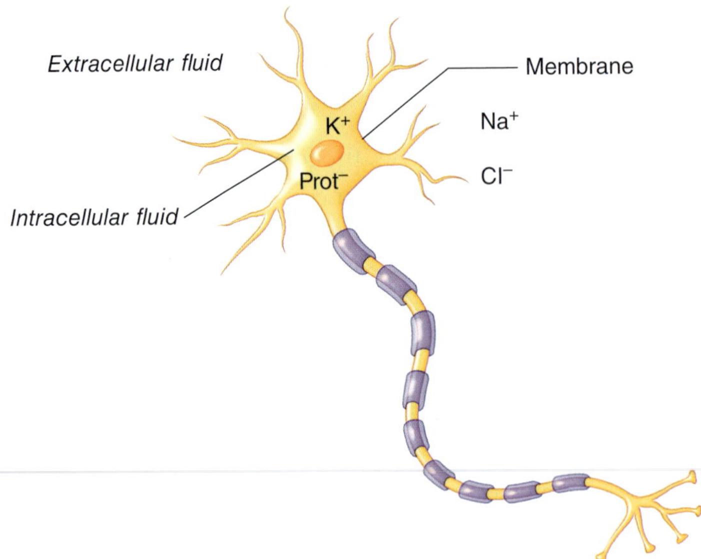

Figure 2.4 Sodium (Na^+) and chloride (Cl^-) ions are concentrated mainly outside the neuron. High concentrations of Na^+ and Cl^- ions are outside the neuron in the extracellular fluid. Large, negatively charged proteins ($Prot^-$), trapped inside, give the interior of the neuron an overall negative charge. The inside also contains high levels of potassium ions (K^+).

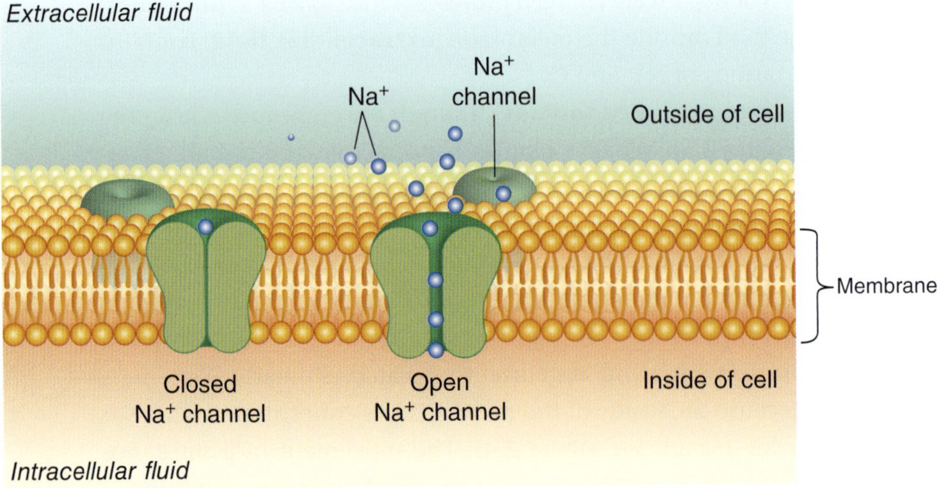

Figure 2.5 Sodium ions (Na^+) pass through channels. Sodium ion channels (green) within the neuronal membrane (orange) permit Na^+ (blue), concentrated in the extracellular fluid, to enter the neuron.

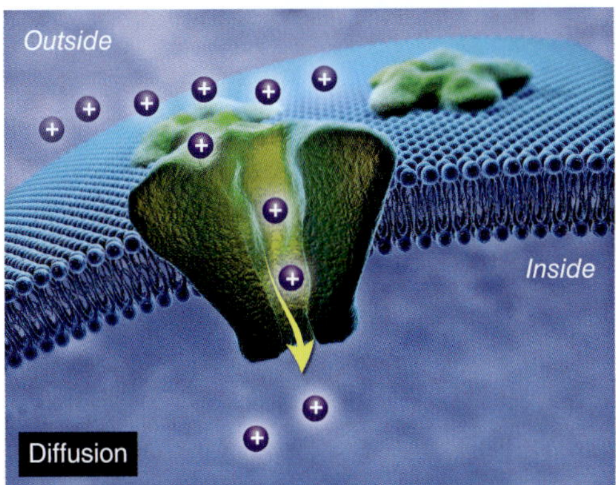

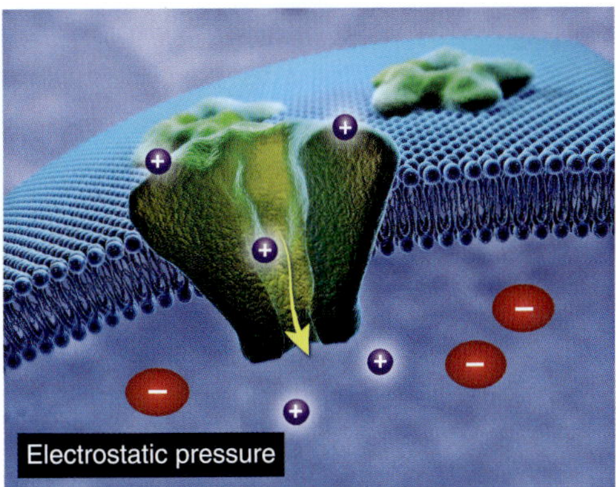

Figure 2.6 Sodium is drawn into the neuron by diffusion and electrostatic pressure. Left: Na^+ (purple circles) is more concentrated outside the neuron, and therefore it moves ("diffuses") to the inside of the neuron. Right: Because Na^+ has a positive charge, it is attracted to the negatively charged interior of the neuron.
(Adapted from image by @Beth LaFrenier/Getty Images.)

charges is called **electrostatic pressure**. Electrostatic pressure drives positively charged Na^+ to the negatively charged inside of the neuron (Figure 2.6, *right*). In summary, two factors drive Na^+ from the outside to the inside of the neuron: (1) diffusion, which moves it to an area of lesser concentration and (2) electrostatic pressure, which moves it toward the opposite charge. Normally, both of these factors combine to exert a powerful force that draws Na^+ inside the neuron.

Let's return now to our earlier example of a "heat-sensitive neuron" in the skin that is activated when you lift a hot cup. The neuron becomes activated because the heat from the cup causes Na^+ channels in the dendrites to open, allowing Na^+ to rush into the neuron. The first step in activating or exciting the heat-sensitive neuron, then, is the entry of Na^+ into the dendrites.

As we saw in the opening scenario, lidocaine prevents pain sensations from the dentist's drill by blocking Na^+ channels. Without Na^+ entry into neurons that normally respond to painful stimuli, the neurons do not become activated, they do not transmit information to the brain, and you feel no pain. If lidocaine were applied to heat-sensitive neurons in your hand, you could lift a hot cup without feeling the heat. Of course, if the drug blocked Na^+ channels in all of the sensory neurons of the hand (not just the ones that respond to heat, but those sensitive to pressure, touch, and so on), you wouldn't feel the cup at all.

We have seen that Na^+ is normally concentrated outside the neuron, entering as the neuron becomes excited and Na^+ channels open. But how does the neuron maintain a higher Na^+ concentration outside compared to inside the neuron, especially if Na^+ has the opportunity to cross through the membrane whenever Na^+ channels open? Embedded within the neuronal membrane, in addition to the Na^+ channels, is a protein that acts like a pump to push Na^+ ions out of the neuron, and to bring K^+ ions in. This **sodium-potassium pump** is continuously active and is responsible for maintaining the high concentrations of Na^+ outside and K^+ inside. However, for every two K^+ ions pulled into the neuron, three Na^+ ions are pumped out. This contributes to the negative charge inside compared to outside the neuron. This mechanism may seem like a small detail in neuronal function, but consider that the neuron can only be activated when Na^+ enters the neuron. Without the activity of the sodium-potassium pump, Na^+ would not enter the neuron because there would be no diffusion to the side of lesser concentration or electrostatic pressure to drive it across the membrane.

2.2.2 Depolarization of the Neuron

The difference in charge inside compared to outside the neuron is called the **membrane potential** or **voltage** (Figure 2.7). As we have seen, large negatively charged proteins trapped inside the neuron make the neuron negative inside compared to outside; the sodium-potassium pump helps

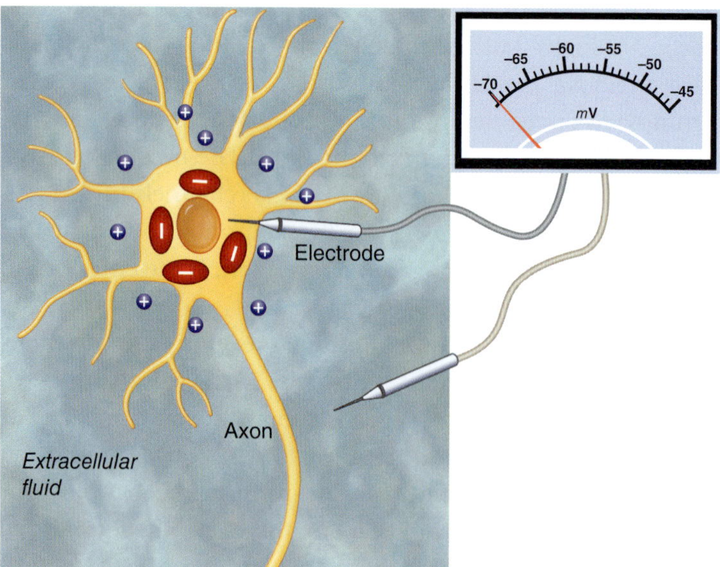

Figure 2.7 **The membrane potential: the difference in charge between the inside and outside of a neuron**. By placing a small wire (an electrode) on the interior side of the membrane and another on the exterior side, a voltmeter calculates the difference in charge across the membrane, i.e., the membrane potential. At rest, the membrane potential is about –70 mV, i.e., 70 mV more negative inside compared to outside the neuron.

to maintain this negativity inside. How much more negative is the inside of the neuron? When a neuron is not firing, it typically has a "resting membrane potential" (or simply **resting potential**) of about –70 mV. The neuron at rest is 70 mV more negative on the *interior side* of the membrane than it is in the extracellular fluid outside the neuron. If the membrane potential were –65 mV, the inside would still be negative compared to outside, but to a lesser extent. What if the membrane potential were +20 mV? The inside would be positive compared to the outside. Remember: the positive or negative sign of the membrane potential tells you the charge *inside* compared to outside the neuron.

Let's return to the heat-sensitive neuron. Assume that its membrane potential at rest is –70 mV. What happens to the membrane potential when the hand comes into contact with a hot object? As positively charged sodium ions enter the neuron, the membrane potential is reduced (it goes from a highly negative to a slightly less negative value). For instance, the membrane potential may change from –70 to –68 mV.

When the inside and outside of a neuron are different in charge, we say that the neuron is **polarized**. Therefore, at rest, when the neuron has a membrane potential of –70 mV, the neuron is polarized. However, as Na^+ enters, and the membrane potential is reduced (moves from –70 mV to a value closer to 0), we say that the neuron is becoming **depolarized**. So, when the hand touches the hot cup, the heat-sensitive neuron becomes depolarized due to the inflow of Na^+.

2.2.3 Reaching the Firing Threshold

In our example, imagine that the heat of the cup caused only a brief opening of a few Na^+ channels, allowing only a small amount of Na^+ to enter. If so, the neuron would have undergone only a slight depolarization, say from –70 to –69 mV, but not enough to cause the neuron to fire (that is, to transmit a signal down the axon). A hotter object would have caused more Na^+ entry and greater depolarization. How much depolarization is needed in order for the neuron to fire? This depends upon the neuron's **firing** (or action potential) **threshold**. For most neurons, firing requires that the neuron be depolarized to about –55 mV. In the case of our hot cup, a change of approximately 15 mV (from –70 to –55) is required to reach the firing threshold.

If heat causes enough Na^+ channels to open and enough Na^+ to enter, the depolarization will be sufficient to reach the firing threshold, and the neuron will "fire." But what does this mean? When the firing threshold is reached, particular types of channels called **voltage-gated** (or voltage-sensitive) channels open. These channels are activated not by heat, but by the increase in positive charge that has entered the neuron in their immediate vicinity. Recall that the "voltage" across the membrane is another way

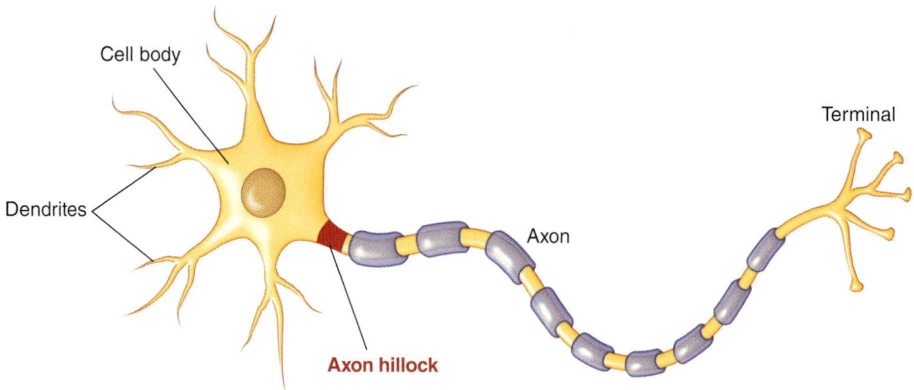

Figure 2.8 The axon hillock. When the firing threshold is reached at the initial segment of the axon, around the axon hillock (indicated in red), the neuron fires an "action potential," which sweeps along the entire axon until reaching the axon terminal.

of referring to the membrane potential. The voltage-gated channels open when the membrane potential is depolarized to approximately –55 mV.

Where are these voltage-gated channels located? They are found along the entire axon, from its initial segment all the way to the axon terminal. For most neurons, the initial segment of the axon begins just beyond the **axon hillock**, where the cell body gives rise to the axon (Figure 2.8). (For sensory neurons, the initial segment of the axon begins just a small distance beyond the dendrites.) In order for the voltage-gated channels to open, the membrane potential must be about –55 mV (firing threshold) *at the initial segment* of the axon.

2.2.4 The Neuronal Signal (Action Potential) Sweeps across the Axon

The opening of these voltage-gated channels permits Na^+ to rush in, depolarizing the neuron a bit further along the axon. This causes adjacent Na^+ channels to open, more Na^+ entry, and the opening of voltage-gated Na^+ channels further along the axon. From the axon's initial segment all the way to the axon terminal, the Na^+ channels open sequentially, like falling dominoes (Figure 2.9). This is what it means to say that the neuronal signal sweeps across the axon.

Recall that the Na^+ channels along the axon are described as "voltage-gated" because their opening is triggered by a change in the membrane potential or "voltage" across the membrane. Imagine yourself to be a voltage-gated Na^+ channel, currently closed, and located somewhere along the axon. A Na^+ channel at the axon's initial segment has just opened, and there are several hundred Na^+ channels between that channel and "you." Now, other Na^+ channels closer to you are opening. When a Na^+ channel

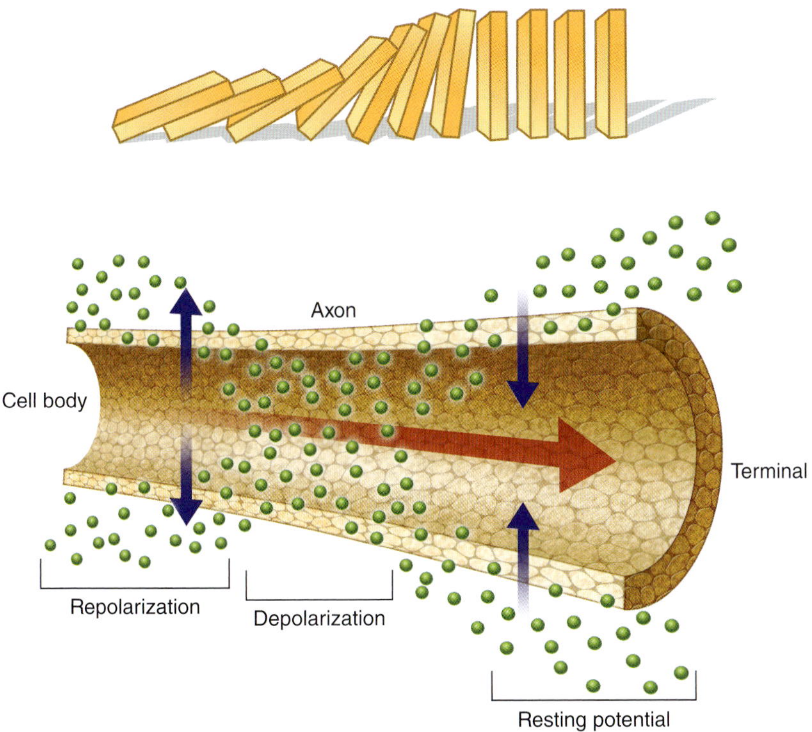

Figure 2.9 The action potential sweeps along the axon. In the bottom image, the action potential (red arrow), traveling from left to right, has not yet arrived to the right side of the axon. The right side of the axon is therefore still at its resting potential. As the action potential sweeps across the axon, voltage-gated Na^+ channels open, one after another, like falling dominoes (top drawing), allowing Na^+ ions (green spheres) to enter. This portion of the axon has therefore become depolarized. The Na^+ that entered initially is pumped out again (left portion of the axon). This repolarizes the axon, permitting the next action potential to occur.

just next to you opens, the membrane potential at your location depolarizes enough to cause you to open (remember, you are a sodium channel). Your shape is changing in a way that allows Na^+ to flow through you! As a result, there is enough depolarization at your location to cause the opening of a neighboring voltage-gated Na^+ channel on the other side of you, closer to the axon terminal. When we say that "a neuronal signal sweeps across the axon," or that "a neuron fires an **action potential**," we are speaking of this successive opening of ion channels, from the initial segment of the axon all the way to the axon terminal.

2.2.5 A Close-up Look at the Action Potential

As we have seen, when a neuron fires an action potential, voltage-gated sodium channels open, one after another, along the axon. Let's look at the membrane potential more closely as the neuronal signal, or action potential, reaches a single point along the axon. Before the signal arrives,

Na^+ channels are closed, and with a voltmeter, you measure a resting potential of about –70 mV. Immediately after the voltage-gated Na^+ channel opens, Na^+ rushes in and depolarizes the neuron to such an extent that the inside of the neuron briefly becomes *positive* compared to the outside (Figure 2.10). However, the neuron quickly becomes repolarized and returns to its resting potential. The action potential is therefore made up of a rapid rise *and* fall in the membrane potential. The action potential is sometimes referred to as a "spike," because in graphs like that shown in Figure 2.10 the rapid rise and fall of the membrane potential measured at a particular point of the membrane has a spike-like appearance.

When you think of an action potential moving from the axon's initial segment to its terminal, it's convenient to think of Na^+ channels opening one after another, with Na^+ rushing in at each point along the axon. However, the action potential involves movement of potassium ions (K^+) as well. At rest, K^+ is more concentrated inside compared to the outside of the neuron. After Na^+ has begun to rush in, positive charge accumulates

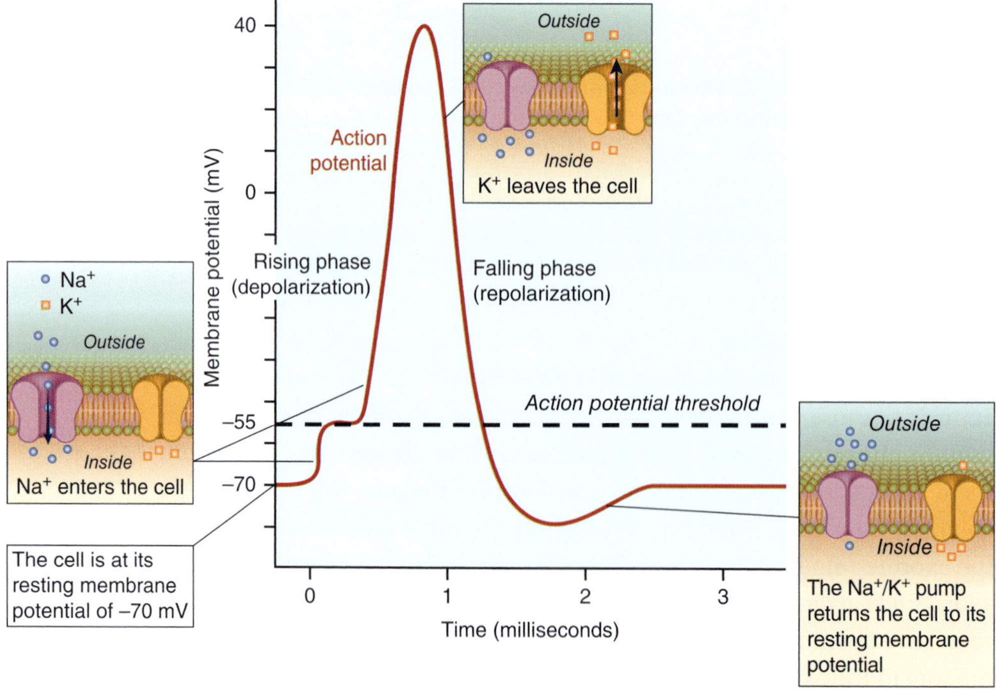

Figure 2.10 The rapid depolarization and repolarization of the action potential. During the rising phase of the action potential, Na^+ gates open, and Na^+ brings its positive charge into the cell (depolarization). During the falling phase, K^+ gates open and K^+ carries its positive charge out of the cell (repolarization). The rise and fall of the action potential typically ocurs in less than 2 milliseconds. The membrane potential usually drops a bit below the resting potential before returning to rest. The Na^+/K^+ pump (not shown in the figure) restores Na^+ and K^+ ions to the outside and inside of the cell, respectively.

inside the neuron and this causes the opening of voltage-gated channels for K^+. K^+ then crosses to the exterior of the neuron where it is less concentrated. While Na^+ carries positive charge into the neuron, K^+'s exit removes positive charge from the interior of the neuron, causing repolarization as illustrated in Figure 2.10. Finally, recall that the sodium-potassium pump returns Na^+ and K^+ to the outside and inside of the neuron, respectively.

After a neuron fires an action potential and undergoes depolarization, there is a delay or **refractory period** (usually about 1 millisecond) during which the neuron cannot fire again. While the neuron is depolarized, the Na^+ channels are unable to operate. After the neuron is repolarized and Na^+ channels return to their voltage-sensitive state, another action potential may occur.

2.2.6 Myelinated Axons Permit Saltatory Conduction

We have seen that as the action potential moves along the axon, a voltage-gated Na^+ channel opens along the axon, Na^+ enters and depolarizes the neuron enough for the neighboring Na^+ channel to open, and so on, until the action potential reaches the axon terminal. In some neurons, however, Na^+ does not need to enter through ion channels at each point along the axon. Neurons that are **myelinated** contain patches of glial cells that form bands of myelin (Chapter 1) surrounding much of the axon (Figure 2.11). Between each patch of myelin are spaces called **nodes of Ranvier**. Na^+ and K^+ can flow through voltage-gated channels at these nodes, but not at the portions of the axon surrounded by myelin. The action potential "jumps" from one node to the next, a process called **saltatory conduction** that considerably speeds the movement ("conduction") of the action potential along the axon. Therefore, the speed of action potential movement across the axon, or its **conduction velocity**, is faster for myelinated compared to unmyelinated axons.

Some nervous systems lack myelin altogether. For instance, neurons in snails, worms, and most other invertebrates are unmyelinated. As a result, information travels relatively slowly along the length of their axons (about one meter per second). This slow transmission of information is not problematic for the survival of very small animals (Zalc, 2006), but as the nervous system grows in size, slow transmission of neural signals leads to slow motor responses, which is disadvantageous to survival. Myelination appears to be an evolutionary adaptation to the increased length of neurons in larger vertebrate nervous systems, speeding the rate of axonal signal conduction by fifty to a hundredfold.

Studies have shown that myelination of axons is subject to environmental influence over the life of an organism (Chang, Redmond, & Chan, 2016). For instance, mice isolated early in life and deprived of interaction

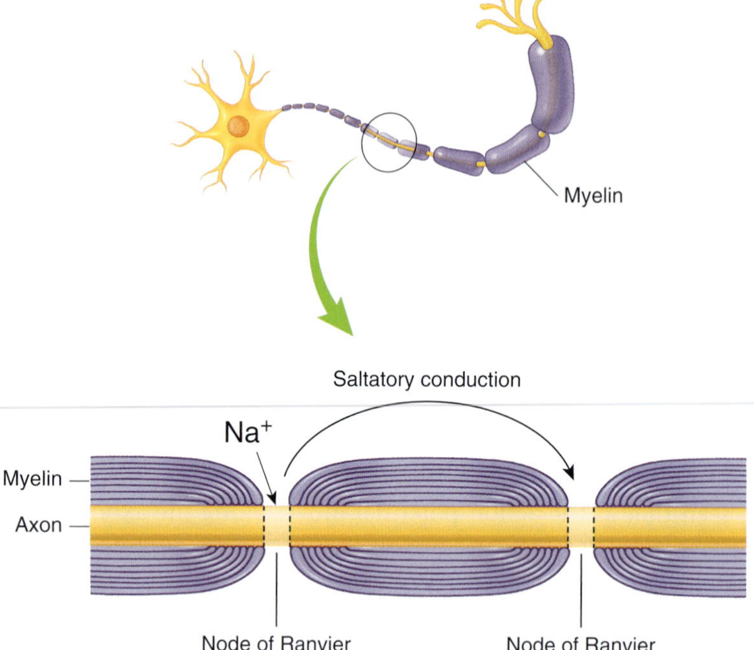

Figure 2.11 **Saltatory conduction**. During saltatory conduction, the action potential "jumps" from one node of Ranvier to the next, greatly speeding the neuron's conduction velocity.

with other mice have less myelin around neurons in the prefrontal cortex and show impairments in sociability and aspects of memory. Even adult mice deprived of social interaction (for eight weeks) undergo a decrease in prefrontal cortical myelin and behavioral deficits. Remarkably, after the mice are allowed to interact with other mice again, myelination of the prefrontal neurons is restored, and behavioral abnormalities disappear. These results suggest that myelination, and the resulting increase in the speed of signal conduction along the axon, not only serves to speed motor responses; myelination also contributes to information processing in brain regions that are critical to memory and complex behaviors.

Before we leave the topic of the action potential and its movement along the axon, it is worth familiarizing yourself with some important terminology (including some terms you've already encountered but can now use in a more precise manner). To say that a neuron **fired** is to say that it produced an action potential (which swept across its axon). To say that a neuron is firing slowly means that it is generating action potentials infrequently (e.g., only once every few seconds). A rapidly firing neuron generates action potentials frequently. A rapidly firing neuron in humans can fire up to about 1,000 times per second. We've seen that an action potential is sometimes called a **spike**. A fast-firing neuron may therefore also be described as "fast-spiking."

A neuron may fire slowly at one moment, and then, in response to some event, it may begin to fire at a faster rate. This doesn't mean that the action potential is sweeping across the axon faster. Its conduction velocity remains the same, and depends upon whether or not the neuron is myelinated as well as on other structural characteristics of the axon. When the neuron fires faster, action potentials are being generated (and each one is sweeping across the axon) at a higher rate (more times per second).

KEY CONCEPTS

- As a neuron becomes activated, sodium ions (Na^+) concentrated on the outside of the cell enter through small openings or "channels," driven by diffusion and electrostatic pressure.
- The charge inside compared to outside the neuron, or "membrane potential," is highly negative when the neuron is at rest. However, as Na^+ ions enter, the neuron is depolarized, i.e., the membrane potential becomes less negative.
- When a neuron's membrane potential reaches a firing threshold at the axon's initial segment, an "action potential," a sequential domino-like opening of Na^+ channels, moves along the axon.
- The speed with which an action potential travels across the axon to reach the terminal is its conduction velocity. Myelinated neurons undergo saltatory conduction, which increases the conduction velocity compared to that of unmyelinated neurons.
- A neuron may generate action potentials more rapidly at one moment than at another. We describe this as a change in the neuron's firing rate.

TEST YOURSELF

1. What two ions are highly concentrated outside the neuron?
2. Why is the inside of a neuron so negatively charged?
3. What is meant when we say that diffusion drives Na^+ into a neuron when Na^+ channels open?
4. What is meant when we say that electrostatic pressure drives Na^+ into a neuron when Na^+ channels open?
5. If the membrane potential of a neuron is –70 mV, that means that the inside of the neuron is 70 mV more ______ than the outside.
6. When the membrane potential is +20 mV, that means that the ______ (inside/outside) of the neuron is 20 mV more positive than the ______ (inside/outside).

7. As the membrane potential of a neuron shifts from –70 to –68 mV, it becomes more ____ (polarized/depolarized). As the membrane potential shifts from –70 to –72 mV, it becomes more _____ (polarized/ depolarized).
8. You touch a hot stove. Dendrites of heat-sensitive neurons in your hand become ____ (depolarized?/polarized?) as Na^{+} ions _____ (flow into/ flow out of) the neuron.
9. Along the axon, what makes each sodium gate open?

2.3 NEUROTRANSMITTERS ARE RELEASED INTO THE SYNAPSE AND BIND TO RECEPTORS

We return once again to our scenario of picking up the hot coffee cup. The hot cup depolarizes heat-sensitive neurons in the hand. The depolarization is sufficient to trigger an action potential. When the action potential reaches the axon terminal, a neurotransmitter is released. The transmitter crosses a synaptic cleft and binds to receptors on a receiving neuron in the spinal cord.

Here, we examine neurotransmitter release, receptor binding, and clearance from the synaptic cleft.

2.3.1 Neurotransmitters Are Released

Neurons take nutrients from the diet and, through several chemical reactions, they **synthesize** (produce) a neurotransmitter. Often, neurotransmitter synthesis begins with an amino acid obtained from dietary proteins. For instance, the amino acid tryptophan is the **precursor** for the serotonin neurotransmitter, and the amino acid tyrosine is the precursor for dopamine. Chemical reactions within the axon terminal convert the amino acid into a neurotransmitter, and neurotransmitters are then packaged into small spherical containers (**vesicles**). Some large neurotransmitters are synthesized in the cell body, packaged into vesicles, and then the vesicles are transported to the axon terminal.

When the action potential arrives at the axon terminal, calcium ion (Ca^{++}) channels open, and calcium rushes into the neuron. The inflow of Ca^{++} causes the neurotransmitter-filled vesicles to fuse with the membrane at the axon terminal (see Figure 2.12). Part of the vesicle then ruptures and releases the neurotransmitter contents into the synaptic cleft. The merging of the vesicle with the membrane and the secretion of the contents into the synaptic cleft is called **exocytosis**.

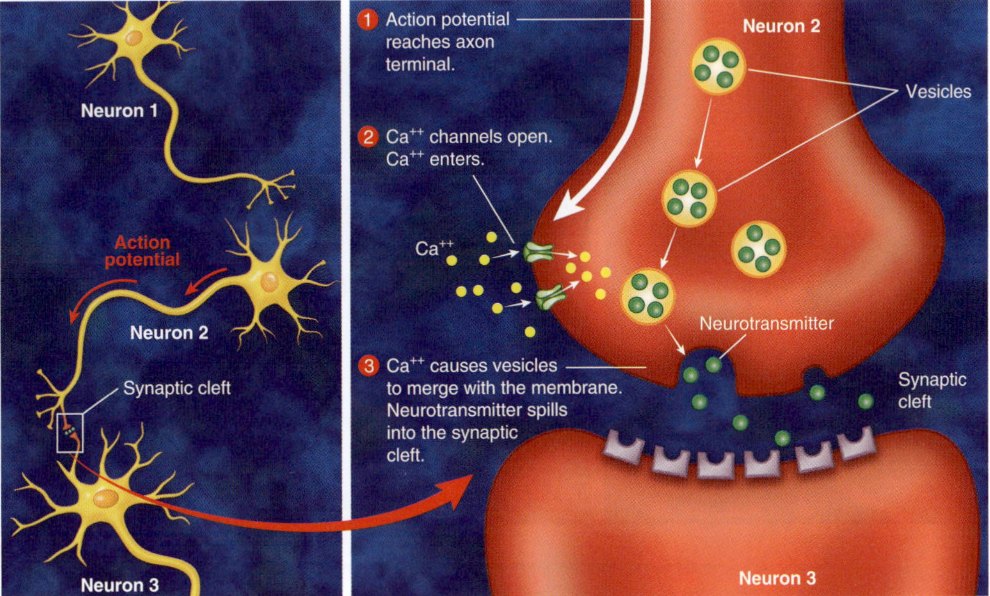

Figure 2.12 Exocytosis of a neurotransmitter. The arrival of the action potential at the axon terminal of Neuron 2 causes exocytosis, the merging of neurotransmitter vesicles with the membrane, and release of neurotransmitter into the synaptic cleft separating Neuron 2 and Neuron 3.

2.3.2 Neurotransmitters Bind to Receptors

After the neurotransmitter is released into the synaptic cleft, it may bind to receptors on another neuron. The neuron that releases a neurotransmitter into a synaptic cleft is called a **presynaptic** neuron. On the other side of the synaptic cleft is a **postsynaptic** neuron with receptors on its cell body and dendrites. In Figure 2.13, a presynaptic neuron releases a neurotransmitter that binds to receptors on a postsynaptic neuron. A part of the neurotransmitter molecule (the "active site") fits into the receptor like a key fits into a lock. Most neuronal communication occurs in this fashion between pre- and postsynaptic neurons.

However, in some cases a neurotransmitter may bind to receptors on the same neuron that released it. These presynaptic receptors are called **autoreceptors**. Transmitter binding at an autoreceptor is analogous to pressing the brakes of a car when it's moving too fast. Imagine that a neuron is firing very rapidly. Each time the neuron fires, it releases neurotransmitter molecules that bind to receptors on a postsynaptic neuron and also bind to autoreceptors located on the presynaptic (releasing) neuron. The autoreceptors will be activated more frequently than usual, which signals the presynaptic neuron to slow down its rate of firing (and consequently of neurotransmitter release). The autoreceptor therefore is part of a **negative feedback loop** that regulates rates of neuronal firing and neurotransmitter release.

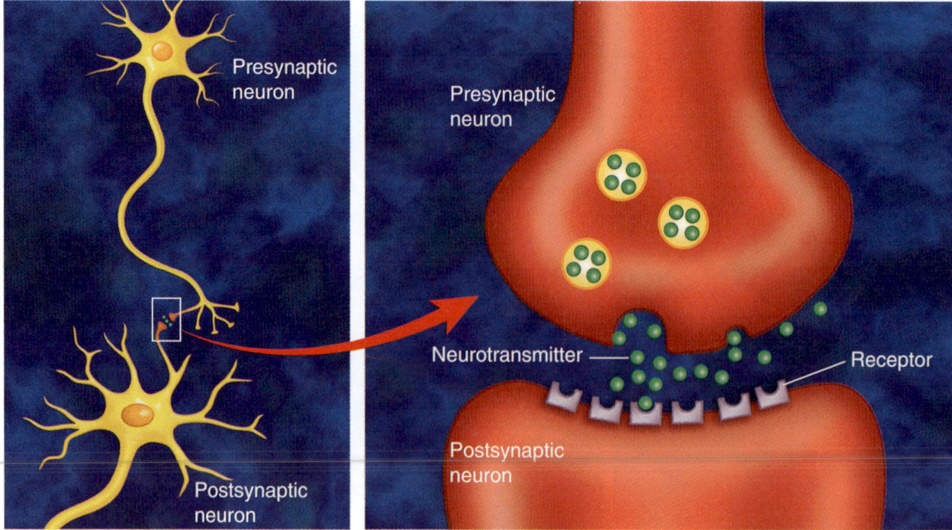

Figure 2.13 **A neurotransmitter is released from the presynaptic neuron, crosses the synaptic cleft, and binds to a receptor on the postsynaptic neuron.**

2.3.3 Neurotransmitters Are Cleared from the Synapse

If neurotransmitters that were released into the synaptic cleft simply accumulated, the synapse would become so clogged with neurotransmitter molecules that all postsynaptic receptors would be bound by neurotransmitters all the time! A recycling mechanism called **neurotransmitter reuptake** prevents this from occurring (Figure 2.14, left). **Transporter** proteins embedded in the presynaptic membrane transport neurotransmitter molecules from the synapse back into the presynaptic terminal so they can be repackaged into vesicles. Neurotransmitter molecules in the synapse or presynaptic terminal may also be inactivated by **enzymes**, which break the transmitter into inactive components (**degradation**) or otherwise inactivate them (Figure 2.14, right). Reuptake and deactivation ensure that neurotransmitters have only a brief period of time to activate their receptors.

KEY CONCEPTS

- **When the action potential reaches the axon terminal, neurotransmitter molecules are released into the synaptic cleft and may bind to receptors on other neurons.**
- **Neurotransmitters, once released, have only a short amount of time to bind to a receptor before they are either cleared away from the synaptic cleft or inactivated.**

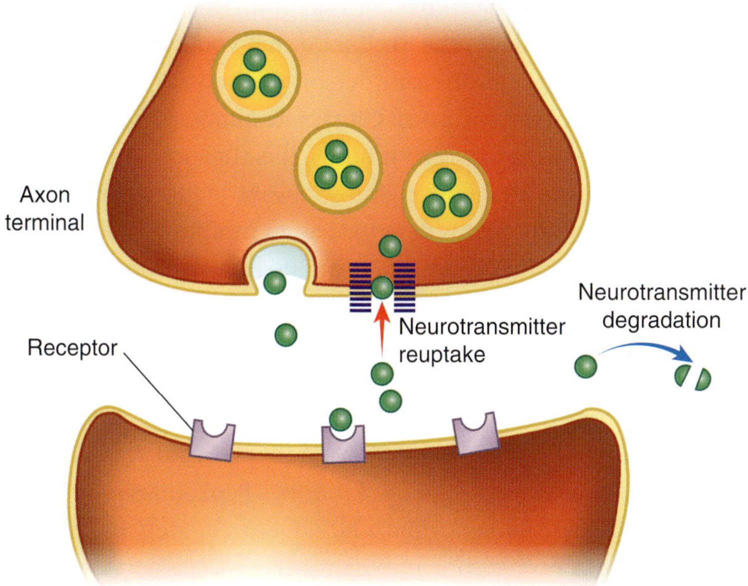

Figure 2.14 Neurotransmitter reuptake and degradation. Neurotransmitters are cleared from the synapse by reuptake and/or degradation by enzymes.

TEST YOURSELF

1. **After a neurotransmitter is released into the synaptic cleft, it may bind to ____ on another neuron.**
2. **The neuron that releases the neurotransmitter into the synaptic cleft is called a _____ (presynaptic/postsynaptic) neuron. The neuron on the receiving side of the synaptic cleft is the ______(presynaptic/postsynaptic) neuron.**
3. **Describe two ways that neurotransmitters are cleared from the synapse.**

2.4 NEUROTRANSMITTERS EXCITE, INHIBIT, OR MODULATE THE ACTIVITY OF NEURONS

A neurotransmitter has an excitatory effect if, when it binds to a receptor on a receiving neuron, it *increases* the activity of that neuron. For instance, when you touch the hot cup, the neurotransmitter released from the heat-sensing neuron excites the postsynaptic neuron in the spinal cord, making you more likely to activate the motor neuron and drop it. Conversely, a neurotransmitter has an inhibitory effect if it reduces the activity of the receiving neuron. A neuron in the cortex that recognizes that the cup is valuable china releases a neurotransmitter from its axon terminal in the spinal cord that inhibits the spinal cord neuron. This makes the neuron less likely to fire, and reduces the likelihood that you'll drop the cup.

The two most abundant neurotransmitters in the brain are **glutamate** and **GABA** (gamma-aminobutyric acid). Glutamate almost always increases the activity of the neurons to which it binds. It is therefore described as an excitatory neurotransmitter. GABA almost always reduces the activity of neurons to which it binds, and is described as an inhibitory neurotransmitter. In the sections that follow, we will examine how neurotransmitters bind to receptors to produce neuronal excitation or inhibition.

An example of glutamate's and GABA's typical actions can be seen in the storm of neuronal activity that occurs during epileptic seizures. The seizures can result from too much glutamate release (During & Spencer, 1993) or insufficient inhibitory actions of GABA (Baulac et al., 2001). Both produce abnormally high levels of neuronal firing. Benzodiazepine drugs like Valium (Diazepam) or Xanax (Alprazolam) reduce anxiety by increasing the effects of GABA on neurons in brain areas that generate fear and anxiety (Del-Ben et al., 2012).

Unlike glutamate and GABA, some neurotransmitters like **dopamine**, **serotonin**, and **norepinephrine** do not simply excite or inhibit other neurons. Their effects on postsynaptic firing are more complex. This subset of neurotransmitters are called **neuromodulators**, for they modulate (alter) the activity of many receiving neurons at once. For instance, we saw in Chapter 1 that some of the dopamine-releasing neurons are located in a small region of the midbrain called the substantia nigra. A relatively small number of dopamine neurons in the substantia nigra send axons to the much larger striatum. When a dopamine neuron fires, it releases dopamine into many synapses, and after release, the dopamine acts not only upon postsynaptic neurons but also upon receiving neurons some distance away. This ability of a neurochemical to act at a distance well beyond its release site is called **volume transmission**. A single dopamine neuron can therefore modulate the activity of many receiving neurons at once (see "Neurons Can Make Recurrent, Divergent, and Convergent Connections" below). As we will see in future chapters, dopamine, serotonin, norepinephrine, and other neuromodulators have profound effects on our ability to move, learn, and experience emotions.

2.4.1 Neuronal Excitation: EPSPs

How does glutamate excite a neuron? In most cases, when an excitatory neurotransmitter binds to a receptor on the postsynaptic neuron, it causes an ion channel within the receptor to open, which permits Na^+ (or another positively charged ion) to enter the neuron (Figure 2.15). The Na^+ channel depicted in the figure is **neurotransmitter-gated** because it *only* opens when a neurotransmitter binds to it. We will see later that not

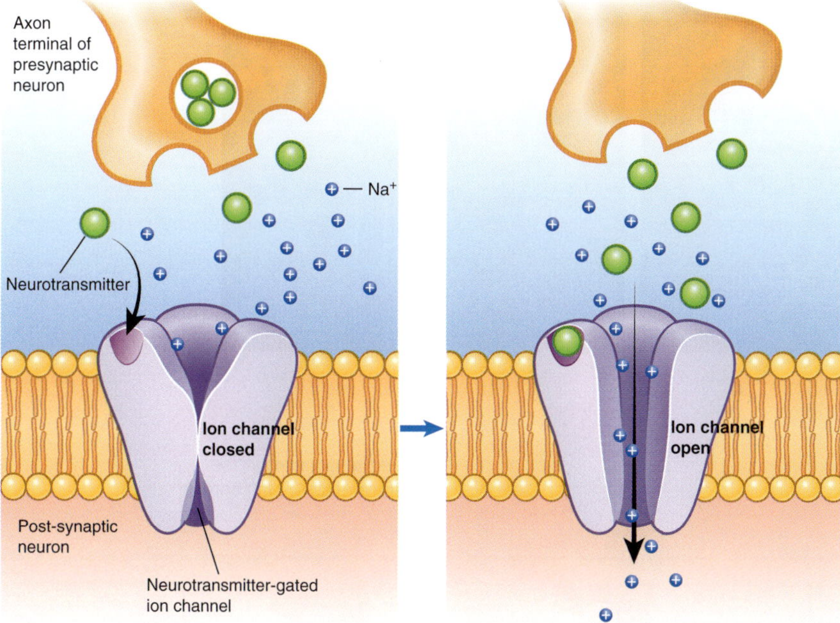

Figure 2.15 **Some receptors contain ion channels**. When the neurotransmitter binds to the receptor, an ion channel at the core of the receptor opens.

all receptors contain ion channels within them. But for the moment, this scenario is useful in order to illustrate neuronal excitation.

Imagine, that the excitatory neurotransmitter glutamate binds to a receptor at a dendrite, the Na^+ channels within the receptor open, and the inflow of Na^+ causes depolarization, bringing the membrane potential from, say, –70 to –68 mV (Figure 2.16). This depolarization of 2 mV is called an **excitatory postsynaptic potential**, or **EPSP**. If the membrane potential went from –70 to –69 mV, the size of the EPSP would have only been 1 mV. Will an EPSP of 1 or 2 mV cause the neuron to fire an action potential? No. As you know, the action potential firing threshold is often close to –55 mV. What would happen if glutamate bound to many different receptors at nearly the same time, and the inflow of Na^+ caused an EPSP of 2 mV at each receptor? The summation, or adding together, of these EPSPs could reach the firing threshold and cause the neuron to fire an action potential.

2.4.2 Neuronal Inhibition: IPSPs

Recall that some neurotransmitters, like GABA, are inhibitory. When GABA binds to a receptor, it causes **hyperpolarization** rather than depolarization. The membrane potential may shift, for example, from –70 to –72 mV. This makes the neuron even more polarized than it was at rest. From this state of hyperpolarization, even more depolarization will be necessary in order for the neuron to reach the action potential (firing) threshold.

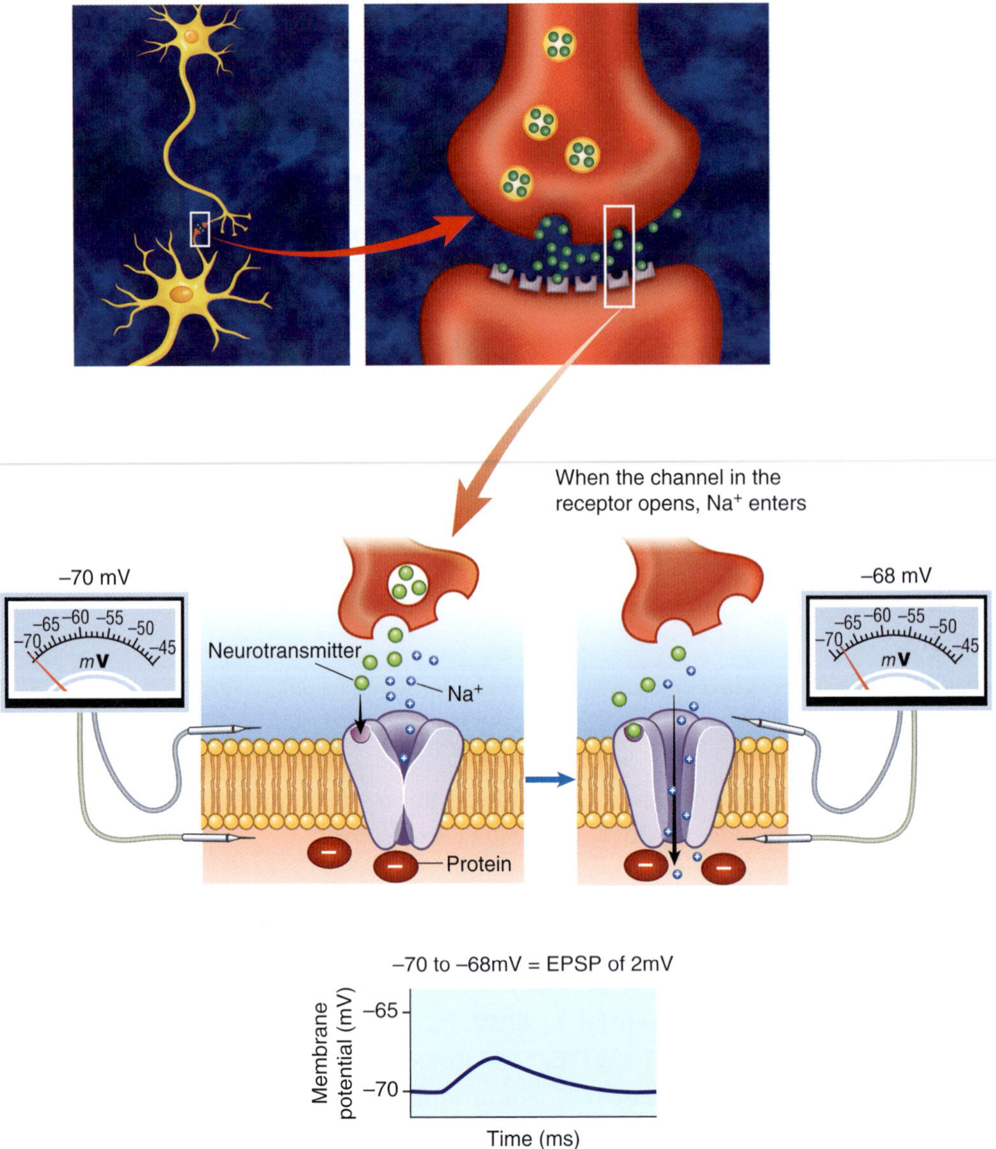

Figure 2.16 An excitatory neurotransmitter (green) is released from a presynaptic terminal and binds to a receptor (purple) on the postsynaptic neuron. When the ion channel in the receptor opens, Na^+ ions enter and carry their positive charge into the postsynaptic neuron. In this example, the membrane potential is depolarized from –70 mV to –68 mV, an EPSP of 2 mV.

A neuron can undergo hyperpolarization when an inhibitory neurotransmitter binds to receptors that cause the opening of Cl^- channels, allowing Cl^- ions to enter the neuron. Alternatively, hyperpolarization can occur when K^+ channels open, causing K^+ to flow out of the neuron. In both cases, the polarization of the neuron increases: The interior of the membrane becomes increasingly negative compared to the exterior.

If a neurotransmitter causes hyperpolarization of a postsynaptic neuron, say from –70 to –72 mV, we say that it has caused an **inhibitory postsynaptic potential** or **IPSP**, in this case an IPSP of 2 mV. Just like EPSPs, IPSPs can add together.

2.4.3 Spatial and Temporal Summation

The EPSPs and IPSPs occurring at different places (i.e., *spatial* locations) on the dendrites and cell body of a neuron may add together (Figure 2.17). This is called **spatial summation**. Two small EPSPs may add together to produce a large depolarization. If spatial summation leads to depolarization that exceeds the firing threshold at the axon's initial segment, voltage-gated Na^+ channels open, and an action potential occurs. Alternatively, IPSPs produced by inhibitory neurotransmitters may add together to strongly inhibit a receiving neuron. Often, EPSPs and IPSPs add together, and the neuron is excited only if the EPSPs are greater than the IPSPs.

Neurotransmitters bind to and then dissociate from (come off) the receptor. Once the transmitter dissociates from the receptor, the receptor becomes available for the binding of another neurotransmitter molecule. It is possible, then, for a neurotransmitter to bind to a receptor, and, then after a very brief delay, for another transmitter molecule to bind to the same receptor. If a neurotransmitter binds to a receptor quickly enough (say two or three times in rapid succession), EPSPs or IPSPs can summate over time (**temporal summation**; again, see Figure 2.17). For instance, a number of small EPSPs – one quickly after the other – can produce a large depolarization, moving the neuron closer to its firing threshold.

The neuron illustrated in Figure 2.17 has only two different synaptic inputs. However, in the real world, neurons undergo spatial and temporal summation at the same time. For instance, some neurons contain thousands of receptors, and neurotransmitters may bind to many of them at once, leading to spatial summation; at some of the receptors, the neurotransmitter may bind quickly enough for the EPSPs to summate over time, producing temporal summation.

2.4.4 Graded Potentials Get Smaller as They Spread along the Membrane

Say that an excitatory neurotransmitter binds to a postsynaptic receptor and causes an EPSP at a dendrite at a point far from the axon's initial segment. Let's say that this caused a 3 mV EPSP, depolarizing the membrane potential from –70 to –67 mV. Note again that this EPSP is observed *at the dendritic location where the neurotransmitter bound to its receptor and opened a* Na^+ *channel*. Will the membrane potential also be –67 mV if we measure

A

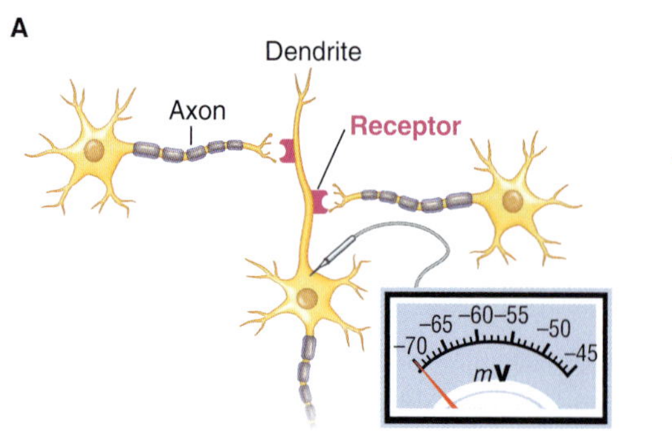

No synapses are active.
The resting membrane potential is –70mV.

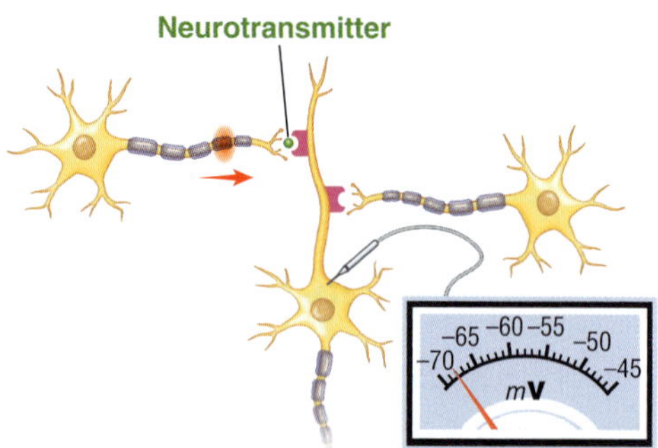

Activation of one excitatory synapse (left) produces a 2mV EPSP, depolarizing the membrane potential from –70mV to –68mV.

B

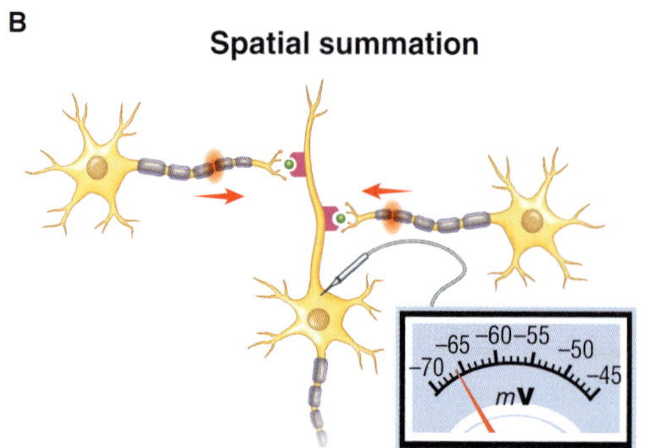

Activation of two different excitatory synapses produces two simultaneous EPSPs of 2mV each, depolarizing the membrane potential from –70mV to –66mV.

C

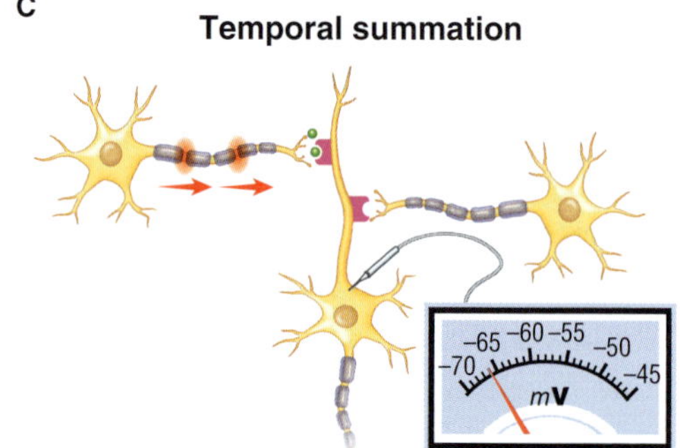

Activation of one excitatory synapse twice in rapid succession produces two EPSPs of 2mV each, depolarizing the membrane potential from –70mV to –66mV.

Figure 2.17 Spatial and temporal summation. Inputs arriving at different spatial locations of a neuron can add together with spatial summation. Inputs arriving quickly in succession at the same location can add together with temporal summation.

it at the axon hillock, or some other location near the initial segment of the axon? No. The magnitude of an EPSP decreases as it spreads along the membrane of the dendrite (and cell body), away from the site of Na^+ entry (Figure 2.18). So, by the time EPSPs (or IPSPs) reach the axon hillock/initial segment, they are smaller than they were at the site where they were generated in the cell body or dendrites. If the EPSP occurs very close to the axon hillock, it will not have to travel far before reaching the initial segment; therefore, the size of the EPSP will not diminish as much as an EPSP generated further away. Recall that a neuron only fires an action potential if the membrane potential exceeds the firing threshold at the initial segment of the axon. So, the closer an EPSP or IPSP is to the axon hillock/initial segment, the larger effect it will have on the firing of the neuron.

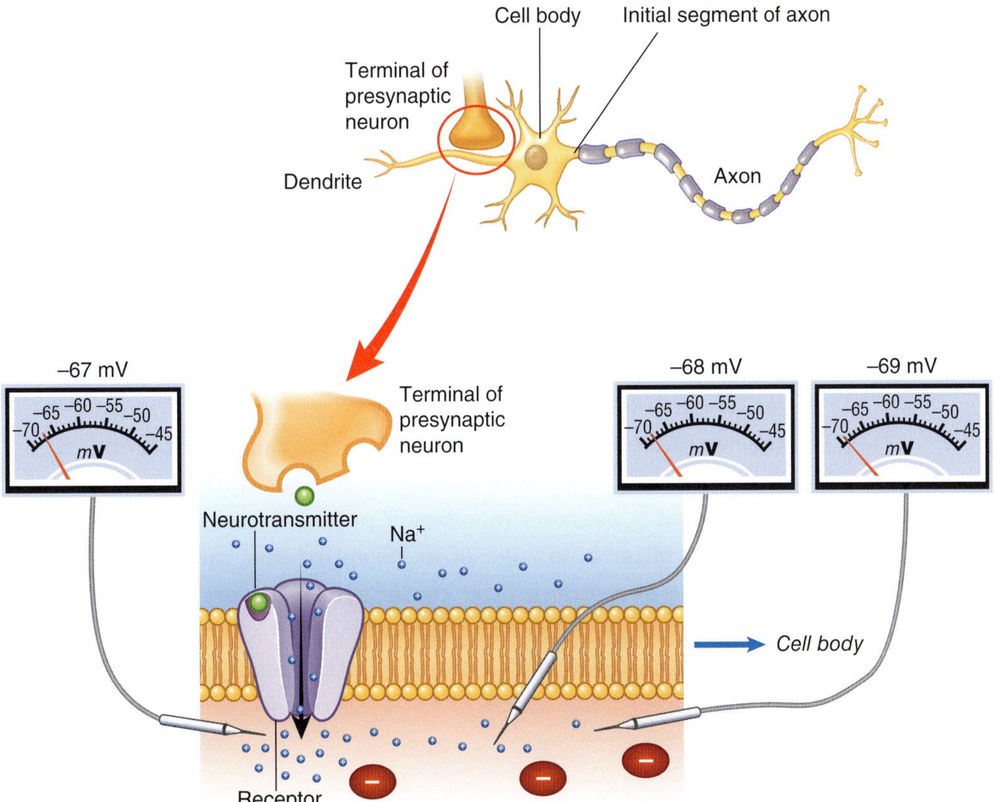

Figure 2.18 A graded potential diminishes as it spreads. At the point of synaptic input, Na^+ concentration and depolarization is greatest. As Na^+ moves along the inner wall of the membrane, further from this point, its concentration decreases. As a result, the EPSP decreases as it spreads along the dendrites and cell body.

Therefore, an important difference exists between (1) EPSPs and IPSPs in the dendrites and cell body of the neuron and (2) action potentials in the axon. EPSPs and IPSPs diminish as they move along the membrane of the dendrites and cell body, and are therefore called **graded** potentials (a potential that is "graded" can have different values from small to large). In contrast, the size of an action potential does not diminish as it moves, because it is generated anew at each point where the voltage-gated channels open and sodium enters along the axon.

KEY CONCEPTS

- **A neurotransmitter is excitatory at a synapse if it interacts with a receptor to produce an EPSP, or depolarization, and increases the neuron's likelihood of firing.**
- **A neurotransmitter is inhibitory at a synapse if it interacts with a receptor to produce an IPSP, or hyperpolarization, and decreases the neuron's likelihood of firing.**

- Those inputs arriving at different spatial locations of a neuron add together with spatial summation and those arriving quickly in succession at the same location add together with temporal summation. If the summation is sufficient to drive the membrane potential above the firing threshold, an action potential is generated.
- In contrast to action potentials, graded potentials (EPSPs and IPSPs) diminish in size as they spread across the membrane.

TEST YOURSELF

1. Say the membrane potential is at –70 mV when an EPSP of 3 mV arrives. The membrane potential is now ____.
2. If the neuron is at –70 mV and an IPSP of 3 mV arrives, it is now at ____ mV.
3. Imagine that a neuron's membrane potential currently = –70 mV. A neurotransmitter binds one of its receptors and causes an EPSP of 2 mV. Did the neurotransmitter cause (a) Na^+ to enter the neuron; (b) Cl^- to enter; (c) K^+ to exit the neuron?
4. Imagine that a neuron's membrane potential currently = –70 mV. A neurotransmitter binds one of its receptors and causes an IPSP of 2 mV. Did the neurotransmitter cause (a) Na^+ to enter the neuron; (b) Cl^- to enter?
5. As an EPSP spreads along the dendrite, does it increase, decrease, or stay the same? How does this differ from an action potential?
6. What would more strongly affect the firing of a neuron, an EPSP that arrives to its cell body near the axon hillock or far from the axon hillock? Explain.

2.5 THERE ARE VARIOUS FORMS OF NEUROTRANSMISSION

Just as there are various types of communication between people, there are also various forms of neurotransmission. You can communicate with another person by tapping him on the shoulder, speaking to him in words, using sign language, and so on. A neuron typically communicates by releasing a neurotransmitter, which binds to a receptor on another neuron. When the neurotransmitter binds, it can affect the receiving neuron in several different ways. In some cases, neurons communicate without releasing a neurotransmitter at all. Let's investigate further.

2.5.1 Ionotropic and Metabotropic Receptors

As you have seen, some neurotransmitters bind to receptors that contain an ion channel. These are called **ionotropic receptors** (Figure 2.19, top).

For instance, when the excitatory neurotransmitter glutamate binds to an ionotropic glutamate receptor, a Na^+ channel within the receptor opens, permitting Na^+ to enter and to depolarize the neuron. Other kinds of ionotropic receptors may have Ca^{++} or Cl^- ion channels that open when a neurotransmitter binds. In all of these cases, the ionotropic receptor contains both a neurotransmitter binding site and an ion channel.

Another type of receptor, a **metabotropic receptor**, contains no ion channel (Figure 2.19, bottom). Like the ionotropic receptor, the metabotropic receptor possesses a site where the neurotransmitter fits like a key fits into a lock. But when the neurotransmitter attaches to the binding site of a metabotropic receptor, a complex molecule called a **G-protein**, located on the interior side of the neuronal membrane, changes shape and becomes activated. The activation of the G-protein leads to activation of other molecules called **second messengers**. The "message" they send is that a neurotransmitter has arrived at the receptor. The results of second messenger activation may include opening of nearby ion channels (shown in Figure 2.19, bottom right), altering protein synthesis, and even altering gene expression (not shown in the figure). Unlike ionotropic changes, which are short-lived (the ion channels remain open for a few milliseconds at the most) and only exert their effects in the immediate vicinity of the receptor, metabotropic changes last longer (seconds to minutes) and can affect the activity of the entire neuron.

2.5.2 Neural Communication without Neurotransmitters

A neurotransmitter, once released, crosses a synapse and binds to a receptor on the postsynaptic neuron. However, a minority of neurons communicate *without* a neurotransmitter. The presynaptic and postsynaptic neurons, in this case, are extremely close to one another, separated only by a very narrow gap called the **gap junction**. When the presynaptic neuron undergoes an action potential and Na^+ enters through its voltage-gated channels, the intracellular Na^+ can pass directly, through gap junction channels, to enter the postsynaptic neuron (Figure 2.20). This direct flow of ions allows excitation (depolarization) to spread between neurons much faster and with greater strength than is possible with traditional chemical synapses that require neurotransmitters to be released, cross a synapse, and bind to receptors before influencing the postsynaptic neuron.

KEY CONCEPTS

- **Ionotropic receptors contain a neurotransmitter binding site and an ion channel. Metabotropic receptors contain a binding site but not an ion channel. Neurotransmitter binding to a metabotropic receptor activates second messenger molecules within the postsynaptic neuron.**

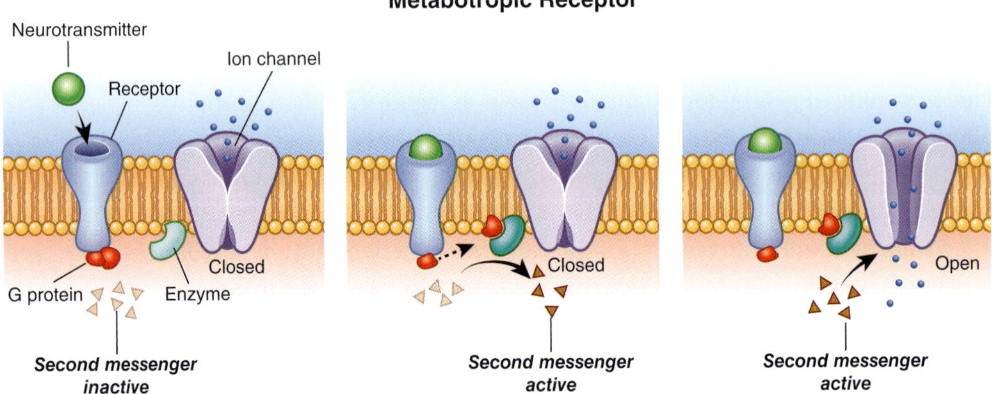

Figure 2.19 Ionotropic versus metabotropic receptor. When a neurotransmitter binds to the ionotropic receptor, an ion channel opens within the receptor itself. In contrast, the metabotropic receptor takes its name from the fact that neurotransmitter binding initiates several metabolic steps (usually involving G-proteins and enzymes) that may lead to opening of ion channels within the membrane, not within the receptor itself.

- **Changes in the postsynaptic neuron are longer-lasting at metabotropic compared to ionotropic receptors.**
- **Gap junctions permit excitation to spread across neurons rapidly without neurotransmitters.**

2.6 BEHAVIOR DEPENDS UPON THE ACTIVITY OF NEURONS: REVISITED

We now return to the example depicted at the beginning of the chapter, in which a hand holds a hot cup, and a spinal cord reflex causes the hand to open and the cup to drop (again, see Figure 2.3). We asked how this reflex can be inhibited, at least for a few moments, when the cup is recognized to be expensive. Through this example, we can now review all of the key principles discussed above.

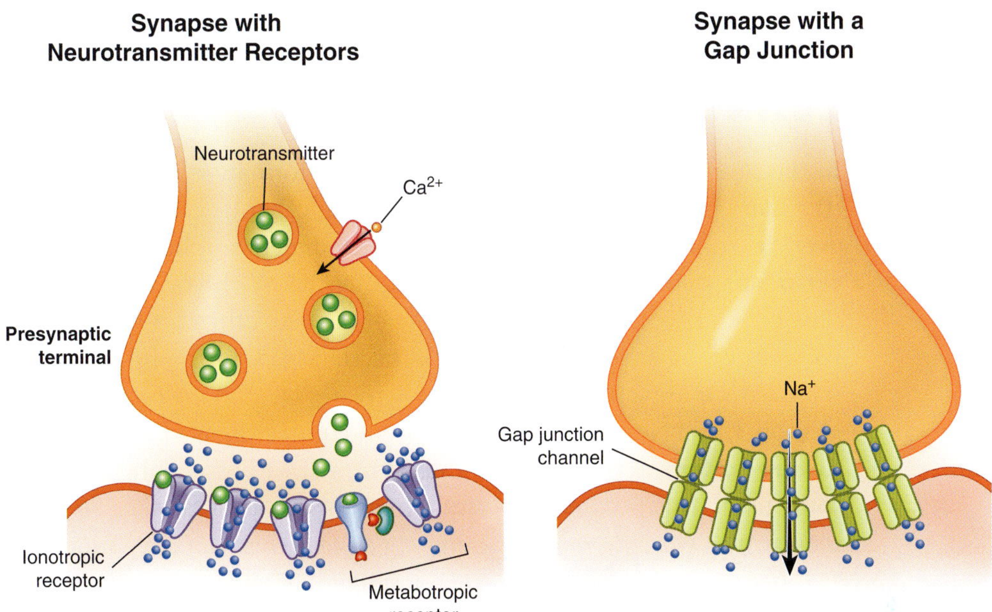

Figure 2.20 The gap junction. Neurons may communicate through synapses with neurotransmitter receptors (left) or with gap junctions (right).

First, the heat of the cup causes the opening of Na^+ channels in the dendrites of the sensory neuron in the hand. Na^+ enters as a result of electrical and concentration forces. Depolarization of the neuron exceeds the firing threshold at the axon's initial segment, triggering an action potential. The action potential moves along the axon to the terminal, triggering the opening of Ca^{++} channels and the release of an excitatory neurotransmitter into the synapse. The transmitter molecules bind to receptors of a local spinal cord neuron, generating EPSPs, small depolarizations in the cell body, and/or dendrites. If the EPSPs summate to exceed the firing threshold at the axon's initial segment (near the axon hillock), then the local spinal cord neuron will also fire and release an excitatory transmitter to activate the motor neuron. The motor neuron releases a neurotransmitter that binds to receptors on a muscle fiber, which activates muscles that open the hand. The cup drops.

But some regions of the brain may recognize the cup is valuable and send inhibitory signals to the spinal cord. Neurons descending the spinal cord from the brain release an inhibitory neurotransmitter that generates IPSPs in the local spinal cord neuron, the same neuron that is receiving EPSPs from the heat-sensing neuron. If the summation of the EPSPs and IPSPs produces enough depolarization to exceed the firing threshold at the initial segment of the axon, the local spinal cord neuron will fire, causing the motor neuron to fire and the cup to drop. If the IPSPs are sufficient to prevent depolarization to the firing threshold, the local spinal cord neuron will not fire. The hand will continue to hold the cup, perhaps long enough to place it safely on a table!

2.7 NEURONS CAN MAKE RECURRENT, DIVERGENT, AND CONVERGENT CONNECTIONS

In the case of the hot cup, neurons carried information from one place (the hand) to another (the spinal cord) to another (the muscles). However, in some cases, sets of interconnected neurons have excitatory **recurrent connections** with one another. Recurrent connections are illustrated in Figure 2.21A, where one neuron activates a second; and the second neuron sends a recurrent connection back to the first, exciting it as well. Or, imagine that Neuron 1 activates Neuron 2 which activates Neuron 3; and Neuron 3 sends a recurrent connection back to Neuron 1. **Reverberatory activity** allows the set of neurons to remain active for some time. This becomes relevant when, for instance, a set of neurons represents a working memory item (e.g., a face that you have in mind). The neuronal ensemble can remain active, allowing you to maintain the working memory representation, even when the external stimulus (e.g., the face) is no longer present in the external world. The frontal and parietal lobes appear to contain arrangements of neurons of this sort that subserve working memory (Leavitt, Mendoza-Halliday, & Martinez-Trujillo, 2017).

In other cases, neurons have **divergent connections**: A small number of neurons broadcast a message to a large number of recipients (Figure 2.21B), like a TV announcer who broadcasts his message to a large audience of listeners. For instance, midbrain dopamine neurons carry a signal to many recipient neurons throughout the forebrain, alerting them when unexpected food, money, or other valued objects appear. In humans, single midbrain dopamine neurons can make synaptic contact with approximately a million postsynaptic neurons (Pissadaki & Bolam, 2013).

In another arrangement, many neurons send **convergent connections** to a small number of recipient neurons. Imagine, for instance, that one of the neurons shown in Figure 2.21C is activated whenever you are seated on your living room sofa, another when you are looking out the window, and still another when you hear the sound of the air conditioner. These inputs may converge upon a recipient neuron that is activated only when you are on the sofa AND looking out the window AND you hear the sound of the air conditioner. The cerebral cortex contains neurons that are activated by particular environmental stimuli and send convergent inputs to neurons in the striatum which only respond to the conjunction (co-occurrence) of these stimuli (Horvitz, 2009; Shipp 2017). Convergent connections between neurons are also seen in the visual system, which we will turn to in the next chapter.

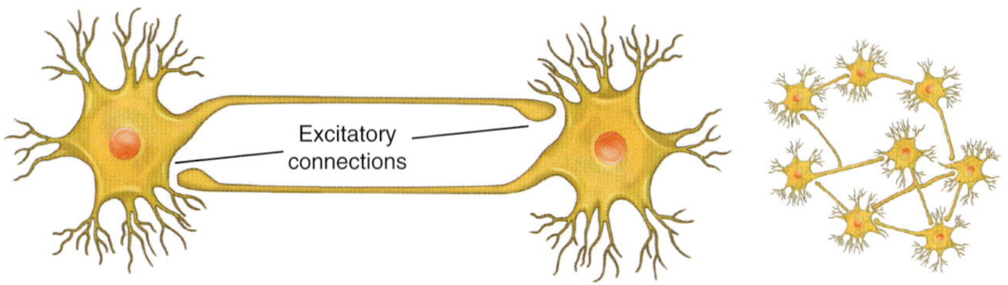

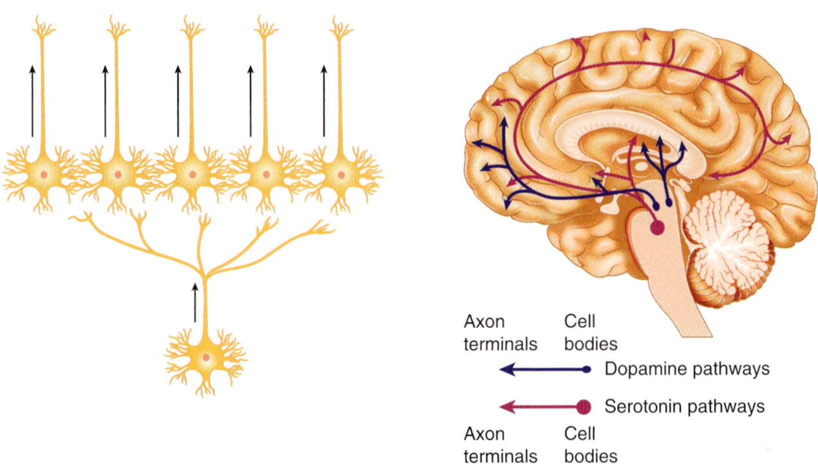

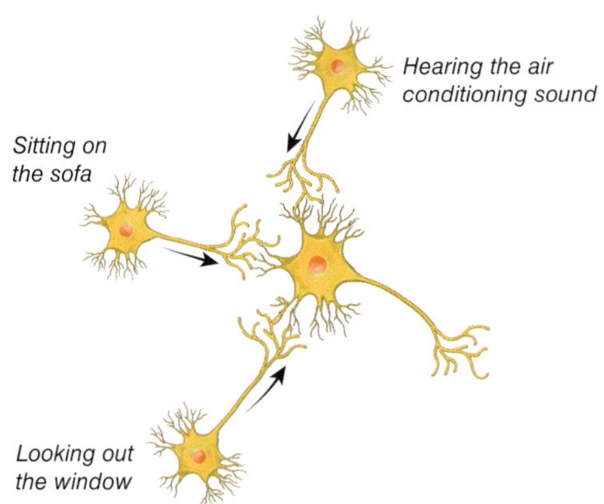

Figure 2.21 **Recurrent, divergent, and convergent connections.** (A) A set of neurons may form recurrent excitatory connections to maintain their activity. (B) One neuron may send divergent signals to many recipients throughout the brain. (C) A large number of input neurons may converge upon a single neuronal recipient.

2.8 PSYCHOACTIVE DRUGS AFFECT NEUROTRANSMISSION

Drugs that pass the **blood–brain barrier** may affect cognition, emotion, and behavior by their interactions on neural activity and chemical communication between neurons. The blood–brain barrier allows only certain substances to reach the brain. This wall of tightly packed endothelial cells surrounds the brain's blood vessels, preventing most substances (nutrients, viruses, chemicals) from passing through. The cells are packed together so tightly that virtually nothing can pass between them. In order to pass from the blood vessels to the brain, a substance must somehow pass *through* the cells. Those that can are either small, uncharged molecules like oxygen, molecules that dissolve in the layers of fat making up the membrane of the endothelial cells, or very important substances such as glucose, which the brain expends energy on actively transporting through the cells and into the brain.

We previously examined several of the steps by which neurons release neurotransmitters to communicate with other neurons (Figure 2.22). Let's now examine how some common psychoactive drugs work by altering these steps.

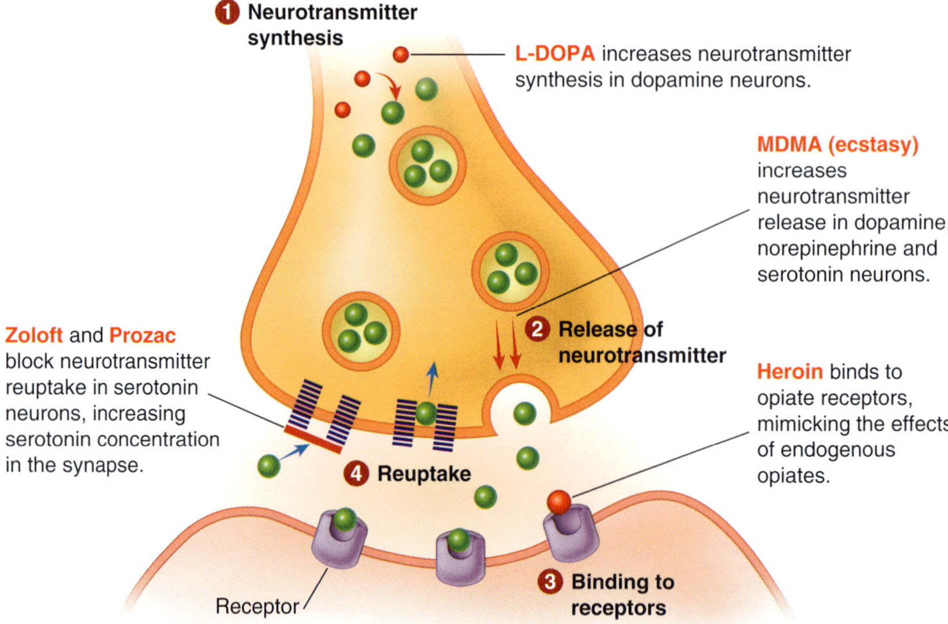

Figure 2.22 **Psychoactive drugs affect neurotransmission in various ways.** Most of the commonly known antidepressant, antipsychotic, and recreational drugs interact with (1) neurotransmitter synthesis, (2) release, (3) receptor binding, and/or (4) reuptake.

1. *Neurotransmitter synthesis.* Drugs may either reduce or increase neurotransmitter synthesis and in this way reduce or increase the amount of neurotransmitter available for release. For instance, L-DOPA, a drug used to treat Parkinson's disease, increases the synthesis of the neurotransmitter dopamine. Parkinson's patients suffer a movement disorder caused by the death of dopamine neurons in the brain, and L-DOPA restores some movement abilities by partially restoring the amount of dopamine available for release in the surviving neurons. Because L-DOPA increases dopamine levels and therefore dopamine transmission at its receptor, it is an example of an **agonist** drug – a drug that mimics or (in this case) *enhances* the activity of a neurotransmitter.

2. *Neurotransmitter release.* Amphetamine produces heightened arousal and alertness by increasing the release of several neurotransmitters, but especially dopamine and norepinephrine. Another neurotransmitter-releasing drug, MDMA ("ecstasy") can produce feelings of empathy and euphoria. MDMA acts primarily by increasing the release of serotonin, norepinephrine, and dopamine. MDMA is therefore a serotonin, norepinephrine, and dopamine agonist.

3. *Neurotransmitter receptor binding.* Some drugs bind directly to receptors, the same receptors to which neurotransmitters normally bind. For instance, heroin exerts both analgesic (pain-reducing) and euphoric effects because it binds to receptors normally bound by the endogenous (produced by the body) opiate neurotransmitters. Think of heroin as a "decoy" that fits into opiate receptors and activates them, tricking the receptor into thinking that it has bound a naturally released opiate transmitter. Heroin is an example of an agonist drug, in this case one that *mimics* the activity of a neurotransmitter.

Another drug that binds directly to receptors is Haldol, an antipsychotic drug used to treat schizophrenic delusions and hallucinations. Haldol binds directly to dopamine receptors but does not activate them. Therefore, when dopamine is released from a presynaptic neuron, it finds fewer dopamine receptor sites available for binding. Imagine a game of musical chairs, but instead of people seated in chairs, neurotransmitters are bound to receptors. If a drug like Haldol occupies many of the dopamine receptors, then some of the dopamine molecules in the synapse will be unable to bind to a receptor. Haldol is an example of an **antagonist** drug, a drug that blocks or reduces the effects of a neurotransmitter.

4. *Neurotransmitter clearance.* Many antidepressant drugs reduce the rate at which serotonin is cleared from the synapse by reuptake into the presynaptic terminal. In the same way that trash begins to accumulate on the street when it is not cleared away by garbage trucks, serotonin accumulates in the synapse when it is not cleared away by the reuptake pump. By disrupting the activity of the serotonin reuptake pump, antidepressants

like Zoloft and Prozac allow synaptic levels of serotonin to rise. With more serotonin in the synapse, more serotonin is available to bind to serotonin receptors.

Of course, there are other ways in which drugs can affect neurotransmission. For instance, lidocaine and other local anesthetics block sodium channels and thereby prevent action potentials. Some antidepressants increase neurotransmitter levels in the synapse by inhibiting the enzymes that normally degrade them. In each of these cases, however, psychoactive drugs interact with the mechanisms that normally subserve neuronal communication, i.e., the mechanisms that we've examined in this chapter.

KEY CONCEPTS

- **Neurons relay information from one nervous system location to another, as we saw in the case of the reflex carrying information about the hot cup.**
- **Neurons can make recurrent, divergent, and convergent connections with other neurons.**
- **Psychoactive drugs can alter (a) the synthesis of neurotransmitters, (b) neurotransmitter release in the synapse, (c) binding to receptors, and (d) clearance from the synapse.**
- **Agonist drugs mimic or enhance the activity of a neurotransmitter, whereas antagonists block or reduce the effects of a neurotransmitter.**
- **Through their effects on neuronal communication in particular brain areas, psychoactive drugs can alter cognition, emotion, and behavior.**

TEST YOURSELF

1. **Some psychoactive drugs affect the** *synthesis* **of neurotransmitters. Describe three other mechanisms in neurotransmission that can be affected by psychoactive drugs. Give an example of a drug that acts via each of these mechanisms.**
2. **Is Prozac an agonist or an antagonist drug? Explain your answer.**

2.9 The Big Picture

As you recall a childhood event, neurons in the memory-related hippocampus generate action potentials and transmit the signal along their axons. This leads to release of neurotransmitters that activate other neurons needed for memory retrieval. Later in the day, as you observe a friend and imagine what she is feeling, neurons in sensory areas of your cortex respond to the sound of her voice and the downward cast of her eyes.

In about 50 milliseconds, they have transmitted signals to neurons in memory-related brain regions which, in turn, bring to mind emotional states that you've associated with these sensory signs in the past.

Neurons communicate with one another, usually by releasing a neurotransmitter that binds to a postsynaptic receptor to transmit a message to the receiving neuron. As we will see in each of the chapters that follow, the interaction between neurons is critical to our sensory, behavioral, cognitive, and emotional states.

In the last chapter, we considered the neuroscience perspective that conscious decisions and other mental events *emerge from neural activity*, and that the very act of deciding arises from neurons interacting with one another. While some neural activity coincides with changes in conscious mental events, other neural activity acts behind the scenes, below the threshold of consciousness. The remainder of this book focuses on how mental, emotional, and behavioral phenomena arise from the activity of, and interactions between, neurons in various brain structures.

2.10 Creative Thinking

1. Why is it important that neurotransmitters are cleared from the synapse? What might happen if they were allowed to accumulate to an abnormal extent?
2. Thoughts are believed to arise as a result of activity of sets of neurons. As we've seen, many neurons become active only when they receive above-threshold excitation from presynaptic neurons. How do you explain a thought that pops into your mind, seemingly out of nowhere, unconnected to anything you were conscious of a moment earlier? Some neurons can fire even when they receive no excitatory input from other neurons. They have internal mechanisms that generate "spontaneous" depolarization. Could such neurons contribute to a thought that "pops" into your mind? Are there other explanations for such thoughts?
3. Return to the opening scenario where the dentist describes lidocaine's effects on pain sensations. Can you now understand everything he says? If so, replace Sarah's responses with different (more knowledgeable) responses.

Key Terms

References

Baulac, S., Huberfeld, G., Gourfinkel-An, I., Mitropoulou, G., Beranger, A., Prud'homme, J. F., ... LeGuern, E. (2001). First genetic evidence of GABA(A) receptor dysfunction in epilepsy: a mutation in the gamma 2-subunit gene. *Nature Genetics*, *28*(1), 46–48.

Chang, K. J., Redmond, S. A., & Chan, J. R. (2016). Remodeling myelination: implications for mechanisms of neural plasticity. *Nature Neuroscience*, *19*(2), 190–197.

Del-Ben, C. M., Ferreira, C. A. Q., Sanchez, T. A., Alves-Neto, W. C., Guapo, V. G., de Araujo, D. B., & Graeff, F. G. (2012). Effects of diazepam on BOLD activation during the processing of aversive faces. *Journal of Psychopharmacology*, *26*(4), 443–451.

During, M. J., & Spencer, D. D. (1993). Extracellular hippocampal glutamate and spontaneous seizure in the conscious human brain. *Lancet*, *341*(8861), 1607–1610.

Horvitz, J. C. (2009). Stimulus–response and response–outcome learning mechanisms in the striatum. *Behavioural Brain Research*, *199*(1), 129–140.

Leavitt, M. L., Mendoza-Halliday, D., & Martinez-Trujillo, J. C. (2017). Sustained activity encoding working memories: not fully distributed. *Trends in Neurosciences*, *40*(6), 328–346.

Pissadaki, E. K., & Bolam, J. P. (2013). The energy cost of action potential propagation in dopamine neurons: clues to susceptibility in Parkinson's disease. *Frontiers in Computational Neuroscience*, *7*, 13.

Shipp, S. (2017). The functional logic of corticostriatal connections. *Brain Structure & Function*, *222*(2), 669–706.

Zalc, B. (2006). The acquisition of myelin: a success story. *Novartis Foundation Symposium*, *276*, 15–21; discussion 21–15, 54–17, 275–281.

3
Sensory Systems

IAN HOOTON / SCIENCE PHOTO LIBRARY / Getty Images

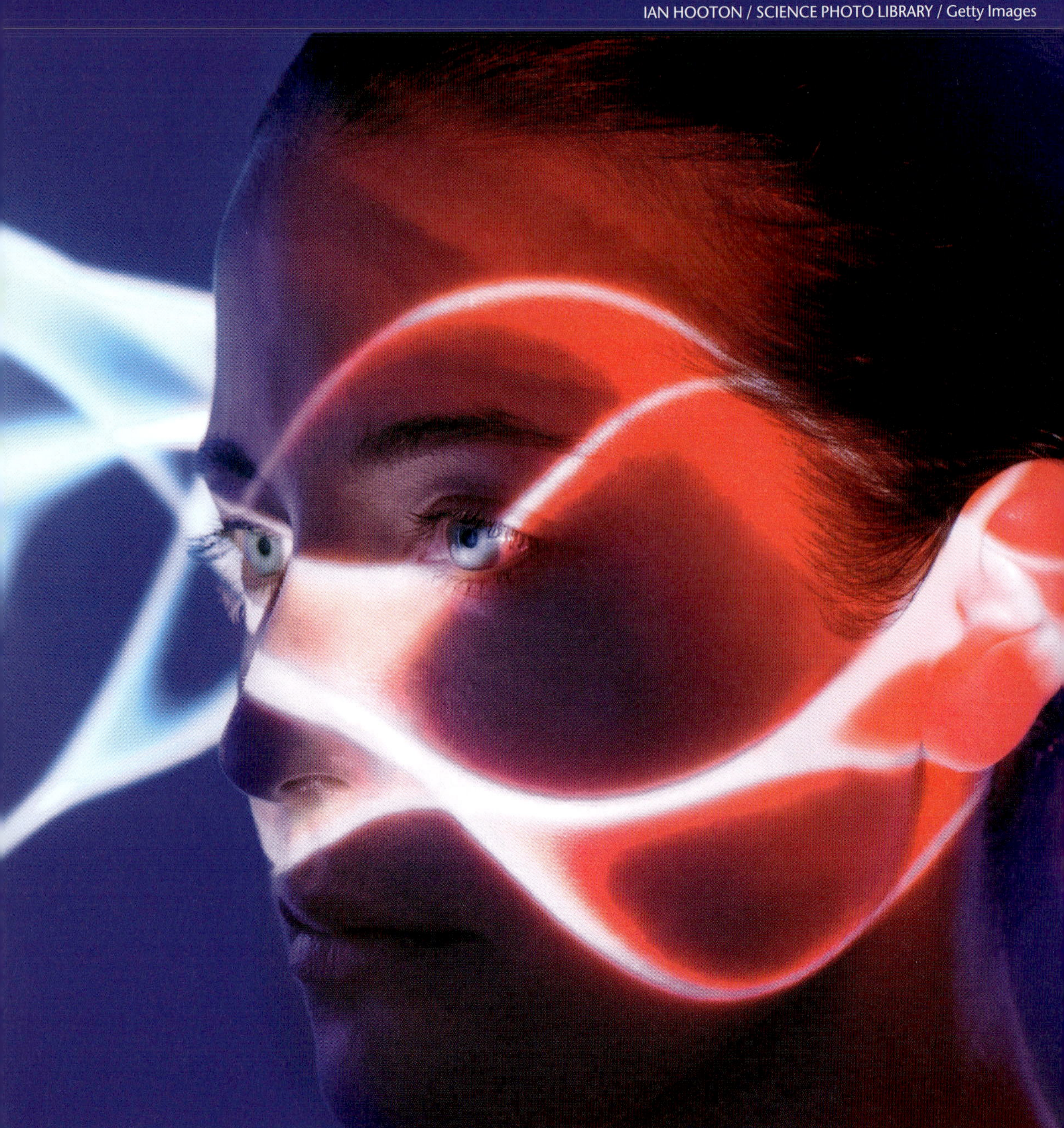

Consider This ...

Peggy was 22 when she was severely injured in a motorcycle accident on a two-lane highway in California. Because she was not wearing a helmet, the impact of the pavement upon the back of her head caused major brain injury. When she woke up in a hospital bed, she realized she couldn't see. The physician conducted a thorough physical examination. Peggy was completely blind, but there was no damage to the eye itself. A brain scan showed that her visual cortex had been damaged.

Unfortunately, Peggy did not recover her sight. However, about six months after the accident, a group of young kids were throwing a football when suddenly the ball was speeding along a path toward Peggy's head. Without being warned, she somehow knew to duck, and her friend watched in amazement as the ball went harmlessly by. The next day, the friend took Peggy to a nearby university where neuroscientists conducted additional tests of her vision.

Peggy was completely blind in the traditional sense, but she had "blindsight," the ability to respond to some visual objects without consciously seeing them. Later in the chapter, we'll return to this bizarre phenomenon.

The brain's sensory processing gives rise to rich sensory experiences. The visual system informs us about shape, size, color, and location of objects that surround us. As Peggy's blindsight illustrates, some of this information is processed in a way that gives rise to conscious awareness, while other sensory information can produce a behavioral response even when the sensory events are not consciously perceived.

3.1 SENSORY SYSTEMS IN GENERAL

It's useful to divide sensory processing into several steps (Figure 3.1). First, changes in the outside world (such as light and sounds) produce forms of energy that impact upon the body, and more specifically upon neurons. How does a change in the physical energy in the outside world change the activity of our neurons? Specialized **sensory neurons**, also called **sensory receptor cells**, respond to visual, auditory, tactile, taste, and other sensory stimuli. For instance, receptor cells in the retina of the eye (photoreceptors) respond to light. Sound activates receptors in the ear; touch activates receptors in the skin. In each case, the physical stimulus changes the electrical activity of the receptor cell, and the amount of neurotransmitter it releases. The conversion of a physical stimulus into changes in the activity of a neuron is called **transduction**. Physical energy from the environment (light, sound waves, pressure on the skin) is "transduced" into changes in neuronal activity.

The sensory receptor communicates with other neurons that send the sensory signal along a pathway that ends in higher brain centers typically located in the cerebral cortex. The difference between a visual and an auditory experience depends upon *which* pathway of neurons is firing, and ultimately which area of the cortex is activated. If you were to artificially stimulate neurons in my visual pathway, I would presumably have a visual experience. Whether or not it resembles a "real-world" visual experience would depend upon whether the pattern of neuronal activity in these neurons resembles a pattern of activity produced by a real-world visual event.

We devote much of this chapter to an in-depth look at vision, the best-understood sensory system. A comprehensive survey and analysis of *all* our sensory systems would require several chapters. However, later in this chapter, we will look briefly at some of the other major sensory systems and consider commonalities in the way different sensory modalities (vision, hearing, touch, smell, and taste) process stimuli.

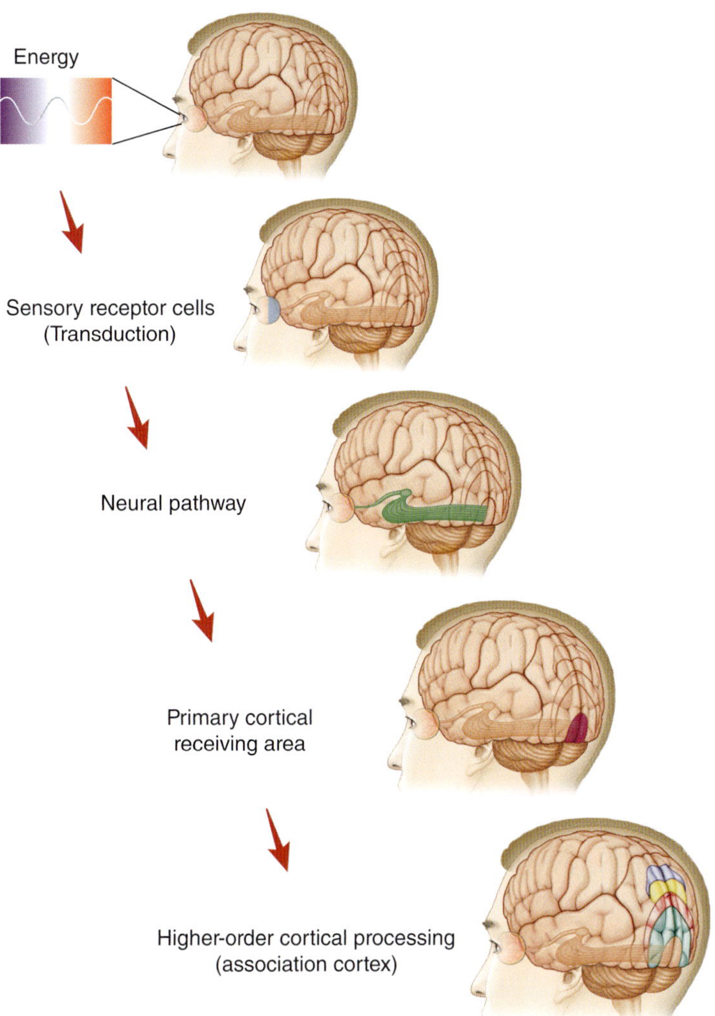

Figure 3.1 Key steps in sensory information processing. The visual and other sensory systems (auditory, tactile, etc.) require these same steps, beginning with a source of energy and ending with perception of the stimulus.

3.2 VISION

Of all our senses, the visual system brings us the most detailed information about the world. It also occupies a larger portion of the human brain (~30 percent of the cortex) than any other sensory system.

A camera stores a record of whatever image passes through its lens. The visual system works differently. In humans and other mammals, the visual system is constantly choosing which parts of the visual world to focus upon. It is selective. Like other parts of the brain, the visual system has been molded through millions of years of evolution to effectively serve the needs of the species. It helps us to navigate through the environment, to locate and manipulate objects, to recognize those stimuli that are valuable as well as those that are harmful.

3.2.1 The Eye Bends Light to Produce a Focused Image on the Retina

In order to see a table, a rose, or any other object, light must shine on it, bounce off at least some parts of it, enter the eye, and reach the retina. The retina is where our light-sensitive neurons are located. Let's begin our exploration of vision by asking how light from external objects reaches the retina at the back of the eye.

Light

The human visual system only responds to a small range of wavelengths within a much larger electromagnetic spectrum (Figure 3.2A). Electromagnetic radiation within this range is called **visible light**. We are insensitive to all other wavelengths of light, from the tiny (high-frequency) wavelengths the size of an atom, to very long wavelengths (low frequency) of hundreds of meters (radio waves) and beyond. If it were evolutionarily advantageous, our visual system could have evolved differently and extended its sensitivity down to lower or higher frequencies on the spectrum, as have the visual systems of other animal species.

Within the narrow spectrum of visible light, different wavelengths of light correspond to different colors. The shorter wavelengths are perceived as "cool" colors such as violet and blue. The longer wavelengths appear as "warmer" colors, yellows and reds (again, see Figure 3.2A). White light is a mixture of all the wavelengths within the visible spectrum, and black is the absence of light. Light consisting of just a single wavelength (such as a pure blue light) is perceived as saturated (rich). Light made up of a mixture of wavelengths is less saturated. Light waves with a higher amplitude (height) are perceived as brighter (Figure 3.2B).

The Eye

The human eye appears at first to be a very simple structure in the shape of a globe. Insects and other species have eyes with a more complex appearance. An insect's eyes are composed of thousands of small components, each of which brings a separate image to its nervous system. However, when it comes to the simple appearance of the human eye, looks can be deceiving. The human eye is so complex that eye doctors (ophthalmologists) often specialize in treating only a single component of the eye, such as the retina.

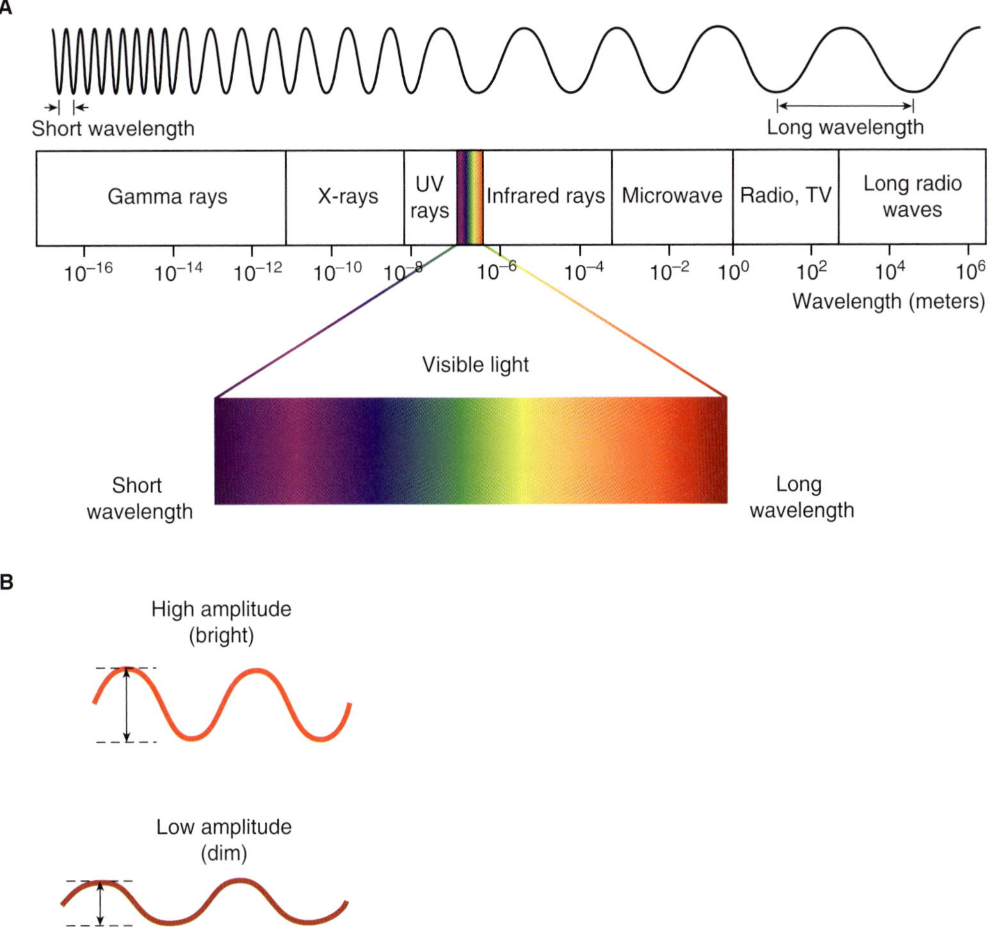

Figure 3.2 Visible light. (A) The human visual system responds to a small range of wavelengths (visible light) within a much larger electromagnetic spectrum. Within this narrow range, we perceive different wavelengths as different colors. (B) Light with a high amplitude is perceived as brighter than light with a low amplitude.

While the visual system does not passively receive information like a camera, the eye itself does have some features similar to a camera (see Figure 3.3). When you take a picture with a camera, an aperture (opening) can be adjusted to allow a particular amount of light to enter. The light then passes through a lens, which focuses the image upon an image sensor (such as film) at the back of the camera. In the human eye, the amount of light that enters is controlled by the diameter of the **pupil**. The **cornea** of the eye **refracts** (bends) the entering light even before it enters the pupil. After the light passes through the pupil, it bends further as it passes through the **lens** of the eye. Tiny muscles can elongate or shorten the lens in order to focus the incoming image upon the **retina**. The shape of the lens flips the image, so the retina actually receives an inverted image of the real-world object. As we will see, the retina is a thin layer of tissue at the back of the eye that contains neurons that transduce light into patterns of neuronal activity.

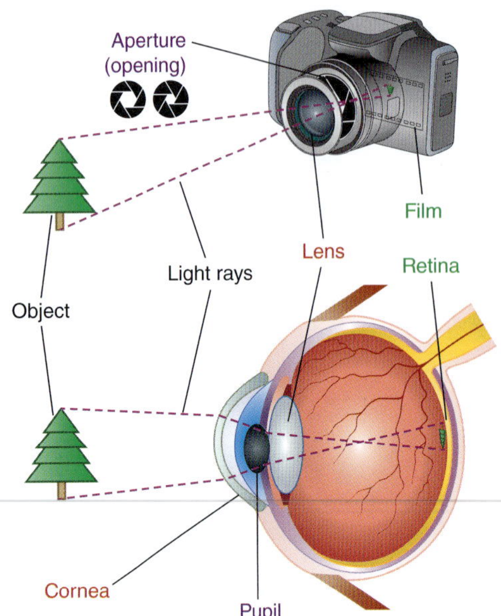

Figure 3.3 **The basic structure of the human eye is very much like a camera.** The eye has an opening for light (pupil), structures that focus the light (the cornea and lens), and a region where light from the image lands (retina). The parts of a camera carry out similar functions.

3.2.2 Photoreceptors: The Light-Sensitive Neurons of the Retina

We have seen so far that light from the outside world bounces off objects and forms images upon your retina. Let us ask how the retina compares to a movie screen, which also receives patterns of light that make up images. Unlike the movie screen, the retina is not a passive recipient of images. The brain constantly directs eye and head movements so that light bouncing off objects of interest lands upon your retina. It is as if you were watching a film and yelling to the cameraman, "Focus on the villain, I want to see his face again!" In the end, the images you are attending to land upon your retina, and this causes changes in the activity of neurons in the retina.

Neurons that detect light are located at the back of the retina; they are called **photoreceptors**. After arriving at the retina, light (almost always) needs to pass several layers of other cells before reaching the light-sensing photoreceptors (Figure 3.4). An exception is a central portion of the retina where light has a direct shot at the photoreceptors with no other cells in the way. Just behind the photoreceptors is a layer of tissue called the **retinal pigment epithelium**. This tissue at the very back of the eye absorbs extra light so that the light does not bounce around the eye. The pigment epithelium also provides nutrients to the photoreceptors. The key idea is that light travels all the way toward the back of the eye and then continues its journey through a forest-like group of cells before finally reaching the photoreceptors, its final destination.

The two types of photoreceptors, **rods** and **cones**, are named for their shapes; the rods are the longer and slightly leaner ones (Figure 3.5). In the

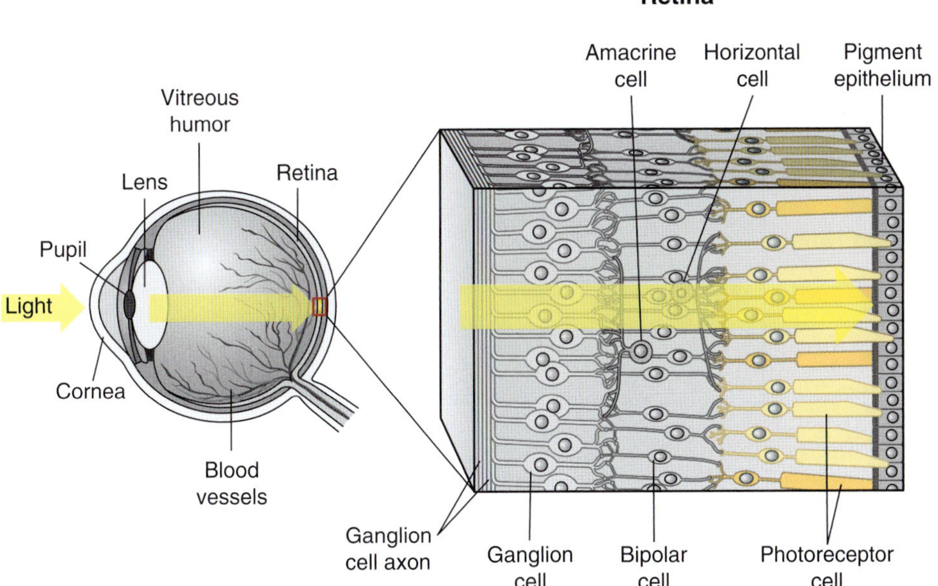

Figure 3.4 Light enters the eye and reaches the photoreceptors in the retina. After light passes through the lens and vitreous humor, it arrives to the retina where it continues through several layers of cells before it reaches the light-sensitive photoreceptors.

human eye, cones are found mostly in a central portion of the retina called the **fovea**, where the lens focuses the images that we look at directly. Imagine you are looking at a scene containing a tree surrounded by bushes and flowers. If you are focusing directly upon the tree, the image of the tree is falling upon your cone-rich fovea. The other parts of the scene, say the bushes and flowers, are falling upon the periphery of your retina, that is, upon your rods.

The retina also contains a portion with no photoreceptors at all. The area, called the **optic disk**, is where axons carrying visual information from the retina leave on their way to the brain. It is also called the **blind spot** because you are unable to see objects that fall upon this retinal location. Carry out the test in Figure 3.6 to demonstrate to yourself that you are unable to see images that fall upon your blind spot.

Rods Respond to Low Levels of Illumination

The rod-filled periphery of the retina is more sensitive to light than the cone-filled center. This is because individual rods respond to very low intensities of light, intensities that would fail to activate a cone. In addition, as seen in Figure 3.7, a large number of rods send their combined output to individual receiving neurons (bipolar cells, described below). Whenever a group of neurons pools its combined output to a smaller number of neuronal recipients, we say that there is **convergence** of information.

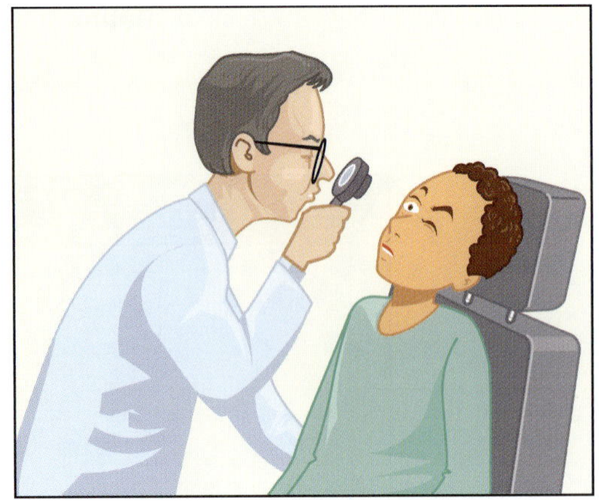

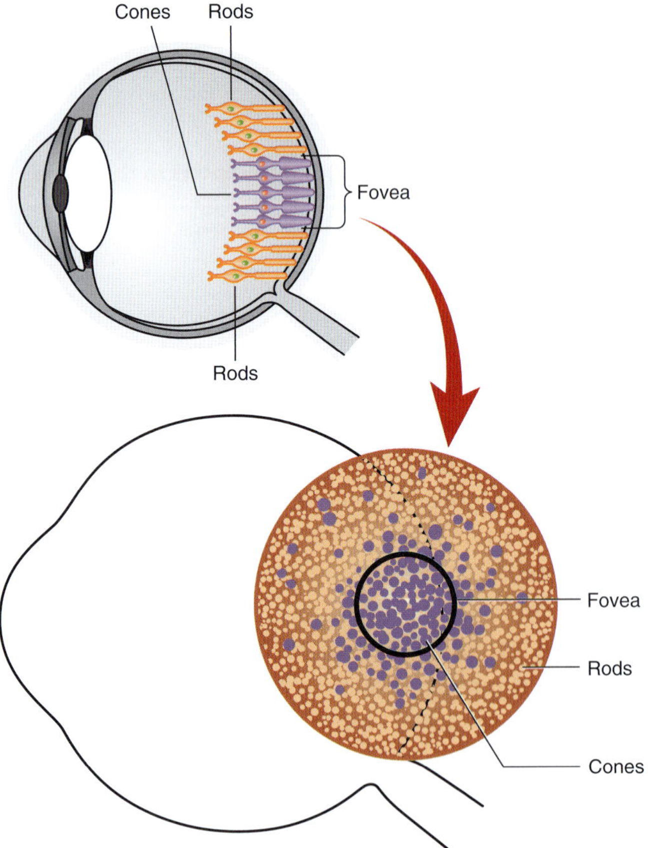

Figure 3.5 Cones are in the fovea. If you were to look straight back at a person's retina, you would see the cones (purple) clustered in the center (fovea) while most of the rods are located in the periphery of the retina. In the drawing of the eyeball (middle), the rods and cones are greatly enlarged. In reality, they'd be tiny, and located within the thin retinal layer at the back of the eye.

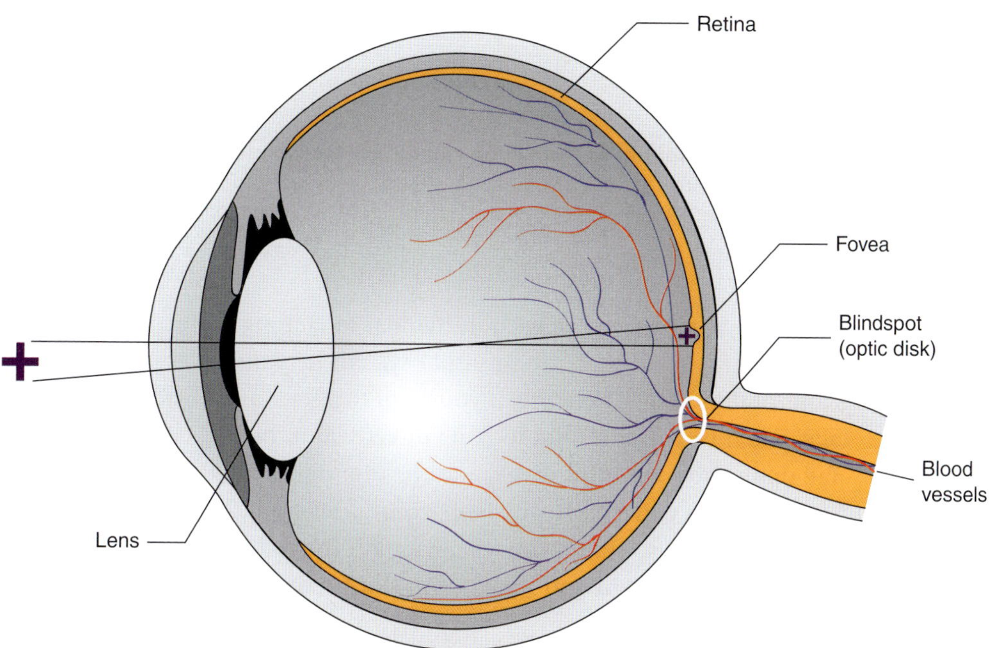

Figure 3.6 **Can you see an image falling upon your blind spot**? How to make an image fall upon the blind spot in the retina of your right eye: With your nose pointing between the cross and the black circle, cover your left eye and stare at the cross with your right eye. Slowly move toward the image. Continue staring at the cross with your right eye. At a certain point, the black circle will disappear. The image of the circle is now falling upon the blind spot of the retina in your right eye. To make an image fall upon the blind spot in the retina of your left eye: Cover your right eye and look at the circle with your left eye. Adjust your head distance. The cross will disappear when its image falls on the retinal blind spot.

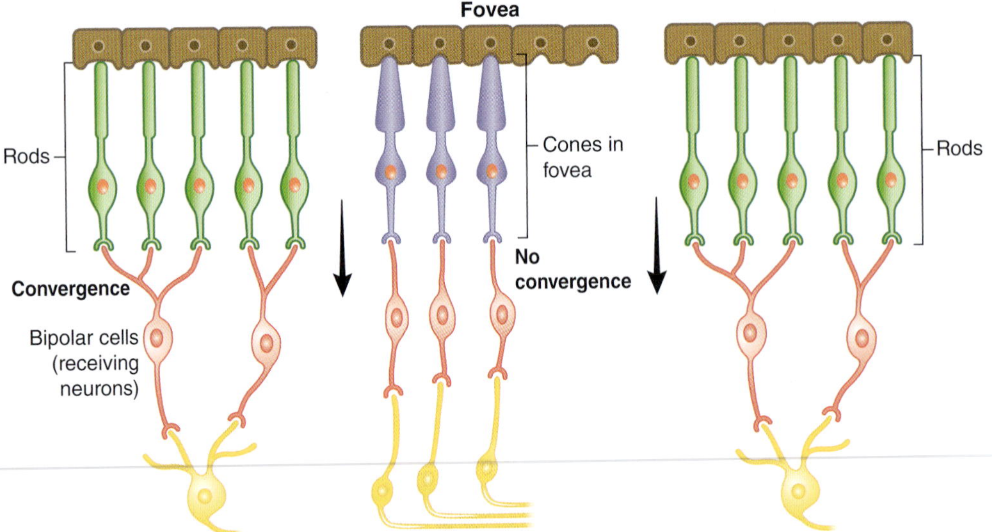

Figure 3.7 **The rod-filled periphery of the retina can detect low levels of light.** Rods respond to small changes in light intensity, and the output of many rods "converge" (add together) to influence the activity of the bipolar cells. This allows the rod-filled periphery of the retina to respond strongly to even low levels of light.

The light sensitivity of each individual rod, along with convergence of rod outputs, leads to a strong visual system response even under conditions of dim light. Therefore, if you want to detect a faint star in the night sky, you'd be better off not looking directly at it, because its image would fall upon the cone-filled fovea, and the dim light would be insufficient to stimulate the cones. Instead, avert your gaze about 20 degrees off to the side of the star, so that its image falls upon the rod-filled periphery of the retina. (Try it tonight and see if a dim star becomes easier to detect.)

Cones Transmit Visual Detail

Cones provide high **acuity** (sharp vision). For this reason, you can best identify the small letters in the eye chart in the eye doctor's office when you stare at them directly so that the image falls upon the fovea. High acuity is attributable to one-to-one connections between cones and the cells that receive the cones' signal (Figure 3.8). Imagine that you are looking at a painting, and you focus upon an area of fine detail. Different parts of the detailed image fall upon different cones. Neurons further along in the visual pathway receive inputs from just a single cone. On the other hand, the visual information reaching a rod combines with the information reaching many other rods when they send their combined output to receiving neurons. Without one-to-one mapping between photoreceptors and receiving neurons, the details are lost.

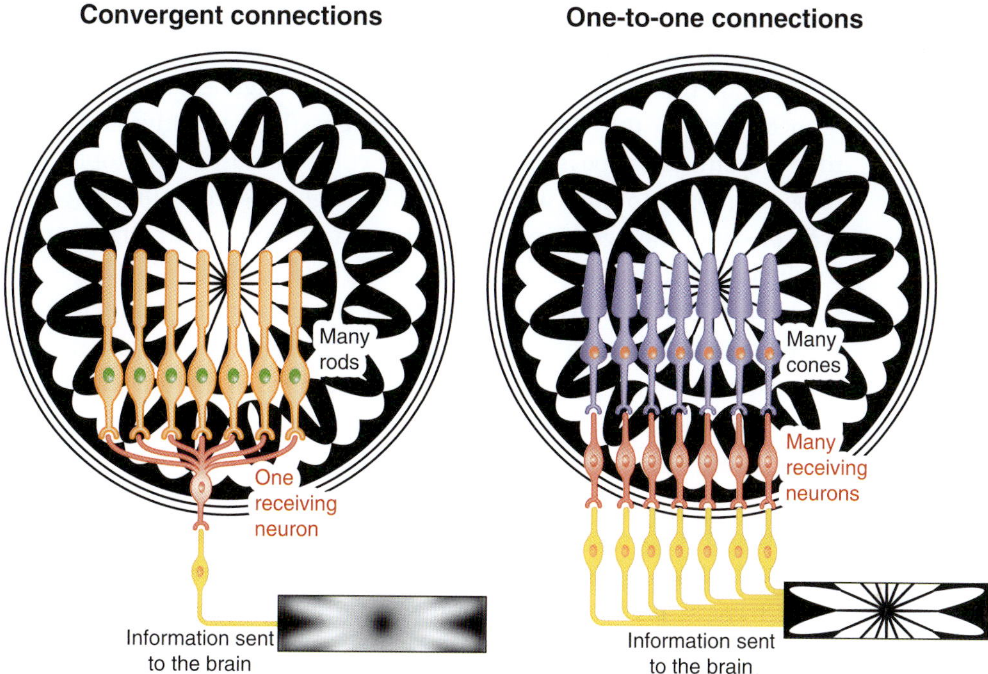

Figure 3.8 The cones transmit details better than rods. Detailed patterns of rod activation are lost when combined output from rods converges upon a small number of receiving neurons. In contrast, detailed patterns of cone activation are maintained as the cones communicate in a one-to-one manner with their receiving neurons.

Figure 3.9 Only the cones transmit color. To the left is a photograph of a carnival scene. The brain "sees" a very different picture. To the right, notice the blurring and loss of color of parts of the scene that fall on the rod-rich periphery of the retina. Normally, our eyes dart around a scene, allowing the cone-rich fovea to capture the details and colors that surround us.
(Adapted from World City, World Party by Michael Elleray.)

Cones Are Sensitive to Color

In addition to their role in visual acuity, cones detect colors. Rods respond only to black and white (gray scale). Figure 3.9 illustrates the sharp color that we see at the center of our field of vision compared to the blurry and colorless periphery, away from the center of our gaze.

There are three kinds of color-sensitive cones (Figure 3.10A). They differ according to the kind of **photopigment** (light-sensitive molecule) they contain. One type is called the "blue cone" because its photopigment responds mostly to short wavelength (blue) light (Figure 3.10B). A second type of cone, the "green cone," contains a photopigment that is most sensitive to medium-wavelength (green) light. Finally, the "red cone" responds best to long wavelengths (red, but also orange and yellow). These three types of cones communicate with other neurons in the visual pathway, and their signal eventually reaches visual areas of the cerebral cortex.

Notice in Figure 3.10B that the "green cone" responds maximally to green. Green is its "preferred" color. But follow the line representing the green cone response as the line descends to the right into the red wavelengths and you'll see that the green cone responds to red light too – just not as much as it responds to green. Similarly, the other two kinds of cones have a "preferred color," but respond to other colors as well to a lesser extent.

When you look at a red tomato versus a green bean, does the "red cone" *only* respond to the light reflected off the tomato and does the green cone *only* respond to the light reflected off the green bean? No. As you can see in Figure 3.10C, red cones respond strongly to the long wavelengths coming from the tomato; but green cones respond too, just to a lesser degree. Green cones respond strongly to the medium wavelengths coming from the green bean; but red cones respond too, just to a lesser degree. Most colored objects stimulate at least two types of cones. In order to tell the color of an object, the visual system compares the response of the red, blue, and green cones to one another. The precise manner in which these comparisons occur remains to be elucidated.

KEY CONCEPTS

- **The human visual system detects wavelengths of light within only a small range of the electromagnetic spectrum.**
- **The two types of photoreceptors, rods and cones, both convert light to neural activity. Rods are specialized for sensitivity to low levels of light. Cones allow visual acuity and sensitivity to different wavelengths of light (colors).**

TEST YOURSELF

1. **What are the major cell types in the retina? Describe their role in visual processing. (What are cones better at detecting? What are rods better at detecting?)**

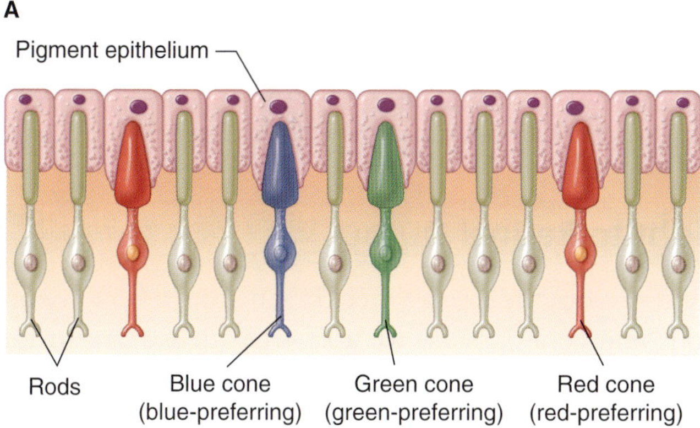

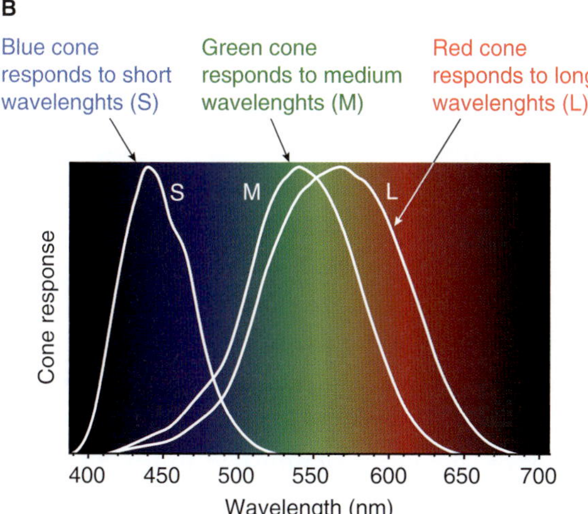

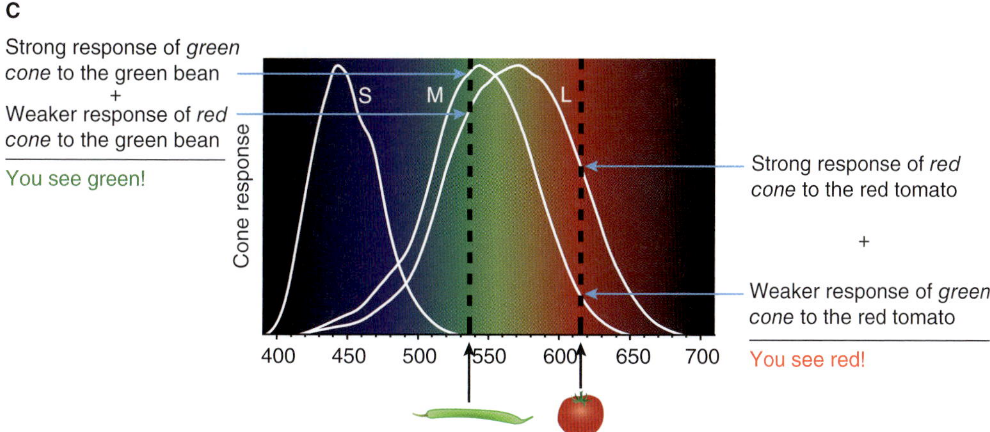

Figure 3.10 Three types of cones and their responses to light. (A) One kind of cone responds preferentially to blue, another to green, and the third to red. (B) The colors in the background represent different colors of light entering the eye, with their wavelengths labeled on the *x*-axis. The three curved lines represent the response of the "blue cones," which respond mostly to short wavelengths of light, "green cones," which prefer medium wavelengths, and "red cones," which respond preferentially to long wavelengths. (C) In order to tell the color of an object, the visual system compares the response of the red, blue, and green cones to one another.

2. Why are cones better able to transmit visual details than rods? Put another way, what is it about rods that make them so *bad* at transmitting detail? (Hint: It has to do with the number of rods or cones that send combined output to receiving neurons in the visual system.)

3.2.3 From Light to Retinal Output

We've seen that light reaches the retina where it generates a response in photoreceptors (rods and cones). Next, we ask: What does it mean for photoreceptors to *respond* to light? *How* do they respond?

Light Inhibits the Activity of Photoreceptors

In Chapter 2, we saw that neurons become depolarized (excited) when positively charged sodium ions (Na^+) enter. You might therefore imagine that when light hits the photoreceptors in the retina, they become depolarized. However, the opposite is true. Na^+ enters and depolarizes both the rods and the cones *in the dark*! This excitatory inflow of Na^+ ions, along with a small inflow of calcium ions, is called the **dark current**. What happens when light arrives?

Recall that photoreceptors contain light-sensitive photopigment molecules. When light hits a rod or a cone, its photopigment undergoes a change in conformation (shape). The conformational change of the photopigment triggers a series of chemical reactions within the photoreceptor that ultimately causes the Na^+ channels to close. The reduced inflow of the positively charged Na^+ leads to hyperpolarization (inhibition) of the photoreceptor (Figure 3.11). (In the dark, K^+ ions exit the neuron while Na^+ enters; so, when light stops Na^+ entry, and K^+ continues to exit, the net effect is hyperpolarization.) In case you need to brush up on the terms "depolarization" and "hyperpolarization," and the factors that drive Na^+ and other positively charged ions into and out of neurons, it might be worthwhile to take a few minutes and review these topics in Chapter 2.

Photoreceptors Send Signals to Bipolar Cells

Photoreceptors communicate with **bipolar cells** (Figure 3.12). Recall that photoreceptors are *inhibited* by light. When light arrives, are the bipolar cells activated or inhibited? The fact is that one class of bipolar cells is activated by light (ON bipolar cells) and another class is inhibited by light (OFF bipolar cells). For our purposes, it will be sufficient to focus only on the bipolar cells that are activated by light. When we refer to "bipolar cells," we will be describing these ON bipolar cells.

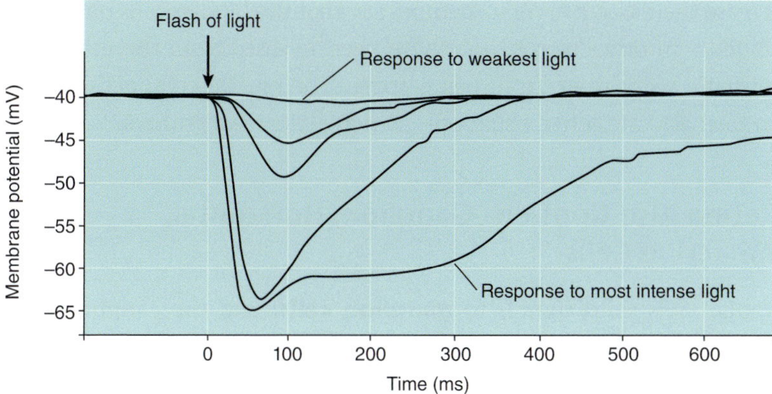

Figure 3.11 Light hyperpolarizes the membrane potential of photoreceptors. The figure shows the change in the membrane potential of a single photoreceptor (a cone) following light flashes of varying intensity. Intense flashes of light cause strong hyperpolarization (e.g., traces dropping from –40 to –65 mV membrane potential). Weak-intensity flashes produce only slight hyperpolarization (the cell remains near its –40 mV resting state).
(Schnapf & Baylor, 1987.)

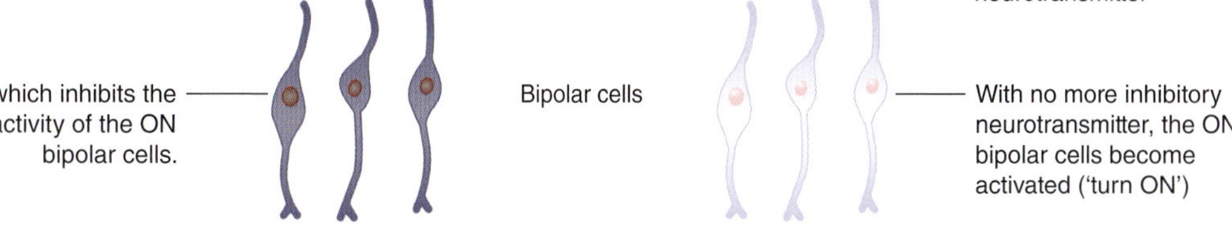

Figure 3.12 Photoreceptors communicate with bipolar cells. In the dark, photoreceptors release their neurotransmitter. The drawing shows the transmitter inhibiting bipolar cells (left panel). When light arrives, the photoreceptors stop releasing their neurotransmitter (right panel), allowing the bipolar cells to become active.

In the dark, when photoreceptors are most active, they release a neurotransmitter that *inhibits* the activity of the bipolar cells. When light arrives and the photoreceptors become inhibited, they stop releasing their neurotransmitter. The bipolar cells are no longer inhibited by the neurotransmitter, and increase their activity. We sometimes say that the bipolar cells have been disinhibited – in other words, they have been released from the inhibition that normally keeps them from being active. The bipolar cells, activated by light, in turn activate other visual cells, which activate still others.

The Retina Also Contains Ganglion, Horizontal, and Amacrine Cells

The bipolar cells send signals to **ganglion cells**, and the ganglion cells pass the information to the brain. The photoreceptor → bipolar cell → ganglion cell completes the three-stage retinal information processing of light (Figure 3.13).

Before we get to the very important ganglion cells, let's consider two other types of neurons in the retina. **Horizontal cells** receive input from photoreceptors and send outputs to several nearby photoreceptors. Imagine that light shines upon photoreceptor E and activates a horizontal cell as depicted at the top of Figure 3.14. That activated horizontal cell sends output to nearby photoreceptors D and F, reducing their response to light. The more photoreceptor E responds to light, the less D and F can respond. This allows nearby photoreceptors to compete with one another in their visual responses. Because the competition involves inhibition of lateral (adjacent) neurons, it is called **lateral inhibition**.

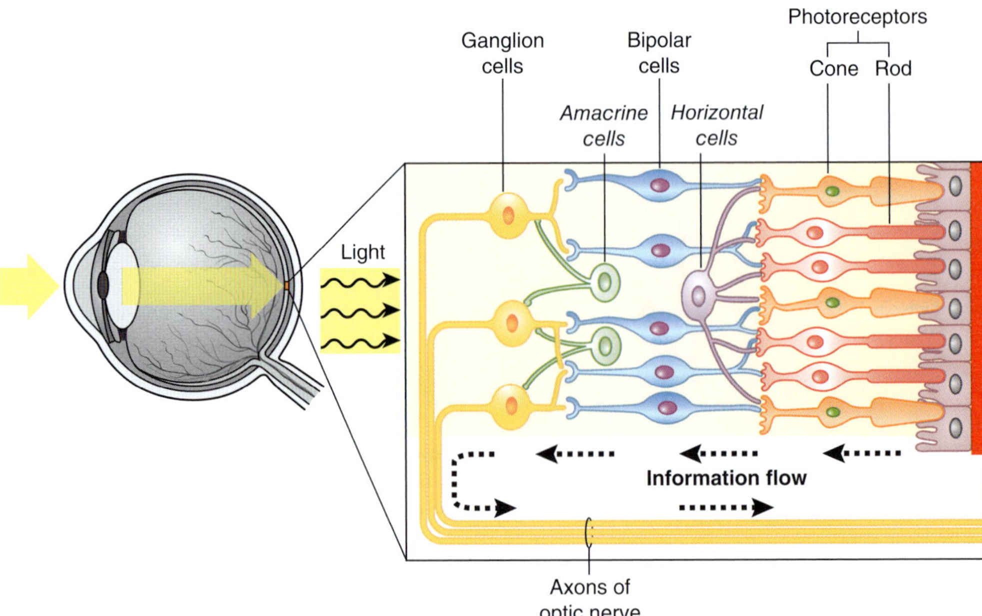

Figure 3.13 Anatomical connections of the five cell types in the human retina. Information flows from the photoreceptors to bipolar cells to ganglion cells. The horizontal cells and amacrine cells modulate this flow of visual information.

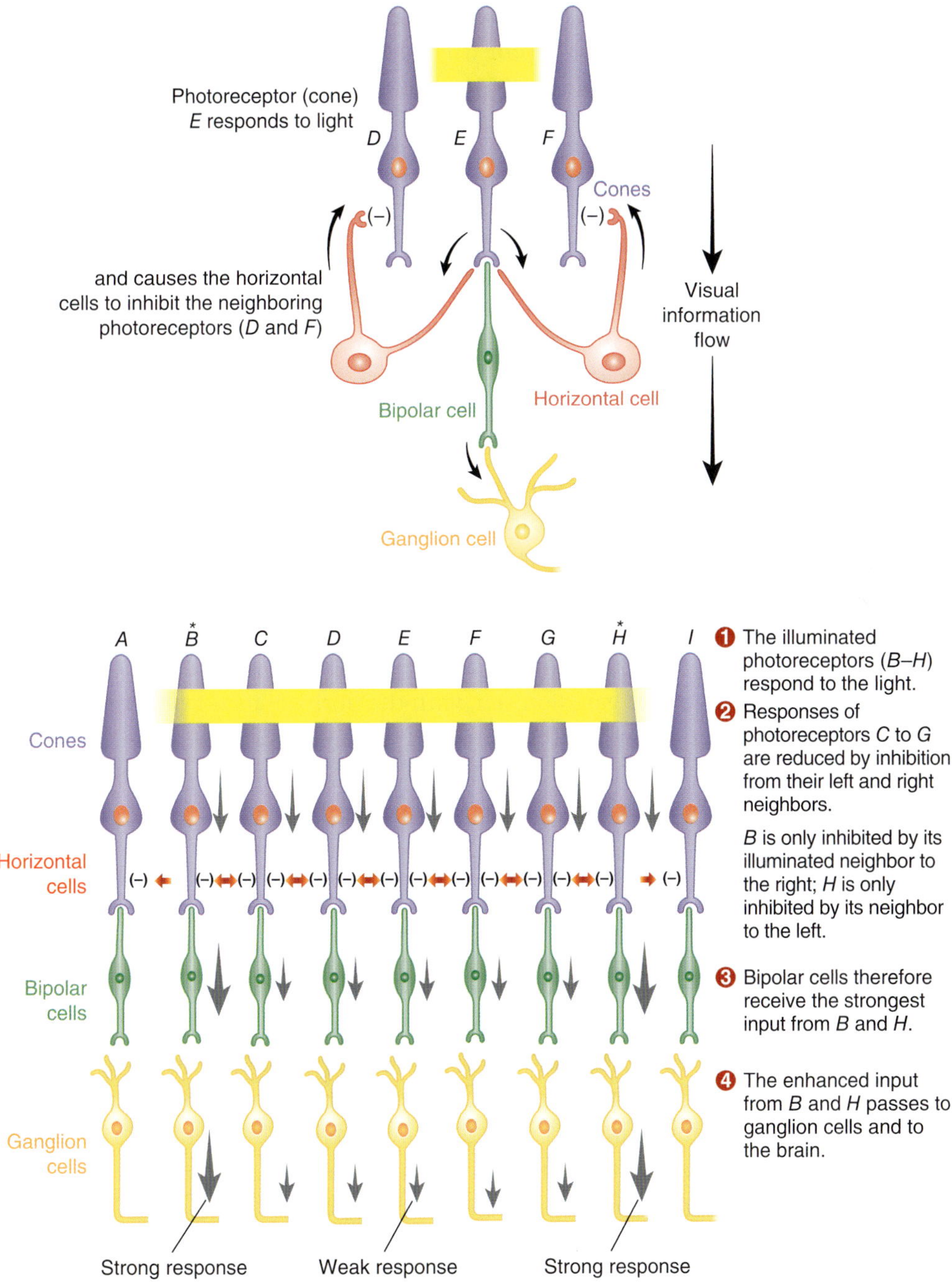

Figure 3.14 Horizontal cells and lateral inhibition. (A) When photoreceptors respond to light, they pass on the information to bipolar cells which pass it on to ganglion cells. But photoreceptors also suppress the visual response of their neighbors via horizontal cells. (B) The cones at the outer edges of the illuminated area (B and H) send a particularly strong visual signal to the brain. This helps to enhance visual detection of edges.

What happens if light falls equally on a large number of photoreceptors? Each photoreceptor will inhibit the response of its neighboring photoreceptors. Almost all the photoreceptors will show a diminished response to the visual stimulus. *Almost* all of them, because the photoreceptors on the edges of the image will be the least inhibited. In the bottom panel of Figure 3.14, light falls upon photoreceptors B through H. Photoreceptors C, D, E, F, and G are each inhibited by the activity of their neighboring photoreceptors on each side of them. But photoreceptor B is only inhibited by photoreceptor C, and photoreceptor H is only inhibited by activity of photoreceptor G. The horizontal cells, by contributing to lateral inhibition among photoreceptors, enhance detection of edges.

Amacrine cells are located between the bipolar and ganglion cells (again, see Figure 3.13). They receive visual input from bipolar cells, and send signals to retinal ganglion cells. This allows ganglion cells to respond to images falling on regions of the retina larger than that which drives the activity of a single bipolar cell.

So far, we have said that visual information is first detected by the rods and cones, that is, the photoreceptors. This visual information moves sequentially along three principal types of cells in the retina: photoreceptor to bipolar cell to ganglion cell, with the horizontal and amacrine cells influencing the ways that the visual signals combine as they move along the three principal cell types. We turn now to the ganglion cells: the neurons in the retina that carry visual information to the brain.

Retinal Ganglion Cells Carry Information to the Brain

Retinal ganglion cells have long axons that bundle together (making up the **optic nerve**) and exit the retina (Figure 3.13). Half of these axons from each eye cross to the opposite hemisphere of the brain, at a point called the **optic chiasm** (Figure 3.15). After the axons of the optic nerve pass through the optic chiasm, we refer to them as the **optic tract**.

Notice in Figure 3.15 that the axons leaving the lateral side of the left eye terminate in the left hemisphere of the brain, while those in the medial portion of the left eye terminate in the right hemisphere. This is because in humans and other mammals, axons from the lateral portion of the eyes (the left side of the left eye and the right side of the right eye) do *not* cross sides as they continue toward the cortex; those axons from the medial portion of the eyes cross to the opposite hemisphere.

Also notice that light coming from the right half of the visual environment projects to the left half of the retina of both eyes, and that both of these retinal regions send axons to the left hemisphere of the brain. Therefore, visual objects in the left visual field are perceived in the right (contralateral) side of the brain, and vice versa for objects in your right

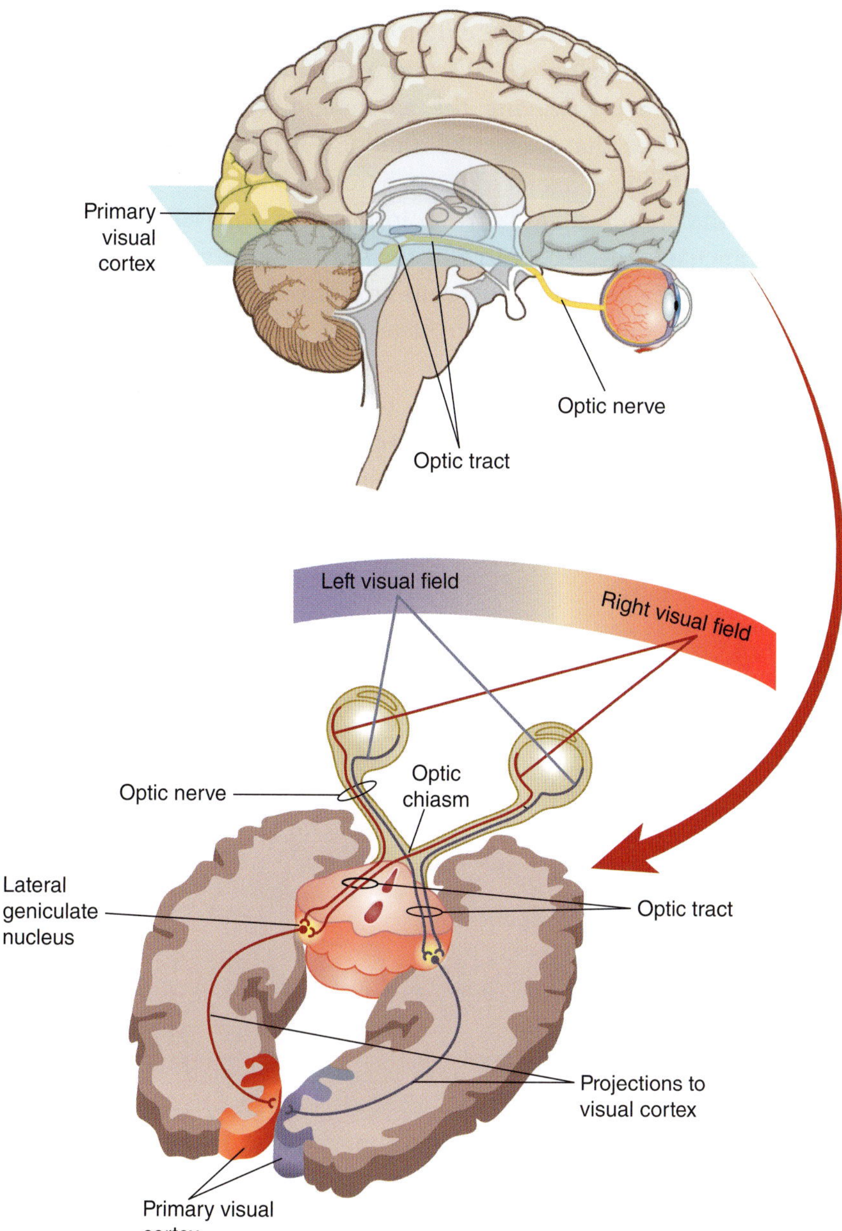

Figure 3.15 The visual pathway, from the eye to the visual cortex. For both eyes, the nerves coming from medial areas of the retina (closest to the nose) cross at the optic chiasm to the contralateral side of the brain. Nerves from lateral parts of the retina (closest to the ears) do not cross. This arrangement explains why objects in the right visual field are perceived by the left visual cortex, and vice versa.

visual field. This is why damage to visual areas of the left hemisphere interferes with seeing objects in the right visual field.

Three key brain regions receive information directly from the retina. One bundle of axons leaving the retina terminates in the **superior colliculus**, an area that looks like a mound sitting atop the midbrain (Figure 3.16). A line going straight back from a point between your eyes back into the brain would reach a point between your left and right superior colliculus. The superior colliculi shift the gaze toward significant visual stimuli. If a bee flies across your field of vision and lands near you, neurons in the superior colliculus detect its location, and send motor commands to the eyes, causing them to track the bee's movement. While neurons in the superior colliculi detect visual objects, they do not contribute to higher-level aspects of visual perception such as objects' color or shape. Visual areas of the cortex are responsible for noticing the yellow color on the bee's body. It makes sense that an area of the midbrain that specializes in fixating your gaze on a stimulus need not take part in detecting such details.

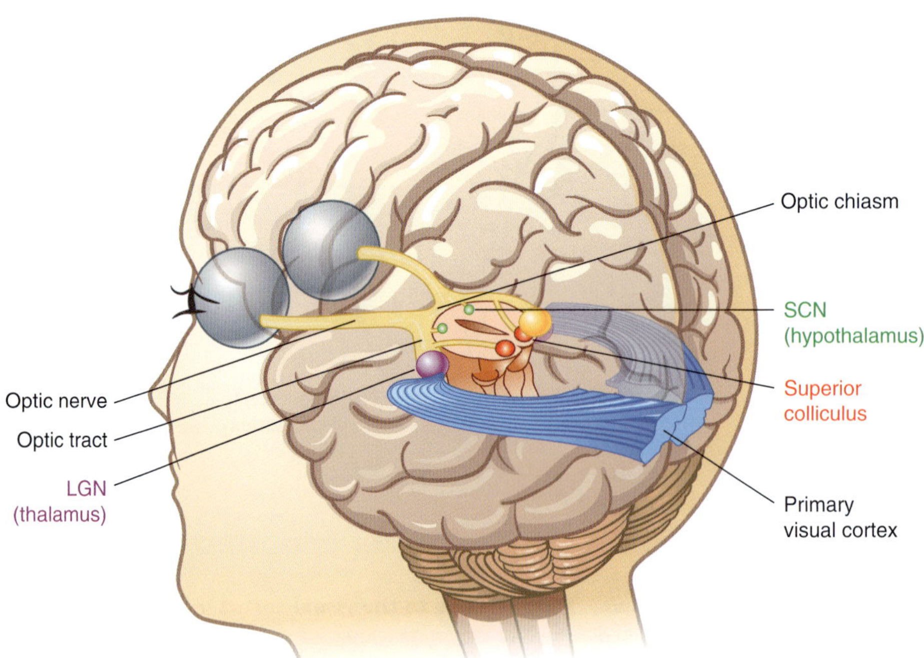

Figure 3.16 **The optic tract carries information from the retina to three key brain regions.** Most of the optic tract axons terminate in the lateral geniculate nucleus (LGN) of the thalamus, which, in turn, sends visual information to the primary visual cortex. Smaller branches of the optic tract terminate in the superior colliculus and the suprachiasmatic nucleus (SCN) of the hypothalamus.

The **suprachiasmatic nucleus** (**SCN**) is another subcortical region that receives input from the retina (Figure 3.16). The optic nerve alerts the SCN, the body's internal clock, that light has arrived to the retina and it's time to wake up. The SCN is a tiny region of the hypothalamus, but it plays a big role in linking our sleep–wake cycles to environmental light cues such as the sun.

The largest portion of the retinal axons travels via the optic tract to the **lateral geniculate nucleus** (**LGN**) of the thalamus. The LGN is the critical way-station connecting the eye and retina to the primary visual cortex where higher-order analysis of visual input begins. The primary visual cortex then sends information to other visual areas of the cortex to give rise to the perception of the colors, shapes, and locations of objects that surround us. The pathway from the retina → optic nerve → optic tract → LGN → primary visual cortex is the one we will principally follow as we continue our exploration of the visual system.

KEY CONCEPTS

- **Visual information is passed along a route involving three principal retinal neurons: photoreceptors, bipolar cells, and ganglion cells. The flow of visual information along these three principal cell types is influenced by the horizontal and amacrine cells.**
- **The principal route by which visual information reaches higher-order visual processing areas is from retina to thalamus to cortex. However, other brain regions such as the superior colliculus and SCN receive visual information as well.**

TEST YOURSELF

1. **Photoreceptors send visual information to ____ cells which send information to retinal ganglion cells.**
2. **What are the key functions of the SCN and superior colliculi?**
3. **A bundle of retinal ganglion cell axons is called the "optic nerve." But once the optic nerve passes beyond the optic chiasm, we refer to these axons as the optic ____.**
4. **If you had damage to the left optic nerve, would you have visual impairment in both eyes, or just the left eye? What if the damage was in the left optic tract (i.e., beyond the optic chiasm)? (Hint: take a look at Figure 3.15.)**

3.2.4 Neurons at Early Stages of the Visual System Respond to Simple Stimuli

We now turn our attention to how the brain processes visual information to produce the rich spectacle of our visual world. As you've seen, light on the retina changes the activity of the photoreceptors, which in turn changes the activity of bipolar cells, which finally changes the activity of retinal ganglion cells. If you were to record the activity of an individual retinal ganglion cell, what type of visual stimuli would make it fire?

Retinal Ganglion Cells

To answer the question, you'd need to insert a thin metal microelectrode (about the shape of a sewing needle) very close to the neuron's cell body where it can detect each of the neuron's action potentials (Figure 3.17A). A wire from the electrode would then inform a computer when the neuron fires at a faster or slower rate. This technique is called **single-neuron recording** or **single-unit recording**.

Using this technique, you first notice that the retinal ganglion cell is firing slowly when the room is dark.This is its background rate. Now you shine a small beam of light upon a portion of the retina (Figure 3.17B). The ganglion cell still fires slowly. Hmmm. Disappointing. Is this as fast as the ganglion cell can fire? Would it fire faster if you moved the beam of light to a different area of the retina? *What area* of the retina needs to be illuminated for this neuron to fire at its maximal rate? In the language of neuroscience, "What is the neuron's **receptive field**?"

You move the beam of light to a nearby region of the retina (Figure 3.17C), and the ganglion cell suddenly responds with a burst of action potentials! The size of the light beam hasn't changed, just the retinal area that's illuminated. You are now stimulating a number of photoreceptors that are connected via bipolar cells to the retinal ganglion cell. You seem to have stumbled upon the neuron's receptive field.

You now widen the circle of light a bit, and the neuron fires even faster. Your light beam is now hitting enough photoreceptors to *strongly* activate the ganglion cell (via the bipolar cells). However, as you continue to widen the circle of light, the ganglion cell starts to respond more slowly! Why does an increase in the illuminated area of the retina produce a reduction in the retinal ganglion cell response?

Retinal ganglion cells have what is called a **center–surround receptive field**. Some ganglion cells are activated when light shines upon a center area and inhibited when light shines upon a surrounding area. We would say that such a ganglion cell has an "on-center" receptive field. If you imagine the cell's receptive field to be the shape of a doughnut located somewhere on the retina, then light falling on the hole of the doughnut (the center) excites the retinal ganglion cell (Figure 3.17C), and light falling on the dough surrounding the hole of the doughnut (the surround) inhibits it (Figure 3.17D). This is because photoreceptors in the center part of the receptive field excite the ganglion cell (via the bipolar cells) and photoreceptors located in the surround area inhibit it.

As the figure shows, a beam of light falling only on the "center" of the receptive field causes the "on-center" ganglion cell to fire maximally. However, when the light beam is broadened to illuminate both the "center" and also some of the (inhibitory) "surround" region, the cell no longer fires maximally (Figure 3.17E). The ganglion cell's rate of firing is therefore a sum of the excitation caused by illumination of the center of its receptive field and inhibition caused by illumination of the surround regions.

Other ganglion cells have the opposite response to light, an "off-center" receptive field. These cells are most strongly activated when the center of the receptive field is dark, and the surround area is illuminated (Figure 3.17F). Both the on-center and the off-center cells share an important key feature: They respond not simply to overall amounts of light but to the contrasts of light and dark falling on their center versus surround regions. The most effective stimuli for driving activity in these neurons are small spots of light (for the on-center cells) or small spots of darkness (for the off-center cells) (Kuffler 1953).

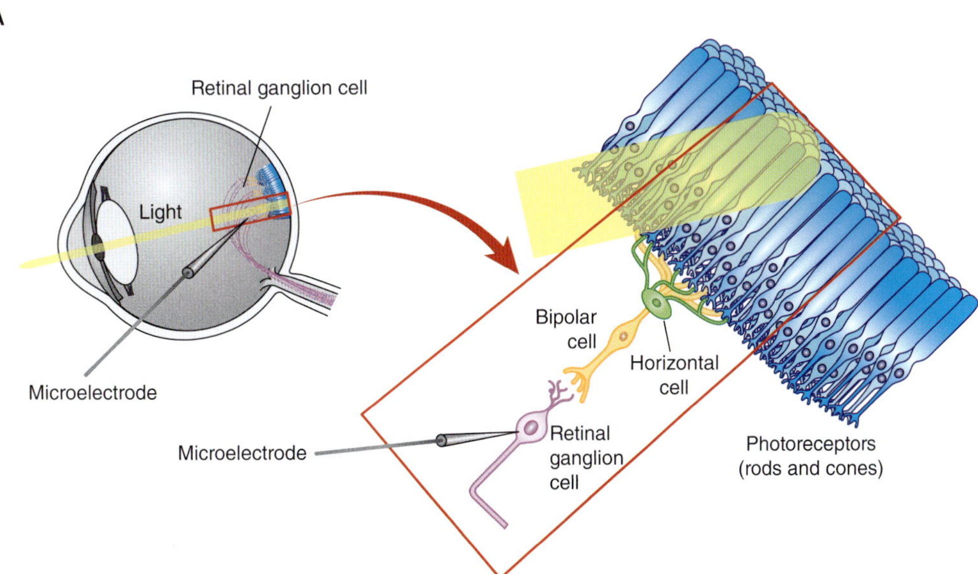

Figure 3.17 **(A) The experimenter records the activity of individual ganglion cells while shining light on various areas of the retina.** (B–C) Retinal ganglion cells with on-center receptive fields fire most rapidly when the center part of the receptive field is illuminated. (D) These cells are inhibited when light shines on their "surround" region. (E) Illumination of both the center and surround areas causes excitation and inhibition to cancel each other out. (F) Retinal ganglion cells with an off-center receptive field fire most rapidly when the surround region is illuminated and the center region becomes dark.

B

Light outside the cell's receptive field has no effect on the firing rate

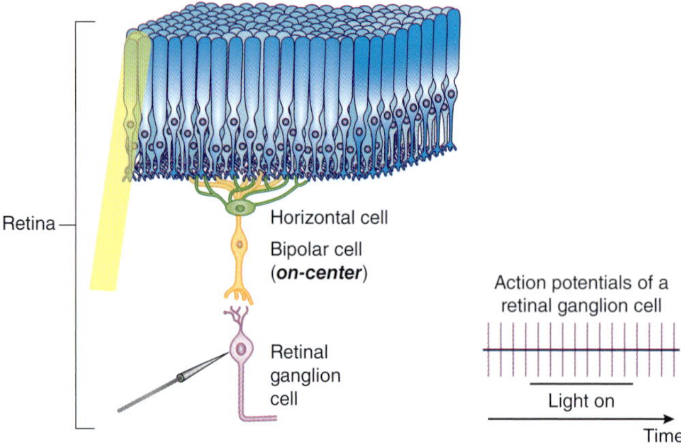

C

Illuminating the center of the receptive field causes the 'on-center' ganglion cell to fire rapidly

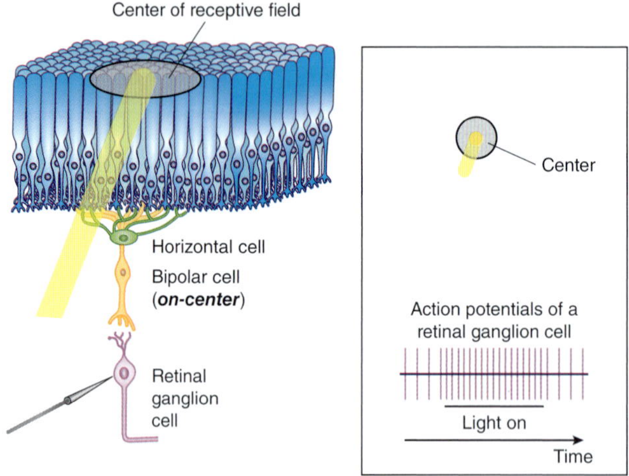

D

Illuminating the surrounding region inhibits the cell's firing

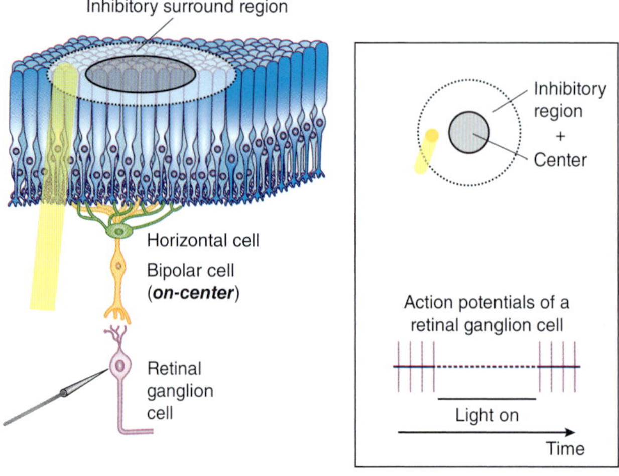

Figure 3.17 (cont.)

E

When a wide beam of light Illuminates both the excitatory center and the inhibitory surround, excitation and inhibition cancel out and the cell fires at its background rate

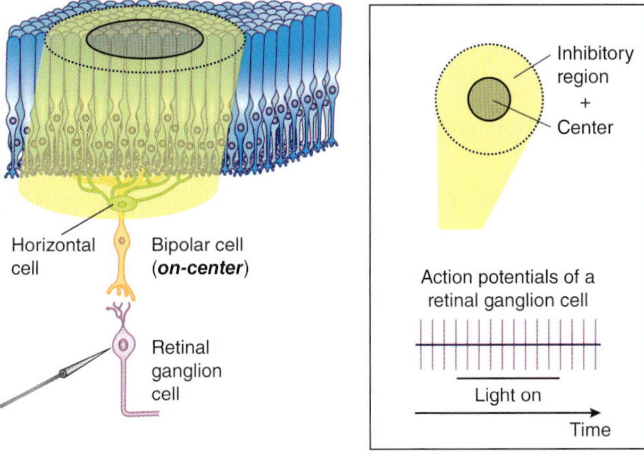

F

In cells with 'off-center' receptive fields:

– Illuminating the center of the receptive field inhibits firing

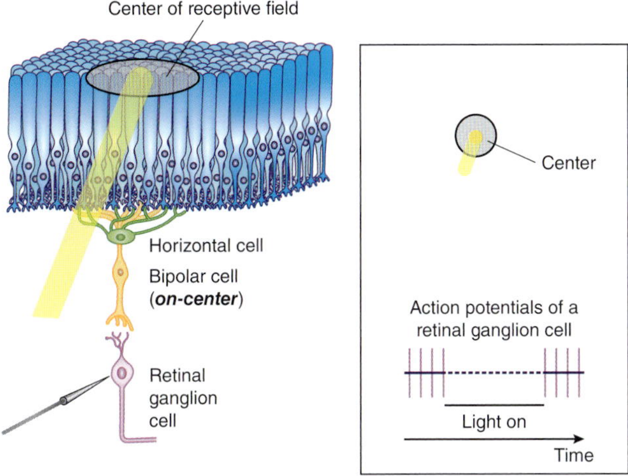

– Illuminating the surround region increases firing

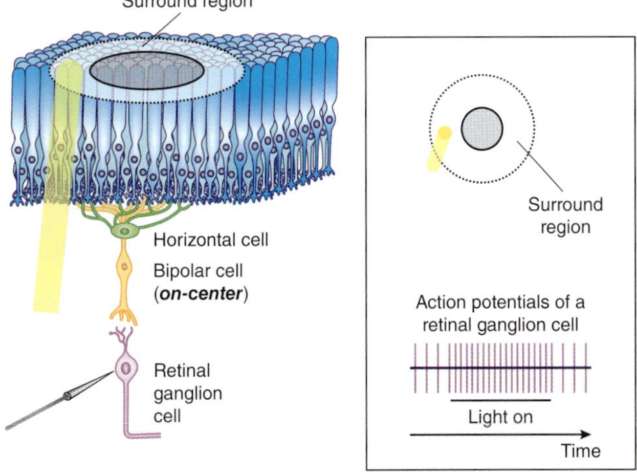

Figure 3.17 (cont.)

In an interesting experiment, researchers gave monkeys a drug that specifically prevents the firing of the on-center ganglion cells, leaving the off-center cells unaffected. They injected the drug into the retina of monkeys during a task where they had to detect spots that appeared on a screen. When the experimenters silenced the on-center ganglion cells, monkeys could no longer detect spots that were brighter than the background but they could still detect those that were darker than the background. The on-center cells appear to be necessary for detecting increases in brightness, while the off-center cells detect when objects become darker (Schiller, 2010).

The receptive field of an individual retinal ganglion cell likely covers only a small portion of the scene falling within your field of vision. However, taken together, the receptive fields of all the ganglion cells cover your entire field of vision (Figure 3.18). The receptive fields of these cells are said to **tile** the retina. Just as a well-tiled kitchen floor has no gaps between tiles, the receptive fields of the ganglion cells cover nearly the entire retina, and therefore nearly the entire field of vision, with virtually no gaps.

Even knowing that the ganglion cells tile the retina, it would be natural to wonder how the activity of these neurons can possibly contribute to the perception of complex visual stimuli such as a steep waterfall, a

Figure 3.18 **Retinal tiling. Each yellow circle represents the receptive field of an individual ganglion cell**. For instance, one cell may respond only to a small portion of the upper left corner of the scene, while the receptive fields of other ganglion cells cover other parts of the scene. Together, the ganglion cell receptive fields cover the entire field of vision.

familiar face, or a car with oil dripping from its exhaust pipe. In later sections, we will return to this question.

Lateral Geniculate Nucleus (LGN)

Recall that the retinal ganglion cells send axon terminals to the LGN of the thalamus. You might have imagined that neurons in the LGN are sensitive to more complex aspects of a visual scene than the mere arrival of light to doughnut-shaped areas of the retina. You might wonder whether some of the neurons will respond to the sight of a table or a flower. However, the receptive fields of neurons in the LGN are virtually identical to those of the retinal ganglion cells, i.e., center–surround. The LGN is a good example of what it means to be a **relay nucleus**: It takes its inputs from the retina, and transmits the information faithfully to the cortex.

If you were to look at a slice of the human LGN, you'd notice that it's made up of six easy-to-see layers (Figure 3.19). These layers are seen in the LGN of many non-human primates as well. The two bottommost layers contain large neurons; they're called the **magnocellular** (large-cell) **layers**. Above these are the four **parvocellular layers** containing the small cells. Tucked between each of these six layers of the LGN are thin regions containing additional neurons. These are the **koniocellular layers**. One magnocellular layer receives input from the left eye and the other from the right. Similarly, the input to successive parvocellular layers alternates between left and right eyes.

Let's take a moment to review. We've seen that light arriving at the retina generates responses in photoreceptors, the rods and cones. The photoreceptors signal to the bipolar cells, which in turn communicate with the retinal ganglion cells. Visual information travels along the axons of the retinal ganglion cells, terminating in the LGN (and to a much lesser extent in the superior colliculus, SCN, and other visual target sites). The LGN contains several magnocellular and parvocellular layers (with koniocellular neurons tucked in between), and a given layer receives input from just one eye.

The Primary Visual Cortex

When the output of the LGN reaches the **primary visual cortex**, also referred to as **V1**, the story of visual information processing gets more interesting. We use the term "primary" to indicate any cortical area that is the *first cortical way-station* for a particular sensory system and which receives its strongest input directly from the thalamus.

The primary visual cortex is found in the most posterior portion of the brain. Like most of the cerebral cortex, it consists of six layers. The

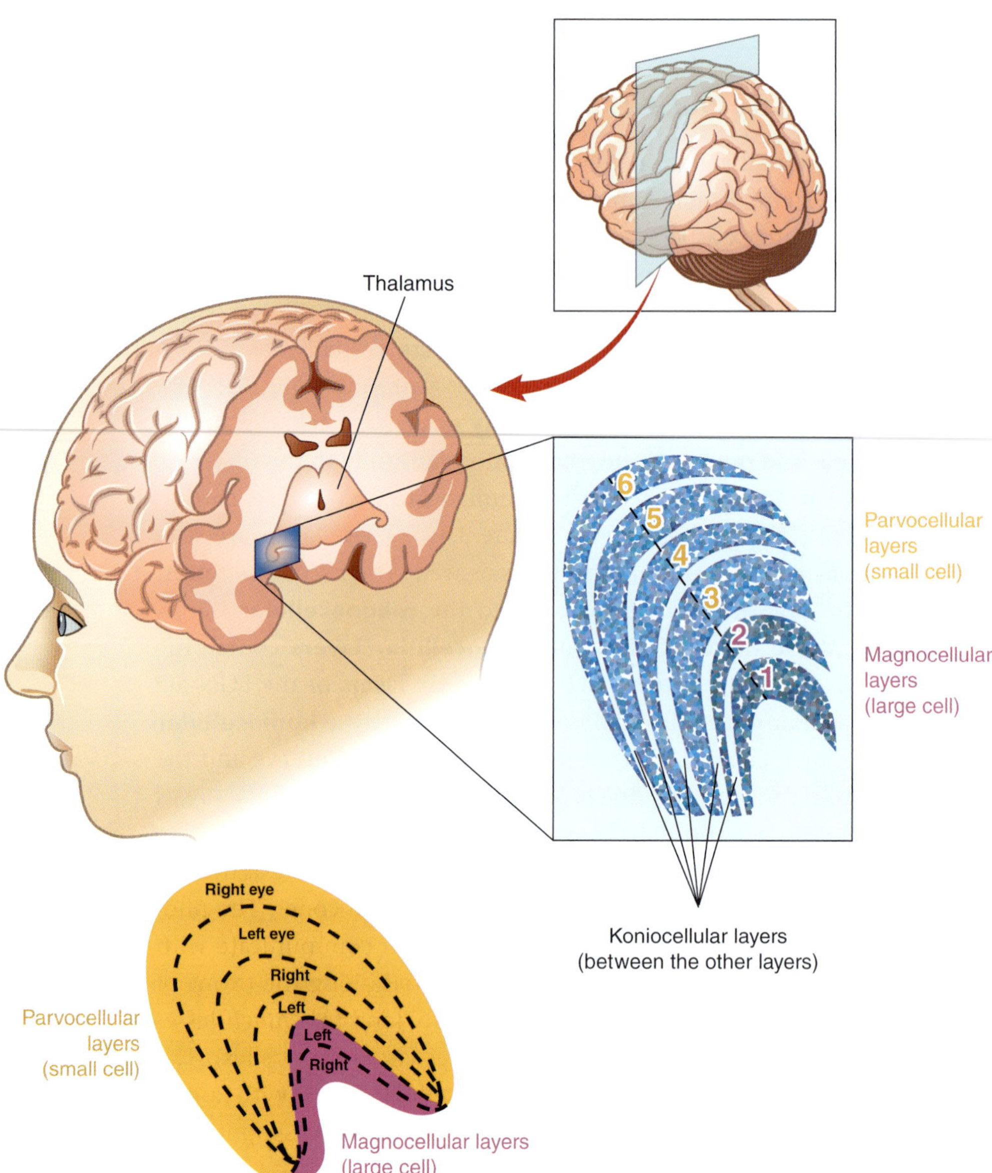

Figure 3.19 The six layers of the LGN. The left lateral geniculate nucleus (LGN) is shaded blue in the brain illustration. A close-up view shows its magnocellular and parvocellular layers, along with koniocellular layers in between. The bottom drawing shows that a particular layer of the left LGN receives information from either the left or the right eye, not both. The same is true for the right LGN.

different layers receive inputs from, and send outputs to, particular brain regions. Here, we focus upon two layers of particular interest, layers 4 and 6. Layer 4 is important because this is where most of the information from the LGN arrives (i.e., axon terminals from the LGN terminate on neurons of this layer).

Cortical layer 6 is interesting from a cognitive point of view. This layer sends outputs back to the LGN of the thalamus. Neuroscientists believe that this **corticogeniculate pathway** (*cortex* to lateral *geniculate* nucleus) plays an important role in attention. When you are hungry, your goal is likely to be finding and eating food. In this case, the most important visual stimuli become those that are edible! Axons from layer 6 of the cortex to the LGN transmit commands to the thalamic region to filter out visual information that is irrelevant to the current goal, e.g., stimuli that are not edible and not associated with anything that is edible (Briggs & Usrey, 2008). This reduces the amount of information that the LGN sends the visual cortex, information that may distract you from detecting those objects of greatest relevance to your current goals.

What kinds of visual stimuli affect the firing of the neurons in the primary visual cortex? David Hubel and Torsten Wiesel, working at Harvard University in the 1960s and 1970s, provided surprising answers to this question and were awarded the Nobel Prize in Physiology or Medicine for their work.

In their experiments, they anesthetized cats, stabilized their heads, and kept their eyes open and focused on a specific point on a screen in front of them. Thin metal microelectrodes were then placed into area V1 to record the activity of individual neurons (Figure 3.20). When they presented circles of light upon the retina, the neurons did not respond. They tried varying the location and size of the circles, expecting to see responses like those seen in the retinal ganglion cells. But the circular light beams had no effect on the V1 cells.

Then they stumbled upon an accidental discovery. In order to present the small circles of light to the retina, they would glue a small circle of metal onto a glass slide, and shine light through it. One day, as they were recording the activity of a neuron in V1, they slid the glass slide into place and the cell starting firing vigorously. But it was not the circle of light that was causing the neuron to fire. The neuron was responding to the movement of the edge of the slide across a particular area of the retina! The edges needed to be in a particular orientation. As shown in Figure 3.20, a particular V1 neuron that responds to a vertical edge does not respond to an edge in another orientation.

These cells in V1, which respond to lines of a specific orientation falling upon a particular region of the retina are called **simple cells**. Let's think about the significance of this. In a small area of the visual cortex (V1) we find cells that respond only to edges of a particular orientation (say vertical or horizontal or some orientation in between) and within a particular location in the visual field (say to the upper right of the center of gaze). Hubel and Wiesel suggested an explanation for how this perception of edges might occur. Suppose that you are looking at the stem of a flower pointing directly upward; its edges are oriented

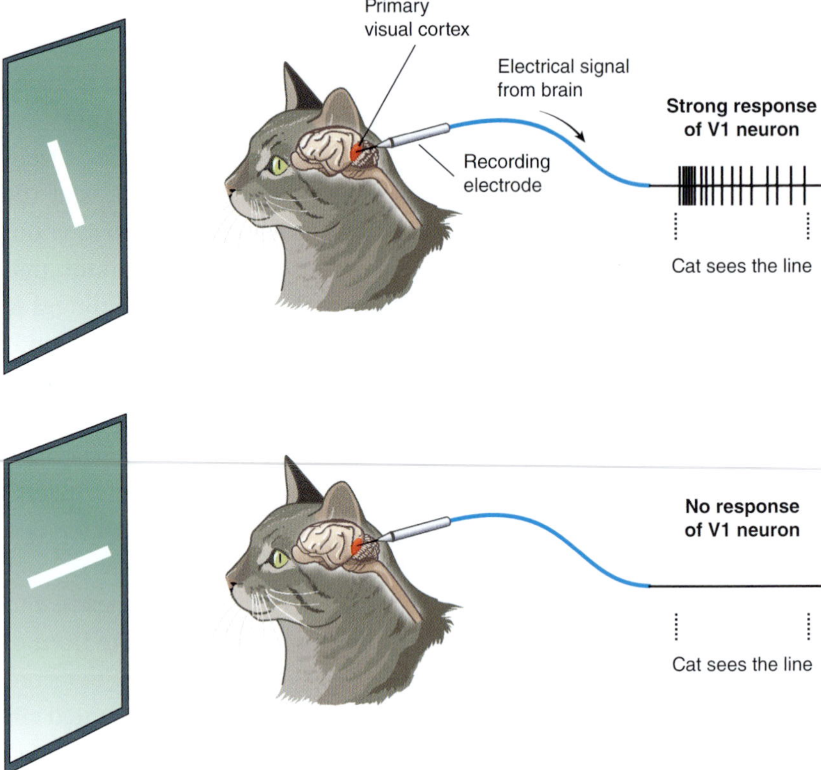

Figure 3.20 **Searching for receptive fields of individual neurons in the primary visual cortex (V1).** Many of the neurons in V1 respond to lines of a particular orientation within a certain region of the visual field. The cell recorded in this example responds to lines with the top edge oriented to the left of vertical (top drawing). The same cell shows no response to horizontal lines.

vertically (Figure 3.21). Now, imagine that the edge of the stem falls upon a small area of the retina that falls within the small circular receptive fields of three LGN cells. As shown in the figure, the receptive fields for each of these LGN cells might be lined up vertically, one on top of the other. If the edge of the stem falls across each of these receptive fields, each of the LGN neurons will be activated. Now, imagine that a single V1 cell receives input from these three LGN cells, and the V1 cell is active when all three of its inputs are active. What would result? The vertically oriented stem, and any other vertical line falling upon the same area of the retina, would excite the V1 cell.

Another type of neuron found in V1 and also in **V2** (**secondary visual cortex**) is the **complex cell**. These cells respond to lines of specific orientation, just like the simple cells. But a complex cell will respond to a line of that orientation no matter where it appears in the visual field. Also, the complex cells respond to *movement* of the line in a specific direction. This gives them the ability to detect when an object is moving.

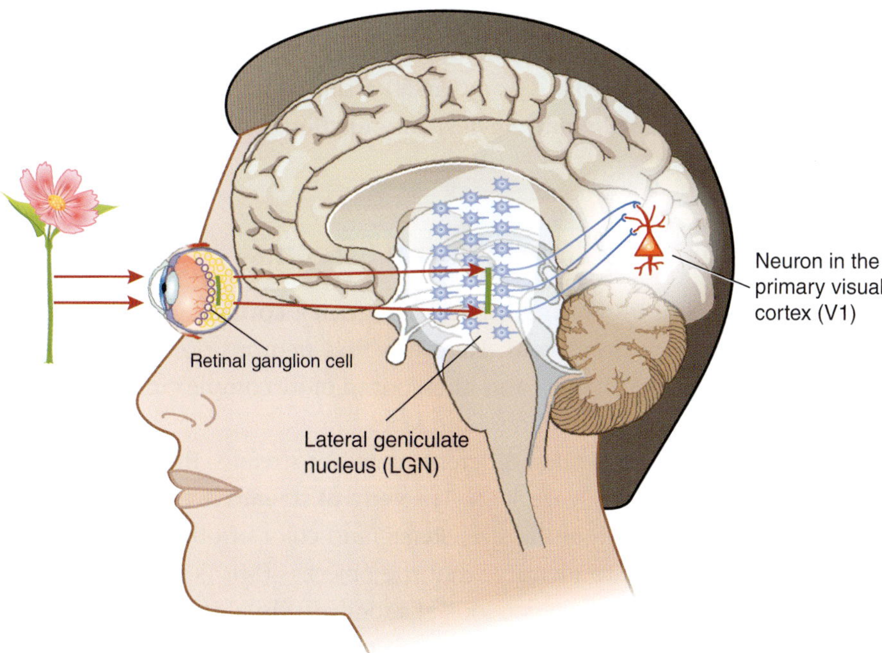

Figure 3.21 **How does a neuron in the primary visual cortex (V1) detect a straight edge**? When a vertical line falls upon the retina (e.g., the edge of the flower stem), it simultaneously activates several retinal ganglion cells and lateral geniculate nucleus (LGN) cells with receptive fields arranged vertically on the retina. The output of the LGN cells activates a neuron in the primary visual cortex, which responds only to lines with a vertical orientation. Other V1 neurons receive input from ganglion cells arranged at other orientations on the retina.

KEY CONCEPTS

- A neuron's visual receptive field is that portion of the visual world to which the neuron responds.
- Ganglion cells and LGN cells have center–surround receptive fields.
- Information at lower levels of the visual system (e.g., LGN) combines to produce more complex visual responses in the visual cortex. Visual information is combined, like building blocks.
- Neurons in V1 respond to lines of particular orientations and to the movement of lines in particular directions.

TEST YOURSELF

1. You're telling a friend about the receptive field of some neuron in the visual system, and he says "But what do you mean by the neuron's receptive field?" How would you explain it (in your own words)?
2. Describe to your friend the receptive fields of retinal ganglion cells. Describe receptive fields of simple cells in V1.

3. **How many cell layers do we generally find in the neocortex? Which layer receives input from the thalamus?**
4. **Is the lateral geniculate body (LGN) a simple relay, or might it play a role in attention? (Hint: Review the function of the corticogeniculate pathway.)**

3.2.5 The Dorsal and Ventral Streams

Beyond V1 and V2 are the higher-order visual cortical areas, referred to as **visual association areas**. Here you find neurons do not respond to simple bright or dark spots and lines, but to more complex environmental stimuli like animals, buildings, and faces.

Visual information takes different routes, or streams, through the higher-order visual areas (Figure 3.22). The **ventral stream** is a group of cortical brain areas that analyze the size, shape, and color of objects, i.e., properties that allow you to identify what the object is (Mishkin & Ungerleider, 1982). For instance, when you look at a football, visual information passing through the ventral stream permits you to distinguish it from a basketball (or from a bird, for that matter). The ventral stream is sometimes called the "what" pathway because it allows you to identify *what* an object is.

But if you are on the field, trying to catch the football, you are mostly concerned with *where* it is. The **dorsal stream** specializes in detecting where things are. Without the dorsal stream, you would be unable to locate the football on its trajectory toward you. It would be little consolation that your ventral stream allowed you to recognize that you just missed a football and not a basketball! Similarly, your ventral stream allows you to recognize that the long, thin, yellow object on your desk is a pencil. But your dorsal stream detects its location, so when you want to pick it up, your motor system can activate the appropriate motor neurons

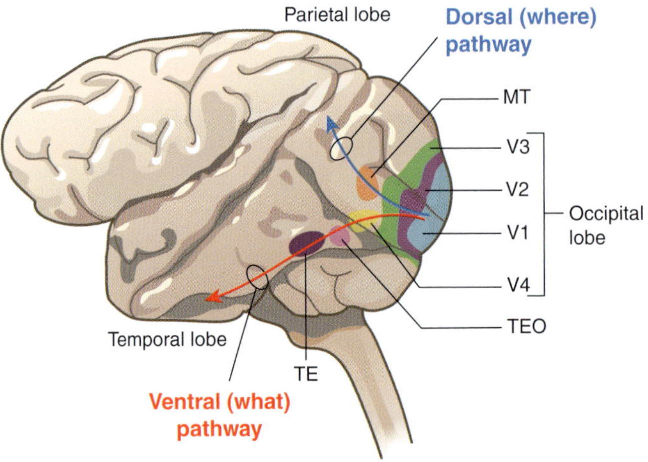

Figure 3.22 Dorsal and ventral streams. Visual information moves along the dorsal and ventral streams to distinct higher-order visual areas. The dorsal stream processes the object location, features that tell us "where" it is. The ventral stream processes details of its color and shape, features that describe "what" it is. Notice that the dorsal stream goes from the occipital lobe to the parietal lobe, while the ventral stream goes from the occipital lobe to the temporal lobe.

and ultimately the correct arm and hand movements that allow you to grasp it. By determining an object's location, information from the dorsal stream helps motor systems to manipulate objects we see around us. The dorsal stream plays such an important role in our interactions with objects that it is sometimes considered to be the link between visual and motor systems of the brain (Goodale & Milner, 1992).

People with damage to the ventral stream are often unable to recognize objects and faces. However, they have no problem grasping objects and can walk around without bumping into things so long as the dorsal stream is functioning normally. On the other hand, a person with damage to the dorsal stream is unable to grasp objects and often bumps into things, but can describe visual objects in great detail and can recognize faces without difficulty.

3.2.6 The Visual Cortex Contains Columns of Neurons with Similar Receptive Fields

Imagine that your electrode is recording the activity of a V1 neuron that responds to horizontal lines. Now, you move the electrode downward a tiny distance, in a vertical direction perpendicular to the surface of the cortex. You find another neuron that responds to lines of the same (horizontal) orientation. There is an entire column of neurons with the same receptive field – horizontal lines! Neurons that respond to lines of the same orientation are found within a particular **orientation column** (Figure 3.23A).

So, you've recorded from an orientation column containing neurons that respond to horizontal lines. Just next to this column is another column containing neurons that respond to a slightly different orientation. Next to these, a slightly different orientation, and so on, until cells representing all orientations are found. In Figure 3.23A, cells in the leftmost column all respond to horizontal lines, and those in the next column respond to lines that are slightly off-horizontal. In fact, the cells in the "horizontal line" column also respond a bit to lines of a slightly off-horizontal orientation. But they respond maximally to horizontal lines. Sometimes we say that those cells "prefer" horizontal lines. Each column of cells "prefers" a particular orientation. Perpendicular to the orientation columns are columns of cells that respond more to input from the left eye than the right, and columns that respond more to the right eye than the left (Figure 3.23B). These are the **ocular dominance columns**. In some layers of V1, the shift from ocular dominance columns with cells responding exclusively to the left eye to those responding only to the right eye is gradual; between the monocular (single-eye) columns are cells that respond equally to both eyes.

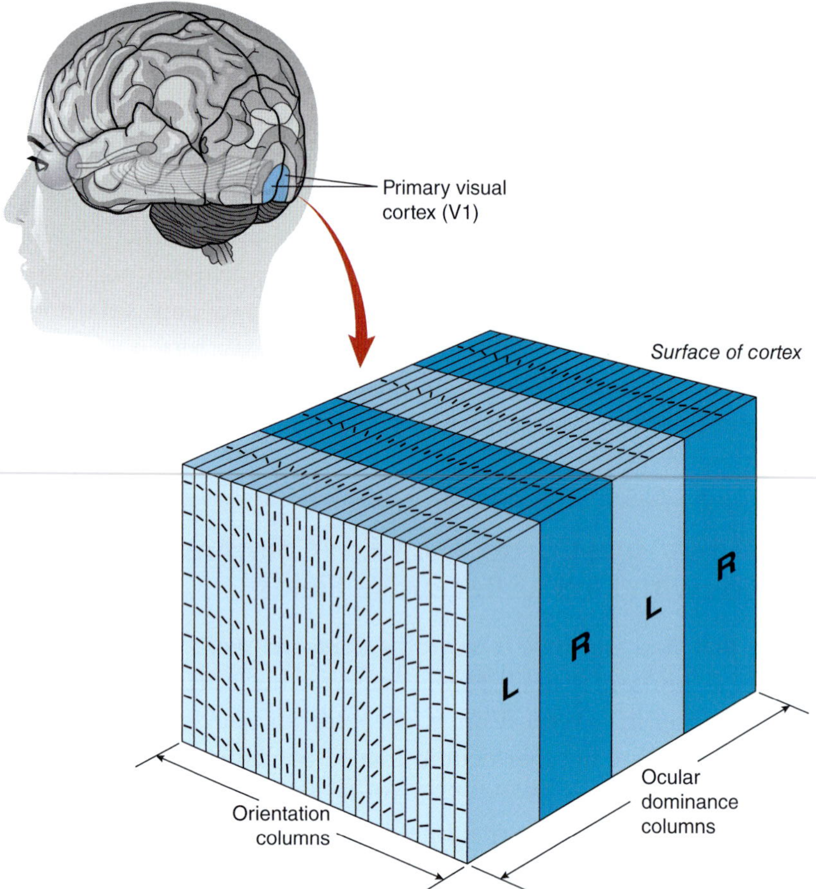

Figure 3.23 **Orientation and ocular dominance columns**. Neurons in a given column of the cortex all respond to lines of the same orientation (orientation columns). Perpendicular to the orientation columns are alternating columns of neurons that receive input mostly from the left versus right eye (ocular dominance columns).

KEY CONCEPTS

- **As visual information passes beyond V1 to higher-order processing areas, it takes different routes or "streams" through the brain.**
- **The ventral stream analyzes object size, shape, and color to assess "what" it is. The dorsal stream analyzes the object's location, i.e., "where" it is.**
- **The visual cortex contains orientation columns, with all neurons in a column responding to lines of the same orientation.**
- **Perpendicular to the orientation columns are ocular dominance columns, which respond best to the left eye or the right eye. In some cases, neurons that respond equally to both eyes are located between the left and right eye columns.**

TEST YOURSELF

1. **Describe the visual processing functions served by the dorsal and ventral streams. Which of these visual pathways is more important for recognizing objects and faces? Which is more important for guiding your hand as you reach to grasp a key?**
2. **Visual neurons within the same orientation column all respond to lines of the same orientation. Draw an example of four neighboring orientation columns, and the lines that might activate neurons in each of the four columns.**
3. **Look around the room for an object that has a vertically oriented line, and a horizontally oriented line (e.g., a chair with a vertical back and horizontal arms). Do those two different parts of the chair activate neurons in the same orientation column or different columns?**

3.2.7 Functional Issues

A large number of cortical areas contribute to the perception of our complex visual world. There are more than twenty separate cortical areas devoted to vision in humans and other higher primates. Here we describe several of the high-level visual processing areas in the cortex.

Cortical Specializations for Color, Movement, and Shape

The dorsal stream area **MT** (Figure 3.22) plays a key role in movement detection. Returning to an analogy used earlier, MT contains cells that would show specific activity patterns when you are watching a football traveling from left to right at an upward angle. Damage to area MT disrupts perception of motion direction.

Ventral stream areas **V4** and **TEO** (again, see Figure 3.22) contain neurons that respond selectively to an object's color. Recall that **color vision** begins with cones in the retina. The cones transmit color information through the visual pathway until they reach V4 and TEO. Neurons in these higher-order visual areas (within the temporal lobe) respond not only to reds, blues, or greens, but to all the different hues (light blue, dark red, pink, and so on). These color-sensitive areas have an orderly arrangement of color preferences: Neurons that respond maximally to pink are near those that respond strongly to red; those that respond to red are near those that respond to orange, these are near those that prefer yellow, and so on (Li, Liu, Juusola, & Tang, 2014).

Ventral stream area **TE** (along with TEO) contains neurons that respond to the shape of objects. Another high-order visual area, the **fusiform face**

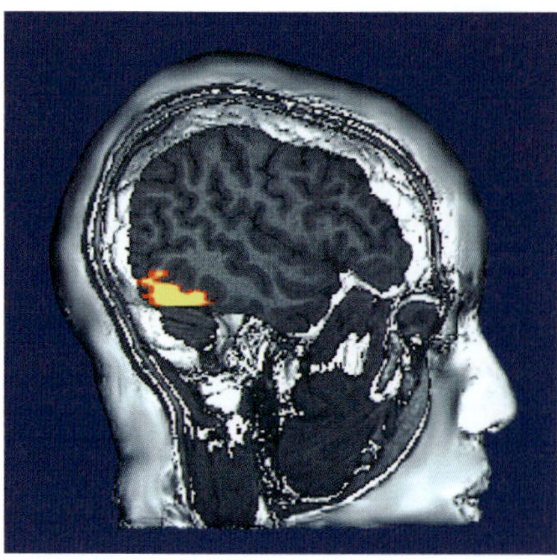

Figure 3.24 The fusiform face area. Neurons in the fusiform face area (yellow) respond to faces, regardless of their shape, color, or orientation. (NIH.)

area (**FFA**) (Figure 3.24), responds to very specific kinds of shapes, such as faces. Individuals with **prosopagnosia** or the loss of the ability to identify individual faces (Benton, 1990) have usually suffered damage to the FFA (Kanwisher, McDermott, & Chun, 1997). Face recognition depends especially upon the FFA in the right hemisphere, and prosopagnosia is more common following damage to the right hemisphere than the left.

Depth Perception

In order to judge the distance of visual objects, the brain relies on several kinds of information. For instance, closer objects block our view of more distant objects; if two objects are the same size (say two identical cups), the one that appears larger is probably closer to you. Such information can be detected with just a single eye, and these are therefore called **monocular cues**.

We also use **binocular cues**, as illustrated by the following example. Cover your left eye and place your forefinger about 4 inches directly in front of your nose. If you now cover your right eye (look at your finger with just your left eye), your finger will appear to jump several inches to the right! Why is that? It's because the image of a nearby object (in this case, your finger) placed in front of your eyes falls on different portions of the retinas of your two eyes. The *difference* between the two different retinal locations is called **retinal disparity**. Now, place your finger further away from your nose, and repeat the experiment. Does your finger jump as much as it did when it was closer? If your finger could be placed 100 feet in front of you and you did the same experiment, this time your finger would not appear to "jump" at all. The retinal disparity is less when objects are further away. Neurons in V1, V2, and some higher-order visual areas compute the amount of retinal disparity of objects. Without these neural calculations, we would have more difficulty telling which objects are closer and which are further from us.

Blindness and Blindsight

Blindness can be caused by disease, genetic malfunctions, or injury at various points along the visual pathway, from the lens of the eye (cataracts cause the lens to become clouded) to visual areas of the cortex. One cause of blindness is a stroke that deprives the brain of blood and oxygen, leading to death of V1 neurons. A patient with damage to V1 on the left side of the brain would suffer blindness for objects in the right visual field (again, review Figure 3.15). The blind part of the visual field is called a **scotoma**. Damage to higher-order visual areas beyond V1 (such as areas MT or V4) typically produces loss of specific function, such as motion perception or color perception, but not total loss of vision.

A strange instance of blindness mentioned at the beginning of this chapter is **blindsight** (Kentridge, Heywood, & Weiskrantz, 1999). Recall the opening story of Peggy who became blind as a result of head injury, but who could nevertheless dodge a flying object that was heading toward her. To undergo examination of her blindsight, the person might be seated in front of a large movie screen. The investigator says, "I would like you to tell me whether a light is on to the upper right, upper left, lower right, or lower left." The patient assures the investigator that she will be unable to see the light at all. "Just guess," says the investigator. Then the process of randomly presenting a light in the various quadrants begins and, surprisingly, the patient points in the correct direction with a probability far above chance levels. However, when asked what she saw, she says, "nothing." This shows that the brain can carry out at least some visual processes without awareness.

Visual awareness is typically lost when, for reasons mentioned above, visual information fails to reach V1. However, recall that the superior colliculus receives visual information relevant to object location and motion. In some cases, an individual who has lost visual awareness following V1 damage may still detect an object's location so long as visual input reaches the superior colliculus (Kato, Takaura, Ikeda, Yoshida, & Isa, 2011). In other cases, an individual who is blind due to V1 damage may have blindsight because information is sent from the LGN directly to motion-detection area MT (Ajina, Pestilli, Rokem, Kennard, & Bridge, 2015). Activation of area MT may allow the individual to detect the location and motion of the object, but without V1 the person has no inner experience of "seeing" the object.

Synesthesia

Synesthesia is a rare condition in which there is a blending or combining of the senses, such as sounds producing colors, or numbers having different colors. It can occur spontaneously in some people, and in others in response to powerful drugs (such as LSD), and occasionally during epileptic seizures. One individual with synesthesia recounted: "A few years ago, I mentioned to a friend that I remembered phone numbers by their color. He said, "So you're a synesthete!" I hadn't heard of synesthesia – I only knew that numbers seemed naturally to have colors: five is blue, two is green, three is red … And music has colors, too: the key of C# minor is a sharp, tangy yellow, F major is a warm brown …" (Raskin, 2003).

Often synesthesia involves a merging between vision and another sensory experience, such as seeing particular colors when listening to particular sounds. Yet some forms of synesthesia involve two non-visual senses, such as feeling tactile sensations in response to sounds.

Various hypotheses have been proposed to explain synesthesia. Perhaps the simplest is that it is due to unusual connections between brain areas – for instance, abnormally strong connections between cortical areas involved in number recognition and those (such as V4) involved in experiencing colors. Many brain imaging studies have been conducted on individuals with synesthesia. However, it has been difficult to identify consistent differences in brain structure or function in synesthetes compared to controls. This may be due, at least in part, to the wide range of different synesthetic experiences, and perhaps even different causes of synesthesia (Hupé & Dojat, 2015; Arend, Yuen, Sagi, & Henik, 2018).

KEY CONCEPTS

- **The visual cortex of humans and other primates contains many visual areas that are specialized for processing particular aspects of visual stimuli, such as movement, color, and shape.**
- **An important part of depth perception depends on binocular cues, i.e., the fact that images of objects close to us fall upon different regions of the retina of the two eyes, while those far away do not. The brain uses this information about retinal disparity to determine which objects in a visual scene are closer or further away.**
- **Blindness can occur because of damage or dysfunction at all levels of the primary visual system pathway, up to V1. Blindsight sometimes**

allows individuals without visual awareness to nevertheless detect simple attributes of a stimulus such as its location. Blindsight may arise from visual connections to brain areas that specifically detect object location and motion, such as the superior colliculus or area MT.

- Synesthesia involves a blending of sensory experience.

TEST YOURSELF

1. What are some visual cues we use for depth perception? Which require only one eye?
2. Say a person has blindness within a particular area of their visual field. That "blind" part of their visual field is called a ______.
3. Sarah is blind, but can dodge a flying object heading toward her. We call this strange condition ______.
4. Give an example of synesthesia.

3.3 OTHER SENSORY SYSTEMS

There is no universal agreement on the exact number of human sensory modalities. The most commonly named are vision, audition (hearing), somatosensation (perception of pressure, heat, and pain), olfaction (smell), and gustation (taste).

3.3.1 Audition

Audition (hearing) depends upon detecting vibrations (sound waves), which arrive through the air (for humans). The frequency of these sound waves determines the pitch we hear, from the low-frequency pitch of the cello to the high-frequency pitch of the flute. Humans can hear sounds of frequencies from approximately 20 to 20,000 hertz (Hz; cycles per second). Age-related hearing loss is greatest for the high frequencies, leading to difficulties detecting high-frequency speech sounds. The sound waves also have an amplitude we hear as loudness.

As sound waves enter the ear, they cause the **eardrum** (the **tympanic membrane**) to vibrate (see Figure 3.25). The vibrating eardrum then causes vibrations in the three small bones called **ossicles**: the hammer, the anvil, and finally the stirrup of the middle ear. The last one, the stirrup, contacts a thin membrane on the **cochlea** (Greek for "snail"), a spiral-shaped structure in the inner ear containing fluid-filled canals. Vibration of the stirrup produces waves in the fluid inside the cochlea.

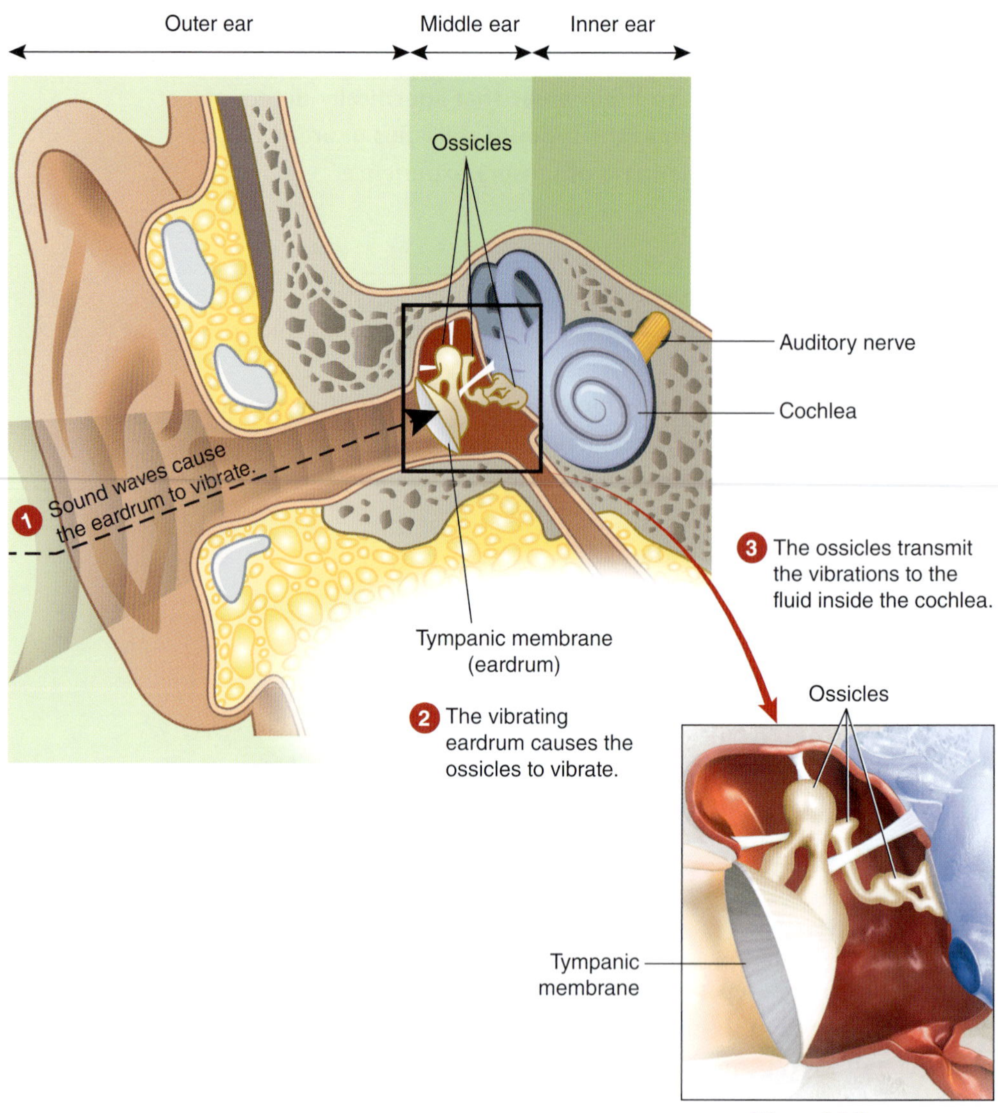

Figure 3.25 Three steps that allow soundwaves to cause fluid to vibrate inside the cochlea.

Imagine that you grab hold of the inner ear and unroll the spiral-shaped cochlea (Figure 3.26). First, you notice the thin, flexible **basilar membrane** running along its entire length. As illustrated in the figure, the vibrating fluid in the cochlea causes the basilar membrane to move in a wave-like fashion. **Hair cells**, sitting on top of the basilar membrane, move up and down with this wavelike movement as if they were surfing the waves. These hair cells are the sensory receptors of the auditory system. As they rise with the movement of the basilar membrane, the hairs (**cilia**) of the cells bump up against the **tectorial membrane** just above. This makes the cilia of the hair cells bend.

A

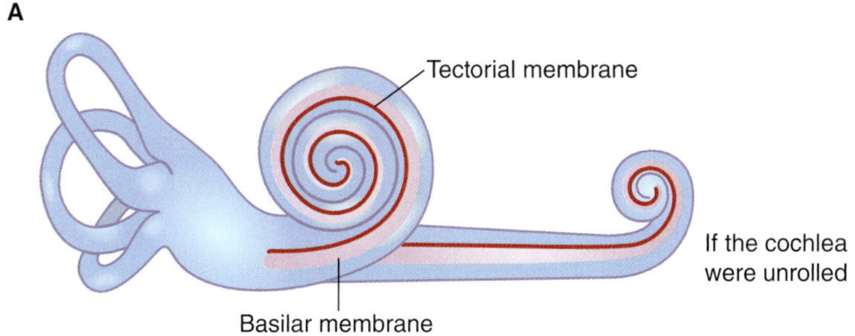

B

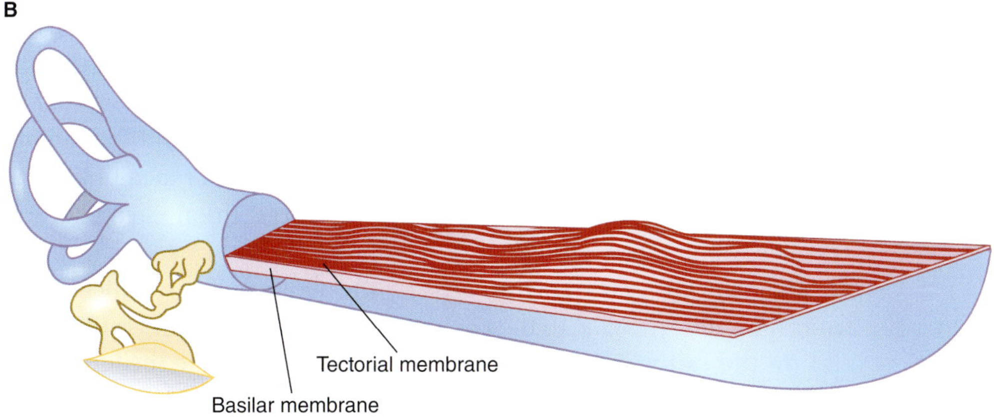

C

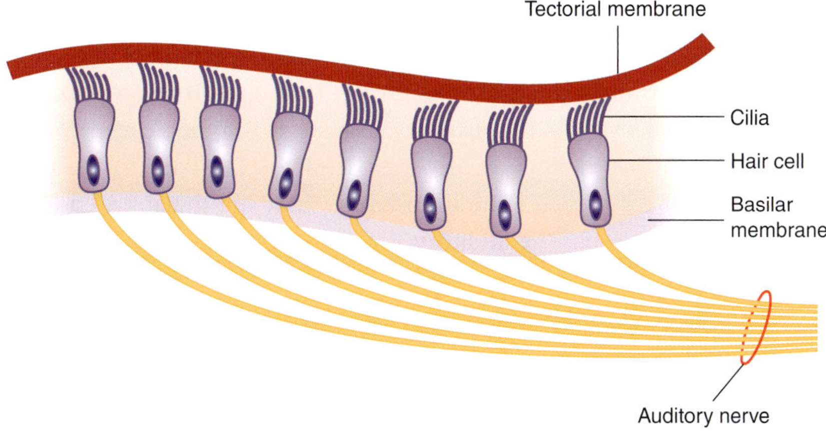

Figure 3.26 **The basilar membrane and its hair cells**. (A) The spiral-shaped cochlea contains a basilar membrane (pink) and a tectorial membrane (red). (B) If the cochlea were flattened out, one would see the membranes moving in a wave-like manner. (C) Hair cells are sandwiched between the basilar and the tectorial membrane. As sound causes wave-like motion of the membranes, the cilia of the hair cells press against the tectorial membrane.

The hair cells are the neurons that transduce physical energy (the sound waves, or more specifically the waves of fluid the sound waves produce in the cochlea) to neural activity for the auditory system, just as the photoreceptors are the transducers for the visual system. When the hair cells bend, positively charged ions pass through their membrane, depolarizing the cells. The depolarized hair cell releases its neurotransmitter to activate its receiving neuron, the **auditory nerve**, which carries a signal to the brain.

Not all hair cells on the basilar membrane respond to all sound frequencies. One end of the basilar membrane vibrates in response to high-frequency waves (Figure 3.27A), allowing the nearby hair cells to detect high-pitched sounds. Low-pitched sounds cause strong vibrations at the other side of the basilar membrane. Because cells that respond to different sound frequencies, from the chirping of a bird to the rumbling of an engine, are located in different places on the basilar membrane, the membrane is said to be **tonotopically organized** (from Greek, tono = frequency and topos = place).

The hair cells in the cochlea activate the auditory nerve, which transmits the auditory signal to the **cochlear nucleus**. Don't confuse the cochlea (in the ear) with the cochlear nucleus (located in the medulla). The sound information is then passed to several other regions of the brainstem before reaching the thalamus and then the cortex (Figure 3.27B). One set of neurons carries the signal from the cochlear nucleus to the superior olive (in the pons); other neurons travel from there to the inferior colliculus (in the midbrain). Still other neurons leave the inferior colliculus to send the auditory signal to the **medial geniculate nucleus** of the thalamus. Finally, neurons in the thalamus project to the **auditory cortex**.

Recall that layer 4 of the visual cortex receives its input from the thalamus, and that layer 6 of the visual cortex sends output back to the thalamus to help "filter" or select the information that the thalamus continues to send to the cortex. The auditory thalamus and cortex have a similar organization. Layer 4 of the auditory cortex receives input from the medial geniculate nucleus of the thalamus, and layer 6 of the auditory cortex communicates back to the thalamus, enabling a filtering of auditory stimuli. In fact, nearly all the other sensory systems (such as touch and taste) have the same organization: Cortical layer 4 receives thalamic input, and layer 6 communicates back to the thalamus.

How do we localize sound? The brain employs two primary mechanisms. First, sound coming from your left will reach your left ear before it reaches your right ear. This difference in timing to arrive at the two ears (**interaural timing difference**) is less than 1 millisecond, but the brain is sensitive to this difference. Second, sound coming from your left will be more intense (louder) when it reaches the left ear than

A. Cochlea

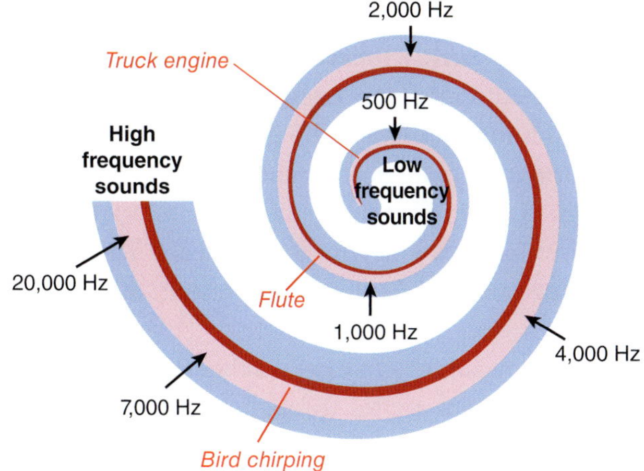

B. Pathway from cochlea to auditory cortex

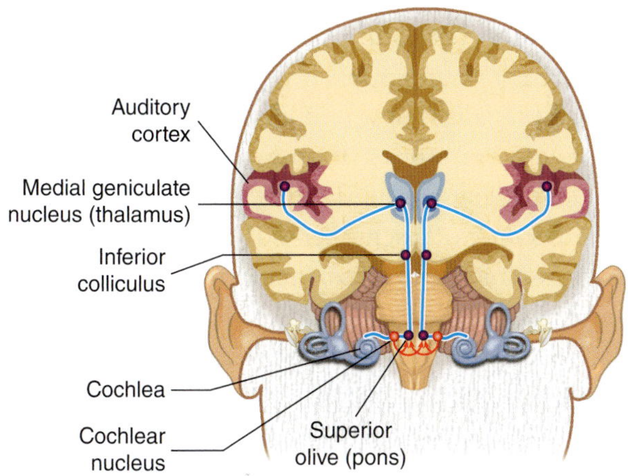

C. Auditory cortex

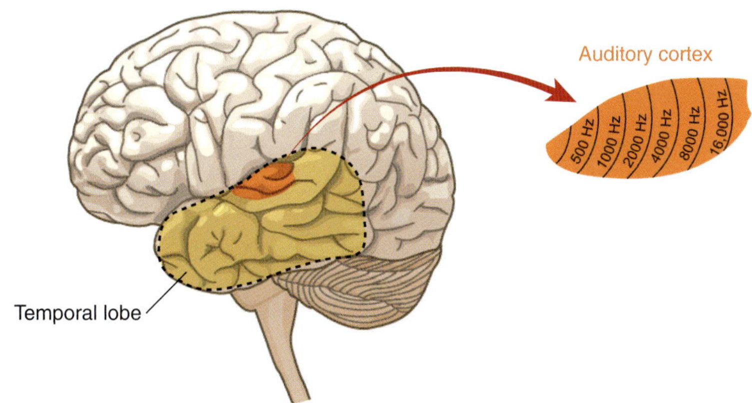

Figure 3.27 **Auditory information travels from the cochlea to the auditory cortex**. (A) The cochlea in the ear responds tonotopically to auditory input. (B) Auditory information travels from the cochlea to the cochlear nucleus in the medulla. From there, the information travels to the superior olive, the inferior colliculus, the medial geniculate nucleus of the thalamus, and finally the auditory cortex. (C) Tonotopic organization is maintained at each auditory relay, including the auditory cortex.

the right. The brain uses both this **interaural intensity difference** and the interaural timing difference to locate auditory events. Notice from Figure 3.27 that the superior olive is the first stage of the auditory pathway to receive information from both cochleas. Individual neurons in the superior olive and in the inferior colliculus respond to differences in timing and intensity of sounds entering the two ears. The neuronal activity in these early-stage auditory structures represents a key code for sound localization.

We saw earlier that, after *visual* information reaches the primary visual cortex, it travels via two different routes through the cortex. A ventral stream analyzes the color, size, and other properties of the visual stimulus to identify *what* the object is; a dorsal stream analyzes *where* it is. Does the auditory system have a similar division of labor? Yes. After auditory information reaches the primary auditory cortex, additional processing in a ventral stream through the cortex identifies the nature of the sound ("what" it is, e.g., a violin, a baby crying, spoken words) (Figure 3.28). In addition to the very early-stage analysis of sound location (e.g., in the superior olive, as noted above) a dorsal stream of information processing in the cortex is dedicated to identifying sound location ("where" it is coming from, the kitchen or the bedroom?) (Rauschecker, 2011).

There are a number of causes for hearing loss, including genetic factors, trauma, disease, aging, and, most often, loud noises. The problems that lead to hearing loss can be divided into three categories. First are those that prevent sound waves from reaching the eardrum, or the vibrations of the

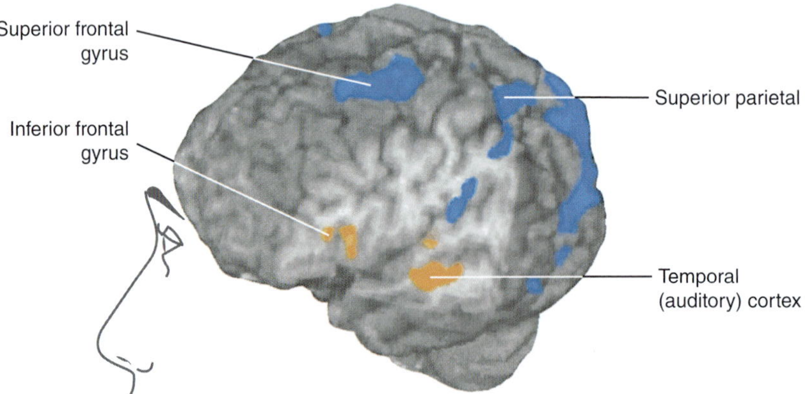

Figure 3.28 Auditory regions for identifying "what" versus "where." Ventral areas of the frontal and temporal cortices (orange) are highly active when human subjects identify the nature of a sound, e.g., a violin versus a baby's cry. Dorsal areas of the frontal and parietal cortices (blue) become active when subjects are locating the source of the sound.
(Adapted from Alain, Arnott, Hevenor, Graham, & Grady, 2001, fig. 2, © (2001) National Academy of Sciences, USA.)

eardrum from moving along the ossicles in the middle ear (**conductive hearing loss**). Causes of conductive hearing loss include infection, tumor, and genetic abnormalities. Second are dysfunctions that disrupt the functioning of the cochlea and its hair cells, or the auditory nerve with which the hair cells communicate (**sensorineuronal hearing loss**). Causes of sensorineuronal hearing loss include loud sounds, head trauma, and aging. Third, when the auditory signal is disrupted somewhere along its route through the brain, **central hearing loss** can occur. Central hearing loss (e.g., from stroke or brain trauma) can result from damage to any part of the auditory pathways through the brain (again, see Figure 3.27), particularly within the brainstem and the auditory cortex.

3.3.2 Somatosensation

Somatosensation refers to sensations coming from the body. The somatosensory system encompasses touch, temperature, body position (proprioception), and pain (nociception). Here, we will focus on touch, temperature, and pain.

When you touch an object with your fingers, you activate receptors located in the skin. More specifically, you activate **mechanoreceptors**, which respond to skin deformation (a change from its usual shape). As depicted in Figure 3.29, there are four major types of mechanoreceptors:

- **Merkel's disks** respond to light touch.
- **Meissner's corpuscles** respond to touch and slow vibrations.
- **Ruffini endings** respond to stretching of the skin (pressure) and warmth.
- **Pacinian corpuscles** respond to brief, deep pressure and rapid vibrations.

Consider a baby in the arms of its mother. Light touch to the baby's fingers, toes, even its lips, activates Merkel's disks and Meissner's corpuscles. When the baby stretches its hand wide to grab the mother's thumb or to pick up a toy, its Ruffini endings are activated by the stretch, while Merkel's disks and Meissner's corpuscles respond to the object within its grasp. As the mother tickles the baby, activation of its Pacinian corpuscles gives rise to the tickle sensation.

Somatosensory receptors are activated by touch at particular areas on the body's surface. The sensory receptors in your fingertips have small receptive fields, giving rise to highly accurate tactile (touch) perception. You can tell if an object is touching the tip of the index finger, or whether it is touching a different part of the finger very close by. In contrast, the receptors in the skin of your back have large receptive fields, making touch perception less accurate.

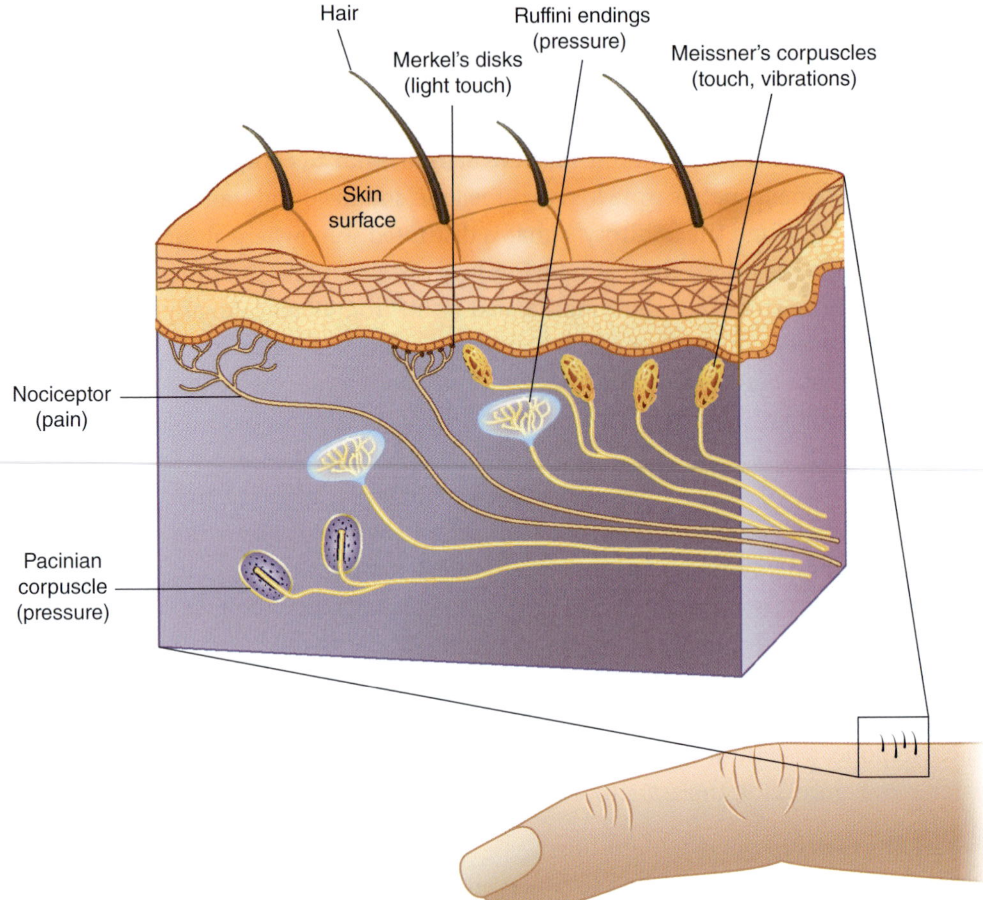

Figure 3.29 The four major skin receptors for touch. Notice that most of the tactile receptors are encapsulated, but Merkel's disks are freely exposed. Nociceptors also have freely exposed nerve endings.

Some somatosensory receptors specifically detect noxious (unpleasant or painful) stimuli. They are called **nociceptors** (again, see Figure 3.29). There are four principal types of nociceptors:

- **Mechanical nociceptors** respond to intense pressure (e.g., from a strong pinch or scratch) or to piercing of the skin (e.g., from a cut).
- **Thermal nociceptors** respond to intense heat.
- **Chemical nociceptors** detect chemical toxins (e.g., from spider venom).
- Receptors that can detect more than one type of noxious stimulus are called **polymodal nociceptors**.

Some nociceptors send pain signals to the CNS via fast-conducting bundles of myelinated axons called **Aδ** (pronounced "A delta") **fibers**. When Aδ fibers are stimulated in humans, subjects report a sharp pain. Other nociceptors send pain information along slow-conducting **C fibers**. These thin, unmyelinated axons transmit a duller, long-lasting pain. In addition to the skin, nociceptors are located in joints (as those with arthritis can attest to) and in the viscera (organs) of the body.

Somatosensory receptors, then, include those that respond to touch (mechanoreceptors) and pain (nociceptors). Another kind of somatosensory receptor responds to non-painful changes in temperature; they are called **thermoreceptors**. Each of these receptor cells has a **nerve ending**, which acts like a dendrite; it receives the incoming somatosensory (touch, pain, temperature) information. Notice in Figure 3.29 that some nerve endings are "encapsulated"; they are enclosed by capsules of connective tissue. Others are not enclosed; they are freely exposed. In either case, stimulation at the skin causes ion channels in the nerve endings to open.

The somatosensory receptor cells are unusual in that they do not have the typical configuration of dendrites → cell body → axon → terminal. Instead they have a long axon, with one end in the skin (the nerve ending), which receives somatosensory input, and the other end in the spinal cord, where neurotransmitter is released. Where are their cell bodies? Just outside the spinal cord in the **dorsal root ganglia** (Figure 3.30).

Let's follow a somatosensory signal from the skin to the brain. Say a sharp needle cuts through the skin of a finger and activates a nociceptor. A signal travels along the axon of a somatosensory neuron terminating in the spinal cord (see Figure 3.30). From there, spinal cord neurons send signals along axons that cross the midline and travel up the contralateral side of the brain, until the somatosensory information reaches the **ventral posterior nucleus** of the thalamus. From the thalamus, the signal is carried to the **primary somatosensory cortex** (Figure 3.31) within the parietal lobe. Non-painful tactile stimuli, which activate mechanoreceptors in the skin, generate signals that travel a similar, although slightly different, route to the ventral posterior thalamus and then to the primary somatosensory cortex.

From the primary somatosensory cortex, information is sent to the secondary somatosensory cortex. This and other high-order somatosensory regions of the parietal cortex carry out analyses of tactile stimuli that allow you to distinguish one object from another (e.g., the feel of a pencil compared to an apple). Some individuals with damage to these high-order somatosensory processing regions lose the ability to recognize objects on the basis of touch, i.e., they suffer from tactile agnosia. Recall that damage to high-order areas of the visual cortex can give rise to *visual* agnosias, the inability to visually recognize faces or other objects. Those with agnosia remain sensitive to sensory input (touch, vision), but lose the ability to use that input to recognize objects.

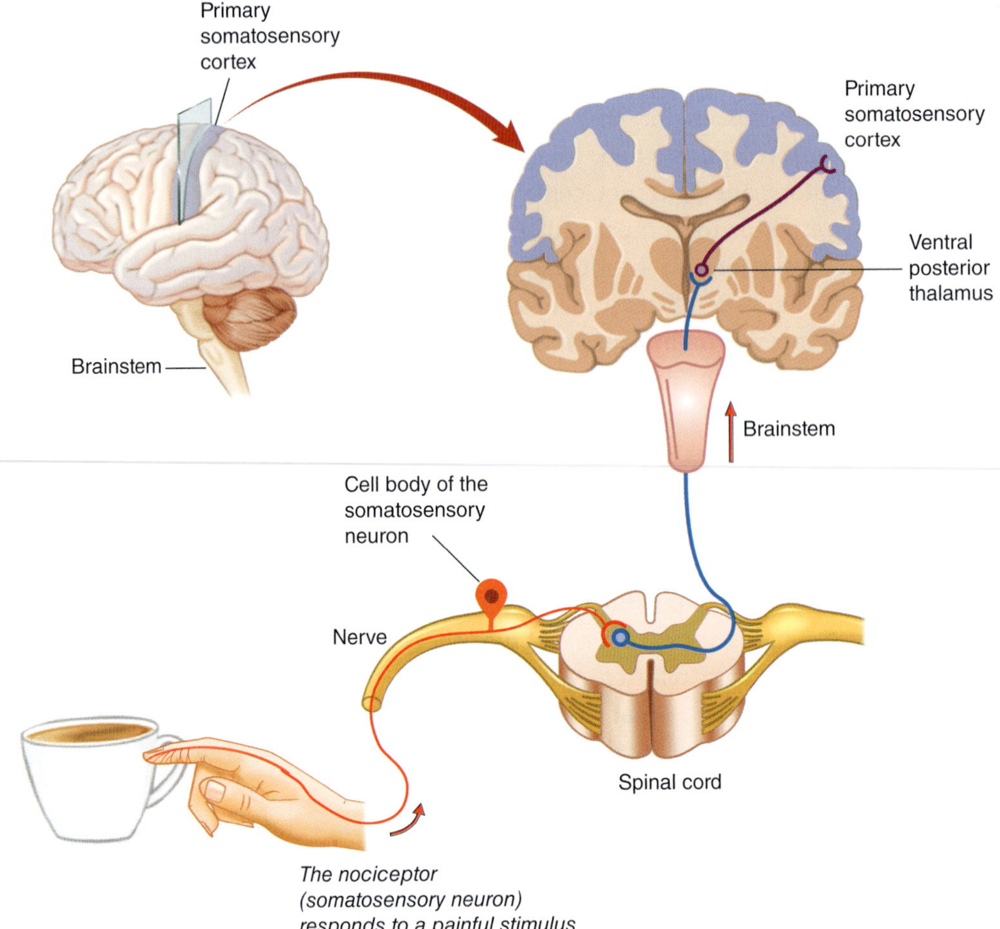

Figure 3.30 Somatosensory system, from the skin to the cortex. The somatosensory signal is carried from the nociceptor in the skin to the spinal cord. A spinal cord neuron then carries the signal through the brainstem to the thalamus. Finally, a thalamic neuron sends the signal to the primary somatosensory cortex.

3.3.3 Smell (Olfaction) and Taste (Gustation)

The olfactory (smell) system detects small molecules in the air (**odorants**), from the smell of delicious soup to the aversive odor of toxic chemicals. The gustatory (taste) system detects molecules in food (**tastants**). Tastants allow us to detect food quality and quantity, from the taste of meat, to the amount of sugar in the coffee. Both smell and taste depend on receptors in the nose, tongue, and other tissues that secrete mucus.

Smell

Humans rely much less on smell for survival, reproduction, and avoiding danger than do many animals. Nonetheless, we can detect a huge number

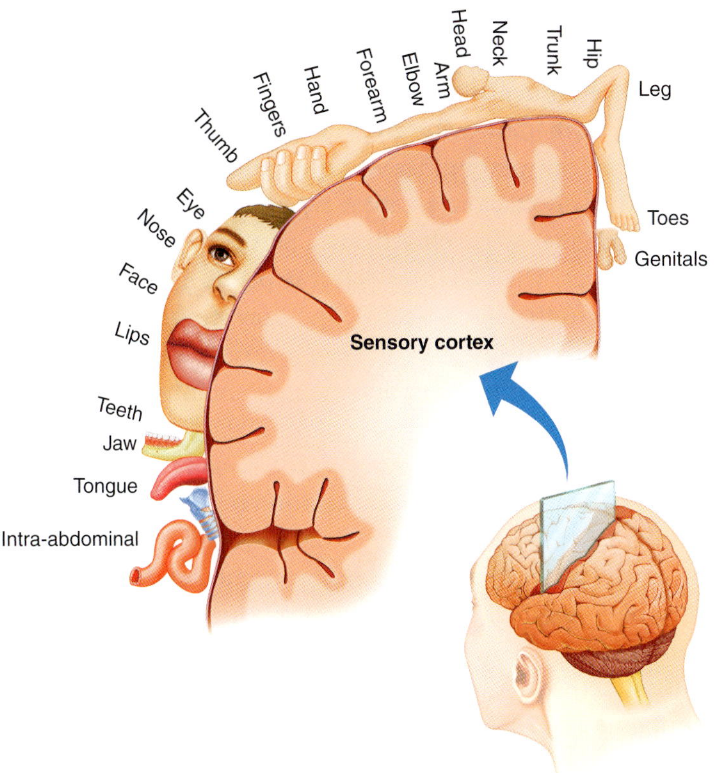

Figure 3.31 Primary somatosensory cortex and body part representations. Notice that large areas of the primary somatosensory cortex are dedicated to the face. Also notice that a much larger area is dedicated to the fingers compared to the toes.

of different odors. Many species are much more sensitive to smells (olfactory stimuli) than are humans. Next time you see a neighbor walking his dog on a leash, watch how frequently the dog stops and investigates his surroundings with his nose.

Odorants enter through the nose or mouth and dissolve in a layer of mucus before landing upon **olfactory receptors** at the top of the nose (Figure 3.32). The receptors are located on very fine hair-like extensions (cilia) of the **olfactory neurons**. Diseases that change the mucus of the nose or mouth can prevent odor molecules from dissolving in, and passing through, the mucus; this prevents the odor molecules from reaching the hair-like cilia, and their olfactory receptors. To summarize, the olfactory neurons contain cilia, which contain the olfactory receptors.

Animals like dogs, with a highly developed sense of smell, have over 1,000 different types of olfactory receptors. Humans have only about 400. However, it has been estimated that we can discriminate over a trillion different odors (Bushdid, Magnasco, Vosshall, & Keller, 2014)! How can a trillion odors be detected with just 400 receptors?

The answer begins with the fact that a single odorant molecule usually activates many different receptors. So, for instance, a single odorant molecule coming from a particular wine activates many different types of olfactory receptors. Further, the wine gives off not only one type of odorant molecule, but ten or twenty different kinds, with each odorant activating a combination of olfactory receptor types. Therefore, a particular wine, or flower, or cheese, will each activate a particular combination of olfactory receptor types. The odor you detect depends upon the combination of receptor types that are activated, and how strongly each of the receptors is activated. With just 400 or so olfactory receptor types, the number of *combinations* is enormous, and so is the number of odors we can distinguish.

Do the cilia of a single olfactory neuron contain many types of olfactory receptors? No. A particular olfactory neuron contains just one type of receptor (Figure 3.32). When an odor activates a particular group of olfactory receptors, the olfactory neurons become excited and send signals to the olfactory bulb, the first brain structure that receives information about the odor.

Now, let's imagine that a particular odorant enters the nose and binds to neurons containing a particular type of olfactory receptor, say those colored green in Figure 3.32. While olfactory neurons with that type of receptor may be scattered throughout the nose, the axons of these neurons all cluster together when they terminate in the olfactory bulb. These small clusters of axon terminals are called **glomeruli**. So, each glomerulus receives inputs from a particular type of olfactory receptor. Because a particular odor activates a particular set of olfactory receptor types, you could theoretically identify the odor that someone is smelling simply by knowing which of her glomeruli are active! (Recording the activity of each of your individual glomeruli at once would be technically challenging, and is not yet possible.)

When the axons of olfactory neurons reach the glomeruli, they make synaptic contact with neurons called **mitral cells** (again, see Figure 3.32). The axons of the mitral cells bundle together to make up the **olfactory tract**. The olfactory tract sends its information to several brain areas including the **primary olfactory cortex** (also called the *rhinencephalon*, or "nose brain") located within the medial part of the temporal lobe. Recall that for other senses (e.g., visual, auditory, somatosensory), information is sent to the thalamus before being transferred to the corresponding primary sensory region of the cortex. But for smell, information goes directly from the olfactory bulb to the olfactory cortex without passing first to the thalamus.

The olfactory cortex, in turn, projects to the **orbitofrontal cortex** (**OFC**), and in humans this is the area believed to give rise to the conscious

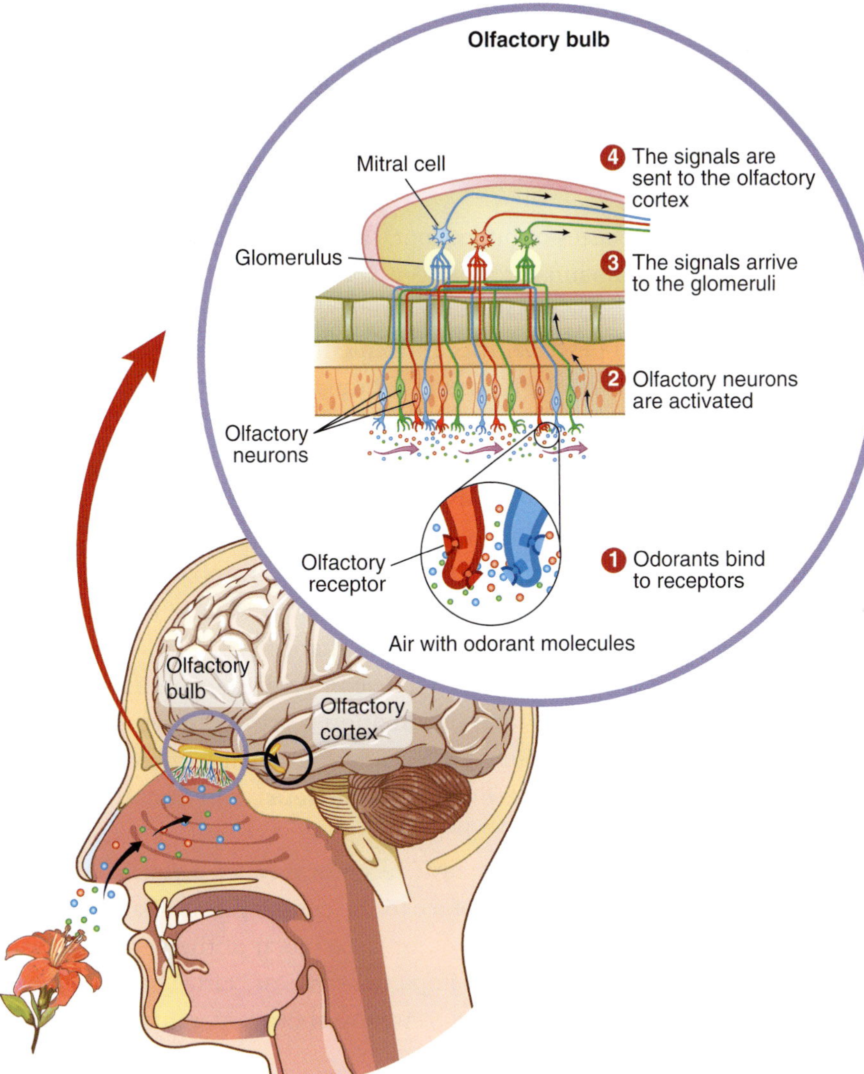

Figure 3.32 From the nose to the olfactory cortex. Odorants enter the nose and bind to receptors on olfactory neurons. Olfactory neurons of the same type (illustrated here as red, green, or blue) cluster together in the glomeruli of the olfactory bulb. The olfactory bulb sends signals to the primary olfactory cortex.

experience of smelling an odor. One patient who suffered damage to the OFC completely lost his sense of smell (Li et al., 2010). Odors continued to activate his primary olfactory cortex, but with damage to his OFC, he was unable to perceive them.

Loss of olfactory sensation is called **anosmia**. We've already seen that it can result from an abnormality in the mucus through which odorants must pass before reaching the olfactory receptors. Another cause of anosmia is damage to the olfactory cortex. One sign of anosmia is that foods become less appetizing. A particularly dangerous consequence of anosmia is the inability to detect odors coming from gas leaks, fire, and other smells that normally serve as important warning signals.

Taste

In addition to the tastes of bitter, sour, salty, sweet, we also detect a fifth basic taste called umami (pronounced "oo-mommy," and meaning "savory" in Japanese). The umami taste, produced by the amino acid glutamate, is difficult to describe. It is an element in the taste of many foods (asparagus, tomato, meat); receptors for umami are directly activated by the flavor-enhancer MSG (monosodium glutamate).

The mouth and throat contain tiny **taste buds** (small organs in the tongue), each of which contains many **taste receptors** (Figure 3.33). Chemicals in food make contact with the taste receptors. For instance, when you chew a strawberry, the fruit's chemicals dissolve in saliva, move through a central pore in the taste bud, and bind to taste receptors. The strawberry activates receptors for both sweet and sour.

The taste receptor cells make synaptic contact with cranial nerves (VII, IX, and X) that carry the taste information to the **solitary nucleus** in the medulla (again, see Figure 3.33). The taste signal is then sent to the thalamus (the **ventral posterior medial nucleus**), and from there to the **gustatory cortex**.

Loss of taste conveyed by the taste receptor is called **ageusia**. This disorder frequently results from damage to the cranial nerves that carry taste information to the brain. However, because much of the perceived taste of food comes from its smell, an impaired sense of "taste" can also result from loss of smell (i.e., reduced response to airborne odorants) rather than from a reduced perception of tastants.

KEY CONCEPTS

- **In each of the senses examined here – vision, audition, somatosensation, olfaction, and gustation – a physical stimulus interacts with a sensory receptor.**
- **The sensory receptor either directly or indirectly transmits sensory information to the brain.**
- **The pathway through the brain almost always includes the thalamus (not so for smell).**
- **Sensory information eventually arrives at a primary sensory region of the cerebral cortex, and undergoes further processing in higher-order processing regions.**

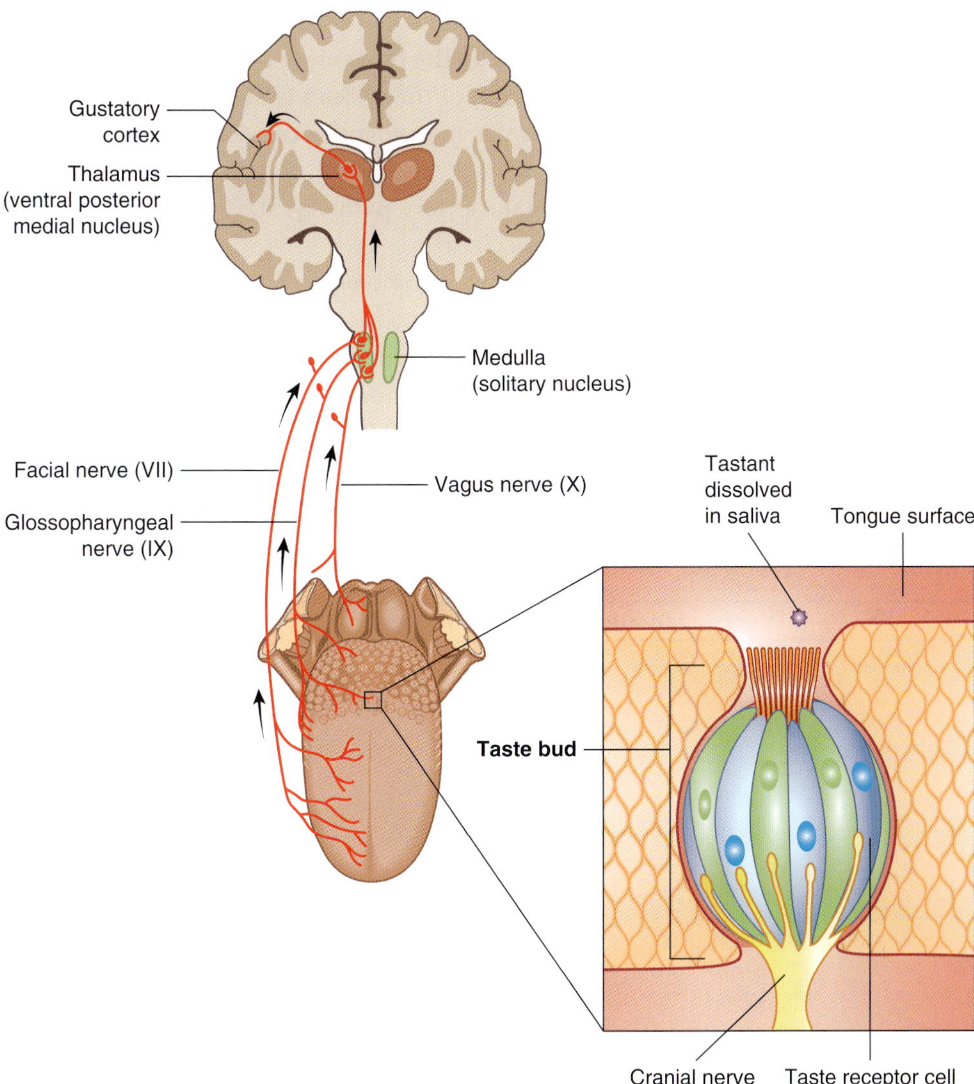

Figure 3.33 From the tongue to the gustatory cortex. Taste buds in the tongue contain taste receptor cells. The taste receptor cells synapse upon cranial nerves (VII, IX, and X), which carry taste signals to the medulla. The signal is then sent to the thalamus, and finally to the gustatory cortex.

- **The specific types of energy, receptor types, and pathways through the brain differ according to the sensory modality, as summarized in Table 3.1.**

TEST YOURSELF

1. **Hair cells in the inner ear play the most important role in the auditory system. What are they, and how do they function?**

2. **Transduction in the visual system is carried out by the photoreceptors, and in the auditory system by the movement of hair cells. Before the hair cells move, the vibration of the ossicles leads to vibration of fluid in the cochlea. Why isn't this movement of cochlear fluid an example of transduction?**
3. **Briefly describe the somatosensory pathway, starting in your big toe and ending in your cortex.**
4. **Describe how 400 olfactory receptor types can give rise to the perception of over a trillion different odors.**
5. **When you take a bite of cake, what must occur in order for its tastant chemicals to reach the taste receptors? What are the neurons that carry the taste information to the brainstem?**

Table 3.1 Summarizing key features of the major sensory systems of the brain.

	Energy (Stimulus)	Receptor Type	Key Pathway
Vision	Visible light	Photoreceptors (rods and cones)	Optic nerve/tract to thalamus to visual cortex
Audition	Sound waves	Hair cells	Auditory nerve to cochlear nucleus to thalamus to auditory cortex
Somatosensation	Touch/pressure/painful stimuli to the skin	Somatosensory receptors (mechanoreceptors, nociceptors)	Axons of somatosensory neurons to spinal cord to thalamus to somatosensory cortex
Olfaction	Odorant molecules	Olfactory receptors	Axons of olfactory neurons to olfactory bulb to olfactory cortex
Gustation	Tastant molecules	Taste receptors	Cranial nerve to medulla to thalamus to gustatory cortex

3.4 The Big Picture

Sensory systems do not provide perfect copies of the external world. Nervous systems have been molded through millions of years of evolution to best attain success in the ecological niche of the given species. Our vision is not as keen as other predators, our olfactory system does not compare with that of canines, and our auditory system is limited to a frequency band that is exceeded in many other animals. Our sensory systems are the way they are because they help us to survive, to procreate, and to pass on to the next generation the genetic instructions for the same sensory systems.

We chose to focus our discussion on the visual because it is the most studied, and therefore the most well understood. However, by comparing vision to other systems such as hearing, touch, smell, and taste, we find that they carry out many of the same steps to convert physical to neural energy, and transmit the neural information to the brain. While our senses may give us great pleasure, they evolved to enable us to successfully respond to our environments through our actions. The brain basis of action is the topic we turn to next.

3.5 Creative Thinking

1. An evil sorcerer removes all of Bob's retinal ganglion cells. You need to build an artificial retina to replace them. What are the key properties your artificial "ganglion cells" will need in order to transmit signals that the (real) LGN of the thalamus will recognize? How should they respond to light on different parts of the artificial retina? (Remember, in order for the LGN to recognize these signals, they must resemble the natural signals generated by real ganglion cells.)
2. How would your visual experience be different if you suffered brain damage that prevented information processing in your dorsal stream? How would this affect your daily life?
3. What, if anything, would be the harm of losing all somatosensory sensation? If you had to give up one sensory system (either vision, audition, somatosensation, olfaction, or gustation), which would you choose?
4. Yesterday, as Michelle noticed the smell of fresh coffee in the kitchen, a particular set of glomeruli in her olfactory bulb were activated. (You were monitoring her glomeruli.) Today, those same glomeruli are activated. Does this mean she's smelling coffee again? Explain your answer.

Key Terms

Aδ (A delta) fibers 130
acuity 94
ageusia 136
amacrine cell 102
anosmia 135
auditory cortex 126
auditory nerve 126
basilar membrane 124
binocular cue 120
bipolar cell 98
blind spot 91
blindsight 121
C fibers 131
center–surround receptive field 106
central hearing loss 129
chemical nociceptor 130
cilia 124
cochlea 123
cochlear nucleus 126
color vision 119
complex cell 114
conductive hearing loss 129
cones, photoreceptors 90
convergence 91
cornea 89
corticogeniculate pathway 113
dark current 98
dorsal root ganglia 131
dorsal stream 116
eardrum 123
fovea 91
fusiform face area (FFA) 119
ganglion cell 100
glomeruli 134
gustatory cortex 136
hair cell 124
horizontal cell 100
interaural intensity difference 128
interaural timing difference 126
koniocellular layers 111
lateral geniculate nucleus (LGN) 105
lateral inhibition 100
lens 89
magnocellular layers 111
mechanical nociceptor 130
mechanoreceptor 129
medial geniculate nucleus 126
Meissner's corpuscles 129
Merkel's disks 129
mitral cell 134
monocular cue 120
MT, visual area 119
nerve ending 131
nociceptor 130
ocular dominance columns 117
odorant 132
olfactory neuron 133
olfactory receptor 133
olfactory tract 134
optic chiasm 102
optic disk 91
optic nerve 102
optic tract 102
orbitofrontal cortex (OFC) 134
orientation column 117
ossicles 123
Pacinian corpuscles 129
parvocellular layers 111
photopigment 96
photoreceptor 90
polymodal nociceptor 130
primary olfactory cortex 134
primary somatosensory cortex 131
primary visual cortex (V1) 111
prosopagnosia 120
pupil 89
receptive field 106
refraction 89
relay nucleus 111

References

Ajina, S., Pestilli, F., Rokem, A., Kennard, C., & Bridge, H. (2015). Human blindsight is mediated by an intact geniculo-extrastriate pathway. *Elife, 4*.

Alain, C., Arnott, S. R., Hevenor, S., Graham, S., & Grady, C. L. (2001). "What" and "where" in the human auditory system. *Proceedings of the National Academy of Sciences, 98*(21), 12301–12306.

Arend, I., Yuen, K., Sagi, N., & Henik, A. (2018). Neuroanatomical basis of number synaesthesias: a voxel-based morphometry study. *Cortex, 101*, 172–180.

Benton, A. (1990). Facial recognition. *Cortex, 26*, 491–499.

Briggs, F., & Usrey, W. M. (2008). Emerging views of corticothalamic function. *Current Opinion in Neurobiology, 18*(4), 403–407.

Bushdid, C., Magnasco, M. O., Vosshall, L. B., & Keller, A. (2014). Humans can discriminate more than 1 trillion olfactory stimuli. *Science, 343*(6177), 1370–1372.

Gonzalez, F., & Perez, R. (1998). Neural mechanisms underlying stereoscopic vision. *Progress in Neurobiology, 55*, 191–224.

Goodale, M. A., & Milner, A. D. (1992). Separate visual pathways for perception and action. *Trends in Neurosciences, 15*(1), 20–25.

Hubel, D. H., & Wiesel, T. N. (1998). Early exploration of the visual cortex. *Neuron, 20*(3), 401–412.

Hupé, J.-M., & Dojat, M. (2015). A critical review of the neuroimaging literature on synesthesia. *Frontiers in Human Neuroscience, 9*, 103.

Kanwisher, N., McDermott, J., & Chun, M. M. (1997). The fusiform face area: a module in human extrastriate cortex specialized for face perception. *Journal of Neuroscience, 17*, 4302–4311.

Kato, R., Takaura, K., Ikeda, T., Yoshida, M., & Isa, T. (2011). Contribution of the retino-tectal pathway to visually guided saccades after lesion of the primary visual cortex in monkeys. *European Journal of Neuroscience, 33*(11), 1952–1960.

Kentridge, R. W., Heywood, C. A., & Weiskrantz, L. (1999). Attention without awareness in blindsight. *Proceedings of the Royal Society B: Biological Sciences, 266*, 1805–1811.

Kuffler, S. W. (1953). Discharge patterns and functional organization of mammalian retina. *Journal of Neurophysiology, 16*(1), 37–68.

Li, M., Liu, F., Juusola, M., & Tang, S. M. (2014). Perceptual color map in macaque visual area V4. *Journal of Neuroscience, 34*(1), 202–217.

Li, W., Lopez, L., Osher, J., Howard, J. D., Parrish, T. B., & Gottfried, J. A. (2010). Right orbitofrontal cortex mediates conscious olfactory perception. *Psychological Science, 21*(10), 1454–1463.

Mishkin, M., & Ungerleider, L. G. (1982). Contribution of striate inputs to the visuospatial functions of parieto-preoccipital cortex in monkeys. *Behavioural Brain Research, 6*(1), 57–77.

Raskin, R. (2003). An interview with Stephanie Morgenstern and Mark Ellis on Remembrance. *P.O.V., a Danish Journal of Film Studies; 15*, 170–184.

Rauschecker, J. P. (2011). An expanded role for the dorsal auditory pathway in sensorimotor control and integration. *Hearing Research, 271*(1–2), 16–25.

Schiller, P. H. (2010). Parallel information processing channels created in the retina. *Proceedings of the National Academy of Sciences, 107*(40),17087–17094.

Schnapf, J. L., & Baylor, D. I. (1987). How photoreceptors respond to light. *Scientific American, 256*(4), 40–47.

4 Movement

SCIEPRO / Science Photo Library / Getty Images

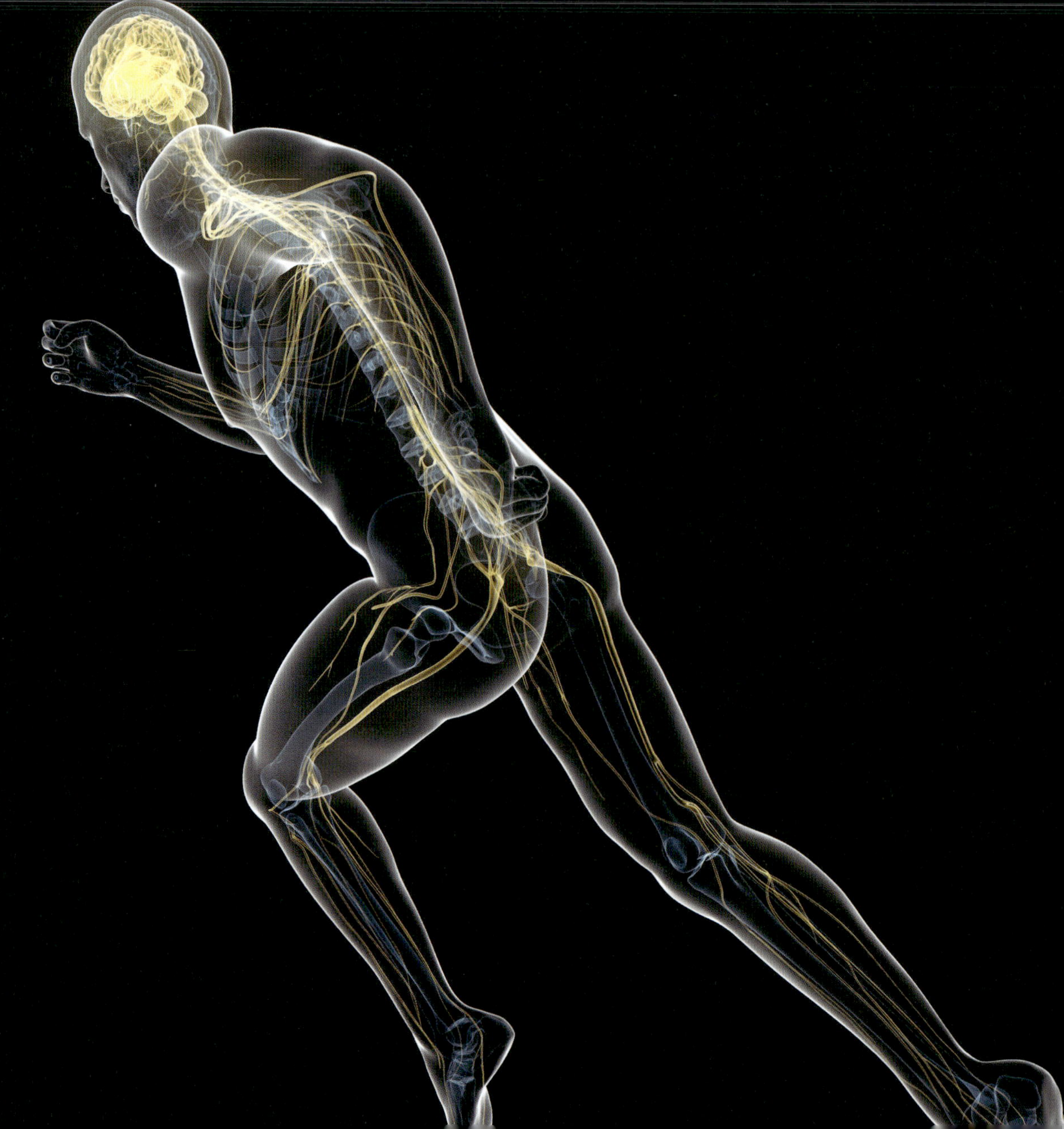

Consider This ...

Jon had just been hired as a new professor of psychology when he met Wayne, a researcher of cognition in his sixties. Wayne was a sweet, gentle man, enthusiastically curious about everything – especially everything related to the brain and thinking.

Jon and Wayne would meet once a week to work on a brain-based model of habit learning. These meetings proceeded slowly. Certain ideas arose, things Jon thought were obvious and not worth thinking much about. But for Wayne, everything was worth thinking about slowly and carefully.

The two had been meeting for about six months when Wayne mentioned that he'd been diagnosed with a motor neuron disease called amyotrophic lateral sclerosis (ALS). He had been limping recently, but he would gradually lose other motor functions. At some point, he would need a cane to walk, then a wheelchair. Eventually, he would even lose the motor neurons that control speech. He was gathering information about different types of wheelchairs. He approached it all methodically and logically.

Wayne's ALS would lead to the degeneration of the upper motor neurons that send signals from the brain to the spinal cord, as well as the lower motor neurons that send signals from the spinal cord to the muscles. Without motor neurons to drive muscle contractions, the muscles weaken and atrophy. Sensory nerves are spared, so vision, hearing, touch, smell, and taste remain normal. Cognitive functions are usually spared too, and Wayne's wonderful mind would remain unaffected. But he would be "locked in," unable to control his body movements.

The friends continued to meet regularly, ultimately moving their meetings to Wayne's home, and eventually by his bed. When he lost his speech, he'd type on a keyboard, and Jon would read his questions from the computer screen. Their work went slowly – after 15 minutes they might cover one sentence – because Wayne typed one letter at a time. Then again, Wayne had always gone slowly and carefully over everything.

Wayne passed away several years later. Like most people with ALS, he died from respiratory problems when he lost control of muscles in the rib cage that support breathing. Some with ALS have a family member with the disease, and there are a number of genes associated with the disease. But for the majority who suffer ALS, the cause is unknown.

Wayne's loss of motor function helps us to appreciate the near-miraculous manner in which our motor systems normally give rise to effortless, accurate body movements. For instance, imagine that you wish to sip coffee from the cup on your desk, and your hand moves to grasp it. To perform this simple movement, brain regions must work together to coordinate muscle activity. And yet your job is merely to think of the goal – take a sip. The body movements seem to take care of themselves.

When you formulate the goal of your movement, to sip coffee, you are likely activating the prefrontal cortex. This brain area holds the goal firmly in mind while other brain areas calculate the body movements needed to accomplish the goal (Figure 4.1). For instance, premotor areas of the frontal cortex take into account the current position of your hand and the location of the cup in order to accurately move your hand to the cup. Other premotor neurons calculate how to shape your hand and fingers to grasp the cup.

The primary motor cortex and nearby motor areas then send commands to the spinal cord, which in turn communicates with the muscles that move body parts. As your arm begins to move, your spinal cord is already receiving commands to curl your hand and fingers to the appropriate shape for grasping the cup. You then lift it with enough force to raise it, but not so much that the coffee flies upward and spills. Your cerebellum helps the frontal cortex to calibrate this movement on the basis of past experiences lifting the cup without spilling.

Throughout the entire movement, neurons in your parietal lobe are receiving sensory feedback from the movement, such as the pressure your fingers are exerting on the handle, and the parietal lobe passes that information to the motor cortex. In this way, if the cup begins to slip, your parietal lobe knows about it, and the motor cortex quickly readjusts the position and pressure of your hand and fingers. Your fingers now grip the handle more tightly, and the cup lifts, gently touching your lips. The cerebellum notes the slip, so that your grasp pressure is more appropriate to the task in the future.

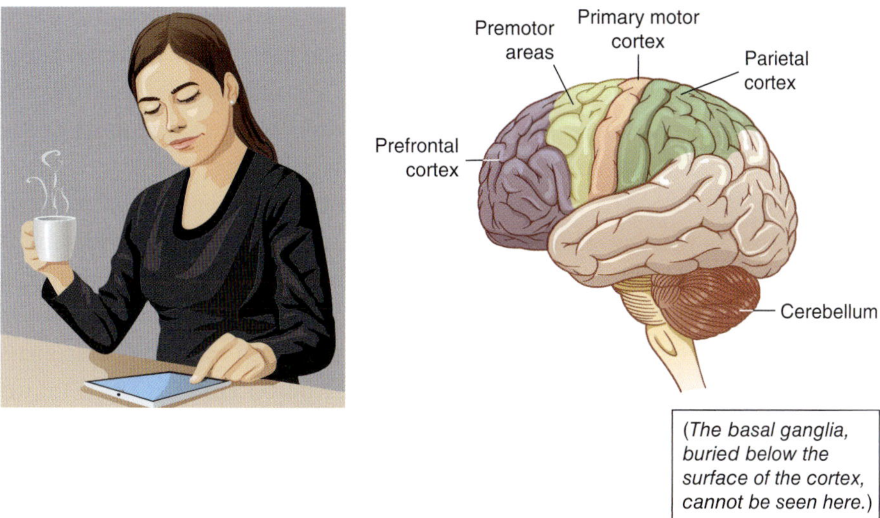

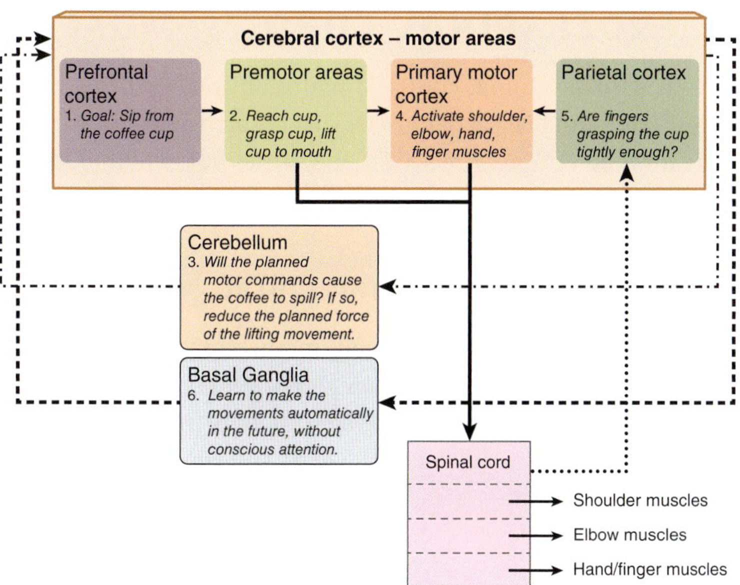

Figure 4.1 An overview of the brain's motor systems. The prefrontal cortex generates goals of a movement. The premotor and primary motor cortex translate these goals into more specific movement commands, and send them to the spinal cord. Neurons exiting the spinal cord communicate directly with the muscles that move body parts. The parietal cortex adjusts movements on the basis of sensory feedback from the body. The cerebellum and basal ganglia modify movement commands to increase accuracy and automaticity of movements. Damage to any one of these regions can cause a severe and unique type of movement disorder.

You began with a goal, to sip some coffee; the only part of the sequence of which you were consciously aware. The rest occurred automatically. Of course, there was a time in early childhood when you had to pay attention to almost every part of this movement sequence. Bringing a cup to your lips was serious business. But the basal ganglia have turned these conscious goal-directed actions into largely automatized (automatic) behaviors. Your mind now jumps from one goal to another, and most of the required bodily movements occur effortlessly, like a gift.

After Wayne's ALS had progressed, he could still generate movement goals just as you can. However, without the neurons that carry movement commands from the brain to the spinal cord or from the spinal cord to the muscles, his intentions would not translate into action. What parts of the brain generate movement goals? How does the brain translate these goals into motor commands to move specific body parts? How are these motor commands sent to muscles to generate body movements? While much of this puzzle remains mysterious, neuroscience is shedding light on how the goals we hold in our minds generate actions.

4.1 FROM SPINAL CORD TO MUSCLE

We begin with the spinal cord and brainstem neurons that activate the muscles. The particular set of muscles that are activated and their sequence of activation determines the action one carries out, whether lifting a cup, typing on a computer keyboard, or swimming in a lake.

4.1.1 Motor Neurons Communicate with Muscles

Alpha motor neurons originating in the spinal cord carry information to the muscles that move limbs and other body parts from the neck down. Other alpha motor neurons that originate in the brainstem (**cranial nerves**) control the muscles of the head and some muscles of the neck.

Alpha motor neurons generally leave the spinal cord at the portion closest to the muscle they target. So, for instance, those exiting the **cervical** division, at the top of the spinal cord, target neck, shoulder, and arm muscles, while those leaving the **sacral** division, at the bottom of the cord, target muscles in the back of the foot (Figure 4.2). This reduces neuronal wiring necessary to reach the muscle. Still, motor neurons that reach the muscles of the foot must travel a long distance. Imagine the length of these axons in the giraffe!

Voluntary movement of a particular body part depends upon communication between the brain and the spinal cord. If Mr. Jones has suffered an accident completely severing his spinal cord within the thoracic division (Figure 4.3), can he still voluntarily move his shoulder? Yes. As Figure 4.3 indicates, cervical nerves are above the cut. The brain can still communicate with cervical nerves that control shoulder muscles. Can he

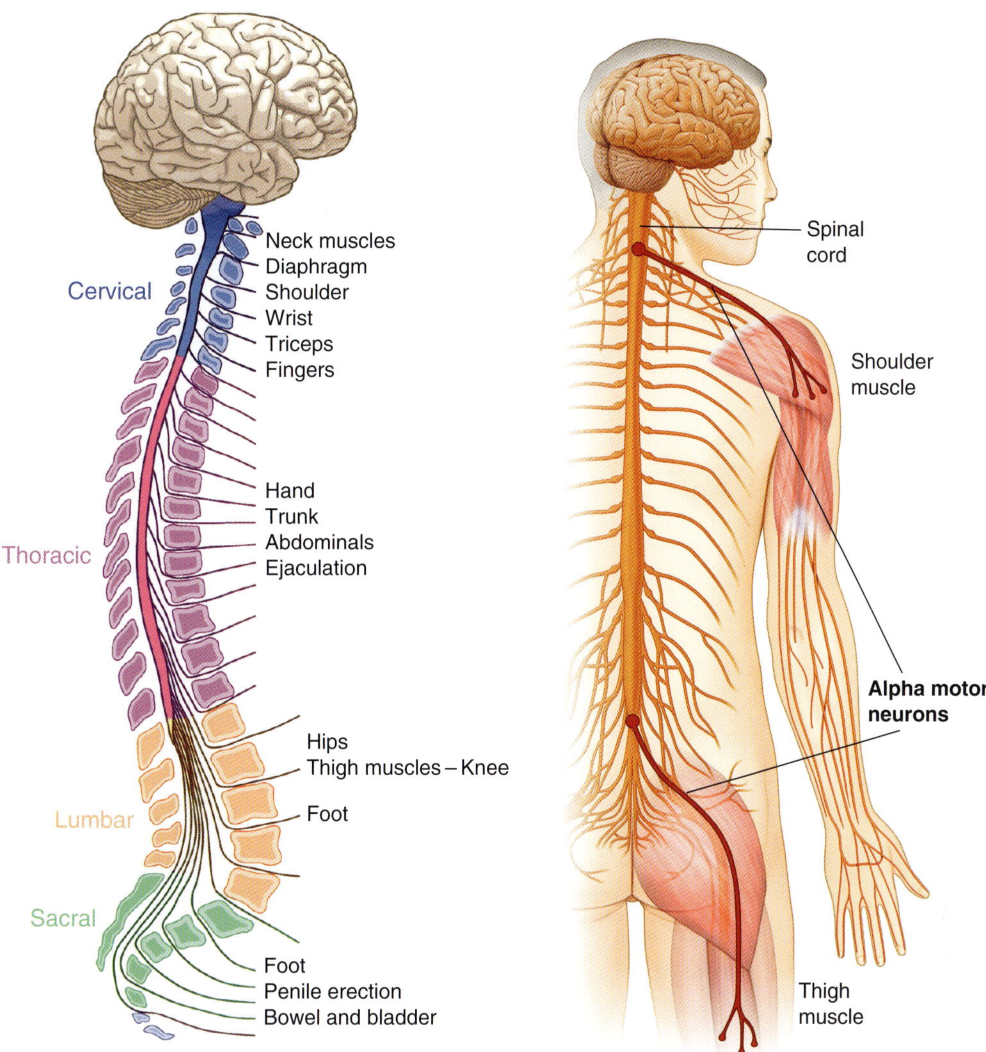

Figure 4.2 **The spinal cord is comprised of four major regions: cervical, thoracic, lumbar, and sacral**. Alpha motor neurons exiting different regions of the spinal cord control movement of different body parts.

still voluntarily move his legs? No. The lumbar nerves controlling the legs are below the cut. Individuals who have lost control of leg movements but maintain control of the arms suffer **paraplegia**. Those who lose control of all of their limbs suffer **quadriplegia** (also called **tetraplegia**). Quadriplegia often results from cuts to the cervical region of the spinal cord. Because cervical nerves target muscles needed for breathing, damage to this part of the cord may require patients to use a ventilator that essentially breathes for them, forcing air in and out of the lungs.

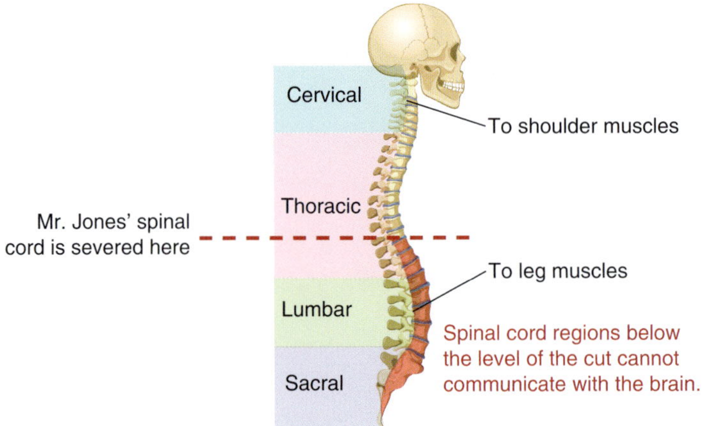

Figure 4.3 A spinal cord cut through the thoracic region. After a cut through the thoracic region of the spinal cord, brain commands no longer reach lumbar nerves controlling leg muscles.

Within the butterfly-shaped gray matter of the spinal cord reside alpha motor neurons (Figure 4.4). Their axons exit from the ventral portion of the gray matter (**ventral horn**) to reach the muscles. The surrounding white matter contains axons traveling between the brain and the spinal cord. These axons carry motor commands from the brain, such as commands necessary to grasp a coffee cup. In this case, the axons of the neurons descending through the spinal cord white matter must target the proper set of alpha motor neurons residing in the gray matter. The alpha motor neurons activate muscles of the hand and fingers to shape the hand so that it complements the shape of the cup handle.

4.1.2 Muscle Contractions Move Body Parts

An alpha motor neuron makes contact with **skeletal muscle**, muscles that move the bones (the skeleton). **Tendons** connect muscles to particular bones, so muscle contraction causes particular bones to move (Figure 4.5). Because skeletal muscle is striped, or *striated*, it is a kind of **striated muscle**. In contrast, **smooth muscle** lacks a striped appearance and generally controls involuntary functions. For example, smooth muscles of the intestines move food through the digestive system, and those in our eyes cause the pupils to expand and contract.

Each muscle is comprised of hundreds of thousands of thread-like cells called **muscle fibers**. The alpha motor neuron exits the spinal cord and it synapses upon a set of muscle fibers within a muscle (Figure 4.6). If the neuron targets many muscle fibers, activation of the neuron can

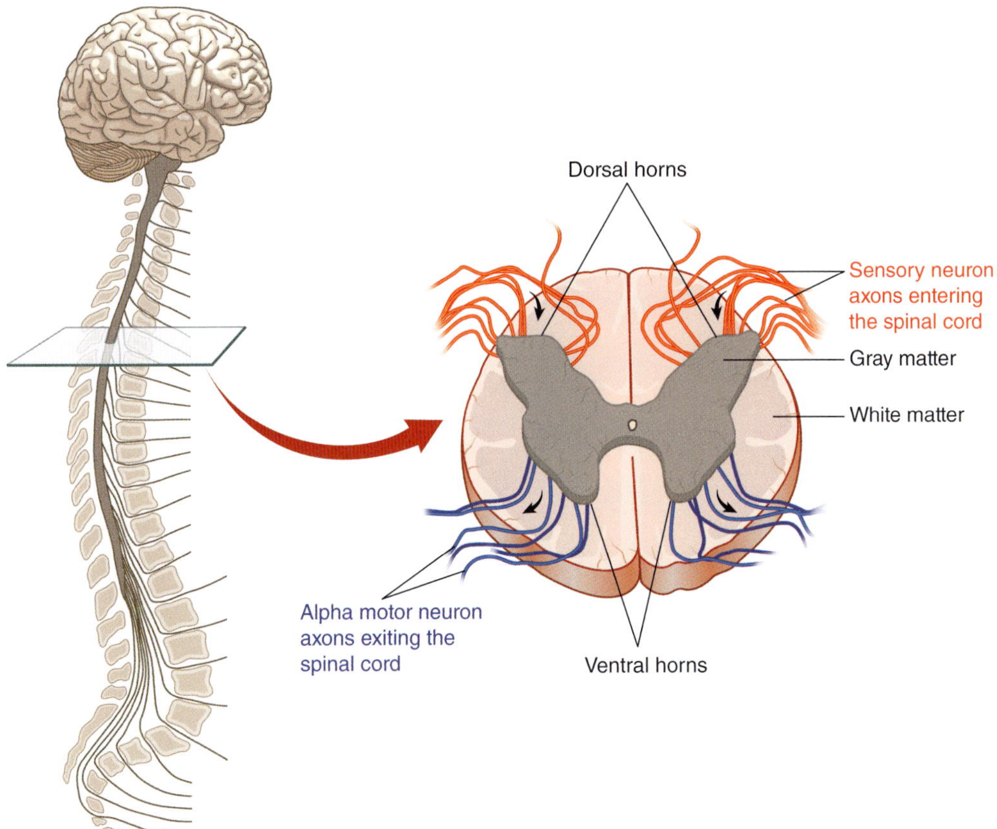

Figure 4.4 Alpha motor neurons originate in the spinal cord gray matter. Their axons (blue) exit the spinal cord from the ventral horn. Axons of sensory neurons (red) enter the spinal cord from the dorsal horn. The surrounding white matter contains the axons traveling from the brain to the spinal cord (and vice versa).

contract (shorten) many muscle fibers at once, driving a very large and powerful movement. This occurs in the muscles at the back of the leg, where branches of a single alpha motor neuron axon target thousands of muscle fibers. Some motor neurons, however, target only ten to twenty muscle fibers. This allows more precise movements, such as those of the fingers and lips.

At the end of its terminal, the alpha motor neuron releases the neurotransmitter **acetylcholine** (ACh), which crosses a synapse (**neuromuscular junction**) to reach a receptor on the muscle fiber (Figure 4.7). The muscle fibers contain **nicotinic receptors**, one of the two types of ACh receptors. When ACh binds to the nicotinic receptor, the receptor's shape changes and a region of the receptor opens to allow sodium (Na^+) to flow in. The opening of these Na^+ channels in the muscle fiber membrane initiates a process that leads to contraction of the muscle fiber.

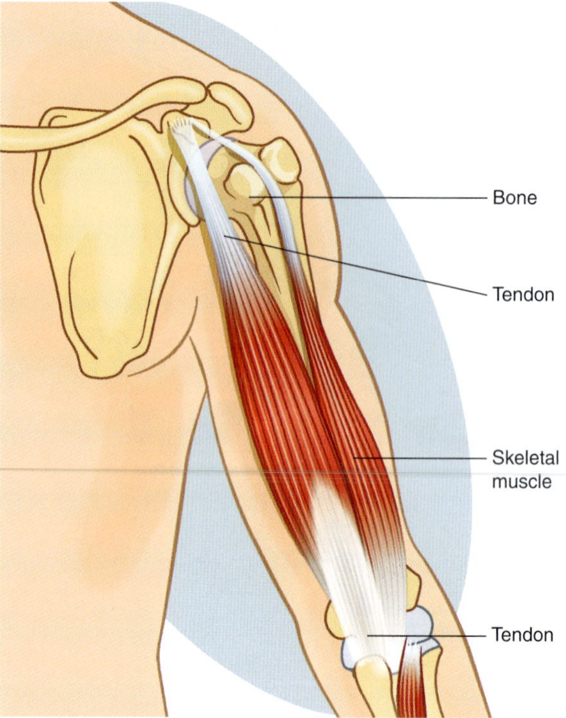

Figure 4.5 **The tendon connects skeletal muscle to bone.**

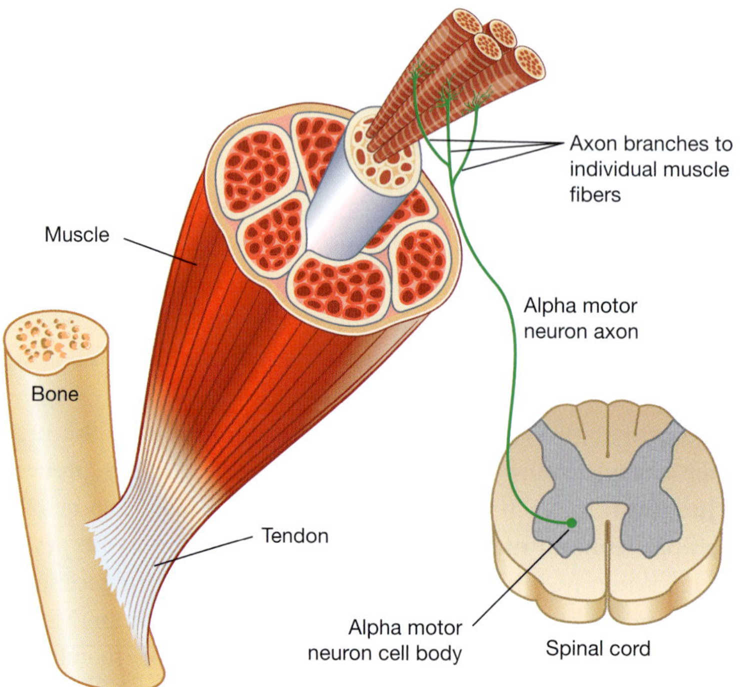

Figure 4.6 **Alpha motor neurons exit the spinal cord and synapse upon muscle fibers.**

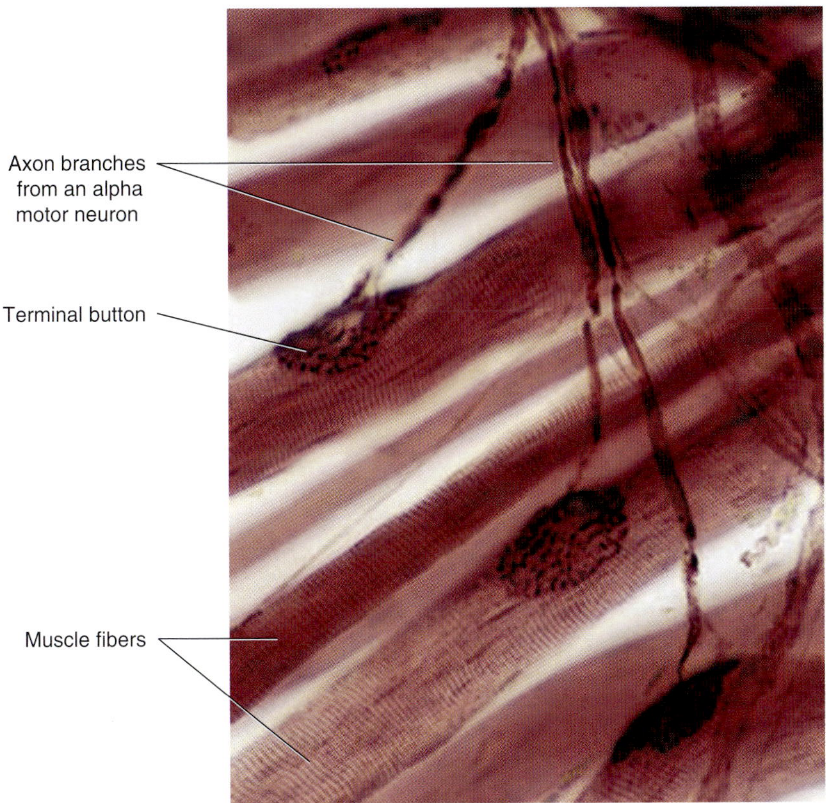

Figure 4.7 Light microscope image of an alpha motor neuron making contact with muscle fibers. In this image, the axon branches of a single alpha motor neuron make contact with several muscle fibers though terminal buttons.
(From Banich & Compton, 2018.)

As the muscle fibers connecting two bones contract, the bones may come closer together to produce a **flexion** movement (Figure 4.8). If these muscle fibers relax, and other muscle fibers contract, the bones move farther apart for an **extension** movement. Extend your right upper and lower arm straight at your side (in a 180 degree angle). Flexion at the elbow now brings them to a 90 degree angle, allowing you to wave hello. Further elbow flexion allows you to scratch your neck. Extension, on the other hand, increases the angle around the joint. Complete extension of the elbow back to a 180 degree angle is customary when we shake hands with another person.

The bicep muscle is a **flexor**: Bicep contraction causes flexion (or bending) at the elbow as the bones of the lower and upper arm move toward each other. In contrast, the triceps is an **extensor** muscle: Contraction of the triceps causes extension around the same joint, as the bones move away from one another. The biceps and triceps are **antagonistic** muscles: They move bones in opposite directions. When you lift your arm, the

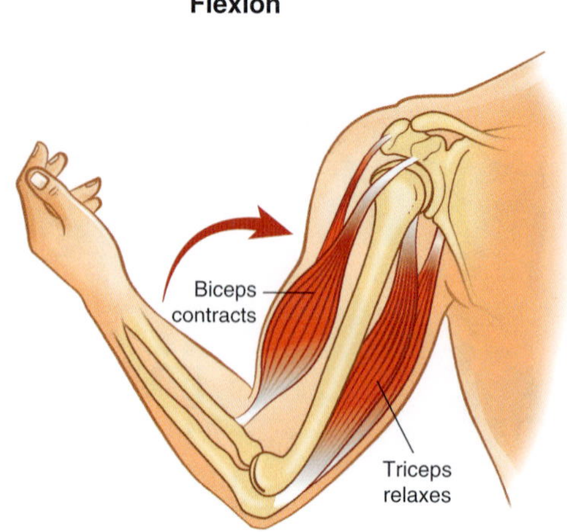

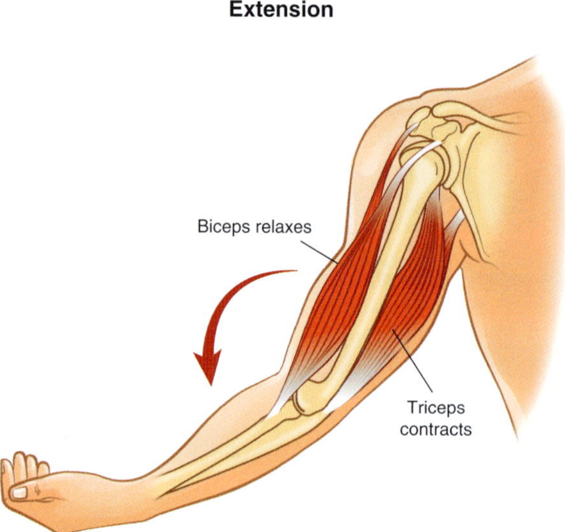

Figure 4.8 **Flexion and extension.**

triceps relaxes while the biceps contracts. If members of an antagonistic pair of muscles contract at the same time, the limb will become more rigidly fixed in position. Activation of antagonist muscle pairs helps us maintain body balance when standing, for it keeps our limbs in a fixed position and minimizes body movements. In contrast to antagonistic muscles, which cause movement in opposite directions, **synergistic muscles** contract together to perform a movement.

We have seen that muscle contraction causes movement of body parts. But suppose you wished to refrain from moving a body part, for instance while hiding from a wild animal. Can a neurotransmitter released into the neuromuscular junction inhibit muscle fiber contraction to prevent movement of a body part? No. There are only two ways to inhibit movement of a body part. One is for the alpha motor neuron to stop firing so that it is no longer releasing ACh into the neuromuscular junction. The muscle will not contract; it will remain flaccid. The second way involves contraction of both members of an antagonist muscle pair. As we saw, this will set the body part in a fixed position, immobile. If your body were to freeze in terror, this is what would happen.

The nervous system monitors the current length and tension of the muscles, allowing for adjustments to be made to the muscles so they can more accurately carry out intended movement. Key to monitoring the state of the muscles are the **muscle spindles**, special sensory receptor cells found within muscles (Figure 4.9). The muscle spindles inform the nervous system about changes in the length of the muscle at each moment in time. In addition, **Golgi tendon organs** are located in the tendons

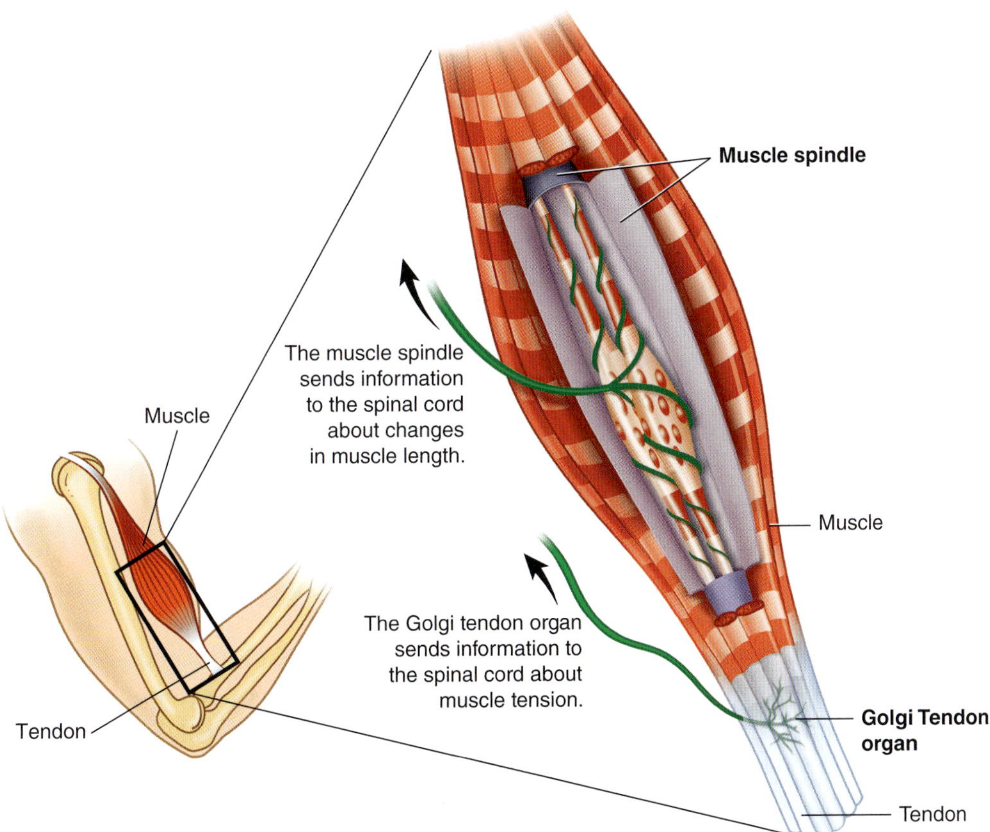

Figure 4.9 **Muscle spindle and Golgi tendon organ**. The muscle spindle and Golgi tendon organ are sensory structures that detect changes in the length and tension of the muscles, permitting the nervous system to make continuous adjustments to muscle state.

(which connect muscle to bone), and they sense muscle and tendon tension. As you lift the coffee cup, the biceps muscle shortens. If it shortens too quickly, the coffee may spill. In this case, muscle spindles and Golgi tendon organs inform the brain and spinal cord about this unexpectedly rapid change in the state of the muscle, allowing corrective body movements. Of course, the brain may not be able to make adjustments rapidly enough to prevent the accident. But areas of the brain that learn from such mistakes (such as the cerebellum discussed below) can use information from the muscle spindles and Golgi tendon organs in order to know about the state of the muscles at the time of the coffee accident (Loeb & Tsianos, 2015). This helps the brain's motor learning systems to plan more successful movements in the future.

4.1.3 The Spinal Cord Controls Reflexes and Some Repetitive Body Movements

When you step on a sharp object, your leg rapidly withdraws as the opposite leg extends to bear your weight (Figure 4.10). Pain-sensing neurons in the foot respond to the sharp object and communicate this information to spinal cord neurons. The message is passed along to several other spinal cord neurons before it reaches the alpha motor neurons. The alpha motor neurons send a signal to flexor muscles in the thigh to contract, lifting the injured leg. As one leg lifts, your opposite leg *extends*, keeping you from falling. This is because motor neurons exiting the side of the spinal cord opposite the injured leg cause contraction of extensor muscles of the other thigh. This is an example of relatively simple coordinated activity of spinal cord neurons. The withdrawal reflex occurs quickly because it does not require motor commands from the brain. On the other hand, if you wish to walk stoically over the sharp object, you would need descending commands from the brain to inhibit this reflex activity within the spinal cord.

You may have heard that a chicken without a head can walk, at least for a short while. The coordinated activity of many body parts seen during walking occurs through communication between spinal cord neurons. **Local spinal cord neurons** have cell bodies, dendrites, and axons contained entirely within the spinal cord. Groups of local neurons can excite and inhibit one another to produce complex patterns of alpha motor neuron activity and coordinated movement of limbs. In some cases, the axons of local neurons cross divisions of the spinal cord to coordinate muscle activity of separate limbs. For this reason, electrical stimulation of neurons within an animal's spinal cord can produce involuntary but coordinated walking movements when the animal is placed on a treadmill, even after the spinal cord is disconnected from the brain (Grillner & Wallen, 1985).

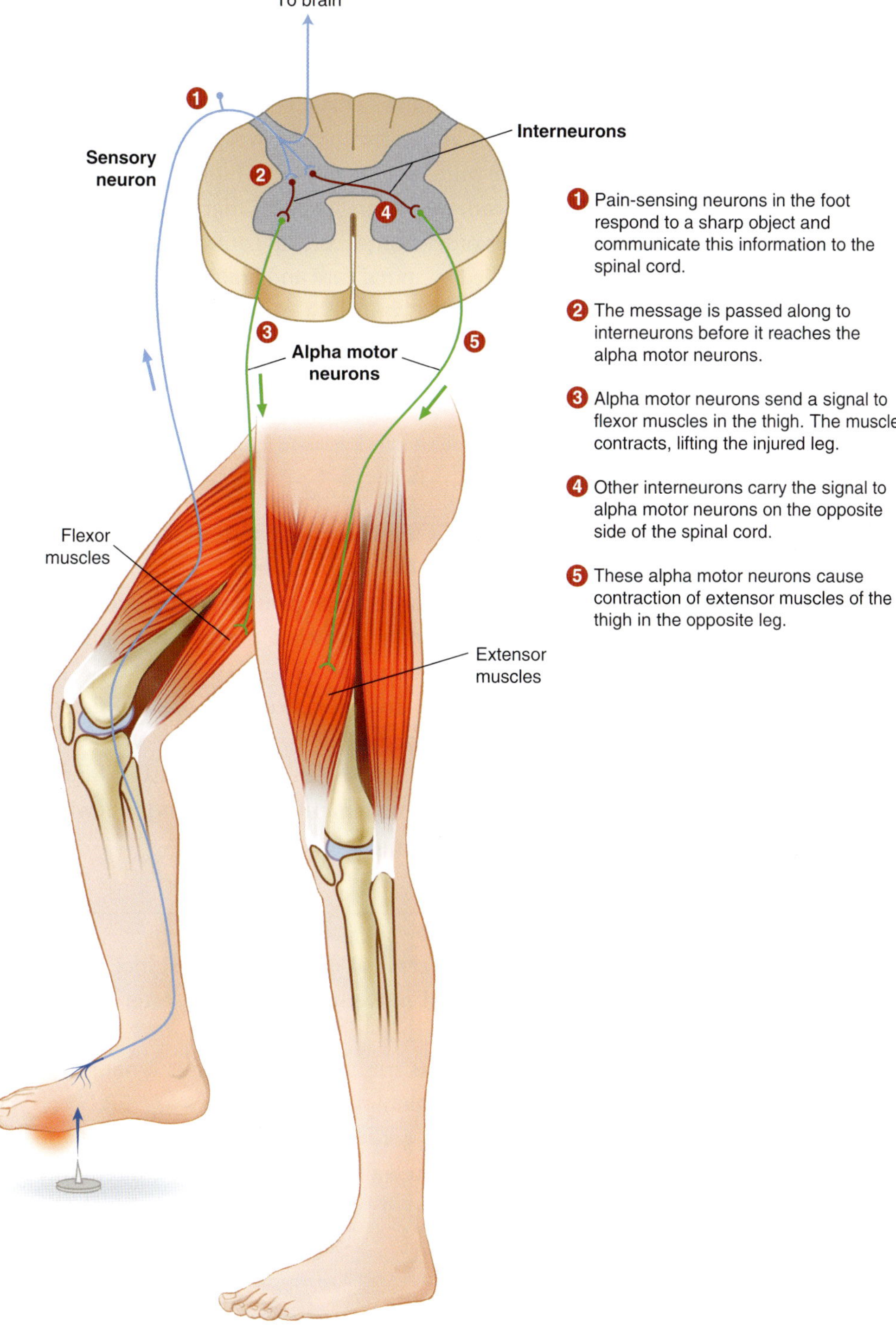

Figure 4.10 Spinal cord leg withdrawal reflex. The leg withdrawal reflex occurs through spinal cord sensory neurons, motor neurons, and interneurons. As one leg lifts, the other extends.

Repetitive behaviors such as walking, chewing, and breathing are controlled by sets of neurons called **central pattern generators** (**CPGs**) located in both the spinal cord and the brainstem. Higher brain regions such as the frontal cortex can control these behaviors if we choose to break their automatic rhythm and exert voluntary control over them. If you choose to chew in rhythm to your favorite song, to walk in a funny way to amuse your friends, or to hold your breath while lying flat (and frightening your mother), you are introducing higher-order frontal cortical control over behaviors that would normally be controlled by spinal cord and brainstem CPGs. When the repetitive behavior is under CPG control, it can sometimes occur without conscious awareness. This frees the higher-order brain regions to contemplate more interesting things, like the way the brain controls movement.

KEY CONCEPTS

- Alpha motor neurons permit the brainstem and spinal cord to activate skeletal muscle and generate body movements.
- An alpha motor neuron that targets many muscle fibers produces large and powerful movements, while one that targets few muscle fibers permits more precise movements.
- Behaviors, whether simple or complex, are composed of flexion and extension movements of the body.
- Central pattern generators (CPGs) within the brainstem and spinal cord control repetitive body movements like walking, chewing, and breathing, sometimes without conscious awareness.

TEST YOURSELF

1. Does a complete cut in the cervical division of the spinal cord impair hand movements? Are hand movements impaired after a cut in the sacral division?
2. The alpha motor neuron exits the spinal cord and it synapses upon a set of muscle ____ (cells) within a muscle.
3. You don't have to pay much conscious attention to putting one foot in front of the other while you walk because walking is a repetitive behavior controlled by ____ ____ ____ located in both the spinal cord and the brainstem.

4.2 PRIMARY MOTOR CORTEX

A long-term goal of neuroscience is to restore movement to those with spinal cord injuries, Parkinson's disease, ALS, and other motor disorders. One exciting and promising approach is to use signals from a patient's own brain to move robotic limbs. Brain signals that represent the person's intended actions may cause an artificial limb to grasp a cup, bring it to the person's lips, and carry out many other desired behaviors. Optimally, such a limb would be as flexible and varied in its movements as a normal limb.

Researchers have made progress using tiny electrodes that record the activity of neurons in the primary motor cortex and nearby regions of the cortex (Ifft, Lebedev, & Nicolelis, 2012; Rajangam et al., 2016). A computer deciphers the individual's intentions from neuronal signals, leading it to generate digital commands that cause the desired movement of artificial limbs or wheelchairs. In some quadriplegic patients, electrodes recording neural activity in the primary motor cortex has been used to decipher their intentions, and translate them into movements of a cursor on a computer tablet. With this technology, patients unable to move their limbs are able to open a browser, scroll through their email, or send a text message simply by thinking of where they wish to move the cursor and when they want to click the mouse (Nuyujukian et al., 2018). Many neuroscientists predict dramatic advances in the use of neural signals to control artificial devices (**brain–machine interface**).

Our focus in this section, however, will not be on how brains interface with machines, but on how brains interface with the spinal cord to produce desired movements. The frontal cortex can be divided into three major regions, each playing important roles in movement: the **primary motor cortex**, the **premotor areas**, and the **prefrontal cortex** (Figure 4.11). We begin with the primary motor cortex, a region of the frontal cortex that communicates directly with the spinal cord.

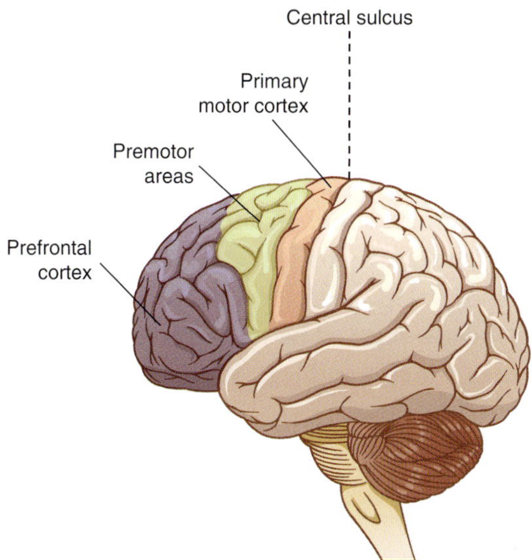

Figure 4.11 **The frontal cortex and control of movement**. Three major regions of the frontal cortex contribute to movement control: the primary motor cortex, the premotor areas, and the prefrontal cortex.

4.2.1 The Primary Motor Cortex Controls Movement of the Opposite Side of the Body

The primary motor cortex sends direct motor commands to the brainstem and spinal cord. **Corticospinal neurons** in the primary motor cortex (and premotor cortex) send motor commands to the spinal cord, where they target either alpha motor neurons or spinal cord interneurons (Figure 4.12). **Corticobulbar neurons** communicate with brainstem alpha motor neurons to control face muscles and some muscles in the neck. Corticospinal and corticobulbar neurons are called **upper motor neurons**, while the alpha motor neurons in the brainstem and spinal cord that directly target the muscles are referred to as **lower motor neurons**.

Neurons in the left primary motor cortex activate muscles mostly on the right side of the body, while neurons in the right motor cortex activate muscles to the left. **Contralateral** (opposite side) control of movement occurs because most corticospinal neurons have axons that cross to the opposite side of the brain before terminating in the spinal cord (again, see Figure 4.12). Most neurons (about 80 percent) cross at the level of the medulla while about 10 percent continue down to the spinal cord before crossing close to the site of axon termination. The remaining 10 percent of neurons do not cross at all, targeting alpha motor neurons on the same (**ipsilateral**) side of the spinal cord from which the corticospinal neuron originated.

The primary motor cortex is located in the **precentral gyrus**, and (like other parts of the cerebral cortex) contains six layers of neurons (Figure 4.13). Counting down from the top, the fifth layer contains the corticospinal neurons. These neurons are also called **pyramidal neurons** because their cell bodies are shaped like pyramids.

4.2.2 Body Parts Are Represented in a Map within the Motor Cortex

The primary motor cortex has a **somatotopic** organization; that is, different regions of the primary motor cortex represent different parts of the body (Ferrier 1874; Penfield & Boldrey, 1937). Electrical stimulation of medial regions of the primary motor cortex, tucked between the left and right hemispheres, activates muscles in the feet and legs; stimulation of more lateral parts of the motor cortex activates muscles in the hands; and stimulation even further lateral causes movement of face muscles including the

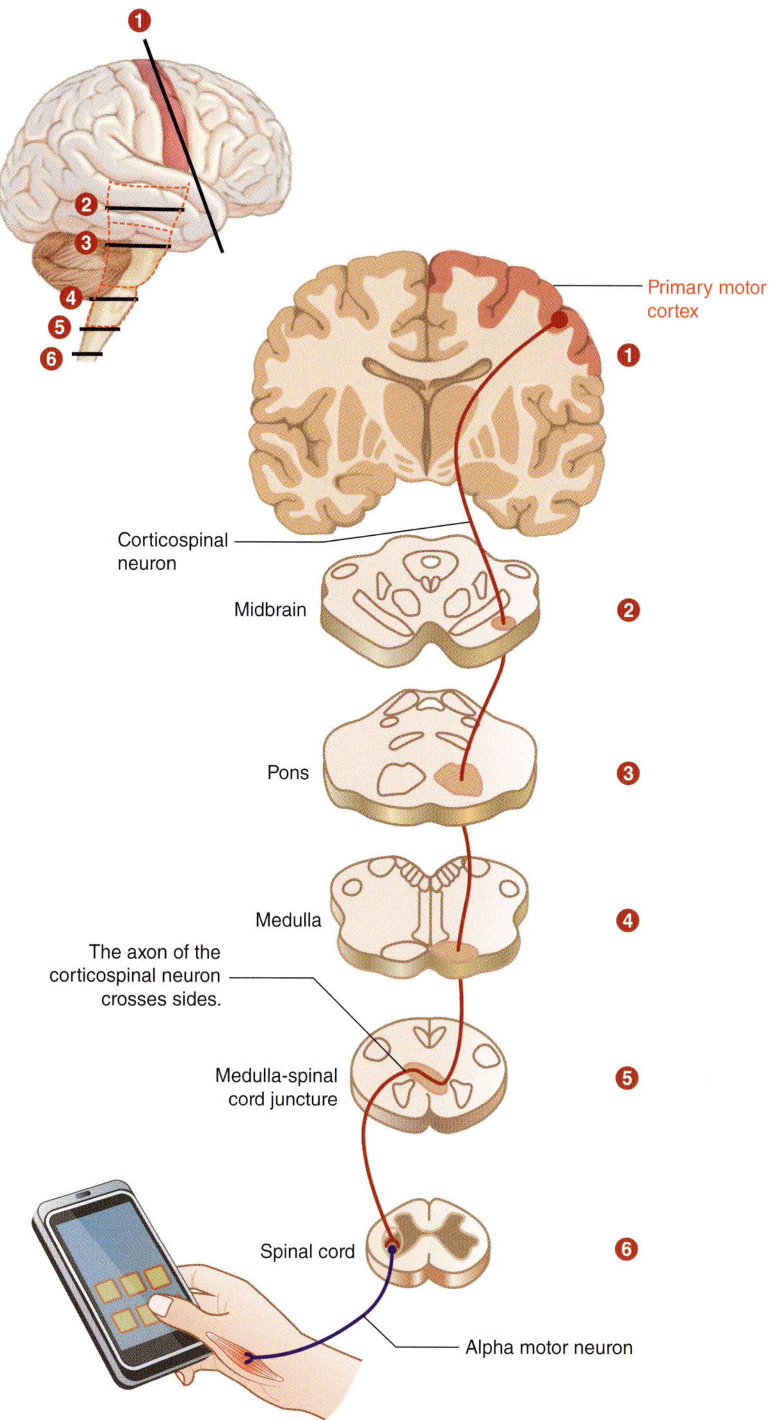

Figure 4.12 Corticospinal neurons send information from the primary motor cortex to the spinal cord. The axons of most corticospinal neurons cross sides in the medulla and continue their path to the spinal cord. This is why the left motor cortex controls right-side body movements, and vice versa.

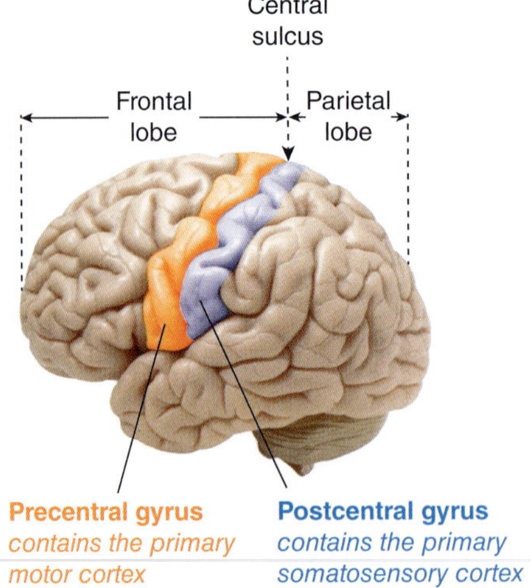

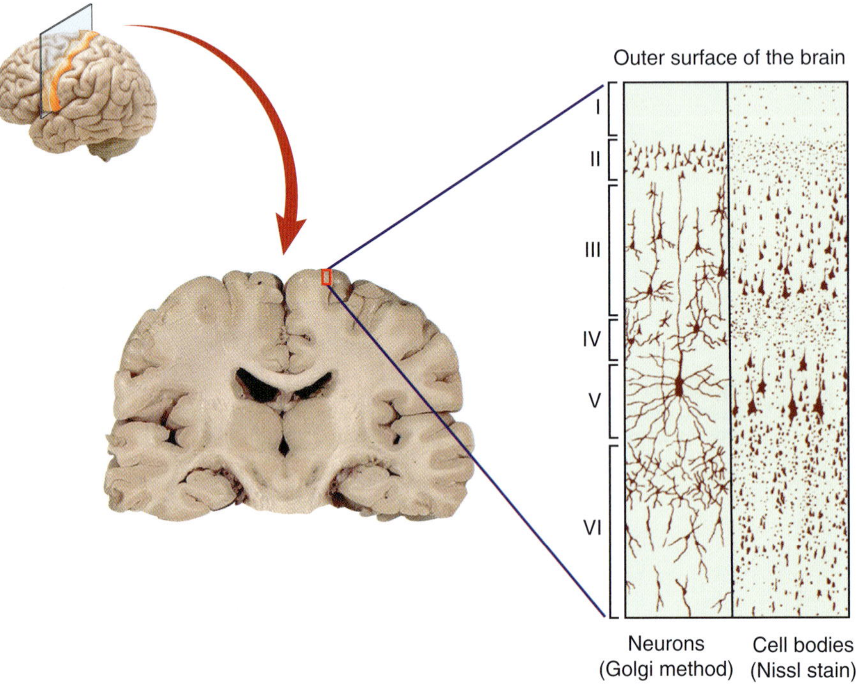

Figure 4.13 The primary motor cortex is in the precentral gyrus. The primary motor cortex lies just anterior to the central sulcus which separates the frontal and parietal lobes. The primary somatosensory cortex lies within the postcentral gyrus. Corticospinal neurons are found in layer V of the motor cortex (the fifth layer counting from the top to the bottom). (Brain slice, John Beal, LSU Health Sciences Center.)

tongue (Figure 4.14A). The amount of the motor cortex that represents a particular body part in the map reflects the amount of control the motor cortex exerts over that part. As can be seen, much of the motor cortex is dedicated to muscles that move the fingers and those needed for speech.

A

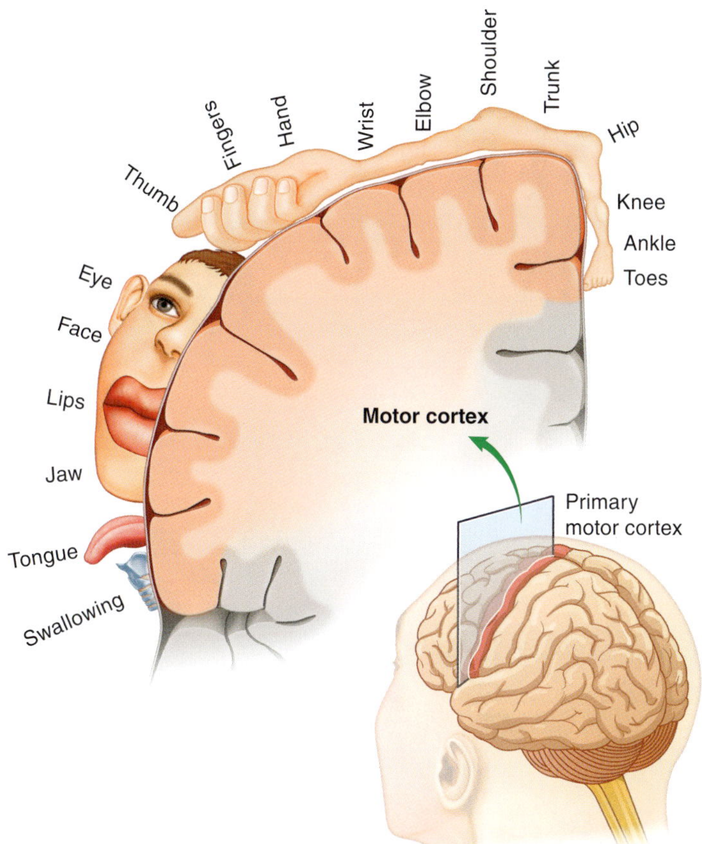

B

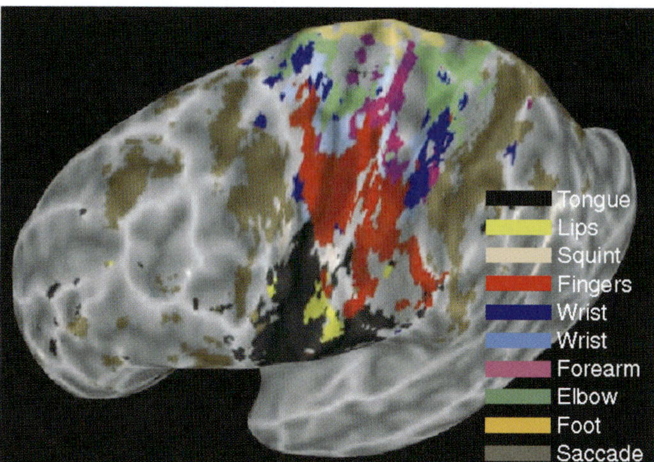

Figure 4.14 Maps of the motor cortex. (A) In the Penfield body map of the human motor cortex, different parts of the primary motor cortex control movement of different body parts. (B) Modern fMRI images show a more complex, patchy, organization of the body map. Note, however, many similarities with the earlier Penfield body map. The tongue representation remains at the bottom of the lateral surface, the foot is represented in a top medial region, and much of the motor cortex is dedicated to finger control. (Adapted from Meir et al., 2008.) (C) Recent maps of the motor cortex link cortical areas to actions rather than body parts. When the areas colored in the illustration were electrically stimulated for half a second, the monkey carried out a particular behavior: hand movement to the mouth as if eating; eyes closed and hand raised as if defending against threat; and other behaviors shown in the illustration. The specific behavior depended upon which cortical area was stimulated.

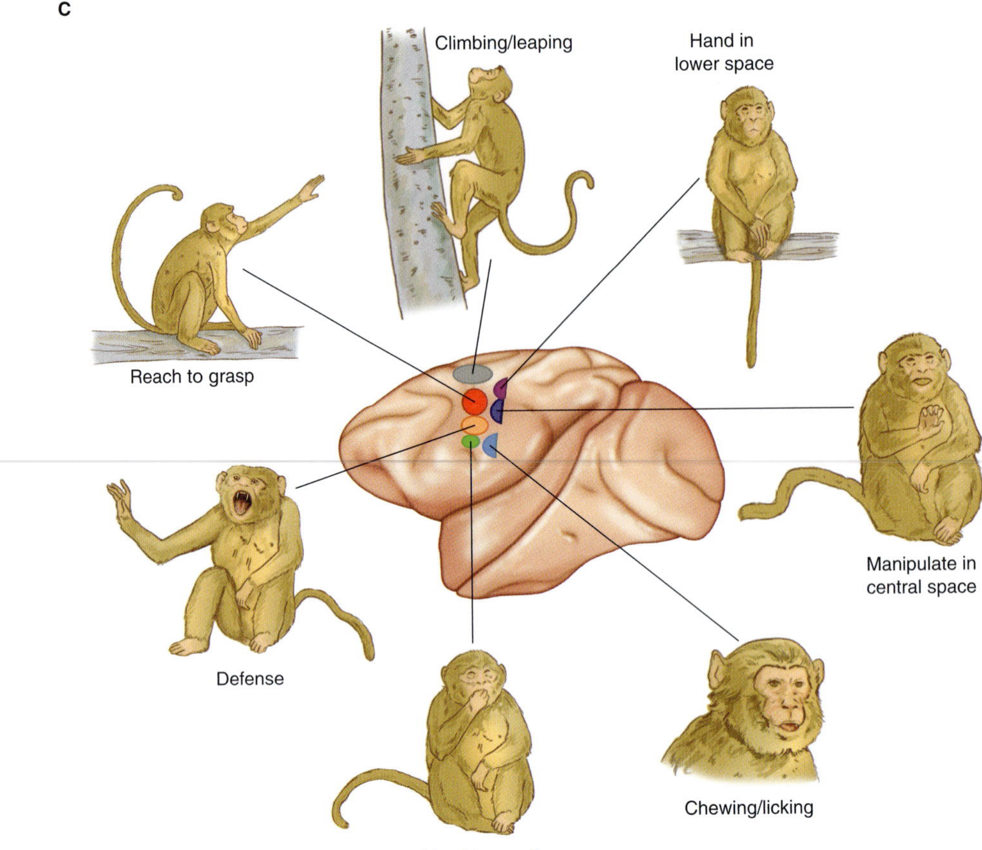

Figure 4.14 (cont.)

While different body parts are represented in particular areas of the motor cortex, fMRI data suggest that the arrangement of body part representations is not quite so orderly as once believed (Park, Belhaj-Saif, Gordon, & Cheney, 2001). As shown in Figure 4.14B, areas representing different body parts are arranged in a splotchy manner, like continents on a map.

When an accident or stroke destroys part of the motor cortex, movements become less accurate, weaker, and slower, and it becomes particularly difficult to move individual fingers. However, the fact that some patients with lesions of the primary motor cortex can still move their fingers and other body parts shows that alternative pathways from brain to muscle exist.

4.2.3 The Parietal Cortex Sends Tactile Feedback to the Primary Motor Cortex

As you write with a pencil, the precision of your finger movements depends upon the tactile feedback you receive as you squeeze the pencil and move it along the paper. Imagine that you had received an anesthetic in your hand and could not feel the pencil between your fingers. As you might imagine, it would be very difficult to produce the precise movements needed to write neatly on the page. You might even drop the pencil. The **primary somatosensory cortex** of the parietal lobe (see Figure 4.13) receives this tactile feedback and passes it to the primary motor cortex. When somatosensory inputs to the primary motor cortex are disrupted, fine motor coordination is impaired. For instance, experimenters injected a drug directly into the brains of monkeys, specifically within the somatosensory cortex. The drug silenced the activity of neurons. When the drug reached the finger area of the somatosensory cortex, monkeys could no longer use their fingers to pick up small pieces of food. They did not lose the ability to move the fingers. But they could no longer coordinate their finger movements in a way that allowed them to grasp the food (Hikosaka, Tanaka, Sakamoto, & Iwamura, 1985).

4.2.4 The Primary Motor Cortex Contributes to Integrated Behaviors

Body maps of the primary motor cortex, such as those shown in Figure 4.14A, give the false impression that activation of neurons in a particular area of the motor cortex causes movement of an individual body part as a piano key sounds a particular note. According to the metaphor, complex movements require activation of many areas of the motor cortex in a particular pattern, just as a piano player presses a sequence of keys in order to produce a melody. However, there are some flaws in this metaphor.

The first problem with the keyboard comparison is that some corticospinal neurons of the motor cortex can simultaneously activate multiple muscles from different body parts. A neuron in the motor cortex that causes movement of various muscles would be like a key on the piano sounding many notes at once. How can a single corticospinal neuron influence movement of multiple body parts? The corticospinal neuron projects to an interneuron of the spinal cord, and the interneuron, in turn, activates multiple alpha motor neurons. Each of the alpha motor neurons activates a different muscle. On the other hand, some corticospinal neurons activate only a single muscle by directly synapsing on an alpha motor neuron of the spinal cord. As you may recall, a single alpha motor neuron often contacts many muscle fibers, but the fibers are all part of the same muscle.

A more dramatic challenge to the piano keyboard metaphor comes from experiments showing that areas of the primary motor cortex control entire behavioral actions, not just limb movements. The traditional map of body parts in the motor cortex (again, see Figure 4.14A) was based upon studies in which very brief (e.g., 20 milliseconds) stimulation of a particular point of the motor cortex in monkeys (and other animals) caused movement of an individual body part (Fritsch & Hitzig, 1870; Leyton & Sherington, 1917). However, when stimulation of the motor cortex lasts longer (about half a second), the monkeys perform coordinated sequences of behavior (Graziano, 2006). For instance, stimulation of one area caused the monkey to first close its hand, then move hand to mouth, and finally open its mouth as if it were going to eat. This hand-to-mouth movement generated by electrical stimulation of the motor cortex occurs in the absence of food. Once the movement begins, it is unaffected by sensory feedback. For example, if an obstacle is placed between the hand and the mouth, the hand will move toward the mouth and bump into the obstacle. When the hand returns to its original position and the stimulation is repeated, the hand will move in the same direction and bump into the obstacle again.

Stimulation at other areas of the primary motor (or premotor) cortex produces other actions, such as turning the head while moving the arm to a defensive posture or moving the hand and fingers within a central space, as if the monkey were examining an object. These data suggest that activation of a particular area of the motor cortex does not simply cause movement of an individual body part, or even a group of nearby body parts, but is capable of coordinated, goal-directed movement. Stimulation of motor cortical regions can produce behavioral melodies, not just notes. These results suggest that the motor cortex may contain an "action map" (Figure 4.14C) in addition to a "body map" (Graziano, 2016).

The long-duration stimulation may have activated complex circuits within the spinal cord that were capable of coordinating the behavioral melody, or perhaps the stimulation activated groups of corticospinal neurons that, together, produced the complex behaviors. Some of these neurons may have been far from the site of electrical stimulation but possessed strong synaptic connections with the directly stimulated neurons. In either case, these data suggest that activation of a particular area of the motor cortex may generate meaningful behaviors, not just movement of individual or nearby body parts.

KEY CONCEPTS

- **The left primary motor cortex produces right-side body movements, and vice versa.**
- **The motor cortex contains a general map of body parts. However, the neurons that control particular body parts spread around the motor cortex in a patchy way rather than group together in distinct regions.**

- Activation of particular areas of the primary motor cortex do not simply move a single body part, but can elicit an entire behavior. For instance, electrical stimulation of one area of the motor cortex causes the hand to move toward the mouth and the mouth to open.

TEST YOURSELF

1. Neurons in the left primary motor cortex activate muscles mostly on the right side of the body. This "opposite-side" control of movement is called ______ control.
2. How do you explain the fact that the motor cortex on one side of the brain primarily controls movement of the other side of the body?
3. Body parts that we can control with great precision are generally those represented by relatively _____ regions of the motor cortex.
4. If you were unable to feel the movement of the computer keys as you press them with your fingers, it would be difficult to type. Explain this phenomenon in terms of the information that is sent from touch receptors to the parietal lobe, and from there to the corticospinal neurons.

4.3 PREMOTOR AREAS

The premotor areas include a number of frontal lobe regions anterior to the primary motor cortex (Figure 4.15), including both the **dorsal** and **ventral premotor areas** and the **supplementary motor area** (**SMA**). The primary motor cortex receives much of its input from the premotor areas. Therefore, as we explore the functions of the premotor areas, we are revealing some of the kinds of information that may be relayed to corticospinal neurons to influence movement.

4.3.1 The Supplementary Motor Area Is Active during the Conscious Desire to Move

Move your right arm sometime in the next 30 seconds. You can decide the direction and moment to move the arm. Wait until you wish to do it.

It is unclear exactly how brain activity produces the conscious decision to move. However, activity within the SMA, a premotor area on the medial surface of the brain, coincides with the feeling of wanting to move. Individuals who elected to undergo brain surgery to treat epilepsy agreed to participate in studies involving stimulation of movement-related brain areas. When the SMA was stimulated, they reported an "urge" or "need" to move a body part (Fried et al., 1991). The urges were usually specific;

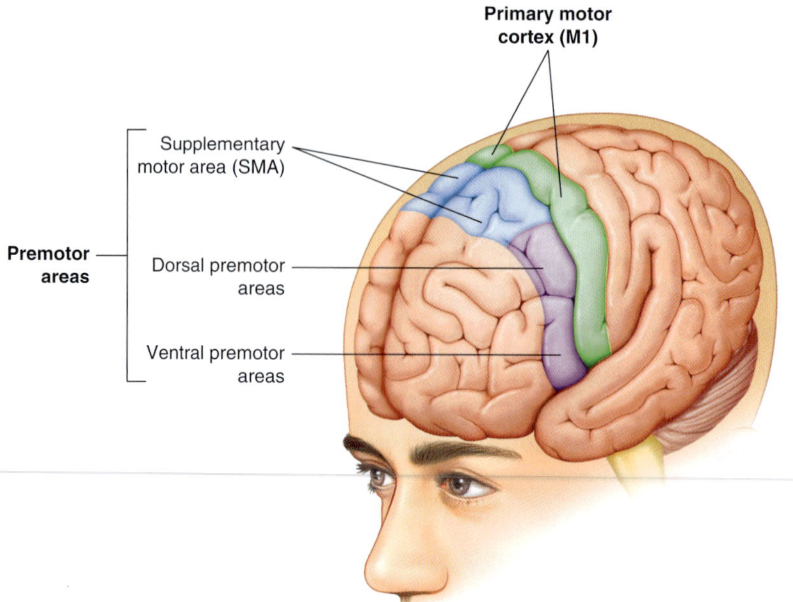

Figure 4.15 Premotor areas. The premotor areas lie just anterior to the primary motor cortex.

for instance, an urge to move the right leg inward. When the stimulation intensity was low, the urge to move occurred but the movement did not. When the stimulation was slightly increased, the movements actually occurred. In this case, the subjects could anticipate the moment when the leg was about to move, but they did not feel as if they had caused the movements themselves (and of course they had not).

Some investigators believe that the desire to move a body part arises from brain activity in the **inferior parietal lobe** (Figure 4.16), a ventral part of the posterior parietal cortex with strong connections to the SMA. When the inferior parietal area is stimulated, subjects report a desire to move a body part. However, the movement urge is less specific than that following SMA stimulation. The subject may identify the limb she wants to move, but usually not how she wants to move it. For instance, one subject described how stimulation of the inferior parietal area made her feel: "I wanted to move my foot," she said. The experimenter asked which foot. "This one," she replied, pointing to the left leg. The experimenter asked how she wanted to move it. "I don't know. I just wanted to move it," she said (Desmurget & Sirigu, 2012, p. 1006). Unlike SMA stimulation, increased intensity of stimulation to the inferior parietal does not cause a movement to occur, simply the desire for the movement. Taken together, the data suggest that conscious movement intentions may arise

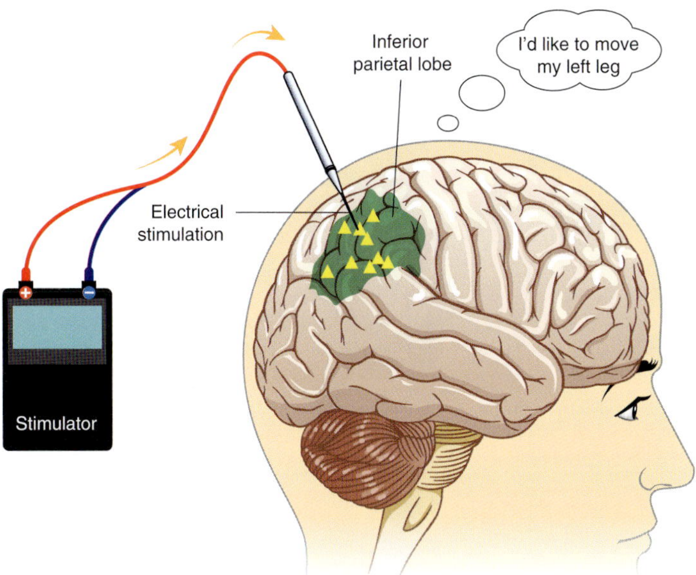

Figure 4.16 The inferior parietal lobe and the desire to move. Electrical stimulation within the inferior parietal lobe (at sites marked by triangles) produces feelings of "wanting to move."

with neuronal activity in the inferior parietal and that this information may pass to the SMA where the intention is refined to a more specific kind of body movement. This hypothesis, of course, leaves open the question of whether these conscious movement intentions might arise from neuronal activity that occurs before one is aware of intending any movement at all (see Box 4.1).

BOX 4.1 Does the brain choose our actions before we become aware of the choice?

The **readiness potential** is a non-invasive measure of brain activity occurring before a movement. It can be recorded with EEG electrodes glued to a subject's scalp. When it first appears, the readiness potential is centered over the SMA. Some moments later, just before the movement occurs, the readiness potential is centered over the primary motor cortex. By observing this readiness potential, an experimenter can anticipate the subject's body movement. But can the experimenter tell that a movement will occur even before the subject has consciously decided to move?

To address this question, Benjamin Libet and colleagues asked subjects to press a button with their finger whenever they "felt the urge" to do so (see Figure 4.17). They were also instructed to keep their eyes on the hand of a clock, and to report its position at the moment they felt the urge to make the movement (Libet, Gleason,

BOX 4.1 (cont.)

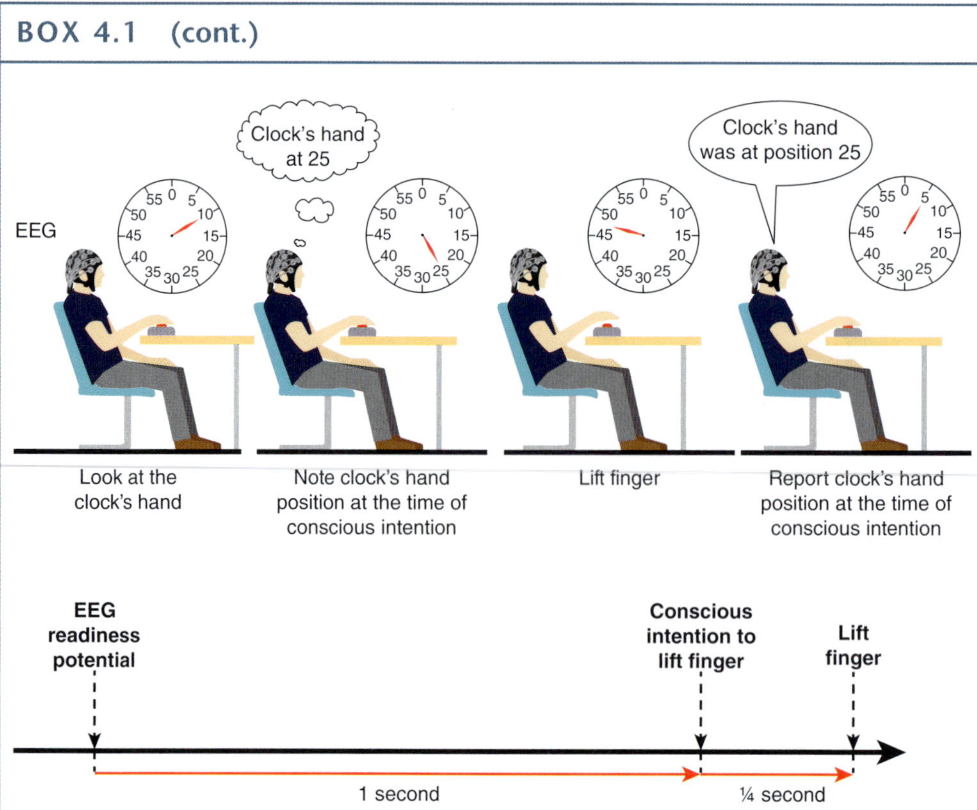

Figure 4.17 Does the brain decide to move before we are conscious of the decision? This illustration depicts Libet's methodology for determining the moment at which a subject "felt the urge" to move the finger. The brain generated a movement-related readiness potential even before the subject was aware of deciding to lift a finger.

Wright, & Pearl, 1983). On average, the urge to move occurred about a quarter of a second before the movement. But the readiness potential began about 1 second earlier. Such findings have been replicated many times. Similar studies using fMRI have observed that activity in the frontal and parietal lobes can predict a subject's decision up to 10 seconds before it enters awareness (Soon, 2008). Some neuroscientists and philosophers interpret such results to suggest that the brain has already decided to take an action before we consciously decide to act. However, others make the following point: Activity in the brain, even in some individual neurons, can partially predict actions several seconds before they occur. Still, one cannot conclude that during the time when this early brain activity is observed, the brain has "decided" upon the upcoming action. The early brain activity may contribute to the later decision, but that does not mean that the brain activity directly caused, or determined, the decision. The ultimate decision may still occur just before the action is performed (Murakami, Vicente, Costa, & Mainen, 2014).

If neuronal activity within the inferior parietal lobe and SMA are involved in our conscious intentions to carry out an action, what happens when these areas are damaged? Individuals with damage to the inferior parietal lobe may show signs of apathy, a reduced desire to carry out any behavior at all (Tumati, Martens, de Jong, & Aleman, 2019). In other patients, damage to either the inferior parietal or the SMA causes **alien hand syndrome**. In this strange disorder, the hand contralateral to the brain damage makes movements that are not consciously intended. For instance, after the person uses his normal (unaffected) hand to place a phone call, the alien hand may hang up the phone before the call has been answered. Without normal activity of the inferior parietal and SMA, the motor system appears to carry out behaviors that are no longer linked to the person's conscious intentions.

One brain-imaging study focused on a participant who had an alien hand that he could sometimes control (Assal, Schwartz, & Vuilleumier, 2007). When he moved his fingers with conscious, voluntary control, his brain showed high neuronal activity levels within the inferior parietal lobe, SMA, and primary motor cortex, as well as nearby brain areas. In contrast, during involuntary finger movements, the primary motor cortex was active, but not the inferior parietal, SMA, or other nearby areas. Taken together, these data suggest the intriguing possibility that the inferior parietal and premotor areas may be associated with the conscious intention to move.

4.3.2 Movement Preparation Is Associated with Premotor Activity

While stopped at a traffic light, you prepare to press the accelerator. In animal studies, the neural activity that accompanies movement preparation can be studied in detail using experimental procedures similar to the traffic light example. For instance, a monkey may see a yellow circle (the "instruction cue") on the screen that instructs it to move its arm to the right in order to receive a juice reward. If its arm moves too soon, it receives no reward. It must wait until the yellow circle turns green (the "go signal"). After the instruction cue, while the monkey is preparing to move its arm, premotor neurons become highly active, particularly within the **dorsal premotor cortex** (Weinrich & Wise, 1982). Different sets of neurons are active depending upon the direction of the upcoming movement (e.g., right or left). If the preparatory activity of these neurons is disrupted, the subjects are slow to begin the movement once the go signal arrives (Churchland & Shenoy, 2007). These results suggest that premotor activity that precedes a movement helps generate a state of readiness to perform the movement once the appropriate moment arrives. Such a state allows us to press the accelerator at the moment the traffic light turns green.

4.3.3 Visuomotor Neurons Prepare the Hand to Grasp Objects

To grasp a coffee cup, you curl your hand and fingers in a way that complements the shape of the cup. You do this on the basis of visual information regarding the cup's shape. The position of your fingers would need to be different in order to pick up keys. Try reaching for a cup, and you will see that your hand assumes the grasp position even before it has reached the target object. **Visuomotor** neurons in the **ventral premotor area** translate visual information about the target object into motor actions. When an animal makes a visually guided movement such as grasping, neurons in the ventral premotor area begin firing as soon as the animal sees the object to be grasped. When the premotor area is inactivated with an anesthetic drug, the monkey loses the ability to make hand movements appropriate for grasping the object in its view (Rizzolatti & Luppino, 2001).

4.3.4 Mirror Neurons Are a Bridge from Observation to Imitation

Mirror neurons become active not only when a monkey grasps an object, but also when it observes another monkey or human performing the same action (Figure 4.18) (Gallese, Fadiga, Fogassi, & Rizzolatti, 1996; Rizzolatti & Luppino, 2001). Mirror neurons are found within premotor and other areas of the cortex. Some mirror neurons are activated when the monkey observes someone manipulating an object by hand; others respond when the monkey sees someone placing an object on a table. Some mirror neurons are more selective than others. The most selective are activated not only by a particular kind of movement, such as gripping an object, but by an even more specific type of movement, such as gripping with the whole hand versus gripping with two fingers.

The key property of mirror neurons is not simply that they respond to observed actions – other neurons do that as well. It is that the same neuron is activated while observing or performing an action. So, as a monkey watches you lift a caramel with two fingers, specific "mirror neurons" in its premotor cortex are activated; these same premotor neurons are activated when the monkey imitates the action. Presumably, activity of those neurons contributes to the monkey's ability to lift the caramel with its fingers. The mirror neuron is special because it provides a bridge between observation and action – a mechanism for imitation.

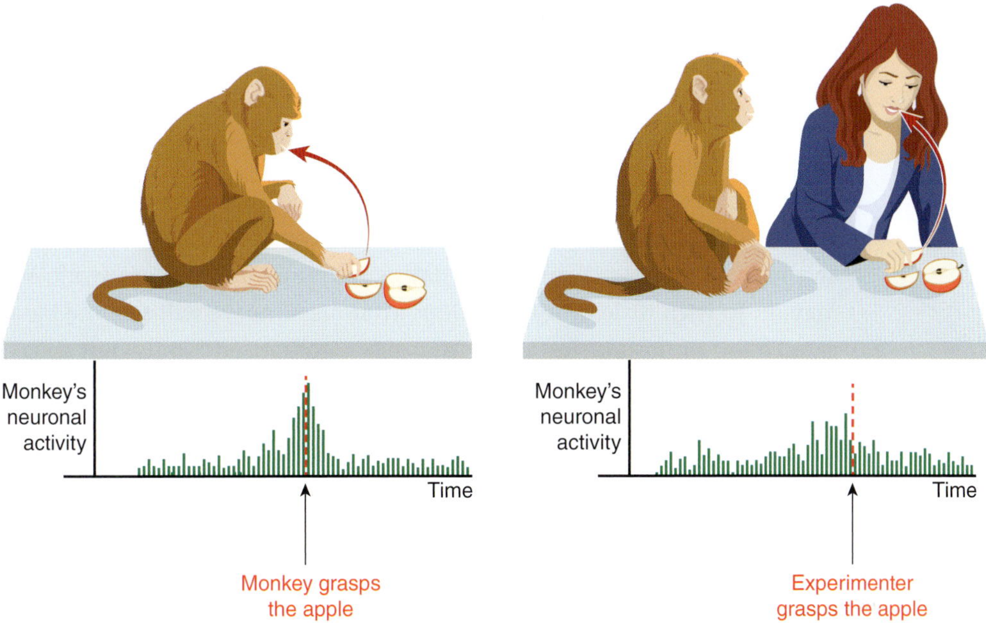

Figure 4.18 Mirror neurons. A mirror neuron shows intense activity when the monkey grasps the apple, and also when the monkey observes the experimenter perform the same grasping movement. The increased activity of the neuron is associated with the grasping movement itself in both cases.

Humans also appear to possess mirror neurons (Jeon & Lee 2018; Montgomery, Seeherman, & Haxby, 2009). For instance, fMRI shows that premotor areas of the human brain become active when a person either smiles or sees someone else smile. It seems likely that mirror neurons in a baby, activated as its mother smiles, permit the baby to imitate the facial expression. Presumably, the baby has another set of mirror neurons that respond when someone sticks out the tongue, allowing the baby to imitate this movement as well.

4.4 PREFRONTAL CORTEX

We will examine cognitive functions of the **prefrontal cortex** (**PFC**) when we discuss attention and working memory in Chapter 10. However, the PFC also plays several important roles in movement.

4.4.1 The Prefrontal Cortex Keeps Movement Goals in Mind

Imagine that your present goal is to prepare coffee, but while pouring the water into the coffee maker you forget the goal and begin to carry out actions appropriate for a completely different goal, like washing the dishes. Your behavior would become fragmented, and, if taken to an extreme, non-functional. Intentional behavior depends upon the brain's representation of a goal. The PFC plays a critical role in representing goals for the purpose of movement control (Miller & Cohen, 2001; Hasselmo, 2005; Mansouri, Koechlin, Rosa, & Buckley, 2017).

In some cases, we carry out complex behavior automatically without a conscious goal. For instance, we may be accustomed to turning right at a particular street corner every day as we return home from work. We may do so with little or no conscious awareness. As we will see, the basal ganglia are important for acquiring such automatized habits. But today, instead of turning right, we may wish to turn left in order to pick up fresh bread at the market. Do we turn left or right? Evidence suggests that ventral regions of the PFC determine which of our goals has the highest value (O'Doherty, 2011). Let us imagine that the PFC calculates that today going to the market is more valuable than going directly home because it will satisfy our desire for fresh bread. In the absence of PFC activity, we would simply have performed our "default" behavior, in this case to turn right as we usually do. Without the prefrontal goal representation, we engage in the behavior that is most habitual, or direct our behavior toward whatever stimulus is brightest and shiniest (Miller & Cohen, 2001). The prefrontal cortex keeps our behavior directed toward those goals we believe are most valuable.

4.4.2 Behavioral Control Sometimes Requires Withholding Actions until a Later Time

You know how to move a cursor on your computer screen to open a document. But you have also learned not to click the mouse while your computer is still starting up. The PFC plays an important role in inhibiting motor acts until the appropriate time.

In one study, human subjects were instructed to press a button as soon as a circle appeared on a screen. However, they were also instructed not to press the button if an X appeared after the circle. This was a difficult task, because the X sometimes appeared just as the subject was about to press the button in response to the circle. On some of these trials, subjects successfully withheld the button press, and on other trials, they could not inhibit the response. fMRI showed that the PFC was highly activated on the trials when they successfully inhibited their behavior (see Figure 4.19) (Li, Huang, Constable, & Sinha, 2006).

Damage to the PFC or to a number of other brain regions can produce a bizarre abnormality called **utilization behavior**. Patients are unable to resist the impulse to use an object that has been placed within reach, even when the object is not needed. For instance, a patient might pick up a

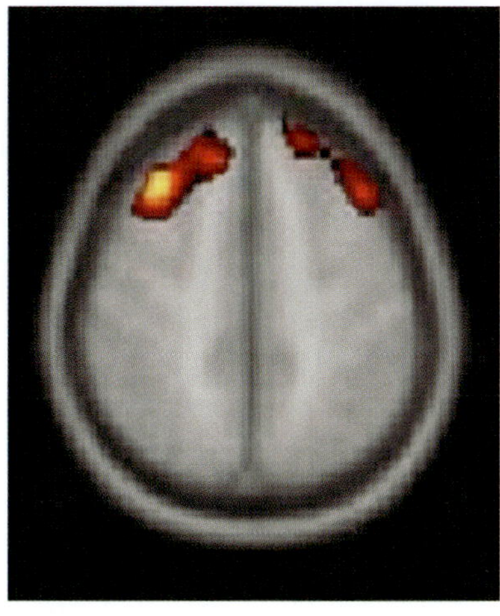

Figure 4.19 **The prefrontal cortex (PFC) and behavioral inhibition**. fMRI showing activation within the PFC as human subjects inhibit their own behavioral responses. A slice of the brain is seen as if you were looking down at it from the ceiling. The front (anterior) part of the brain is at the top.
(Adapted from Li, Huang, Constable, & Sinha, 2006, fig. 1, © 2006 Society for Neuroscience.)

pair of spectacles, put them on, then see another pair on the table and put them on too! The patients are compelled to take and use the object, and they continue to do so even after the experimenter has asked them to stop. One explanation of utilization behavior is that we, as ordinary people, are also unconsciously driven to grab objects we see, but, without our realizing it, inhibitory processes involving the PFC and other brain regions prevent these impulses from inappropriately influencing behavior. Damage to the PFC may interrupt the inhibitory processes that normally prevent us from acting on these impulses.

4.4.3 Frontal Eye Fields Locate Objects Relevant to the Current Goal

The **frontal eye fields** (FEF) are located in a small strip of the PFC. They play a role in the control of voluntary eye movements. **Visual saccades** are quick, simultaneous movements of both eyes in the same direction toward a visual object. Saccades allow the visual object of interest to land directly on the fovea, permitting the visual system to view it with the greatest focus and highest resolution. The FEF generate saccades purposefully to track an object relevant to current goals. For instance, if a cat is stalking a mouse, the FEF generate saccades that allow the cat to track the mouse's movements. Sometimes, the FEF even generate saccades to the location where a goal object is expected to arrive. Because of activity in the FEF, the cat can move its eyes to the location where it knows the mouse will be a moment later, improving the cat's chances of leaping and capturing the mouse as soon as it enters the cat's field of vision.

In contrast to the FEF, which generates eye movements in order to achieve particular goals (e.g., to catch a mouse), eye fields in the parietal lobe and within the superior colliculi control visual saccades in a more reflexive manner, e.g., moving the eyes to an object simply because it is new or shiny and bright. The FEF controls eye movements in the service of some larger goal that one wishes to achieve.

KEY CONCEPTS

- **Activity in the supplementary motor area is associated with the conscious desire to move.**
- **Premotor neurons play a critical role in reaching for and grasping objects.**
- **Mirror neurons are activated while observing or performing an action, and may contribute to our ability to imitate the actions of others.**
- **The prefrontal cortex is important for deciding which actions to perform, inhibiting behavior until the optimal time to act, and directing eye movements toward stimuli relevant to the current goal.**

TEST YOURSELF

1. **Robert has damage to his right supplementary motor area. While holding the phone with his right hand and talking to his friend, his left hand grabs the phone and ends the call. This type of action without conscious intention is seen in people with _____ _____ syndrome.**
2. **Mirror neurons become active when you observe another person performing an action. What makes mirror neurons different from neurons in the visual cortex that may also become active when you're watching another person's actions?**
3. **Many areas of the brain can generate rapid eye movements (saccades) toward visual objects, including the parietal cortex and superior colliculus. How do the saccades generated by the frontal eye fields differ from those generated by these other areas?**

4.5 BASAL GANGLIA

The basal ganglia are important in choosing which behavior is most valuable given your current **state**. Your state includes environmental stimuli, such as the visual, auditory, tactile, and olfactory stimuli that make your bedroom recognizably different from your kitchen. Inputs from the cerebral cortex inform the basal ganglia about these sensory conditions, your current body position, and other information about your current state. From past experience, the basal ganglia have learned which actions are most useful when you are in this (or a similar) state, and the basal ganglia communicate with the frontal cortex to select which behaviors to perform at the present moment. When a particular behavior has been successful many times in the past, the basal ganglia help to convert the behavior into a habit – that is, an action that occurs automatically whenever you are in a particular "state" (Yin, Knowlton, & Balleine, 2004; Ashby, Turner, & Horvitz, 2010; Shan, Christie, & Balleine, 2015). For instance, the basal ganglia may have learned that when you are facing your front door with the key in your hand and the intention of entering the house, a certain pattern of hand and arm movements has often been successful in unlocking the door in the past. The basal ganglia may direct you to carry out these movements with little or no thought about the action you are carrying out.

4.5.1 The Basal Ganglia Form a Looped Circuit

The subcortical structures that make up the basal ganglia are linked together to form a circuit with the cerebral cortex (Figure 4.20). In the first stage of the circuit, virtually all areas of the cortex (including visual, tactile, auditory, proprioceptive, and motor) send information to the **striatum**, the input region of the basal ganglia. This information defines the individual's current state, the stimuli she currently perceives, her body position, the movements she intends to make, and those she has just executed. Striatal neurons send information to the **globus pallidus**, the basal ganglia's output structure. Information from the globus pallidus goes to the ventral thalamus, and finally back to the cortex. Because information travels in a circuit that begins and ends in the cerebral cortex, information passing through the basal ganglia gives rise to **looped circuits**. While information begins the route from *all* areas of the cerebral cortex, the final destination (i.e., the recipient of the thalamic output) is the frontal cortex. The basal ganglia therefore permit the flow of information from the entire cerebral cortex to the movement-related frontal lobes (and to some brainstem areas that control movement as well).

4.5.2 Dopamine Influences the Initiation of Behavior

In addition to input from the cerebral cortex, the striatum also receives dopamine (DA) input from the **substantia nigra**, a region of the midbrain (Figure 4.21). The DA-releasing neurons projecting from the substantia nigra to the striatum are the **nigrostriatal** DA neurons. In Chapter 13, we will learn that the death of these nigrostriatal DA neurons is responsible for motor abnormalities seen in Parkinson's disease, including difficulties initiating voluntary movements.

Drugs that reduce dopamine transmission produce **catalepsy** (muscle rigidity) and a lack of movement similar to that of Parkinson's patients (Gerlach & Riederer, 1996). In contrast, increases in striatal DA

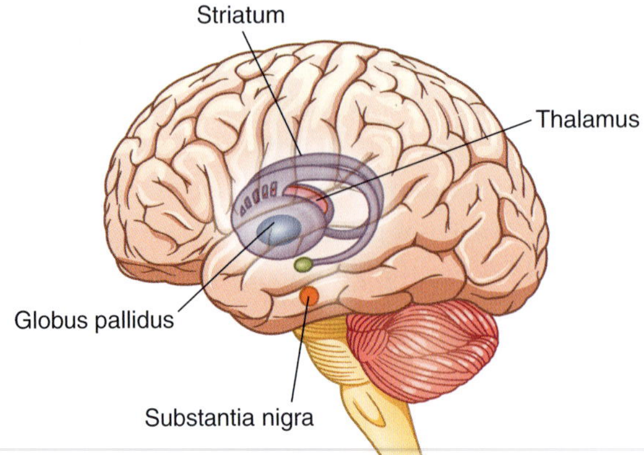

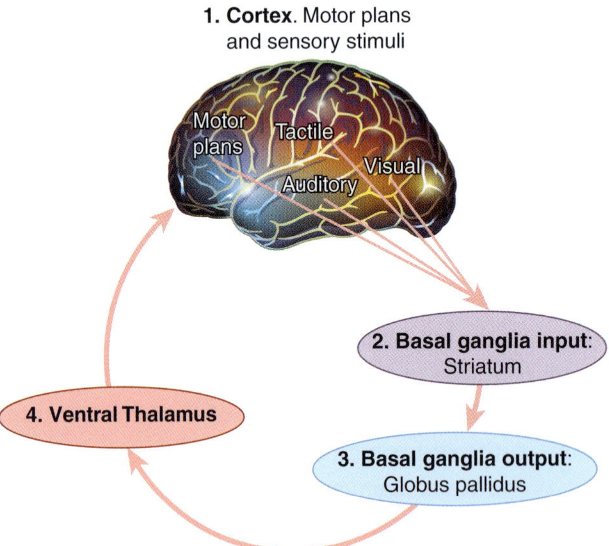

Figure 4.20 The basal ganglia. The basal ganglia are a group of subcortical brain regions (top panel) that send information around a "looped circuit" that originates in the cerebral cortex and ends in the cortex as well (bottom panel).

concentrations cause animals and humans to produce bizarre, purposeless movements. A rat administered a DA agonist drug might continually lick or bite the walls of the cage, repeatedly sniff one corner of the cage, or groom itself for long periods without pause (Joyce & Iversen, 1984). Because the behavioral routines are repeated again and again in a uniform stereotyped manner, this is called behavioral stereotypy. Notice that the behaviors themselves – sniffing, biting, licking, grooming – are not abnormal. For a

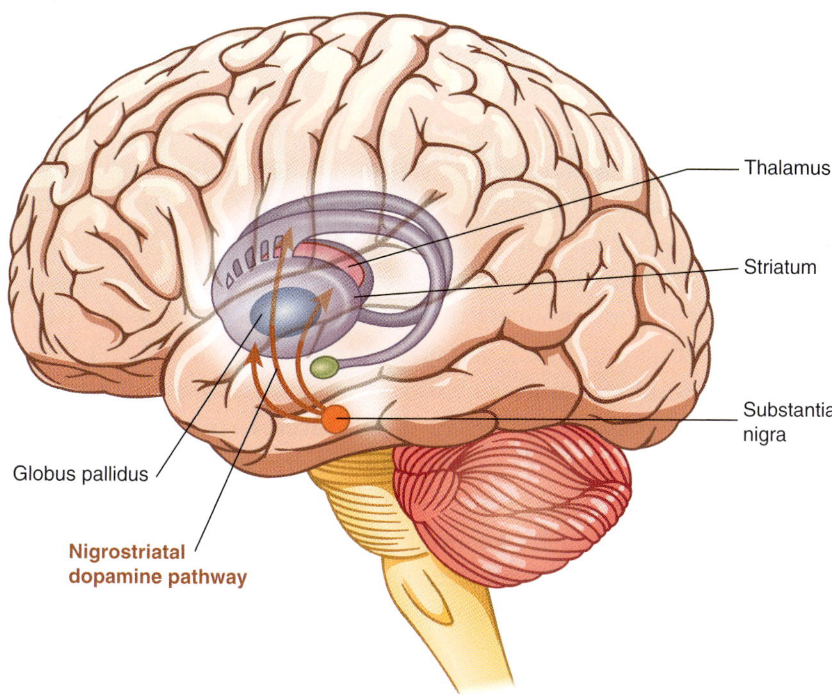

Figure 4.21 Nigrostriatal dopamine input to the striatum. Dopamine neurons found within the substantia nigra send axons to the striatum.

rat, sniffing is a typical response to encountering novel stimuli, and biting is an appropriate component of eating. The abnormality is that the pieces of behavior are no longer tied to the animal's environmental circumstance. Humans also show abnormal behavioral movements when dopamine levels are too high. Parkinson's patients receive **levodopa** (**L-DOPA**), which raises their dopamine levels and restores some of their lost movement abilities. However, the drug can sometimes produce a terrible side effect called levodopa-induced dyskinesia in which the patient makes uncontrollable body movements such as swinging the head violently from one side to another, or wiggling the arms and legs (Niccolini, Loane, & Politis, 2014). In summary, when dopamine levels are high, behaviors occur intensely and repetitively, regardless of environmental conditions. When dopamine levels are low, behaviors fail to occur.

4.5.3 Some Areas of the Striatum Are Necessary for Automatized Behavior

Imagine entering your kitchen and opening the refrigerator door. Just before opening the door, you are thinking about pouring yourself a nice, cool glass of milk. In this case, your behavior is goal-directed. We have seen that the PFC is important in representing the goal (e.g., drinking milk). However, imagine that you have performed this behavior so often, perhaps thousands of times in this same kitchen, that when you pass the refrigerator you automatically open it even if you're not in the mood for milk or anything else. Environmental stimuli have come to trigger the behavior automatically. Habitual behaviors can occur without the brain representing the desired goal. Behaviors change from a goal-directed to an automatized mode after many repetitions.

Goal-directed and automatized behaviors depend upon different regions of the striatum. The striatum is divided into medial and lateral parts. The **medial striatum**, which receives strong input from the PFC, is necessary for goal-directed behavior. The **lateral striatum**, which receives strong input from the primary motor cortex and nearby premotor areas, is necessary for automatized behavior.

In rats as well as humans, goal-directed behaviors that are frequently repeated may become automatized (Dickinson, 1985). When a rat first learns to press a lever for food, the behavior is goal-directed. The rat takes into account whether or not it desires food before it presses the lever, just as a person considers whether she desires milk before opening the refrigerator. However, with repeated experience of pressing for food, the rat will eventually press the lever even if it is not hungry. That is, the goal-directed behavior becomes automatized. However, the behavior does not become automatized in rats with lesions to the lateral striatum (Yin et al., 2004). These animals continue to take into account the value of the food when pressing the lever; their behavior remains goal-directed. On the other hand, animals with lesions of the medial striatum come to perform the behavior in a habitual manner even more quickly than do normal (non-lesioned) animals (Yin, Ostlund, Knowlton, & Balleine, 2005).

In summary, information about one's current state arrives at the basal ganglia via inputs from the cortex to the striatum. On the basis of the current state, the basal ganglia choose an appropriate action. In some cases, this action selection takes current goals into account, while in other cases, the environmental stimuli trigger behaviors automatically. Selected actions are communicated to the motor system via the basal ganglia output from the thalamus to the frontal lobes.

4.6 CEREBELLUM

The cerebellum lies at the base of the brain, just behind the pons (Figure 4.22). It contains more than half the brain's neurons. Historically, it was believed to serve purely motor functions, but is now understood to

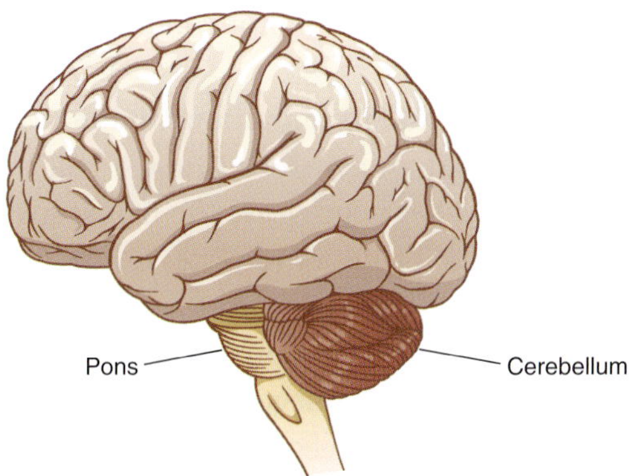

Figure 4.22 **Cerebellum.** The cerebellum lies just behind the pons.

contribute to cognition and emotion as well. In Chapter 9, we examine cerebellar involvement in learning. Here, we will discuss the cerebellum's contribution to movement accuracy, and how the cerebellum helps us to avoid carrying out movements that were unsuccessful in the past.

4.6.1 The Cerebellum Predicts Movement Consequences

According to one theory, the cerebellum predicts the consequence of a movement before the movement occurs (Ito, 2008). Imagine you are playing pool. You must hit the white cue ball with your stick at the angle that will make it strike another ball in just the right way to knock the second ball into a pocket. You begin by imagining how the cue ball will move if you hit it at one angle. If you don't like the imagined results, you make an adjustment. You know that once you have hit the white ball at an incorrect angle, it is too late for adjustments. So, you must predict the consequences of the movement of your cue stick before you make the movement itself. The cerebellum is believed to be critical in predicting movement consequences. Now imagine that you wish to lift a coffee cup from the table with enough force to raise it to your lips, but not so much force that the coffee goes flying onto the floor. In this case, you may not consciously need to picture the consequences of lifting your arm. But the cerebellum nevertheless anticipates the consequences of the movement commands before they are sent to the spinal cord to ensure that they are appropriate for lifting the cup to your lips.

Before a movement is initiated, the cerebellum receives copies of motor commands from the frontal cortex. After the movement has occurred, the cerebellum receives information about the tactile, visual, auditory, and proprioceptive results. So, it has all the information needed to learn to predict consequences of intended movements. As the cerebellum becomes expert at predicting whether your intended behavior is on target for your desired result, it can adjust frontal cortical motor commands before they are sent to the spinal cord.

Other views of cerebellar function emphasize its importance in the timing of behavior. Imagine, for instance, that you wish to throw a ball to someone. A successful throw will require that you release the ball at just the right moment. If you release the ball too soon or too late, it may fall directly at your feet. Patients with cerebellar damage typically show great impairment in throwing a ball accurately, and other problems in movement accuracy. When patients with cerebellar damage are asked to tap along with a regularly spaced tone, their tapping becomes atypically variable as soon as they are required to continue the tapping rhythm on their own after the tone stops (Ivry, Spencer, Zelaznik, & Diedrichsen, 2002). A problem with timing might account for at least some of their movement problems.

4.6.2 Cerebellar Damage Impairs the Coordination and Accuracy of Movements

One sign of cerebellar damage is abnormal **gait** (walking). Individuals make small shuffling steps with their feet abnormally wide apart. Patients may also slur their speech due to difficulties controlling the muscles of the mouth.

When asked to touch the tip of the nose with the finger, some patients will begin to move the finger toward the nose but stop the movement too soon, undershooting the target. In other cases, the finger may move too far, overshooting, and passing the tip of the nose. If you did not know the person had cerebellar damage, you might think he was failing a roadside drunk-driving test. As the patient brings the finger to touch the tip of the nose, it is common for the hand to shake back and forth in a **tremor**. Such patients are unable simply to bring the finger directly to the target. These deficits in movement illustrate the cerebellum's role in the accuracy of body movements. As you might have guessed, alcohol impairs function of the cerebellum (Hanchar, Dodson, Olsen, Otis, & Wallner, 2005).

Cerebellar damage can also produce abnormal eye movements. Patients may have difficulty tracking a slowly moving object with the eyes (smooth pursuit), and when they try to look straight ahead, they will make small, jerky eye movements. During visual saccades, they will sometimes over- or undershoot the object, failing to land the eyes directly upon the target. This, of course, resembles the problem with finger-to-nose touch. In general, when the cerebellum is damaged, it is difficult to adjust body movements in a precise manner that matches the demands of the task.

4.6.3 The Anatomy of the Cerebellum Allows Fine-Tuning of Movements before They Occur

The anatomy of the cerebellum permits it to fine-tune motor commands. Most of its input comes from **mossy fibers** (Figure 4.23), axons that carry copies of the movement plans of the frontal cortex, as well as sensory information (tactile, visual, balance-related) about external stimuli and the position of one's own body parts. The mossy fibers send this information to **granule cells**, which in turn communicate with **Purkinje cells**. Purkinje cells therefore receive information about the motor plans of the frontal cortex and the sensory results of your movements once they are executed. If you are playing pool, it is likely that the Purkinje cell will receive information about how you plan to hit the white ball before you actually hit it. A few moments later, the Purkinje cell will receive information about the results of hitting the ball.

The cerebellum receives a second major source of input from axons called **climbing fibers** (they appear to "climb up" Purkinje cells like a vine climbs up a tree trunk). According to some theories, these climbing fibers fire when an error in movement has occurred. When you strike the ball in a way that fails to achieve the outcome you had expected, the climbing fibers begin to fire. The result of this climbing fiber "error" signal is to weaken the mossy fiber and granule cell inputs that were active when the error occurred. In the future, when the frontal cortex prepares to hit the ball in the same way, the mossy fibers carrying information about the intended movement will be unable to activate the cerebellum. The key idea is that movement instructions that led to poor outcomes in the past can be 'canceled' on their way to the cerebellum. In this case, the frontal cortex must generate a new set of planned movements, which might be more successful.

Purkinje cells carry information to neurons in the **deep cerebellar nuclei**. The cerebellar nuclei are the final outputs of the cerebellum. They carry information from the cerebellum back to the cortex and to other areas of the forebrain, brainstem, and spinal cord.

KEY CONCEPTS

- **The basal ganglia receive information from the cerebral cortex about current internal and external stimuli. Output from the basal ganglia helps to select actions that will be useful under the current conditions.**
- **The basal ganglia are important for converting goal-directed actions into habits.**
- **The anatomy of the cerebellum permits it to evaluate and fine-tune our intended movements even before the movement occurs.**

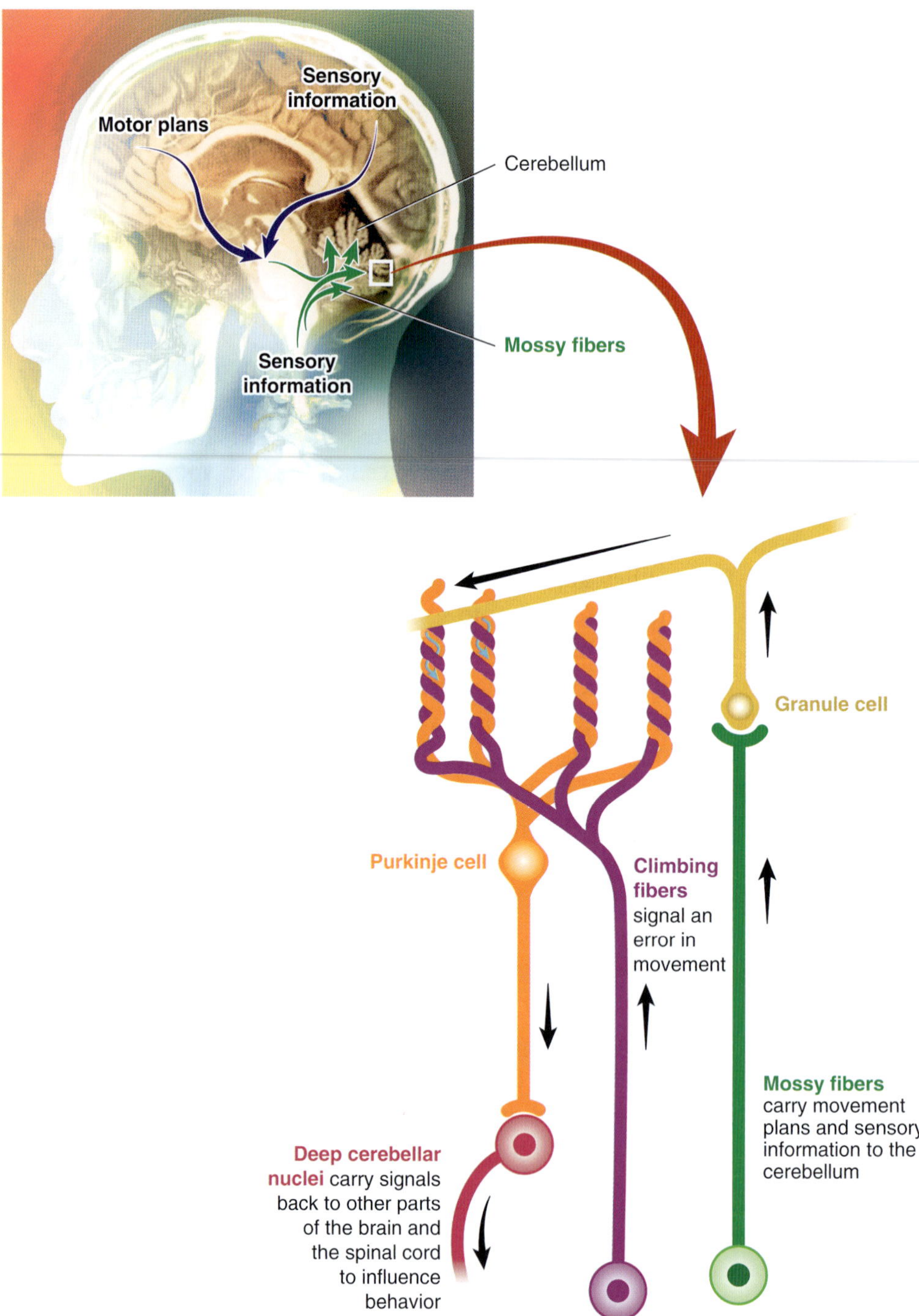

Figure 4.23 Neuronal circuitry in the cerebellum. Mossy fibers carry information about movement plans and sensory information to granule cells, which in turn transmit this information to Purkinje cells, and finally to the cerebellar nuclear cells. Cells in the cerebellar nuclei send signals to other brain regions. In addition, climbing fibers wrap around the dendrites of Purkinje cells. According to some theories, climbing fibers are activated when a movement leads to unintended results.

TEST YOURSELF

1. **What does it mean to say that the basal ganglia make a looped circuit? At what anatomical site within the circuit does dopamine exert its primary effects on motor behavior? Describe these effects of dopamine on behavior.**
2. **You lift a glass of juice with just enough force to bring it to your lips, but not so much that the juice spills to the floor. Describe the kinds of information the cerebellum is likely to receive before and after your arm movement. If you do lift the glass too quickly and the juice spills, which axons send the "error" information to the cerebellum (hint, they wrap around the Purkinje cells)? And, how does the cerebellum use this error signal to fine-tune motor commands for lifting the glass in the future?**

4.7 The Big Picture

Much of our movement occurs without conscious awareness. We select goals, and the movements needed to obtain them are often selected automatically as a result of complex processing of information in frontal cortical, parietal, basal ganglia, cerebellar, and spinal motor processing circuits.

Our movement goals, which might be to take a stroll in the park, to prepare coffee, or to type an essay, depend upon activity in the prefrontal cortex. To carry out these goals, the premotor and primary motor cortex must plan the specific limb movements needed and send motor commands to the spinal cord, which activates muscles. Ultimately, our behaviors require flexion and extension of body parts in the proper sequence for achieving the goal.

Frontal cortical control of movement is refined by the basal ganglia and the cerebellum. Both communicate continuously with the frontal cortex. The basal ganglia are important for selecting movements appropriate to our current state. The cerebellum takes advantage of our clumsy behaviors in the past to ensure that our present movements are more accurate. Many brain areas work together to translate the goals we hold in our minds into actions that occur in the external world.

4.8 Creative Thinking

1. Brain imaging shows that wrist, shoulder, and hand representations in the motor cortex do not line up in the orderly fashion suggested by earlier body maps. Instead, neurons corresponding to these body parts

are intermixed on the cortical surface. Why might this intermixing be advantageous? (Hint: Imagine that each of these neurons is capable of activating other nearby neurons.)

2. Lesions of the primary motor cortex lead to weak, slow movements, but not a complete loss of movement. In light of these observations, is it possible that all communication between brain and muscle must pass through the primary motor cortex? Explain. Suppose that neuroscientists had found instead that lesions of the primary motor cortex always produce a complete loss of movement, how would this have changed your conclusion?
3. As you've read, the brain generates a readiness potential before the conscious decision to act. While we are conscious of the decision to act, we are not conscious of the earlier readiness potential. When you decide to take a break from studying, do you believe that your conscious decision to pause was caused by earlier brain activity of which you had no conscious awareness?

Key Terms

acetylcholine (ACh) 151
alien hand syndrome 171
alpha motor neurons 148
antagonistic muscles 153
brain–machine interface 159
catalepsy 177
central pattern generator (CPG) 158
cervical spinal cord 148
climbing fibers 183
contralateral 160
corticobulbar neurons 160
corticospinal neurons 160
cranial nerves 148
deep cerebellar nuclei 183
dorsal premotor areas 167
dorsal premotor cortex 171
extension movement 153
extensor muscle 153
flexion movement 153
flexor muscle 153
frontal eye fields (FEF) 175
gait 182
globus pallidus 177
Golgi tendon organs 155
granule cells 183
inferior parietal lobe 168
ipsilateral 160
lateral striatum 180
levodopa (L-dopa) 179
local spinal cord neurons 156
looped circuits 177
lower motor neurons 160
medial striatum 180
mirror neurons 172
mossy fibers 183
muscle fibers 150
muscle spindles 155
neuromuscular junction 151
nicotinic receptors 151
nigrostriatal dopamine neurons 177
paraplegia 149
precentral gyrus 160
prefrontal cortex (PFC) 173
premotor areas 167
primary motor cortex 159
primary somatosensory cortex 165
Purkinje cells 183

References

Ashby, F. G., Turner, B. O., & Horvitz, J. C. (2010). Cortical and basal ganglia contributions to habit learning and automaticity. *Trends in Cognitive Sciences, 14*(5), 208–215.

Assal, F., Schwartz, S., & Vuilleumier, P. (2007). Moving with or without will: functional neural correlates of alien hand syndrome. *Annals of Neurology, 62*(3), 301–306.

Churchland, M. M., & Shenoy, K. V. (2007). Delay of movement caused by disruption of cortical preparatory activity. *Journal of Neurophysiology, 97*(1), 348–359.

Desmurget, M., & Sirigu, A. (2012). Conscious motor intention emerges in the inferior parietal lobule. *Current Opinion in Neurobiology, 22*(6), 1004–1011.

Dickinson, A. (1985). Actions and habits: the development of behavioural autonomy. *Philosophical Transactions of the Royal Society of London B: Biological Sciences, 308*, 67–78.

Ferrier, D. (1874). Experiments on the brain of monkeys.–No. I. *Proceedings of the Royal Society of London, 23*, 409–430.

Fried, I., Katz, A., McCarthy, G., Sass, K. J., Williamson, P., Spencer, S. S., & Spencer, D. D. (1991). Functional organization of human supplementary motor cortex studied by electrical stimulation. *Journal of Neuroscience, 11*(11), 3656–3666.

Fritsch, G., & Hitzig, E. (1870). *Electric Excitability of the Cerebrum*, trans. G. v. Bonin. Springfield, IL: Thomas.

Gallese, V., Fadiga, L., Fogassi, L., & Rizzolatti, G. (1996). Action recognition in the premotor cortex. *Brain, 119*, 593–609.

Gerlach, M., & Riederer, P. (1996). Animal models of Parkinson's disease: an empirical comparison with the phenomenology of the disease in man. *Journal of Neural Transmission, 103*(8–9), 987–1041.

Goodale, M. A., & Humphrey, G. K. (1998). The objects of action and perception. *Cognition, 67*(1–2), 181–207.

Graziano, M. (2006). The organization of behavioral repertoire in motor cortex. *Annual Review of Neuroscience, 29*, 105–134.

(2016). Ethological action maps: a paradigm shift for the motor cortex. *Trends in Cognitive Sciences, 20*(2), 121–132.

Grillner, S., & Wallen, P. (1985). Central pattern generators for locomotion, with special reference to vertebrates. *Annual Review of Neuroscience, 8*, 233–261.

Hanchar, H. J., Dodson, P. D., Olsen, R. W., Otis, T. S., & Wallner, M. (2005). Alcohol-induced motor impairment caused by increased extrasynaptic GABA(A) receptor activity. *Nature Neuroscience, 8*(3), 339–345.

Hasselmo, M. E. (2005). A model of prefrontal cortical mechanisms for goal-directed behavior. *Journal of Cognitive Neuroscience, 17*(7), 1115–1129.

Hikosaka, O., Tanaka, M., Sakamoto, M., & Iwamura, Y. (1985). Deficits in manipulative behaviors induced by local injections of muscimol in the first somatosensory cortex of the conscious monkey. *Brain Research, 325*(1–2), 375–380.

Ifft, P. J., Lebedev, M. A., & Nicolelis, M. A. L. (2012). Reprogramming movements: extraction of motor intentions from cortical ensemble activity when movement goals change. *Frontiers in Neuroengineering, 5*, 16.

Ito, M. (2008). Control of mental activities by internal models in the cerebellum. *Nature Reviews Neuroscience, 9*(4), 304–313.

Ivry, R. B., Spencer, R. M., Zelaznik, H. N., & Diedrichsen, J. (2002). The cerebellum and event timing. *Annals of the New York Academy of Sciences, 978*, 302–317.

Jeon, H., & Lee, S. H. (2018). From neurons to social beings: short review of the mirror neuron system research and its socio-psychological and psychiatric implications. *Clinical Psychopharmacology and Neuroscience, 16*(1), 18–31.

Joyce, E. M., & Iversen, S. D. (1984). Dissociable effects of 6-OHDA-induced lesions of neostriatum on anorexia, locomotor activity and stereotypy: the role of behavioural competition. *Psychopharmacology* (Berl), *83*(4), 363–366.

Leyton, A. S. F., & Sherington, C. S. (1917). Observations on the excitable cortex of the chimpanzee, orangutan, and gorilla. *Quarterly Journal of Experimental Physiology, 11*, 135–222.

Li, C. S. R., Huang, C., Constable, R. T., & Sinha, R. (2006). Imaging response inhibition in a stop-signal task: neural correlates independent of signal monitoring and post-response processing. *Journal of Neuroscience, 26*(1), 186–192.

Libet, B., Gleason, C. A., Wright, E. W., & Pearl, D. K. (1983). Time of conscious intention to act in relation to onset of cerebral activity (readiness-potential). The unconscious initiation of a freely voluntary act. *Brain, 106*(3), 623–642.

Loeb, G. E., & Tsianos, G. A. (2015). Major remaining gaps in models of sensorimotor systems. *Frontiers in Computational Neuroscience, 9*.

Mansouri, F. A., Koechlin, E., Rosa, M. G. P., & Buckley, M. J. (2017). Managing competing goals – a key role for the frontopolar cortex. *Nature Reviews Neuroscience, 18*(11), 645–657.

Meir, J. D., Aflalo, T. N., Kastner, S., & Graziano, M. S. A. (2008). Complex organization of human primary motor cortex: a high-resolution fMRI study. *Journal of Neurophysiology, 100*, 1800–1812.

Miller, E. K., & Cohen, J. D. (2001). An integrative theory of prefrontal cortex function. *Annual Review of Neuroscience, 24*, 167–202.

Montgomery, K. J., Seeherman, K. R., & Haxby, J. V. (2009). The well-tempered social brain. *Psychological Science, 20*(10), 1211–1213.

Murakami, M., Vicente, M. I., Costa, G. M., & Mainen, Z. F. (2014). Neural antecedents of self-initiated actions in secondary motor cortex. *Nature Neuroscience, 17*(11), 1574–1582.

Niccolini, F., Loane, C., & Politis, M. (2014). Dyskinesias in Parkinson's disease: views from positron emission tomography studies. *European Journal of Neurology, 21*(5), 694–E643.

Nuyujukian, P., Albites Sanabria, J., Saab, J., Pandarinath, C., Jarosiewicz, B., Blabe, C. H., ... Henderson, J. M. (2018). Cortical control of a tablet computer by people with paralysis. *PLOS ONE, 13*(11), e0204566.

O'Doherty, J. P. (2011). Contributions of the ventromedial prefrontal cortex to goal-directed action selection. *Annals of the New York Academy of Sciences, 1239*, 118–129.

Park, M. C., Belhaj-Saif, A., Gordon, M., & Cheney, P. D. (2001). Consistent features in the forelimb representation of primary motor cortex in rhesus macaques. *Journal of Neuroscience, 21*(8), 2784–2792.

Penfield, W., & Boldrey, E. (1937). Somatic motor and sensory representation in the cerebral cortex of man as studied by electrical stimulation. *Brain, 60*(4), 389–443.

Rajangam, S., Tseng, P. H., Yin, A., Lehew, G., Schwarz, D., Lebedev, M. A., & Nicolelis, M. A. (2016). Wireless cortical brain–machine interface for whole-body navigation in primates. *Scientific Reports, 6*, 22170.

Rizzolatti, G., & Luppino, G. (2001). The cortical motor system. *Neuron, 31*(6), 889–901.

Shan, Q., Christie, M. J., & Balleine, B. W. (2015). Plasticity in striatopallidal projection neurons mediates the acquisition of habitual actions. *European Journal of Neuroscience, 42*, 2097–2104.

Soon, C. S., Brass, M., Heinze, H. J., & Haynes, J. D. (2008). Unconscious determinants of free decisions in the human brain. *Nature Neuroscience, 11*(5), 543–545.

Tumati, S., Martens, S., de Jong, B. M., & Aleman, A. (2019). Lateral parietal cortex in the generation of behavior: implications for apathy. *Progress in Neurobiology, 175*, 20–34.

Weinrich, M., & Wise, S. P. (1982). The premotor cortex of the monkey. *Journal of Neuroscience, 2*(9), 1329–1345.

Yin, H. H., Knowlton, B. J., & Balleine, B. W. (2004). Lesions of dorsolateral striatum preserve outcome expectancy but disrupt habit formation in instrumental learning. *European Journal of Neuroscience, 19*(1), 181–189.

Yin, H. H., Ostlund, S. B., Knowlton, B. J., & Balleine, B. W. (2005). The role of the dorsomedial striatum in instrumental conditioning. *European Journal of Neuroscience, 22*(2), 513–523.

5 Sleep–Waking and Circadian Rhythms

Sam Edwards / OJO Images / Getty Images

Consider This …

A 38-year-old man suffered a severe traumatic brain injury from an assault that put him in a "minimally conscious state." He was not asleep, yet neither was he fully awake. When asked a question, he could sometimes communicate "yes" or "no" by blinking in a certain way. Sometimes, when asked to move his hand, his hand would move. Occasionally, he would move his mouth as if to speak, but the sounds from his mouth were unintelligible. Rehabilitation programs that included physical, occupational, and speech therapies were unsuccessful. Most of the time, he remained unresponsive and uncommunicative, with his eyes closed. He passed six years in this manner.

One day, neurosurgeons implanted electrodes into his brain in order to stimulate the central thalamus. Studies in rats and monkeys suggested that stimulation of this area could activate brain arousal systems. After he recovered from surgery, the central thalamus was stimulated bilaterally (on both sides of his brain). He could suddenly keep his eyes open for much longer periods of time. He could pick up objects and look at them for the first time since his accident. He could speak a little, not much, but enough to be understood for the first time in six years.

This medical procedure of implanting electrodes, or neurostimulators, to send electrical impulses to a particular brain area is called **deep brain stimulation**. The effectiveness of deep brain electrical stimulation of the thalamus suggests that this structure is necessary in order to be awake and alert. As we will see later in the chapter, waking requires that the thalamus sends information to the cerebral cortex. As you might imagine, when we fall asleep, thalamocortical communication is disrupted, and it is restored when we wake each day. In this chapter, we will examine the brain changes that occur as we lose conscious awareness every night during sleep, and then (thankfully) as we enter a state of waking consciousness in the morning.

Sleep remains among the most mysterious aspects of our daily lives. During sleep, we are unaware of the world around us. Why do we "have to" sleep? Why do infants sleep so much? Is sleep a time when particular brain and bodily processes occur? What happens if we do not get enough sleep? What brain mechanisms underlie dreaming? What happens if these brain mechanisms malfunction?

These and many related issues have fascinated scientists, philosophers, and writers since time immemorial. A simple, commonsense definition of sleep is a state of fairly continuous and long-lasting unconsciousness that can be reversed rapidly and relatively easily. The scientific study of sleep received its jump-start in 1953 with a revolutionary report that while subjects slept in the laboratory they periodically exhibited episodes of *rapid eye movements* interspersed within longer periods of sleep without such eye movements (Aserinsky & Kleitman, 1953). When awakened during the rapid eye movement episodes, subjects typically reported dreaming, whereas when awakened during inactive periods, they rarely reported dreaming. Several years later, other researchers confirmed and extended these findings and coined the term rapid eye movement (**REM**) sleep (Dement & Kleitman, 1957). The REM/dream period of sleep seemed to constitute a third state of existence along with waking and non-rapid eye movement (**non-REM**) sleep.

The remarkable scientific progress in the past half-century caused a field of research that was in the dark and "asleep" to come into the light and "awaken." Today, "sleep" has its own panel for scientific investigation in the National Institutes of Health, and thousands of sleep doctors and clinics exist throughout the world.

5.1 CIRCADIAN RHYTHMS

One of the obvious characteristics of sleep is that it occurs in regular daily cycles. You may not become tired at precisely the same time every night, but neither do you fall asleep at random moments (unless you have a sleep disorder). Our cycles of waking and sleeping have a rhythm.

Many aspects of life on earth occur in a regular, repeatable manner. Some events repeat quickly, while others cycle more slowly. For instance, the intervals between heartbeats of the hummingbird are measured in milliseconds. On the other hand, some insects (such as certain cicada species) emerge from the ground every seventeen years.

Two dominant natural cycles affect life on our planet: annual cycles and daily cycles. Annual cycles reflect the fact that the earth orbits the sun once a year. This gives rise to yearly changes in the seasons, yearly bird migration and reproduction, and yearly cycles of plant growth. Sleeping and waking are controlled by a 24-hour cycle – this is called a **circadian** cycle (from the Latin *circa*, "about," and *dies*, "day"). Circadian cycles, like annual cycles, also have a planetary cause. The earth rotates on its axis every 24 hours, and this produces a recurring transition from day to night.

The day-to-night variation leads to daily changes in environmental temperature, daily opening and closing of flowers, and daily cycles of sleep and waking. Of course, some cycles that affect our lives were invented by humans simply as a matter of convenience, e.g., the seven-day week and the thirty-day month. In contrast, the circadian rhythms that control our sleep cycles are biologically programmed; they are adaptations to living on a planet where the morning light appears every 24 hours.

5.1.1 If You Lived in a Cave, Cut Off from the Outside World, Would You Still Wake Up Every Morning at the Same Time?

If our patterns of sleep and waking are linked to the 24-hour cycle of sun exposure to the earth, what would happen to our sleep patterns in the absence of all light cues? In 1962, a French geologist, Michel Siffre, went into an underground cave in France for two months in order to close himself off from all information about the outside world. He was unaware of daily changes in light, sound, temperature, or any other environmental stimuli. These external cues that normally allow us to know what time it is are called **zeitgebers** (meaning "time-givers" in German). In the absence of all zeitgebers, Siffre had no way to know what time it was. He reported on the events of his daily life to his aboveground colleagues via a telephone. Much of his physiology and behavior remained cyclic even in the absence of zeitgebers. However, some of his cycles were longer than 24 hours. For instance, instead of falling asleep on average every 24 hours, he fell asleep approximately every 25 hours.

Of course, strong and valid conclusions cannot be based on a study employing only one subject. But in the laboratory, we can study the sleep–wake cycles of humans and other animals under tightly controlled conditions. Imagine a hamster in a cage with food, water, and a running wheel.

Say the lights turn on and off on a 24-hour cycle: on for 12 hours then off for 12 hours every day. Once the hamster gets used to this schedule, it will begin running around the time the lights go off (it's a nocturnal animal) and will continue running until a few hours before the lights come on 12 hours later (Figure 5.1).

So long as the hamster expects the light to go off and on at the same time every day, it starts and stops running at nearly the same time every day. The hamster's behavior has become **entrained** (synchronized) to the 24-hour light–dark cycle. What would happen if the lighting conditions did not change? Suppose that, like the geologist in the cave, the hamster remained in a dark environment for days? Under these conditions, the hamster's behavior *remains* rhythmic, running approximately the same number of hours each day. However, its rhythm is no longer tied to environmental cues; it becomes **free running.** It becomes active at a slightly later time each day (again, see Figure 5.1). The animal no longer starts its active waking time every 24 hours, for its free-running activity cycle is closer to 25 hours.

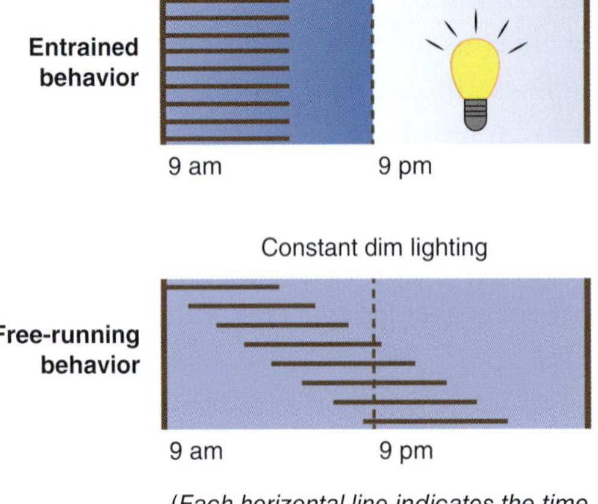

Figure 5.1 Circadian activity rhythms. In the "entrained" condition (with light going on and off at specific times), the hamster becomes active at the same time every night. In constant dim light, where the environment no longer provides time cues (a "free-running" condition), the hours when the animal is active begin to drift, starting a little later every day. This reflects the animal's internal ("endogenous") biological clock. (Top, © George Eason/Alamy Stock Photo.)

Instead of being governed by the onset of light, or some other zeitgeber, the hamster's behavior, along with much of its physiology, is now controlled by an internal or **endogenous biological clock**. Almost any life form on earth will show the same result: In the absence of environmental cues, regular sleep–wake cycles still occur, but the free-running rhythms are either slightly more than 24 hours, or slightly less than 24 hours – depending upon the animal.

5.1.2 The Suprachiasmatic Nucleus Is the Brain's Master Clock

Where is the biological clock that drives these rhythms? If we could find it, what would happen if it were destroyed? By the early 1970s, researchers had discovered a neural pathway that connected the retina to an area of the hypothalamus called the **suprachiasmatic nucleus** (SCN – lying "supra" or just above the optic "chiasm") (Figure 5.2). When experimenters lesioned the SCN in the brains of laboratory rats, the rats' daily periods of

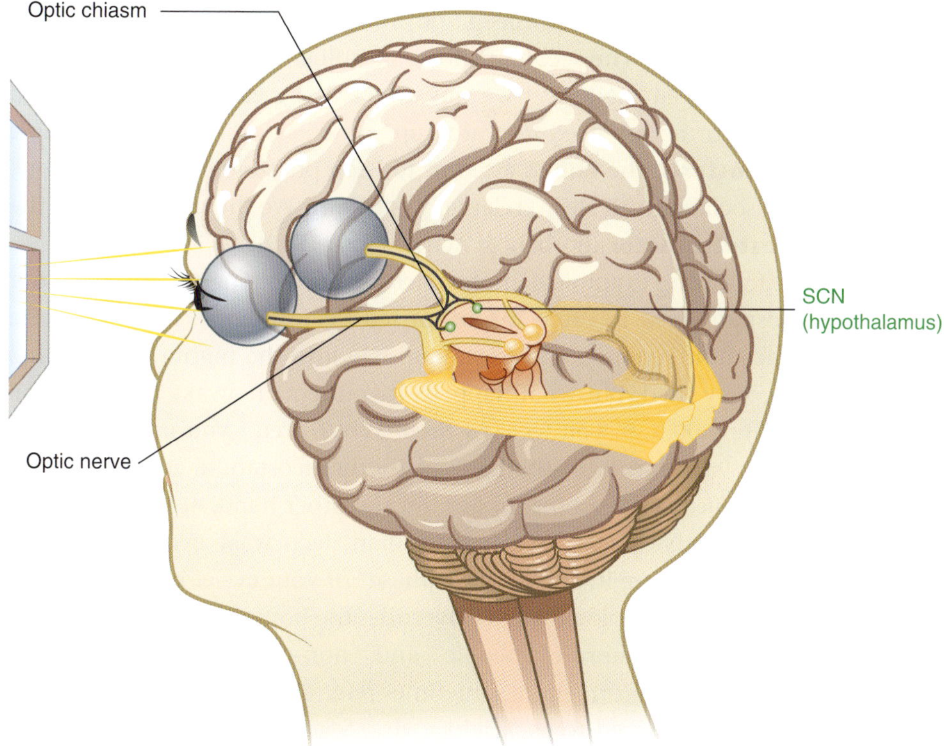

Figure 5.2 The anatomical location of the suprachiasmatic nucleus. The suprachiasmatic nucleus (SCN) lies just above the optic chiasm. It detects light and entrains (synchronizes) daily biological and behavior rhythms to the onset of light from the environment.

running (as well as water intake and other daily activities) were no longer entrained to the light–dark cycle. Their free-running behavior occurred at entirely random periods of the day and night (Stephan & Zucker, 1972; Moore & Eichler, 1972).

Other clocks controlling various physiological functions are localized throughout the body, but they are all under the influence of this master SCN clock. Many genes have been discovered that influence various aspects of **circadian rhythms**. One of the most important of these is a gene named CLOCK whose protein product affects the length of the circadian cycle. Discovery of the CLOCK gene opened up an entirely new area of research into the genetic and molecular aspects of circadian rhythms (King et al., 1997), which may provide new avenues for the treatment of sleep disorders (Jagannath, Taylor, Wakaf, Vasudevan, & Foster, 2017).

5.1.3 Two Factors Influence the Sleep–Wake Cycle

Two factors control our sleep–waking cycle. The first factor, as we have already seen, is the endogenous clock that strongly influences the time that we and other animals fall asleep and wake up. This is referred to as the **circadian factor**. The second factor that influences our sleep time is the obvious fact that the longer we stay awake, the greater we feel the need to sleep. Our body's need to "catch up" on delayed sleep is an example of **homeostasis**, the body's attempt to keep physiological factors (here, those associated with sleep) relatively constant. We therefore call this the **homeostatic factor** (Borbély & Achermann, 1999).

The following example demonstrates how our biological clock and our homeostatic need to catch up on missed sleep interact. Imagine that a work deadline required you to stay up late into the night. At 3:00 a.m., you are very tired. But what happens if you remain awake for another 6 hours? By 9:00 a.m. you feel *less* tired. Why? Aren't you more sleep deprived at 9:00 a.m.? On the basis of the homeostatic factor alone, you should be sleepier at 9:00 a.m. But, on the other hand, at 9:00 a.m., you are in an "active phase" of your circadian sleep–wake cycle, whereas at 3:00 a.m., you were in an "inactive phase" of your cycle. In this case, the influence of your biological clock overrides the homeostatic drive to sleep.

We all know "morning people" and "non-morning people." Using poetic license, the former are sometimes referred to as "early birds" while the latter are referred to as "night owls." Some think of the night owls as a bit lazy or disorganized, or that they want to leisurely take in the day's news over a cup of coffee. However, research suggests that early birds show strong and rapid physiological responses to the onset of the morning light, while others (night owls) respond much later. Some genetic evidence suggests that these characteristics may run in families.

The study of circadian rhythms also helps us to understand jet lag. Say that your flight departs New York City at 8:00 p.m. and lands in Rome at 8:00 a.m. local time on the following day. In your excitement, you want to rush out immediately to see the Coliseum. However, it's still only 2:00 a.m. in New York. With your sleep–wake cycle still entrained to New York zeitgebers, your biological clock tells you that you should be in bed. Exposure to the bright Roman morning sunshine will cause your internal clock to reset in a few days, i.e., your sleep–wake cycle will eventually entrain to the time cues in Rome.

KEY CONCEPTS

- **Virtually all life on earth is influenced by a circadian cycle of approximately 24 hours.**
- **While typically influenced by external cues such as periods of light and darkness, a biological clock operates in the absence of any external signals.**
- **In mammals, the brain mechanism controlling circadian rhythms is located in the suprachiasmatic nucleus of the hypothalamus.**
- **The degree to which you feel tired depends on an interaction between your biological clock and how long you have been awake.**

TEST YOURSELF

1. **If you were in a cave with no external cues about time of day, would you still show a circadian rhythm? Would you begin to sleep at random times during the day and night?**
2. **What brain structure is considered the brain's master clock?**
3. **Sleep is said to be governed by circadian and homeostatic factors. Explain what this means.**
4. **After a night without sleep, a person may be very tired at 4:00 a.m. Surprisingly, they may feel less tired at 9:00 a.m., even though they have had 5 additional hours without sleep! Why?**

5.2 STAGES OF SLEEP

In the sleep laboratory, researchers employ several physiological measures as the individual sleeps. Three key measures are examination of brain waves, muscle activity, and eye movements. As we will see, these measures can reveal the stage of sleep that the subject has entered.

(1) Brain waves arise from the electrical activity of the brain. To record this activity, electrodes are applied to the scalp and the **electroencephalogram** (**EEG**) is recorded (Figure 5.3A). Brain waves revealed

A

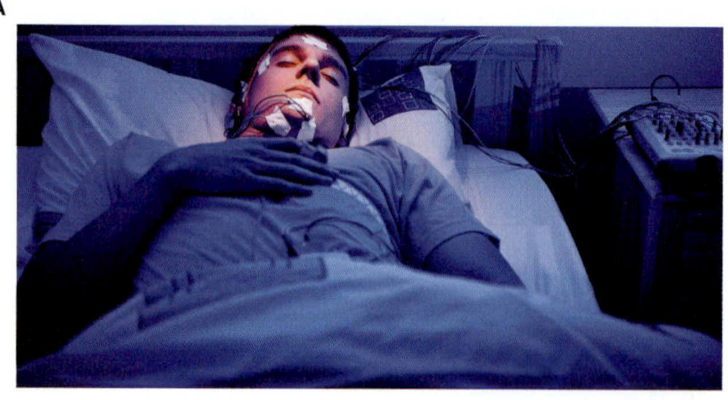

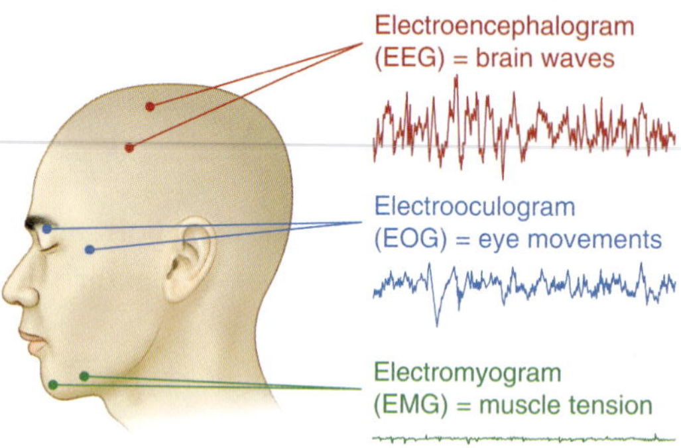

B

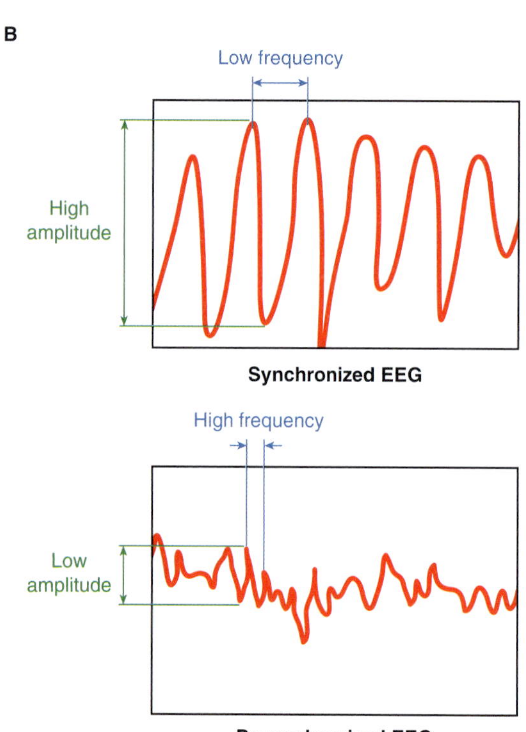

Figure 5.3 Recording EEG, EOG, and EMG. (A). Prior to an all-night sleep study, a patient is wired up for recording of the EEG, EOG, and EMG. (B). When an individual is drowsy, neurons fire in synchrony with one another and generate "synchronized" EEG of high amplitude and low frequency. When the person becomes alert, the neurons fire out of synch with one another and generate a "desynchronized" EEG with low amplitude and high frequency. (Photo, © wunkley/Alamy Stock Photo.)

through EEG do not give detailed information regarding the activity of individual neurons in the brain, but reflect the summed activity of small electrical currents (primarily EPSPSs and IPSPs) from billions of cortical neurons. By analogy, if you were to place a microphone over the top of a baseball stadium, you would not be able to tell who is on first and who is on second base. But when a batter hits a home run, you would hear the crowd roar. Similarly, the EEG gives relatively general information about the overall activity of many neurons, mostly in the cortex.Two key measures of the brain waves displayed in the EEG are the **amplitude** and **frequency**. As seen in Figure 5.3B, the amplitude of the EEG (the height of the waves) is greatest when neurons are **synchronized** with one another. (Imagine the crowd all cheering in unison) (Steriade, Nunez, & Amica, 1993). During the synchronized EEG, the high amplitude waves are cycling up and down with a low frequency (as if the crowd were cheering together slowly). On the other hand, when neurons are **desynchronized**, i.e., firing "out of sync" with one another, EEG shows low-amplitude waves cycling up and down rapidly (i.e., with high frequency). Imagine many small waves in the ocean splashing together out of sync and creating lots of small ripples in the water. As we will see below, when a subject becomes alert, her EEG becomes desynchronized.

(2) To study muscle activity during sleep, electrodes are often attached to the chin and neck. When muscles contract, the electrodes pick up the electrical activity generated by the muscle fibers. The recording of this muscle activity is called an **electromyogram** (**EMG**). The larger the amplitude of the EMG waves, the greater the muscle contractions.

(3) For eye movements, electrodes are placed on the facial skin surrounding the eye in order to record the electrical potential across the eyeball. This measurement produces the **electrooculogram** (**EOG**). When the eyes are not moving, the amplitude of the EOG is flat.

Let us follow these three measurements as a person goes from a state of alertness to drowsiness, and through the various stages of sleep. We'll begin with an individual who is awake, and first examine his EEG, that is, the combined activity of neurons in the cortex.

When we are awake and in an alert state, neurons in different areas of the cortex are firing independently; perhaps some are engaged in verbal thought, others in visual attention, and still others in working memory. During the moments when some neurons are firing rapidly, other neurons are firing slowly, or are silent. At a certain moment, silent neurons may begin to fire. The EEG is therefore recording activity of neurons which are "out of sync" with one another, or desynchronized. Notice in Figure 5.4

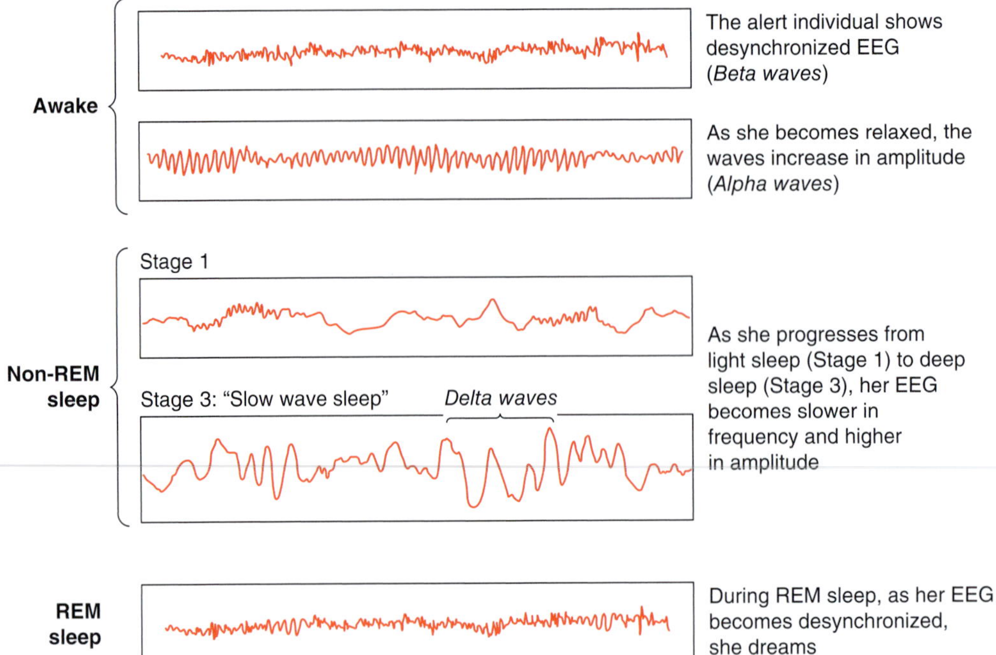

Figure 5.4 EEG activity during waking, drowsiness, and sleep. As the person becomes drowsy and then enters progressively deeper stages of sleep, EEG waves become progressively higher in amplitude and lower in frequency. In contrast, during REM sleep, the person shows EEG of low amplitude and high frequency, resembling that while awake and alert.

that an individual who is alert shows desynchronized (high-frequency, low-amplitude) EEG. These "ripple-like" EEG waves seen when we're alert and concentrating are called **beta waves**. While awake and alert, the individual occasionally makes body movements reflected in large-amplitude EMG. EOG shows eye movements as the person scans her environment.

As the person becomes relaxed or drowsy, EEG waves increase in amplitude and become slower in frequency, producing **alpha waves**. These same alpha waves are seen during peaceful states of meditation (Takahashi et al., 2005; Bing-Canar, Pizzuto, & Compton, 2016). The relaxed individual also shows reduced movements of the body (reductions in EMG activity) and eyes (reductions in EOG activity).

The first stages of sleep are labeled from lightest (Stage 1) to deepest (Stage 3) (Berry et al., 2017). From the moment of sleep onset, the progressive transition from Stage 1 through Stage 3 may take 30 to 60 minutes. During that time, the EEG frequency steadily slows and the amplitude steadily increases (Figure 5.4). As sleep progresses from Stages 1 to 3, breathing slows, body and brain temperature decrease, heart rate and blood pressure decline, and bodily activity and eye movements cease (EMG and EOG amplitudes decrease). During these non-REM stages of sleep, the parasympathetic branch of the autonomic nervous system becomes dominant. Brain blood flow and metabolism are low, and in most areas of the brain there is decreased neuronal activity. It is very difficult to wake someone up from deep (Stage 3) sleep, and if you do, they feel particularly sleepy and disoriented.

Stage 3 sleep is characterized by very large and slow waves in the EEG called **delta waves**. Due to these slow-cycling EEG waves, the sleep that occurs during Stage 3 is sometimes called **slow-wave sleep**. When a subject's slow-wave sleep is disrupted, she typically feels unrefreshed and unrested the next day. This deep stage of sleep is therefore considered the most restorative. One might imagine that sleepwalking should occur while a person is dreaming; however, sleepwalking, sleep talking, and bed wetting all occur mostly during non-REM stages of sleep.

If you were observing the EEG and EOG of an individual in REM, you might think she was awake. She would show the low-amplitude, high-frequency (desynchronized) EEG characteristic of a person who is awake. The EEG seen during REM includes a mixture of the beta waves otherwise seen when we are awake and concentrating, and the alpha waves that are associated with our quieter more relaxed waking moments. Her EOG would indicate that the eyes were rapidly moving about. A closer look at the EOG, however, would show that eye movements during REM were more rapid than normally seen during waking.

The REM period is largely dominated by sympathetic nervous system activation: rapid twitching of many of the small muscles of the body; increased and irregular heart rate, blood pressure, and respiration; a dramatic increase in brain metabolism to an active waking level; and penile erections in men and clitoral engorgement in women. If this were not unusual enough, two other dramatic changes occur. Intense and vivid dreaming takes place during REM sleep, and the large muscles of the body completely lose their tone. We are literally paralyzed during REM sleep. The EMG therefore shows a nearly completely flat line indicating the near complete absence of muscle contractions (**muscle atonia**).

Figure 5.5 shows all-night sleep recordings of a typical subject as he moves from one sleep stage to another. Four key things to notice in the figure are:

(1) Over the course of the night, individuals alternate between non-REM (Stages 1–3) and REM sleep (REM is marked in red).
(2) Subjects typically enter REM for the first time after about 1½ hours of non-REM sleep.
(3) Periods of REM begin about every 90 minutes.
(4) The amount of time spent in REM increases over the course of the night.

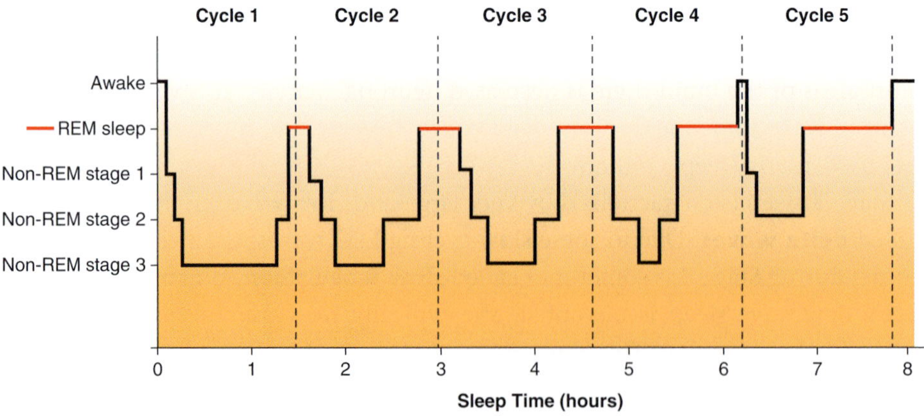

Figure 5.5 **Sleep cycles for a subject during an all-night sleep recording**. The length of the horizontal lines in the image represents the duration of time in a particular stage of sleep. Notice that deep sleep stage 3 is dominant during the first several hours. REM episodes recur about every 90 minutes, growing longer as the night progresses.

KEY CONCEPTS

- **Progressing through Stages 1–3 of non-REM sleep, brain activity becomes synchronized, with EEG waves showing increased amplitude and decreased frequency. This is especially true during Stage 3. Without time in Stage 3, sleepers do not feel refreshed.**
- **EEG during REM resembles that seen during alert waking. Most vivid dreaming occurs in REM sleep.**
- **REM sleep episodes occur in a rhythmic manner about every 90 minutes, with increased duration of REM periods as sleep progresses.**

TEST YOURSELF

1. **During REM sleep, what happens to cortical EEG, muscle tone, and eye movements? What other physiological changes occur during REM sleep?**
2. **If neurons are firing with high frequency and low amplitude, are they synchronized or desynchronized? What if they are firing with low frequency and high amplitude?**
3. **Do sleepwalking and sleeptalking occur during REM or non-REM sleep?**

5.3 SLEEP VARIES WITH AGE AND SPECIES

Apparently, all animals, down to the tiny fruit fly, consistently exhibit daily alternating patterns of sleep and waking. However, there are vast differences in the brains, bodies, and ecological niches of the thousands of animal species that populate the earth. Even within a species, sleep patterns may change over the individual's lifetime. Let us briefly consider how sleep patterns change over the human lifespan and how they vary across animal species.

5.3.1 The Amount of Time Spent Sleeping Changes over the Lifespan

At birth, human babies wake and sleep at nearly random times. Their sleep is said to be **arrhythmic**. Ask any parent of a newborn: It is difficult to predict when the baby will fall asleep and the duration of the sleep period. This begins to change around 2–3 months of age and (if the parents are fortunate) a clear daily rhythm of sleep and waking is typically present by 4–6 months.

Just prior to birth, the fetus may be in REM continuously! This discovery has led researchers to suggest that the time spent in REM sleep is critical for early brain development. As displayed in Figure 5.6, newborns sleep 60–70 percent of the time, and approximately half that sleep time

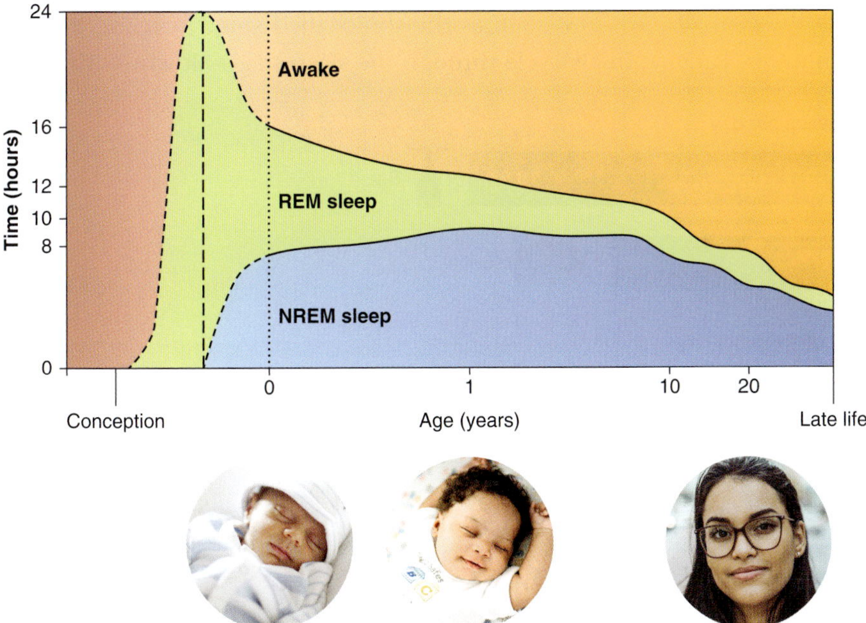

Figure 5.6 Amount of time humans spend awake, in non-REM and in REM sleep. During early months after conception, the fetus spends all of its time in REM sleep. The newborn (age "0") spends about 16 hours sleeping, with over half this time in REM. Over the years, we spend more of our daily hours awake.

(Graph adapted from Hobson, 2009, © 2009 Nature Publishing Group, a division of Macmillan Publishers Limited. All rights reserved; photos adapted from Vera Kratochvil (left), NICHD/NIH (middle), Pixels.com (right).)

is spent in REM sleep. By 2 years of age, babies are sleeping 50 percent of the time, and approximately 30 percent of that time is spent in REM sleep. From this point until adolescence, there is a gradual decline in both the total time spent asleep and the percentage of that total sleep time spent in REM sleep. From young adulthood into old age there is moderate reduction in time spent sleeping, with most healthy adults sleeping 6–8 hours, and with about 20 percent of that time spent in REM sleep.

5.3.2 Sleep Patterns Vary across Species

When trying to understand a complex behavioral process, such as sleep, researchers often find it useful to examine it across a variety of species. Is it similar in all animals? Is it observed even in very small animals such as the fruit fly? (See Box 5.1.)

Large animals generally sleep less than small ones. Giraffes, horses, cows, and many other large mammals sleep only about 3–4 hours a day. Humans and other intermediate-sized mammals sleep about 8–10 hours per day. Some of the smaller mammals, such as the bat, sleep 18–20 hours a day (Figure 5.7). The long total sleep duration of small animals typically involves quick cycling between non-REM and REM sleep, with some of these small creatures (such as the short-tailed shrew) cycling every 8 minutes. Large animals cycle through the sleep stages slowly, with some

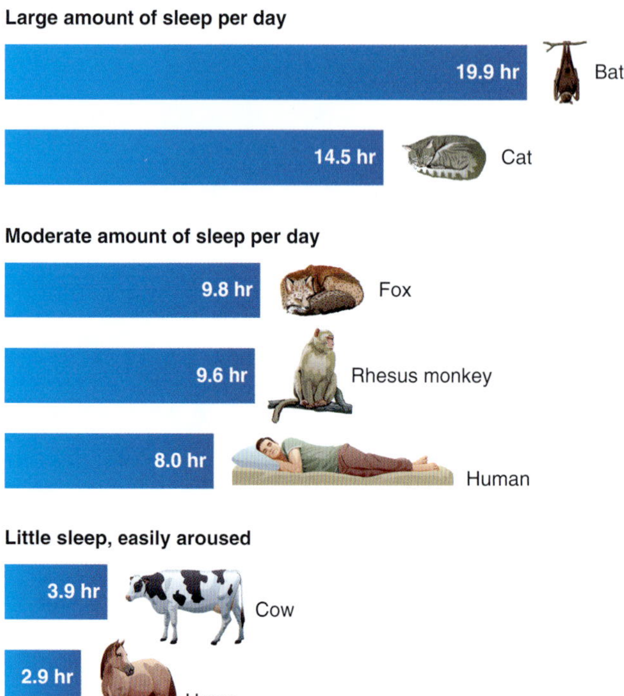

Figure 5.7 The amount of time spent in sleep per day in various species. The large variation ranges from nearly 20 hours in the bat to less than 3 hours in the horse.

elephants taking about 2 hours to complete a single non-REM/REM cycle. We do not know why some animals sleep more than others, but one possibility is that those that sleep most are those that most need to conserve and restore energy. From this point of view, small animals sleep a lot because they have high metabolic rates, expend a lot of energy, and restore energy during sleep. Large animals generally have low metabolic activity, expend less energy (per pound), and therefore have less need for sleep.

REM sleep is confined almost exclusively to mammals and birds, with mammals spending 10–20 percent of total sleep time in REM sleep and birds spending a smaller percentage in REM sleep. Somewhat surprisingly, there is no solid evidence for the existence of REM sleep in aquatic mammals (whales, dolphins, and porpoises).

Killer whales and dolphins have particularly unique and interesting sleep behaviors (Siegel, 2008). They remain awake for several weeks after birth. When they sleep, only one side of the brain enters slow-wave sleep at a time. The other side of the brain remains awake. This allows them to swim and even avoid obstacles while one side of the brain sleeps (Figure 5.8). Some birds also manifest sleep in a single hemisphere at a time, for example during long-distance migratory flight.

Slow Wave Sleep (SWS) in the Dolphin

Left hemisphere	Right hemisphere
Slow wave sleep	Awake
Awake	Slow wave sleep
Slow wave sleep	Awake
Awake	Slow wave sleep

Figure 5.8 The dolphin sleeps one hemisphere at a time. While one hemisphere of the brain enters slow-wave sleep, the other stays awake. When the left hemisphere is awake, it takes in visual information from the open right eye, and vice versa. This allows the animal to navigate while resting half the brain.
(Dolphin photo by torange.biz.)

BOX 5.1 Sleep in the Fruit Fly

Let's examine a study that revolutionized the sleep field. If someone told you that fruit flies go through periods of sleep and waking, you might not be surprised, but you certainly would wonder how we know. You cannot attach electrodes to the head of the fly and record its EEG. Instead, experimenters placed individual flies in small glass tubes and measured their activity with movement sensors (Figure 5.9). In an environment with 12 hours of light alternating with 12 hours of dark, flies display almost all of their activity during the light period. When experimenters vibrated the fly's "home" (i.e., its tube) at a low intensity while the flies were active, they responded to this vibration. However, when the same stimulus was applied while the flies were "resting," they showed no behavioral response to the vibration. When the vibration intensity was increased, the flies now responded (Shaw, Cirelli, Greenspan, & Tononi, 2000). Conclusion 1: It is hard to arouse a fly during its inactive period (they have a high "arousal threshold"); this is true of other animals while they are asleep, and suggests that the flies may have been sleeping. Next, the experimenters gently tapped the tubes for 12 hours during what was normally the flies' rest period. The idea was to prevent them from resting (possibly sleeping). When flies were observed during the subsequent 12-hour active phase, they exhibited a large increase in resting (possibly sleeping). Conclusion 2: The rest phase appears to be homeostatically regulated in what looks like a recovery of the sleep that was lost: like us, fruit flies must "catch up" on lost sleep. In further experiments comparing fly behavior to the well-known patterns of mammalian sleep, supporting parallels were found in drug studies (e.g., "caffeinated" flies remain active for longer), in development (very young flies rest more), and in expressed genes that had previously been shown to be involved in sleep and circadian rhythm regulation. Besides being remarkable in its own right, by using fruit flies this study throws open the door to exploration of the genes that regulate sleep and waking. The fruit fly has a relatively small genome, which was fully sequenced (its entire DNA code revealed) in 2000. It also has a short life cycle and many offspring. Together, these factors make the fruit fly a very good model organism for identifying and manipulating genes that may be relevant to sleep.

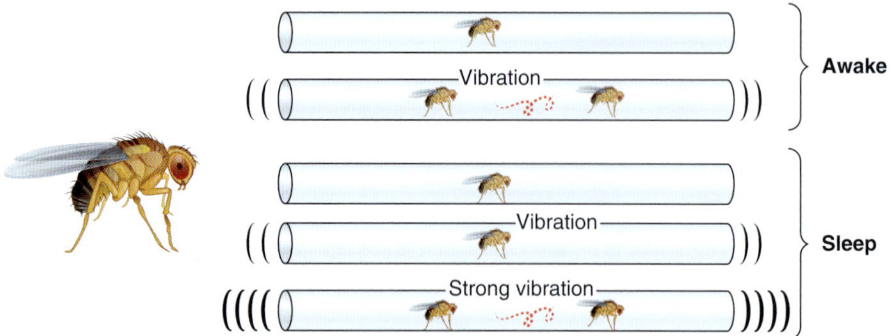

Figure 5.9 Are the flies sleeping? Experimenters measured the behavioral activity levels of fruit flies in response to a vibration. During periods of rest, the flies were unresponsive; they would not move unless exposed to a very strong vibration. The strong vibration woke them up from sleep.

5.4 DREAMS

Are dreams profound, or random and largely meaningless? Are they oracles that prophesy the future? Why do signs of sexual excitement often emerge in the dream state? When animals enter REM sleep, are they dreaming? How about human infants? These and other questions about dreams remain controversial. Dreams also provide a potential treasure trove for the brain scientist. For example, how can we be asleep and unconscious of the hustle and bustle of the world around us while simultaneously partaking of an inner psychedelic adventure? What neural mechanisms mediate this process?

Even though pet owners swear that their dogs dream and new parents are sure that their babies are dreaming, the only real assurance of the occurrence of a dream is a human report delivered upon awakening. Although everyday thinking is known to occur during the various stages of non-REM sleep, the intense mental events that most of us would consider dreaming occur almost exclusively in REM sleep. Thus, based on observing their eyes darting about under closed lids and seeing their faces and extremities twitching during REM, we can speculate that mammals and some birds, including newborns of these species, are dreaming. What they dream about is a question for philosophers and poets to ponder and not, at least at present, open to scientific inquiry.

When we dream, visual and movement-related imagery predominate. Dreams are delusions in the sense that we strongly believe we are awake, when there is much evidence to tell us we are not. We may think we are awake even when faced with impossible sequences and/or timing of events (walking through the door of a house and immediately finding ourselves in a place far away), or with unlikely physical capabilities (flying). Dreams are bizarre; ideas are often linked to one another through loose associations, rather than the logic that normally ties together our waking thoughts. Sometimes, the transitions from one part of a dream to another are consistent and logical, even though the entire scenario may be strange and foreign. Dreams are also creative: Themes and images from many different aspects of our life may be combined to create an episode that is unusual and imaginative (Domhoff, 2003; Hobson, 2009).

Dreams are sometimes filled with strong emotions such as elation, anxiety, or anger. About 75 percent of the emotions described in dreams are negative; they often include the desire to escape from danger. Why is that? Perhaps this emotionality and negativity is a response to the storms of autonomic nervous system activity (sympathetic responses associated with fight or flight) going on during REM sleep.

In contrast with memory of events in our waking lives, dream content disappears from our memory with amazing ease and speed. While people and events from our past are often incorporated into our dreams, we are rarely aware that we are thinking of the past while we are dreaming. Similarly, a dream may incorporate our fears and hopes about the future, but while dreaming we aren't usually aware that we are thinking about the future. More generally, the dreamer often loses the ability to distinguish past, present, and future. It may be significant that while sensory areas of the cortex (particularly visual areas) are active during dreaming, frontal lobe brain regions associated with tracking the order of events in time are notably inactive during dreaming.

Recall that while these dramatic cognitive events called dreams occur, we are paralyzed. One might speculate that this paralytic mechanism has evolved in order to protect dreamers from "acting out" their dreams and potentially harming themselves or others. (Of course, we can never do more than guess why something has evolved.) We'll return to this notion later.

We cannot specify with certainty what gives rise to dreams or what the functions of REM sleep and dreaming are. We can, however, indicate what brain events are associated with REM sleep and dreaming. For instance, during REM sleep, neurons in the brainstem are activated. Some of these brainstem neurons are involved in sympathetic nervous system activation, and their activity may act as emotional triggers for dream events. Even if this is the case, it is difficult to know whether the sympathetic nervous system activity causes dream emotionality or whether the emotional experience of the dream activates the sympathetic nervous system. When you have a frightening dream of being chased, is your cortex weaving a story to account for your brainstem activation of the sympathetic nervous system (elevated heart rate, high blood pressure, and so on)? Or is it the frightening dream content that causes the brainstem to activate your sympathetic nervous system?

One widely held speculation about dream content is that dreams are confabulations, stories made up in response to the ongoing, random brain activity. This is based in part on the idea that a critical general function of the brain that has emerged through evolution is the ability to create integrated stories or hypotheses from limited pieces of information. According to this point of view, during REM sleep the brainstem generates random inputs to the cortex, and the cortex creates an "interpretation" of these random signals. Fabulous, but often meaningless, stories emerge from this raw material. This is not to deny that if you are fearful over some upcoming event in your life that you will be more likely to have a dream filled with anxiety. However, according to this view, the detailed scenes and specific dialog in your personal dream movie do not represent premonitions or personal moral lessons, but rather the brain's attempt to weave together brainstem signals with fragments of recent memories and emotions.

One of the most exciting and interesting aspects of the study of dreams is the investigation of the brain regions involved in dreaming. Researchers recorded EEG activity in sleeping subjects whom they woke at various stages of sleep and asked whether they had been dreaming (Siclari et al., 2017). The brain activity was monitored using a large number of electrode sensors (high-density EEG), providing a higher level of anatomical precision than that obtained with traditional EEG recordings. Dreaming was associated with activation (high-frequency waves) in posterior regions of the cortex, largely involving the occipital and posterior parietal lobes (Figure 5.10). While most dreams are accompanied by activation of posterior cortical areas, frontal lobe activation is sometimes observed, particularly when subjects report having had "thoughts" during the dream (Siclari et al., 2017), or during **lucid** dreaming, where the individual is aware that she is dreaming, and may have some control over her dream content (Dresler et al., 2012).

KEY CONCEPTS

- **Across the lifespan, the largest change in sleep in humans occurs between fetal development, a time of continuous REM, and the first one or two years after birth, where about half the time is spent sleeping, and only a portion of this is dedicated to REM.**
- **Sleep appears to be a universal feature of animal life. It is seen in animals from the elephant to the human to the fruit fly.**
- **The vivid experience during sleep that we refer to as dreaming is mostly confined to REM sleep.**

TEST YOURSELF

1. **Describe the changes that occur to sleep cycles as humans age.**
2. **Which animal sleeps more hours in a day, an elephant or a bat? What is the likely explanation for this?**
3. **Activation in the ______ and ______ lobes is strongly associated with dreaming, although frontal lobe activity is often observed during lucid dreams.**

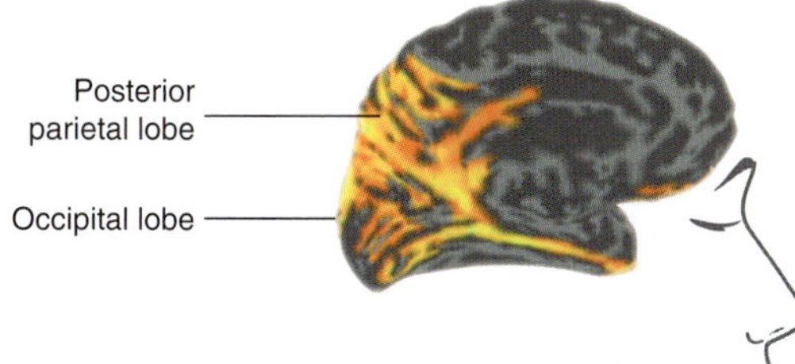

Figure 5.10 Posterior regions of the cortex activated during dreaming.
(Adapted from Siclari et al., 2017, fig. 56D.)

5.5 BRAIN MECHANISMS

We have described the states of waking, non-REM sleep, and REM sleep. Let us now ask how the brain gives rise to these states.

5.5.1 Activation of the Thalamus and Cerebral Cortex Is Key to the Waking State

We begin with a brief discussion of the neurobiology of waking, that is, the period when we are conscious, aware, and responsive to external stimuli. Recall the case of the young man described in the opening of this chapter. He was in a minimally conscious state for years until he received electrical stimulation of the central thalamus. Following recovery from the operation, the thalamus was stimulated, and he suddenly showed long periods when he could keep his eyes open, and a greatly increased responsiveness to verbal commands. For the first time since his injury, he was able to use objects and speak in an understandable manner (Schiff et al., 2007).

The fact that deep brain stimulation of the thalamus restored this man's conscious awareness and behavioral responsiveness suggests that regions of the thalamus play a key role in the waking state (Figure 5.11). The thalamus is the gateway to the cerebral cortex, where our waking consciousness resides. Perhaps it is not surprising then that low cortical arousal, whether due to accident, stroke, or disease, can compromise our waking lives. Stimulation of the **intralaminar nucleus**, a central region of the thalamus, is particularly effective in producing cortical arousal and wakefulness (Gent, Bandarabadi, Herrera, & Adamantidis, 2018).

Waking is also associated with activation of several clusters of neurons in the brainstem and hypothalamus (Figure 5.12). The cells within these nuclei are continually active during waking and thus continuously release

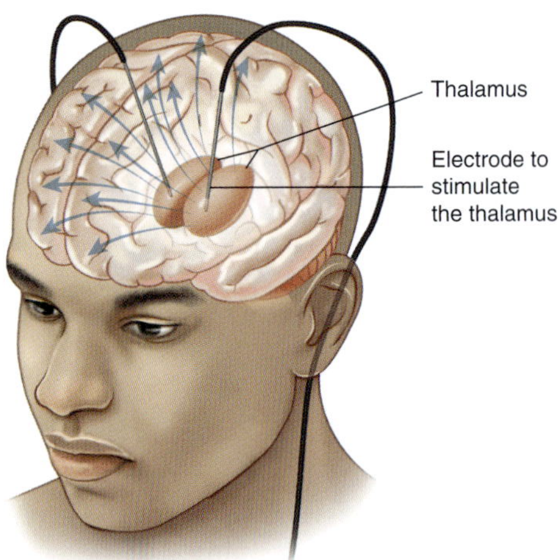

Figure 5.11 Stimulation of the thalamus wakes up the cortex. The thalamus sends projections to the entire cerebral cortex. Stimulation of the thalamus can produce cortical arousal and wakefulness in individuals who have been minimally conscious for years.

A

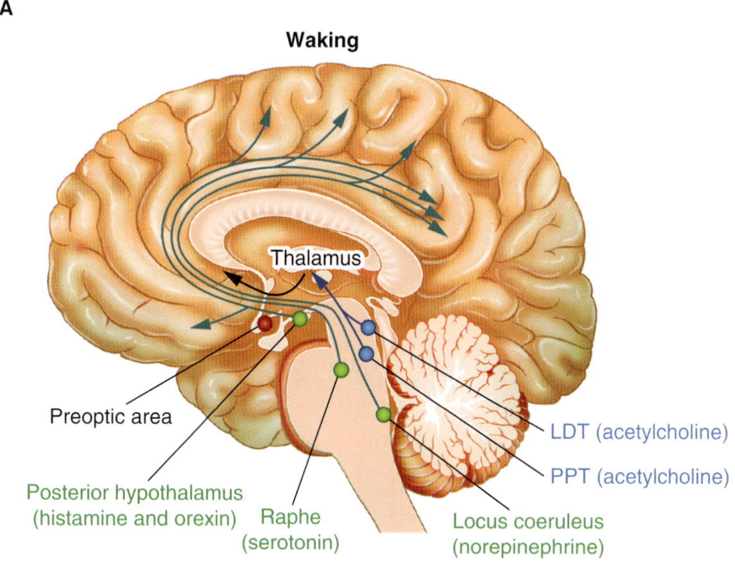

B

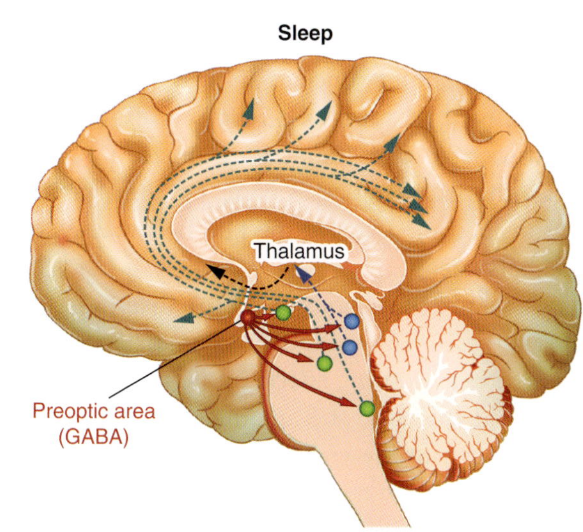

Figure 5.12 Neurochemicals important for arousal. (A) Several clusters of neurons are activated during waking. Many (green circles) send projections to the cortex, where they release serotonin, norepinephrine, histamine, or orexin. Others (blue circles) release acetylcholine to the thalamus. Neurons in the thalamus, in turn, send axons to the cortex. (B) In order to initiate sleep, the preoptic area (red) releases GABA to turn off the waking-on neurons.

their neurotransmitters at their axon terminal sites throughout the brain and spinal cord (McGinty & Szymusiak, 2011). The most important of these neurons (and the neurotransmitters they release) are:

- brainstem raphe nuclei (serotonin)
- brainstem locus coeruleus (norepinephrine)

- brainstem pedunculopontine/laterodorsal tegmental nuclei (PPT/LDT) (acetylcholine)
- posterior hypothalamus (histamine and orexin).

As you can see from Figure 5.12A, these brain regions refer to the location where the cell bodies of these arousal-related neurons reside, but their neurotransmitters are often released within the cerebral cortex or thalamus. Scientists do not yet know why we need so many types of wake-maintaining neurons. Evolution works in ways that are often a mystery to us.

These neurons are sometimes called "waking-on" neurons because they are "on" (activated) during waking. A key feature of these neurons is that they lead to excitation of the cerebral cortex. As seen in Figure 5.12, most of these waking-on neurons release neurochemicals which act upon the cortex directly.

Other waking-on neurons release their neurochemicals to the thalamus, where they activate other sets of neurons which, in turn, activate the cortex. We saw earlier that a key area for waking and arousal is the intralaminar nucleus of the thalamus. Many of the brainstem PPT/LDT neurons release acetylcholine to the intralaminar nucleus of the thalamus, permitting the intralaminar neurons to activate the cerebral cortex. Activity of the PPT/LDT neurons is associated with the desynchronized (low-amplitude, high-frequency) EEG that characterizes waking. On the other hand, when the PPT/LDT neurons become inactive the EEG becomes synchronized and the individual falls asleep.

Many stimulant drugs enhance the actions of neurotransmitters found in waking-on neurons. The best-known stimulants are cocaine and the amphetamines, which exert their arousing effects primarily by increasing levels of norepinephrine, and therefore the amount of norepinephrine available to bind to its receptors in the cortex and other brain regions. Nicotine is a potent stimulant found in tobacco products. It works through activation of the nicotinic receptor, one of the acetylcholine receptor subtypes.

5.5.2 Neurons within the Hypothalamus Trigger Non-REM Sleep

As we have seen, during normal waking the brain is in an active state of readiness for reacting or responding, and the EEG is desynchronized (low-amplitude, high-frequency waves). At bedtime, as we relax and close our eyes, the EEG becomes a bit more synchronized and alpha waves appear. With the onset of sleep, we observe an even more synchronized EEG. What happens in the brain during this transition from waking to sleep?

The onset of sleep is accompanied by activation of neurons within a region of the anterior hypothalamus called the **preoptic area**. As shown in Figure 5.12B, these preoptic area **sleep-on neurons** inhibit the brainstem and hypothalamic neurons that produce a state of wakefulness. This inhibition is mediated primarily by the release of the neurotransmitter **GABA**. In the 1920s, an Austrian neurologist and psychologist, Constantin von Economo, discovered that patients with damage to the part of the hypothalamus now known to contain these sleep-on neurons lost the ability to sleep (von Economo, 1929)! He also found that many patients with damage to parts of the brainstem now known to contain wake-on neurons became lethargic and, in some cases, comatose (unconscious). Subsequent animal research that lesioned very specific areas within the brainstem and hypothalamus confirmed von Economo's findings, and more precisely identified anatomical areas that are active during sleep versus waking (i.e., illustrated in Figure 5.12).

Several factors activate the "sleep-on" neurons. Below are three critical factors.

- The circadian clock in the SCN activates sleep-on neurons in the anterior hypothalamus.
- Increases in body temperature activate sleep-on neurons. This explains why we may become sleepy in warm environments.
- During long periods of wakefulness, a molecule called **adenosine** accumulates, and promotes sleepiness. It does this, in part, by binding to adenosine receptors that activate sleep-on neurons. If a build-up of adenosine leads to sleepiness, what would be the effect of a drug that blocks adenosine's actions? Have a cup of coffee and find out. A key effect of caffeine is to block adenosine receptors and prevent its sleep-inducing effects.

Normally, neurons in particular areas of the thalamus transmit sensory (visual, auditory, tactile) information to their respective processing areas of the cortex. The thalamic neurons that transmit or relay this sensory information to the cortex are called **thalamic relay neurons**. However, during non-REM sleep, neurons in a part of the thalamus called the **reticular nucleus** produce synchronized bursts of firing. (In other words, the reticular neurons all fire together as a group, pause, fire again, and so on.) Firing of the reticular neurons inhibits the thalamic relay neurons (Figure 5.13), preventing them from transmitting sensory information to the cortex (Sherman, 1998). This is the primary reason why it is so difficult to arouse us from deep non-REM sleep. As soon as the reticular nucleus is inhibited, animals wake up (Herrera et al., 2016).

Cortical neurons in the non-REM sleeping brain rarely engage in their normal tasks of thought, memory, visual imagery, and other kinds of

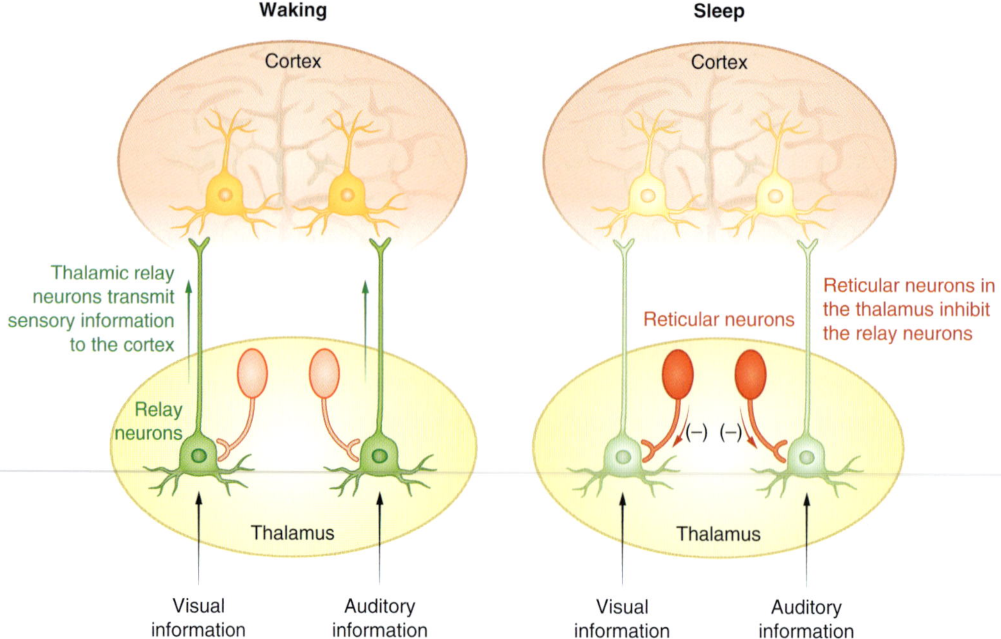

Figure 5.13 Disconnection between thalamus and cortex during sleep. Neural connections from the thalamus to the cortex transmit sensory information during waking. This sensory information is suppressed during sleep, depriving the cortex of environmental input.

information processing. The cortex effectively goes "off-line," unreceptive to incoming sensory information and unable to process information on its own. As we shall see, something happens to drastically change the mode of brain activity from this non-REM state to the state of REM sleep, when EEG suggests that the brain has entered a state resembling wakefulness.

5.5.3 REM Sleep Depends upon Activation of Neurons in the Brainstem

A remarkable series of experiments in the 1950s and 1960s carried out in France revealed that REM sleep is initiated by neurons in the brainstem. The lead researcher, Michel Jouvet, cut into the brain of cats, leaving the thalamus, cortex, and other parts of the forebrain on one side of the cut and the posterior brainstem (pons and medulla) and spinal cord on the other (Figure 5.14B, left panel). The forebrain, now divorced from the posterior brainstem could no longer enter REM sleep. The animals showed no rapid eye movements and the cortex showed no desynchronized (fast, low-amplitude) EEG waves. For the most part, the cortex and the rest of the forebrain appeared to be almost continually stuck in slow-wave sleep.

However, when Jouvet examined the neural tissue in the posterior brainstem and spinal cord, he found signs of REM including loss of

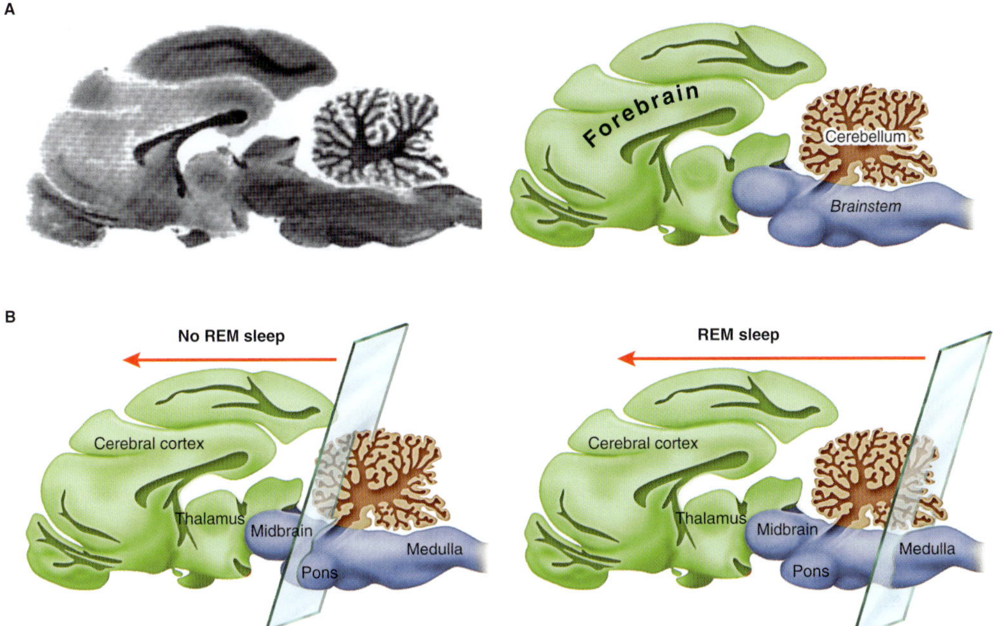

Figure 5.14 Surgical separation of the brainstem from the forebrain prevents REM sleep. (A) A cat's brain seen in front-to-back (sagittal) section. Notice that the cortex is to the left, and the brainstem is to the right. (B) The forebrain cannot enter REM sleep when it is disconnected from the pons.

muscle tone (atonia) in the large muscles of the body. Thus, while the part of the brain anterior to the cut was not in REM sleep, the part posterior to the cut showed normal signs of REM. This finding suggested that the brain region necessary for initiating REM sleep was somewhere posterior to the cut. A more specific identification of the critical regions for REM came from later studies.

The experimenter wondered what would happen if the cut was made posterior to the pons (Figure 5.14, right panel). This would allow the pons to communicate with the forebrain. In this case, the forebrain showed signs of relatively normal REM sleep! This result suggested that the brain can enter a REM state so long as it receives input from the pons. In support of this hypothesis, later research showed that discrete, localized lesions in the pons and portions of the medulla abolish REM sleep without significantly affecting non-REM sleep. While the pons is said to generate the REM state, it does not alone produce dreaming. The visual scenes, events, emotions, and other characteristics of dreams require much more than activity of the pons, but importantly involve activity of the thalamus and cerebral cortex.

As we discussed above, a number of neurotransmitter-specific neurons are active while we are in the waking state. These "waking-on" neurons release various neurochemicals, which help us to maintain our waking state. Most of the waking-on neurons are silent during REM sleep. There is an exception, however. One group of waking-on neurons in the brainstem, the PPT/LDT neurons (again, see Figure 5.12), become strongly activated during REM sleep. When we discussed waking, we saw that these neurons release acetylcholine to the thalamus and activate thalamocortical neurons. The similarities in the activity of the cortex during waking and REM sleep are due, in part, to the thalamocortical activation that occurs in both states.

Another important aspect of REM sleep depends on a group of neurons within the pons that send axons down to the medulla. The medulla neurons, in turn, powerfully inhibit spinal cord motor neurons and paralyze large groups of torso and limb muscles. Strong evidence for the importance of the pons in muscle paralysis during REM is that animals with destruction of small regions within the pons fail to become paralyzed during REM sleep, and instead move about, apparently acting out their dreams (Figure 5.15).

Interestingly, during REM sleep not only is motor output blocked, but sensory inputs from the external world are also suppressed. Thus, we have

Figure 5.15 **This cat is in REM sleep!** Normally, the brainstem inhibits motor neurons, preventing the cat from acting out its dreams. After lesioning the pons, the cat enters REM without muscle paralysis, and moves about, apparently acting out a dream. (From Morrison, Sanford, Ball, Mann, & Ross, 1995, © 1995, American Psychological Association.)

a state in which the subject is isolated from its world in terms of both input and output, and yet generates mental activity of often fascinating content.

Figure 5.16 summarizes the regions of the brainstem, hypothalamus, thalamus, and cortex that are important for waking, non-REM sleep, and REM sleep.

	Waking	Non-REM Sleep	REM Sleep
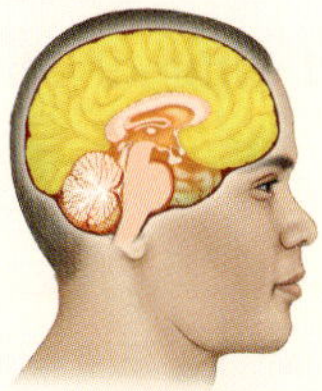 Cortex	Desynchronized cortical activity (alpha and beta waves)	Synchronized cortical activity (delta waves)	Desynchronized cortical activity (alpha and beta waves)
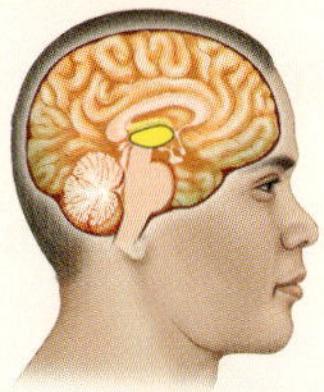 Thalamus	Intralaminar nucleus of the thalamus	Reticular nucleus of the thalamus	
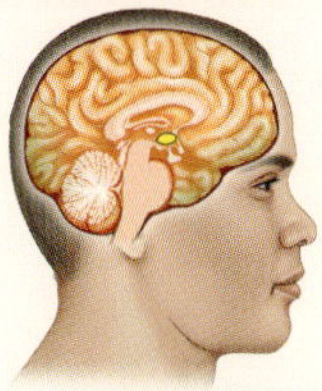 Hypothalamus	Posterior hypothalamus	Anterior hypothalamus (preoptic area)	
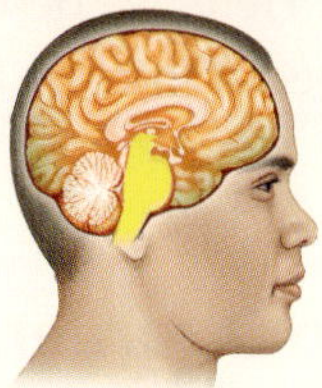 Brainstem	• Raphe nucleus • Locus coeruleus • PPT/LDT		• PPT/LDT • Brainstem neurons that inhibit spinal motor neurons
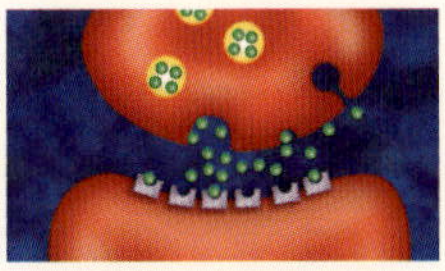 Neurochemicals	Serotonin, norepinephrine, acetylcholine, histamine, orexin	GABA, adenosine	Acetylcholine

Figure 5.16 Summary of brain areas and neurochemicals critical for waking and sleep. Waking and sleep are characterized by changes in cortical activity, activation of thalamic, hypothalamic, and brainstem regions, and neurochemical release. This table summarizes information discussed throughout this chapter.

KEY CONCEPTS

- **During waking, the brain generates adenosine, the most important sleep inducer.**
- **Waking depends upon activation of the thalamus and cerebral cortex.**
- **Waking also depends upon activity of waking-on neurons in the brainstem and hypothalamus.**
- **Sleep requires that sleep-on neurons in the preoptic area of the hypothalamus inhibit the waking-on neurons.**
- **REM sleep depends upon activity of neurons located within the brainstem, particularly in the pons.**

TEST YOURSELF

1. **What is meant by "waking-on" neurons? (In other words, why are they *called* that?)**
2. **Most waking-on neurons release neurochemicals that excite the _____.**
3. **What is meant by "sleep-on" neurons?**
4. **Most sleep-on neurons inhibit waking-on neurons by releasing the inhibitory neurotransmitter _____.**
5. **What are three factors that initiate sleep?**
6. **How are muscles paralyzed during REM (Describe the role of neurons in the pons and medulla.)**

5.6 DISEASES AND DISRUPTIONS

There is a large variety of sleep disorders. Some are quite common while others, such as familial genetic diseases, are quite rare. Here, we describe several sleep disorders that are either common or of special interest from a neuroscience perspective.

5.6.1 Insomnia, the Most Common Sleep Disorder, Is an Inability to Sleep

Insomnia is an inability to fall or remain asleep. It accounts for over 75 percent of clinical sleep complaints and affects almost 30 percent of the population in the USA. There are varous consequences of this lack of sleep. Foremost among them is an unrefreshed feeling and an inability to perform at a high cognitive level. Other negative consequences include confusion, memory lapses, irritability, emotional instability, increased blood pressure, and increased stress hormones. These detrimental effects of sleep loss can often be attributed to a failure to attain the restorative effects of Stage 3 sleep.

Common causes of insomnia are stress and anxiety. Insomnia can result from air travel to another time zone; use of stimulant drugs such as caffeine, especially in the evening; various mental disorders, such as depression; frequently changing work hours; and finally, environmental conditions such as noise and light. Insomnia is much more frequent in the aged. This is at least partly attributable to their higher incidence of painful conditions, such as arthritis, which can interfere with sleep.

It is difficult to treat insomnia with any degree of specificity. The most productive initial action is frequently a session with the family physician or a therapist, and, if a follow-up is needed, a visit to a specialist trained in sleep medicine.

Treatments for insomnia include sleep medications and behavioral treatments (Cheung, Ji, & Morin, 2019). Sleep medications, generally known as hypnotics, include the widely used benzodiazepines, such as Librium and Valium. Along with other hypnotics, these drugs also act as muscle relaxants and anxiolytics (anxiety-reducing drugs). These features add to their sleep-inducing efficacy. Insomnia, anxiety, and muscle tension all interact to exacerbate one another, and benzodiazepines reduce all three. When compared to hypnotic drugs of the previous era, such as barbiturates, benzodiazepines are much safer in cases of accidental overdose or attempted suicide. Nevertheless, the benzodiazepines still have the common side effect of morning drowsiness and impaired coordination, effects that can increase the risk of auto accidents.

The primary mechanism of action of benzodiazepines is to activate **$GABA_A$ receptors**. These receptors are found in many brain regions, and we do not know precisely where the benzodiazepines act to induce sleep. However, many neuroscientists suspect that benzodiazepines activate $GABA_A$ receptors in several of the "waking-on" regions of the brain that are seen in Figure 5.12. By increasing actions at the inhibitory GABA receptor, these drugs may be "turning off" the waking-on neurons. Following the introduction of Librium and Valium, other sleeping pills were developed as modifications of these compounds, designed to be more short-acting (in order for the sleeper to awaken without feeling drowsy) and to have fewer side effects.

One problem with sleep medications is that, especially at high doses, drug tolerance may develop, which leads to the need for additional amounts of the drug. Another danger is the development of dependence on the drug, often making it difficult to abstain from continued use. Finally, when a person stops taking the drug, especially suddenly, there can be significant rebound effects of anxiety and troubling dreams.

Many other drugs have been used as sleep aids, and even though they are often effective in that regard, they typically have some important shortcoming (Mendelson, 2007). Opioid drugs induce sleep, but they are dangerous because of the ease of overdosing. **Antihistamines** also produce sleepiness, as you may know if you've used an antihistamine for a runny nose. Antihistamines block the action of histamine, a neurochemical mentioned earlier for its role in wakefulness. However, their usefulness for insomnia is limited because they produce daytime sleepiness. Some derive benefits from the use of the pineal hormone **melatonin** as a sleep aid. Melatonin increases sleepiness and sleep duration (Dollins, Zhdanova, Wurtman, Lynch, & Deng, 1994), and has not been associated with serious side effects following either short- or long-term use (Andersen, Gogenur, Rosenberg, & Reiter, 2016).

Finally, cognitive behavioral therapy is an effective treatment for insomnia (Koffel, Koffel, & Gehrman, 2015; Cheung et al., 2019), and has the obvious advantage of being free of the side effects associated with drug treatments. The cognitive behavioral approach to treating insomnia typically involves three key elements. First, the client is encouraged to only spend time in bed when it is time to go to sleep, and to avoid interspersing sleep periods throughout the day. This consolidation of sleep is designed to increase sleepiness at bedtime. Clients are also encouraged not to use the bed for working, reading, or other activities aside from sleep (or sex). In this way, a strong association is formed between the bed and sleep. Finally, the therapist helps the client to challenge his own anxiety-provoking beliefs about sleep. For instance, the person may become anxious as soon as he has trouble falling asleep because he focuses upon thoughts about danger to his health (or other "awful consequences") that will result from failing to fall asleep. Reevaluating dysfunctional and unrealistic beliefs (cognitive restructuring) can help reduce the anxiety that is counterproductive to sleeping.

5.6.2 Narcolepsy Involves Intense Sleepiness during the Daytime

Even a superficial examination indicates that narcolepsy may result from a malfunction of REM sleep. It appears that several phenomena normally confined to REM sleep have "escaped" into the waking state. Narcolepsy involves excessive, sometimes irresistible, *daytime sleepiness*. Along with this, those with narcolepsy often enter REM sleep within a few minutes after falling asleep, instead of after the typical 90-minute delay of the first REM period. Narcolepsy is of course very dangerous because of the possibility of automobile accidents. Additional symptoms that may be present in those with narcolepsy include the following:

(1) **Cataplexy** is a sudden loss of muscle tone often brought on by emotional situations and typically lasting only for a few minutes or less.

Many non-narcoleptic, healthy people may experience a mild version of this when they report being "weak with laughter," or "weak in the knees." Unlike REM sleep and its accompanying paralysis, subjects remain awake during an episode of cataplexy. A major danger of cataplexy is the possibility of injury from a fall when the muscle paralysis intrudes with little warning.

(2) **Sleep paralysis** is the inability to move for several minutes following awakening or, less frequently, just prior to sleep onset. Sleep paralysis is often experienced as scary or disturbing.

(3) **Hypnagogic hallucinations** can best be considered as having a dream while awake, again occurring typically just prior to sleep onset or upon awakening. The individual sees, hears, or feels something that appears vivid and real, but which is not present. For instance, the individual may hallucinate the image of a person or a strange shape, or believe she is hearing something knocking or crashing. Like sleep paralysis, the hallucinations can be frightening. Sometimes sleep paralysis and hypnagogic hallucinations may occur at the same time.

Recent progress in the understanding and treatment of narcolepsy has been dramatic (Nishino & Mignot, 2011). It was not until the early 1970s that William Dement at Stanford University carried out the first study to estimate the prevalence of narcolepsy. Narcolepsy is much rarer than insomnia, affecting less than 0.1 percent of the adult population. It typically begins after puberty, is a chronic condition, and likely involves genetic factors.

There have been two major advances in understanding narcolepsy. The first was the demonstration of its heritability in dogs found through inbreeding of dogs that displayed the canine form of the disorder (Nishino & Mignot, 2011). This suggested the possibility that scientists could discover the genes that contribute to narcolepsy. And, indeed, the brains of afflicted dogs lack the receptor for orexin, one of the neurochemicals released by waking-on neurons. The second finding was the evidence that most cases of human narcolepsy are strongly associated with a near-complete loss of orexin-containing neurons (Thannickal et al., 2000). It is possible that narcolepsy results from a degenerative process that leads to the death of orexin neurons (Mahoney, Cogswell, Koralnik, & Scammell, 2019).

The most general treatment of narcolepsy is the use of stimulant drugs, such as amphetamine and methylphenidate (Ritalin), which act to enhance the actions of brain norepinephrine, one of the transmitters released by waking-on neurons. More recently, the drug modafinil (Provigil) has proved to be the single most effective treatment. Modafinil increases neuronal activity in areas of the hypothalamus associated with waking and arousal. Given the loss of orexin in those with narcolepsy, you might wonder whether treatments that increase orexin activity may have therapeutic benefits. Current research is examining the benefits (and side effects) of orexin supplements in treating narcolepsy (Nepovimova et al., 2019).

5.6.3 Sleep Apnea Deprives the Sleeper of Oxygen

A person with sleep apnea suffers a disruption of breathing during sleep. A collapse and blockade of the upper airway deprives the sleeper of oxygen, which, in turn, produces a brief arousal from sleep (not necessarily strong enough to produce awakening). Loud snoring typically accompanies these episodes, which may occur hundreds of times during a single night of sleep. Individual episodes may last only for seconds or even up to a minute or two. Due to this frequent sleep disruption, patients fail to get a full and deep night of sleep and are therefore sleepy and fatigued the next day. This pattern is repeated daily if untreated. Sleep apnea occurs predominantly in adult males, especially in those who are obese and therefore have increased pressure on their chest and increased tissue around the upper airway. Currently, the most effective treatment is the application of **continuous positive airway pressure** (**CPAP**) (Figure 5.17). CPAP is a mask that fits over the nose and/or mouth and blows air into the throat so that the airway remains open (rather than collapsing) during sleep.

In addition to daytime sleepiness and fatigue, chronic sleep apnea carries other health risks due to sleep loss and repeated instances of lost oxygen. Among the more serious consequences are hypertension, increased risk of stroke, and structural brain damage.

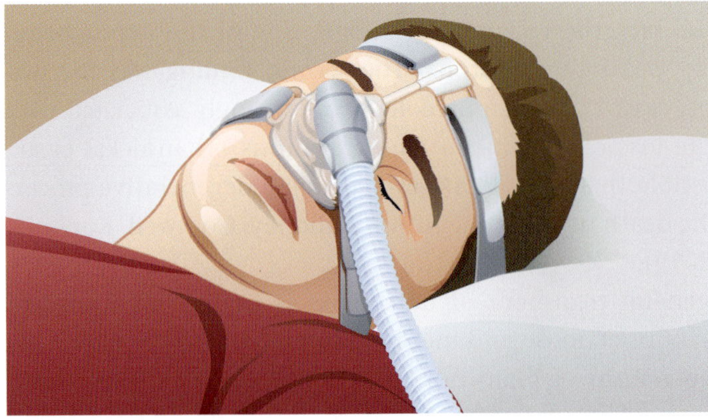

Figure 5.17 **A patient undergoing CPAP treatment for sleep apnea**. Continuous positive air pressure (CPAP) into the respiratory system treats sleep apnea by keeping the airways open during sleep.

5.6.4 In REM Sleep Behavior Disorder (RBD), the Sleeper Can Act Out His Dreams

As we have noted earlier, normal REM sleep is characterized by the complete loss of muscle tone (paralysis or atonia) for large muscles. We also saw that destruction of an area of the pons in experimental animals produces REM sleep *without* paralysis. As these animals transition to REM sleep, they stand, begin to move about, and even walk, all while remaining asleep. It was only natural to suggest that they were "acting out their dreams." More than twenty years after these laboratory experiments, a similar syndrome was reported in humans, especially in elderly males (Schenck, Bundlie, Patterson, & Mahowald, 1987). Because the observed behavior was immediately followed by the opportunity to interview the subjects, it was clear that in many cases they were indeed acting out their dreams. The individual may sometimes shout, scream, and punch while dreaming. This can obviously be dangerous for the sleeping individual and for their bed partner. The disorder, which afflicts less than 1 percent of the population (Boeve, 2010), is termed **REM Sleep Behavior Disorder** (**RBD**).

The direct cause of this syndrome is not known, but there is reason to believe that there may be underlying destruction of the pons or of the pathway descending from there to motor neurons in the spinal cord. Currently, there is no known treatment, but muscle relaxant drugs can sometimes provide help.

Probably the most unexpected and important finding related to RBD is that the disorder can signal the impending onset of Parkinson's disease. In one study, approximately 40 percent of the RBD patients were later diagnosed with Parkinson's disease! Currently, it is hypothesized that in many instances, both RBD and Parkinson's disease and some forms of dementia derive from the same basic neurological disorder, the development of abnormal clumps of protein within neurons. These protein clumps, called Lewy bodies, disrupt normal neuronal functioning (Chapter 13).

5.7 BENEFITS OF SLEEP

When we ask why sleep or any other behavior evolved, we are in dangerous territory. We can speculate, but in the end we cannot truly know the answer. On the other hand, when it comes to determining the *benefits* of sleep, we have a better chance of getting definitive answers through experimental research.

Sleep is not a random event simply there to pass time. The brain ensures that sleep occurs. As we have seen, when we are deprived of sleep, we are driven to make up the deficit. This suggests that it may serve an important purpose. Scientists have several commonly held beliefs regarding why we sleep.

- To save energy by reducing the behavioral activity that occurs when we are awake.
- To restore brain function. During non-REM sleep, the brain is processing very little information, and evidence suggests that sleep has restorative effects on our mood and cognition. But why then do we enter REM sleep, an active state when the brain uses a great deal of energy? One proposal is that intermittent interruption of non-REM sleep with REM keeps the brain in a state of readiness to act (Siegel & Rogawski, 1988). Were it not for REM sleep, the subject in a long, continuous period of deep non-REM sleep might lapse into a state of torpor (like hibernation) where they would be incapable of rapidly reacting to environmental or physiological emergencies.

Whether or not restoration of energy and/or brain function are the core reasons why sleep evolved, they are benefits that come from our time sleeping. Several other benefits to sleep are listed below. Any or all of these benefits may have been associated with adaptive advantages that contributed to the evolution of sleep.

- The immune system is strengthened during sleep. Sleep deprivation weakens the immune system, making us more susceptible to disease.
- Sleep, especially REM sleep, promotes brain development and maturation.
- During sleep, the brain may consolidate memories acquired during the day. There is evidence to suggest that REM sleep is particularly important for consolidation of skills, while non-REM sleep is important in memory of events we experienced during the day (episodic memory) (Grønli, Soulé, & Bramham, 2013). Chapter 9 will return to the role of sleep in consolidation of episodic memories.
- During sleep, the brain's internal plumbing system, called the glymphatic system, efficiently flushes out toxins accumulated during waking hours. We might have imagined that waste, which accumulates in one region, say the lateral hypothalamus, would be somehow disposed of in that area, while waste that accumulates in another area, say the pons, is disposed of there. But instead of many local systems for waste disposal, the glymphatic system flushes waste products into fluid-filled compartments that leave the brain and eventually enter the liver and kidneys, where they are filtered out of the body along with other bodily waste. Experiments in mice have recently shown that during sleep the brain eliminates waste products, including accumulated toxic proteins, at more than twice the elimination rate during waking. Without sleep, toxic proteins began to accumulate in the brains of the mice, including proteins associated with Alzheimer's disease in humans (Nedergaard & Goldman, 2016).

KEY CONCEPTS

- Insomnia is the most common complaint regarding sleep. Both pharmacological and cognitive/behavioral approaches can be effective in treating it. Most drugs used to treat insomnia interact with brain GABA receptors.
- Narcolepsy involves intense daytime sleepiness. Some of its symptoms (cataplexy, hypnagogic hallucinations, and sleep paralysis) can be characterized as REM sleep that has escaped into the waking period. Loss of orexin neurons has been identified as a major causal factor leading to narcolepsy.
- Those with sleep apnea suffer a loss of oxygen while sleeping due to a blockade of airway passages. This is effectively treated by introducing additional air into the sleeper's throat.
- REM Sleep Behavior Disorder includes a return of muscle tone during REM sleep, which allows the individual to "act out" dreams. This may be dangerous to the sleeper and others. Recent evidence indicates that RBD may be an initial sign of a larger brain pathology that includes Parkinson's disease and dementia.
- Sleep is not merely a passive state that interrupts our waking activities. Many critical processes and functions occur during sleep, including restoration and repair of brain and body, immune system strengthening, memory consolidation, and disposal of the brain's waste products.

TEST YOURSELF

1. How do benzodiazepines work to help overcome insomnia?
2. Why do those with sleep apnea fail to get a full night of deep sleep?
3. What are four important benefits that occur during sleep?

5.8 The Big Picture

Sleep appears to exist in all animals. Sleep and waking are controlled, in part, by an endogenous biological clock, but also by external cues like the rising sun, which tells the brain when it's time to wake up. Between the biological clock and these zeitgebers, we stay, more or less, on a 24-hour sleep–wake cycle. As we fall asleep, we first enter non-REM sleep, when slow synchronized neuronal firing produces EEG of progressively higher amplitude. As we enter the dream state of REM sleep, cortical activity becomes desynchronized, and EEG resembles that of the alert waking state.

Disorders of sleep range from the common difficulty of insomnia to the bizarre acting out of dreams. Scientists constantly seek better medical treatments, and, in some cases, behavioral therapies for these disorders. We are also learning of new benefits that derive from sleep, including positive effects on immune function, consolidation of learning and memory, and clearance of toxic waste that has accumulated in the brain during waking.

5.9 Creative Thinking

1. Imagine that you have your own sleep laboratory, outfitted with any equipment you desire. A new drug has been discovered to treat a particular disease, and you have been asked to make sure that it does not have any strange side effects on sleep cycles. What types of experiments would you conduct? What would you want to observe?
2. A genie offers to change your brain function so that you can sleep with just one hemisphere at a time, like a killer whale or a dolphin can. (You could maintain your human form and other aspects of brain function.) Would you ask the genie to do this? Why or why not?
3. Why do you think human babies spend so much of their sleep time in REM?
4. If your mother were suffering from insomnia, what would you recommend as treatment? What would be the first thing (or combination of things) to try? The second? Explain your reasoning.

Key Terms

adenosine 213
alpha waves 200
amplitude (EEG) 199
antihistamines 220
arrhythmic 203
beta waves 200
cataplexy 220
circadian 193
circadian factor 196
circadian rhythm 196
continuous positive airway pressure (CPAP) 222
deep brain stimulation 192
delta waves 201
desynchronized EEG 199
electroencephalogram (EEG) 197
electromyogram (EMG) 199
electrooculogram (EOG) 199
endogenous biological clock 195
entrained behavior 194
free-running rhythm 194
frequency (EEG) 199
GABA 213
$GABA_A$ receptors 219
homeostasis 196
homeostatic factor 196
hypnagogic hallucinations 221
intralaminar nucleus of the thalamus 210
lucid dreams 209
melatonin 220
muscle atonia 201

References

Andersen, L. P. H., Gogenur, I., Rosenberg, J., & Reiter, R. J. (2016). The safety of melatonin in humans. *Clinical Drug Investigation, 36*(3), 169–175.

Aserinsky, E., & Kleitman, N. (1953). Regularly occurring periods of eye motility, and concomitant phenomena, during sleep. *Science, 118*, 273–274.

Berry, R. B., Brooks, R., Gamaldo, C. E., Harding, S. M., Marcus, C. L., Vaughn, B. V., & Tangredi, M. M. (2017). *The AASM Manual for the Scoring of Sleep and Associated Events: Rules, Terminology and Technical Specifications.* Darien, IL: American Academy of Sleep Medicine.

Bing-Canar, H., Pizzuto, J., & Compton, R. J. (2016). Mindfulness-of-breathing exercise modulates EEG alpha activity during cognitive performance. *Psychophysiology, 53*, 1366–1376.

Boeve, B. F. (2010). REM sleep behavior disorder: updated review of the core features, the RBD-neurodegenerative disease association, evolving concepts, controversies, and future directions. *Annals of the New York Academy of Sciences, 1184*, 15–54.

Borbély, A. A., & Achermann, P. (1999). Sleep homeostasis and models of sleep regulation. *Journal of Biological Rhythms, 16*, 557–568.

Brown, R. E., Basheer, R., McKenna, J. T., Strecker, R. E., & McCarley, R. W. (2012). Control of sleep and wakefulness. *Physiological Reviews, 92*. 1087–1187.

Carter, M. E., Yizhar, O., Chikahisa, S., Nguyen, H., Adamantidis, A., Nishino, S., & de Lecea, L. (2010). Tuning arousal with optogenetic modulation of locus coeruleus neurons. *Nature Neuroscience, 13*(12), 1526–1533.

Cheung, J. M. Y., Ji, X. W., & Morin, C. M. (2019). Cognitive behavioral therapies for insomnia and hypnotic medications considerations and controversies. *Sleep Medicine Clinics, 14*(2), 253–265.

Dement, W., & Kleitman, N. (1957). Cyclic variations in EEG during sleep and their relation to eye movements, body motility, and dreaming. *Electroencephalography and Clinical Neurophysiology, 9*(4), 673–690.

Diekelmann, S., & Born, J. (2010). The memory function of sleep. *Nature Reviews Neuroscience, 11*, 114–126.

Dollins, A. B., Zhdanova, I. V., Wurtman, R. J., Lynch, H. J., & Deng, M. H. (1994). Effect of inducing nocturnal serum melatonin concentrations in daytime on sleep, mood, body-temperature, and performance. *Proceedings of the National Academy of Sciences of the United States of America, 91*(5), 1824–1828.

Domhoff, G. W. (2003). *The Scientific Study of Dreams: Neural Networks, Cognitive Development, and Content Analysis* (1st ed.). Washington, DC: American Psychological Association.

Dresler, M., Wehrle, R., Spoormaker, V. I., Koch, S. P., Holsboer, F., Steiger, A., … Czisch, M. (2012). Neural correlates of dream lucidity obtained from contrasting lucid versus non-lucid REM sleep: a combined EEG/fMRI case study. *Sleep, 35*(7), 1017–1020.

Gent, T. C., Bandarabadi, M., Herrera, C. G., & Adamantidis, A. R. (2018). Thalamic dual control of sleep and wakefulness. *Nature Neuroscience, 21*(7), 974–984.

Grønli, J., Soulé, J., & Bramham, C. R. (2013). Sleep and protein synthesis-dependent synaptic plasticity: impacts of sleep loss and stress. *Frontiers in Behavioral Neuroscience, 7*, 224.

Herrera, C. G., Cadavieco, M. C., Jego, S., Ponomarenko, A., Korotkova, T., & Adamantidis, A. (2016). Hypothalamic feedforward inhibition of thalamocortical network controls arousal and consciousness. *Nature Neuroscience, 19*(2), 290–298.

Hobson, J. A. (2009). REM sleep and dreaming: towards a theory of protoconsciousness. *Nature Reviews Neuroscience, 10*(11), 803–813.

Jagannath, A., Taylor, L., Wakaf, Z., Vasudevan, S. R., & Foster, R. G. (2017). The genetics of circadian rhythms, sleep and health. *Human Molecular Genetics, 26*(R2), R128–R138.

King, D. P., Zhao, Y., Sangoram, A. M., Wilsbacher, L. D., Tanaka, M., Antoch, M. P., … Takahashi, J. S. (1997). Positional cloning of the mouse circadian clock gene. *Cell*, 89(4), 641–653.

Koffel, E., Koffel, J., & Gehrman, P. (2015). A meta-analysis of group cognitive behavioral therapy for insomnia. *Sleep Medicine Reviews, 19*, 6–16.

Mahoney, C. E., Cogswell, A., Koralnik, I. J., & Scammell, T. E. (2019). The neurobiological basis of narcolepsy. *Nature Reviews Neuroscience, 20*(2), 83–93.

Massimini, M., Ferrarelli, F., Huber, R., Esser, S. K., Singh, H., & Tononi, G. (2005). Breakdown of cortical effective connectivity during sleep. *Science, 309*(5744), 2228–2232.

McGinty, D., & Szymusiak, R. (2011). Neural control of sleep in mammals. In M. H. Kryger, T. Roth, & W. C. Dement (Eds.), *Principles and Practice of Sleep Medicine* (5th ed., pp. 76–91). St. Louis, MO: Elsevier.

Mendelson, W. B. (2007). Combining pharmacologic and nonpharmacologic therapies for insomnia. *Journal of Clinical Psychiatry, 68* (Suppl. 5), 19–23.

Moore, R., & Eichler, V. (1972). Loss of a circadian adrenal corticosterone rhythm following suprachiasmatic lesions in the rat. *Brain Research, 42*(1), 201–206.

Morrison, A. R., Sanford, L. D., Ball, W. A., Mann, G. L., & Ross, R. J. (1995). Stimulus-elicited behavior in rapid eye movement sleep without atonia. *Behavioral Neuroscience, 109*(5), 972–979.

Nedergaard, M., & Goldman, S. A. (2016). Brain drain. *Scientific American, 314*(3), 44–49.

Nepovimova, E., Janockova, J., Misik, J., Kubik, S., Stuchlik, A., Vales, K., ... Kuca, K. (2019). Orexin supplementation in narcolepsy treatment: a review. *Medicinal Research Reviews, 39*(3), 961–975.

Nishino, S., & Mignot, E. (2011). Narcolepsy and cataplexy. *Handbook of Clinical Neurology, 99*, 783–814.

Saper, C. B., Fuller, P. M., Pedersen, N. P., Lu, J., & Scammell, T. E. (2010). Sleep state switching. *Neuron, 68*(6), 1023–1042.

Schenck, C. H., Bundlie, S. R., Patterson, A. L., & Mahowald, M. W. (1987). Rapid eye movement sleep behavior disorder. A treatable parasomnia affecting older adults. *JAMA, 257*(13), 1786–1789.

Schiff, N. D., Giacino, J. T., Kalmar, K., Victor, J. D., Baker, K., Gerber, M., ... Rezai, A. R. (2007). Behavioural improvements with thalamic stimulation after severe traumatic brain injury. *Nature, 448*(7153), 600–603.

Shaw, P. J., Cirelli, C., Greenspan, R. J., & Tononi, G. (2000). Correlates of sleep and waking in Drosophila melanogaster. *Science, 287*(5459), 1834–1837.

Sherman, S. M., & Guillery, R. W. (1998). On the actions that one nerve cell can have on another: distinguishing "drivers" from "modulators." *Proceedings of the National Academy of Sciences of the United States of America, 95*(12), 7121–7126.

Siclari, F., Baird, B., Perogamvros, L., Bernardi, G., LaRocque, J. J., Riedner, B., ... Tononi, G. (2017). The neural correlates of dreaming. *Nature Neuroscience, 20*(6), 872–878.

Siegel, J. (2008). Do all animals sleep? *Trends in Neurosciences, 31*(4), 208–213.

Siegel, J. M., & Rogawski, M. A. (1988). A function for REM sleep: regulation of noradrenergic receptor sensitivity. *Brain Research, 472*(3), 213–233.

Stephan, F. K., & Zucker, I. (1972). Circadian rhythms in drinking behavior and locomotor activity of rats are eliminated by hypothalamic lesions. *Proceedings of the National Academy of Sciences of the United States of America, 69*(6), 1583–1586.

Steriade, M., Nunez, A., & Amica, F. (1993) A novel slow (< 1 Hz) oscillation of neocortical neurons in vivo: depolarizing and hyperpolarizing components. *Journal of Neuroscience, 13*, 3252–3265.

Takahashi, T., Murata, T., Hamada, T., Omori, M., Kosaka, H., Kikuchi, M., ... Wada, Y. (2005). Changes in EEG and autonomic nervous activity during meditation and their association with personality traits. *International Journal of Psychophysiology, 55*, 199–207.

Thannickal, T. C., Moore, R. Y., Nienhuis, R., Ramanathan, L., Gulyani, S., Aldrich, M., ... Siegel, J. M. (2000). Reduced number of hypocretin neurons in human narcolepsy. *Neuron, 27*(3), 469–474.

Von Economo, C. (1929). Schlaftheorie. *Ergebnisse der Physiologie, 28*, 312–339.

Vyazovskiy, V. V., Cirelli, C., Pfister-Genskow, M., Faraguna, U., & Tononi, G. (2008). *Nature Neuroscience, 11*, 200–208.

6
Hunger

stanley45 / E+ / Getty Images

Consider This …

Penelope was a 13-year-old girl living in an affluent suburb of Minneapolis. Popular among her classmates, she was also an outstanding, highly motivated student who never seemed satisfied with her performance. Her mother was a successful corporate lawyer, and her father was a physician. They had recently begun to see a marriage counselor, and this made Penelope feel anxious.

When she was younger, she was content with her body image. However, when she was around 13 years old Penelope started to compare herself to some of the other girls in school whose bodies were leaner than hers. Although her body weight of about 100 pounds was perfectly normal for a girl her age and height, she became distressed about fat she noticed around her thighs and stomach. She decided to give up her afternoon cracker and cheese snack. When this appeared to have little effect, she signed up for her school's track team. The image she saw in her bedroom mirror was that of an overweight girl in spite of the fact that her weight had decreased to 95 and then to 90 pounds.

Over the next year, Penelope began to avoid carbohydrates, and eventually began to skip breakfast or lunch. At dinner she would say she was not very hungry. Sometimes, she would even self-induce vomiting after a meal. During the next season on the track team, she was running 3 to 5 extra miles each day and exercising at the gym. Her body weight had now dropped to about 75 pounds. She looked emaciated, her once shiny hair had become thin and stringy, and she had stopped menstruating. Her mother took her to the primary care physician who referred her to a psychiatrist. The psychiatrist strongly advised that she be hospitalized so that she could recover her weight in a controlled environment and undergo therapy. The doctor emphasized that Penelope's life was in jeopardy.

With support from her family, regular therapy sessions, and dietary counseling, she was able to start a long road toward recovery from **anorexia nervosa**. The process took years. During that time, she suffered several setbacks requiring re-hospitalization. But by the time she was 23, she was able to maintain a healthy weight.

In this chapter, we will examine anorexia, which remains difficult to prevent and treat. How could something so seemingly simple, like eating and weight regulation, become a life-threatening problem?

Normally, the feeling of hunger arises from physiological processes that inform the brain that energy resources are low. In the state of hunger, you are likely to seek out and consume available food. You might even feel the urge to eat for emotional reasons, like feeling sad, or because you are in a situation where you are in the habit of eating. However, as Penelope's case illustrates, complex psychological factors such as body image and self-esteem may also affect this motivational system of eating. This chapter will examine both physiological and psychological factors that influence whether, when, and how much, we eat.

6.1 COMPLEX PHYSIOLOGICAL PROCESSES KEEP NEUROBIOLOGICAL VARIABLES IN SAFE RANGES

Many motivational states come from the need to maintain a stable level of some critical factor like food or water. The deprivation produces arousal that *drives* you to restore the basic resting physiological state. Hunger (eating), thirst (drinking), thermoregulation (cooling and heating), oxygenation (breathing), and fatigue (sleep) all reflect a drive to restore a physiological state of one kind or another.

A major factor involved in regulating such behaviors is **homeostasis**, the action of a physiological (or mechanical) system to maintain internal stability when faced with a disturbance of its normal condition. As we will see below, hunger is sometimes considered a homeostatic system that maintains a relatively stable energy state. Let us begin, however, by considering a thermostat (Figure 6.1), a simple home device that works by homeostasis, and which we often take for granted. In the winter in New York City, you set it for a comfortable 70 degrees and forget about it.

Say a storm blows in from the north, bringing strong winds, snow, and plummeting outdoor temperatures. The thermostat senses a chill in your living room; the temperature has fallen below a set point. A signal is sent to the heating system to warm the air. As the temperature reaches 70, the heating system turns off. You don't have to do anything to make this happen; the homeostatic heating system is designed to maintain a

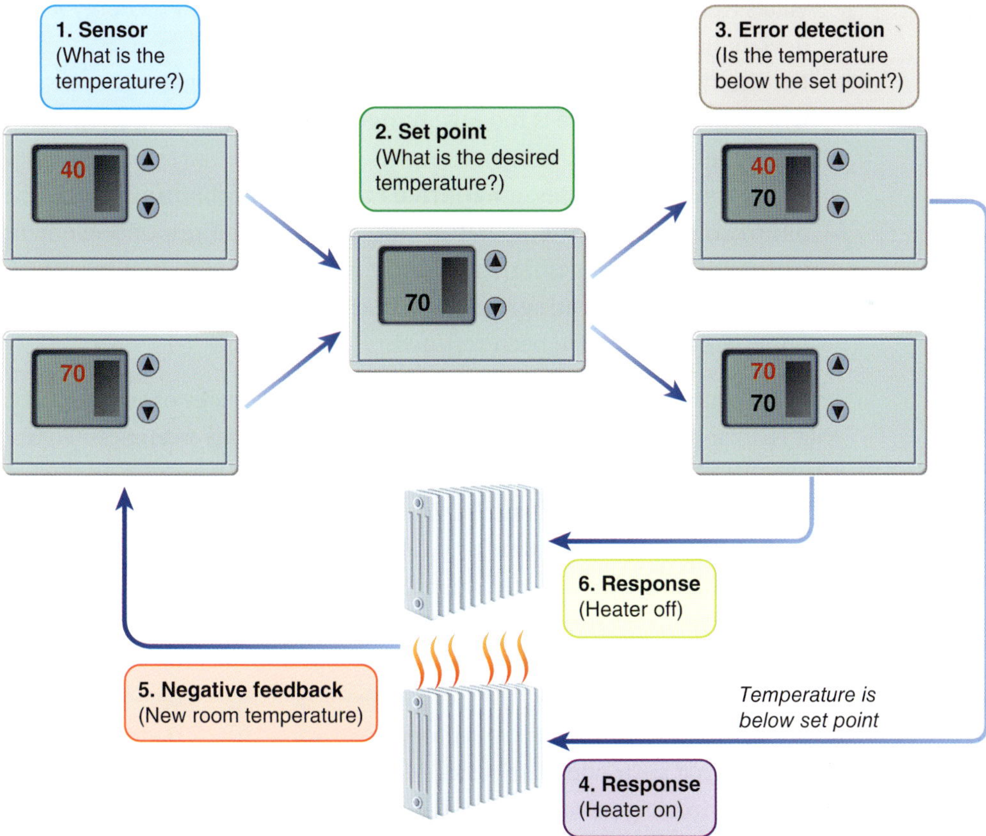

Figure 6.1 Homeostatic control. The heating system shown here is an example of a homeostatic device for it possesses a sensor (to detect temperature), a set point (a target temperature), error detection (it can tell when the temperature is below the set point), and a response (turn on the heater) that brings the room temperature back to the set point. As we will see, eating is at least partly controlled by homeostatic mechanisms in the brain.

relatively constant temperature. So too, the homeostatic systems in your body maintain your levels of glucose and other biological variables at desired levels.

Let's take a closer look at the basic elements the thermostat uses to regulate room temperature and see if we can derive some general principles that apply to the body's regulation of its own energy supply.

- A **sensor** that monitors the process we are interested in. As a thermometer monitors temperature, the body (often the brain) tracks many physiological variables, including current levels of glucose in the blood, the fullness or emptiness of the stomach, and other indicators of available energy.
- The system maintains a target or **set point**. Seventy degrees may be the set point for room temperature. Similarly, the brain systems that control eating may have a set point for desired energy levels.
- For the thermostat, **error detection** occurs when the temperature deviates from the set point; similarly, the brain detects when energy levels deviate from a set point.
- For the thermostat, a **response element** such as a heater is activated when the temperature is too low; hunger and eating are triggered when energy levels are low.
- As the temperature rises, a **negative feedback** mechanism detects the return to the desired temperature and turns off the response element (the heater); as the brain detects a rise in energy levels, it reduces feelings of hunger and eating. (As we will see, sometimes we eat even when our energy levels have been restored.)

Homeostatic bodily processes always display some degree of automaticity; that is, to some extent, they occur without our conscious awareness. For instance, life would be difficult if you had to remember to breathe, including while you were sleeping. Homeostatic physiological systems control breathing automatically. Second, basic physiological processes, like respiration and thermoregulation, come closest to being purely homeostatic. As we learn about complex processes, such as eating and body weight regulation in humans, we find that homeostatic mechanisms play a smaller role than initially believed.

Behaviors can be driven by factors other than direct bodily needs. If you eat so that your body can restore energy levels to an appropriate level, your behavior is guided by a homeostatic process. However, when you reach for a piece of cake after finishing a full meal, your behavior may be guided by the pleasurable taste sensation that you expect to enjoy, that is, by the incentive properties of the cake. Behaviors may therefore be driven not only by homeostasis, but also by environmental rewards (Chapter 11). Nonetheless, in trying to understand mechanisms underlying physiology and behavior, it is useful to begin with simple homeostatic models and see how real-world processes deviate from them.

6.2 DIGESTION OF FOOD PROVIDES NUTRIENTS AND ENERGY FOR USE AND STORAGE

The body requires a large variety of nutrients, in addition to water, oxygen, minerals, and vitamins. Carbohydrates, fats, and proteins are responsible for the energy, repair, and growth of the body. The following list shows some of the common foods in which these nutrients are found.

- Carbohydrates, the source of simple sugars such as glucose, are found in fruits, vegetables, and grains.
- Fats, which provide fatty acids, come from meat, fish, poultry, dairy products, oils, and shortenings.
- Proteins, the source of amino acids, come from lean meat and fish, low-fat dairy products, nuts, and legumes (peas, beans, lentils).

As shown in Figure 6.2, digestion begins in the mouth and terminates with the excretion of the waste products at the end of the large intestine. The major way-stations of the process are:

1. Mouth. Site of chewing of food into smaller pieces and addition of saliva that acts as a lubricant and contains enzymes to begin the digestive process.

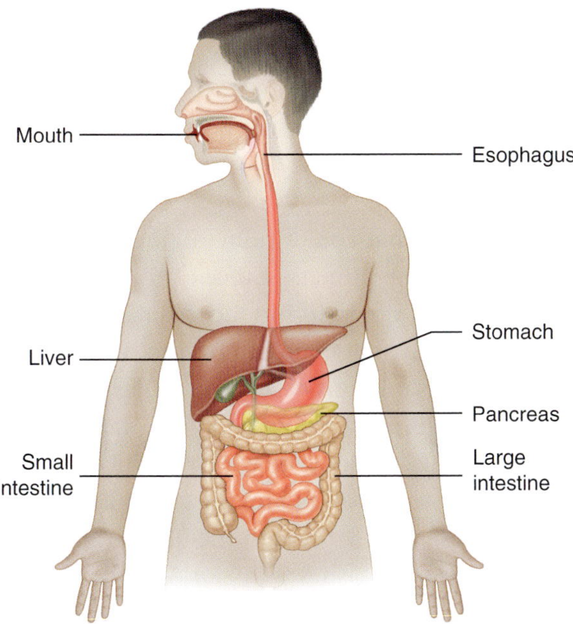

Figure 6.2 Digestion. Food enters the mouth and passes through the esophagus on the way to the stomach. After breakdown by acid in the stomach, the food moves to the small intestine where enzymes (including those from the pancreas) help digest fats, carbohydrates, and protein. The nutrients enter the bloodstream to reach cells throughout the body. Water and some minerals are absorbed in the large intestine.

2. Esophagus. A tube to transport the food from the mouth to the stomach.
3. Stomach. An initial storage area for food. Acids in the stomach begin the breakdown of food (and destroy most bacteria). The acidity in the stomach is so strong that if you were to place your finger inside the stomach, it would be broken down as well. The partially digested food is sent from the stomach to the small intestine.
4. Small intestine. A number of enzymes, including those supplied by the *pancreas*, help to break down food particles in the small intestine into even smaller particles. In this way, carbohydrates, fats, and protein are digested as they pass through the stomach and small intestines. Nutrients from the digested food pass from the small intestine into the bloodstream so that they can be transported throughout the body.
5. Large intestine. Water and some minerals are absorbed here, and the waste material from the digestive process is stored here until it is excreted from the body.

Since the brain and much of the rest of the body are continuously active, whether waking or asleep, there is a constant need for energy. Eating provides us with energy for immediate use and for storage. Most of the energy used by the body in a typical day is used just for **basal metabolism**, that is, to keep all of the cells of the body functioning and to keep the body warm while we are at rest. (We will return to consider basal metabolism when we consider weight loss strategies below.) Additional energy is used when we are physically active. When we take in more energy (calories) from food than we spend in basal metabolism and physical activity, the body can store energy for future use. The body stores energy in different ways for use in the short-term (within hours) versus longer-term storage.

6.2.1 Short-Term Storage

The brain runs on **glucose**, a sugar that comes primarily from carbohydrates in the diet. Glucose provides the primary source of energy to cells. Once inside a cell, glucose is broken down to produce a small molecule called **ATP**, which provides the energy that maintains the activity of cells, including neurons. A single cell uses millions of ATP molecules every second! Each molecule of glucose that is broken down provides the cell with many ATP molecules. To use a money analogy, imagine the glucose molecule as a $10 bill, an ATP molecule as a quarter, and the cell as a machine that can only use quarters. Glucose travels through the bloodstream and enters cells. But once it enters, the cell "cashes it in" for ATP, the form of energy that it can use.

Notice that glucose can only provide energy after it has moved out of the bloodstream and *entered* a cell. For cells outside the brain, glucose can only enter the cell with the help of the hormone **insulin**. As shown in Figure 6.3A, the membrane surrounding cells contains receptors for insulin, and insulin traveling through the bloodstream can bind to the insulin receptor. When it does, the cell sends a signal instructing its own DNA to produce more glucose transporter proteins. The glucose transporters insert themselves into the cell membrane and help move glucose from the bloodstream into the cell. When insulin levels are high and many glucose transporters are produced, glucose enters cells rapidly, providing them with large amounts of energy (ultimately, ATP).

But where does the insulin come from? There is always at least a low level of insulin in the blood, enough for small amounts of glucose to enter cells. However, after you eat a carbohydrate-rich meal (say, a large stack of pancakes) and blood glucose levels surge, the pancreas senses the glucose elevation, and releases extra insulin into the bloodstream (see Figure 6.3B). High insulin levels are glucose's "ticket" to enter the cells. Under these conditions of high glucose, the liver stores excess glucose as large molecules of **glycogen**, which is made of many branches of sugar. Glycogen is a way of efficiently saving up extra glucose.

After about 5 hours without eating, the pancreas senses a drop in glucose levels and releases the hormone **glucagon** into the bloodstream (again, see Figure 6.3B). When glucagon arrives to the liver, it essentially announces: "energy sources are low, so let's dip into our savings." Specifically, glucagon signals the liver to convert glycogen back to glucose, and to release glucose into the bloodstream so it can provide other cells with energy. An advantage of glycogen for short-term energy storage is that it is quickly converted back to glucose. This allows the body to maintain relatively stable levels of glucose in the bloodstream even during delays between meals.

Glucose moves from the blood directly into brain cells without the help of insulin. In this sense, the brain is a *privileged* site – it's first at the glucose dinner table. Of all parts of the body, the brain uses the most energy and can least afford to go without energy. Therefore, even when blood glucose levels are low and the pancreas stops releasing insulin, the brain is still able to consume glucose. Insulin is only needed for glucose to enter peripheral cells, not brain cells.

6.2.2 Long-Term Storage

Most of the body's energy is stored as fat. A disadvantage of fat for energy storage is that, compared to glycogen, fat is only slowly converted to usable forms of energy. But fat also has some advantages for energy storage.

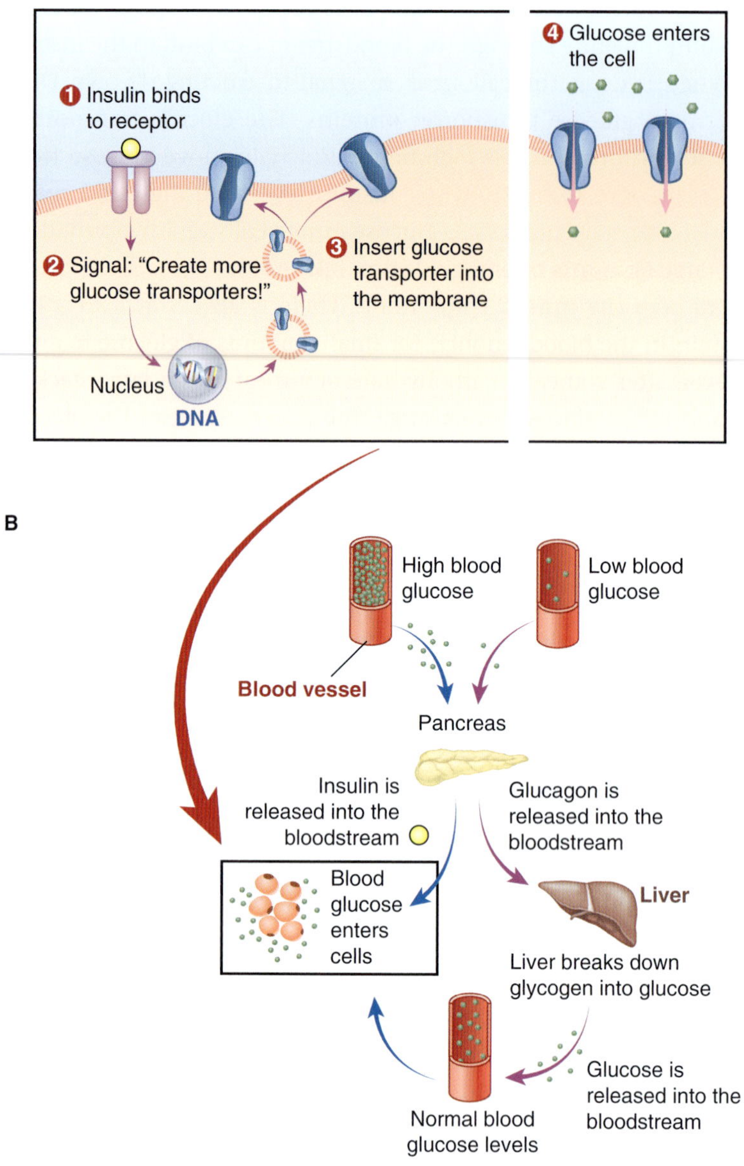

Figure 6.3 Insulin and glucagon regulate glucose entry into cells. (A) Insulin receptors are located on the cell membrane. When insulin (yellow circle) binds to its receptor, the cell increases production of glucose transporters, which permit glucose to enter the cell. (B) When glucose levels are high, the pancreas releases insulin, promoting glucose entry from the bloodstream into cells. When glucose levels are low, the pancreas releases glucagon, promoting breakdown of glycogen to glucose in the liver, and release of glucose into the blood.

A single gram of fat stores twice as much energy (ATP molecules) as a gram of glycogen. In addition, glycogen attracts a great deal of water, and the water and glycogen are stored together. This combination of glycogen with water adds weight to the stored molecules. If you were to depend upon glycogen to store all the energy you currently store as fat, you would weigh hundreds of additional pounds. Despite its slow conversion to energy, fat is therefore a highly efficient form of energy storage. It is for this reason that migrating birds accumulate large fat reserves before they begin their journey across continents.

Molecules of fat are stored inside **adipose cells** or "fat cells." Inside these cells, **fatty acids** bind with a glycerol molecule, and together they make up a **triglyceride**. Most cells outside of the brain can use free fatty acids as fuel, but this requires that the fatty acids be freed from the glycerol (Figure 6.4). This is what happens when glucose is low. Sensing low blood glucose, the pancreas releases glucagon (as we saw earlier), which sends a signal to the adipose cells to break their triglycerides into free fatty acids, and to release the free fatty acids into the bloodstream.

The free fatty acids enter the bloodstream but do not pass the blood–brain barrier (or pass only in extremely small quantities), and the brain lacks enzymes needed to extract energy from the fatty acids. As we saw earlier, the brain gets its energy almost entirely from glucose. However, there is an exception. During starvation, when no glucose is available, the liver begins to produce **ketones**, molecules formed from the breakdown of fatty acids. While fatty acids don't readily pass the blood–brain barrier, ketones do. They can be used by the brain (both neurons and glia) when no glucose is available.

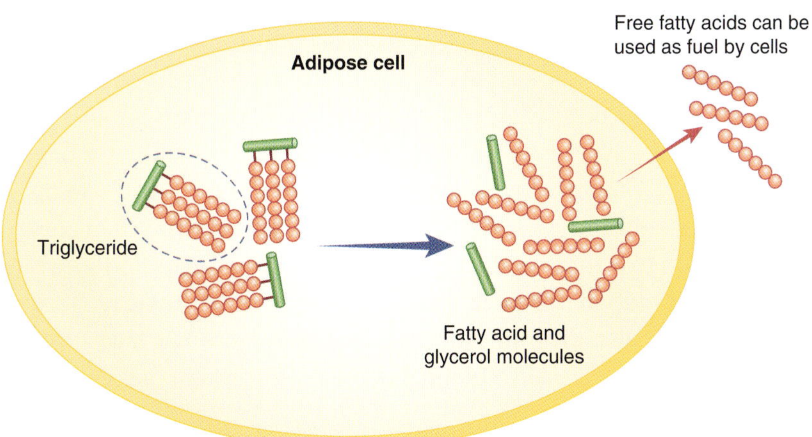

Figure 6.4 The breakdown of fat into fatty acids. Adipose (fat) cells store fat as triglycerides. When energy resources are low, triglycerides are broken down, liberating free fatty acids, which can be used as fuel by many cells outside the brain.

KEY CONCEPTS

- Beginning in the mouth and ending in the large intestine, a series of processes permit food to be digested and absorbed into the bloodstream.
- The brain and the rest of the body require energy to function. Most of the body's energy comes from the breakdown of glucose derived from carbohydrates. Inside the cells, glucose is broken down to produce energy-rich ATP molecules.
- In the short term, glucose can be stored in the liver as glycogen, and easily converted back to glucose when needed.
- For longer-term usage, excess glucose is stored as triglycerides inside adipose cells throughout the body. When energy is needed, fatty acids are liberated from the triglycerides and used as fuel in the periphery of the body.

TEST YOURSELF

1. What are the main sites of the digestive process, and what functions are carried out at each of them?
2. Glucose can only provide energy after it has moved out of the bloodstream and *entered* a cell. For cells outside the brain, the hormone _____ helps glucose to enter cells. *How* does this hormone increase glucose entry into cells?
3. Why is fat such an efficient form of long-term energy storage?

6.3 DOES HOMEOSTASIS COMPLETELY DETERMINE WHEN WE EAT?

From what we've just discussed, it might seem simple to formulate a homeostatic theory of feeding and body weight regulation. For instance, the body might sense levels of glucose circulating through the bloodstream as a thermometer senses heat. When glucose is low (*error detection*), the organism might receive a signal to eat (*response element*). When energy levels are raised to a threshold level (*set point*), eating might end (*negative feedback*). That's when the organism would experience **satiety** (feeling full). This idea that a drop in blood glucose below normal levels causes hunger and that an increase in blood glucose produces satiety is called the **glucostatic theory**.

The **lipostatic theory** also holds that the brain monitors energy levels and triggers hunger when energy levels drop. But according to this homeostatic theory, hunger is triggered by a drop in energy stored as fat (*error *detection*). When fat storage is restored to its *set point*, eating stops (*negative feedback*) and the individual feels full. Evidence exists to support both the glucostatic and lipostatic theories. As we will see below, changes in both glucose and fat levels *do* influence hunger and satiety. The brain must therefore have some way of knowing whether glucose and fat levels are high, low, or at their normal set point. In the next section, we will discuss some of the signals that inform the brain about energy needs.

However, homeostatic theories alone cannot explain all conditions that lead us to eat. From a purely homeostatic perspective, your desire for a calorie-filled piece of strawberry shortcake should only occur when energy resources are low. But imagine that you have finished a large meal of steak, potatoes, and salad. Your blood is now filled with glucose, and your adipose cells have full stores of fat. In this case, you eat dessert for reasons other than homeostasis. You expect it to taste good, and you sometimes eat for pleasure. Another reason may be that your friends have gone to the trouble of baking the cake and you don't want to disappoint them by passing on it. Sometimes, we eat for reasons that have nothing to do with either homeostasis or reward expectation. For instance, if we customarily eat dessert after dinner, we may eat a piece of cake placed in front of us merely out of habit. We will explore some of the physiological and psychological, or cognitive, reasons for eating (or refraining from eating) in the next section.

6.4 PHYSIOLOGICAL, EMOTIONAL, AND COGNITIVE SIGNALS TELL THE BRAIN TO START OR STOP EATING

Why do we eat at the moments we eat? Do we wait for physiological hunger signals to tell the brain that we are low on nutrients? Do we eat at lunchtime when others eat, regardless of our physiological state? Do we eat when we see or smell our favorite food regardless of hunger level or time of day? As we will see, physiological, emotional, and cognitive signals can combine to regulate when we eat and when we refrain from eating.

6.4.1 Physiological Signals

Neurons in some brain regions sense levels of glucose. Many of these glucose-responsive neurons are in the hypothalamus. Some become activated when glucose concentrations increase; others fire more when glucose drops. However, glucose levels in the brain are not the same as those in the periphery of the body. In order to know whether we should eat, the brain also needs to know about energy levels in the periphery of the body, and whether or not the stomach is filled with new sources of energy (food) on their way to the body.

When the stomach is empty, a peptide hormone called **ghrelin** is released from the stomach into the bloodstream (Figure 6.5). Ghrelin is sometimes called "the hunger hormone" (Williams & Elmquist, 2012). After several hours without eating, levels of ghrelin in the bloodstream correlate with feelings of hunger, and injections of ghrelin produce feelings of hunger (Klok, Jakobsdottir, & Drent, 2007). The hypothalamus contains ghrelin receptors. When these receptors are activated in rodents,

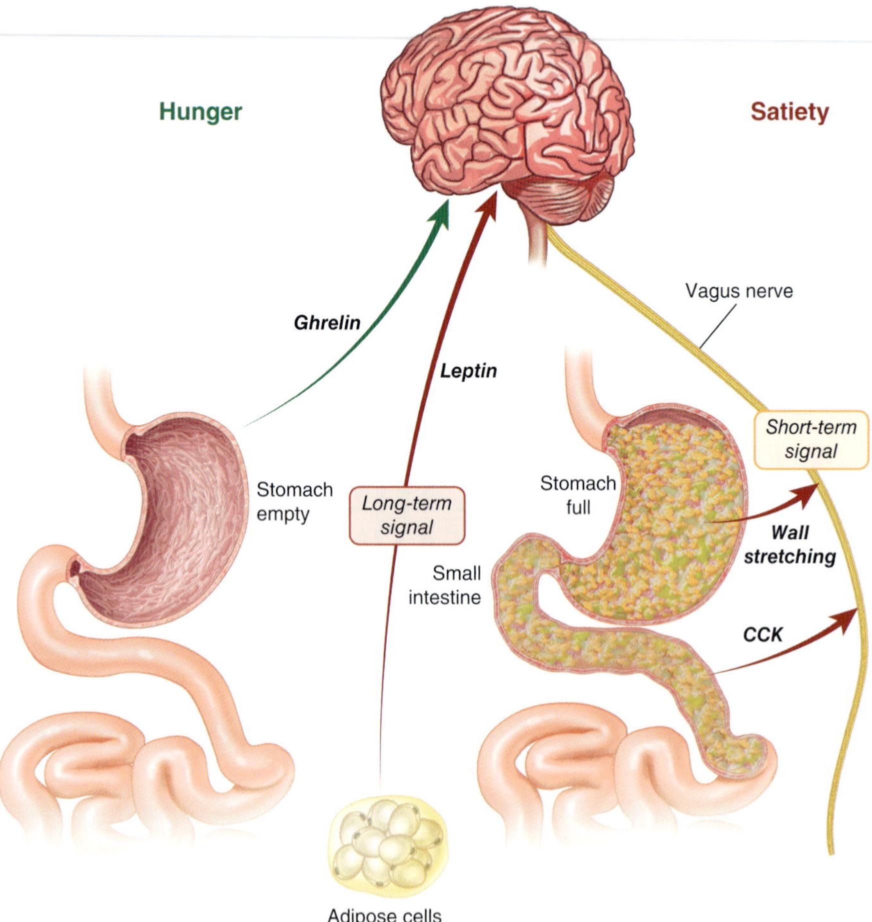

Figure 6.5 **Peripheral signals communicate with the brain's hunger and satiety circuits**. When the stomach is empty, ghrelin carries a hunger signal to the brain. When the stomach is full, the stomach wall stretches and sends a satiety signal through the vagus nerve to the brain. As food enters the small intestine, cholecystokinin (CCK) is released, carrying an additional satiety signal to the brain through the vagus nerve. A longer-term satiety signal comes from the hormone leptin which is released in response to fat accumulation in adipose cells.

the animals begin to eat. Mice lacking ghrelin receptors eat relatively little and are lean. As you might expect, individuals on a diet release higher levels of ghrelin into the bloodstream. This physiological signal, and the resulting hunger sensations, are likely factors that make dieting difficult.

If ghrelin triggers hunger and eating, how does the brain know when to *stop* eating? As food fills the stomach, it stretches, stimulating receptors in the stomach wall. This provides one of the initial signals for satiety: "I feel like I'm going to burst if I eat any more!" The vagus nerve, which transmits many signals between the internal organs and the brain, informs the brain about the stretch of the stomach and contributes to feelings of satiety (Figure 6.5).

However, the amount of stretch does not carry the complete message about when it's time to stop eating. You would not be satisfied if your dinner tonight consisted of a half-gallon of water, which would certainly stretch the stomach and provide that "full feeling." There are also a large number of satiety signals sent to the brain regarding the type of nutrient and the nutritional value of the food you consume. One of the most important chemical signals is released by food entering the small intestine. As food enters the intestines for digestion, the peptide hormone **cholecystokinin (CCK)** stimulates the vagus nerve to send a satiety signal to the brain. The vagus nerve is therefore sensitive to stomach distension and CCK levels, as well as other factors related to food consumption. It communicates these satiety signals to the brain, and reduces food consumption.

Other satiety signals operate over a longer time scale. The most important of these is the hormone **leptin** (Zhang et al., 1994), which is released mostly from adipose cells (again, see Figure 6.5). The more fat in the cells, the more leptin is released into the bloodstream. When leptin reaches the brain, it signals that enough fat is stored throughout the body. However, fat accumulates gradually over time, so leptin cannot be responsible for feeling full immediately after eating a meal. While the vagus nerve responds to stomach stretch and CCK to generate a rapid satiety signal to the brain, the leptin signal for satiety operates over a longer time scale. As leptin levels rise, food consumption decreases and energy metabolism (calories burned) increases. Leptin prevents fat accumulation from getting out of control.

Humans born with a leptin deficiency (*congenital leptin deficiency*) are constantly hungry and become obese. Treatment with leptin reduces their hunger, increases their physical activity and metabolism, and allows them to lose weight (Klok, Jakobsdottir, & Drent, 2007). Similarly, mice lacking the gene for leptin gain more than three times the weight of normal mice (Figure 6.6). The missing gene is referred to as the *ob* or obesity gene. (The symbol or abbreviation for a gene is always in italics

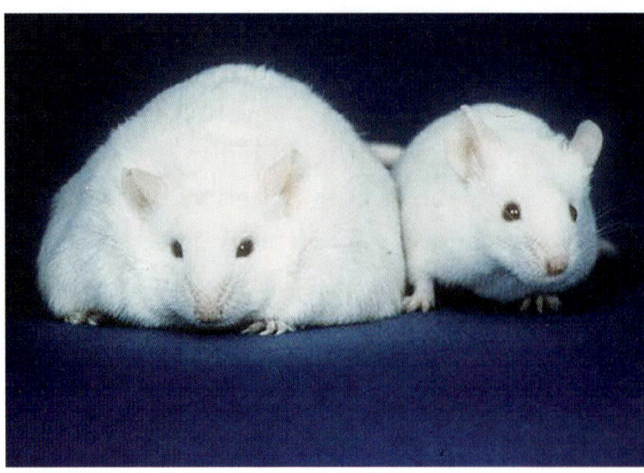

Figure 6.6 Mice lacking the *ob* gene become obese. The mouse on the left is missing the *ob* gene that normally produces leptin. Without leptin, fat accumulates because the animal receives no long-term satiety signal. (commons.wikimedia.org/wiki/File:Fatmouse.jpg.)

and lowercase.) Just remember that the *ob* gene normally releases leptin, and leptin normally reduces fat accumulation. When the *ob* gene is missing (or disrupted), the lack of leptin leads to obesity. Leptin is produced in adipose cells, but it travels to the brain and binds to receptors on cells in the hypothalamus where it tells the hypothalamus that "Peripheral stores of fat are in plentiful supply. We can stop eating now!" Like humans deficient in leptin release, mice lacking leptin receptors become obese (Williams & Elmquist, 2012).

6.4.2 Emotional and Cognitive Signals

Eating does not depend only on the powerful brain signals for hunger and satiety discussed above. As mentioned earlier, we also eat foods that we expect to be palatable (tasty, rewarding). We may describe eating for enjoyment as an emotional rather than physiological cause of eating, but of course the experience of reward also depends upon neurobiological processes (examined in Chapter 11).

We may also acquire the habit of eating when exposed to particular cues (environments, times of day, smells) that we associate with eating. If we often eat (say cookies) in a train, the sights, sounds, and smells of the train may become *conditioned stimuli* that trigger eating. (See Chapter 11 for further discussion of conditioned stimuli.) More precisely, the conditioned stimuli of the train may trigger a *desire* or *craving* for the cookies, and it is that strong desire that leads you to eat. When a heroin user is exposed to a particular street corner previously associated with taking the drug, the cue may become a conditioned stimulus that triggers a drug craving. In the same way, cues associated with eating may come to trigger a food craving (Jansen, 1998).

We sometimes exert cognitive control to restrain ourselves from eating, for instance when on a diet. It may be more difficult to restrain ourselves when we feel sad, angry, or anxious (Cardi, Leppanen, & Treasure, 2015). Even positive emotions can reduce self-restraint and increase food consumption. In general, those trying to *restrain* themselves from eating, so-called "restrained eaters," eat more when they are emotional. On the other hand, emotions may have no effect on eating or even reduce it in people who simply eat when hungry and stop eating when satiated ("non-restrained eaters"). Strong emotions may cause restrained eaters to eat more because it distracts them from the self-control they need to keep from eating (Lattimore & Caswell, 2004).

KEY CONCEPTS

- **A key trigger for hunger is the release of ghrelin from the gut.**
- **Short-term satiety signals include increased stomach contents, and the release of CCK by the intestines.**
- **Longer-term satiety depends upon leptin released from fat cells in the body.**
- **We also eat for cognitive and emotional reasons. For instance, the pleasurable qualities of certain foods motivate us to eat even when we're not hungry. Also, emotional stimuli may distract us from the self-control that normally restrains eating.**

TEST YOURSELF

1. **What are the glucostatic and lipostatic theories of hunger? These kinds of theories do not account for some factors that drive us to eat. Explain.**
2. **How does the brain know when the stomach is empty?**
3. **Describe some evidence that ghrelin provides a "hunger signal" to the brain.**
4. **What abnormalities are seen in people born with a leptin deficiency? How do you explain these abnormalities?**
5. **Give two examples of how cognitive and/or emotional signals may influence eating.**

6.5 THE HYPOTHALAMUS IS A KEY BRAIN STRUCTURE FOR HUNGER AND SATIETY

Up to this point, we have discussed digestion, nutrients, and some of the important physiological and cognitive factors that influence hunger and satiety. We now turn our attention to the critical role of the brain in our motivation to eat. Much of the important processing of hunger and satiety signals is carried out by evolutionarily older portions of the CNS. Neurons in the brainstem and hypothalamus are particularly important in these basic motivational states (Woods, 1964; Lyon, Halpern, & Mintz, 1968). The continued involvement of these brain regions through evolution should come as no surprise because of the dependency on eating for the maintenance of life.

Research in the first half of the twentieth century established that the hypothalamus was critical for several aspects of eating and weight regulation. Destruction of the lateral portion of the hypothalamus resulted in dramatic reductions in eating, weight loss, and death (Anand & Brobeck, 1951), while destruction of other areas of the hypothalamus led to overeating (hyperphagia) and weight gain (Hetherington & Ranson, 1940). These results suggested that the lateral hypothalamus was important for hunger and eating and other hypothalamic areas were important for satiety; scientists of that era did not know what physiological mechanisms underlay these changes.

Discoveries from the 1970s to the end of the twentieth century showed that molecules such as ghrelin, CCK, and leptin are released from the periphery of the body during hunger or satiety. As we saw, some of these substances enter the bloodstream and bind to receptors in the hypothalamus. Others indirectly signal to the hypothalamus via the vagus nerve. Most researchers now agree that the hypothalamus is the primary brain region responsible for regulating feeding. Let's consider how peripheral signals for hunger and satiety interact with hypothalamic and brainstem regions to influence the motivation to eat.

Imagine that you have been invited to your friend's house for a 6:00 p.m. dinner to celebrate her birthday. Her father has prepared a five-course meal. At the start of dinner, your stomach is empty and blood glucose levels are low. Glucose-sensitive neurons in various areas of the hypothalamus detect your low glucose levels. In the meantime, your empty stomach releases high levels of ghrelin into your bloodstream. The **arcuate nucleus** of the hypothalamus contains receptors for ghrelin, and it interprets the current flood of ghrelin molecules as a message that your stomach contains no food. The arcuate nucleus, in turn, communicates with another area of the hypothalamus called the **lateral hypothalamus** (**LH**), which is important in stimulating hunger, food-seeking behaviors, and eating (see Figure 6.7).

When you have finished the meal and can't eat another bite, the vagus nerve sends satiety signals to the **solitary nucleus** in the medulla. From there, the information is passed to the arcuate nucleus, which, in turn, signals the **paraventricular nucleus** (**PVN**) of the hypothalamus, which is important in satiety (again, see Figure 6.7).

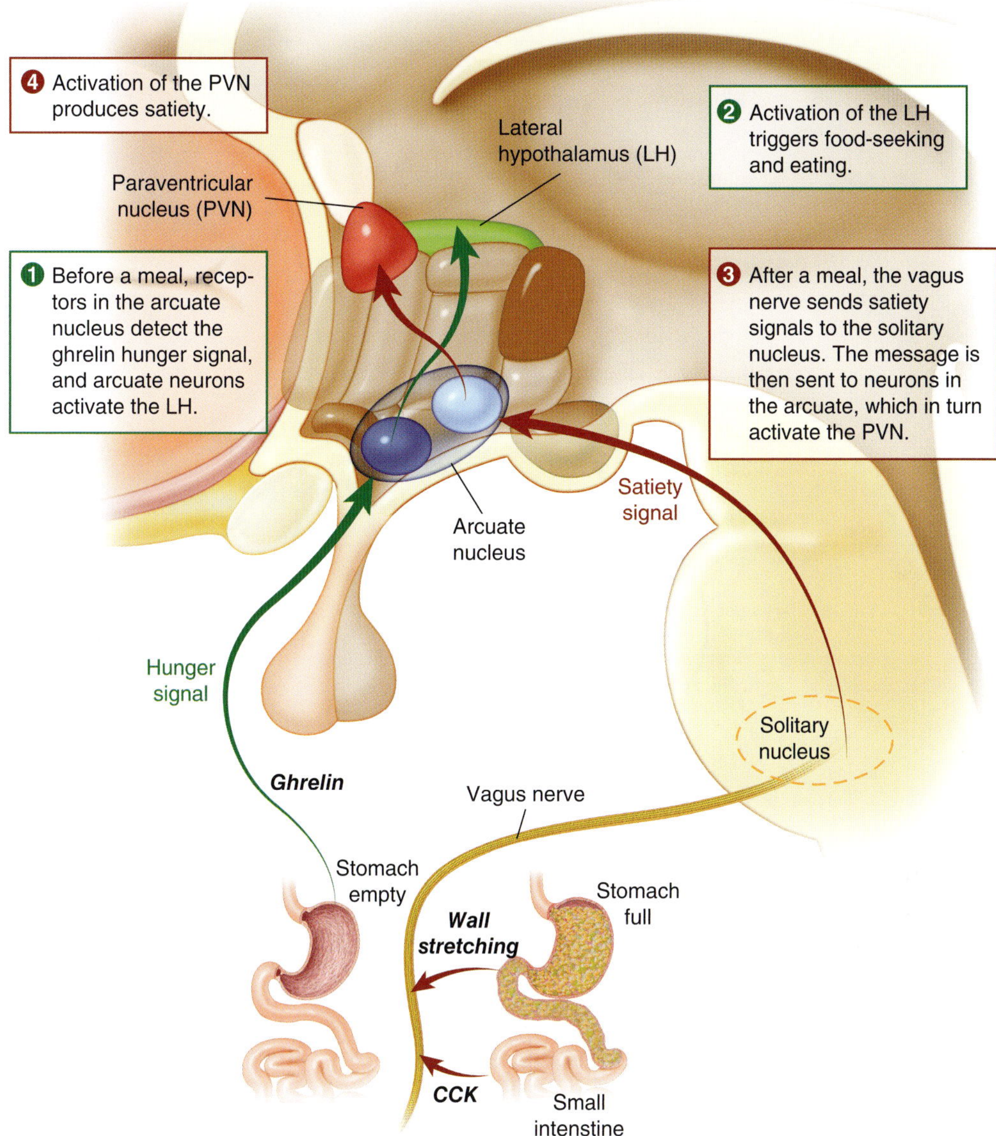

Figure 6.7 Hypothalamic signals of hunger and satiety. A set of neurons in the arcuate nucleus of the hypothalamus activates the lateral hypothalamus (LH) before a meal to signal hunger. A separate set of arcuate neurons activates the paraventricular nucleus (PVN) after a meal to signal satiety.

The arcuate nucleus therefore contains one set of neurons that signals the LH to start eating (let's call these the arcuate "hunger" neurons), and another set that signals to the PVN to stop eating (let's call these the arcuate "satiety" neurons). As shown in Figure 6.8, the arcuate "hunger" neurons release **neuropeptide Y** (**NPY**). This neurochemical excites the LH neurons, increasing the urge to eat. But notice in the figure that

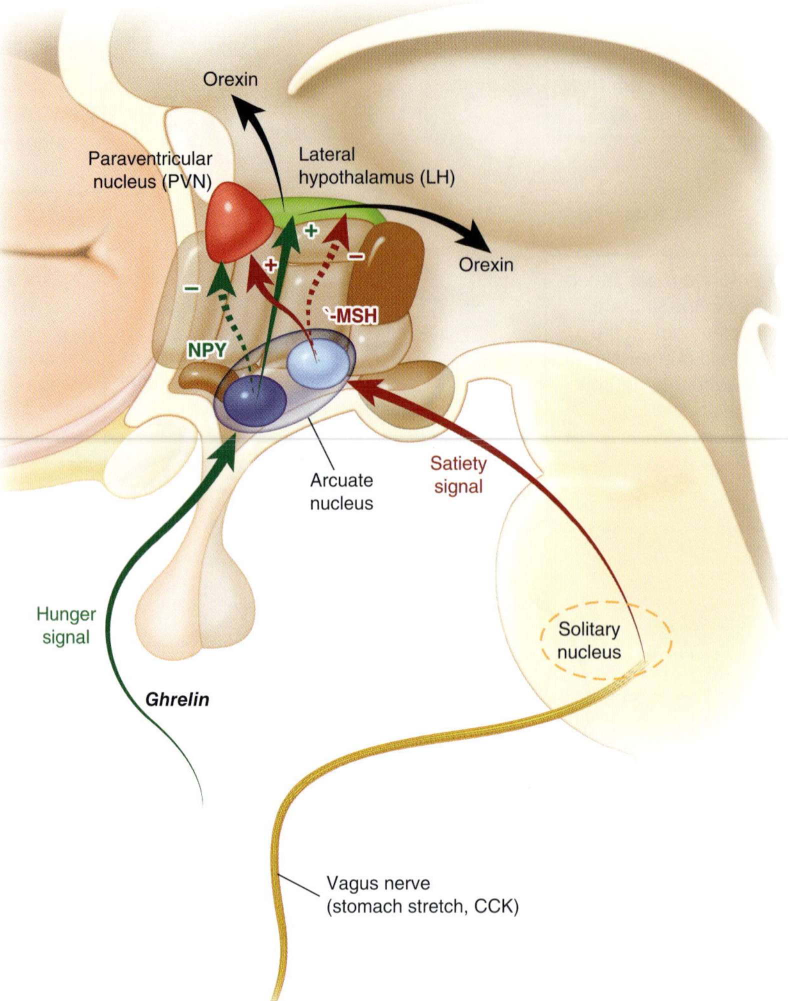

Figure 6.8 Neurochemicals signaling hunger and satiety. One set of arcuate neurons responds to peripheral hunger signals by releasing neuropeptide Y (NPY), which excites the lateral hypothalamus (promoting eating) and inhibits the paraventricular nucleus (reducing satiety). Another set of arcuate neurons responds to peripheral satiety signals by releasing alpha-melanocyte-stimulating hormone (α-MSH) to activate the paraventricular nucleus and inhibit the lateral hypothalamus. The lateral hypothalamus neurons contain the hunger-producing neurotransmitter orexin.

neuropeptide Y inhibits the PVN. The arcuate "hunger" neurons therefore activate the LH to stimulate hunger, and also inhibit the PVN to turn off satiety circuits. The arcuate "satiety" neurons have a similar dual action. They release **alpha melanocyte-stimulating hormone** (**α-MSH**) to excite the PVN (satiety) neurons. At the same time, they release α-MSH to the LH to inhibit hunger.

Another chemical that increases eating is the peptide **orexin**. The appetite-stimulating orexin is contained within neurons of the LH. (This same neurochemical was later discovered to also be important in states of waking and arousal, as we saw in Chapter 5). "Orexis" means appetite in Greek, and anorexia means lack of appetite. Orexin and other neurochemicals that stimulate hunger are referred to as **orexigenic**. Those that reduce appetite are referred to as **anorexigenic**. We have seen that ghrelin, neuropeptide Y, and orexin are orexigenic neurochemicals, while CCK, leptin, and α-MSH are anorexigenic.

Let us return once again to the hunger and satiety signals occurring before and after dinner (Figure 6.8). Ghrelin released from your empty stomach activates "hunger" neurons in the arcuate nucleus of the hypothalamus. These arcuate neurons activate the LH. Many of the LH neurons contain orexin, and release the peptide to a number of other brain areas that contribute to your drive to eat. Now, bread is placed on the table. Despite your hunger, and the high activation of LH neurons releasing orexin, you try not to fill up on the bread. You may need to use your prefrontal cortex to inhibit eating when hunger signals are strong (see Chapter 4). After you have eaten, arcuate "satiety" neurons inhibit the LH neurons, while simultaneously activating the PVN. Their combined effects reduce your drive to eat more. As you've seen, leptin also reduces hunger, but leptin levels won't rise until about 4 hours after the meal. So, leptin won't signal that the meal has filled you up, but it may reduce your urge to eat in the middle of the night.

Before leaving the physiological mechanisms that influence the state of hunger, let us review the two branches of the autonomic nervous system (ANS) which exert overarching, modulatory control on these processes. Eating and digestion of food is one of the major functions of the parasympathetic branch of the ANS (often referred to as the "rest and digest" functions, see Chapter 1). Parasympathetic activity is associated with food consumption, which permits the body to fuel up on energy, and in some cases, to store it as fat for future use. In contrast, when there is an increased need for energy, for example during exercise or a looming threat, the sympathetic branch of the ANS, often termed "fight or flight" (or, in humans, "fight, flight and worry") is called to action. The sympathetic nervous system shuts down the processes related to feeding and digestion. Have you ever noticed that you lose your appetite when you become anxious or frightened? When your brain believes a threat is imminent, the sympathetic nervous system tells the body that this is no time for a meal. While stress reduces eating in most animals, an exception to this was noted above for humans actively restraining themselves from eating (stress can cause a person to fall off their diet and therefore to eat more). This exception aside, activity of the sympathetic nervous system reduces food consumption.

KEY CONCEPTS

- **Some neurons in the arcuate nucleus of the hypothalamus contain receptors for the orexigenic (appetite-stimulating) hormone ghrelin. These "hunger" neurons in the arcuate release neuropeptide Y to activate the lateral hypothalamus.**
- **Other neurons in the arcuate nucleus respond to satiety signals and release α-MSH to stimulate the PVN and reduce eating.**
- **The autonomic nervous system also modulates eating and digestion. The sympathetic nervous system reduces these activities in response to emergency situations.**

TEST YOURSELF

1. **Describe the key hypothalamic nuclei involved in hunger and satiety.**
2. **Which hypothalamic nucleus releases neuropeptide Y and alpha melanocyte-stimulating hormone? How do these neurochemicals contribute to hunger and satiety?**
3. **Describe how autonomic nervous system (ANS) activity influences hunger and satiety.**

6.6 VARIOUS FACTORS INFLUENCE BODY WEIGHT

Simple math gives us an insight into body weight maintenance: Calories consumed – calories expended = remaining calories (which are mostly stored in fat cells). However, weight regulation is more complex than it seems. People trying to lose weight often find it difficult to do so. Some studies in animals and humans attempted to have subjects either gain or lose weight by overfeeding or underfeeding them. When the subjects resumed their normal diet, body weights returned precisely to their pre-experimental level (Cohn & Joseph, 1962; Sims & Horton, 1968). This gave rise to the idea that body weight has a set point. Despite temporary increases or decreases, bodily mechanisms kick in to return our weight to its set point. These mechanisms may include complex interactions between nutrient selection, the functioning of the digestive organs, and metabolic responses that turn nutrients from the diet into energy. These, in turn, depend upon a combination of hormonal, environmental, and genetic factors (Harris, 1990).

An interesting perspective on weight regulation was proposed by Wirtshafter and Davis (1977). They argued that weight is *not* fixed rigidly at a set point. After all, body weight can change considerably under some natural conditions such as pregnancy, hibernation, and migration. If weight hovered around a "set point" before these events, these and other life events were able to move the set point considerably. In contrast to the predictions of set point theory, various factors can shift body weight away from its current level to another level.

Imagine a person who eats a healthy, balanced diet (including moderate amounts of protein, carbohydrate and fat, with plenty of fruits and vegetables), and his weight stabilizes at a particular level. Now, he changes his diet so that it consists largely of McDonald's Whoppers, French fries, and soda, with a high-fat, high-sugar dessert at the end. If he sticks with this kind of diet for a while, his weight will move far from what seemed to be his "set point." Wirtshafter and Davis argued that the most important factor involved in weight gain is the palatability of the diet. Studies in rats clearly show that a chronic, high-fat, highly palatable diet leads to a long-term and potentially stable elevated weight level.

This leads us back to the issue of seeking out food rewards that we encountered earlier. How can we feel full and satisfied at the end of a meal and then long for a slice of chocolate layer cake? Our desire to eat is not governed by homeostatic processes alone; it is also influenced by the reward value we expect to receive from the foods available to us. As discussed in Chapter 11, dopamine and opioid systems in the brain play a key role in motivating us to search for palatable foods, and in the pleasurable (hedonic) experience of consuming them.

6.7 OBESITY IS A MODERN EPIDEMIC WITH MANY CAUSES AND FEW EASY CURES

So far, we have discussed some of the factors that contribute to the initiation and cessation of eating. We turn now to an issue of relevance for human health, obesity. While cultural factors influence our views of the "ideal" body weight and what it means to be "overweight," there are nevertheless clear health risks associated with too much body weight.

6.7.1 How Much Body Weight Is Too Much?

Standards for body weight vary across historical periods and are influenced by social factors (as with other physical attributes like being tall

Figure 6.9 Ideals of female body weight are subject to cultural influence. Compare the ideal feminine body shape depicted by the seventeenth-century painter Peter Paul Rubens to that represented by a more recent model.
(Left, Rubens' *The Three Graces*; right, © CoffeeAndMilk/Getty Images.)

or hairy). For example, look at the many paintings of nude women by the seventeenth-century Flemish artist Peter Paul Rubens (Figure 6.9, left). These depictions of beautiful women of the day certainly don't look like most of today's models, actresses, or women featured in ads. Today, heavy body weight may be considered a positive attribute in some professions such as weightlifting. Body weight standards also vary in people of different races, nationalities, religions, or regions. Throughout history, being overweight was often a feature of royalty and indicative of belonging to the leisured class. These and many other examples show that there is no absolute, universally accepted standard for ideal body weight.

This does not mean, however, that heavy body weight is never a cause for concern. Obesity is increasing rapidly in the USA and throughout most of the industrialized world (World Health Organization, 2019). Why worry? The many adverse health consequences of obesity are serious. Obesity compromises the normal functioning of many organs and other physiological processes of the body. It is therefore not surprising that obesity shortens life expectancy. Next to tobacco use, it is the second leading cause of preventable death in the United States. Consider the leading cause of death in the USA – heart disease. In coronary heart disease (the most common form of heart disease), plaque builds up in the arteries of the heart. Over time, the plaque hardens and narrows the arteries, reducing the flow of oxygen-rich blood. In some cases, blood flow may be blocked completely. Obesity increases the risk of coronary heart disease by over 70 percent (Rimm et al., 1995). Obesity also increases the risk of high blood pressure, type 2 diabetes, and other diseases.

The **body mass index** (**BMI**) is the scale currently used by the USA and the World Health Organization to categorize an individual as underweight, normal weight, overweight, or obese. In Figure 6.10, the numbers in each box show the healthy BMI values for individuals of various heights in green, and BMI values for those who are underweight (yellow), overweight (purple), and obese (light purple and orange). To calculate BMI, weight (in kilograms) is divided by the square of the person's height (in meters). For countries that do not use the metric system (USA, Liberia, and Myanmar) the equation is: weight (pounds) ÷ height^2 (inches) × 703. If you know your weight and height, you can calculate your BMI. (Try it now, but don't forget to convert your height to the correct unit such as inches, and to square that number.)

There are cases in which the BMI taken alone can lead to misleading conclusions about body fat. For instance, a well-muscled body builder is likely to have a high BMI despite having little body fat. A more objective measure of body fat, such as amount of fat as a percentage of total body weight, might be more useful.

BMI Chart

Underweight | Overweight | Healthy | Obese | Extremely obese

Weight (*lbs*)	105	115	125	135	145	155	165	175	185	195	205	215
(*kgs*)	47.7	52.3	56.8	61.4	65.9	70.5	75.0	79.5	84.1	88.6	93.2	97.7
Height (*ft'in" – cm*)												
5'0" – 152.4	20	22	24	26	28	30	32	34	36	38	40	42
5'2" – 157.4	19	21	22	24	26	28	30	32	33	35	37	39
5'4" – 162.5	18	19	21	23	24	26	28	30	31	33	35	37
5'6" – 167.6	17	18	20	21	23	25	26	28	29	31	33	34
5'8" – 172.7	16	17	19	20	22	23	25	26	28	29	31	32
5'10" – 177.8	15	16	18	19	20	22	23	25	26	28	29	30
6'0" – 182.8	14	15	17	18	19	21	22	23	25	26	27	29
6'2" – 187.9	13	14	16	17	18	19	21	22	23	25	26	27
6'4" – 193.0	12	14	15	16	17	18	20	21	22	23	25	26

Figure 6.10 Body mass index (BMI). The chart indicates BMI associated with low body weight, healthy body weight, and obesity. Notice that healthy BMI ranges differ according to an individual's height (rows).

6.7.2 Industrialization and Technology Have Contributed to Obesity

Across the animal kingdom, most species are in a near-constant quest for food. Depending on available food sources, some fail to find sufficient sources of nutrition. These unfortunate ones may live in a constant malnourished state or even die of starvation. Many species developed an adaptive response to this danger by maintaining reserve fat stores for energy in times of need. Although this energy storage process was highly adaptive, in the present day it contributes to human obesity in the industrialized world.

A broad survey of the nations of the world indicates that obesity is directly related to the dietary availability of calories. For most people in industrialized countries, food is abundantly available. Couple this with high palatability of commercially available food, ubiquitous advertising, and high-calorie content, and you have the "perfect banquet" for obesity.

In addition to ready availability of high-calorie foods, the energy expenditure required for daily work has declined. The industrial revolution in Europe beginning in the late eighteenth century freed the worker from long days spent in the fields, and provided more time and income to devote to personal enjoyments. However, it also produced a sedentary lifestyle for many people. Workers may sit for hours at typewriters or telephones. Others will sit and watch products roll off conveyor belts. The advent of television encouraged people to sit back and enjoy what was offered. Public transportation and the automobile freed people from having to walk or ride horses.

During recent decades, there has been a particularly dramatic rise in childhood and adolescent obesity in developed countries (Lee & Yoon, 2018). In the USA over the past thirty years, obesity has doubled in children, and tripled for adolescents and teenagers (Ogden, Carroll, Kit, & Flegal, 2014). Many factors have been linked to this rise. From 1994 to 2006, children and teenagers (2–18 years of age) increased the amount of calories from fast food by more than 10 percent (Vikraman, Fryar, & Ogden, 2015). The US population takes in an average of 300-plus more calories than it did in the 1970s. In fact, in the first quarter of 2016, individuals in the USA spent an average of about 10 hours daily in front of computers, televisions, video game devices, cell phones, and tablets. Beyond the reduction in physical activity associated with these sedentary activities, screen time is also linked to metabolic changes that themselves promote weight gain (Mark & Janssen, 2008).

We live in a time of increased calorie consumption and reduced calorie expenditure. It is not surprising that the obesity epidemic is a modern problem. However, genetic and neurobiological factors also seem to affect an individual's chance of becoming obese.

6.7.3 Genetic, Neurobiological, and Interpersonal Factors May Contribute to Obesity

Obesity is heritable, meaning that it is passed down through generations of families. Sorenson and Stunkard (1993) reported that familial resemblance of obesity using the BMI is mainly due to genes. To separate the influence of genes from environment, they looked at adoption data. Obesity in adopted sons and daughters was unrelated to that of their adoptive parents, but was strongly related to obesity in their biological parents, particularly their biological mothers. When the contributions of genes and family environment are separated, genes appear to play the larger role in obesity (but certainly not the only role!). The influence of genes on obesity is generally assumed to be polygenetic, that is, it is the result of interactions among multiple genes. In addition, one's genetic predisposition may be influenced by eating habits and exercise (Lee & Yoon, 2018).

Further, food consumption activates midbrain dopamine neurons and high levels of dopamine release within motivation-related brain regions such as the nucleus accumbens. As you will learn in Chapter 11, drugs like cocaine and other addictive substances activate these same neurochemical pathways, which are associated with reward processing. Obesity is associated with hyper-responsiveness of these reward-related brain regions. For instance, when obese subjects were shown pictures of high-calorie foods, they showed high levels of nucleus accumbens activation compared to control subjects (Stoeckel et al., 2008). In addition to this abnormal activation of brain reward circuits while anticipating rewarding food, some obese individuals also show reduced activation of the brain's inhibitory control systems (described in Chapter 4). These inhibitory control systems normally allow us to withhold particular behaviors at times of our choosing. Drug and other addictions are similarly associated with disruption in inhibitory control systems. The neurobiology of obesity may therefore overlap with that of addictive behavior (Volkow, Wang, Fowler, & Telang, 2008).

In addition to genetic and neurobiological factors, interpersonal factors may contribute to obesity. For instance, interpersonal violence (such as physical abuse, sexual abuse, and bullying by peers) is a risk factor for the later development of obesity (Midei & Matthews, 2011). Because obese children are also more prone to bullying, it is possible that interpersonal violence increases the risk of obesity, and that obesity, in turn, increases the risk for interpersonal violence in a kind of vicious cycle.

Low self-esteem is also associated with obesity (Lee & Yoon, 2018). Again, it is possible that a vicious cycle exists in which low self-esteem contributes to obesity, which in turn lowers self-esteem. Many psychological and environmental factors are linked to obesity, but it can be difficult to disentangle those that are causes of obesity from those that are effects.

6.7.4 Treatments for Obesity

As you can tell by the large numbers of ads in the media and by the proliferation of health clubs and gyms, weight loss is a major concern and billions of dollars are spent on it every year in the USA. You might intuit that all of this effort has not been terribly effective. In general, it is relatively easy to lose weight in the short term, but harder to maintain that loss. It requires a strong commitment to a change in lifestyle that many people find difficult.

Treatment for eating disorders such as anorexia, bulimia, and binge-eating disorder typically involves psychological approaches, as discussed below. In some cases, psychological therapy may be useful as a therapy for obesity as well. However, the four approaches most often used to help obese individuals lose weight are diet, exercise, pharmacological treatments, and, in extreme instances, surgery. Let's explore these.

Diet

The simplest way to lose weight is to eat less and to eat more selectively. In most cases, weight gain results when caloric intake exceeds caloric expenditure. Several kinds of diets have been shown to be safe and effective for weight loss. These include low-carbohydrate diets (such as the Atkins diet), low-fat diets (see American Heart Association dietary guidelines), and the Mediterranean diet (rich in vegetables, low in red meat, a moderate amount of mostly monounsaturated fat, with restricted calories). Studies of the relative effectiveness of low-carbohydrate, low-fat, or Mediterranean diets in obese and moderately overweight individuals suggest that a similar amount of weight loss can be achieved with any one of these types of diets (Johnston et al., 2014; Shai, 2008). One advantage of the Mediterranean diet is that it has been shown to reduce the risk of cardiovascular disease (Bray, Fruhbeck, Ryan, & Wilding, 2016).

Health professionals recommend that those wishing to lose weight monitor food portion sizes, calories, fat intake, and body weight with common sense. It is also important to avoid using food to regulate one's own moods (Strychar, 2006). Altering one's diet is a difficult process to maintain over the long term. A universal piece of advice is to avoid extreme dietary restriction without a physician's guidance because of the potential health risks of doing so.

Exercise

Most obesity prevention strategies involve a combination of diet with increased physical activity (World Health Organization, 2019). When we refer to exercise, we mean use of muscles. When muscles contract, especially when they are used over an extended period, they derive the necessary energy from breakdown of stored fat and glycogen. The larger the muscles used, the greater the energy expended.

Let's return once again to the fundamental idea that weight gain occurs when more calories are consumed than expended. This energy imbalance can be addressed by reducing calories, increasing energy expenditure, or both. While some of the energy you expend each day comes from physical activity, you also use energy when you are not physically active. During periods of rest, your body still needs to burn calories to carry out physiological functions like pumping the heart, breathing, and maintaining the activity of neurons. How much energy is required for this background activity of the body? It depends upon your **basal metabolic rate** (**BMR**); the higher the rate, the more calories you burn while at rest. Your basal metabolic rate is responsible for most (60–75 percent) of the energy you expend each day. After about 20 years of age, basal metabolic rate declines by 1–2 percent per decade.

The basal metabolic rate depends mostly upon what is called the fat-free mass of your body. The fat-free mass includes everything in your body except for fat: internal organs, bone, muscle, water, and connective tissue. The more fat-free mass, the higher the basal metabolic rate (Cunningham, 1991). As we saw earlier, fat is an excellent source of energy *storage*. But because it burns energy very slowly, an individual with a large amount of fat will generally have a lower basal metabolic rate than a person whose body composition is made up of a larger proportion of fat-free mass. This means that exercise can contribute to weight loss in two fundamental ways. First, energy is spent through physical activity. But second, by building muscle, you increase your fat-free mass and therefore raise your basal metabolic rate. This means that you burn more calories even during periods of inactivity.

Drugs

The market for diet drugs in the USA runs into billions of dollars annually. Thousands of these drugs have been used to treat obesity but few, if any, remain successful in the long run. Because most drugs carry health risks and unwanted side effects, employing drugs chronically for weight loss should be considered only when diet and exercise have failed. A major problem with drug use is targeting the drug exclusively to the place where it is needed. Most drugs are taken systemically (orally or by injection) and therefore travel through the bloodstream to all parts of the body. Therefore, it is difficult to limit their action to a particular neuron type (say neurons in the arcuate nucleus of the hypothalamus that release α-MSH) or a particular aspect of the feeding process like satiety.

Remember that "supplements" available without a prescription do not have to prove safety or efficacy in order to be sold in stores. Some weight loss pills have been shown to be carcinogenic, some cause damage to the heart and liver, and others may present other health risks. It is therefore important to always consult with your physician before using a weight loss supplement obtained in a store or over the internet, no matter how harmless it looks from the label.

Some of the earliest diet drugs were similar to amphetamines. They increased norepinephrine and dopamine activity and reduced hunger. However, they sometimes produced cardiovascular crises, and carried the risk of addiction. They were eventually taken off the market.

Since a large body of research shows that activation of brain dopamine is a key component in the brain's reward circuitry, the idea emerged that the blockade of dopamine, by decreasing the reward (pleasurable) value of food, could act as a diet drug (Volkow et al., 2008). The problem that arises here is that we would not want to administer a drug that would reduce the reward value of *all* positive things. In addition, while drugs that block dopamine receptors strongly reduce the amount of effort an individual will exert in order to obtain food, they don't have much effect on food consumption itself (Salamone & Correa, 2012). Therefore, dopamine antagonists seem unlikely to hold promise as a diet drug.

Some diet drugs exert their effects by modulating brain serotonin activity. The drug fenfluramine, which causes the release of serotonin into the synapse, made a big splash as an effective appetite suppressant in the 1990s (Hainer, Kabrnova, Aldhoon, Kunesova, & Wagenknecht, 2006). Unfortunately, it had to be withdrawn because it produced cardiovascular problems. While other drugs targeting brain serotonin have come and gone from the marketplace, a currently approved serotonin-acting drug may hold promise for reducing weight without serious health risk.

There are currently several classes of medications that have been approved in the USA for long-term management of weight with demonstrated safety and efficacy (Pilitsi et al., 2019). The drugs interact with receptors for serotonin (Lorcaserin), opioids (Naltrexone), norepinephrine (Phentermine), and digestion-related enzymes (Liraglutide, Orlistat). Like other medications, they come with potential side effects, and no one medication works for all individuals. Those considering medication for weight management should consult their physician.

More recently, the search for diet drugs has been enlightened by the progress in the deeper understanding of specific neural mechanisms mediating feeding and satiety. This provides more localized and specific drug targets, including orexin, ghrelin, CCK, neuropeptide Y, α-MSH, and their receptors. A major disappointment to this field is the fact that while leptin plays a role in satiety and reduces eating in obese rodents and humans with genetically based leptin deficiency, leptin treatment is not effective in treating human obesity. At least for the present, the search for the elusive magic bullet continues.

Weight-Loss (Bariatric) Surgery

In cases where other treatment options have failed in persons with BMIs of 35 kg/m^2 or more, surgery is the final choice. In general, this has been shown to be quite successful, with typical weight loss of 40–50 kg (about 90–110 lb) and a relatively long-lasting result. By lowering body weight and fat stores, the surgery can also decrease type 2 diabetes and hypertension, and can lower mortality rates. But, of course, there are always dangers to undertaking any invasive surgery requiring general anesthesia.

The most common form of bariatric surgery is **gastric bypass** (see Figure 6.11). It works in two ways. First, the surgeon decreases the storage

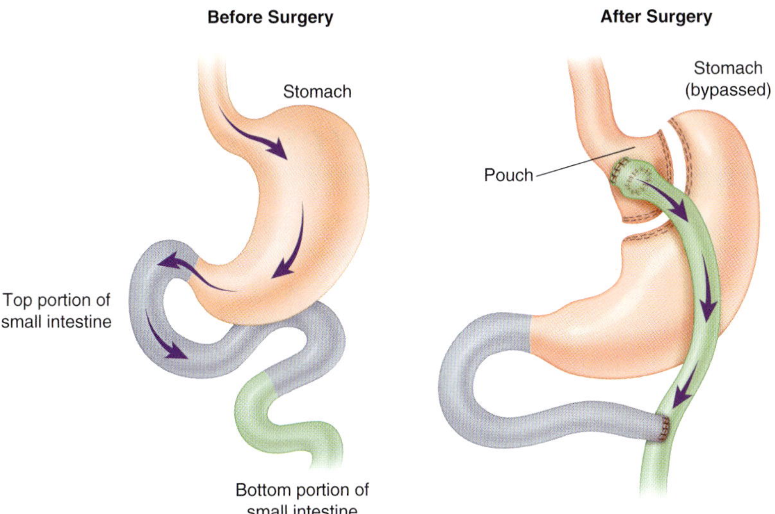

Figure 6.11 Weight loss (bariatric) surgery. In gastric bypass, the most common form of bariatric surgery, the surgeon divides a small part of the stomach (the "pouch") from the rest of the stomach. This small stomach pouch is then connected to a bottom portion of the small intestine, bypassing the rest of the stomach and much of the upper portion of the small intestine.

size of the stomach. This causes the individual to feel full sooner, and therefore to reduce meal size. Second, the surgeon connects this small stomach area (the pouch) to the bottom portion of the small intestine. In doing so, she bypasses most of the stomach and much of the upper portion of the small intestine. Because the "bypassed" part of the intestine no longer has food passing through it, few nutrients and calories are absorbed.

KEY CONCEPTS

- Societal and genetics factors play a role in obesity.
- In some obese individuals, anticipation of highly appealing food may trigger brain circuits associated with addictive behavior.
- Diet and exercise can help with weight loss.
- Many drugs have been marketed for weight loss, but most have had dangerous side effects.
- Surgery to reduce the capacity of the digestive system is effective, but there are always risks that accompany major surgery.

TEST YOURSELF

1. Describe some of the cultural factors that may contribute to obesity today.
2. Describe two ways in which exercise may help to reduce body weight.
3. What lines of evidence suggest that obesity is in part genetically controlled?

6.8 THE THREE MAIN TYPES OF EATING DISORDERS ARE ANOREXIA, BULIMIA, AND BINGE-EATING DISORDER

While many people strive to achieve a healthy weight, for some the quest becomes harmful. There are a number of disorders of body weight regulation and feeding. The three most commonly known are anorexia nervosa, bulimia nervosa (referred to here as anorexia and bulimia), and binge-eating disorder.

6.8.1 Anorexia

The case study of Penelope, which began this chapter, provides an illustrative description of this disorder. Anorexia is an intense fear of gaining weight and a disturbed body image. The fear of gaining weight motivates the person to reduce caloric intake and often to engage in excessive exercise (American Psychiatric Association, 2013). The individual with anorexia weighs less than 85 percent of that expected for someone of his or her age and sex. The severity of anorexia depends upon the individual's body mass index, ranging from mild (BMI of 17–18 kg/m^2), to moderate (BMI 16–17 kg/m^2) to extreme (BMI less than 15 kg/m^2) (again, see Figure 6.10). Despite this low body weight, the person with anorexia maintains the perception of being overweight (Figure 6.12).

It is difficult to predict who will become anorexic, and many important aspects of anorexia remain beyond our grasp:

- The cause of anorexia remains unknown. Its psychology and biology are both poorly understood.
- It is difficult to treat the disorder effectively.
- It can persist for years, with recovery often followed by relapse.

Anorexia can affect individuals of all ages, sexes, sexual orientations, and races, but adolescent girls and young adult women have the greatest risk of developing the disorder (Smink, van Hoeken, & Hoek, 2012; Nagl et al., 2016). Its prevalence is about 1 percent in women and less than 0.5 percent in men. The majority suffering from anorexia also suffer from major depressive, anxiety, and/or obsessive compulsive disorder during their lifetime.

The mortality rate is high, especially in those not receiving treatment. About 2 percent of children and 5 percent of adults suffering from anorexia die from it, usually as a result of either starvation-related medical complications or suicide. The death rate for those with anorexia is higher than for any other psychological disorder. For those diagnosed with anorexia in

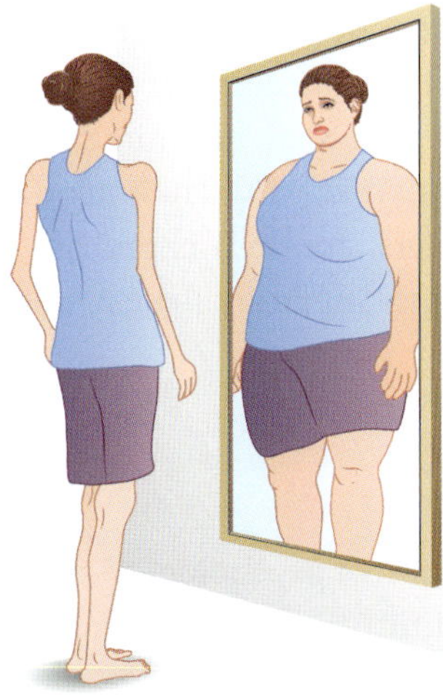

Figure 6.12 Anorexia is associated with body image distortions.

their twenties, the death risk is eighteen times that of healthy people their age (Arcelus, Mitchell, Wales, & Nielsen, 2011).

What Causes Anorexia?

Eating disorders, including anorexia, are significantly less common in non-industrialized countries, and are most common in cultures that idealize thinness (Makino, Tsuboi, & Dennerstein, 2004; Keel & Forney, 2013), suggesting that social pressures may be powerful influences on the development of the disorder. However, some individuals are more vulnerable to these influences than others. Childhood personality traits of anxiety, obsessions, and perfectionism are risk factors for anorexia (Kaye, Wierenga, Bailer, Simmons, & Bischoff-Grethe, 2013).

In searching for neurobiological factors that may underlie anorexia, a major difficulty is the fact that existing data come from patients who are already suffering from the disorder. Since there are no definitive signs for predicting who will become anorexic, it is difficult to track the psychological and biological changes that precede its development. When studying neurobiological characteristics of those currently ill or recovering from anorexia, neurobiological abnormalities associated with the disease could be causes, but they could also be effects of malnourishment.

Cognitive testing shows that those with anorexia are often highly focused upon detail at the expense of noticing more global features (big-picture perspective) of visual scenes (Zipfel, Giel, Bulik, Hay, & Schmidt, 2015). The fact that this focus upon detail is also seen in healthy sisters of people with anorexia suggests that the cognitive trait of over-focusing is not simply a byproduct of malnourishment, but may be part of a genetic predisposition.

Evidence for a genetic component for anorexia comes from twin studies in which one twin has the disorder and the researchers determine the likelihood of the other also having it. The rate of concordance (both having anorexia) in monozygotic twins (twins with identical genes) is four times higher than it is in dizygotic twins (whose genes are no more similar than that between any siblings) (Kipman, Gorwood, Mouren-Siméoni, & Adès, 1999). As with many behavioral disorders, anorexia is probably due to the interaction of a number of psychological, neurobiological, and genetic factors.

Treatments for Anorexia

Most treatments for anorexia involve a combination of psychological therapy with supervised weight gain. In cases of malnutrition, hospitalization (often lasting several weeks) may be required, followed by outpatient treatment to monitor progress. The individual with anorexia may be reluctant to begin treatment due to anxiety about gaining weight even when in a state of life-threatening malnourishment.

Once in treatment, recovery can be a prolonged process requiring years of therapy, and with periods of improvement followed by relapse of symptoms. In some cases, anorexia can be a life-long illness, requiring the individual to battle their anxieties about eating and weight gain, and to remain vigilant against unhealthy food avoidances. While many of us give little thought to exactly what we eat and how much, those with anorexia may need to follow rules of healthy eating in a conscious and systematic manner in order to maintain progress in battling this difficult disorder. With treatment, about 40 percent of those with anorexia make a full recovery. The outcome is best for those who receive treatment within the first few years of their illness (Zipfel et al., 2015).

Family-based therapy has a particularly high rate of success in treating anorexia in adolescents (Stiles-Shields, Hoste, Doyle, & Le Grange, 2012; Lock, 2015). Parents often blame themselves for causing their child's eating problem. A key aspect of family-based therapy is inclusion of parents, helping them to let go of their feelings of guilt and responsibility, and encouraging them to participate in the plan for helping their child return to a normal weight. The therapy also focuses on promoting healthy relationships between the adolescent and the parents.

An effective treatment approach in adults is cognitive-behavioral therapy (CBT), which works to help the patient identify and challenge their own irrational beliefs about eating and body shape. For instance, irrational beliefs such as "I will only be happy if I can lose this weight" or "unless I lose a great deal of weight I will be a worthless person" may be replaced eventually with healthier beliefs such as "my self-worth doesn't depend upon my size or shape." Positive outcomes have also been shown with psychoanalytic approaches that help the patient to gain insights about their own thoughts and feelings associated with eating. This might include associations between family relationships, self-esteem, and body weight. Although many different types of drug-based therapies have been tried, none has consistently been shown to be successful in treating anorexia.

6.8.2 Bulimia

People with **bulimia** binge-eat; that is, they consume unusually large amounts of food and feel unable to stop. Shortly thereafter, they engage in behaviors to **purge** (remove) the food from their system by making themselves vomit, or by misuse of laxatives or other drugs. Individuals may also compensate for their binges by engaging in extreme exercise or extreme food restriction. The prevalence of bulimia in the USA is approximately 1.5 percent in women and 0.5 percent in men.

Patients with bulimia are in many ways similar to those with anorexia. Both disorders are most prevalent in young women, both involve an abnormal focus upon food, both involve distorted body image, and both are associated with anxiety, perfectionism, and obsessive behavior. These similarities have led to a continuing debate regarding whether bulimia and anorexia are both aspects of a more general disorder.

A major difference between them is that those with anorexia are extremely underweight, while those with bulimia are typically normal weight or even overweight. (Eating a large amount at once appears to promote weight gain, even with purging.) In addition, patients with bulimia differ from those with anorexia in that they have gross and varied damage and inflammation of the entire digestive tract, from mouth to intestines. This is especially attributable to vomiting and the associated gastric acids.

What Causes Bulimia?

Like anorexia, a variety of factors can contribute to bulimia. The evidence for a genetic contribution comes once again from twin studies where the concordance rate is 23 percent for monozygotic twins and 9 percent for dizygotic twins (Kendler et al., 1991). The biological factors that have been considered include all of the neurochemicals discussed in early sections of this chapter as being involved in eating and satiety. Psychological factors that may predispose an individual to bulimia include anxiety, obsession, perfectionism, and depression. The person's self-image and self-evaluation are strongly influenced by their body shape or weight. Finally, the social environment, including public media, social media, peer groups, and family, appears to play important roles. Like anorexia, bulimia is most common in cultures where thinness is a social ideal (Keel & Forney, 2013).

Treatments for Bulimia

As with anorexia, family-based therapy is an effective treatment for adolescents with bulimia. The treatment of choice for adults with bulimia is cognitive behavioral therapy (Svaldi et al., 2019). Antidepressant drugs, especially those like Prozac that elevate brain levels of serotonin at the synaptic level, have shown some positive results. Finally, there is some evidence that combining psychotherapies with drug treatment may provide additive benefits for patients with bulimia (see Hay & Claudino, 2010 for a review).

6.8.3 Binge-Eating Disorder

Individuals with **binge-eating disorder** (**BED**), like those with bulimia, eat large amounts of food at once, and experience a loss of control. But because those with BED do not purge, individuals with this disorder are often overweight or obese. The prevalence of BED over a lifetime is about 3.5 percent for females and 2 percent for males in the USA, greater than that of either anorexia or bulimia. In contrast to anorexia and bulimia, which primarily affect adolescents and young adults, BED occurs with similar frequency across the adult lifespan (Hudson, Hiripi, Pope, & Kessler, 2007).

What Causes Binge-Eating Disorder?

The causes of binge-eating disorder are not known. Risk factors include a family history of the disorder, low self-esteem, and a history of depression. Some report that their episodes binging are triggered by negative emotions such as sadness or anger (Cardi et al., 2015). Like other eating disorders, causes are likely to involve combinations of genetic, psychological, and interpersonal factors.

Treatments for Binge-Eating Disorder

Among psychological treatments, cognitive behavioral therapy has the highest success rate for BED (Grilo, Reas, & Mitchell, 2016). In addition, an amphetamine-like drug, lisdexamfetamine dimesylate (LDX), is FDA-approved for treatment of BED, although, like other stimulant drugs, it carries some risk of abuse and dependence.

KEY CONCEPTS

- **Anorexia is a dangerous disorder in which individuals severely restrict their eating. Weight loss and malnourishment can become a serious health risk and may even be fatal.**
- **Various psychological treatments including family-based therapies are effective in treating anorexia. So far, drug treatments for anorexia have not been shown to be effective.**

- **Individuals with bulimia eat in binges and then purge. Unlike those with anorexia, they are not usually underweight. Some forms of psychological and pharmacological therapy are effective in treating bulimia.**
- **As the name implies, those with binge-eating disorder engage in binging, but they do not purge and may therefore become overweight or obese. Both psychological and pharmacological treatments can be effective for binge-eating disorder.**

TEST YOURSELF

1. **Describe factors that contribute to anorexia and bulimia.**
2. **Distinguish the symptoms of anorexia, bulimia, and binge-eating disorder.**

6.9 The Big Picture

When energy resources are low, signals from the periphery send signals to the brain, leading to hunger, food consumption, and restoration of energy. However, we may also eat for other reasons – out of habit, for pleasure, for social reasons, and so on. Imagine that Bob is in an airplane and hasn't eaten for hours. His stomach is empty, ghrelin levels are high, hunger circuits in the hypothalamus are activated, and he feels a strong desire to eat. The next time he flies, he's prepared. He puts a chocolate bar in his carry-on bag. On the plane, when his hypothalamic hunger circuits kick in, he eats his delicious chocolate, and next time he's on a plane, he craves that chocolate regardless of whether or not he's hungry (independent of his ghrelin levels and hypothalamic circuits).

In societies with an increased availability of high-calorie foods and reduced daily energy expenditure, obesity has become an increasing problem with serious health risks. In addition, anxieties about gaining weight and distortions in body image can lead to life-threatening reductions in weight, or anorexia. These and other eating disorders demonstrate that eating in humans is a complex phenomenon in which homeostatic processes interact with psychological, social, and cultural influences.

6.10 Creative Thinking

1. You are tasked with inventing a drug that reduces eating through actions in subregions of the hypothalamus. How would your drug affect

particular regions of the hypothalamus? (You might review Figure 6.7 to answer this.)

2. As a parent, if you were concerned that your child was becoming obese, what actions would you take (if any)?
3. If you were concerned that a friend was anorexic, what actions would you take (if any)?
4. If the US president named you surgeon general, what would you do to help reduce obesity? Are there steps you would take to help prevent young women from developing anorexia?

Key Terms

adipose cells 239
alpha melanocyte-stimulating hormone (α-MSH) 248
anorexia nervosa 232
anorexigenic 249
arcuate nucleus of the hypothalamus 246
ATP 236
basal metabolic rate (BMR) 257
basal metabolism 236
binge-eating disorder (BED) 265
body mass index (BMI) 253
bulimia 263
cholecystokinin (CCK) 243
error detection 234
fatty acids 239
gastric bypass 259
ghrelin 242
glucagon 237
glucose 236
glucostatic theory 240
glycogen 237
homeostasis 233
insulin 237
ketones 239
lateral hypothalamus (LH) 246
leptin 243
lipostatic theory 240
negative feedback 234
neurochemicals 247
neuropeptide Y (NPY) 247
orexigenic 249
orexin 249
paraventricular nucleus (PVN) 246
purge 263
response element 234
satiety 240
sensor 234
set point 234
solitary nucleus 246
triglyceride 239

References

American Psychiatric Association. (2013). *Diagnostic and Statistical Manual of Mental Disorders* (5th ed.). Washington, DC: American Psychiatric Publishing.

Anand, B. K., & Brobeck, J. R. (1951). Localization of a "feeding center" in the hypothalamus of the rat. *Proceedings of the Society for Experimental Biology and Medicine, 77*, 323–324.

Arcelus, J., Mitchell, A. J., Wales, J., & Nielsen, S. (2011). Mortality rates in patients with anorexia nervosa and other eating disorders: a meta-analysis of 36 studies. *Archives of General Psychiatry, 68*(7), 724–731.

Bray, G. A., Fruhbeck, G., Ryan, D. H., & Wilding, J. P. H. (2016). Management of obesity. *Lancet, 387*(10031), 1947–1956.

Cardi, V., Leppanen, J., & Treasure, J. (2015). The effects of negative and positive mood induction on eating behaviour: a meta-analysis of laboratory studies in the healthy population and eating and weight disorders. *Neuroscience and Biobehavioral Reviews, 57*, 299–309.

Cohn, C., & Joseph, D. (1962). Influence of body weight and body fat on appetite of "normal" lean and obese rats. *Yale Journal of Biology and Medicine, 34*, 598–607.

Cunningham, J. J. (1991). Body composition as a determinant of energy expenditure: a synthetic review and a proposed general prediction equation. *American Journal of Clinical Nutrition, 54*(6), 963–969.

Grilo, C. M., Reas, D. L., & Mitchell, J. E. (2016). Combining pharmacological and psychological treatments for binge eating disorder: current status, limitations, and future directions. *Current Psychiatry Reports, 18*(6).

Hainer, V., Kabrnova, K., Aldhoon, B., Kunesova, M., & Wagenknecht, M. (2006). Serotonin and norepinephrine reuptake inhibition and eating behavior. *Annals of the New York Academy of Sciences, 1083*, 252–269.

Harris, R. B. (1990). Role of set-point theory in regulation of body weight. *FASEB Journal: Official Publication of the Federation of American Societies for Experimental Biology, 4*, 3310–3318.

Hay, P. J., & Claudino, A. M. (2010). Bulimia nervosa. *BMJ Clinical Evidence.*

Hetherington, A. W., & Ranson, S. W. (1940). Hypothalamic lesions and adiposity in the rat. *Anatomical Record, 78*, 149–172.

Hudson, J. I., Hiripi, E., Pope, H. G., & Kessler, R. C. (2007). The prevalence and correlates of eating disorders in the National Comorbidity Survey Replication. *Biological Psychiatry, 61*, 348–358.

Jansen, A. (1998). A learning model of binge eating: cue reactivity and cue exposure. *Behaviour Research and Therapy, 36*(3), 257–272.

Johnston, B. C., Kanters, S., Bandayrel, K., Wu, P., Naji, F., Siemieniuk, R. A., … Mills, E. J. (2014). Comparison of weight loss among named diet programs in overweight and obese adults: a meta-analysis. *JAMA, 312*(9), 923–933.

Kaye, W. H., Wierenga, C. E., Bailer, U. F., Simmons, A. N., & Bischoff-Grethe, A. (2013). Nothing tastes as good as skinny feels: the neurobiology of anorexia nervosa. *Trends in Neurosciences, 36*(2), 110–120.

Keel, P. K., & Forney, K. J. (2013). Psychosocial risk factors for eating disorders. *International Journal of Eating Disorders, 46*(5), 433–439.

Kendler, K. S., MacLean, C., Neale, M., Kessler, R., Heath, A., & Eaves, L. (1991). The genetic epidemiology of bulimia nervosa. *American Journal of Psychiatry, 148*, 1627–1637.

Kipman, A., Gorwood, P., Mouren-Siméoni, M. C., & Adès, J. (1999). Genetic factors in anorexia nervosa. *European Psychiatry: The Journal of the Association of European Psychiatrists, 14*, 189–198.

Klok, M. D., Jakobsdottir, S., & Drent, M. L. (2007). The role of leptin and ghrelin in the regulation of food intake and body weight in humans: a review. *Obesity Reviews: An Official Journal of the International Association for the Study of Obesity, 8*(1), 21–34.

Lattimore, P., & Caswell, N. (2004). Differential effects of active and passive stress on food intake in restrained and unrestrained eaters. *Appetite, 42*(2), 167–173.

Lee, E. Y., & Yoon, K.-H. (2018). Epidemic obesity in children and adolescents: risk factors and prevention. *Frontiers of Medicine, 12*(6), 658–666.

Lock, J. (2015). An update on evidence-based psychosocial treatments for eating disorders in children and adolescents. *Journal of Clinical Child & Adolescent Psychology, 44*, 707–721.

Lyon, M., Halpern, M., & Mintz, E. (1968). The significance of the mesencephalon for coordinated feeding behavior. *Acta Neurologica Scandinavica, 44*, 323–346.

Makino, M., Tsuboi, K., & Dennerstein, L. (2004). Prevalence of eating disorders: a comparison of Western and non-Western countries. *Medscape General Medicine, 6*, 49.

Mark, A. E., & Janssen, I. (2008). Relationship between screen time and metabolic syndrome in adolescents. *Journal of Public Health, 30*(2), 153–160.

Midei, A. J., & Matthews, K. A. (2011). Interpersonal violence in childhood as a risk factor for obesity: a systematic review of the literature and proposed pathways. *Obesity Reviews, 12*(501), e159–e172.

Nagl, M., Jacobi, C., Paul, M., Beesdo-Baum, K., Hofler, M., Lieb, R., & Wittchen, H. U. (2016). Prevalence, incidence, and natural course of anorexia and bulimia nervosa among adolescents and young adults. *European Child & Adolescent Psychiatry, 25*(8), 903–918.

Ogden, C. L., Carroll, M. D., Kit, B. K., & Flegal, K. M. (2014). Prevalence of childhood and adult obesity in the United States, 2011–2012. *JAMA, 311*(8), 806–814.

Petrovich, G. D. (2018). Lateral hypothalamus as a motivation-cognition interface in the control of feeding behavior. *Frontiers in Systems Neuroscience, 12*, 14.

Pilitsi, E., Farr, O. M., Polyzos, S. A., Perakakis, N., Nolen-Doerr, E., Papathanasiou, A. E., & Mantzoros, C. S. (2019). Pharmacotherapy of obesity: available medications and drugs under investigation. *Metabolism: Clinical and Experimental, 92*, 170–192.

Rimm, E. B., Stampfer, M. J., Giovannucci, E., Ascherio, A., Spiegelman, D., Colditz, G. A., & Willett, W. C. (1995). Body size and fat distribution as predictors of coronary heart disease among middle-aged and older US men. *American Journal of Epidemiology, 141*, 1117–1127.

Salamone, J. D., & Correa, M. (2012). The mysterious motivational functions of mesolimbic dopamine. *Neuron, 76*(3), 470–485.

Shai, I., Schwarzfuchs, D., Henkin, Y., Shahar, D. R., Witkow, S., Greenberg, I., ... Stampfer, M. J. (2008). Weight loss with a low-carbohydrate, Mediterranean, or low-fat diet. *New England Journal of Medicine, 359*(3), 229–241.

Sims, E. A., & Horton, E. S. (1968). Endocrine and metabolic adaptation to obesity and starvation. *American Journal of Clinical Nutrition, 21*, 1455–1470.

Smink, F. R., van Hoeken, D., & Hoek, H. W. (2012). Epidemiology of eating disorders: incidence, prevalence and mortality rates. *Current Psychiatry Reports, 14*(4), 406–414.

Sørensen, T. I., & Stunkard, A. J. (1993). Does obesity run in families because of genes? An adoption study using silhouettes as a measure of obesity. *Acta Psychiatrica Scandinavica*, Supplementum, *370*, 67–72.

Stiles-Shields, C., Hoste, R. R., Doyle, P. M., & Le Grange, D. (2012). A review of family-based treatment for adolescents with eating disorders. *Reviews on Recent Clinical Trials, 7*, 133–140.

Stoeckel, L. E., Weller, R. E., Cook, E. W., 3rd, Twieg, D. B., Knowlton, R. C., & Cox, J. E. (2008). Widespread reward-system activation in obese women in response to pictures of high-calorie foods. *NeuroImage, 41*(2), 636–647.

Strychar, I. (2006). Diet in the management of weight loss. *Canadian Medical Association Journal, 174*, 56–63.

Svaldi, J., Schmitz, F., Baur, J., Hartmann, A. S., Legenbauer, T., Thaler, C., ... Tuschen-Caffier, B. (2019). Efficacy of psychotherapies and pharmacotherapies for Bulimia nervosa. *Psychological Medicine, 49*(6), 898–910.

Vikraman, S., Fryar, C.D., & Ogden, C. L. (2015). Caloric intake from fast food among children and adolescents in the United States, 2011–2012. *National Center for Health Statistics Data Brief*, no. 213. Hyattsville, MD: National Center for Health Statistics.

Volkow, N. D., Wang, G.-J., Fowler, J. S., & Telang, F. (2008). Overlapping neuronal circuits in addiction and obesity: evidence of systems pathology. *Philosophical Transactions of the Royal Society of London B: Biological Sciences, 363*, 3191–3200.

Williams, K. W., & Elmquist, J. K. (2012). From neuroanatomy to behavior: central integration of peripheral signals regulating feeding behavior. *Nature Neuroscience, 15*(10), 1350–1355.

Wirtshafter, D., & Davis, J. D. (1977). Set points, settling points, and the control of body weight. *Physiology & Behavior, 19*, 75–78.

Woods, J. W. (1964). Behavior of chronic decerebrate rats. *Journal of Neurophysiology, 27*, 635–644.

World Health Organization: Obesity and overweight fact sheet. www.who.int/mediacentre/factsheets/fs311/en/

Zhang, Y., Proenca, R., Maffei, M., Barone, M., Leopold, L., & Friedman, J. M. (1994). Positional cloning of the mouse obese gene and its human homologue. *Nature*, *372*, 425–432.

Zipfel, S., Giel, K. E., Bulik, C. M., Hay, P., & Schmidt, U. (2015). Anorexia nervosa: aetiology, assessment, and treatment. *Lancet Psychiatry*, *2*(12), 1099–1111.

7
Sex

Ben Cranke / DigitalVision / Getty Images

Consider This ...

By the time she was 4 years old, she knew that she was not a boy. She remembers the day her grandmother saw her running around the yard playing in the dress belonging to the little girl next door and scolded her. "Little boys should not wear girls' clothing," her grandmother said. That was when she knew that others saw her differently than she saw herself. In high school in Hawaii, she began hormone therapy and soon gained the confidence to wear women's clothing to school. At eighteen, she underwent sex change (gender reassignment) surgery.

Janet Mock is now Contributing Editor for *Marie Claire*, a host for MSNBC, correspondent for *Entertainment Tonight*, and author of the memoir *Redefining Realness: My Path to Womanhood, Identity, Love & So Much More*. "I have a boyfriend whom I love, friends who love me just as I am despite my past, despite everything. And I have a career as a writer that gives me meaning, and gives me real purpose." Janet's change in gender was particularly difficult for her father. "He had to process it in his way. And I always say there's a mourning for him. He had a baby boy that he loved, and that

Janet Mock.
(© Pacific Press/Getty Images.)

he had dreams for. And you know, I had to give him that time to mourn that. You know, I'm just so blessed and so happy that through the years, you know, I transitioned – I started transitioning 13 years ago. So with my father, he's had 13 years to come around, and he came around in about four or five years, you know, to embrace me as his new baby girl. And it's beautiful, and I love him" (Martin, 2011).

The sense of one's own gender (**gender identity**) does not come from one's sexual anatomy, for there are individuals, like Janet, whose gender identity does not match the sexual characteristics of the body. Where does gender identity come from? Can a person have a brain with female characteristics and the sex organs of a male, and vice versa? In this chapter, we will ask how genes and sex hormones contribute to the development of the sexual organs, the brain, and gender identity.

7.1 HORMONES INFLUENCE SEXUAL DEVELOPMENT AND SEXUAL BEHAVIOR

The body contains **endocrine glands** that release hormones directly into the bloodstream (Figure 7.1). The hormones can travel long distances through the bloodstream before reaching their receptors in the brain or

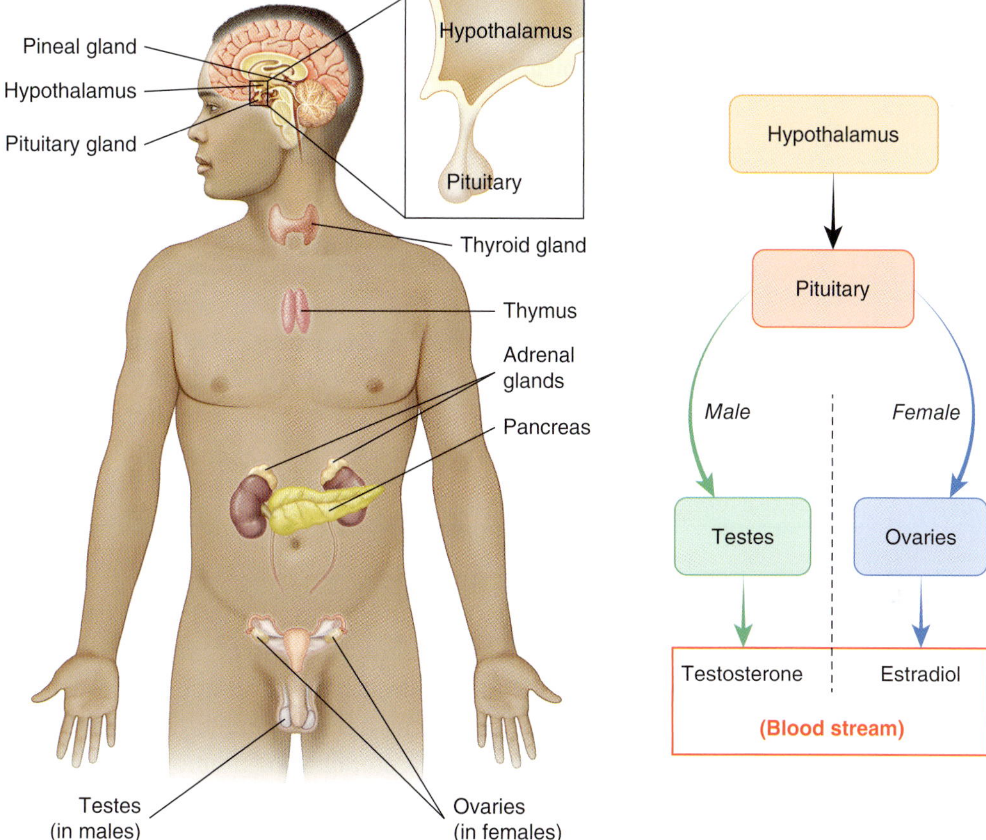

Figure 7.1 The testes, ovaries, and other endocrine glands. Endocrine glands release hormones into the bloodstream, such as testosterone released by the male testes, and estradiol released by the female ovaries. Like other endocrine hormones, gonadal hormone release is under the control of the hypothalamus.

the periphery. Endocrine hormones influence growth, mood, sleep, sexual behavior, and other functions. As we will see in later sections of this chapter (and in Chapter 12: Stress, Fear, and Anxiety), the release of hormones from endocrine glands in the body is sometimes influenced by activity of the brain. For instance, the hypothalamus releases hormones that travel a short distance to the pituitary gland; the pituitary gland, in turn, releases hormones that travel long distances through the circulatory system to reach endocrine glands in the periphery of the body, and increase their release of hormones into the bloodstream.

Two of the endocrine glands of particular interest to us for this chapter are the **testes** in males and **ovaries** in females (again, see Figure 7.1). They are the **gonads**, and they produce and release the major sex hormones (**gonadal hormones**). The primary gonadal hormone in males (released by the testes) is **testosterone**, a member of the **androgen**

Table 7.1 Sex hormones.

Hormone group	Functions	Key members	Produced primarily in	Receptor
Androgens	• Development of male sexual organs and secondary sex characteristics • Sexual arousal	• Testosterone • Androstenedione • Dihydrotestos-terone (DHT)	• Testes (males) • Various tissues that convert testosterone to DHT	• Androgen receptor
Estrogens	• Development of secondary sex characteristics • Menstrual cycle • Sexual arousal	• Estradiol • Estrone (during and after menopause)	• Ovaries (females)	• Estrogen receptor (ER-α; ER-β)

family of hormones (see Table 7.1). In females, the ovaries release high levels of **estradiol**, a member of the estrogen group of hormones.

All androgen hormones bind to androgen receptors and therefore exert similar effects on the body. Androgens have a number of physiological functions, including inhibition of fat storage and promotion of muscle growth. In fact, testosterone and other androgens (androstenedione and dihydrotestosterone (DHT)) have been banned from use in the Olympics because athletes use them to promote muscle growth despite severe health risks. Like the androgens, estrogens have several important physiological functions, including protecting neurons from death (neuroprotection) and protecting against some degenerative diseases (Behl, 2002). In this chapter, however, we will focus on the role of these gonadal hormones, androgens and estrogens, on sexual development and arousal.

Testosterone and estradiol molecules have closely related structures. In fact, only a single enzyme (the aromatase molecule) inside the ovaries is needed to convert testosterone to estradiol (Figure 7.2). While testosterone is the primary gonadal hormone released by the male, and estradiol by the female, male and female gonads release the other hormone as well in smaller quantities. Females deficient in the aromatase enzyme have abnormally high levels of testosterone and low levels of estradiol (again, see Figure 7.2). For reasons that will become clear in later sections, this can lead to abnormalities in the development of female sexual organs.

Both the androgens and the estrogens are **steroids**, that is, small, fat-soluble hormones capable of crossing cell membranes to enter the interior of cells (Figure 7.3). Inside the cell, the hormone binds to an intracellular receptor in the cytoplasm. The receptor and hormone

Ovary

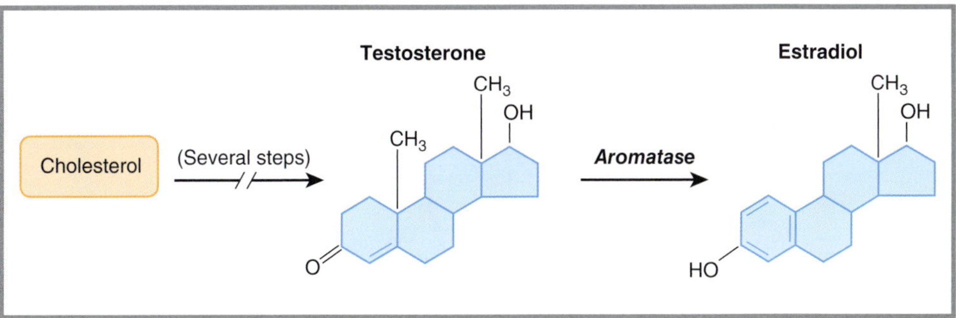

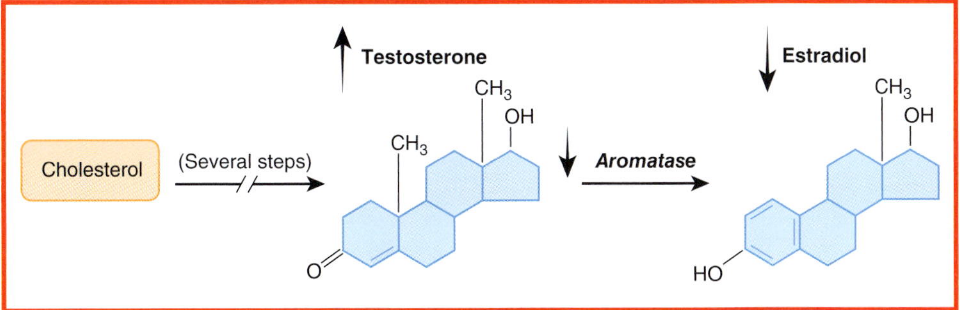

Figure 7.2 Testosterone and estradiol are closely related molecules. In the ovaries, cholesterol is converted to testosterone. Just a single enzyme, aromatase, is needed to convert testosterone to estradiol (top). Deficiencies in aromatase cause an abnormal build-up of testosterone and low levels of estradiol (bottom).

together (steroid-receptor complex) move into the cell nucleus, where the receptor attaches to DNA and initiates the expression (transcription and translation) of genes that produce long-lasting changes in cell function. For instance, during early periods of development, steroid sex hormones can enter cells, bind to receptors, and activate genes that direct the cells to develop into those of particular sex organs. In adulthood, the steroid hormones may act upon the brain to heighten sexual arousal. Steroids typically remain active for long periods of time, sometimes for many hours, while other hormones are typically degraded within minutes.

Sex hormones, particularly testosterone and other androgens, play first **organizing** and later **activating** roles in sexual behavior. These roles are analogous to the relation between constructing a musical instrument and later playing it. The way that an instrument is constructed limits or constrains the sounds that it can produce when played in the future. Similarly, the *organizing* effects of hormones on the early development of sexual anatomy and brain circuits can influence the sexual feelings and behaviors that are *activated* when sex hormones are released in later years.

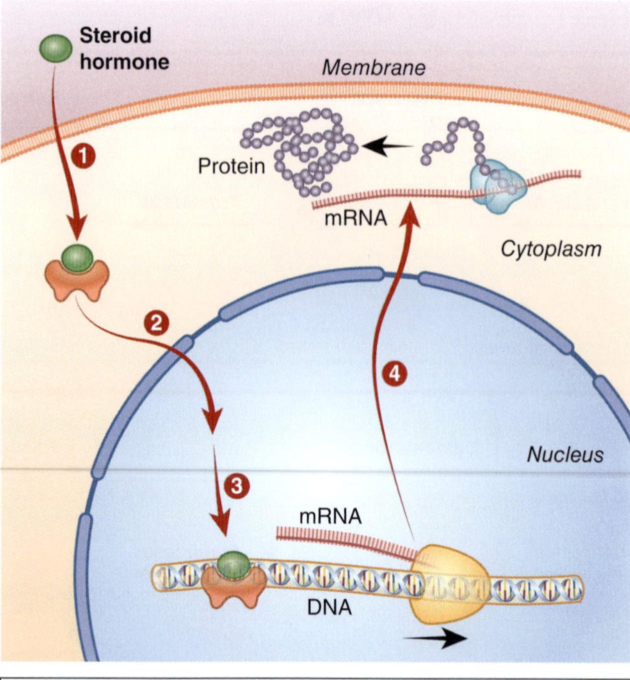

1. The steroid hormone binds to a receptor inside the cell
2. The steroid-receptor complex moves to the nucleus of the cell
3. The steroid-receptor complex binds to DNA
4. Genes are expressed and new proteins are generated

Figure 7.3 **Steroid hormones**. Steroid hormones are capable of binding to receptors within the cell cytoplasm, producing long-lasting effects on the cell.

KEY CONCEPTS

- **The testes and ovaries are endocrine glands that release high levels of testosterone and estradiol, respectively.**
- **Like all steroid hormones, testosterone and estradiol are small, fat-soluble molecules capable of crossing cell membranes and binding to receptors located within the cytoplasm of the receiving cell.**
- **Steroid hormones can bind to DNA in the cell's nucleus and alter gene expression, producing lasting changes in the cell's functioning.**

TEST YOURSELF

1. **What are the male and female gonads? What is the major sex hormone released by each?**
2. **What is the distinction between organizing and activating effects of gonadal sex hormones?**

7.2 SEXUAL DIFFERENTIATION BEGINS WITH THE SRY GENE

When a **sperm** fertilizes an egg (**ovum**) it produces a single cell called the **zygote** (Figure 7.4). If you were to closely examine a zygote that will become male and one that will become female, the only difference would be

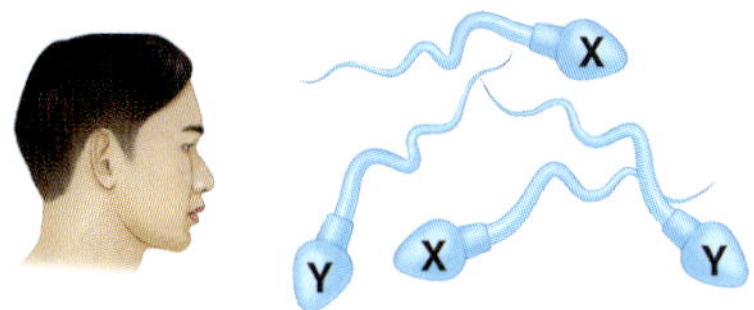

Each sperm cell contains either an X or a Y chromosome

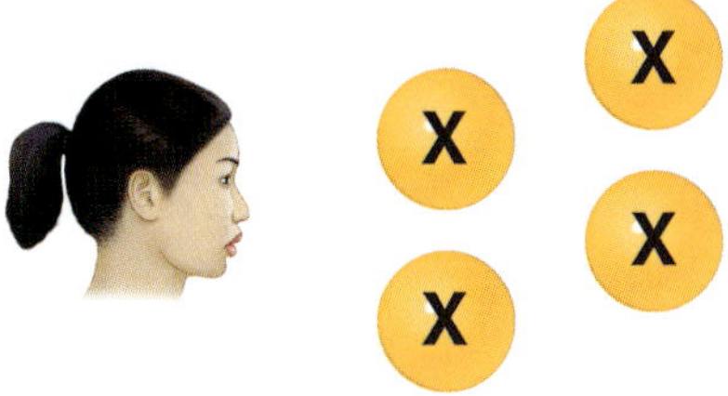

Each egg cell contains an X chromosome

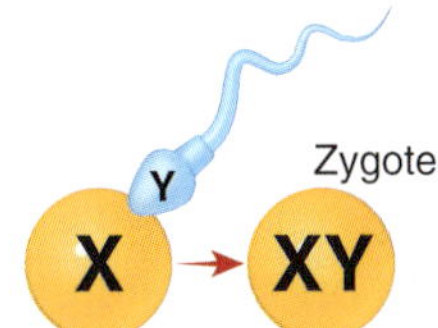

When a sperm containing a Y chromosome fertilizes an egg, the zygote develops into a male

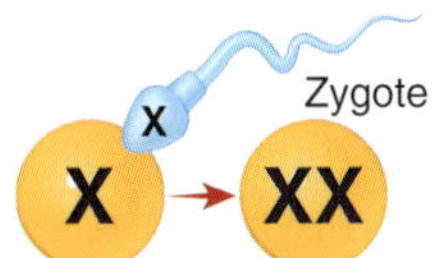

When a sperm containing an X chromosome fertilizes an egg, the zygote develops into a female

Embryo

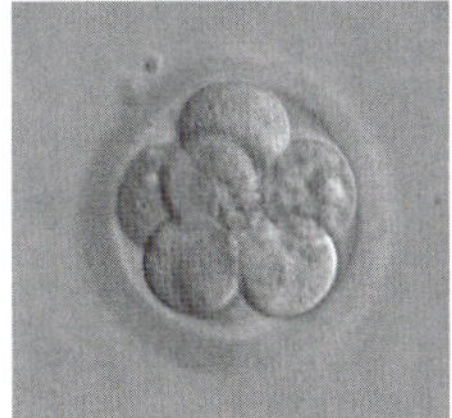

The human embryo on day 3, after several cell divisions.

Figure 7.4 When a sperm fertilizes an ovum, the single-celled zygote is created. The zygote divides to become an embryo.
(© ekem, courtesy RWJMS IVF Program.)

in the chromosomes (the strands of DNA in the cell containing the genes). Specifically, only one of the twenty-three pairs of chromosomes would differ, the sex chromosomes. The sex chromosomes are of two types, X and Y. Females have two X chromosomes, while males have an X and a Y. During the first six weeks of development, the gonads have not yet become either testes or ovaries; they are still **undifferentiated**. They have not yet undergone the changes that will make them distinct, and so at this stage, the gonads can theoretically become either testes or ovaries.

But in the sixth week of pregnancy, a key event occurs in the male embryo. A gene on the Y chromosome called the **SRY gene** is expressed. Expression of SRY leads to the creation of a molecule called **sex-determining protein**. (In other words, cells of the gonads read instructions in the DNA of the Y chromosome, and then use those instructions to create the sex-determining protein.) The sex-determining protein plays a critical role in causing the undifferentiated gonads to become testes. Because females do not possess a Y chromosome, they have no SRY gene. In the absence of the gene, the undifferentiated gonads become ovaries rather than testes. Female gonads develop as a default condition. The testes and ovaries can first be distinguished between the sixth and eighth weeks of **gestation**. Gestation is usually calculated as an approximate age of the fetus measured since the mother's last menstrual period.

While the SRY gene is normally localized on the Y (male) chromosome, there are rare instances in which the gene is located on an X chromosome, and the female (with two X chromosomes) may possess the SRY gene. In such cases, the gene produces its normal developmental effect of promoting growth of the testes. As a result, the female develops either two testes, a testis and an ovary, or a mixture of ovary and testis on each side. This condition is called XX male syndrome, for it leads to male characteristics in a genetically female (XX) individual.

7.3 HORMONES RELEASED BY THE TESTES MASCULINIZE THE SEX ORGANS

Much of the female reproductive system (including the upper vagina and uterus) develops from a pair of tube-like structures in the embryo called the **Müllerian ducts** (Figure 7.5). The internal structures of the male reproductive system (including the seminal vesicles and ejaculatory duct) develop from the **Wolffian ducts**. Before the reproductive systems have differentiated, the male and female embryos contain both of these ducts.

Testosterone released from the testes **masculinizes** the sex organs. The hormone enters the cells of the Wolffian ducts and triggers expression of genes that lead to development of the internal parts of the male reproductive system. Testosterone (and other androgens) also trigger development of the scrotum and penis. Another hormone is released from the testes, **Müllerian-Inhibiting Factor** (also called Anti-Müllerian hormone), which causes the Müllerian ducts to degenerate. This defeminizes the male's internal sexual anatomy. In other words, it prevents the male from developing a uterus and other female internal reproductive structures.

Because the female gonads have become ovaries, and ovaries do not produce Müllerian-Inhibiting Factor, she maintains her Müllerian ducts, which develop into female sexual organs. In addition, because the ovaries do not produce high levels of testosterone, her Wolffian ducts degenerate instead of forming male sexual organs. In the absence of the gonadal hormones, testosterone and Müllerian-Inhibiting Factor, genes trigger development of female sex organs, that is to say, the anatomy is **feminized**. The male and female organs typically become distinguishable between weeks 8 and 12 of gestation (again, see Figure 7.5).

In very rare cases where the testes release abnormally low amounts of androgens or where androgen receptors are insensitive to the hormones, the penis and other male genitals fail to develop (Misrahi et al., 1997). Although genetically male, the individual develops a female appearance or, in some cases, an **intersex** appearance intermediate between a male and a female. A medical condition (congenital adrenal hyperplasia) that exposes girls to unusually high testosterone levels during prenatal (before birth) and early postnatal development can also lead to the development of ambiguous genitals such as an enlarged clitoris that resembles a penis. Ambiguous genitals are also seen in the rare cases where females lack the aromatase enzyme that converts testosterone to estradiol. Girls with **aromatase deficiency** fail to develop breasts or undergo menstruation during puberty. Overall, about 1 in 2,000 individuals are born with genitalia that are clearly atypical for their genetic sex, although more are born with subtler variations in sexual anatomy. As we will see later in this chapter, the presence or absence of sex hormones during early stages of development can influence not only an individual's sexual anatomy, but their future gender identity as well.

Much of the development of sexual anatomy takes place prior to birth. However, important steps also occur during puberty when the brain sends signals to the gonads to trigger additional sexual development. In females, puberty usually begins at 10–11 years of age, and includes development of secondary sexual characteristics such as growth of the breasts, triggered mostly by estradiol release from the ovaries. About a year later, progesterone causes ovulatory cycles to begin. In males, beginning at 11–12 years of age, the secondary sexual characteristics such as facial hair, muscular growth, and deepening of the voice are triggered by release of testosterone

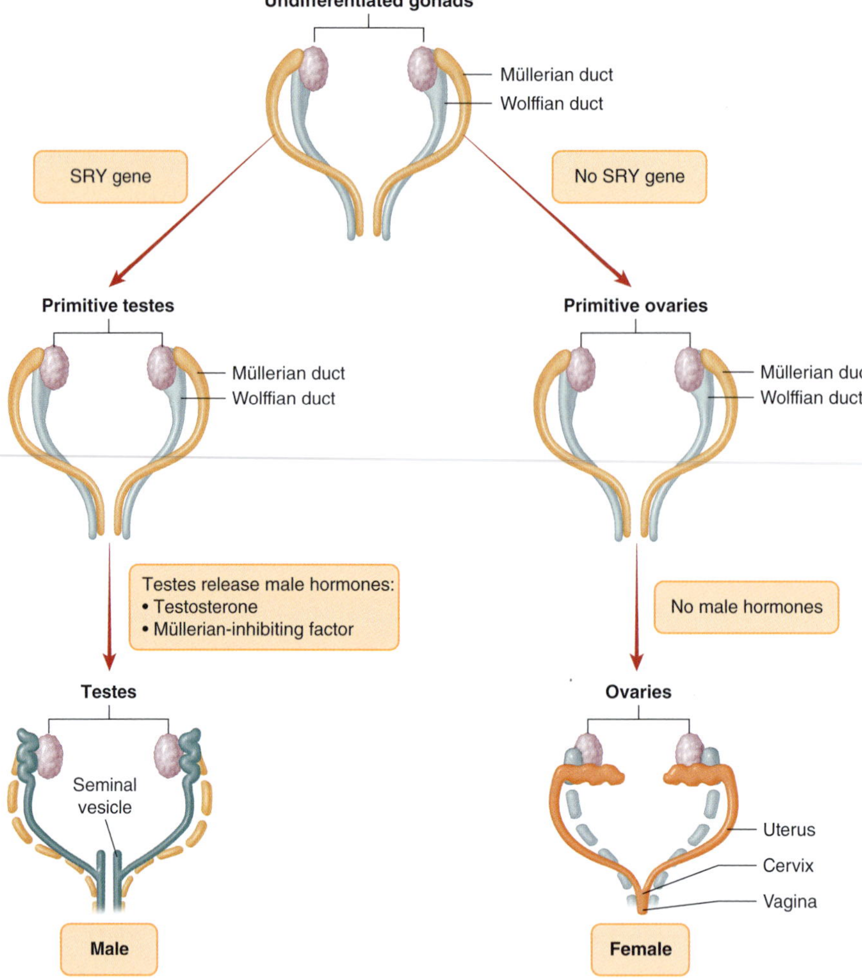

Figure 7.5 **The SRY gene and male hormones lead to male reproductive anatomy**. The SRY gene causes gonads to become testes rather than ovaries. Testes release testosterone, which causes the Wolffian duct to survive and develop into male sexual structures. The testes also release Müllerian-Inhibiting Factor, which causes the Müllerian duct to degenerate, preventing development of female sexual structures.

from the testes (and also by the actions of DHT). For both boys and girls, the growth of pubic/body hair results from hormones released from the adrenal glands (Shirtcliff, Dahl, & Pollak, 2009).

KEY CONCEPTS

- **Sexual differentiation begins with expression of the SRY gene on the male's Y chromosome. This gene expression leads to development of testes; without SRY, ovaries develop.**

- **The testes release high levels of testosterone, which masculinizes the reproductive structures, and Müllerian-Inhibiting Factor, which prevents development of female reproductive structures. In the absence of these hormones, the reproductive anatomy becomes female.**
- **Males with unusually low testosterone activity and females with high testosterone during early development can develop ambiguous sexual anatomy.**

TEST YOURSELF

1. **How does the SRY gene contribute to development of male versus female sex organs?**
2. **Describe the roles of testosterone and Müllerian-Inhibiting Factor in the masculinization and feminization of sex organs.**
3. **Describe developmental effects seen in girls exposed to unusually high testosterone levels during prenatal and early postnatal development.**

7.4 ARE MALE AND FEMALE BRAINS DIFFERENT?

Under the influence of testosterone and other androgen hormones, human sex organs are masculinized between weeks 6 and 12 of pregnancy. Androgens also masculinize the brain, but not until the second half of pregnancy and continuing for the first three months after birth (Swaab & Garcia-Falgueras, 2009). In the absence of testosterone and other androgens, the brains (like the peripheral sex organs) of humans and other animals develop largely as females. In addition, estradiol contributes to female brain development.

Male/female differences, or **sexual dimorphisms**, are seen in many brain areas. When we say that brain area X is sexually dimorphic, we mean that, on average, the region is different (e.g., larger) in one sex or the other. But individuals within a sex may vary greatly with respect to the size (or other sexually dimorphic characteristic) of the structure. Even within a single individual, some sexually dimorphic brain regions may be highly masculinized or feminized, while other such regions may not be (McCarthy & Arnold, 2011).

Researchers have focused particularly upon sexual dimorphisms in the hypothalamus, which plays a key role in sexual behavior. A region of the hypothalamus, the **medial preoptic area** (**mPOA**), contributes especially to sexual behavior in males. Researchers found that a portion of the mPOA is larger in the brains of males compared to females. This area of the mPOA has been named (appropriately) the **sexually dimorphic**

nucleus (**SDN**). Another region of the hypothalamus, **anteroventral periventricular nucleus** (**AVPV**) plays a role in the female ovulatory cycle. The AVPV is larger in females than males (Lenz & McCarthy, 2010).

How does the SDN become larger in males and the AVPV larger in females? During a sensitive period of brain development, just before and after birth, neurons in the female SDN undergo a high rate of cell death (apoptosis) while those in males survive (Figure 7.6). Researchers believe that high levels of androgens in males during this period protect the male SDN cells from death. Consistent with this hypothesis, female mice injected with androgens during this period develop a male-sized SDN and engage in male sexual behavior as adults (e.g., they mount other females from behind). Cells in the AVPV survive in females while they undergo a high rate of cell death in males (McCarthy & Arnold, 2011). In this case, the high androgen levels in males appear to *cause* cell death.

Here is a strange fact revealed in rodent studies: The rise in testosterone sometimes masculinizes the brain via estrogen receptors. How can a rise in testosterone lead to *estrogen* receptor activation? After all,

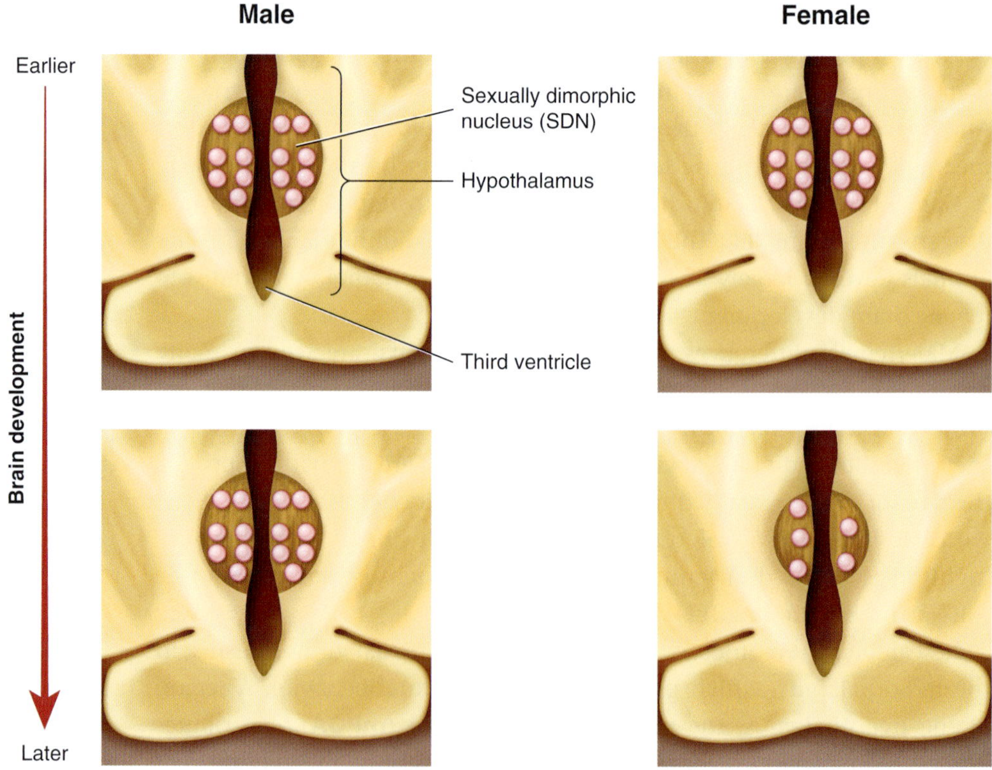

Figure 7.6 The mPOA is larger in males than females. Early in brain development, the mPOA of males and females is similar. However, males maintain their mPOA cells (pink) over the course of brain development, while the female mPOA undergoes a high rate of cell death.

testosterone binds to androgen receptors, not estrogen receptors. The answer is that some cells of the brain contain the aromatase enzyme that converts testosterone to estradiol. Testosterone therefore becomes estradiol, and estradiol then binds to estrogen receptors and produces brain masculinization.

But this leads to another question: If estrogen receptors can masculinize the brain, why is the female brain not masculinized by the high levels of estradiol released from the ovaries? The answer is that during this stage of development the female bloodstream contains a molecule called alpha-fetoprotein, which binds estradiol and prevents it from entering (and masculinizing) the developing female brain. On the other hand, testosterone is released from the testes into the bloodstream, and successfully enters the brain.

To recap this complex scenario: During male development, testosterone enters cells in the brain that contain the aromatase enzyme, which converts the testosterone into estradiol. Estradiol then binds to estrogen receptors. Other testosterone molecules enter cells, and without converting to estradiol, they bind to androgen receptors. Therefore, both androgen and estrogen receptors can masculinize the brain during development. During female development, brain estrogen receptors are not activated because estradiol is bound to alpha-fetoprotein and unable to reach the brain.

Compared to these data from rodent studies, the relative contributions of estrogen and androgen receptors on brain development in humans is harder to assess. For ethical reasons, one cannot manipulate these receptors in the fetus for experimental purposes. The precise roles of estrogen and androgen receptors in masculinization and feminization of sex-related areas of the human brain remain poorly understood.

Not all differences between male and female brains are the result of hormone actions. Some brain cells of the rat fetus undergo sexual differentiation even without hormone influences. There are many genes, including SRY, that are expressed at different levels in male compared to female brains during periods of development. Differences in gene expression are likely to account for brain differences between males and females observed even before hormones have had a chance to influence brain development (Swaab & Garcia-Falgueras, 2009). The precise role of genes in guiding sexual dimorphisms of the brain also remains to be determined.

An area of great interest is whether and how male and female brains differ in other regards, that is, apart from sexual functions. Sexual dimorphisms have been reported not only for hypothalamic regions that directly drive sexual behavior, but also for the lobes of the cerebral cortex, the corpus callosum, and the amygdala – brain areas associated with thought and emotion (Cahill, 2006; Shiino et al., 2017; Denley, Gatford, Sellers,

& Srivastava, 2018). Some caution is required in interpreting such data, however. First, as noted earlier, even when a neuroanatomical difference between sexes is significant, the variability within one sex may be large. Second, studies differ in how they compare the size of brain areas. For instance, imagine that Mary's hippocampus takes up a larger proportion of her brain than Bob's does. But what if Bob has a larger brain than Mary overall? Even if Mary's hippocampus is larger than Bob's as a percentage of their brain sizes, the volume of their hippocampi may be the same. Even when hundreds of male and female brains are compared to one another, disagreement about the correct methodology for comparing brain regions can lead to disagreements about whether a given region is sexually dimorphic or not (Tan, Ma, Vira, Marwha, & Eliot, 2016). Third, as we'll see in the next chapter, brain regions may expand as a result of experience. The violinist, who becomes expert in using particular fingers to produce melodies, shows an increase in the size of the parts of the somatosensory cortex that receive sensations from these fingers. Therefore, while some sexually dimorphic brain regions are likely to reflect influences of sex hormones during early brain development, others may result from differences in experiences common to males versus females, and may therefore be subject to social and cultural influences.

7.5 HORMONES GUIDE THE DEVELOPMENT OF SEXUAL BEHAVIOR IN ANIMALS

In order to understand how sex hormones act during sensitive periods of development to produce differences in adult behavior, scientists have examined the behavior of both humans and animals that were previously exposed to hormone conditions typical of the opposite sex. In the next section, we will ask how unusual hormone conditions during brain development affect later gender identity (an individual's self-identification as male or female) and behavior in humans. However, our understanding of human sexual development has been strongly influenced by studies that have examined the neurobiology of sexual behavior in non-human mammals. We therefore turn first to the question of how exposure to sex hormones during brain development affects sexual behavior in other animals.

Some of the important investigations of hormonal influences on sexual development have been conducted in rats. What is "typical" sexual behavior in rats? Female rats initiate copulation (sexual intercourse) by hopping and darting around the male, running away, and waiting for the male to pursue them. While waiting for the male, the female adopts a posture called **lordosis**, in which her spine is curved downward and her hips and pelvis are elevated. This posture, which facilitates penetration by the male, is a signal of her receptivity to intercourse. The male mounts the female from behind, engages in intercourse, dismounts, and the female runs away. The female then once again hops and darts around the male, restarting the cycle, which is repeated several times until the male ejaculates (Pfaus, 2009).

If female rats are injected with testosterone during sensitive periods of brain development, they will later show masculinized sexual behavior, mounting female partners, as males typically do. Their behavior is also defeminized. They will not engage in lordosis or other female-typical sexual behaviors. These effects are seen only if the high testosterone exposure occurs during periods of brain development (McCarthy & Arnold, 2011). Similarly, if male rats are deprived of testosterone during sensitive periods of brain development, they will later show female-typical behavior (Figure 7.7).

Masculinization and defeminization are two separate processes that occur at different stages of brain development. Male rats deprived of normal testosterone during both periods of masculinization (when circuits for male sexual behavior normally develop) and also periods of brain defeminization (when brain circuits for female sexual behavior are normally prevented from developing) show female and not male sexual behavior. However, if the males are exposed to *normal* testosterone levels during the

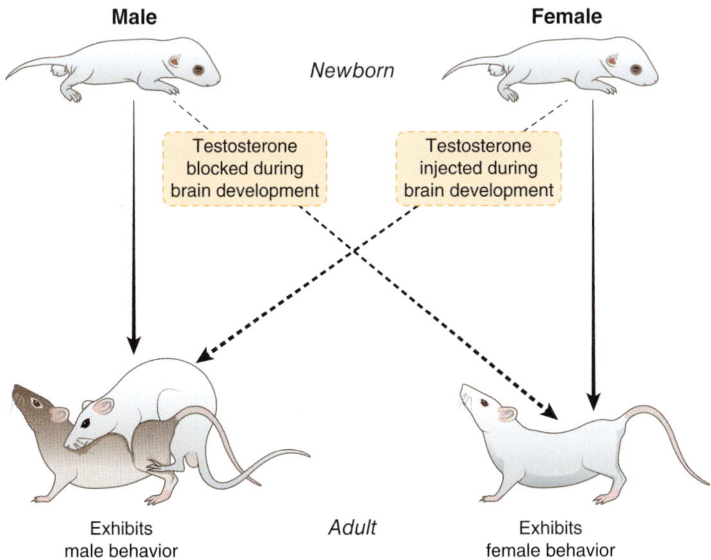

Figure 7.7 **The presence or absence of testosterone during brain development shapes the sexual behavior that will be seen in adulthood.**

period of brain masculinization but deprived of testosterone during periods of feminization, they will show both male-typical and female-typical sexual behavior (Lenz & McCarthy, 2010).

KEY CONCEPTS

1. **Several areas of the male and female brains are anatomically different.**
2. **Animal studies point to a sensitive period of brain development during which testosterone, normally released by the testes, organizes the brain for later male-typical sexual behavior. The absence of high testosterone levels leads to feminization of behavior.**

TEST YOURSELF

1. **Give examples of sexual dimorphism in the human brain.**
2. **Describe evidence supporting a role for testosterone in the development of male versus female sexual behavior in animals.**

7.6 EARLY HORMONE EXPOSURE AND GENETICS AFFECT GENDER IDENTITY AND HUMAN SEXUAL BEHAVIOR

While research in animals can shed light on neurobiological factors that influence the sexual development of the brain and behavior, human sexuality also has facets that are not easily examined using animal subjects. Scientists have great interest in understanding how neurobiological factors might influence gender differences in behavior, the gender with which we identify, and the gender to which we are attracted.

7.6.1 Gender Identity and Gender-Related Behavior

There is a wide range of toy preference among boys and girls, but, on average, boys are more likely to choose non-social or mechanical toys such as cars and balls, while girls more often choose toys such as dolls that resemble people and allow them to have imaginary social interactions. Researchers sometimes examine the amount of time the children spend playing with different items, or the kind of playthings the children choose, or in very young children the amount of time they spend simply looking at the toys. The differences in the kinds of toys boys and girls prefer are surprisingly large; in terms of their statistical reliability, mean differences in toy preference are as large as or larger than the differences between men and women's average heights (Hines, Constantinescu, &

Spencer, 2015). A question of obvious interest is the extent to which these differences are caused by environment or biology.

Clearly, the environment plays a role; family, friends, and television all communicate expectations regarding the ways that boys and girls should act. However, the fact that gender differences in toy preference are seen in infants as young as 6 months of age, with boys spending more time looking at a truck and girls spending more time looking at a doll, suggests the possibility that innate factors may play a role as well (Alexander & Wilcox, 2012). One cannot rule out the possibility that, even by 6 months of age, different familial or other environmental influences might shape preferences. However, even among infant boys of 3–4 months of age, those with the highest androgen levels showed the greatest preference for looking at male-typical toys (Alexander & Wilcox, 2012).

The psychologist and researcher John Money hypothesized that biology does not determine gender traits or gender identification. He believed that, with the proper environment, anyone can be raised as either a boy or a girl, regardless of genetic sex (Money, 1975). This view is difficult to maintain, however, in light of evidence from a group of boys who were raised as girls since birth. Like other boys, they possessed XY chromosomes and were therefore exposed to male levels of androgens during fetal development. But because of a developmental disorder called cloacal exstrophy that caused the penis to be partly or completely absent (along with abnormalities of the bladder and intestines), they were given surgery at birth for female-sex assignment. Parents were instructed not to reveal to the children information about their sex at birth, since this might adversely affect psychological development. Despite parental encouragement to play with dolls and other girl-typical toys, nearly all of the children showed male-typical toy preferences. All developed sexual attraction toward women, not men, and most later developed a male gender identity (Reiner & Gearhart, 2004). In dramatic contrast to Money's prediction, most adopted the gender that corresponded to their male genes and male-typical hormone exposure, not the female gender with which they were raised. Because the surgery that these children underwent soon after birth included removal of the testes, these results suggest that gender identity is related to organizational changes in the brain that occur prior to birth.

As we saw earlier, genetic males who lack sensitivity to testosterone and other androgens often show anatomy that is intersexed. These are boys whose brains were not exposed to the hormones that normally produce masculinizing effects during brain development. If it is true that testosterone exposure during brain development contributes to male gender identity, these individuals should not show male gender identity despite their XY genes. Consistent with this prediction, they almost always identify as female and develop sexual attraction to males (Swaab & Garcia-Falgueras, 2009).

Finally, evidence for testosterone's developmental influence on gender-typical behavior comes from cases of genetic females exposed to abnormally high prenatal testosterone levels. Compared to other girls, they show more preference for boy-typical toys. As adolescents, they read fewer fashion magazines and more sports magazines compared to girls on average. They do not typically develop a male gender identity; however, as adults they are more likely than other women to be in male-dominated occupations (e.g., auto mechanic). The effects of testosterone on future interests appears to depend upon exposure to the hormone both prenatally and during the first few months after birth (Berenbaum & Beltz, 2016). Such findings, which have been replicated in over a dozen studies in several different countries, strongly suggest a developmental influence of sex hormones on later behavior (Reiner & Gearhart, 2004; Berenbaum & Beltz, 2016).

7.6.2 Transsexual and Transgender Individuals

Transgender people do not identify with the gender that corresponds to their sexual anatomy. They include a diverse group that includes those who express their identity by wearing clothes of the other gender (cross-dressers), those who impersonate the opposite sex (drag queens and kings), and those who identify with both genders (bigender) or neither. The group also includes **transsexuals**, for whom the mismatch between their gender identity and sexual anatomy produces enough stress and unhappiness to motivate them to undergo medical procedures (surgery or hormone therapy) to change their sex. About 1.4 million adults in the USA identify as transgender, or about 0.6 percent of the adult population (Flores, Herman, Gates, & Brown, 2016).

Caitlyn Jenner, formerly Bruce Jenner, a winner of an Olympic gold medal for decathalon (a combination of track and field events), is anatomically and genetically male (XY chromosomes). However, like Janet Mock (in the story that opened this chapter), she felt herself to be female even when she was a child. Jenner recalls getting involved in sports as "a way to prove your masculinity," and entered college on a football scholarship before switching to decathalon (Steinmetz, 2015).

Throughout her life, she suffered **gender dysphoria** (Sawyer, 2015), the distress that often comes from a mismatch between the gender assigned at birth and the individual's gender identity. Gender dysphoria includes feelings of loneliness, anxiety, and depression, and carries a high risk for suicide. A shocking 41 percent of transgender men and women in the USA attempt suicide, compared to a rate of 4.6 percent for the overall US population (Haas, Philip, & Herman, 2014). In Jenner's attempt to make her outward appearance more closely match her gender identity, she took hormone replacement therapy and engaged in cross-dressing, but has not undergone a sex change operation.

In earlier sections, we considered animal studies that shed light on how sex hormones contribute to the development of sexual anatomy, the brain, and sexual behavior. When considering human sexual identity, higher levels of complexity come into play. Gender identity, physical appearance, and concerns about how others may perceive us interact in complex ways. Part of this complexity involves the way that biological factors have shaped our bodies and brains. Let us ask, then, how biological factors might influence human gender identity.

While androgens contribute to the development of sexual organs of the body, it is the influence of androgens on *brain* development that seems more likely to influence gender identity. Androgens masculinize the sexual organs at a relatively early period of development compared to their actions on the brain. Some researchers have theorized that if androgen levels are high during development of the sexual organs and low during development of the brain, or vice versa, gender identity may not match the sex of the sexual organs (Swaab & Garcia-Falgueras, 2009). Female-like brain structures may be seen in individuals with male sexual anatomy, and male-like brain structures may be seen in persons with female anatomy.

For instance, portions of the **bed nucleus of the stria terminalis**, a structure that provides communication between emotion-related areas of the amygdala and sex-related areas of the hypothalamus, are, on average, twice as large in men compared with women. However, in males with female gender identity, who elect to undergo a sex change procedure, the average size of these brain regions is similar to that of females. Similarly, a portion of the anterior hypothalamus implicated in sex is normally larger in males than females. However, the average size of the brain region in males who choose to become female is similar to that of females. In the case of females who choose to become males, the bed nucleus and areas of the anterior hypothalamus are male-typical in size. These differences appear to result from brain development prior to birth rather than hormonal effects in adulthood (Swaab & Garcia-Falgueras, 2009). While there are controversies regarding which specific brain regions contribute to gender identity (Guillamon, Junque, & Gomez-Gil, 2016), evidence from the brains of individuals who do not identify with their anatomical sex suggests that gender identity is likely linked to characteristics of the brain rather than the anatomy of the body.

7.6.3 Sexual Orientation

All of the great apes (which include humans) have been observed to engage in sexual behavior with a member of their own sex. Homosexual behavior is particularly common among the bonobo great apes (Figure 7.8), where about 60 percent of all sexual behavior is between females. Homosexual behavior is also seen in elephants, giraffes, bottlenose dolphins, and other species.

A person's sexual orientation refers to the gender to which they are attracted. Approximately 1–3 percent of men, and a similar proportion of women, say they are primarily, or only, attracted to the same sex (Laumann, Gagnon, Michael, & Michaels, 1994; Chandra, Mosher, Copen, & Sionean, 2011). A larger percentage (about 6 percent of men and 8 percent of women) report having had at least one sexual partner of the same sex since they were 18 years old, although these figures rise and fall over the years (Wienke & Whaley, 2015). Social factors appear to have little impact upon homosexuality. Being raised by homosexual parents does not affect the sexual orientation of the child. Many methods have historically, and tragically, been used to try to change a homosexual to a heterosexual, including castration, psychoanalysis, various drug treatments, brain surgery, electroshock treatment, and imprisonment. Attempts to change an individual's sexual orientation by persuasion or coercion have been notoriously unsuccessful. Sexual orientation appears to be largely fixed by adulthood.

Efforts to change an individual's sexual orientation have historically arisen from stigmas attached to homosexuality, including the belief that same-sex attraction constitutes a mental disorder. In addressing such

Figure 7.8 Bonobo great apes.
(© Anup Shah/Getty Images.)

misconceptions, the American Psychological Association states their conclusion that "same-sex sexual and romantic attractions, feelings, and behaviors are normal and positive variations of human sexuality regardless of sexual orientation identity" (Anton, 2010).

If sexual orientation is resistant to environmental/social change, is it subject to biological influences? A great deal of evidence suggests that it is. Recall our earlier discussion of genetically male individuals (XY chromosomes) who were exposed to male levels of androgens during fetal development, but received surgery at birth for female-sex assignment (due to their condition of cloacal exstrophy). All developed sexual attraction toward women, not men, despite being raised as girls (Reiner & Gearhart, 2004). This suggests that their XY genes and/or exposure to prenatal hormones played a key role in their sexual orientation. Evidence that hormone exposure may be a critical determinant of sexual preference comes from the fact that genetically male individuals who lack sensitivity to androgens (complete androgen insensitivity syndrome) nearly all show sexual attraction to men, not to women (Hines, Constantinescu, & Spencer, 2015). (In this case, environmental influences on sexual orientation cannot be ruled out, for individuals with androgen insensitivity syndrome are typically raised as girls.)

Homosexuals and heterosexuals do not differ in their levels of sex hormones circulating through the bloodstream as adults. However, sex hormones may act during sensitive periods of brain development to affect the individual's later sexual orientation. For instance, girls exposed to high testosterone levels before and shortly after birth (due to congenital adrenal hyperplasia) are several times more likely than other girls to later experience bisexual or lesbian fantasies or to identify as bisexual or lesbian (Meyer-Bahlburg, Dolezal, Baker, & New, 2008).

In order to gauge the genetic contribution to homosexuality, studies have examined the likelihood of homosexuality in one twin given that the other twin is homosexual (the concordance rate among twins). The concordance rate varies across studies, but is consistently higher for monozygotic twins (who share all the same genes) compared to dizygotic twins (with gene similarity no greater than brothers and sisters generally). Taken together, twin studies suggest an approximately 50 percent contribution of genes to sexual orientation (Bao & Swaab, 2010).

The specific genes that contribute to homosexual orientation are not yet known. However, there are clues to suggest that the relevant genes are mostly passed on by the mother. For instance, uncles and cousins of homosexual men have a high likelihood of being gay as well, but this is only true for the mother's side of the family (Hamer, Hu, Magnuson, Hu, & Pattatucci, 1993). There is no elevation in homosexuality among fathers or paternal relatives of gay men. Recall that males receive their single X chromosome exclusively from their mothers. This suggests that key genes contributing to male homosexuality may lie on the X chromosome. Examinations of the DNA of gay siblings have revealed a region of the X chromosome called Xq28 that appears to be linked to male, but not female, homosexuality (Hu et al., 1995; Sanders et al., 2015). Genes contribute to female homosexuality as well, for identical twins are more likely to both be lesbians than fraternal twins. Again, however, little is known about the precise contribution of specific genes to homosexuality in either men or women, and it is likely that many genes are involved (Bao & Swaab, 2010; Roselli, 2018).

Male and female homosexuality appear to differ in significant ways. Women are more likely than men to report sexual desire for both sexes rather than for one sex exclusively. Studies measuring genital responses to sexual stimuli similarly find that women are much more likely than men to show signs of arousal to both sexes. Female reports of same- versus other-sex attraction, while relatively stable, vary over time to a larger extent than those of either heterosexual or gay men. This heightened variability suggests the possibility that environmental factors (such as interpersonal relationships and cultural norms) may play a larger role in the sexual orientation of women compared to men (Diamond, 2012).

KEY CONCEPTS

- **In humans, early masculinization or feminization of the brain can bias an individual toward male or female gender identity and/or gender-typical behavior.**
- **Human gender identity and sexual behavior involves a complex interplay between one's self-concept, biological predispositions, and social norms.**
- **The precise contributions to gender identity are not known, although it likely involves the influence of sex hormones during brain development.**
- **Homosexuality is seen across the animal kingdom. In humans, it appears to be fixed by adulthood, and involves hormonal and genetic components.**

TEST YOURSELF

1. **Describe evidence that supports a role for testosterone in the development of male versus female gender identity in humans.**
2. **How do the brains of male-to-female transsexuals resemble those of females?**
3. **What evidence supports a genetic contribution to homosexuality? What evidence supports a contribution of environmental factors?**

7.7 SEXUALLY AROUSING STIMULI ACTIVATE THE BRAIN

Neuroscientists examining how the brains of men and women respond during sexual arousal is, of course, limited in their ability to observe these responses under natural conditions. After all, subjects in such studies must enter a laboratory setting and place their head into a tube-shaped opening while stimuli (usually visual) are presented and brain responses recorded. Nevertheless, such studies have found that presentation of sexual stimuli produces reliable activations of particular brain regions.

As we will see below, dopamine is released into the nucleus accumbens in animal subjects anticipating the opportunity for sexual contact. Similarly, humans viewing images or videos with sexual content show activations in the nucleus accumbens, as well as other motivation-related brain regions including the hypothalamus and amygdala (see Figure 7.9). The nucleus accumbens is the same brain region that is activated by other rewards such as food, money, and cocaine (see Chapter 11).

In one study, heterosexual men and women viewed photographs of sexually attractive opposite-sex nudes (and also of heterosexual couples engaged in sexual activity). Both the men and the women showed activation of the hypothalamus and amygdala, but the activity was higher in men than women. Even in cases where arousal levels were greater in women, these brain areas responded more strongly in the male subjects

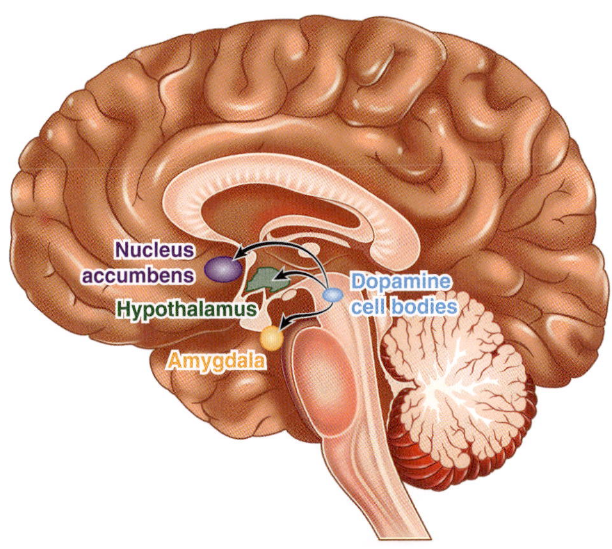

Figure 7.9 **Nucleus accumbens and other regions activated by sex-related stimuli**. Dopamine neurons project to the nucleus accumbens and other motivation-related brain regions. Humans looking at sexual images show activations in the nucleus accumbens, amygdala, and hypothalamus.

(Hamann, Herman, Nolan, & Wallen, 2004). This suggests that activation of these brain regions may play a larger role in sexual arousal of males compared with females.

While heterosexual men show hypothalamic brain activations when viewing erotic stimuli related to the opposite sex, they did not show activations in response to homosexual content. Homosexual men similarly show brain activations that are selective to their sexual preference, i.e., hypothalamic responses to erotic homosexual but not heterosexual content (Paul et al., 2008). On the other hand, female subjects show brain activations that discriminate less with respect to the sexual orientation of the content. This is true of both heterosexual and homosexual women (Sylva et al., 2013). Heterosexual women showed stronger hypothalamic activations to erotic photos of men than women, but the difference in activation produced by photos of men versus women was relatively small compared to the difference in hypothalamic activation for male heterosexuals viewing erotic photos of women compared to men. These results are consistent with the findings described in the previous section, that women are more variable than men with respect to the potential for arousal by same-sex stimuli.

Behavioral data point to other important differences in the conditions that generate sexual arousal in males and females. For instance, compared to men, who frequently report spontaneous sexual urges, women more frequently experience sexual arousal only after exposure to sexual stimuli and in particular contexts often involving intimate interpersonal attachment (Basson, 2000; Diamond, 2012). It can be difficult to study the neural underpinnings of such factors using brain imaging in a laboratory setting, and little is known about how human interpersonal factors and sexual arousal interact from a neurobiological perspective.

In many animal species, sexual responses can be strongly elicited by odorless airborne chemicals called **pheromones**. The fruit fly, for instance, only mates with flies that carry a specific pheromone (Billeter & Levine, 2012). In mammals, the **vomeronasal** organ detects pheromones and sends neural signals to specific areas of the hypothalamus, allowing pheromones to strongly influence the animal's choice of a sexual partner. It is located at the base of the nasal cavity, the large air-filled space above and behind the nose. There is controversy regarding whether a region analogous to the vomeronasal organ exists in humans (Krajnik, Kollndorfer, Nenning, Lundstrom, & Schopf, 2014). While pheromone chemicals have been shown to activate the hypothalamus and some frontal cortical regions in humans (Georgiadis, 2015), there is little evidence that they affect human sexual behavior.

7.8 SEX HORMONES AND OTHER NEUROCHEMICALS CAN STRONGLY AFFECT SEXUAL BEHAVIOR

Testosterone and other sex hormones play a role in the development of brain circuits relevant to sexual behavior (see the earlier section, "Are Male and Female Brains Different?"). After the brain has matured, these hormones continue to play an *activational* role. This does not mean that hormones activate sexual behavior in the sense that a light activates a moth's automatic flight toward it. Hormones can enhance sexual arousal, increasing the expectation of pleasure from sex with a potential partner. Hormones can also make a sexual experience more pleasurable by increasing the sensitivity of the penis, vagina, and cervix to sexual stimulation.

The activational effects of gonadal hormones begin in puberty, when the brain signals the testes to release androgens in males or the ovaries to release estrogens in females. In both cases, the signal begins in the hypothalamus. As seen in Figure 7.10, the hypothalamus releases **gonadotropin-releasing hormone**, which travels a short distance through a network of blood vessels to reach the anterior pituitary. The anterior pituitary then responds by releasing **luteinizing hormone** and **follicle stimulating hormone**. (Both hormones are released by the pituitary in men as well as women.) In turn, these pituitary hormones travel through the bloodstream to the testes to release androgens (in males) or to the ovaries to release estrogens (in females). During puberty, these gonadal hormones lead to development of secondary sexual characteristics as described in an earlier section; but they also interact with the brain to affect sexual arousal and behavior.

The brain contains complex networks of structures related to various aspects of sexual behavior, and the sex hormones interact with these structures to promote sexual behavior. For instance, testosterone has been shown to act within the mPOA of the hypothalamus to promote sexual behavior in male rats. While castration eliminates most testosterone and sexual behavior, a castrated rat will engage in sex again if testosterone is restored specifically within the mPOA (Pfaus, 2009). Testosterone also plays a role in human sexual arousal, and loss of testosterone can diminish libido in both men and women (Buvat, Maggi, Guay, & Torres, 2013; Ingram, Payne, Messore, & Scovell, 2020).

Sexual arousal and behavior in females are strongly affected by estrogen levels (Pfaus, 2009). In the female rat, a loss of estrogen following removal of the ovaries greatly reduces sexual behavior. The behavior, however, can be restored by replacement with estradiol combined with testosterone. These data suggest that estradiol and the small quantities of testosterone

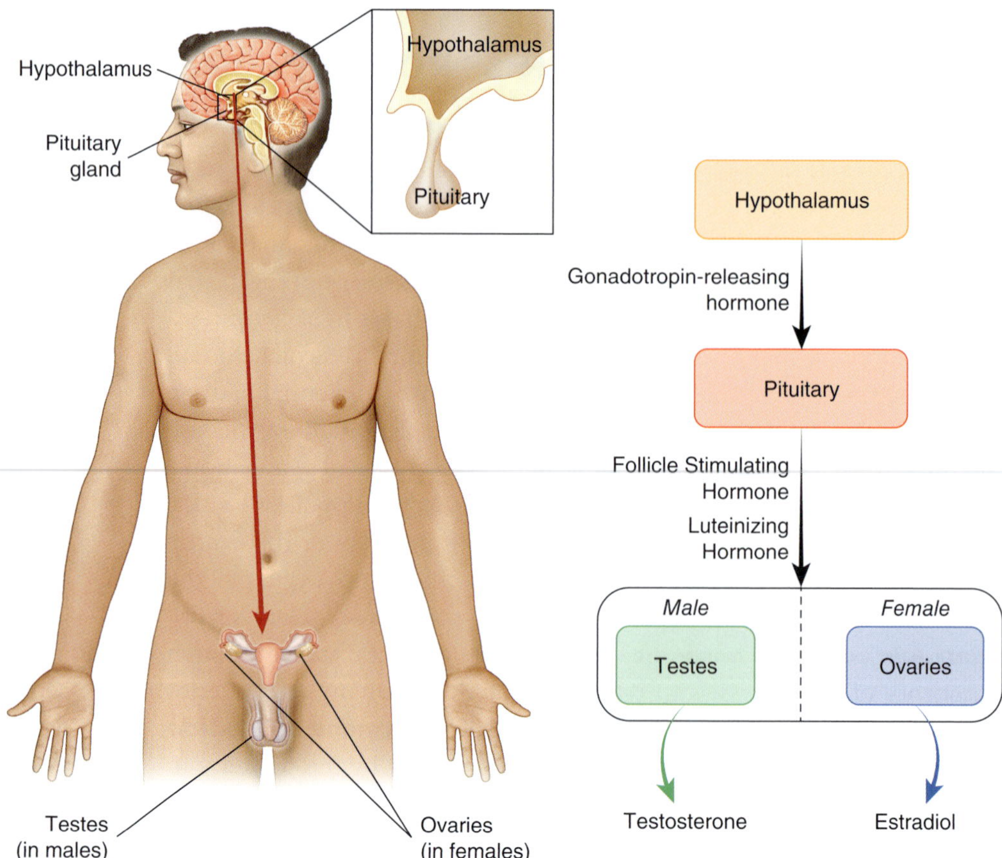

Figure 7.10 Puberty marks the starting point for the activational effects of gonadal hormones. Beginning at puberty, the hypothalamus releases gonadotropin-releasing hormone. Gonadotropin-releasing hormone stimulates the anterior pituitary to release follicle-stimulating hormone and luteinizing hormone. In turn, these pituitary hormones travel to the testes to increase release of testosterone or to the ovaries to increase release of estradiol.

that are normally released from the ovaries are both important in female sexual behavior. Estrogens also play a role in sexual behavior of non-human primates. Female monkeys, for instance, increase their approaches and sexual solicitations to males during periods of peak estrogen levels.

In humans, female estrogen levels rise during the week before ovulation, peak just before ovulation, and then fall rapidly over the following days. Women report an increase in sex drive during the periods of high estrogen levels and a sudden drop as estrogen levels fall after ovulation. During the time of high estrogen levels and maximum fertility, women are most likely to initiate sexual activity either with a partner or through masturbation.

In addition to the gonadal sex hormones, the hormone **oxytocin** plays a role in sexual behavior. Released from the hypothalamus and the pituitary gland, oxytocin serves a number of functions, including release of milk during breast feeding and bonding between mother and infant. Oxytocin is also released in men and women during orgasm. In male rats, oxytocin release in the mPOA increases sexual behavior. In addition, as male rats gain sexual experience, they undergo an increase in the number of oxytocin receptors located on neurons in the mPOA (Gil, Bhatt, Picotte, & Hull, 2013).

Oxytocin has also been linked to bonding of sexual partners (Jurek & Neumann, 2018). After mating, prairie voles (Figure 7.11) form bonds that can last a lifetime. They become monogamous partners, build nests together, and share in parental responsibilities. Compared to voles that have not yet formed a bond, the monogamous voles have high levels of oxytocin receptors. When other kinds of voles with promiscuous behavior patterns (multiple sex partners) receive oxytocin injections, they, too become monogamous. Therefore, oxytocin appears to play a key role in exclusive bonding.

Several neurotransmitters play a role in sexual behavior as well. Dopamine is released in the nucleus accumbens, hypothalamus, and several other motivation-related brain regions during anticipation of sex (Pfaus, 2009). When a male rat notices a receptive female behind a barrier, dopamine levels surge. The more dopamine released, the more likely the male is to copulate with the female when given the opportunity. Dopamine is involved in sexual anticipation for both males and females.

Serotonin inhibits sexual activity, and many antidepressant drugs that increase serotonin activity also decrease sexual arousal and inhibit orgasm in both men and women. Serotonin-elevating drugs similarly reduce aspects of sexual behavior in rats, including ejaculation. There is some evidence suggesting that serotonin's inhibitory effects on ejaculation are due

Figure 7.11 After mating, some prairie voles form life-long bonds.
(@Zuoxin Wang, © 2013, Springer Nature.)

to its disruption of oxytocin activity, and oxytocin restores normal ejaculation in rats under the influence of a serotonin agonist (Cantor, Binik, & Pfaus, 1999). This raises the possibility that oxytocin may be helpful in reversing the sexual side effects of antidepressants.

Impotence, the inability to have or maintain an erection, can occur as a result of reduced activity in brain regions related to sexual arousal. However, it is often the result of insufficient blood flow to the penis. The gas molecule **nitric oxide** increases the diameter of (dilates) blood vessels and increases blood flow to the penis during erection. The drug Viagra (sildenafil), used in the treatment of impotence, increases and prolongs the actions of nitric oxide. This allows nitric oxide to exert larger and more sustained effects on blood flow to the penis, facilitating erection.

KEY CONCEPTS

- In humans, sexually arousing visual stimuli can activate brain areas such as the hypothalamus that play a role in sexual behavior.
- Many hormones and neurotransmitters activate or inhibit sexual arousal and behavior. The sex hormones testosterone and estradiol are critical in the sexual motivation of humans and other animals.

TEST YOURSELF

1. How do heterosexual and homosexual men differ in terms of hypothalamic brain activations when viewing erotic stimuli related to the opposite sex?
2. Are these differences also seen in heterosexual and homosexual women?
3. Describe evidence pointing to a role for dopamine in sexual motivation.

7.9 The Big Picture

During early stages of fetal development, the presence of testosterone leads to physical characteristics of the male anatomy, while its absence leads to the characteristics of the female anatomy. During brain development, both testosterone and estradiol guide the maturation of brain circuits that will influence the adult's sexual attention and behavior toward either male or female partners, and apparently even gender identity. Beginning in puberty and continuing through adulthood, the hypothalamus orchestrates the release of sex hormones from the gonads, which in turn may enhance sexual responsiveness and the excitement of sexual anticipation.

However, sexual attraction, sexual behavior, and gender identity also occur within the context of cultural norms. As Janet Mock's story illustrates, human experience of gender involves the construction of a self-concept, and concern about how those in our social world perceive us.

Genes and sex hormones, as well as socialcultural factors, interact to give rise to gender identity, sexual orientation, and behavior. The complex interplay between these factors remains a topic of great interest to neuroscientists.

7.10 Creative Thinking

1. Is gender identity determined primarily by biology or by culture? Explain your reasoning.
2. If you felt like a man and your body was female, or vice versa, would you take steps to change your gender? How? Would you consider a sex-change operation, hormone therapy, cross-dressing? If so, how might your life change as a result of these steps? Could you live happily without any change in your sexual appearance?
3. Female rats exposed to high testosterone levels during brain development later come to show sexual interest in other females. Is this strong evidence that human female homosexuality is due to high testosterone exposure during brain development? Explain why or why not.

Key Terms

activating role, sexual behavior 277
androgen 275
anteroventral periventricular nucleus (AVPV) of the hypothalamus 284
aromatase deficiency 281
bed nucleus of the stria terminalis 291
endocrine glands 274
estradiol 276
feminized 281
follicle stimulating hormone 297
gender dysphoria 290
gender identity 274
gestation 280
gonads 275
gonadal hormones 275
gonadotropin-releasing hormone 297
impotence 300
intersex 281
lordosis 287
luteinizing hormone 297
masculinize 280
medial preoptic area (mPOA) of the hypothalamus 283
Müllerian ducts 280
Müllerian-Inhibiting Factor 281

References

Alexander, G. M., & Wilcox, T. (2012). Sex differences in early infancy. *Child Development Perspectives*, *6*(4), 400–406.

Anton, B. S. (2010). Appropriate affirmative responses to sexual orientation distress and change efforts. Proceedings of the American Psychological Association for the Legislative Year 2009: Minutes of the annual meeting of the Council of Representatives and minutes of the meetings of the Board of Directors. *American Psychologist*, *65*, 385–475.

Bao, A. M., & Swaab, D. F. (2010). Sex differences in the brain, behavior, and neuropsychiatric disorders. *Neuroscientist*, *16*(5), 550–565.

Basson, R. (2000). The female sexual response: a different model. *Journal of Sex & Marital Therapy*, *26*(1), 51–65.

Behl, C. (2002). Oestrogen as a neuroprotective hormone. *Nature Reviews Neuroscience*, *3*(6), 433–442.

Berenbaum, S. A., & Beltz, A. M. (2016). How early hormones shape gender development. *Current Opinion in Behavioral Sciences*, *7*, 53–60.

Billeter, J.-C., & Levine, J. D. (2013). Who is he and what is he to you? Recognition in Drosophila melanogaster. *Current Opinion in Neurobiology*, *23*(1), 17–23.

Buvat, J., Maggi, M., Guay, A., & Torres, L. O. (2013). Testosterone deficiency in men: systematic review and standard operating procedures for diagnosis and treatment. *Journal of Sexual Medicine*, *10*(1), 245–284.

Cahill, L. (2006). Why sex matters for neuroscience. *Nature Reviews Neuroscience*, *7*(6), 477–484.

Cantor, J. M., Binik, Y. M., & Pfaus, J. G. (1999). Chronic fluoxetine inhibits sexual behavior in the male rat: reversal with oxytocin. *Psychopharmacology* (Berl), *144*(4), 355–362.

Chandra, A., Mosher, W. D., Copen, C., & Sionean, C. (2011). Sexual behavior, sexual attraction, and sexual identity in the United States: data from the 2006–2008 National Survey of Family Growth. *National Health Statistics Reports* *36*(36), 1–36.

Denley, M. C. S., Gatford, N. J. F., Sellers, K. J., & Srivastava, D. P. (2018). Estradiol and the development of the cerebral cortex: an unexpected role? *Frontiers in Neuroscience*, 12.

Diamond, L. M. (2012). The desire disorder in research on sexual orientation in women: contributions of dynamical systems theory. *Archives of Sexual Behavior, 41*(1), 73–83.

Flores, A. R., Herman, J. L., Gates, G. J., & Brown, T. N. T. (2016). How many adults identify as transgender in the United States? http://williamsinstitute.law.ucla.edu/wp-content/uploads/How-Many-Adults-Identify-as-Transgender-in-the-United-States.pdf

Georgiadis, J. R. (2015). Functional neuroanatomy of human cortex cerebri in relation to wanting sex and having it. *Clinical Anatomy, 28*(3), 314–323.

Gil, M., Bhatt, R., Picotte, K. B., & Hull, E. M. (2013). Sexual experience increases oxytocin receptor gene expression and protein in the medial preoptic area of the male rat. *Psychoneuroendocrinology, 38*(9), 1688–1697.

Guillamon, A., Junque, C., & Gomez-Gil, E. (2016). A review of the status of brain structure research in transsexualism. *Archives of Sexual Behavior, 45*(7), 1615–1648.

Haas, A. P., Philip L. R., & Herman, J. L. (2014). *Suicide Attempts among Transgender and Gender Non-Conforming Adults*. Los Angeles, CA: The Williams Institute and American Foundation for Suicide Prevention. http://williamsinstitute.law.ucla.edu/wp-content/uploads/AFSP-Williams-Suicide-Report-Final.pdf

Hamann, S., Herman, R. A., Nolan, C. L., & Wallen, K. (2004). Men and women differ in amygdala response to visual sexual stimuli. *Nature Neuroscience, 7*(4), 411–416.

Hamer, D. H., Hu, S., Magnuson, V. L., Hu, N., & Pattatucci, A. M. (1993). A linkage between DNA markers on the X chromosome and male sexual orientation. *Science, 261*(5119), 321–327.

Hines, M., Constantinescu, M., & Spencer, D. (2015). Early androgen exposure and human gender development. *Biology of Sex Differences, 6*, 3.

Hu, S., Pattatucci, A. M., Patterson, C., Li, L., Fulker, D. W., Cherny, S. S., ... Hamer, D. H. (1995). Linkage between sexual orientation and chromosome Xq28 in males but not in females. *Nature Genetics, 11*(3), 248–256.

Ingram, C. F., Payne, K. S., Messore, M., & Scovell, J. M. (2020). Testosterone therapy and other treatment modalities for female sexual dysfunction. *Current Opinion in Urology, 30*(3), 309–316.

Jurek, B., & Neumann, I. D. (2018). The oxytocin receptor: from intracellular signaling to behavior. *Physiological Reviews, 98*(3), 1805–1908.

Krajnik, J., Kollndorfer, K., Nenning, K. H., Lundstrom, J. N., & Schopf, V. (2014). Gender effects and sexual-orientation impact on androstadienone-evoked behavior and neural processing. *Frontiers in Neuroscience, 8*, 195.

Laumann, E. O., Gagnon, J. H., Michael, R. T., & Michaels, S. (1994). *The Social Organization of Sexuality: Sexual Practices in the United States*. Chicago: University of Chicago Press.

Lenz, K. M., & McCarthy, M. M. (2010). Organized for sex – steroid hormones and the developing hypothalamus. *European Journal of Neuroscience, 32*(12), 2096–2104.

Martin, M. (2011). Transgender Writer Shares Her Powerful Journey to Womanhood. NPR News, Tell Me More. Interview with Janet Mock, June 3, 2011. www.npr.org/2011/06/03/136921779/transgender-shares-her-powerful-journey-to-womanhood and http://janetmock.com/bio/

McCarthy, M. M., & Arnold, A. P. (2011). Reframing sexual differentiation of the brain. *Nature Neuroscience, 14*(6), 677–683.

Meyer-Bahlburg, H. F., Dolezal, C., Baker, S. W., & New, M. I. (2008). Sexual orientation in women with classical or non-classical congenital adrenal hyperplasia as a function of degree of prenatal androgen excess. *Archives of Sexual Behavior, 37*(1), 85–99.

Misrahi, M., Meduri, G., Pissard, S., Bouvattier, C., Beau, I., Loosfelt, H., ... Bougneres, P. (1997). Comparison of immunocytochemical and molecular features with the phenotype in a case of incomplete male pseudohermaphroditism associated with a mutation of the luteinizing hormone receptor. *Journal of Clinical Endocrinology & Metabolism, 82*(7), 2159–2165.

Money, J. (1975). Ablatio penis: normal male infant sex-reassigned as a girl. *Archives of Sexual Behavior, 4*(1), 65–71.

Paul, T., Schiffer, B., Zwarg, T., Kruger, T. H., Karama, S., Schedlowski, M., ... Gizewski, E. R. (2008). Brain response to visual sexual stimuli in heterosexual and homosexual males. *Human Brain Mapping, 29*(6), 726–735.

Pfaus, J. G. (2009). Pathways of sexual desire. *Journal of Sexual Medicine, 6*(6), 1506–1533.

Reiner, W. G., & Gearhart, J. P. (2004). Discordant sexual identity in some genetic males with cloacal exstrophy assigned to female sex at birth. *New England Journal of Medicine, 350*(4), 333–341.

Roselli, C. E. (2018). Neurobiology of gender identity and sexual orientation. *Journal of Neuroendocrinology, 30*(7).

Sanders, A. R., Martin, E. R., Beecham, G. W., Guo, S., Dawood, K., Rieger, G., ... Bailey, J. M. (2015). Genome-wide scan demonstrates significant linkage for male sexual orientation. *Psychological Medicine, 45*(7), 1379–1388.

Sawyer, D. (2015). Bruce Jenner: The interview. ABC News' 20/20 with Diane Sawyer. April 24, 2015. http://abcnews.go.com/2020/fullpage/bruce-jenner-the-interview-30471558

Shiino, A., Chen, Y. W., Tanigaki, K., Yamada, A., Vigers, P., Watanabe, T., ... Akiguchi, I. (2017). Sex-related difference in human white matter volumes studied: inspection of the corpus callosum and other white matter by VBM. *Scientific Reports, 7*.

Shirtcliff, E. A., Dahl, R. E., & Pollak, S. D. (2009). Pubertal development: correspondence between hormonal and physical development. *Child Development, 80*(2), 327–337.

Steinmetz, K. (2015). Caitlyn Jenner on privilege, reality TV and deciding to come out. Time. http://time.com/4142000/time-person-of-the-year-runner-up-caitlyn-jenner-interview/

Swaab, D. F., & Garcia-Falgueras, A. (2009). Sexual differentiation of the human brain in relation to gender identity and sexual orientation. *Functional Neurology*, *24*(1), 17–28.

Sylva, D., Safron, A., Rosenthal, A. M., Reber, P. J., Parrish, T. B., & Bailey, J. M. (2013). Neural correlates of sexual arousal in heterosexual and homosexual women and men. *Hormones and Behavior*, *64*(4), 673–684.

Tan, A., Ma, W., Vira, A., Marwha, D., & Eliot, L. (2016). The human hippocampus is not sexually-dimorphic: meta-analysis of structural MRI volumes. *NeuroImage*, *124* (Pt A), 350–366.

Wienke, C., & Whaley, R. B. (2015). Same-gender sexual partnering: a re-analysis of trend data. *Journal of Sex Research*, *52*(2), 162–173.

8

Brain Development and Plasticity

JUAN GAERTNER / SCIENCE PHOTO LIBRARY / Getty Images

Consider This ...

At the end of nine months, the majority of human pregnancies end with the birth of a beautiful, healthy newborn. Given the complexity of this process, this result can be seen as nothing short of miraculous. Although the genetic program laid down for this typically runs its course in a smooth and trouble-free manner, a vast number of factors can produce developmental malformation. Before we describe normal, healthy brain development and function, let's take a look at the consequences when one of these processes is disrupted.

Alcoholic beverages – wine, beer, and spirits – have become staples of adult life in many societies. Alcohol may serve some positive functions such as facilitating social interaction and relaxation. However, overindulgence or inappropriate usage can have negative consequences. Alcohol can be addictive, can produce liver damage, and may be responsible for highway deaths. But there is another especially devastating consequence of alcohol misuse: It can produce birth defects.

When Rosemary was a college freshman, she was introduced to alcohol at campus parties. Her use of alcohol became habitual, even in her own dorm room, and she often drank heavily. She met her husband, Frank, in college, and they married when she was 24. Her heavy drinking remained a regular part of her life. Two years later, she became pregnant and lowered her alcohol consumption. However, she continued to drink and now hid it from her friends and husband. Frank, Jr. was born when Rosemary was 27. It was immediately evident from his below-average height and weight, his small head, and his long, thin upper lip that Frank, Jr. was a victim of Fetal Alcohol Syndrome (FAS).

By the time Frank, Jr. began kindergarten, he displayed a variety of behavioral and sensory-motor problems including deficits in cognitive and executive function, impulse control, memory, and attention. He also showed signs of speech delay, problems with hearing and vision, and below-average fine motor skills.

The brains of those with FAS show widespread damage to all parts of the nervous system (CNS and PNS). A few of the brain structures consistently found to display major damage are the cerebellum, corpus callosum, basal ganglia, and vestibular system. Alcohol exposure produces disruptions in all stages of neural development. Individual brain cells exposed to alcohol show abnormalities in proliferation (too many or too few cells are born), differentiation (cells develop abnormally), and survival (they die too easily) (Gupta, Gupta, & Shirasaka, 2016). This chapter first explores the development of the nervous system under normal conditions, and sheds light on what can go wrong when normal processes of development are interrupted. Second, we turn to neural plasticity, the ability of the nervous system to continually modify its connections in response to experience.

8.1 DEVELOPMENT

8.1.1 The Nervous Systems of Mammals, Birds, Reptiles, and Fish All Develop According to a Similar Plan

It is almost beyond comprehension that the union of two cells, an egg and a sperm, can ultimately produce a fully formed organism made up of tens of trillions of cells. This development all begins when the sperm fertilizes the egg to produce a tiny single-cell organism, the **zygote**. Its width (0.1 mm diameter) is five times smaller than a grain of sand. Residing within the zygote are the blueprints for creating adult organisms based upon instructions from the 20,000 genes in the human genome. The cells divide over and over and over again, reaching a rate of tens of thousands of divisions per minute at its peak. With each division, the complete complement of genetic instructions is transferred to each new cell. This rapid growth in the number of cells is called **cell proliferation**.

Following conception, the zygote begins to divide within 12 hours. Within a week, three distinct layers of tissue have formed. The inner layer (endoderm) and middle layer (mesoderm) together give rise to the lungs, digestive system, muscle, blood cells, and other parts of the body. However, our focus here is on the development of the nervous system, which arises from the outer layer of embryonic tissue, the **ectoderm** (*ecto* meaning "outer" + *derm* meaning "skin"). The ectoderm also gives rise to the skin. Looking at Figure 8.1, it's not difficult to visualize how the outer tissue of the embryo gives rise to the outer covering of the body. But how is it that the ectoderm also gives rise to the nervous system?

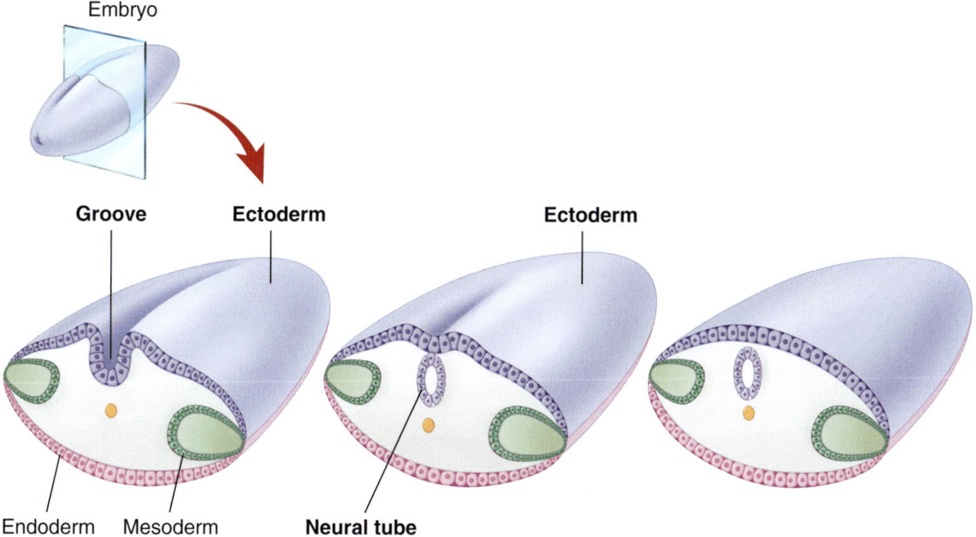

Figure 8.1 The ectoderm folds in to produce the neural tube. The neural tube will eventually give rise to the brain and spinal cord.

As shown in Figure 8.1, during the third week, the outer (ectoderm) layer begins to form a groove, which closes in upon itself to form a tube-like structure called the **neural tube**. The neural tube is of course elongated; it extends anterior (forward) and posterior (backward). (It's a tube after all!) The anterior part will become the brain, and the posterior part will become the spinal cord. The hollow center of the tube will become the ventricles of the brain and the central canal of the spinal cord.

By the fourth week after fertilization, the anterior part of the tube shows three swellings, which will become the forebrain, midbrain, and brainstem (Figure 8.2). As you can see in the figure, the anterior part of the tube bends like the handle of a cane. The other end of the tube closes and forms the spinal cord. This pattern is repeated in all vertebrate species (mammals, birds, reptiles, fish, and all other animals with a backbone) and can be considered the general vertebrate plan for the CNS. The similarity of this plan across the animal kingdom is one of the strongest, fundamental pieces of evidence for the process of evolution.

The brain of the fetus grows rapidly during the nine months of gestation (the time between conception and birth), reaching approximately one-third the size of the adult brain. At birth, the brain takes on the general look of the adult brain primarily because of the characteristic appearance of the gyri and sulci in the cerebral cortex (Figure 8.2). By the end of the second year, it is an amazing 80 percent of the adult brain size, and has taken on the basic structure of the adult brain (Gilmore, Knickmeyer, & Gao, 2018).

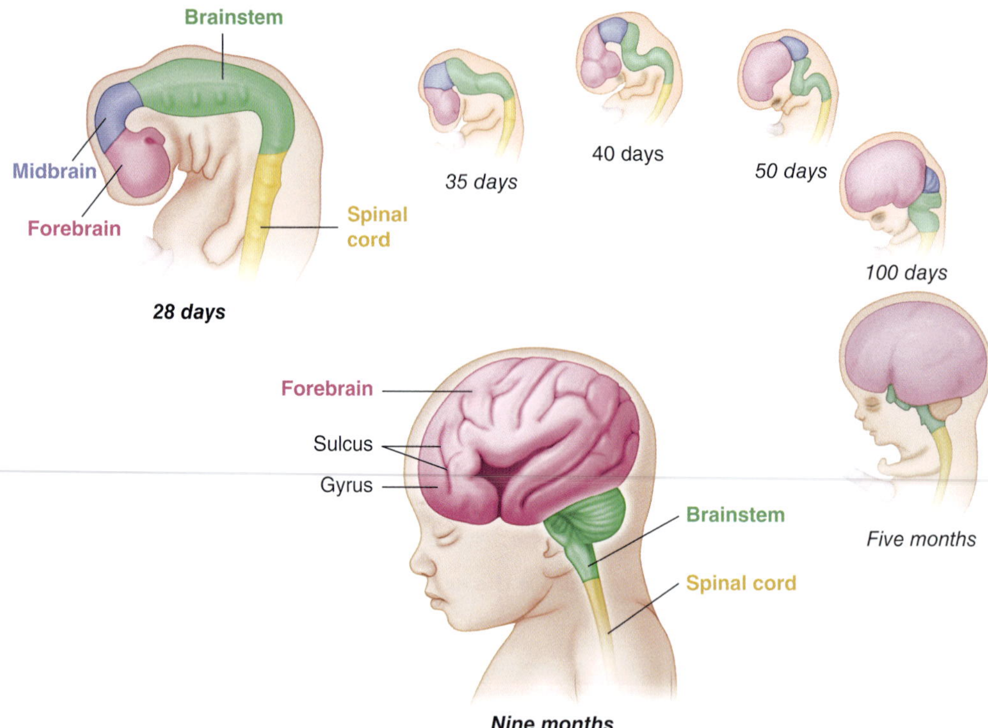

Figure 8.2 Three swellings of the neural tube. Three parts of the anterior neural tube begin to swell (like balloon art) and bend (like the handle of a cane). The swelling at one end (pink) will become the forebrain, the middle will become the midbrain, and the other end (green) will become the brainstem. At nine months, the brain takes on the shape of an adult brain including gyri (hills) and sulci (valleys/grooves) of the cerebral cortex.

8.1.2 Neurons Pass through Five Developmental Phases

The initial cells present during early stages of development divide and eventually produce neurons, bone, blood, heart, and the other of the cells of the body. Once a cell has differentiated and become, say, a neuron, it cannot normally divide and produce blood cells. However, **stem cells**, present at the earliest stages of development, have the potential to produce any kind of cell. A cell with this potential is said to be **pluripotent**. Stem cells are frequently in the news these days because they can, at least theoretically, be used to repair damage to any organ or structure in the body. Some stem cells remain in the adult body and may be capable of unlimited numbers of cell divisions (immortal cells). However, as development progresses, some stem cells receive a signal which leads them down a particular biological path. (Essentially, they are told to grow up, and leave their immature state.) For instance, a stem cell may turn into cells that are capable of producing the neurons and glia of the nervous system.

These cells have reached the next stage of development and are termed **progenitor** cells. If the cells are destined to become neurons (or glia), they are called **neural progenitor cells**.

The process of neural development can be divided into five overlapping phases: cell birth, migration, differentiation, axon growth, and cell death. To examine the birth of the cells destined to become neurons, we return to the neural tube just three weeks after conception, when a human embryo is only 2–3 mm in length (about the size of a flea).

Cell Birth

When you think of the neural tube, it's useful to distinguish between the hollow fluid-filled center of the tube and the wall that surrounds the center. You can see in Figure 8.3 that the part of the wall closest to the center is the **ventricular zone**. This is where the cells destined to make up the nervous system are born. These cells are not the pluripotent stem cells we just spoke of in the previous section; instead, the cells in this zone are the neural progenitor cells that are already destined to become cells of the nervous system (neurons and glia). These neural progenitor cells can divide about fifty times. Early on, they divide just to produce more progenitor cells. Later in the developmental process, they divide to produce another progenitor cell and either a neuron or a glial cell. At its peak, this process of cell division generates several hundred million new neurons per day.

Migration

The neural progenitor cells soon leave the place of their birth, the ventricular zone, and migrate outward. The cells, still in a primitive state

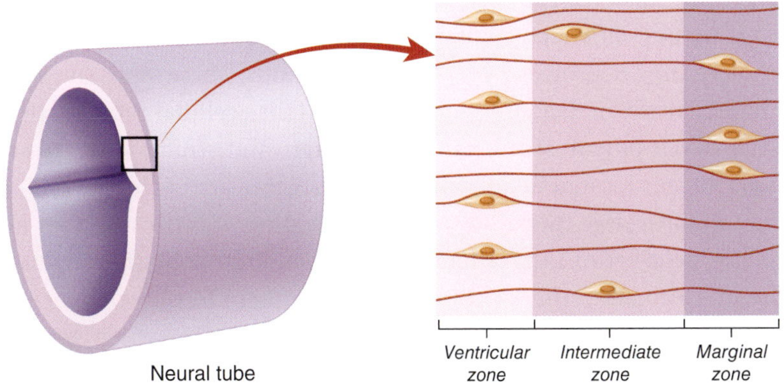

Figure 8.3 The ventricular zone. The ventricular zone, the inner portion of the neural tube wall (light pink), contains the newly born cells that will give rise to the neurons and glia of the nervous system.

lacking axons or dendrites, pass through an intermediate zone of the neural tube and continue to move outward to an exterior layer that adds to the outside of the neural tube. A particularly interesting example of this migration takes place in the development of the cerebral cortex. In leaving the ventricular zone, and passing through the intermediate zone, the cells are guided to the cortex by **radial glia** (Figure 8.4). Radial glia are the first cells produced by cell division, and they act as a kind of scaffolding, providing a temporary structure for other cells to crawl over as they make their way toward their destined locations in the cerebral cortex. The first cells to leave the ventricular zone will form neurons of the lower layer of the cortex; successive waves of cells travel along the radial glia to reach the next higher (more superficial) level, and so on, until the process of forming the six-layered cerebral cortex is complete.

Not all migrating cells glide along the radial glia. Some of them migrate by moving from one radial glial cell to another (like a Mario Brothers figure moving horizontally past columns of a building rather than climbing a column). Whether a cell is climbing a glial guide or moving across glial cells, it needs to know which way to move. Migrating cells encounter chemicals called **chemoattractants**, which provide a trail for the cells to follow. In some cases, the cells encounter **chemorepellants** that they move away from. We will return to attractant and repellant signals below when we ask how axons grow in the correct direction to find their target cells.

Differentiation

Once a cell arrives at its destination, it begins the process of forming the appearance and functions of other cells in the region. As it becomes a specialized *type* of cell, we say that the cell is undergoing **differentiation**. For instance, some layers of the cortex contain specialized neurons with very small cell bodies. Other layers have medium-sized neurons. Still others contain very large neurons in the shape of pyramids. These kinds of structural characteristics depend upon the actions of intracellular proteins that guide the development of the cell's size, shape, and structure (its **morphology**). If cells located in a particular brain region are of the same type (say they all have large, pyramid-shaped cell bodies), it is because they all possess the same set of intracellular proteins guiding their structural development. Ultimately, the set of intracellular proteins in the cell depends upon which of the cell's genes have been expressed (i.e., which genetic instructions have been used to create the proteins).

Let's take a step back. Imagine a bunch of primitive (**undifferentiated**) cells in a particular location of the nervous system. Their neighboring cells have already differentiated into a particular cell type. These

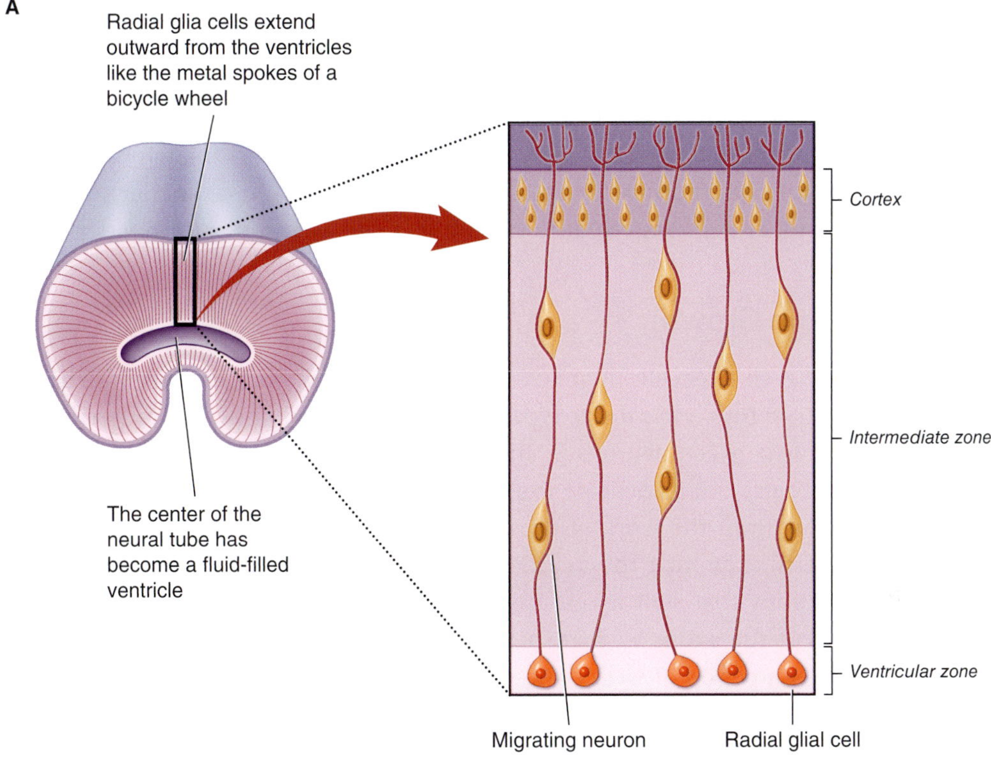

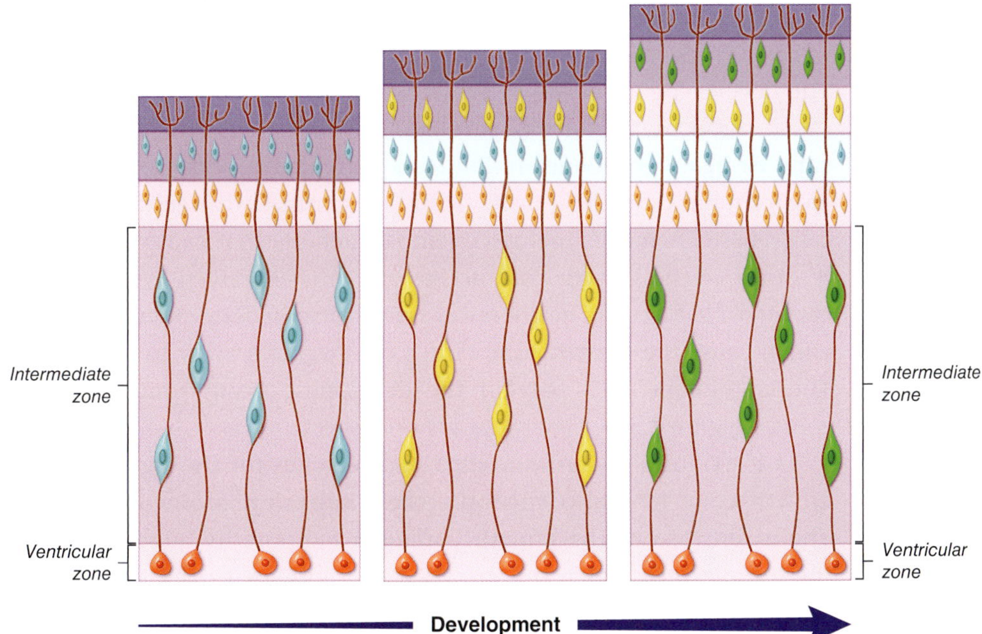

Figure 8.4 Cell migration. (A) Cells that will soon become neurons (yellow) exit the ventricular zone along the long thin processes of the radial glial cells (red) to reach their destination. (B) Each wave of new cells moves past the older ones to form a new layer of cells. Notice, for instance, that the cells migrating away from the ventricular zone (left panel, blue cells) move to the top layer of the cortex. The same can be seen for each wave of migrating cells (yellow and green).

specialized neighbors release a chemical called an **inductive signal** that triggers the undifferentiated cells to express the unique set of genes that cause it to become a cell with a particular morphology. Other cells turn on the genes needed to create their unique identity without any help from environmental signals. Like individualists who "march to the beat of their own drum," they act independently of the cells that surround them, and are said to differentiate in a **cell-autonomous** manner.

Axon Growth

But even after cells migrate to their target destination, and begin to differentiate into a particular type of cell, how can trillions of connections be made between neurons in an orderly manner so that the nervous system can carry out its delicate work? A key advance in answering this question came from the work of the Nobel Prize-winning scientist Roger Sperry. Sperry examined the neurons of the frog retina, and particularly those neurons that sent axons from the retina to the midbrain. He surgically cut the axons so that they no longer reached their midbrain targets. After a period of weeks, the severed axons found their way back to their original target and formed functional connections (Sperry, 1963). He hypothesized that this was due to a complex chemical signaling mechanism, perhaps chemicals that attracted the end of the axon and guided it toward its target neurons.

Later work led to the discovery of many axon guidance molecules. The developing axon senses these chemicals through an area at its tip called the **growth cone** (Figure 8.5A). Thin extensions of the growth cone elongate and bend, like fingers searching around to explore the environment. Sometimes, they come in contact with guidance chemicals. These chemicals include chemoattractants that cause the thin extensions of the growth cone to stretch in their direction, stimulating growth of the axon. The chemical signals also include chemorepellants, which cause the growth cone (and axon) to bend away to avoid them. The chemorepellants prevent the developing axon from veering off course (Figure 8.5B).

As it explores its surroundings and searches for the right path, the growth cone may also encounter **cell adhesion molecules** (**CAMs**). The extensions of the growth cone can temporarily adhere (stick) to these molecules. Once the growth cone adheres to the CAM (which itself may be bound to a neighboring tissue), the growth cone extensions contract, and pull the growth cone (along with its axon "tail") in a forward direction. Chemoattractants, chemorepellants, and CAMs work together to guide developing axons (and dendrites) in the correct direction (Figure 8.5C).

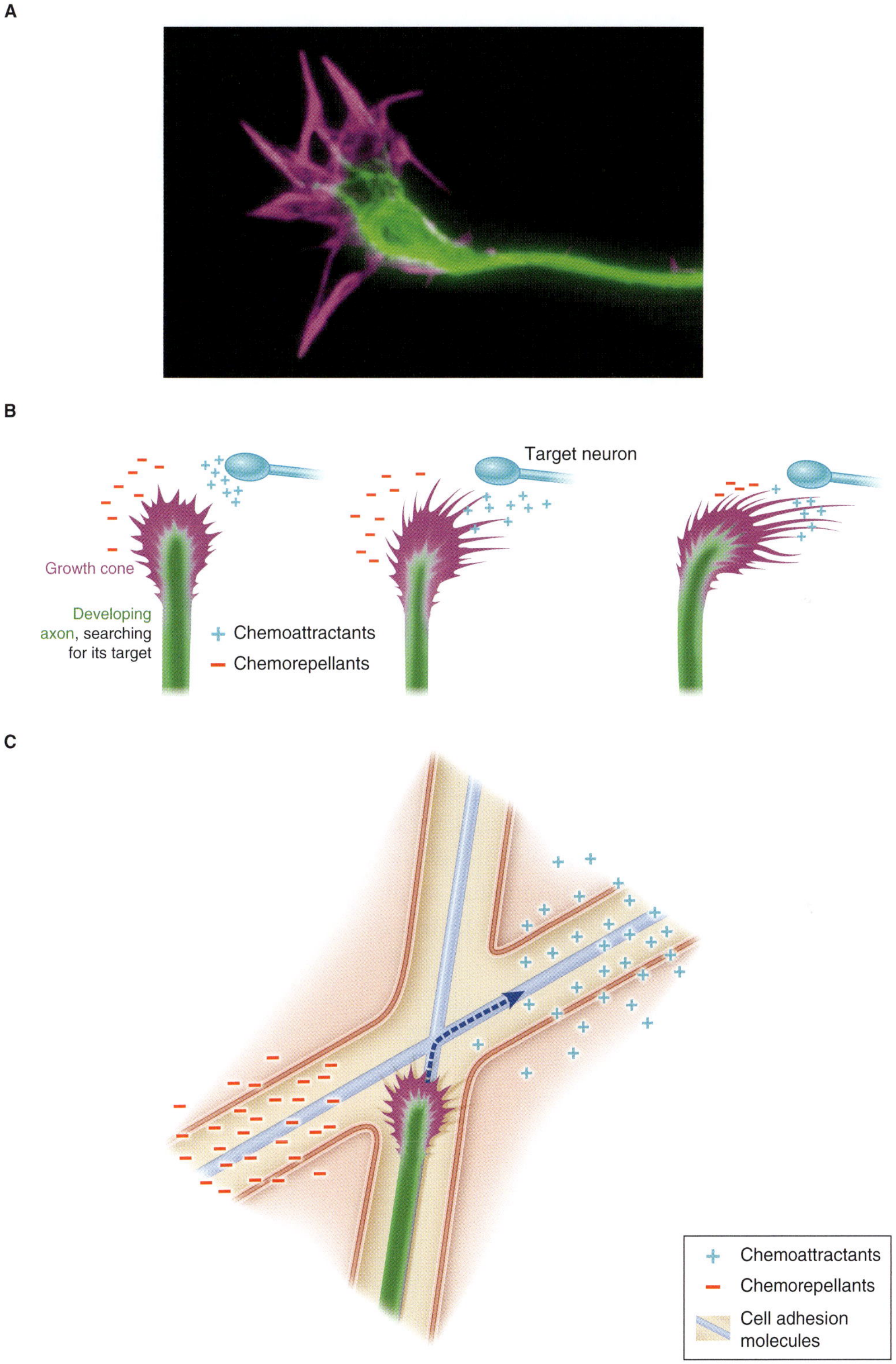

A

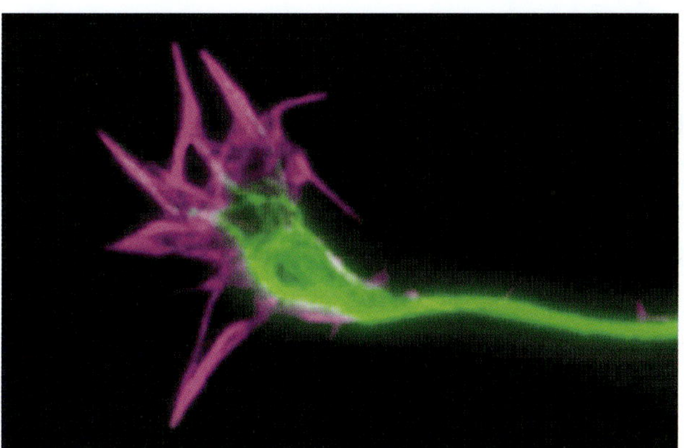

B

Target neuron

Growth cone

Developing axon, searching for its target

+ Chemoattractants

– Chemorepellants

C

+ Chemoattractants

– Chemorepellants

Cell adhesion molecules

Figure 8.5 Growth cones. (A) The growth cone (purple) is located at the tip of the developing axon (green). (Adapted from photo by Paul Letourneau, University of Minnesota.) (B) Chemoattractants (+) and chemorepellants (–) signal to the developing axon which direction to move and which to avoid. (C) Chemoattractant and chemorepellant signals combine with cell adhesion molecules to guide the movement of the growth cone and its axon.
(Adapted from Lowery & Vactor, 2009, fig. 1.)

Cell Death

All of the preceding mechanisms could be described as "positive" in the sense that they are part of constructing nervous systems. By contrast, the process of programmed cell death could be called negative or destructive. To a person unfamiliar with neuroscience, the idea that there is a built-in condition whereby cells in the developing brain are programmed to die might seem strange indeed. Wouldn't this be wasteful of energy and resources that a young brain could ill afford?

Programmed cell death is also called **apoptosis** (from the Greek, "falling off"). All of the cells in the body contain the genes for triggering apoptosis. During development up to early childhood, the brain overproduces neurons and then allows those not being used to die, a survival contest often referred to as "use it or lose it."

While a huge number of neurons are born in the developing fetus, between 20 and 80 percent of them are lost, with the percentage depending on the specific part of the nervous system (Oppenheim, 1991). In the fetus of the mouse, interference with cell death causes the animal to grow a brain so large it will not fit in the skull (Depaepe et al., 2005)! A general principle in the nervous system is to create a large number of neurons, and then to kill off many of them, like a gardener who pulls out the excess plants that sprout up in the garden (Figure 8.6). On the other hand, too much cell death can lead to developmental abnormalities. In the opening story, we considered the effects of alcohol exposure on the developing fetus. Alcohol has many adverse effects on CNS development; one of these is uncontrolled apoptosis, which produces too much cell death and resulting abnormalities in brain development (Gupta, Gupta, & Shirasaka, 2016).

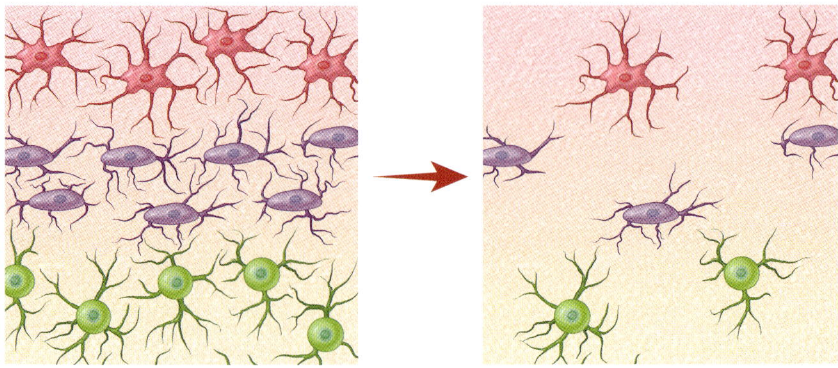

Figure 8.6 Programmed cell death. During brain development, a large number of cells are created (left) and then many of them are lost through programmed cell death (right).

The nervous system not only begins by generating more cells than it needs, the neurons also normally develop more than the necessary number of axons and dendrites, and an excessive number of synapses. It is not uncommon for individual neurons to send out many different axonal branches that form synapses with thousands of other neurons. In the first few years of life, about 700 new connections are formed every second. At certain points in development, the space between neurons is cluttered with axons and dendrites that have formed new connections with one another. But, again, the normally developing nervous system gets rid of a large proportion of these connections, **pruning** (trimming) the axons and dendrites.

KEY CONCEPTS

- The nervous system develops according to the same basic plan in all vertebrate species.
- Development of the central nervous system can be divided into five phases: cell birth, migration, differentiation, axon growth, and cell death.

TEST YOURSELF

1. What is the neural tube, and what is its relation to the brain and spinal cord?
2. What is the difference between a pluripotent cell and a neural progenitor cell?
3. Briefly describe the five stages of neural development.
4. The part of the neural tube wall closest to the center is the _____ zone. This is where the cells destined to make up the nervous system are born.
5. How do radial glia contribute to migration of neurons during development of the nervous system?
6. How do chemoattractants and chemorepellants contribute to cell migration and axon growth during brain development?
7. During development, the CNS overproduces neurons. Those that make successful functional contact with targets survive. The others undergo programmed cell death, also called "_____."

8.1.3 Neurotrophic Factors Allow Neurons to Survive and Grow

While apoptosis controls the death of neurons during development, the Italian neurologist and neuroscientist Rita Levi-Montalcini and her colleagues made the key discovery of a chemical that prevents apoptosis

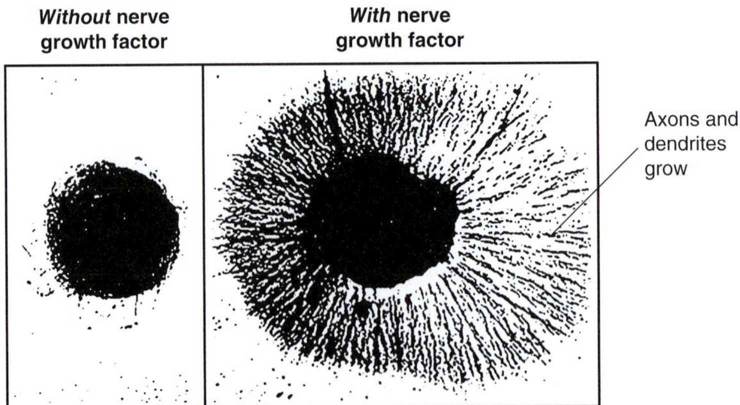

Figure 8.7 **Nerve growth factor**. Clusters of developing neurons exposed to nerve growth factor undergo explosive outward growth of axons and dendrites. (Levi-Montalcini & Calissano, 1979.)

and promotes neuronal growth, called **nerve growth factor** (**NGF**). They showed that the presence of this factor determined whether neurons grow or die. In a dramatic demonstration, Levi-Montalcini and colleagues squirted nerve growth factor into a dish containing clumps of developing neurons taken from a chick embryo. The cells soon underwent explosive growth of axons and dendrites (Figure 8.7). In the absence of NGF, the neurons died.

As a historical note, Rita Levi-Montalcini's parents discouraged their daughters from attending college, fearing that it would interfere with their path to becoming wives and mothers. Nevertheless, Rita graduated from medical school and became an anatomy researcher. In 1938, she lost her position when the dictator of Italy passed a law barring Jews from academic and professional careers. In 1986, she was awarded the Nobel Prize in Medicine for her discovery of growth factors (along with her collaborator Stanley Cohen). She died at the age of 103, and was the longest-living Nobel Laureate.

Levi-Montalcini's research on nerve growth factor opened the floodgates for the study of many other growth factors, now gathered under the general name of **neurotrophic factors** (substances that feed and nourish brain cells). An overabundance of neurotrophic factors can lead to uncontrolled cell proliferation (as occurs in cancer), whereas too little can contribute to one of several neurodegenerative diseases.

8.1.4 Behavioral Abilities Advance as the Nervous System Develops

As we have seen, development of the nervous system proceeds in an orderly and predictable manner. The same can be said for the development of behavioral abilities from birth to adulthood. The newborn infant's response repertoire is initially limited to simple sensory responses and movements (escaping from a painful stimulus or employing simple sucking and grasping reflexes). Following this, in the first two years, there is a universal sequential elaboration of behavior: rolling over, crawling, standing, walking (moving through the world on one's own), and the beginnings of language (communicating with others). These complex behaviors develop gradually and involve many parts of the nervous system. They are accompanied by a vast overproduction of synapses needed to accommodate these seismic transformations in the infant's life, and then a pruning of connections to preserve those most relevant to the necessary behaviors.

Other behavioral changes occur later in development. For instance, the prefrontal cortex, a brain area important in impulse control and aspects of cognition (Chapter 14), continues to mature even after puberty (Figure 8.8). Like other brain regions, the prefrontal cortex increases its synaptic connections and then dramatically prunes them as the adult brain matures. But compared to other brain regions, the prefrontal cortex is delayed in this maturation process. It doesn't reach its maximum number of connections until four years after birth (compared to four months after birth for the visual cortex), and then undergoes a long period in which synaptic connections are pruned. Some neuroscientists have proposed that adolescents' high vulnerability to injuries and drug abuse may reflect the fact that the prefrontal cortex has not yet reached the stage of maturation that will eventually allow better impulse control and decision making (Casey, Jones, & Hare, 2008).

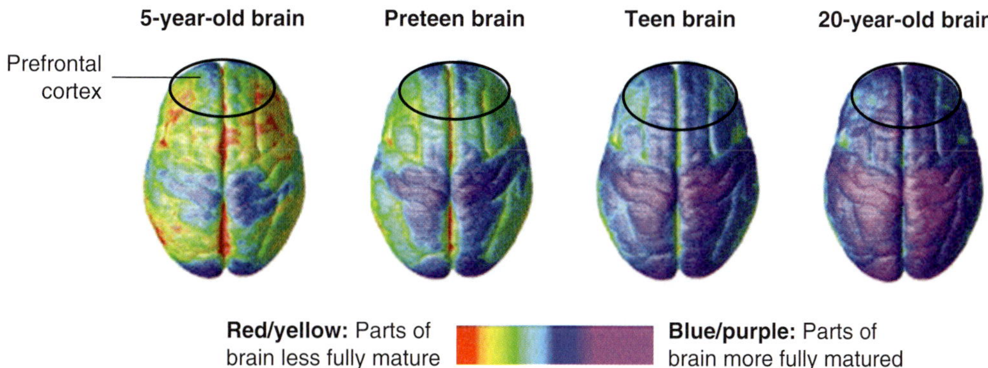

Figure 8.8 The late-developing prefrontal cortex. Images show brains as they would appear if you were looking down at them from the ceiling. The darkest colors (blue and purple) represent the areas that are most fully developed. The bright green color of the prefrontal cortex in the teen brain shows that it is not yet fully developed.

(Adapted from Lenroot & Giedd, 2006, fig. 6, © 2006, published by Elsevier Ltd.)

In discussing changes in brain and behavior across development, we come to the topic of aging. Many healthy people in their eighth or ninth decades of life show minimal, if any, changes in cognitive capacities. In fact, changes in the brain of healthy individuals during aging can be quite limited or even difficult to discern. The picture is different in those with mild cognitive impairment or dementia (Chapter 13 will explore Alzheimer's dementia). Individuals vary greatly in terms of genetic, environmental, and nutritional factors, making it difficult to undertake studies that permit strong scientific conclusions regarding the effects of aging on the non-diseased brain. In addition, individuals may vary in terms of which of the huge number of brain structures, circuits, and biochemical factors undergo age-related changes, making generalizations even more difficult. At best, we can say that a typical change in the brain of the average healthy person over 75 is a 1 percent reduction per year of brain volume. Nevertheless, as noted above, changes in the brain and behavior of healthy older individuals are relatively slow to occur and subtle to discern.

8.1.5 The Brain Produces New Neurons Even in Adulthood

We saw that a key feature of brain development is the birth of neurons, or **neurogenesis**. Are neurons created only during development, or does the adult brain continue to generate neurons? The great Spanish neuroanatomist (and Nobel Prize winner) Santiago Ramon y Cajal was adamant in his belief that no new neurons could be produced by the adult brain in vertebrates. The brain was rigid, fixed, and permanent! He wrote that, in the adult brain, everything may die, and nothing may be regenerated. This position dominated the field for decades and discouraged research that might have provided contrary evidence.

In the 1960s, Joseph Altman, working at MIT, published a series of papers suggesting an alternative view. He reported that new neurons and glia were continually being produced in the brain of adult rats, and, somewhat surprisingly, this production was limited to just two regions of the brain, the hippocampus and the olfactory bulb (Altman & Das, 1965). We now know that the new cells in the hippocampus come from stem cells in the dentate gyrus (Figure 8.9). Those in the olfactory bulb come from stem cells in the walls of the lateral ventricles. The hippocampus and olfactory bulb are the principal areas that receive new neurons in adulthood, although there are also reports of neurogenesis in a few other brain regions. As we will see in Chapter 9, neurogenesis during adulthood plays a role in the storage of new memories.

A

Hippocampus

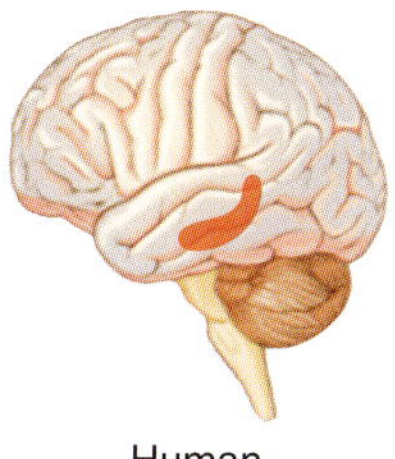

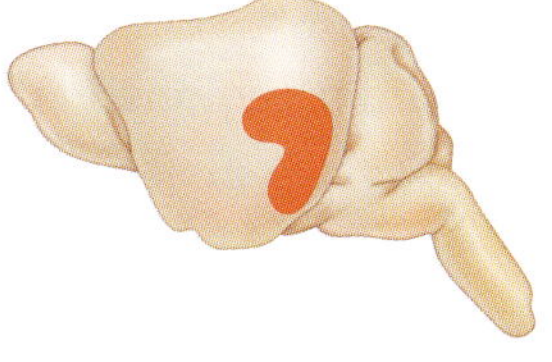

B

New cells in the dentate gyrus of the hippocampus

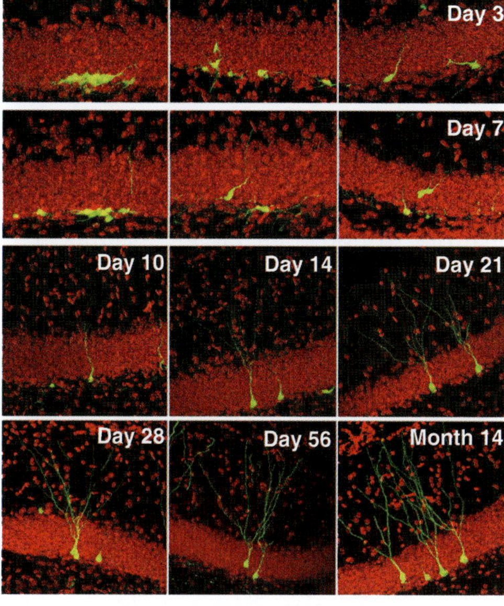

Figure 8.9 Neurogenesis. (A) The hippocampus (red) is depicted in a human and rat brain. (Adapted from Strange, Witter, Lein, & Moser 2014, fig. 1B, © 2014, Nature Publishing Group, a division of Macmillan Publishers Limited. All rights reserved.) (B) New neurons grow in the adult brain within the dentate gyrus of the hippocampus. Newly born cells in the dentate gyrus are labeled in green. The top row shows the first several days after the new neurons are born. By the fourteenth day, dendrites (threadlike extensions) can be seen growing from the new cells. At fourteen months after their birth, the new cells are still alive, and making synaptic contact with other neurons of the hippocampus. (Adapted from Zhao, Teng, Summers, Ming, & Gage, 2006, fig. 1, © 2006, Society for Neuroscience.)

KEY CONCEPTS

- **Nerve growth factor and other neurotrophic factors are critical for the growth and sustenance of developing neurons.**
- **In mammals, some brain regions have the capacity to produce new neurons in adulthood.**

TEST YOURSELF

1. **What is meant by a neurotrophic factor?**
2. **What brain area is among the latest to fully develop after birth?**
3. **What is adult neurogenesis?**

8.2 PLASTICITY

Neural plasticity refers to changes in the nervous system, such as the formation of new connections between neurons, or the strengthening of existing connections. As we have seen, a great deal of plasticity occurs during early nervous system development when the developing axons of neurons invade new territory to find their targets. Neural plasticity also occurs in response to brain injury and disease; sometimes the plasticity is functional and helps us to recover. Plasticity of neuronal connections is also what allows us to acquire new skills, and to recall events that occurred to us years in the past (Chapter 9). Without plasticity, our behavioral responses to events would be fixed, inflexible, like a moth's approach to light. We wouldn't learn from our experiences. In short, if the brain didn't change with experience, it wouldn't be of much use to have one!

8.2.1 Increased Use of a Brain Region Results in Its Expansion

Even without studying neuroscience, there's a good chance that you've read about increases in the size of particular brain areas as individuals gain a particular skill. Perhaps the report of this type that gained the most public attention involved London taxi drivers. In order to be licensed to drive a taxi in London, applicants must memorize the streets of London well enough to be able to recite the precise and most efficient automobile route from point A to point B, which may be many miles apart. It can take up to two years of study to absorb this mental map. As you will see in Chapter 9, the hippocampus is a critical structure in laying down memories of spatial locations. Accordingly, a group of British scientists decided to investigate whether the hippocampi of London cabbies differed from those of a well-matched control group (Maguire et al., 2000). Using MRI to measure the size of brain structures, the researchers found that a portion of the hippocampus in the cabbies was significantly larger than that of the control group. This was not true for any other brain areas in these two groups. Additional analysis of these data demonstrated that there was a positive correlation between years on the job as a cabbie and size of the hippocampus. The experience of driving a cab led to observable plasticity of the hippocampus. Whether the expansion of the hippocampal volume was due to a greater number of neurons, or to a greater density of axons and dendrites, or both, is not known.

In a poignant example of plasticity, let's consider the case of Frank R., an American soldier injured in Iraq. He sustained serious shrapnel wounds to his arm that required surgical removal of the arm below the elbow. During his recovery, besides reporting pain due to the surgery, he described something else quite strange. He said that he felt pain coming from his missing hand and forearm. This is known as **phantom limb pain**, and it occurs in more than half the individuals requiring amputation. The mechanisms producing this pain still remain somewhat of a puzzle. However, some surprising findings have emerged from the study of patients like Frank. For instance, rubbing the patient's face around the jaw can produce a sensation of touch or pain in the missing arm. Rubbing to the left of the jaw seemed to come from the left arm, while rubbing to the right of the jaw seemed to come from the right arm. What is responsible for this apparent cross talk of connections in the brain?

We saw in Chapter 3 that the somatosensory cortex contains a kind of "map" of the body surface. In other words, some regions of the somatosensory cortex are activated by touch to the hands, other areas by touch to the arms, and so on. These areas of the cortex are said to "represent" the hands, arms, and other body parts. As you can see in Figure 8.10, the cortical area representing the face is adjacent to the area representing the arm and hand. Examination of the body representation in the cortex of individuals after amputation of an arm showed that the area receiving input from the hand and arm shrank. The hand and arm regions of the somatosensory cortex were now receiving expanded input from the face. In fact, areas receiving face input had shifted several centimeters across the cortical surface! Now, stimulation of portions of the face activated neurons that had previously received input from the hand and arm (Yang et al., 1994). Because activation of neurons in what had been the hand and arm region continued to give rise to arm and hand sensations, touch to the face produced a sensation that the person perceived to have occurred in his (missing) limb.

Another amazing example of the brain's plasticity is seen after a dramatic and rare surgical treatment for childhood epilepsy. Epilepsy is a devastating brain disorder, like a massive electrical storm in the brain.

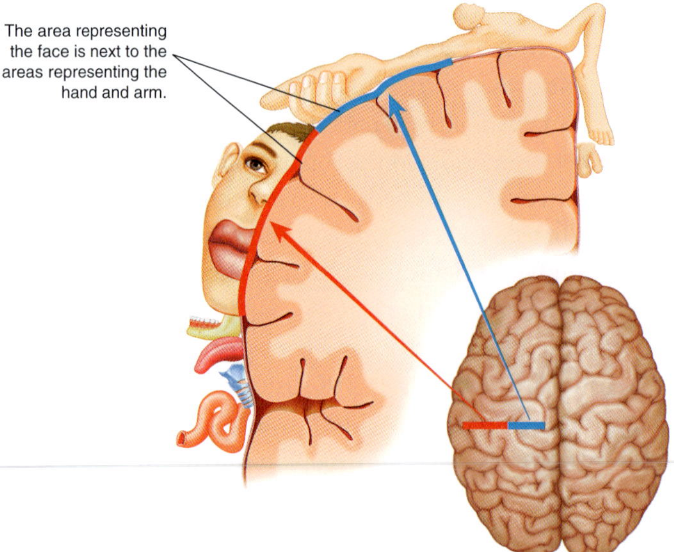

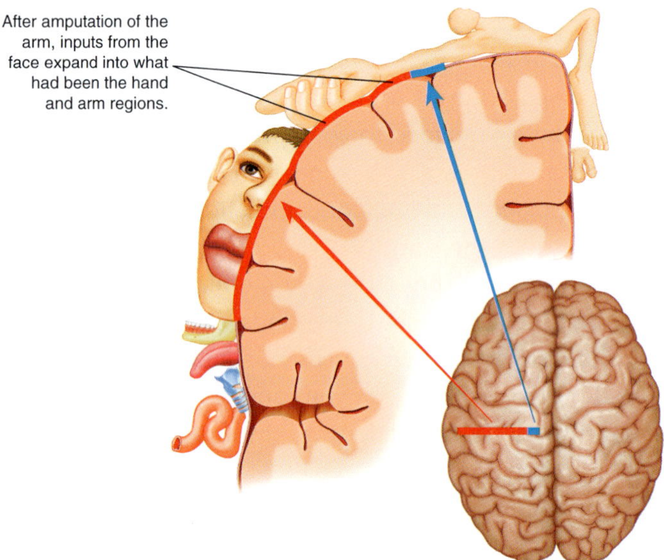

Figure 8.10 Phantom limb. Top: Parts of the somatosensory cortex that respond to touch to the face (red) are next to the areas that respond to touch to the arm and hand (blue). Bottom: After amputation of the arm, regions of the somatosensory cortex that used to respond to touch of the arm or hand now respond to touch to the face. As a result, touch to the face produces a sensation that the individual perceives to have occurred in his (missing) arm.

Rasmussen's disease is a childhood epilepsy, which develops from a failure of the cortex to develop fully in the fetus. The child's frequent and debilitating seizures make a normal and productive life impossible. However, anti-seizure drugs are not effective in treating the disorder.

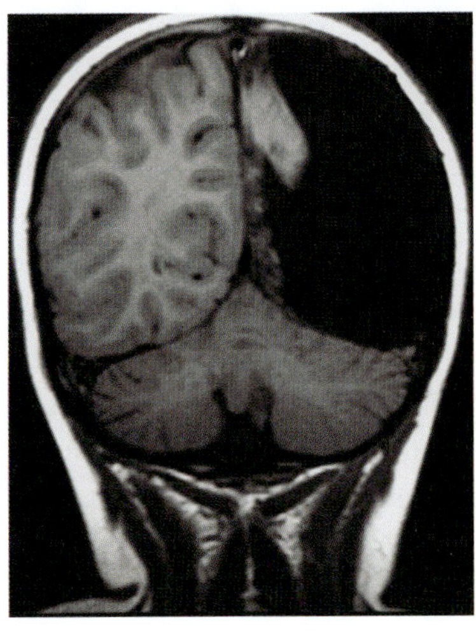

Figure 8.11 Removal of half the brain. In an extreme case of childhood seizures, surgeons removed the hemisphere of the brain where the seizures originated. The remaining hemisphere of the child's brain took over many of the functions normally carried out by the other hemisphere. (From Borgstein & Grootendorst, 2002, © 2002 Elsevier Ltd. All rights reserved.)

Because it is well known that the nervous system is more plastic in the young, it is recommended that surgery be carried out as soon as possible after the brain has largely developed. A drastic but effective surgery for reducing or even abolishing seizures in Rasmussen's disease involves a **hemispherectomy**, where one-half of the entire forebrain is removed (Figure 8.11). An obvious concern is how the surgery will affect cognitive capacities (such as memory, language, and IQ) and motor functions. The most comprehensive report comes from patients from the Johns Hopkins Medical School, one of the major institutions carrying out these surgeries (Vining et al., 1997). The surgery significantly reduced the number of seizures. In addition, not only did the surgery leave their movement and cognitive capacities intact, but most of the children showed an improvement in intellectual ability (likely because their seizures were reduced and they no longer needed to take anti-seizure medications). The authors of the report wrote, "We are awed by the apparent retention of memory after removal of half the brain, and the retention of the child's personality and sense of humor" (Vining et al., 1997, p. 170).

This is as dramatic an example of brain plasticity as can be imagined: young children whose lives are improved following removal of half their forebrain. While we cannot point to the specific sites of plasticity, somehow the remaining hemisphere was able to take over many of the cognitive and motor functions that would normally have been carried out by the other half of the brain.

8.2.2 Brain Areas Adapt to Changes in Their Inputs

The first study to provide anatomical evidence for brain plasticity at the cellular level was considered so revolutionary that many scientists did not believe it.

In the key experiment, a British investigator destroyed some of the neurons that project to a brain area called the septal nuclei (Raisman, 1969). The septal nuclei normally receive inputs both from the hippocampus and from the hypothalamus (Figure 8.12, top). The researcher hypothesized that by destroying the inputs from the hypothalamus to the septal nuclei, the hippocampal inputs to the septal nuclei would expand. He used a high level of magnification provided by an electron microscope in order to study what he expected to be subtle anatomical changes. When he lesioned the inputs from the hypothalamus, axons from the hippocampus reoccupied the space where the hypothalamic inputs had been (Figure 8.12, middle). In other animals, he destroyed the hippocampal axons that normally project to the septal nuclei, and observed new inputs from the hypothalamus. In both cases, the axons of the surviving neurons sprouted additional branches, or offshoots, that grew toward the now-unoccupied target area. The investigator, Geoffrey Raisman, introduced a term to refer to this newly discovered capability of adult brains to undergo anatomical change. He called it "plasticity."

This work has an interesting implication for researchers attempting to help patients recover normal functions after brain damage. Imagine that Mr. Smith suffers damage to neurons that connect the hippocampus to the septal nuclei. In order to restore normal brain function, let's say he would need those *hippocampal inputs to the septal nuclei* to grow back. Raisman's experiments suggest a potential problem. As soon as input from the hippocampus (or some other brain area) is lost, other inputs (e.g., from the hypothalamus) will take over the empty space. So, even if the damaged hippocampal neurons were to send new axons to the septal nucleus, other axons (e.g., from the hypothalamus) would be likely to have invaded the location of their former synaptic inputs. The loss of the normal inputs to neuronal targets leads not simply to reconnections from the original sites, but also to connections from new neuronal sources. There is no reason to expect that these new connections will function in the original, correct manner. We will return to this topic of response to injury later in the chapter.

Another important experiment examining plasticity involved cutting connections from the retina of the eye to the thalamus (Sur, Garraghty, & Roe, 1988). As you may recall from earlier chapters, visual information travels from the retina to an area of the thalamus called the lateral geniculate nucleus, or LGN. Auditory information normally reaches a different compartment of the thalamus called the medial geniculate nucleus, or MGN. (In case you need to quickly review this, say "LGN is visual, MGN is auditory" five times fast.) What would happen if the LGN were destroyed so that axons carrying visual information from the retina were unable to reach their normal thalamic target? Might these "visual"

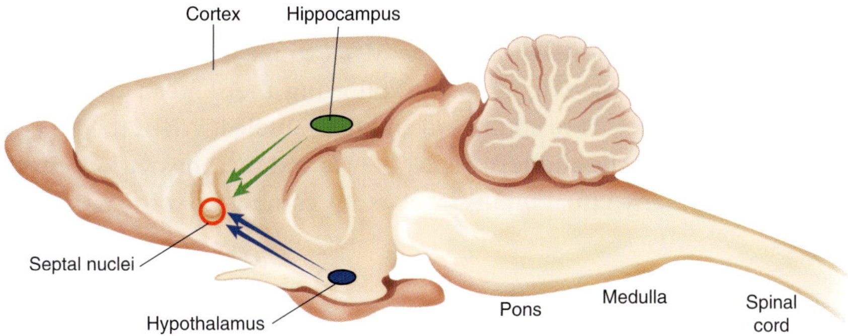

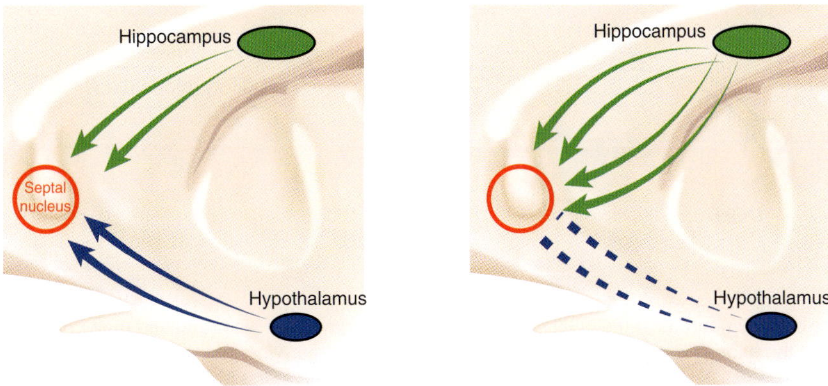

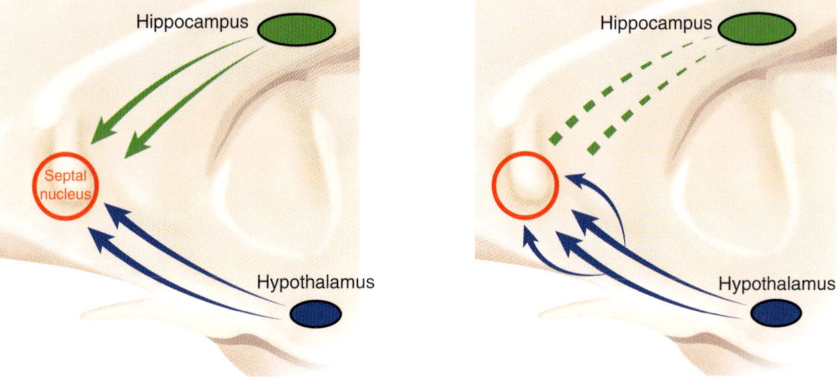

Figure 8.12 **Hippocampal inputs expand when hypothalamic inputs are destroyed, and vice versa**. When one set of inputs to a brain region is damaged, inputs from another area may expand and occupy the space from the lost connections.

neurons develop contacts with the MGN of the thalamus instead? Well, not if the MGN was already crowded with the auditory neurons that terminate there. The experimenters therefore destroyed large portions of the LGN of newborn ferrets, and also cleared away most of the auditory neurons that normally target the MGN to make room just in case visual neurons arrived (Figure 8.13). Following the surgery, the ferrets were allowed to mature to adulthood and then studied. When the experimenters examined the auditory MGN, they found that the neurons there now received many visual inputs from axons coming from the retina.

1. Normally, visual information from the retina goes to the LGN of the thalamus. Auditory information goes to the MGN.

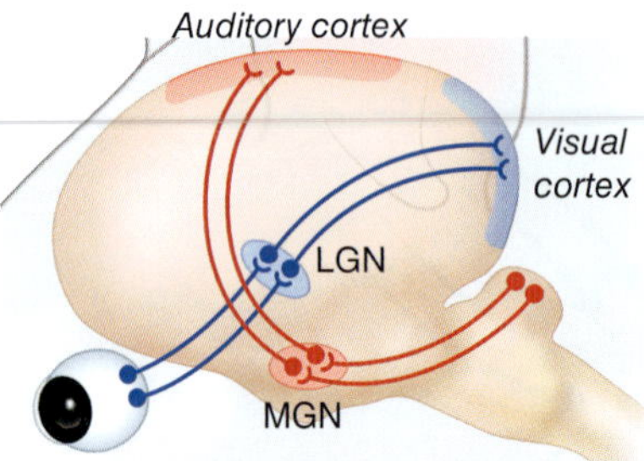

Visual information
Auditory information

2. Experimenters destroy neurons in the LGN, leaving many of the axons from the retina without targets.

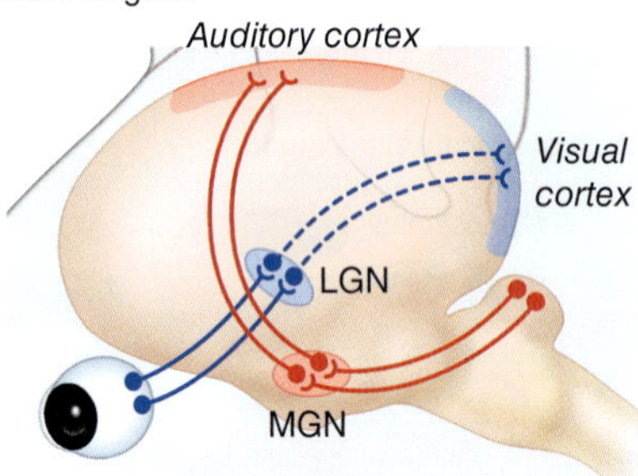

3. Experimenters also removed many of the neurons carrying auditory information and terminating in the MGN.

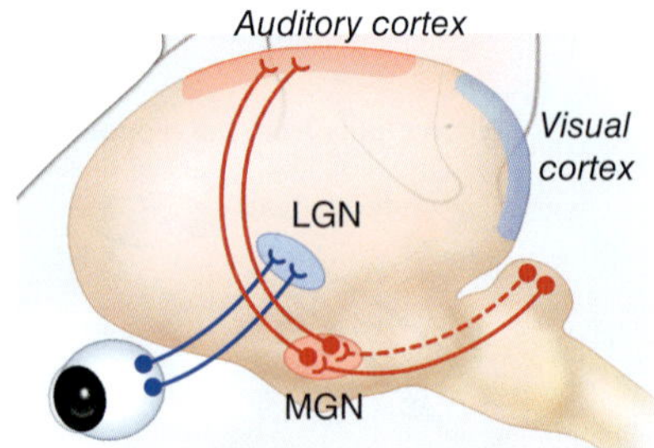

4. Axons terminating in the LGN sprouted new branches, which terminated in the MGN.

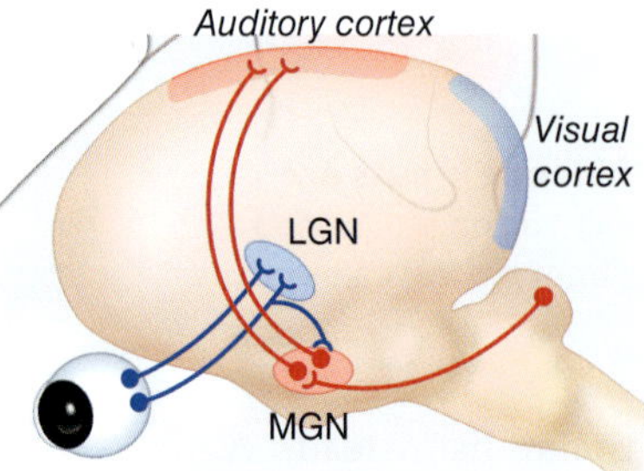

5. A visual stimulus (e.g., a flashing light) that normally activates neurons in the visual cortex now activates neurons in the auditory cortex.

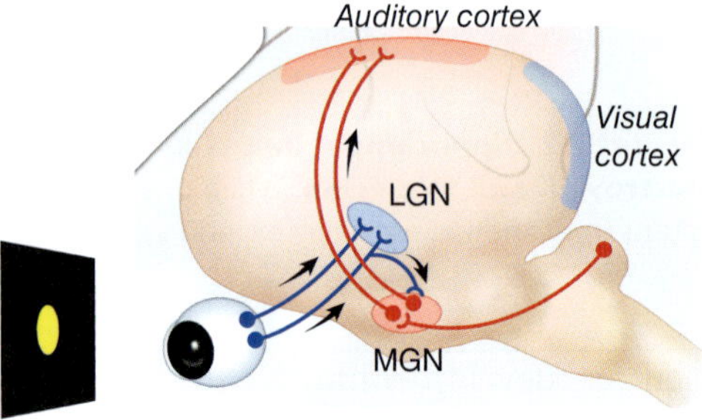

Figure 8.13 **Visual neurons can grow connections to the auditory system.**

When the experimenters later presented the animals with visual stimuli, neurons in the MGN responded, and so did neurons in the *auditory cortex*! The visual stimuli had traveled from the retina to the auditory thalamus (MGN), and then traveled the normal route from the MGN to the auditory cortex where they produced "visual responses" in neurons that would normally have responded to sounds.

The experiments above showed that when a brain area is destroyed the axons that normally send inputs to that region are rerouted to new targets. We now turn to an experiment that examines how the brain adapts to unusual changes in the environment. Very young kittens were raised with goggles that contained three horizontal lines over one eye and three vertical lines over the other eye (see Figure 8.14). For the first three months of their life, the kittens' visual experience was restricted to just these horizontal and vertical lines. How would the visual cortex of these kittens adapt to this restricted visual experience during development?

In kittens exposed to normal environments, a particular cell in the visual cortex will respond mostly to one particular line orientation (horizontal, diagonal, vertical, or another orientation in between). But whatever orientation you present, there will be some visual cortical neurons that respond to it. However, in the kittens who grew up seeing only vertical and horizontal lines, the neurons of the visual cortex only responded to vertical or horizontal lines (Hirsch & Spinelli, 1970). If a vertical line was presented to the eye that had been exposed to vertical lines, cells in the visual cortex would respond; but other line orientations presented to that eye would produce no visual cortical response. So, too, for the eye exposed to horizontal lines. The environment shapes the way our sensory systems respond to the world.

The studies we've looked at in this section so far have shown neural plasticity as a result of unusual conditions – destruction of neurons and sensory deprivation. But can exposure to *natural* environmental stimuli produce changes in the brain that are evident at the level of individual neurons? If so, what kinds of changes in neural structure might be seen?

In a key study, young male rats (22–25 days old) were housed in one of three conditions for four weeks:

- single, small metal cages
- the same cages, but with another rat, and
- an "enriched" condition in which twelve rats were housed together in a large cage and given daily exposure to a varied set of "toys."

First 3 months of life

In adulthood

A diagonal line is shown to the adult cat. Visual cortical neurons do not respond when the diagonal line is presented to either the left or right.

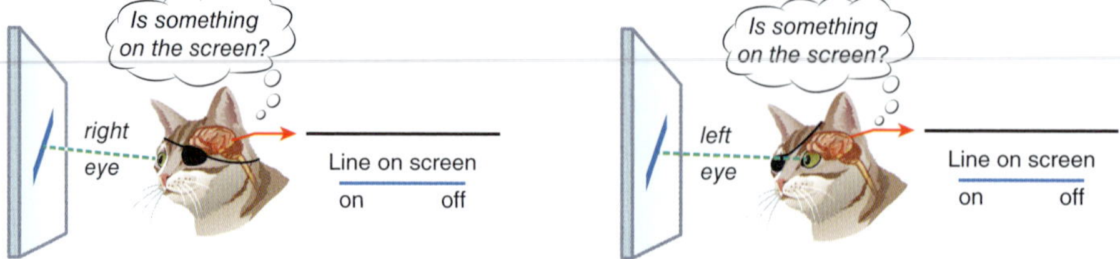

A horizontal line is shown to the adult cat. Visual cortical neurons only respond when the horizontal line is presented to the right eye (i.e., the eye that saw horizontal lines during development).

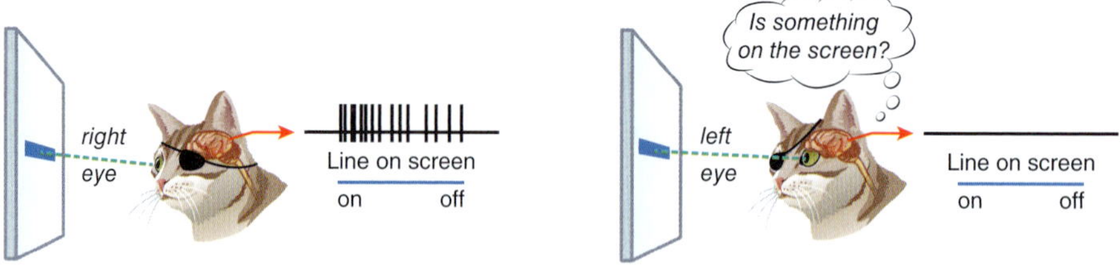

A vertical line is shown to the adult cat. Visual cortical neurons only respond when the vertical line is presented to the left eye (i.e., the eye that saw horizontal lines during development).

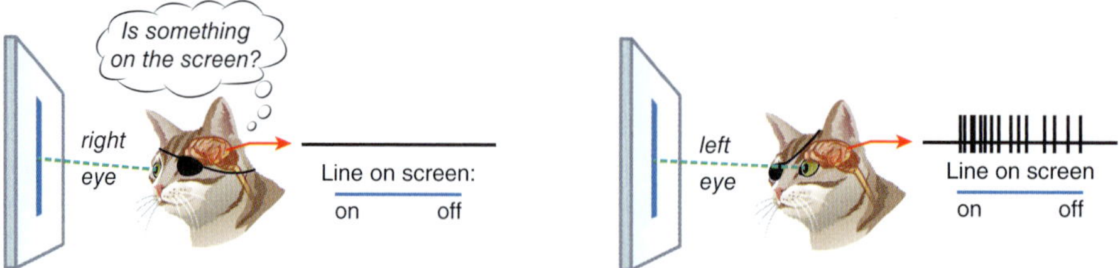

Figure 8.14 **Environmental experience shapes development of the visual system**. After early life exposure to just vertical lines with one eye and horizontal lines with the other, neurons in the visual cortex do not respond to lines of other orientations. Neurons respond to vertical lines only when viewed by the eye that had been exposed to vertical lines earlier in life. So, too, for horizontal lines.

The study employed anatomical techniques to examine the complexity of dendrites in the visual cortex of rats raised under one of these three conditions (Volkmar & Greenough, 1972). Complexity was defined as the number of branches that were found on the dendrites of individual cortical neurons (Figure 8.15). The hypothesis was that an expansion or shrinkage of the dendrites in the visual cortex would be a measure of a corresponding change in synaptic connections. The results clearly showed a significant increase in the number of branches of the dendrites in rats from the enriched condition compared to the single-housed rats.

Other similar studies have pointed to the important interaction between the novel stimuli in the environment (the toys) and the presence of other rats in the cage. The combination of novel objects and social interaction is necessary in order for rats to gain the maximal effects of environmental enrichment. While enriched conditions may produce an expansion of dendrites, the solitary confinement of single-housed rats can also produce shrinkage of dendrites. The more dendritic branches a neuron possesses, the more synaptic connections it can form with other neurons. Other anatomical effects of enrichment include increases in the size of the cell body of the neurons and an increase in the number of glial cells surrounding the neurons. Anatomical effects of enrichment have been observed in many brain regions, including the frontal cortex (important for the animal's behavioral movements) and the hippocampus (important for memory).

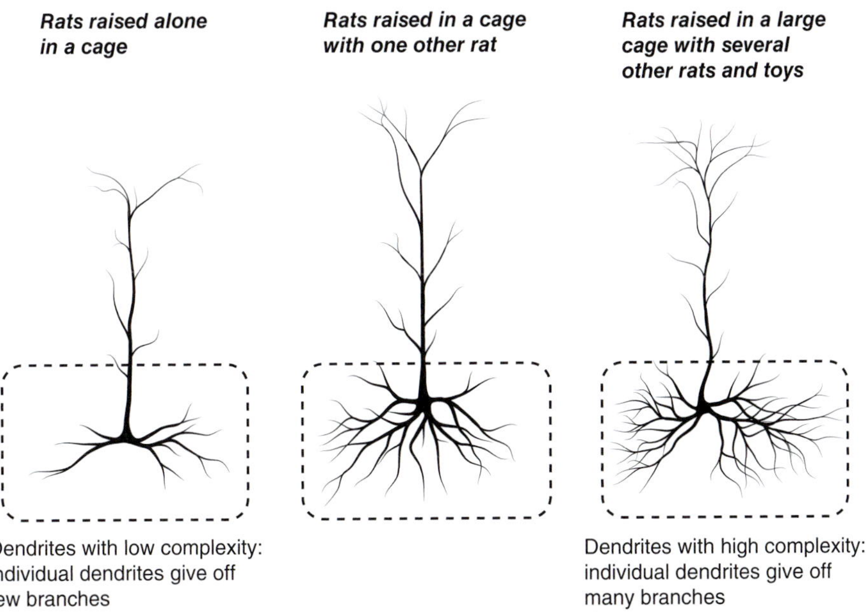

Figure 8.15 An enriched environment increases dendritic branching.

KEY CONCEPTS

- **The structure and function of the brain is continually changing throughout life.**
- **The size of a brain area may increase with use.**
- **If a cortical region is destroyed, its normal input (e.g., from the eye) may be re-routed to another brain area (auditory cortex).**

TEST YOURSELF

1. **Give examples of behavioral experiences that might expand the size of a particular motor cortical area. In your example(s), describe the experience and the part of the motor cortex that you think might expand (e.g., hand region, thumb region, shoulder region, etc.).**
2. **Describe the brain changes seen in London cab drivers.**
3. **What is the effect of an enriched environment versus sensory isolation on neurons in the brain?**

8.2.3 What Gets Plasticity Going?

One of the key contributors to plasticity, nerve growth factor, was explored earlier in the chapter when we talked about the growth of axons toward their targets. We saw that exposure to nerve growth factor is critical for developing neurons to survive and to grow. We also noted that nerve growth factor is one of a large family of proteins referred to as neurotrophic factors. Another important neurotrophic factor is called **brain-derived neurotrophic factor** (**BDNF**). Neurotrophic factors contribute not only to nervous system development, but also to neural plasticity in the adult organism where they play a role in:

- guidance of axons
- growth and branching of axons and dendrites
- development of synapses between neurons.

As we've seen in earlier chapters, most neurochemicals are released from a presynaptic neuron, and they cross a synapse to influence the activity of postsynaptic neurons.

However, neurotrophic factors are often released from a *postsynaptic neuron* to exert a **retrograde** (backward) influence on presynaptic neurons. For instance, imagine that the axons of neurons from the hypothalamus are sprouting additional axon branches to target the septal area. In order to contribute to the growth of the hypothalamic axons, neurons in the septal area would release neurotrophic factors that move retrogradely to promote the growth of the incoming axons.

The most-studied and best-understood form of plasticity in the adult nervous system involves changes in the strength of synaptic connections between neurons. Imagine that Neuron 1 has an axon that terminates at Neuron 2, with a synapse between them. Neuron 1 is presynaptic to Neuron 2, and we sometimes say that Neuron 1 "communicates" with Neuron 2. If Neuron 1 releases an excitatory neurotransmitter we can say that Neuron 2 "responds" to Neuron 1 by becoming excited, maybe even firing an action potential. In some cases, Neuron 2 hardly responds at all to the neurotransmitter released from Neuron 1 because the synapse between them is weak. If the synapse between the neurons is weak, we can say metaphorically that even when Neuron 1 is speaking loudly (releasing lots of neurotransmitter) to Neuron 2, Neuron 2 doesn't hear the message (Neuron 2 doesn't respond). However, in some cases, the synapse can become stronger. This is called **long-term potentiation** (**LTP**).

LTP turns a weak synapse into a stronger one. One way for this to occur is for Neuron 1 to release such a large burst of excitatory neurotransmitter onto Neuron 2 that Neuron 2 becomes activated and fires an action potential, even though the synapse is still weak. In some parts of the brain, this can be enough to produce a long-lasting change in the synapse linking the pre- and postsynaptic neurons. If this produces LTP, then in the future even a small excitatory input from Neuron 1 will be enough to activate Neuron 2 (see Figure 8.16). (The key to generating LTP in many parts of the nervous system is simply for the presynaptic neuron to activate the postsynaptic neuron; a useful phrase for understanding LTP is that "Neurons that fire together, wire together.")

Let's reexamine the scenario in the last paragraph. Imagine again that there is a weak synaptic connection between Neurons 1 and 2, and Neuron 1 releases the excitatory neurotransmitter glutamate. Glutamate from Neuron 1 binds to and activates a glutamate receptor on Neuron 2. Specifically, glutamate activates a kind of glutamate receptor called an AMPA receptor. This allows sodium ions to enter Neuron 2, producing a short-lasting excitation in the neuron. It is likely, however, that this small excitation fails to cause Neuron 2 to fire. What happens when a larger, powerful burst of glutamate from Neuron 1 reaches Neuron 2, causing Neuron 2 to fire? Glutamate will activate not only Neuron 2's AMPA-type glutamate receptors, but also another kind of glutamate receptor called an NMDA receptor. This will cause more sodium ions to enter the neuron and, in addition, it will allow calcium ions to enter. The influx of calcium ions interacts with intracellular biochemical pathways to activate proteins, which carry out a number of processes in the cell, including causing changes in gene expression (Malenka, Kauer, Zucker, & Nicoll, 1988). Here, we're leaving out some details about how the NMDA receptor

1. The neurotransmitter released from Neuron 1 activates AMPA receptors in Neuron 2. Neuron 2 responds with very little excitation because the synapse is weak. (There are so few AMPA receptors, the neurotransmitter may not even find an AMPA receptor to bind to.)

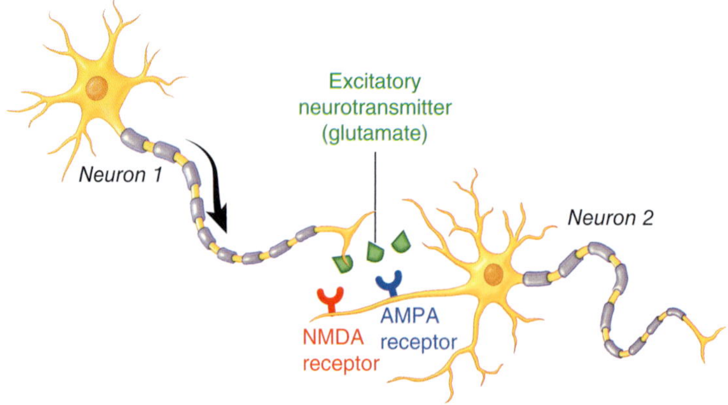

2. If Neuron 1 releases a large amount of neurotransmitter, Neuron 2 becomes excited despite the weak synapse. The neurotransmitter now activates both AMPA and NMDA receptors.

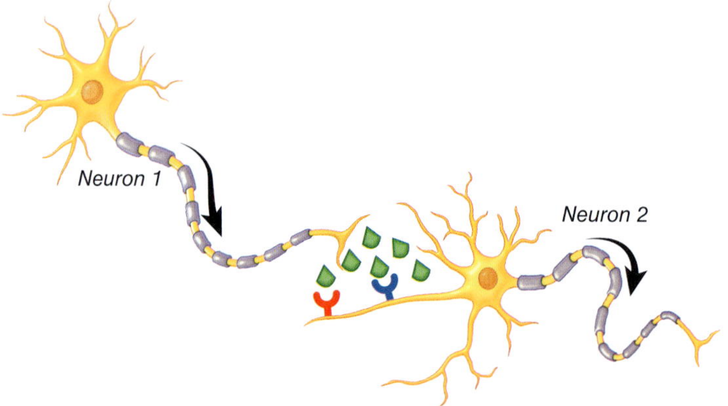

3. As a result of NMDA receptor activation (in 2), additional AMPA receptors pop out onto the postsynaptic dendrite of Neuron 2. Now, even a small amount of neurotransmitter released from Neuron 1 can easily bind to AMPA receptors and strongly activate Neuron 2. The synapse has strengthened through LTP.

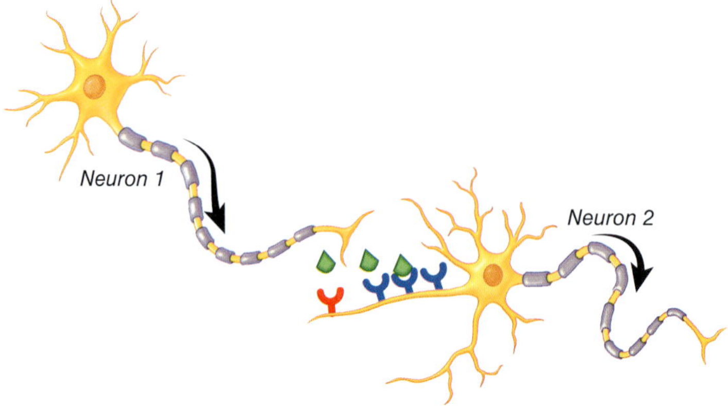

Figure 8.16 **Long-term potentiation: synapses become stronger**. Notice that in steps 1 and 3, Neuron 1 releases only a small amount of neurotransmitter. Before LTP (step 1), Neuron 2 hardly responds to the neurotransmitter. After LTP (step 3), Neuron 2 responds strongly (black arrow along its axon). Often this strong response is the result of many AMPA receptors now available for the neurotransmitter to bind to.

becomes activated; we'll fill them in when we consider LTP's role in learning and memory in Chapter 9.

LTP causes changes in both the pre- and postsynaptic neurons which result in long-lasting increases in the strength of the synapse between them. These changes include:

- greater production of AMPA-type glutamate receptors expressed in the postsynaptic membrane
- an increase in the amount of sodium that flows through ion channels to enter the postsynaptic neuron whenever glutamate binds to a glutamate receptor.

Such changes strengthen the synaptic connection between the neurons. Under some conditions, the synaptic connections between neurons can undergo weakening, or **long-term depression** (**LTD**). LTD involves changes that are opposite to those seen during LTP. For instance, during LTD, a synaptic connection may weaken because the number of postsynaptic AMPA receptors has decreased.

8.2.4 The Central Nervous System Is Susceptible to Injury

Many things can cause damage to the CNS. Plasticity plays a key role in the nervous system's response to injury. Let's begin by considering some of the most common causes of neural damage.

- **Stroke** is an interruption of blood flow to the brain. There are two forms of stroke. In ischemia, a clot blocks a blood vessel. This prevents oxygen and nutrients from reaching part of the brain. The other case is hemorrhage, where a blood vessel ruptures or bursts and, again, the brain is deprived of oxygen and nutrients. Both of these factors can cause brain cells to degenerate. The effects of stroke depend upon the area and size of the damaged brain tissue. In some cases, a person suffering a stroke may lose sensory function (e.g., partial blindness) or language. If the brainstem becomes damaged, the stroke may be fatal due to the death of neurons mediating basic physiological function, such as breathing.
- **Trauma** to the brain is sometimes the result of a major auto accident. When a passenger is thrown against the interior of the car, the rigid skull stops moving at the point of impact, but the soft brain continues to move, striking the interior of the skull and causing brain bruising and bleeding. Other common causes of brain trauma include gunshot wounds and sports injuries (e.g., from boxing, ice hockey, and American football).

- **Tumors**. A tumor is a mass of tissue caused by an accumulation of abnormal cells. Tumors in the brain are of two general types: malignant (cancerous) and benign (non-cancerous). A growing cancerous tumor of the brain may directly damage and destroy neurons and glia. As a benign tumor grows, it takes up limited space within the skull, producing increased pressure on and destruction of otherwise healthy brain cells.
- **Toxins**. Toxins in many forms can harm the CNS. Perhaps the most common is ethyl alcohol, which is a major component of all recreational alcoholic beverages. Other sources of toxins include exposure to radiation; heavy metals in the environment such as lead and mercury; and exposure to pesticides commonly used in agriculture and residential lawn care. The degree of CNS damage is dependent on both the concentration of the toxin and one's level of exposure to it.

Neurons are damaged or die when they are injured, but what is the actual cellular mechanism that produces this? The simple answer is that they die of overexcitement (**excitotoxicity**). This is caused by an unusually high level of synaptic release of glutamate acting at one or both of the major types of glutamate receptors, AMPA and especially NMDA. Overactivation of the glutamate receptors allows a massive amount of $Ca2^{+}$ to enter into the cell body of the neuron via the glutamate receptor ion channels. The excess of intracellular calcium activates a variety of enzymes that damage critical cellular processes, especially those regulating proteins, membranes, and DNA (Choi, 1992). The irony of this situation should not be lost on us because these same events involving glutamate, its receptors, and $Ca2^{+}$ are critical processes in virtually all positive forms of plasticity, including learning and memory. So, here we have the classical case of too much of a good thing!

KEY CONCEPTS

- **Neurotrophic factors are released by target neurons to promote the growth and survival of incoming axons.**
- **Long-term potentiation is the strengthening of synaptic connections between neurons. Changes in synaptic strength play an important role in learning and memory.**
- **In addition to trauma to the brain, the environment contains agents that are potentially harmful to the cells of the nervous system.**
- **Excessive neuronal excitation is the primary mechanism underlying cell death.**

TEST YOURSELF

1. **Long-term potentiation turns a weak ______ into a stronger one.**
2. **LTP often involves an increase in the number of ______ receptors on the receiving neuron. (Hint: It's a type of glutamate receptor.)**
3. **Describe how a stroke can damage neurons. What are two other causes of neuronal damage?**

8.2.5 Biological Processes and Technologies Offer Hope for CNS Recovery

There is an intense interest in developing treatments that will promote recovery after injury to the nervous system from disease or accidents. When we ask about nervous system recovery, there are several questions of interest. Can the damaged neurons reestablish their connections with their targets? If not, can other neurons that are *not* damaged take over some of their functions?

Even if the damaged neurons fail to reestablish normal connections and healthy neurons do not substitute for them, the person may learn strategies to compensate for the movement difficulties or other disrupted functions. For instance, if brain damage causes paralysis of one arm, the person may gain skill in using the unaffected arm to carry out more tasks. If elbow movements are no longer possible, the person may learn to carry out tasks by moving other joints in ways that compensate for the lost abilities.

We begin with a brief discussion of the peripheral nervous system, where damaged neurons can often spontaneously reestablish their connections. We'll then examine promising new treatments under development to promote recovery from central nervous system damage.

Recovery from Damage Is Greater in the PNS than the CNS

Because the peripheral nervous system has a greater capacity for recovery compared to the CNS, studying recovery of nerves in the periphery of the body may help unlock the secrets for aiding CNS recovery. Consider an axon in the arm that has been cut. Changes will occur on both sides of the injury: the part of the axon beyond the cut that's connected to the axon terminals (the distal portion), and the portion of the axon that's still connected to the cell body (the proximal portion) (Figure 8.17). The distal portion will completely degenerate within days following the injury. However, the proximal portion may remain viable due to its continued

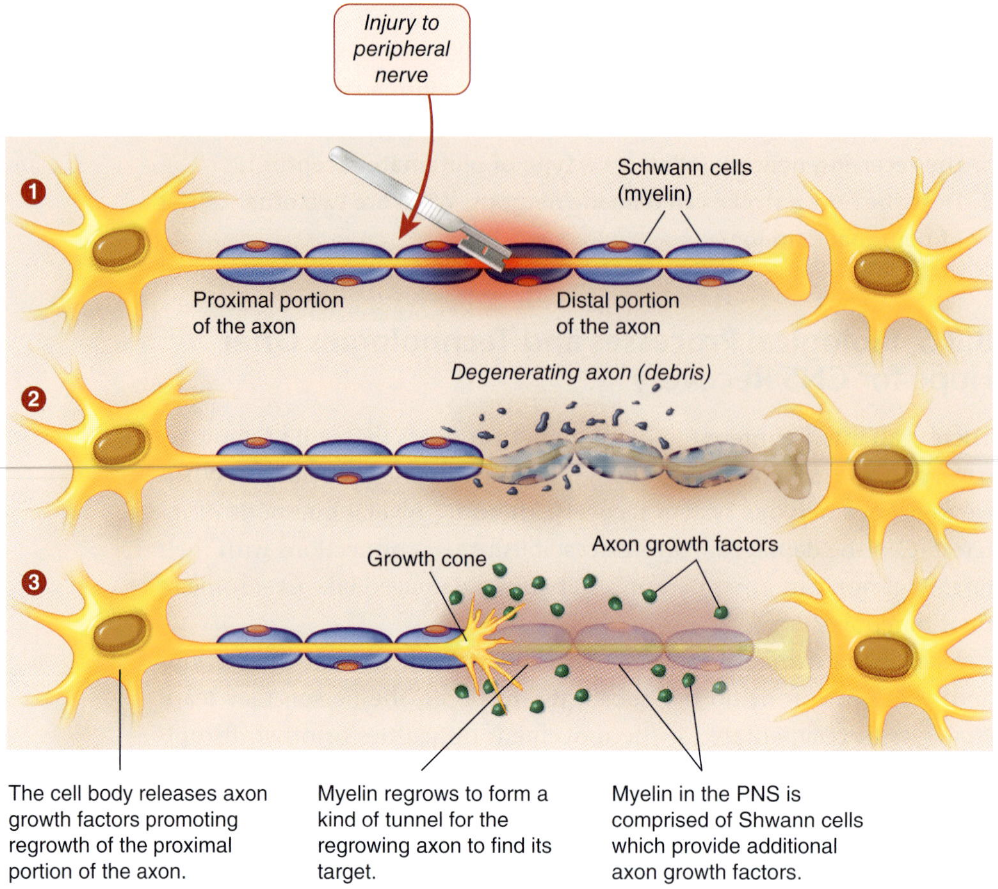

Figure 8.17 Regeneration of a peripheral nerve.

connection to the cell body, which provides the axon with nutrients. The cell body also produces biochemicals that promote regrowth of the axon. This helps the proximal portion of the damaged axon in the periphery to reconnect with its target cell (a muscle, a gland, or another neuron).

The regrowing axon in the PNS extends at the rate of 2–4 mm a day. The leading edge of the regenerating axon contains a growth cone (recall that the growth cone is also seen in developing axons searching for their targets). Regeneration occurs best if the myelin sheath that originally covered the axon is maintained as a regrowth pathway. In the peripheral nervous system, myelin comes from a type of glial cell called **Schwann cells**. Besides providing mechanical support for axonal growth, myelin from the Schwann cells provides an additional source of axonal growth factors.

Many neurons in the CNS are also surrounded by myelin. However, in this case the myelin doesn't come from Schwann cells, but from another kind of glial cell, **oligodendrocytes**. Oligodendrocytes do not produce the growth-promoting chemicals that enable regrowth of peripheral nerves. Neither do they form tunnels for regrowth that help the cells find their targets. Myelin from oligodendrocytes therefore does not provide damaged axons in the brain and spinal cord assistance for axonal regrowth and synaptic reconnection.

This doesn't mean that no CNS recovery occurs. Individuals may show a great deal of improvement in sensory and motor function after brain damage such as a stroke, especially during the first three months of recovery. To some degree, this may reflect recovery of neuronal function in the CNS.

Earlier in the chapter, we saw several examples of neuronal regrowth in the CNS. You may recall that when inputs to a brain region are lost, they may receive new inputs from branches of other axons. Such evidence for CNS regrowth after injuries holds some promise for recovery from brain damage. A difficulty is that the new growth of neuronal connection after brain damage is not necessarily normal or "functional" regrowth. An important question is whether CNS regrowth can be controlled in a way that will provide greater benefits to the patient.

Assistance from Technology

Progress in brain–computer interface (BCI) may be one of the most important advances for people disabled from brain injury. To give you a feeling for this, we'll explore a few cases.

Detailed EEG of brain activity is recorded while a paraplegic patient is asked to picture himself walking steadily. He is then asked to imagine himself standing still. After thousands of repetitions, the computer figures out the patterns of brain activity that are unique to his imagined "walking," and sends signals to a robotic device capable of moving the person's legs, or prosthetic (artificial) legs (Figure 8.18). Preliminary results of this system are encouraging, allowing the individual with paralysis of the legs to walk by simply imagining himself walking (Do et al., 2013). At the moment, the system only permits walking on a treadmill, and occasionally makes the mistake of triggering "walking" at inappropriate times, a potentially dangerous occurrence.

In a considerably more complex example of BCI, scientists placed an array of electrodes in motor areas of a monkey's brain and trained the monkey to move a joystick (with its arm) in order to move a cursor to a mark on a computer screen. It was rewarded with food when it moved the cursor correctly. As it learned this task, the investigators used computer analyses of the monkey's brain activity in order to identify the patterns of neuronal activity that accompanied its arm movements. The computer was also able to send electrical signals that controlled the movements of

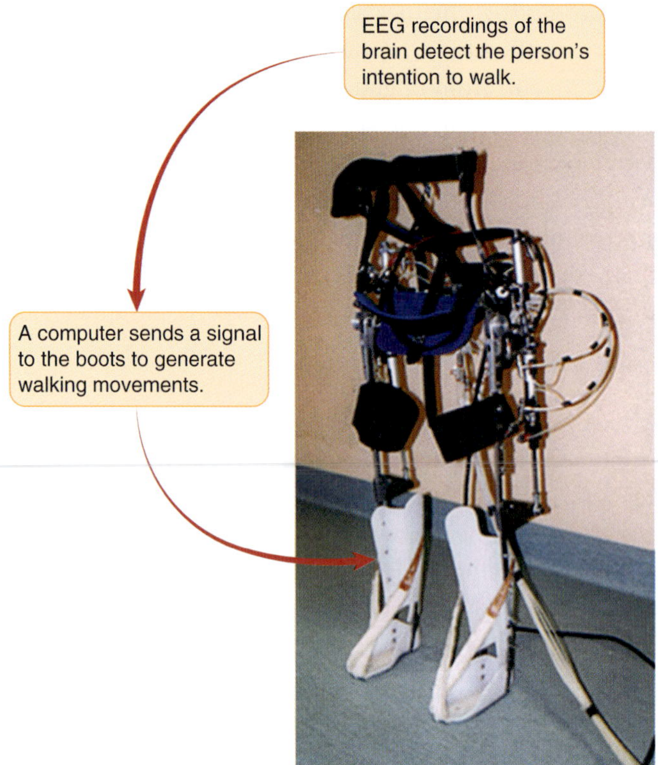

Figure 8.18 **Artificial control of leg movements by brain–computer interface.** (Adapted from Sacco et al., 2011, fig. 1.)

a robotic arm. When the monkey's brain produced the pattern of activity that accompanied its left arm movement, the computer recognized the pattern and signaled to the robotic arm to move to the left. When the monkey's neurons generated the "move right" pattern, the computer caused the robotic arm to move right, and so on. Then, they changed the task. The monkey could still earn food rewards by moving the cursor, but instead of using its arm and hand to move the joystick, it merely needed to generate brain activity that caused the robotic arm to move the joystick. The monkey was quickly able to control the robotic arm with its own brain activity (reviewed in Lebedev & Nicolelis, 2006).

BCI research in animals is opening the door to many possibilities for humans with spinal injuries or degenerative diseases leading to paralysis. For instance, using approaches similar to those described above, monkeys can learn to control the movement of a wheelchair without moving a limb (Rajangam et al., 2016). BCI technology is quickly advancing to allow paralyzed individuals to control aspects of their world simply by thinking about doing it. As we saw in Chapter 4, a BCI allows patients unable to move their limbs to open a browser, scroll through their email, or send a text message simply by thinking of where they wish to move the cursor and when they want to click the mouse (Nuyujukian et al., 2018).

Behavioral Therapy

Physical therapists are trained in helping people to overcome behavioral deficits caused by neural injury. Practice, practice, practice of the disrupted desired behavior can enhance recovery from brain damage. This may be due to activation and training of neural circuits that survived the damage, or to new behavioral strategies that enable the person to compensate for the damage, e.g., adapting to their impairment by carrying out tasks in new ways, using different joints or muscles (Dobkin & Carmichael, 2016). Many other behavioral interventions may be a part of behavioral therapy, depending upon the type of damage the person has suffered. These include general fitness training, biofeedback, mental practice of the impaired movement, and language training (in the case of aphasias).

When the goal is to restore function of an affected body part, one of the most successful approaches is **constraint-induced movement therapy**. The idea is to get the person to use the impaired limb (say the right arm and hand) to carry out a task (say lifting a plastic cup to the mouth), and to repeat the task again and again. The person's tendency may be to grab the cup with the other (unaffected) hand, but they're encouraged not to do this (e.g., by having them sit on the good hand while performing the task).

On the other hand, if the limb is severely impaired, the person may make more improvements by working on **compensatory strategies** instead. For instance, if the person is unable to extend the elbow, the person may learn to reach objects by bending forward with the trunk of the body and elevating the shoulders. In this case, they are compensating for their motor loss rather than reducing the impairment.

The choice of strategies depends upon assumptions about how likely it is that neural plasticity will restore the disrupted cognitive or behavioral function. Given the evidence that behavioral therapy may stimulate neural plasticity (Sterling et al., 2013; Zhai & Feng, 2019), some scientists have argued that it would be advantageous to focus on recovery of function (e.g., using constrain-induced movement therapy) rather than compensating for lost functions (Levin, Kleim, & Wolf, 2009).

CNS Surgery

Often the last thing patients turn to for repair of CNS damage is surgical intervention. There are a large number of possible options, depending upon the type of injury. Many variables should be considered in making an informed decision, including probability of success (what does the record show for patients who have undergone this treatment?), danger of harmful side effects or even mortality, and cost. Let's look at a couple of examples of surgery, ranging from the simple to the complex.

Parkinson's disease is a serious neurological disorder involving tremors and great difficulty initiating movements (Chapter 13). The disease is caused by the death of dopamine neurons in the substantia nigra. Many treatments have had limited success, and there are no known cures. Early on, the idea emerged that a possible effective treatment might be the surgical transplantation of new, healthy dopamine neurons from a donor. Two significant issues immediately arose. First, it seemed unlikely that the axons of the new dopamine neuron transplanted in the substantia nigra (in the midbrain) would find their way to the distant site in the striatum (in the forebrain) where dopamine plays its normal functional role in bodily movements. Second, neurons taken from a recently deceased adult donor's brain would probably be lacking in plasticity. So, the idea arose to take high-plasticity tissue from aborted human fetuses and transplant them directly into the striatum. In the end, many attempts were made, but results concerning the effectiveness of the treatment were inconclusive (Barker, 2013; Elkouzi, Vedam-Mai, Eisinger, & Okun, 2019).

This topic provides an opportunity for us to consider an important, major advance in the general field of tissue restoration. It has always been a dream to use pluripotent stem cells, immature cells capable of developing into any type of adult cell, to replace injured or dead cells anywhere in the body, including the nervous system. However, the issue always becomes where to find the supply of such cells. A group of Japanese scientists have made a huge step in this process. They have taken mature human skin cells and successfully reversed them developmentally to produce a supply of pluripotent cells (Takahashi et al., 2014; Elkouzi et al., 2019). These cells hold out the possibility of being employed clinically to treat brain injuries or neurological diseases where new cells might replace the brain cells that have died.

The next study follows up on this theme. A 38-year-old man from Poland suffered a traumatic injury that severed his spinal cord, leaving about a ½ inch gap in the spinal cord between the nerves that had become disconnected, and paralysis of his lower limbs. About two years after his injury, with no realistic prospect of recovery, he elected to undergo an experimental surgical procedure to restore sensory and motor function in his legs. The cost of the surgery ($10,000 in US dollars) was prohibitive for the man, and the people of his village contributed together to pay for it. Animal studies had shown that the olfactory system has a special ability for regrowth of neurons. The ability comes largely from cells called olfactory ensheathing cells that can form tiny tunnel-like structures to guide the growth of other neurons. This is similar to what the Schwann cells can do in the peripheral nervous system. Could these olfactory cells be transplanted to the spinal cord to permit neuronal recovery?

The surgery involved removal of his olfactory bulbs to serve as a source for the olfactory cells. In a culture (a dish), the olfactory ensheathing cells were allowed to divide for several weeks, to produce enough cells for the surgery. The cells were then injected into the man's spinal cord, into hundreds of locations above and below the wound. The hope was that they would help the damaged neurons make their way across the severed area to form functional connections. In addition, the surgeon removed a small strip of nerve tissue taken from the man's leg and inserted it into the severed area, crossing the gap caused by the wound. More olfactory cells were sprinkled onto this strip of tissue. Weeks after the surgery, the man showed no recovery. However, within about five months, he started to feel sensations in his leg and he could move one of them a bit. A year later, he could walk using a walker and with assistance from another person. This is not full recovery, but he is no longer paralyzed. Neurophysiological exams and MRI scans of his spinal cord provided anatomical evidence consistent with the behavioral improvement (Tabakow et al., 2014). One might rightly say that this is miraculous.

KEY CONCEPTS

- **Damage to the brain can activate stem cells to generate neurons and glia that migrate to the injury site.**
- **Brain–computer interface (BCI) is a rapidly emerging field employing computer technology to allow the brains of paralyzed individuals to control robotic movements.**
- **Behavioral approaches to recovery include those aimed at inducing plasticity and recovery of lost function. Other approaches focus upon training new behavioral strategies to compensate for the functions that have been lost.**
- **Novel surgical approaches are aimed at CNS repair and recovery.**

TEST YOURSELF

1. **Why does neuronal recovery in the PNS occur more readily than that in the CNS? What are some specific limitations of recovery in the CNS?**
2. **Give an example of how a brain–computer interface can be used to help a paralyzed individual to control movements of a prosthetic body part.**
3. **Give two examples of surgical approaches to repair CNS damage.**

8.3 The Big Picture

The brain remains plastic, or modifiable, throughout our lives. Neural plasticity occurs whenever we form a new memory or learn a new skill. In fact, a brain that was not rapidly alterable would be of limited use to us. Without neural plasticity, we would be unable to learn from our mistakes. Fundamental discoveries about the mechanisms underlying early brain development, such as cell birth, cell death, and the growth factors that guide axons to make new connections, provide clues about other forms of neural plasticity, such as those underlying learning, memory and recovery from brain damage.

8.4 Creative Thinking

1. If you were to inactivate all the radial glia in the neural tube, what kind of problems would you expect to observe in brain development?
2. What differences in the human brain would you expect to see between a person maintained in solitary confinement for years and a control subject allowed to live a full, free life in the outside world? If there were differences, would they be irreversible?
3. We saw that the hippocampus of taxi drivers expands with their experience navigating the streets of London. Do you think that a bird watcher who becomes expert at recognizing particular kinds of birds might undergo similar enlargement within the visual cortex?
4. You have just been appointed director of the National Institutes of Health. You are tasked with solving the problem of recovery from brain and spinal cord damage. It's up to you to decide what kinds of research to fund. What five research questions would you list as priorities?
5. Why discuss the processes of brain development and neuronal plasticity in the same chapter?

Key Terms

apoptosis 316
brain-derived neurotrophic factor (BDNF) 332
cell adhesion molecules (CAMs) 314
cell-autonomous 314
cell proliferation 308
chemoattractants 312
chemorepellants 312
compensatory strategies 341
constraint-induced movement therapy 341
differentiation 312
ectoderm 308
excitotoxicity 336
growth cone 314
hemispherectomy 325
inductive signal 314
long-term depression (LTD) 335
long-term potentiation (LTP) 333

References

Altman, J., & Das, G. D. (1965). Autoradiographic and histological evidence of postnatal hippocampal neurogenesis in rats. *Journal of Comparative Neurology, 123*, 319–335.

Andersen, S. L. (2003). Trajectories of brain development: point of vulnerability or window of opportunity? *Neuroscience & Biobehavioral Reviews, 27*, 3–18.

Barker, R. A., Barrett J., Mason, S.L., & Björklund, A. (2013). Fetal dopaminergic transplantation trials and the future of neural grafting in Parkinson's disease. *Lancet Neurology, 12*, 84–91.

Borgstein, J., & Grootendorst, C. (2002). Clinical picture: half a brain. *Lancet, 359*, 473.

Casey, B. J., Jones, R. M., & Hare, T. A. (2008). The adolescent brain. *Annals of the New York Academy of Sciences, 1124*, 111–126.

Choi, D. W. (1992). Excitotoxic cell death. *Journal of Neurobiology, 23*, 1261–1276.

Depaepe, V., Suarez-Gonzalez, N., Dufour, A., Passante, L., Gorski, J. A., Jones, K. R., ... Vanderhaeghen, P. (2005). Ephrin signalling controls brain size by regulating apoptosis of neural progenitors. *Nature, 435*(7046), 1244–1250.

Do, A. H., Wang, P. T., King, C. E., Chun, S. N., & Nenadic, Z. (2013). Brain–computer interface controlled robotic gait orthosis. *Journal of NeuroEngineering and Rehabilitation, 10*, 111.

Dobkin, B. H., & Carmichael, S. T. (2016). The specific requirements of neural repair trials for stroke. *Neurorehabilitation and Neural Repair, 30*(5), 470–478.

Elkouzi, A., Vedam-Mai, V., Eisinger, R. S., & Okun, M. S. (2019). Emerging therapies in Parkinson disease – repurposed drugs and new approaches. *Nature Reviews Neurology, 15*(4), 204–223.

Gilmore, J. H., Knickmeyer, R. C., & Gao, W. (2018). Imaging structural and functional brain development in early childhood. *Nature Reviews Neuroscience, 19*(3), 123–137.

Gupta, K. K., Gupta, V. K., & Shirasaka, T. (2016). An update on fetal alcohol syndrome – pathogenesis, risks, and treatment. *Alcoholism: Clinical and Experimental Research, 40,* 1594–1602.

Hamburger, V. (1934). The effects of wing bud extirpation on the development of the central nervous system in chick embryos. *Journal of Experimental Zoology, 68,* 449–494.

Hayashi, Y., Jinnou, H., Sawamoto, K., & Hitoshi, S. (2018). Adult neurogenesis and its role in brain injury and psychiatric diseases. *Journal of Neurochemistry, 147*(5), 584–594.

Hirsch, H. V., & Spinelli, D. N. (1970). Visual experience modifies distribution of horizontally and vertically oriented receptive fields in cats. *Science, 168*(3933), 869–871.

Lebedev, M. A., & Nicolelis, M. A. (2006). Brain–machine interfaces: past, present and future. *Trends in Neuroscience, 29,* 536–546.

Lenroot, R. K., & Giedd, N. J. (2006). Brain development in children and adolescents: insights from anatomical magnetic resonance imaging. *Neuroscience & Biobehavioral Reviews, 30*(6), 718–729.

Levi-Montalcini, R., & Calissano, P. (1979). The nerve-growth factor. *Scientific American, 240,* 44–53.

Levin, M. F., Kleim, J. A., & Wolf, S. L. (2009). What do motor "recovery" and "compensation" mean in patients following stroke? *Neurorehabilitation and Neural Repair, 23*(4), 313–319.

Lowery, L. A., & Vactor, D. V. (2009). The trip of the tip: understanding the growth cone machinery. *Nature Reviews Molecular Cell Biology, 10,* 332–343.

Maguire, E. A., Gadian, D. G., Johnsrude, I. S., Good, C. D., Ashburner, J., Frackowiak, R. S., & Frith, C. D. (2000). Navigation-related structural change in the hippocampi of taxi drivers. *Proceedings of the National Academy of Sciences of the United States of America, 97,* 4398–4403.

Malenka, R. C., Kauer, J. A., Zucker, R. S., & Nicoll, R. A. (1988). Postsynaptic calcium is sufficient for potentiation of hippocampal synaptic transmission. *Science, 242,* 81–84.

Max, D. T. (2016). One small step: a paraplegic undergoes pioneering surgery. The New Yorker. www.newyorker.com/magazine/2016/01/25/one-small-step-annals-of-medicine-d-t-max

Miller, D. J., Duka, T., Stimpson, C. D., Schapiro, S. J., Baze, W. B., McArthur, M. J., & Sherwood, C. C. (2012). Prolonged myelination in human neocortical evolution. *Proceedings of the National Academy of Sciences of the United States of America, 109,* 16480–16485.

Nuyujukian, P., Albites Sanabria, J., Saab, J., Pandarinath, C., Jarosiewicz, B., Blabe, C. H., ... Henderson, J. M. (2018). Cortical control of a tablet computer by people with paralysis. *PLOS ONE, 13*(11), e0204566.

Oppenheim, R. W. (1991). Cell death during development of the nervous system. *Annual Review of Neuroscience, 14,* 453–501.

Raisman, G. (1969). Neuronal plasticity in the septal nuclei of the adult rat. *Brain Research, 14,* 25–48.

Rajangam, S., Tseng, P. H., Yin, A., Lehew, G., Schwarz, D., Lebedev, M. A., & Nicolelis, M. A. (2016). Wireless cortical brain–machine interface for whole-body navigation in primates. *Scientific Reports, 6*, 22170.

Sacco, K., Cauda, F., D'Agata, F., Duca, S., Zettin, M., Virgilio, R., ... Geminiani, G. (2011). A combined robotic and cognitive training for locomotor rehabilitation: evidences of cerebral functional reorganization in two chronic traumatic brain injured patients. *Frontiers in Human Neuroscience, 5*, 146.

Sperry, R. W. (1963). Chemoaffinity in the orderly growth of nerve fiber patterns and connections. *Proceedings of the National Academy of Sciences of the United States of America, 50*(4), 703–710.

Sterling, C., Taub, E., Davis, D., Rickards, T., Gauthier, L. V., Griffin, A., & Uswatte, G. (2013). Structural neuroplastic change after constraint-induced movement therapy in children with cerebral palsy. *Pediatrics 131*, e1664–1669.

Strange, B. A., Witter, M. P., Lein, E. S., & Moser, E. I. (2014). Functional organization of the hippocampal longitudinal axis. *Nature Reviews Neuroscience, 15*(10), 655–669.

Sur, M., Garraghty, P. E., & Roe, A. W. (1988). Experimentally induced visual projections into auditory thalamus and cortex. *Science, 242*, 1437–1441.

Tabakow, P., Raisman G., Fortuna, W., Czyz, M., Huber, J., Li, D., ... Jarmundowicz, W. (2014). Functional regeneration of supraspinal connections in a patient with transected spinal cord following transplantation of bulbar olfactory ensheathing cells with peripheral nerve bridging. *Cell Transplantation, 23*, 1631–1655.

Takahashi, K., Tanabe, K., Ohnuki, M., Narita, M., Sasaki, A., Yamamoto, M., ... Yamanaka, S. (2014). Induction of pluripotency in human somatic cells via a transient state resembling primitive streak-like mesendoderm. *Nature Communications, 5*, 3678.

Vining, E. P., Freeman, J. M., Pillas, D. J., Uematsu, S., Carson, B. S., Brandt, J., ... Zuckerberg, A. (1997). Why would you remove half a brain? The outcome of 58 children after hemispherectomy – the Johns Hopkins experience: 1968 to 1996. *Pediatrics, 100*, 163–171.

Volkmar, F. R., & Greenough, W. T. (1972). Rearing complexity affects branching of dendrites in the visual cortex of the rat. *Science, 176*, 1445–1447.

Yang, T. T., Gallen, C., Schwartz, B., Bloom, F. E., Ramachandran, V. S., & Cobb, S. (1994). Sensory maps in the human brain. *Nature, 368*, 592–593.

Zhai, Z. Y., & Feng, J. (2019). Constraint-induced movement therapy enhances angiogenesis and neurogenesis after cerebral ischemia/reperfusion. *Neural Regeneration Research, 14*(10), 1743–1754.

Zhao, C., Teng, E. M., Summers Jr., R. G., Ming, G., & Gage, F. H. (2006). Distinct morphological stages of dentate granule neuron maturation in the adult mouse hippocampus. *Journal of Neuroscience, 26*(1), 3–11.

9
Long-Term Learning and Memory

SEAN GLADWELL / Moment / Getty Images

Consider This ...

In the 1930s, a neurosurgeon performed brain surgery on patients with epileptic seizures. The seizures, storms of electrical activity spreading rapidly through the brain, could not be controlled with medication. The surgeon's approach was to identify the brain areas from which the seizures originated, and to remove the tissue. But before removing brain tissue, he would electrically stimulate specific regions of the cerebral cortex to identify areas involved in speech, movement, or perception. He wanted to ensure that these critical brain areas were not damaged during the epilepsy surgery. When electrical stimulation was applied to regions of the temporal cortex overlying the hippocampus (Figure 9.1), patients had sudden memories of past events. These "flashbacks" would stop as soon as the stimulation ended.

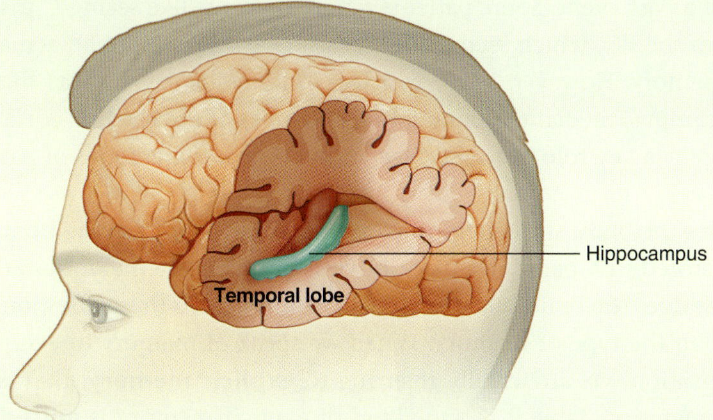

Figure 9.1 **The hippocampus is buried within a medial region of the temporal lobe**. When the surface of the temporal lobe near the hippocampus was stimulated, patients reported flashback memories.

The surgeon, Dr. Wilder Penfield, took notes as the patients described the memories produced by the stimulation. "There was a piano there and someone playing," said one patient. "I could hear the song, you know." Penfield stimulated the same point again, and the patient said, "Someone speaking to another." When the point was stimulated again, she said, "Yes, Oh Marie, Oh Marie! – Someone is singing it."

Penfield then moved the stimulating electrode to a nearby point. "Something brings back a memory. I can see the Seven-Up Bottling Company ... Harrison Bakery." The surgeon then told the patient that the electrical stimulation was beginning again, but he did not really turn on the stimulator. The patient replied, "Nothing."

Another patient heard a popular song as though it were being played by an orchestra. Every time the same temporal lobe location was stimulated, he heard the same music.

The stimulation was restricted to the outer layers of the temporal lobes, the temporal cortex. However, it is possible that the activation also spread to areas deep below the temporal cortex in the **medial temporal lobes**. The medial temporal lobes, unseen when viewing the outer surface of the brain, contain memory-related regions, including the **hippocampus**.

Had the surgeon stimulated neurons that stored memories of past experiences? Penfield's patients often described hearing a song, a piece of a conversation, or seeing a vague image; rarely did they describe an entire memory of a past event. Some patients reported events like seeing Christ appear from the sky, which seems unlikely to have been part of an actual episodic memory. However, as we will see, other evidence suggests that the hippocampus, medial temporal lobes, and areas of the cerebral cortex do in fact play a key role in the storage and retrieval of memories of past experiences.

How does the brain store memories? Is your memory of leaving home yesterday stored in a particular place in your brain? Once memories are stored, how does the brain retrieve them? The answers to these questions depend upon the type of memory. When we speak of memory in everyday conversation, we are usually referring to **explicit memory**, that is, conscious memory (Table 9.1). One kind of explicit memory is **episodic memory**, conscious memories of personal experiences, such as your memory of seeing a movie last weekend, or of having dinner at a restaurant last night. Another type of explicit memory, **semantic memory**, is memory of facts that you have learned ("Paris is the capital of France").

Table 9.1 Summarizing forms of explicit and implicit memory.

Explicit versus implicit	Type of memory	What is remembered	Example
Explicit	Episodic memory	Personal experience	Last night's dinner
Explicit	Semantic memory	Facts	The capital of China
Implicit	Skill learning	Movements	Riding a bicycle
Implicit	Classical conditioning	Associations between two events	Dentist's drill is associated with pain

Other memories are **implicit**, that is, they are not conscious, but they affect behavior. For instance, riding a bicycle involves implicit memories about how to adjust your balance and how to use the brakes. If I asked you how you do these things, you might not be able to tell me. That's because these **skill memories** are implicit; you don't have conscious access to them, but they can (luckily) influence your behavior when you're riding a bike. Implicit memories can also be formed through **classical conditioning**, an association between two events. If you've formed an association between the large yellow McDonald's sign and a hamburger, the sight of the McDonald's sign may put you in the mood for a burger, regardless of whether you have an explicit memory of eating a burger at McDonald's in the past. Whenever a past experience affects our behavior without leaving a conscious trace, we say that we have formed an implicit memory. Some forms of psychotherapy are founded upon the belief that if we can make our implicit memories more accessible to the conscious mind, our behavior will become more flexible, less rigid (see Figure 9.2).

This chapter begins by discussing the storage and retrieval of *episodic* memories. We will then discuss skill learning, classical conditioning, and even simpler forms of learning in a simple organism. (We will mention semantic memory only in passing, for its brain underpinnings are poorly understood.) Each of these different types of memory depends upon different brain circuits. Nevertheless, you will find that some fundamental brain processes are shared by all of these types of memory and learning.

9.1 MEMORY OF EXPERIENCES

The hippocampus is a key memory region, but it is not critical for *all* kinds of memory. The hippocampus is particularly important for storing conscious memories of past experiences (episodic memories). What would life be like without the hippocampus?

"And then it hit me: I'm salivating over a goddam bell."

Figure 9.2 Making an implicit association explicit. After several repetitions of hearing a bell ring before receiving food, Pavlov's dogs began to salivate as soon as they heard the bell. In the cartoon, the dog realizes that this unconscious association was affecting its behavior. Unconscious, or what behavioral scientists would call implicit, associations strongly influence our behavior and thoughts. According to some schools of psychotherapy, there can be therapeutic value to making implicit associations explicit, or "conscious."
(© Robert Leighton/ Cartoon Stock.)

9.1.1 Damage to the Medial Temporal Lobes Produces Amnesia

As a child, Henry Molaison had a bicycle accident that caused brain trauma. He later suffered epileptic seizures. Like Penfield's patients, his epilepsy could not be controlled by medication. At the age of 27, he underwent a surgical procedure to remove large regions of his medial temporal lobes, including much of the hippocampus in both hemispheres. The procedure, carried out in the 1950s, did successfully control his seizures, but also produced unexpected and permanent memory impairment.

Henry's memory loss was obvious within days of his surgery. He could no longer remember what he'd eaten for breakfast. He could not find his way around the hospital or recognize the hospital staff. When someone entered his hospital room, Henry would introduce himself politely and engage in normal conversation. But when the person left the room for a few minutes and reentered, Henry would not remember having met the person, and would reintroduce himself as if for the first time. After reading a magazine article, he would not remember what the article was about, or even having read it. Henry and other patients with bilateral damage to the medial temporal lobes may also show impairment in semantic memory.

However, their greatest impairments are in storing memories of personal experiences, that is, episodic memory.

Henry's general intellectual abilities were normal; there was no drop in his IQ. However, he could not create memories of new experiences. Here is how Henry described his amnesia:

> Every day is alone in itself, whatever enjoyment I've had, and whatever sorrow I've had. Right now, I'm wondering, have I done or said anything amiss? You see, at this moment everything looks clear to me, but what happened just before? That's what worries me. It's like waking from a dream. I just can't remember. (Milner, 1970)

Henry lost so much brain tissue within the medial temporal lobes that it is hard to pinpoint the precise areas of damage responsible for his memory loss (Figure 9.3). However, patients with medial temporal lobe damage

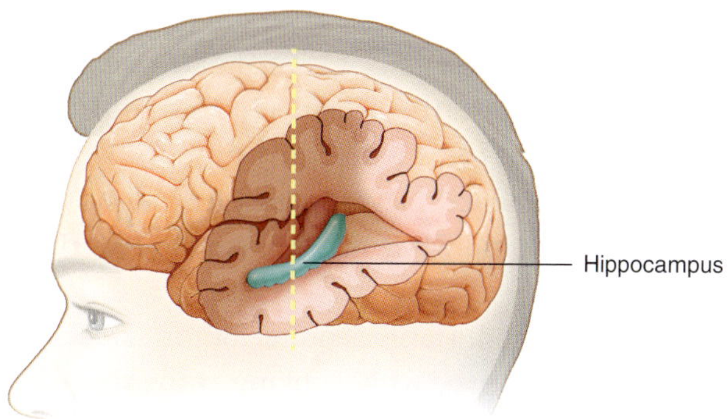

The images below show the brain as if it were sliced along the yellow line in the top image. (The front of the brain is facing you.)

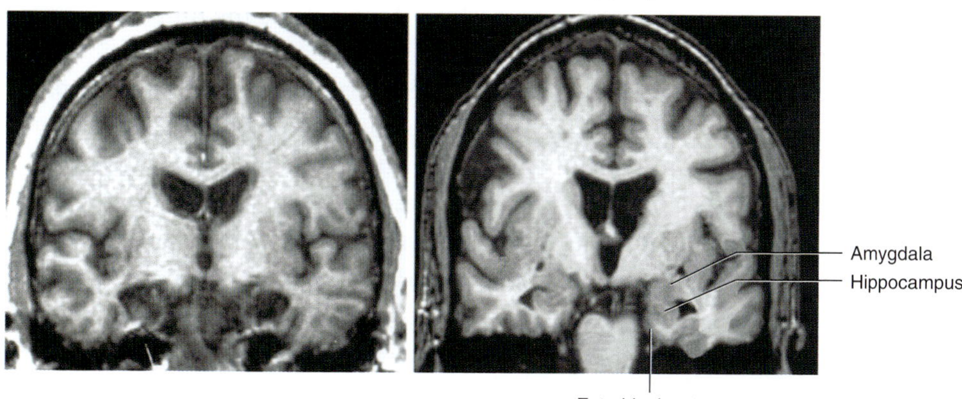

Figure 9.3 The brain after removal of the hippocampus. Henry Molaison's brain is to the left; the brain of a healthy male of the same age is to the right. Notice that neural tissue normally seen in the hippocampus is largely absent (black) in Molaison's brain.
(Adapted from Squire & Wixted, 2011, fig. 1.)

largely restricted to the hippocampus (Vargha-Khadem et al., 1997) suffer similar memory abnormalities, suggesting that the hippocampus is a critical area for episodic memory.

In 1957, neuropsychologist Brenda Milner published a report of her careful cognitive examination of Henry Molaison. Despite his dramatic loss of episodic memory, she found that other aspects of his memory survived the surgery. For instance, his **working memory** was normal. In other words, he could actively keep information like a phone number in mind so long as he wasn't distracted. When asked to remember the number 584, he still remembered it 15 minutes later. He explained how he kept the number in mind: "You just remember 8. You see, 5, 8, and 4 add to 17. You remember 8, subtract it from 17, and it leaves 9. Divide 9 in half and you get 5 and 4, and there you are, 584. Easy." But a moment later, after his attention had shifted, he forgot the number as well as the entire test experience. Without the hippocampus, he was unable to **consolidate** memories about the test session (i.e., he couldn't store them in a long-term manner). He could not consolidate memories about the room he was in during the test, the person administering the test, the number 584, or his own efforts to remember the number. Therefore, he could not later recall the experience. Nevertheless, he had no trouble keeping the number actively in mind while he was being tested. His working memory was fine.

Henry Molaison could also acquire motor skills such as learning to trace the outline of a shape while looking at the shape in a mirror. Due to his episodic memory loss, he believed each training session to be his first. Nevertheless, he made fewer errors each day. His improvement demonstrates that skill learning was not disrupted by damage to the hippocampus. Henry could presumably have learned to ride a bicycle or to swing a tennis racket. As we will see, brain regions outside the hippocampus are important for skill learning.

In summary, medial temporal lobe damage prevents consolidation of episodic memories, that is, explicit memories about past events. However, the damage leaves skill memory and working memory intact. Of course, *some* brain regions are critical for these other kinds of memories. We'll examine the brain basis of skill memory in a later section of this chapter, and working memory will be discussed in Chapter 10.

9.1.2 Old, Recent, and New Memories

The inability to remember events that occur after a brain injury is called **anterograde amnesia**.

Head trauma can produce brain damage that causes anterograde amnesia. Fortunately, the memory loss is usually temporary. On the other hand, the loss of the hippocampus produces anterograde amnesia that is severe and permanent.

Anterograde amnesia can arise from a number of other causes, including stroke, Alzheimer's disease, and a severe deficiency in vitamin B-1. Individuals who abuse alcohol over many years often have reduced B-1 intake in the diet, reduced absorption of the vitamin from the gastrointestinal tract, and decreased availability of B-1 for brain cells. Extreme B-1 deficiency can cause **Korsakoff syndrome**, a neurological disorder that disrupts the ability to store new memories.

Individuals who lose memory for events that occurred *prior* to their brain damage are said to suffer **retrograde amnesia**. Medial temporal lobe damage can cause not only anterograde amnesia, but also retrograde amnesia. Interestingly, the longest-held memories are the least affected (see Figure 9.4). For instance, Henry Molaison had retrograde amnesia for

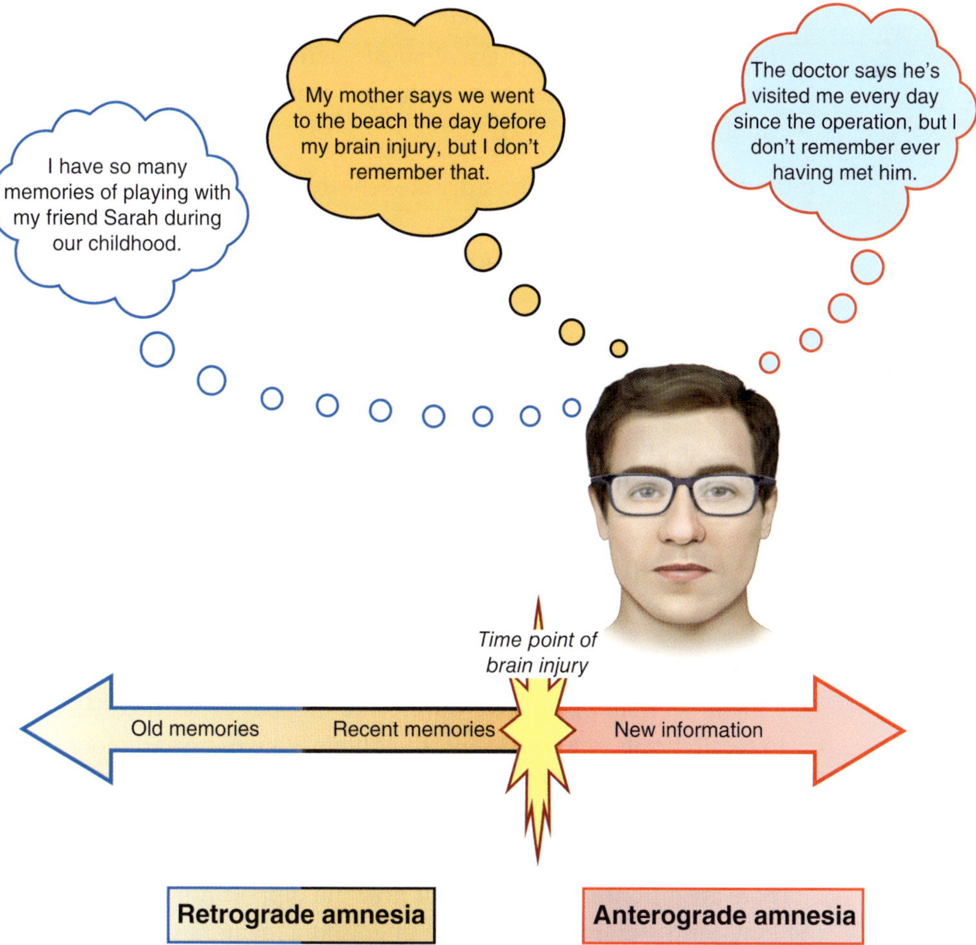

Figure 9.4 Anterograde and retrograde amnesia. Henry Molaison had anterograde amnesia, an inability to recall events that occurred after his brain injury. He also had partial retrograde amnesia which impaired his ability to remember events that occurred during several years before the injury.

events that occurred during the years just before his operation, but he recalled childhood events.

Below is a quote from a patient with both anterograde amnesia and also some retrograde amnesia. Nevertheless, he remembered early childhood events in great detail.

> Dad had 3½ acres of property in Castro Valley and the back property would just grow and would be dry and for some reason, I didn't do it, but somehow or other the next thing we knew is that it was starting to burn. I told dad and he called the Castro Valley fire department. They came up and they got it out real quick. However it started I don't know. He had 3½ acres of property and he just let it grow. It would be grass or whatever. Who knows how it started, but it started to burn. Dad called the Castro Valley fire department and they came up and all the volunteers came in and they got it out in a matter of 10–15 minutes. They stamped it out. They don't know how it started. I was 16–17, in that bracket. Dad had 3½ acres of property. It was summer time, 1938. Those sort of things I think you remember. (Bayley, Hopkins, & Squire, 2003)

Notice that some parts of the story are repeated. It is likely that the patient has difficulty remembering which details he has already related to the interviewer due to his anterograde amnesia. Nevertheless, he has a memory of this childhood event.

Patients with medial temporal lobe loss, then, show both anterograde amnesia and some retrograde amnesia. The retrograde amnesia is usually **temporally graded**, that is, the severity of the memory loss depends upon the age of the memory. Long-held memories are remembered better than more recent ones.

9.1.3 The Hippocampus and Cortex Interact during Memory Recall

When you remember having dinner last night, you reactivate many of the same neurons that were active during the original experience. As people try to recall details of a past event, their brain state more and more closely resembles its state at the time of the original event (Polyn, Natu, Cohen, & Norman, 2005). The more closely a person can reactivate that original brain state, the more vivid the memory (Dijkstra, Bosch, & van Gerven, 2017).

There are differing theories about how the hippocampus contributes to the long-term storage and retrieval of episodic memories, but most share these four key ideas (Moscovitch et al., 2005; Squire & Wixted, 2011):

1. During an experience, the things that we see, hear, and touch activate particular neurons in the cerebral cortex. Without this activation,

the events would not be perceived. Seeing a table *requires* that certain neurons in visual areas of the cortex are activated. In Figure 9.5A, the red-filled circles represent neurons in the cortex that are activated by auditory, visual, and other sensory events you perceive at the moment. If you are in a restaurant with a friend, your active sensory neurons may include visual neurons representing the look of the restaurant, auditory neurons activated by the sound of your friend's voice, and so on.

2. The sensory neurons activated in the cerebral cortex during a particular episode send neural signals down to a smaller number of neurons in the hippocampus.
3. Neurons in the cortex and the hippocampus have excitatory connections, which are **reciprocal**, i.e., neurons in the cortex excite those in the hippocampus, and neurons in the hippocampus activate neurons in the cortex. And so the neuronal activity reverberates back and forth between the two brain regions. This allows the connections between the cortical and hippocampal neurons to grow stronger. But *how*, really, does the connection between neurons grow stronger? This is one of the most important questions in the neuroscience of learning and memory, and we will consider it when we ask *how memories rewire the brain*.
4. A few days after visiting the restaurant, you may encounter a memory **retrieval cue**, something in the environment that brings the memory to mind. According to the theory, a retrieval cue such as seeing a commercial for that restaurant reactivates some of the cortical neurons that were active when you were in the restaurant. These cortical neurons activate some of the hippocampal neurons to which they developed strong connections. Those hippocampal neurons, in turn, reactivate the other cortical neurons that were associated with the dinner experience (episode).

Notice that, according to this view, the hippocampus is necessary in order to reactivate the cortical neurons that correspond to the details of the remembered event. When a memory is recalled, you reactivate (more or less) the same neurons in the cerebral cortex that were active during the original experience. In a sense, the hippocampal neurons can be considered **pointers** to the cortical neurons that represent the details of the remembered event. This theoretical model is called the **hippocampal memory indexing theory** (Teyler & DiScenna, 1986). As the theory predicts, both the hippocampus and regions of the cerebral cortex are activated during memory recall (Squire & Wixted, 2011).

From this perspective, Henry Molaison could not store new episodic memories because he lacked the hippocampal neurons that "link together" memory details stored in the cortex to create a unified memory of an episode. Misremembering an event, according to this theory, involves

A

In the restaurant last night . . .

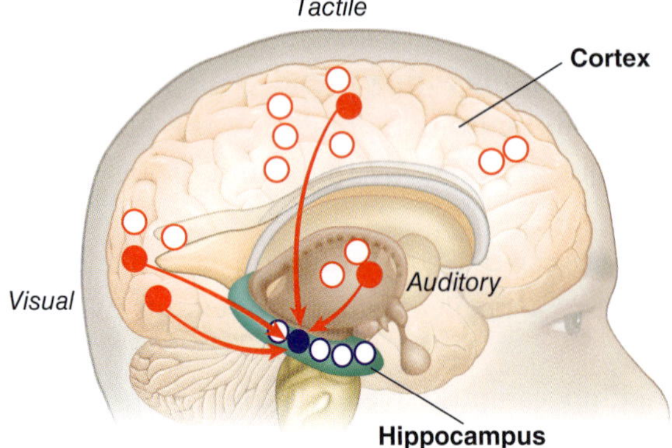

❶ Neurons activated in the cortex (red-filled circles) transmit the sensory details of your experience to neurons in the hippocampus (blue-filled circle).

Some time later . . .

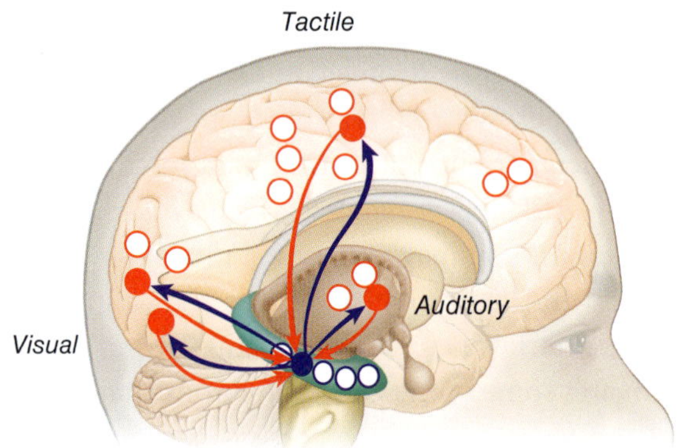

❷ The connections between the cortex and hippocampus are reciprocal, like a 2-way street. Cortical neurons activate hippocampal neurons, which activate cortical neurons, and so on. This allows the neurons to stay active for long periods of time, and to develop strong connections with one another.

In the near future, you recall the restaurant experience . . .

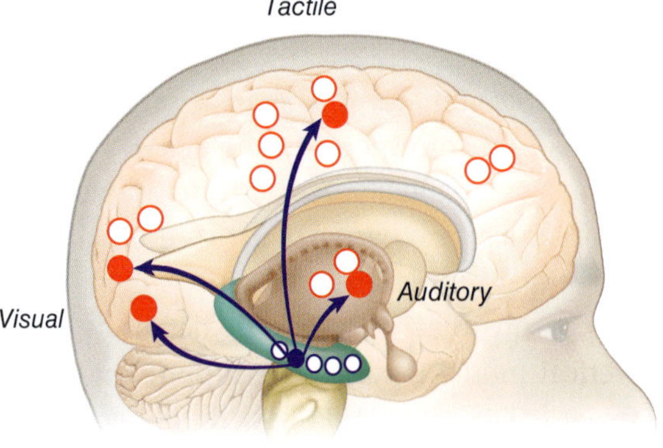

❸ If the hippocampal neurons that were activated during the earlier experience become reactivated in the future, they will reactivate the cortical neurons to which they have strong connections. This allows you to recall the experience.

Figure 9.5 **How does the hippocampus contribute to memory storage and retrieval?**

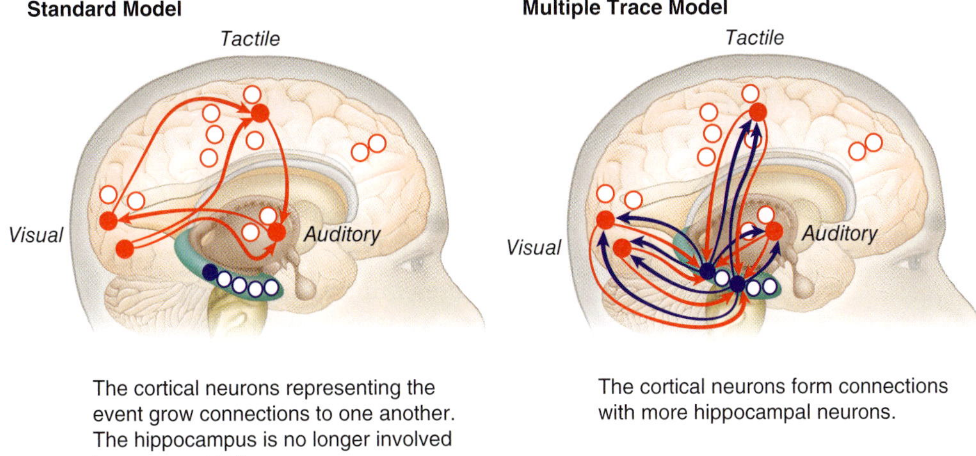

Figure 9.5 (cont.)

activation of cortical neurons that were not active during the original event. A sketchy memory involves reactivation of a subset of the originally active cortical neurons, but too few to recall the memory in much detail. Understanding how the brain produces incomplete or false memories is of particular importance within the legal system, for if an eyewitness incorrectly recalls the details of a crime, the consequences for the accused may be drastic. In fact, in the majority of cases where individuals were falsely convicted of crimes and later exonerated on the basis of forensic DNA testing, the false conviction was due to errors in eyewitness testimony (Garrett, 2011).

Psychologist Elizabeth Loftus has carried out pioneering work since the 1970s examining the vulnerability of memories to distortion. In one study, after viewing an event on film and then receiving misinformation about what occurred, some subjects later remembered the misinformation as part of the event (Schacter & Loftus, 2013). Even the way that a lawyer (or anyone else) asks you questions about an event can affect your recollection. In some cases, individuals confuse events that occurred with those that are imagined. This may be related to the fact that the hippocampus contributes both to memory recall and to imagining new experiences (Hassabis, Kumaran, Vann, & Maguire, 2007).

Before we leave the hippocampus and episodic memory, let us return to the intriguing observation that hippocampal damage often leaves early childhood memories intact. Why is it that these long-held memories survive after hippocampal damage? According to the **Standard Model**

of Memory Consolidation, neurons in the cerebral cortex holding the details of the remembered event become connected to one another directly, through strengthened synapses, over the course of years (Squire & Wixted, 2011). This allows the entire set of cortical neurons representing the episode to eventually become activated *without* hippocampal involvement (Figure 9.5B, left panel). According to the Standard Model, Henry Molaison could recall childhood memories despite loss of the hippocampus because cortical neurons representing various details of the memories had already developed strong connections with one another. According to the model, a retrieval cue such as a childhood photo of your brother can now activate cortical neurons representing Thanksgiving dinner of many years ago, even without hippocampal involvement.

A second theory provides a different explanation for these intact early childhood memories. According to the **Multiple Trace Model**, the hippocampus is needed for retrieval of any episodic memory, even if it is a long-held memory from childhood (Nadel & Moscovitch, 1997; Moscovitch et al., 2005). According to this theory, older memories are less vulnerable to hippocampal damage because they have been retrieved more often over the years. Each time a memory is retrieved, new hippocampal neurons become connected to the cortical neurons holding the memory information (Figure 9.5B, right panel). By analogy, imagine that a single road leads to a city. If an earthquake were to cause damage outside the city, the road might be destroyed, and access to the city would be lost. In contrast, imagine that five different roads lead to the city. The same earthquake is now much less likely to prevent access to the city, because even if a few of the roads are damaged, it is likely that one still remains. In the same way, if an older memory has more neuronal connections from the hippocampus to the memory represented in the cortex, it is less likely that brain damage will destroy all of the hippocampal neurons pointing to that cortical memory trace. According to the multiple trace theory, so many connections had been formed between the hippocampus and the cortical neurons representing Henry Molaison's oldest memories that some of those connections remained intact even after much of his hippocampus was removed.

9.1.4 Information Travels through the Hippocampus

In the previous section, we spoke of memory-related information traveling from the cerebral cortex to the hippocampus, and from the hippocampus to the cortex. By what anatomical route does the information travel? The hippocampus is comprised of three major regions: (1) the **dentate gyrus** (DG), (2) area **CA3** (Cornu Ammonis), (3) and area **CA1** (Figure 9.6). Before

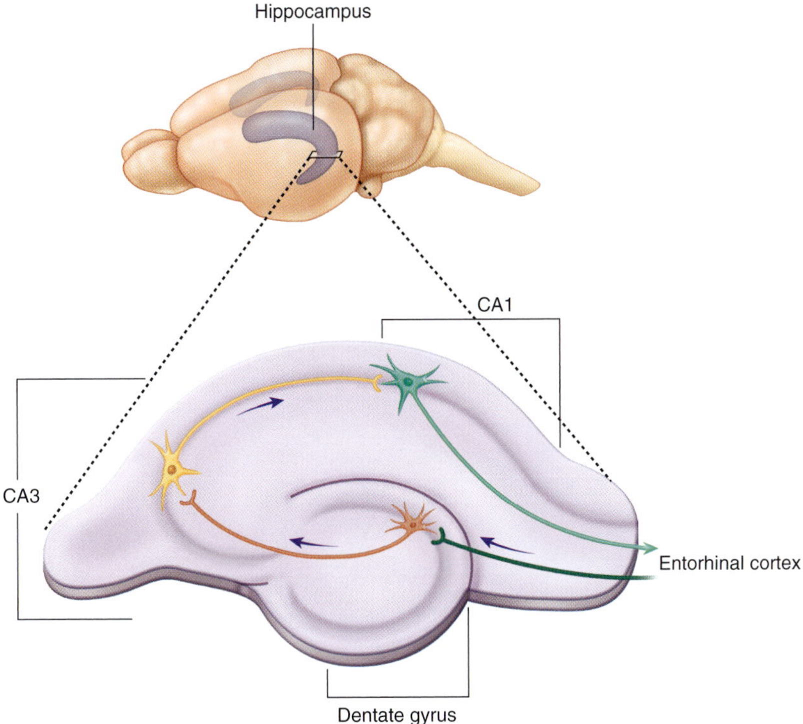

Figure 9.6 **Information flows through three major regions of the hippocampus.** The drawing depicts a slice taken from the hippocampus of the rat brain. A neuron in the dentate gyrus of the hippocampus (red) receives memory-related information from the entorhinal cortex. From the dentate, information travels to neurons in CA3 (orange) and CA1 (green), and finally back to the entorhinal cortex.

entering the hippocampus, information passes through the **entorhinal cortex**. Information from the entorhinal cortex passes through the dentate gyrus, CA3, and CA1, usually in that order, and then arrives back at the entorhinal cortex.

According to the models of memory storage described above, information travels from the cortex to the hippocampus and back again. However, we now see that, before entering the hippocampus, information must first pass through the entorhinal cortex. In fact, memory-related information from the cortex is sent to several regions of the medial temporal lobes before reaching the entorhinal cortex and finally the hippocampus (Figure 9.7). So, when you see illustrations such as those in Figure 9.5 depicting communication between the cortex and the hippocampus, you now know that the connections are not actually direct between the two brain areas. The cortex and hippocampus communicate, but they do so indirectly, via the entorhinal cortex and other medial temporal lobe structures.

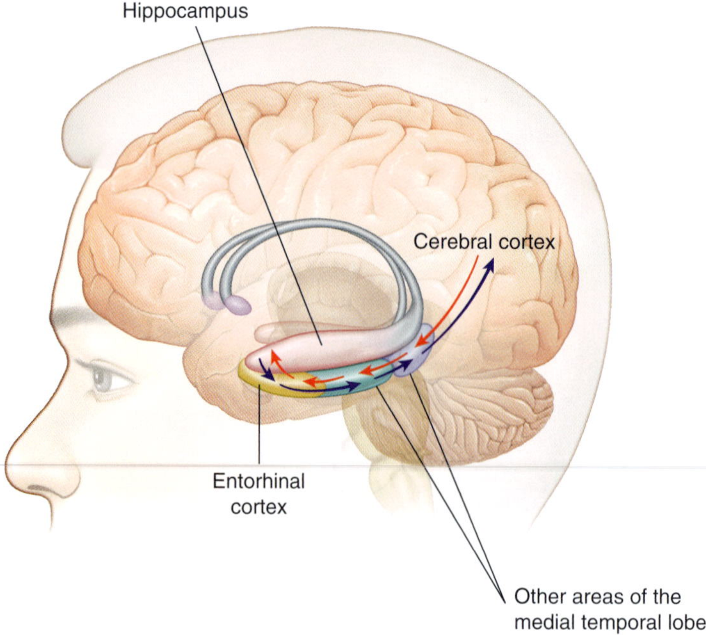

Figure 9.7 **The cortex and hippocampus communicate indirectly**. The cerebral cortex sends perceptual information (about things that are seen, heard, and so on) to several areas within the medial temporal lobe (red arrows). The information eventually arrives at the entorhinal cortex, and finally the hippocampus. The hippocampus also sends information back to the cortex (blue arrows).

9.1.5 Can the Activity of Individual Neurons Reveal What Someone Is Recalling?

If you were to observe the activity of your own individual hippocampal neurons while you remember an event, what would you expect to observe? Say you remember going to a restaurant with your friends Tom and Maria. Are particular neurons activated when you recall Tom sitting next to you, others when you think of Maria, and still others when you recall the way the restaurant looked?

For the sake of illustration, imagine that your memory of Tom, Maria, and the appearance of the restaurant depended upon the activity of just nine neurons (Figure 9.8). Imagine that when neurons 1, 3, 6, and 9 are activated you think of Tom; when neurons 1, 3, 4, and 8 are activated you think of Maria; and when neurons 4, 6, 8, and 9 are activated you think of the restaurant. This is a **distributed network** model. No particular neuron represents Tom versus Maria versus the restaurant. The code for a specific piece of information depends upon the *pattern* of neurons that are activated. According to a distributed network model of memory, information about any particular person, place, or thing is distributed across many neurons (McClelland, Rumelhart, & Group, 1986). In order to know

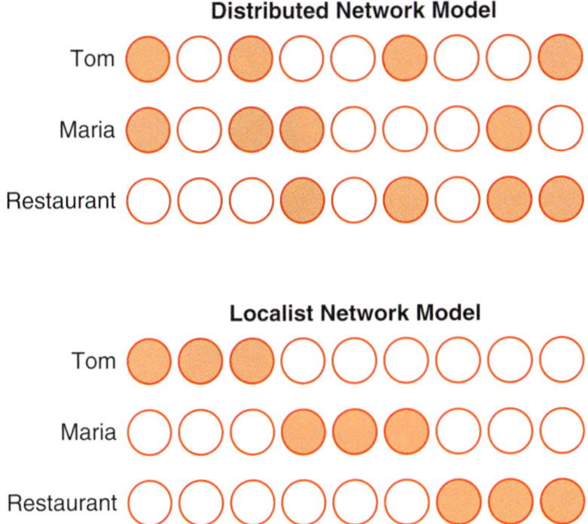

Figure 9.8 **Distributed and localist network models**. Each circle represents a neuron. In the distributed network model, a memory of Tom versus Maria versus the restaurant (each in a different row) produces different patterns of activity across the neurons. But one cannot tell which of these is being remembered based on an individual neuron's activity. In the localist network model, one can observe an individual neuron and know who or what the person is remembering.

who or what you are recalling, an observer would need to examine the pattern of activity across many memory-related neurons.

In contrast, **localist network** models (Bowers, 2009) assume that neurons coding for Tom (say neurons 1, 2, and 3) are different from those that code for Maria (say neurons 4, 5, and 6), which are different than those that code for the restaurant (say neurons 7, 8, and 9). The set of neurons that codes for one particular person, place, or thing does not overlap with the set of neurons coding for something else. In this case, if someone observes that Neuron 1 is firing in your brain, he or she would know that you are recalling Tom. A vivid example of the localist network idea is that, somewhere in your brain, a neuron represents your grandmother. For many years, this localist idea of a "grandmother cell" seemed ridiculous. As we will see, it seems less ridiculous today. This section will first examine experiments in rats and humans that ask whether individual neurons in the hippocampus can represent remembered locations. Then we will ask whether individual neurons can represent remembered people and things. At the end of this section, we will return to the question, "Do grandmother cells exist?"

9.1.6 Memory of Familiar Places

Say a rat explores an environment while a neuroscientist records the activity of several individual neurons within the rat's hippocampus (Figure 9.9A). As the rat passes through a particular region of the environment, a hippocampal neuron becomes activated. Such a neuron is called a **place cell**. The region of the environment that activates the neuron is the neuron's **place field**. In Figure 9.9B, the squares represent the floor of the test environment. The colored area in the boxes represents the place field of individual neurons, with red representing the location where the

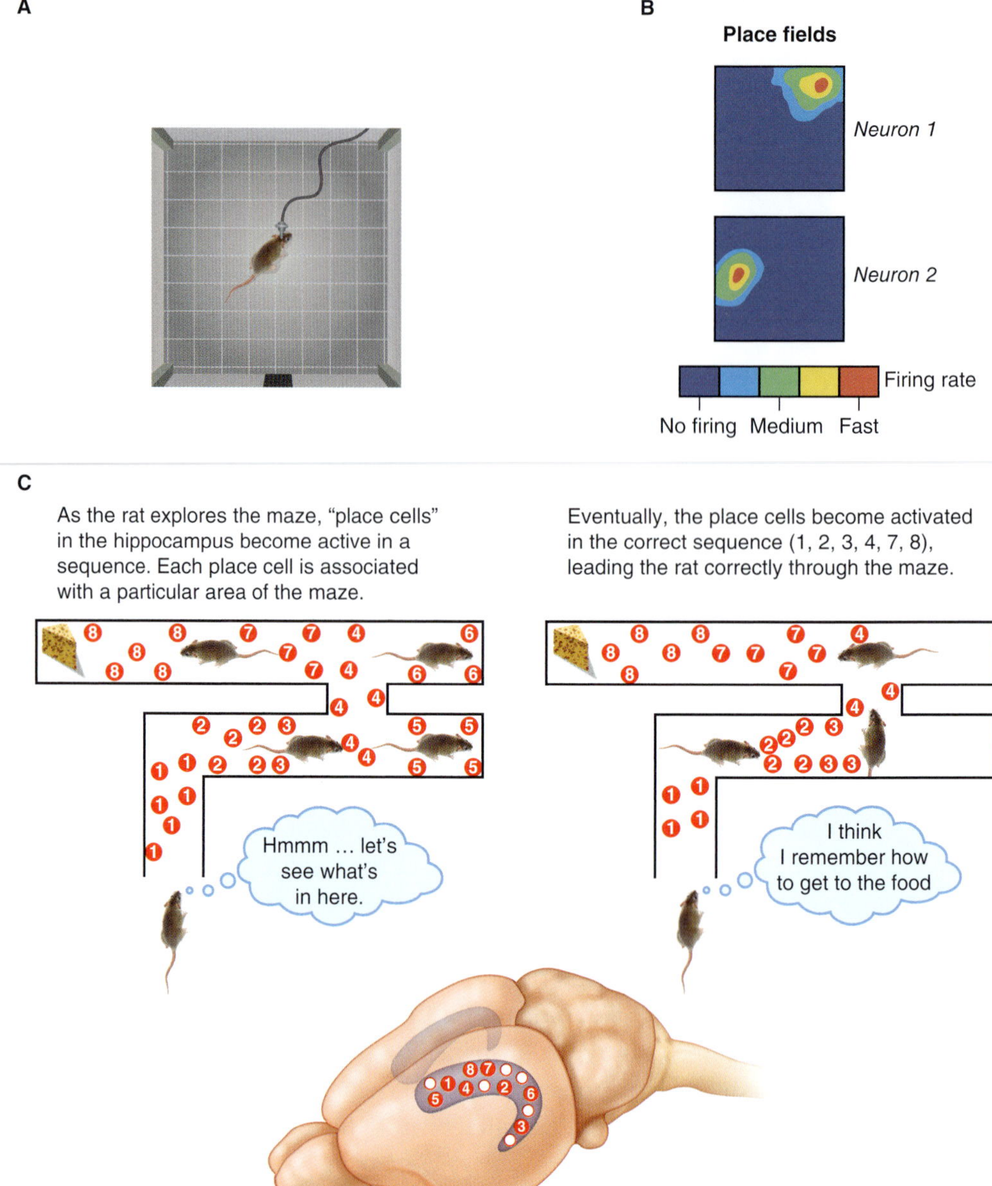

Figure 9.9 Place cells. (A) A rat explores a box while the experimenter records the activity of neurons in its hippocampus. Place cells within the hippocampus fire when the rat passes through a particular region of the box. (B) Place fields for two different hippocampal neurons are shown. The regions in red represent the rat's location in the box when that cell's firing rate is greatest.
(Adapted from Lever, Wills, Cacucci, Burgess, & O'Keefe, 2002, fig. 1, © 2002 Macmillan Magazines Ltd.)
(C) After learning the maze (left), the rat finds its way to the end by moving in the direction signaled by the active place neurons (right).

neuron's firing rate is greatest. When the rat leaves the place field, the neuron stops firing. When the rat returns to the same region, the neuron begins to fire again. Different portions of the environment can cause different place cells to fire. A place cell can therefore be said to represent a particular location of an environment.

If you record a large enough number of place cells and identify the place field of each cell, you can closely predict the rat's location within the environment, and its direction of movement. Together, the activity of hippocampal place neurons appears to provide a "cognitive map" that allows the animal to track its location within a familiar environment.

When a rat walks along a particular path, certain place cells become activated in a specific order. The sequence of place cell activations represents the rat's position as it moves along the path. In Figure 9.9C, let's say that place cell #1 is activated when the rat enters the maze. The next place cells that become active as the rat moves along the path we'll call cell #7, cell #3, and so on. In this example, place cell #8 is activated at the end of the maze where the rat finds food. Later, when the rat is resting, the sequence of place cells is replayed (1, 7 ... 2, 8), often in reverse order (8, 2 ... 7, 1), as if the hippocampal neurons were rehearsing the stored memory of the successful path (Foster & Wilson, 2006). Some neuroscientists believe that this place cell replay is part of a memory consolidation process, allowing each place cell to become more permanently linked to the next one in the sequence (Carr, Jadhav, & Frank, 2011; Drieu & Zugaro, 2019). When rats find a very large food reward at the end of the maze, they spend more time later replaying the maze activity of the hippocampal cells (Michon, Sun, Kim, Ciliberti, & Kloosterman, 2019). (Can you blame them?) Remarkably, while rats are sleeping, some of the place cells that were activated during an exploration session earlier that day are reactivated (Ji & Wilson, 2007). This replay occurs mostly during slow-wave sleep, usually within a few hours of exploring an environment (Diekelmann & Born, 2010).

Later, when the rat is placed in the same environment, before it chooses a direction to walk, the place cells are reactivated (in their original order) as if the rat were retrieving a memory of its previous path (Figure 9.9C). Compared to their activation during the original exploration, place cells' replay occurs on a faster time scale, like a film being played in fast-forward.

Humans also have place cells in the hippocampus and surrounding regions of the medial temporal lobe. Patients implanted with hippocampal electrodes prior to epilepsy surgery played a "taxi driver" game in which they moved through a virtual town using keys on a computer keyboard, searched for passengers who appeared at random locations, and delivered passengers to particular stores. Many of the hippocampal neurons fired selectively to particular spatial locations within the virtual environment (Ekstrom et al., 2003).

One might assume from this section that hippocampal neurons in the rat and the human are dedicated exclusively to representing places. However, some hippocampal neurons fire only when the rat is in a particular location that contains food, others only when the rat is in a particular location, say, the far-right corner of a red box, but not when it is in the far-right corner of a blue box. These data suggest that hippocampal neurons in the rat represent more than just spatial locations. As we will see in the next section, hippocampal neurons in humans clearly represent information beyond spatial location.

9.1.7 Memory of Familiar People and Things

The human hippocampus and surrounding medial temporal lobe regions contain neurons that represent not only places, but also particular people. For example, a neuron might respond only to images of Barack Obama's face – and not to other pictures of people, animals, or places. In a subject who was well-acquainted with the TV series *Friends*, a neuron responded to seven different pictures of Jennifer Aniston (the actress who portrayed a lead character) but not to eighty other pictures of known and unknown people, animals, and places (Quiroga, 2012). In fact, subsequent testing showed that the neuron did respond to one other person – another actress in the same TV show. Most of the hippocampal neurons selectively activated by people are activated by pictures of oneself, family members, or celebrities. Hippocampal neurons do not become activated by all faces, only by familiar faces. *Particular* neurons in the hippocampus represent *particular* familiar people (Figure 9.10). A smaller number of neurons are activated by pictures of places a subject recognizes, such as the Taj Mahal.

Hippocampal neurons that respond to photos of a particular person or place may also respond to the person or place's written or spoken name. A "Barack Obama" neuron would respond not only to the face of Barack Obama, but also to his spoken name. Amazingly, a neuron that responds selectively to the image or name of a particular person is also activated when the subject simply *thinks* of that person (Cerf et al., 2010). Such neurons are often called **concept neurons**. Jennifer Aniston, Barack Obama, and your mother are not what we traditionally think of as *concepts*. These hippocampal neurons represent concepts in that they respond in the same way to different types of physical stimuli related to that particular person or thing. How can a neuron respond to both sounds and images that relate to a particular person or place? Do these neurons receive input coming from both auditory regions and visual regions of the cerebral

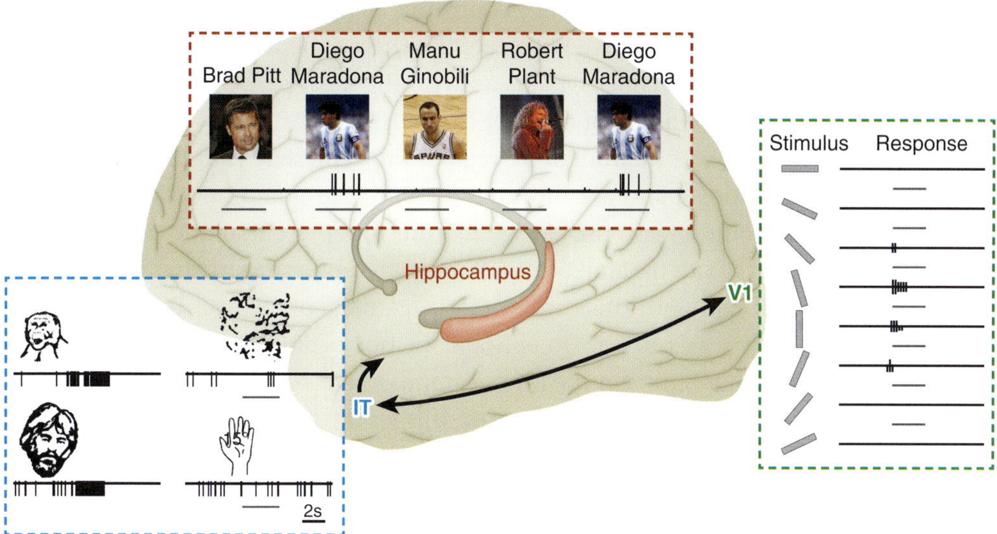

Figure 9.10 Particular neurons in the hippocampus are activated when a subject views a particular familiar person. Neurons in occipital lobe area V1 respond selectively to lines of particular orientations (see Chapter 3), while neurons in the inferotemporal cortex (IT) respond to faces and not to other types of stimuli. However, IT neurons do not fire differentially to particular faces. Neurons in the hippocampus and other medial temporal lobe regions fire selectively to the faces of particular people. In this illustration, a hippocampal neuron fires only when the subject views a picture of Argentinian soccer star Diego Maradona.

(Adapted from Quiroga, 2012, fig.1,

cortex? We do not yet know. We do know that these concept neurons respond to events of personal relevance to the individual, and some investigators believe that these cells may be critical to our memories of past experiences (episodic memories) and facts about the world (semantic memories) (Rutishauser, 2019).

When we recall an episodic memory, are we activating concept neurons to represent the people in the remembered event and place neurons to represent its location? Do some neurons fire specifically in response to abstract concepts like *democracy*, or only to people and things that we've seen or heard in the past? The answers to these questions remain to be solved.

Earlier, we asked whether "grandmother cells" exist. The data described above certainly suggest that individual neurons can represent something as specific as one's grandmother. However, your grandmother is probably not represented by a single neuron, for neurons in the brain die (and new ones are born) all the time. Most neuroscientists believe that if a memory of a particular person or thing depended upon the activity of a single neuron, the memory would be too vulnerable to such changes occurring within the brain. It is possible, however, that a specific set of (say 1,000) neurons are activated when you think of your grandmother. The results above suggest that, to a large extent, different neurons would be activated as you think of Barack Obama and, for the most part, a different set would be activated when you think of Donald Trump.

If one set of neurons were required to represent your grandmother in her blue dress, and another to represent your grandmother in her white dress, wouldn't you run out of neurons to represent all the things you remember? Data obtained from concept neurons suggest that a given neuron will represent the same person regardless of changes in context such as his or her clothing. Do episodic memories emerge from the combined activity of neurons in the hippocampus and cerebral cortex, as theories of memory suggest? If so, how does this work? Neuroscientists continue to explore these intriguing questions.

KEY CONCEPTS

- **Damage to the hippocampus impairs the storage and retrieval of episodic memories.**
- **Memories stored long before the hippocampus is damaged are generally preserved.**
- **The hippocampus and cortex interact during memory storage and retrieval.**
- **The hippocampus contains neurons called place cells, which represent specific information about familiar spatial locations.**
- **The hippocampus and surrounding areas contain neurons called concept neurons, which represent information about specific people and things.**

TEST YOURSELF

1. **Could someone with brain damage like that of Henry Molaison remember (a) having met a person a few days ago? (b) a phone number for a few minutes if he actively rehearsed it? (c) how to use a tricky key to open the door to his apartment, assuming he was experienced in using the key to open the door? (d) whether or not he locked the door to his apartment this morning?**
2. **According to most theories of episodic memory, where are the sensory features of an episodic memory represented? According to these theories, what role does the hippocampus play in memory retrieval?**
3. **Despite anterograde and partial retrograde amnesia, Henry Molaison and other patients with hippocampal loss nevertheless show normal recall of childhood memories. How does the Standard Model of Memory Consolidation explain this observation?**

4. **During episodic memory retrieval, information travels from the cerebral cortex to the hippocampus and back to the cerebral cortex. However, the cerebral cortex does not send axons directly to the hippocampus. Describe the anatomical route by which information from the cortex arrives at the hippocampus.**
5. **The sequence of firing in hippocampal place cells is sometimes "replayed." What does this mean? When is this replay observed? What memory functions might this replay serve?**
6. **What is a "concept neuron"? Give an example of the kinds of stimuli you would expect to activate a concept neuron that represents your mother? What kinds of stimuli would activate a concept neuron representing your father?**

9.2 MEMORIES REWIRE THE BRAIN

Much of learning involves associating one thing with another: a name with a face; good food with a particular restaurant; one hallway of a building with the hallway around the corner. Connections *between* neurons must undergo changes in order to form such associations.

9.2.1 Synaptic Plasticity and Learning

Because we want to understand how one "thing" becomes associated with another, we would like to know how the activity of one set of neurons can activate another set. Here's a hint: when two neurons become activated one after the other, the link between them grows stronger.

Imagine that Neuron 1 releases the excitatory transmitter glutamate, which binds to receptors on Neuron 2. If the synapse is weak, the firing of Neuron 1 may produce only a small excitation of Neuron 2. If the same firing of Neuron 1 later produces a larger excitation of Neuron 2, we say that the synapse has strengthened. When Neuron 1 fires, Neuron 2 is now more likely to fire as well. In Figure 9.11, the synapse between Neuron 1B and Neuron 2 has been strengthened, so that in the future Neuron 1B will strongly activate Neuron 2, while Neurons 1A and 1C will not. The ability of the synapse between two neurons to change in strength is called **synaptic plasticity**. Our discussion of synaptic plasticity will include the terms "ion channels" and "depolarization"; if you need a refresher on these terms, you might briefly review them in Chapter 2.

Imagine that you apply a small amount of electrical stimulation to Neuron 1 (call this amount of stimulation the *test pulse*). This causes the neuron to fire and release the excitatory neurotransmitter glutamate. Glutamate crosses the synaptic cleft and binds to a glutamate receptor

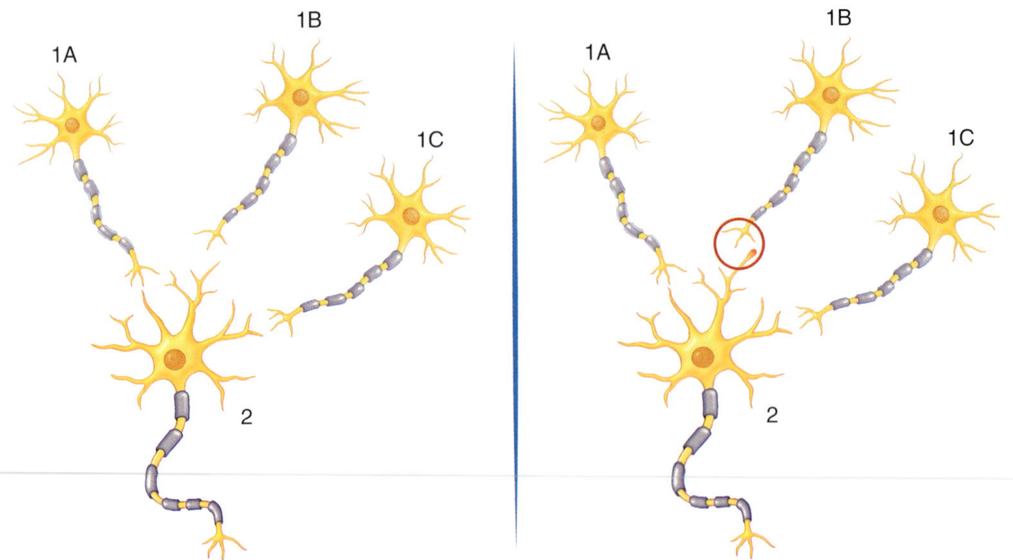

Figure 9.11 Synapses can strengthen. Three presynaptic neurons (1A, 1B, and 1C) send inputs to a postsynaptic neuron (2). The right panel depicts a strengthening of the synaptic connection between neurons 1B and 2. The swelling on the dendrite of synapse 2 represents an increase in the number of neurotransmitter receptors. Activation of neuron 1B is now more likely to activate neuron 2. Activation of neuron 1A or 1C is unlikely to activate neuron 2 because their synaptic connections to neuron 2 remain weak.

on Neuron 2. As a result, Neuron 2 undergoes a small depolarization – not enough for Neuron 2 to fire (Figure 9.12, top). Next, you carry out a procedure to *strengthen the synapse*. The first step in this procedure is to stimulate Neuron 1 again. Glutamate is released, and binds to its postsynaptic receptor. But this time, just after you stimulate Neuron 1 you apply electrical stimulation directly to Neuron 2, forcing it to fire as well (Figure 9.12, middle). During this procedure, you are forcing Neuron 1 and Neuron 2 to *fire* one after the other in quick succession. Do this several times. What is the result of this procedure? If you look at the synapse between Neurons 1 and 2, you will find that Neuron 2 (the postsynaptic neuron) now has an increased number of glutamate receptors. You have just strengthened the synapse between the two neurons!

But how can you be *sure* that the synapse between the two neurons has become stronger. To test the strength of the synapse, you stimulate Neuron 1, using the same small *test pulse* of stimulation that you used at the very beginning of the experiment. You now observe a large excitatory response in Neuron 2 (Figure 9.12, bottom). The small input from Neuron 1 that had earlier produced only a small postsynaptic response (i.e., in Neuron 2) now produces a large postsynaptic response! (Compare the heights of the curved lines at the bottom versus the top of Figure 9.12.) This strengthening or **potentiation** of the synapse can last hours, weeks,

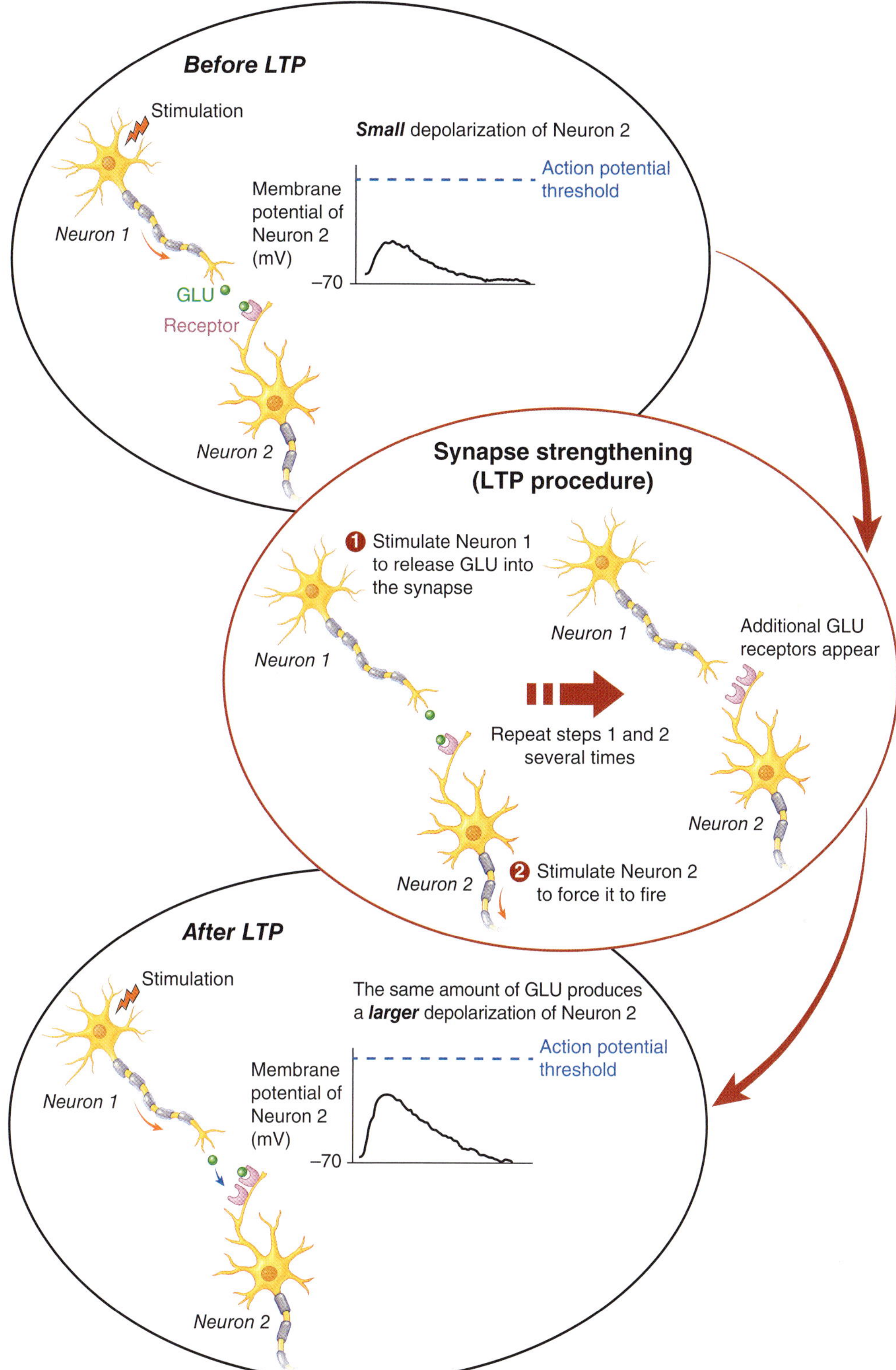

Figure 9.12 Measuring long-term potentiation. Before LTP (top), stimulation of Neuron 1 causes release of the excitatory neurotransmitter glutamate, which binds to a receptor on Neuron 2. After LTP (bottom), Neuron 2 expresses an increased number of receptors for glutamate. The stimulation of Neuron 1 that produced a small depolarization in Neuron 2 before LTP now produces a much larger depolarization.

or, in some cases, months, and is therefore called **long-term potentiation** (**LTP**) (Lomo, 1966).

In order to understand how the synapse strengthens, we must zero in on the glutamate receptors located on the postsynaptic neuron. We notice that there are two types of glutamate receptors present: the **AMPA receptor** and the **NMDA receptor**. When glutamate binds to an AMPA receptor, a channel in the receptor opens and sodium ions (Na^+) flow into the neuron, causing depolarization (Figure 9.13, top). Recall that when we applied our small test pulse to Neuron 1 in the example above, we observed a small depolarization in Neuron 2. That was because glutamate bound to AMPA receptors on Neuron 2, which allowed Na^+ to flow into the neuron *through* those AMPA receptors. (The positive charge of Na^+ entering the neuron causes a small depolarization.) But this Na^+ inflow through AMPA receptors won't strengthen synapses.

In order to strengthen a synapse, the NMDA receptor must become involved. To understand what this means, you need to know that the NMDA receptor possesses a channel not only for Na^+ but also for the positively charged calcium ion (Ca^{++}). When GLU binds to an NMDA receptor, the ion channel opens, but the ions cannot flow through the channel because a large magnesium ion (Mg^{++}) is lodged in the channel blocking Na^+ and Ca^{++} from passing through and entering the cell (Figure 9.13, bottom; see left and middle panels). In order for Na^+ and, more importantly, Ca^{++} to enter through the NMDA receptor, Mg^{++} must first move out of the way.

We say "more importantly" Ca^{++}, because Ca^{++} is the magical ingredient (metaphorically speaking) that causes the synapse to strengthen. But how can Ca^{++} enter if it must enter through the NMDA receptor, and if the ion channels in the NMDA receptor are blocked by Mg^{++}? Let's say you electrically stimulate Neuron 1, causing glutamate release into the synapse. Glutamate binds to the NMDA receptor site and opens the NMDA receptor's ion channel (Figure 9.13, bottom; middle panel). At this point the ion channel is open but it is blocked by Mg^{++}. Then when you electrically stimulate Neuron 2, the neuron becomes strongly depolarized, which allows Mg^{++} to move away from the NMDA receptor ion channel. Now Ca^{++} (and Na^+) can enter the neuron (Figure 9.13, bottom; right panel). The influx of Ca^{++} through NMDA receptor channels activates particular enzymes within the cell, and some of these molecules can trigger gene expression in the cell nucleus, producing proteins that strengthen the synapse (Figure 9.14).

How does this gene expression and protein synthesis strengthen the synapse? In some cases, the synthesized proteins allow more AMPA receptors to appear on the surface of the postsynaptic membrane (depicted earlier in Figure 9.12). The increase in postsynaptic AMPA receptors makes it more likely that, in the future, glutamate, when released, will bind to

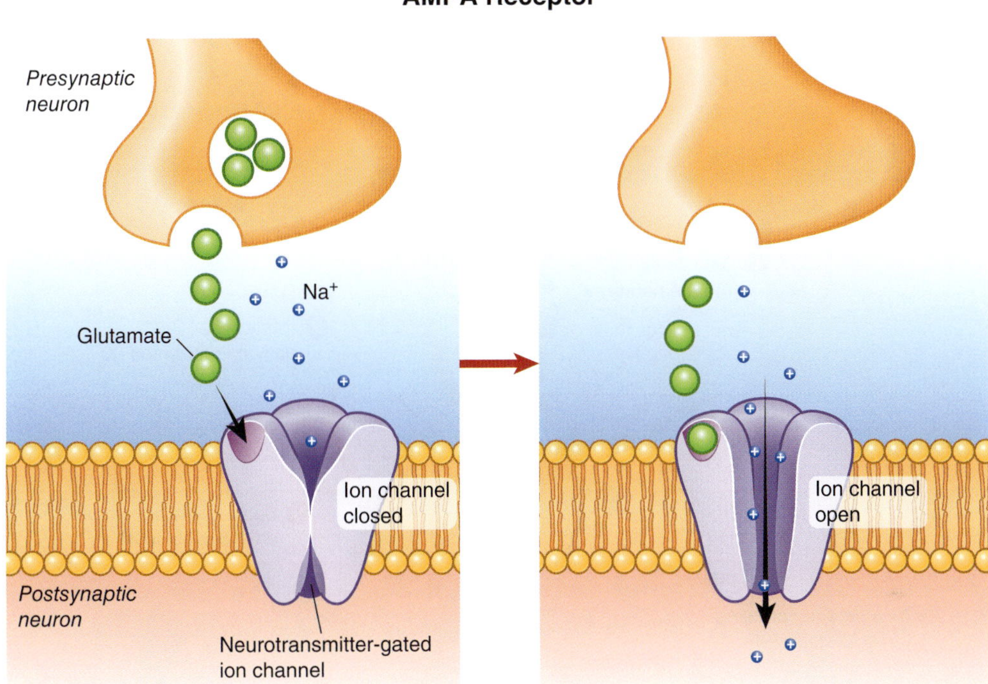

NMDA Receptor

Presynaptic neuron

Na^+

Glutamate

Ca^{++}

Mg^{++}

Ion channel closed

Postsynaptic neuron

Neurotransmitter-gated ion channel

Ca^{++}

Mg^{++}

Ion channel open

When GLU binds, the ion channel opens

Mg^{++}

Ca^{++}

Depolarization liberates Mg^{++}, permitting Ca^{++} to enter

Figure 9.13 AMPA- and NMDA-type glutamate receptors.

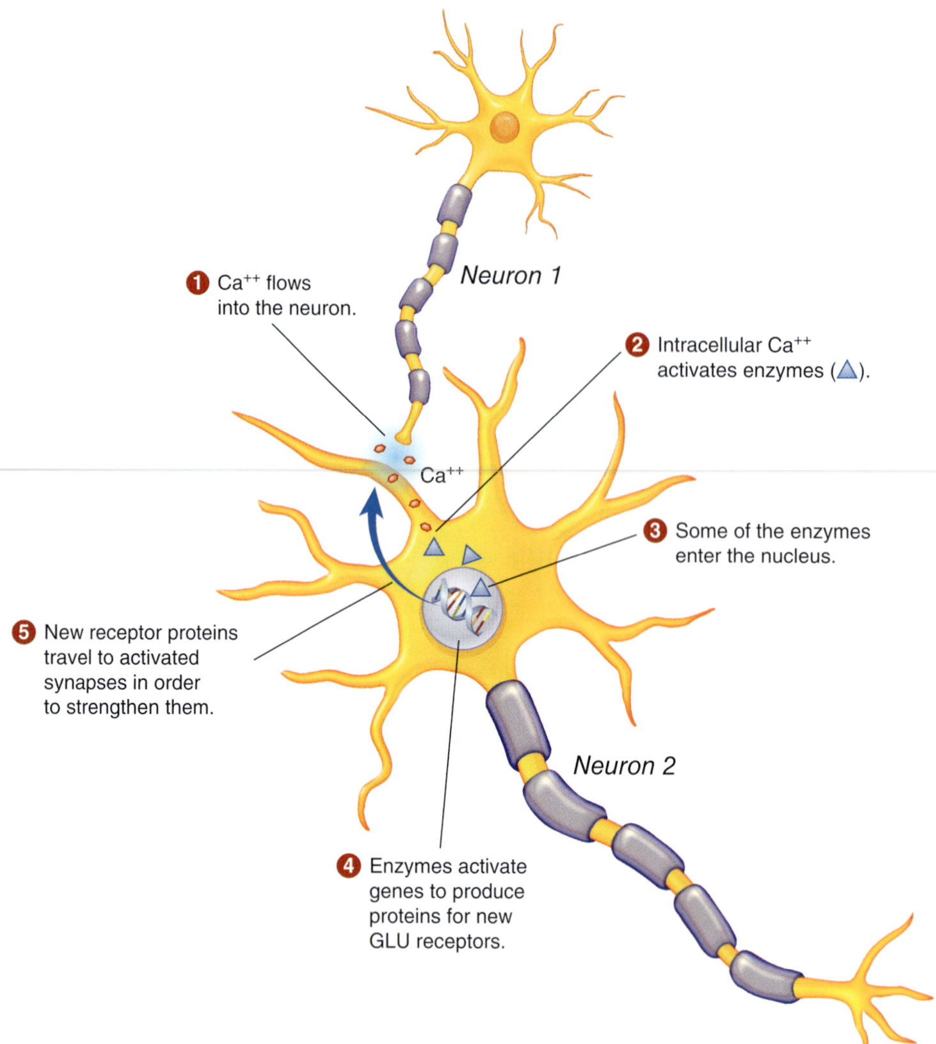

Figure 9.14 Activation of enzymes and genes produces synapse-strengthening proteins.

an AMPA receptor and depolarize the postsynaptic neuron. In other cases, existing postsynaptic AMPA receptors may become more sensitive to glutamate. A third mechanism involves an increase in the future *release* of glutamate by the presynaptic neuron. This third mechanism is particularly interesting for, as you recall, it is the NMDA receptor on the postsynaptic neuron that triggers synaptic plasticity. In order to increase future glutamate release, the postsynaptic neuron must send a **retrograde messenger**, that is, a chemical that moves backwards across the synapse to the presynaptic neuron. The retrograde messenger tells the presynaptic neuron to release more glutamate in the future. Any of these changes will increase the strength of the synaptic connection between the pre- and postsynaptic neuron. All are examples of synaptic plasticity.

Of course, the LTP described above was produced under unnatural conditions. It was produced by applying electrical charges to artificially stimulate neurons. Why should we believe that this type of synaptic plasticity is related to learning and memory? First, rats with poor memory, show weak LTP. Second, the synaptic strengthening produced by LTP decays more quickly in aged compared to younger rats (Barnes & McNaughton, 1980), and the rate of forgetting in aged rats is correlated with the rate of decay in hippocampal LTP. Third, drugs that block NMDA receptors, or prevent LTP in other ways, impair learning in rats and mice (Morris, Anderson, Lynch, & Baudry, 1986; Minichiello, 2009). Finally, a genetic modification in mice that increases the strength of LTP also enhances learning (Martin, Grimwood, & Morris, 2000). Some forms of LTP do *not* depend upon activation of the NMDA receptor; but these are beyond the scope of our discussion.

Synapses can also weaken, or undergo **long-term depression** (**LTD**). This synaptic weakening involves changes that are opposite to those produced by LTP: a decrease in the number or sensitivity of AMPA receptors, or a decrease in neurotransmitter released from the presynaptic neuron. Both LTP and LTD contribute to alter the strength of connections between neurons, and both play important roles in learning. Both LTP and LTD can produce long-term changes in the nervous system, changes necessary for memory lasting days, months, or years. So far, it may be difficult to imagine how changes in synaptic strength produced, say, by an increase in AMPA receptors, relate to memory and learning. The hypothetical example below describes how strengthening particular synapses between neurons might allow you to associate a person's name with her face.

9.2.2 A Hypothetical Example

Imagine a hippocampal concept neuron that fires when you think of a particular woman, Susan. Imagine further that the neuron receives input from two presynaptic neurons (Figure 9.15). One of the inputs is activated when you hear her name; we'll call this the "name neuron." It sends input to the concept neuron through the "name synapse." The other is activated when you see her face, the "face neuron." It sends input to the concept neuron through the "face synapse." In our example, you start off recognizing her face, but not her name. This is because the face synapse starts off strong (it contains many AMPA receptors), and the name synapse starts off weak (it has few AMPA receptors). So the concept neuron initially responds to Susan's face and not to her name.

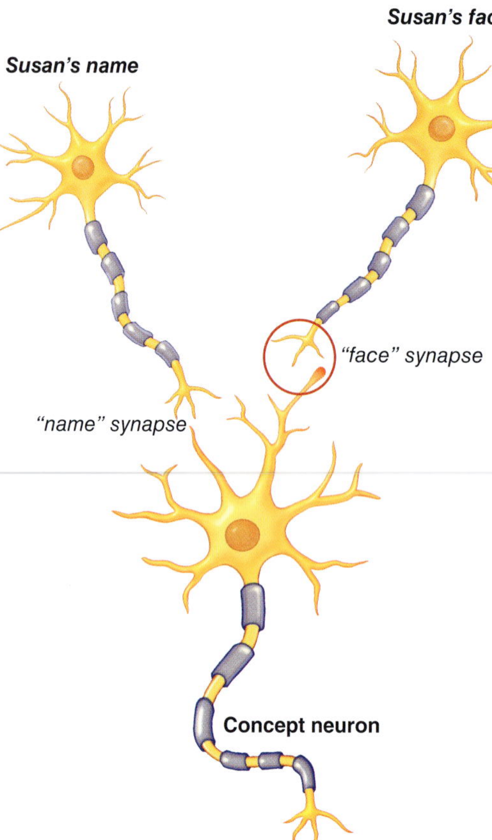

Figure 9.15 A hypothetical example of plasticity and human memory. A concept neuron receives input from a neuron that responds selectively to Susan's name and from a neuron that responds selectively to her face. The red dendritic enlargement represents the many AMPA receptors that currently permit her face to activate the concept neuron. Plasticity at the name synapse will be required in order for the neuron to respond to her name as well.

The neuron responds to the sight of Susan's face, because glutamate released by the face neuron crosses a synapse and binds to the many AMPA receptors that permit this input to strongly activate the concept neuron for Susan. However, no matter how many times you hear her name alone, the neuron never fires. The name synapse currently lacks the AMPA receptors that would be necessary for name input to activate the neuron that represents Susan. Why does the name synapse never strengthen when her name is repeated? After all, glutamate can *bind* to NMDA receptors. Recall that the NMDA receptor channel is blocked by Mg^{++} unless the postsynaptic neuron is depolarized. So long as the NMDA receptor channel is blocked, Ca^{++} cannot enter the neuron. Without Ca^{++} entry into the neuron, the enzymes needed for plasticity are not activated, the critical genes do not produce synapse-strengthening proteins, and more AMPA receptors cannot appear at this synapse. The key idea is that it is not enough for glutamate to bind to the NMDA receptor on the postsynaptic neuron. The neuron must be depolarized at the same time that glutamate binds to the NMDA receptor in order to trigger plasticity at the synapse.

Now, when you hear Susan's name at the same time that you see her face, the input from the face neuron strongly depolarizes the concept neuron representing Susan. This depolarization spreads from the neuron's region of face input throughout the cell body and other dendrites of the neuron, and eventually reaches the name synapse. Now when her name is spoken, glutamate binds to the NMDA receptor at the name synapse at a time when the neuron is already depolarized and the Mg^{++} ion has been liberated from the NMDA receptor channel. Ca^{++} can now pass through the NMDA receptor channel at the name synapse, triggering gene expression and protein synthesis, and setting in motion the structural changes, such as increased AMPA receptor number, that will allow the name *Susan* alone to activate the neuron in the future.

Although this is a hypothetical example, it helps us to think concretely about synaptic plasticity during learning. In order to experimentally examine how plasticity contributes to learning, neuroscientists have investigated simpler forms of learning in animal subjects. In these circumstances, plasticity can be experimentally manipulated as learning occurs. We will examine these investigations of plasticity and learning later in this chapter.

9.2.3 Learning and the Birth of New Neurons

New neurons are born not only during the development of the embryo, but also after birth, even during adulthood (**adult neurogenesis**). Adult neurogenesis is known to occur in the hippocampus (within the dentate gyrus). Adult neurogenesis also occurs within the walls of the lateral ventricles, giving rise to new neurons that then migrate to take their place in the olfactory bulbs. There is debate regarding the existence of adult neurogenesis in other brain regions (Snyder, 2019). In both humans and rodents, neurons continue to be born even in old age, although the rate of neurogenesis declines.

In a key study linking neurogenesis to learning, rats were injected with a chemical that permitted visualization of newly born neurons within the hippocampus. The animals were then given the opportunity to learn one of several tasks. Animals engaged in tasks that depend upon the hippocampus, such as spatial learning, had many more new neurons in the hippocampus compared to rats that had learned tasks not requiring the hippocampus. It's not that learning increased the number of new neurons *produced* through neurogenesis. Of the new neurons that are born each day, many normally die within a few weeks. In the animals that engaged in learning tasks involving the hippocampus, more of the newly born neurons *survived* (Gould, Beylin, Tanapat, Reeves, & Shors, 1999).

Animals living in an **enriched environment** filled with novel objects to explore also show an increased number of neurons created through neurogenesis compared to animals living in a standard laboratory environment (Kempermann, Kuhn, & Gage, 1997). Again, the number of newly born neurons increased because more of them survived. If the new neurons receive synaptic input from other nearby neurons, that is, if the new neurons become part of active neural circuits, they are more likely to survive (Deng, Aimone, & Gage, 2010).

Taken together, these findings suggest that neurons generated through adult neurogenesis become part of networks of hippocampal neurons, and that those that survive are those that play a role in new learning. How is learning affected if an animal does not have the benefit of neurogenesis? A toxin that specifically attacks newly born neurons in the rat impairs learning of hippocampal-dependent tasks (Shors et al., 2001). These and other data suggest that newly born neurons play a critical role in learning and memory.

KEY CONCEPTS

- **Changes in the strength of synaptic connections are an example of the *plasticity*, or changeability, of the brain as a result of experience.**
- **In many parts of the brain, plasticity depends on activation of a particular type of neurotransmitter receptor, called the NMDA receptor. Activation of a neuron's NMDA receptor ultimately leads to increases in gene expression and protein production which are necessary for long-term changes in synaptic strength.**
- **Learning can produce the birth of new neurons, or *neurogenesis*, in several brain regions, including the hippocampus.**

TEST YOURSELF

1. **NMDA glutamate receptors play an important role in synaptic plasticity. What are the conditions necessary in order to open ion channels within the NMDA receptor?**
2. **Describe evidence that long-term potentiation is related to learning.**
3. **Define adult neurogenesis. Describe evidence that learning can increase neurogenesis. Describe evidence that neurogenesis can increase learning.**

9.3 SKILL LEARNING

So far, we've discussed the neurobiology of memory, particularly the kinds of memory that depend on the hippocampus. We turn now to skill learning, which also involves certain kinds of memories. For instance, *learning* to ride a bicycle requires that you store a *memory* of the motor behaviors that help you to steer while keeping your balance, and to retrieve that memory the next time you get on your bicycle. Here we are not necessarily talking about explicit (conscious) memories. Learning to ride a bicycle involves storage of implicit (unconscious) memories. As we practice the task, the brain leaves a record in the form of long-term changes in the connections between neurons. Even though we may be unable to consciously describe what has been stored, the stored information is a form of memory.

9.3.1 Neuronal Assemblies in the Motor Cortex Grow Larger

Recall that after his hippocampal loss Henry Molaison showed episodic memory impairment, but was able to acquire skills. This demonstrated that different types of memory and learning depend upon different brain circuits. Skill learning depends upon plasticity within the frontal cortex, including the primary motor cortex, as well as some areas below the cortex, i.e., subcortical regions.

When human subjects practice a sequence of finger movements for 15 minutes per day over several weeks, regions of the motor cortex activated by the finger movements expand (Karni, Meyer, Jezzard, Adams, Turner, & Ungerleider, 1995). Presumably, this reflects the increased number of neurons in the motor cortex that participate in the execution of the well-practiced movement (Dayan & Cohen, 2011). Activated regions of the motor cortex also expand even when subjects frequently *imagine* performing the sequence of finger movements (Pascualleone et al., 1995).

But how do regions of the motor cortex expand with motor skill training? Neurons in the motor cortex make synaptic connections with other motor cortical neurons; sometimes these are long-distance connections with other neurons a considerable distance away (Sanes & Donoghue, 2000). When groups of neurons possess strong excitatory synaptic connections with one another, they are said to form **neuronal assemblies**. Neuronal assemblies may become activated during performance of skilled motor acts.

The increased regions of the motor cortex activated during performance of a well-practiced skill are believed to reflect an increase in the number of neurons that have been incorporated into active neuronal assemblies. The top panel of Figure 9.16 depicts an assembly of neurons with strong excitatory connections between Neurons A, B, C, and D. The synapses between the neurons are so strong that activation of one of these neurons (say Neuron A) causes activation of the others (B, C, and D). Neuron E remains inactive because none of the neurons in the assembly

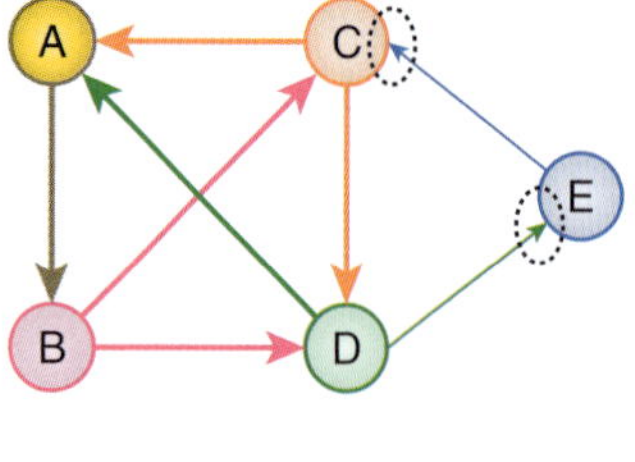

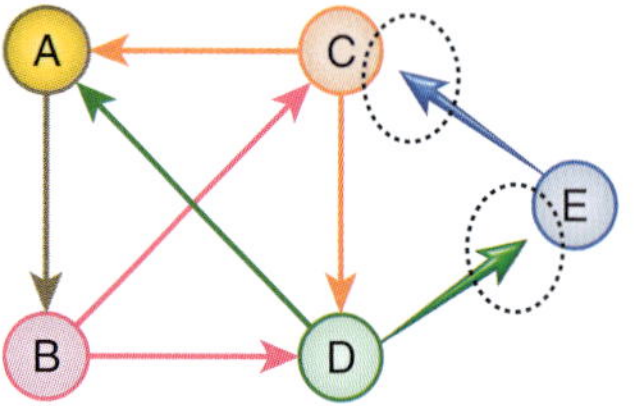

Figure 9.16 Neuronal assemblies. The top panel shows four neurons (A, B, C, D) with strong connections to one another, and a fifth neuron (E) that is only weakly connected. In the bottom panel, neuron E now forms strong connections with other members of the assembly.

has strong synaptic connections with it. The bottom panel of Figure 9.16 shows a strengthening of the connections between Neuron E and some of the neurons in the assembly. The size of the neuronal assembly has grown, thanks to this synaptic plasticity.

Strengthening of learning through practice appears to be based on the inclusion of additional neurons into the assembly of neurons mediating task performance, like adding soldiers to an army. As shown in Figure 9.16, this involves strengthening of connections between neurons, that is to say, synaptic plasticity. Synaptic plasticity in the motor cortex accompanies the acquisition of new skills (Peters, Liu, & Komiyama, 2017). Increases in plasticity lead to enhanced skill learning (Fritsch et al., 2010), while reductions in plasticity in the motor cortex lead to impairments in skill learning (Censor, Sagi, & Cohen, 2012).

But how are particular neurons selected to be added to an assembly? What functions were these neurons serving before they were recruited to the assembly? Were they "uncommitted" and waiting to be assigned a function? Were they previously serving another motor function? If so, was some ability lost when expertise in the practiced task was gained? Answers to these questions remain to be discovered.

9.3.2 Automaticity of Well-Learned Behaviors

The **prefrontal cortex**, located in the most anterior region of the frontal cortex (Figure 9.17) and associated with attention, becomes highly active during early stages of learning a motor skill (Shadmehr & Holcomb, 1997). After a great deal of practice, as behaviors become **automatized** (habitual), activity in the prefrontal cortex diminishes. This makes intuitive sense, for habits do not require much attention. In fact, you may have

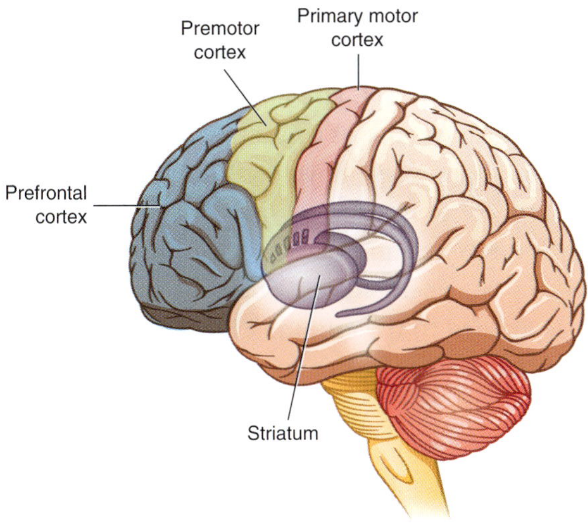

Figure 9.17 Key brain areas involved in acquiring motor skills. During early stages of motor learning, the prefrontal cortex shows high levels of activation. As a motor skill becomes automatized, activity shifts to more posterior parts of the frontal lobe and to the striatum.

noticed that paying close attention to your body movements during an automatized behavior like walking or driving a car can interfere with natural performance.

During motor learning there is a shift in activity from anterior regions of the frontal cortex, such as the prefrontal cortex, to more posterior frontal cortical areas (premotor and primary motor cortex). As this shift is occurring, changes are also occurring within a subcortical structure called the **striatum** (again, see Figure 9.17). The striatum is part of a larger circuit of brain regions called the **basal ganglia**, which is critically involved in habit formation (Rueda-Orozco & Robbe, 2015; Perrin & Venance, 2019). While driving a car and riding a bicycle are useful habits, other habits such as gambling and drug abuse can have unfortunate consequences. A brain-based understanding of how habits are acquired and how they might be reversed is an active area of neuroscience research. In Chapter 11 we discuss the role of the striatum and the neurotransmitter dopamine in habit formation.

9.3.4 The Cerebellum and Refinement of Skilled Movements

The cerebellum, a cabbage-shaped structure behind the pons, helps maintain our balance while we walk (Chapter 4). It also controls precise, rapid body movements. However, the cerebellum does not simply send out motor commands to the spinal cord. Instead, it keeps track of our past errors in performing particular behaviors. When the behavior is repeated in the future, the cerebellum helps the brain's motor systems avoid making the same errors (Caligiore et al., 2017).

For instance, imagine that you want to lift a cup of coffee and bring it to your mouth, but the weight of the cup is lighter than expected. Without prior experience lifting such a light cup, you might accidentally lift it with the force appropriate to a heavier cup. As a result, you lift it too high and too fast. By the time you adjust your movement, bringing the cup back down toward your mouth, coffee has already spilled. The cerebellum learns from such experiences. It receives information regarding the weight of the cup and, as a result of past experience, instructs the motor cortex to alter the amount of force applied to the arm muscles. This allows you to lift the cup to the appropriate height at an appropriate speed without spilling the coffee.

In the illustration above, the cerebellum learns to foresee the outcome of various motor commands and generates a **forward model**. A forward model predicts what will happen in the future. The cerebellum predicts how the body parts will move in response to the motor command currently being sent to the muscles. If the cerebellum predicts that the current motor commands will make the coffee cup rise too fast, it can send its own commands to the frontal cortex to adjust the movement before it is performed. This generally occurs outside of conscious awareness.

KEY CONCEPTS

- As a motor skill is acquired, its performance activates an increased area of the motor cortex. This is believed to reflect an increase in the size of neuronal assemblies devoted to the skill.
- The prefrontal cortex is highly active during early stages of motor learning, and less active as the skill becomes automatized. The basal ganglia plays a key role in the acquisition of automatized skills.
- The cerebellum learns to predict the consequences of planned movements, and helps the frontal cortex to generate motor commands that will achieve a desired outcome (e.g., lifting a cup gently to the lips without spilling the contents).

TEST YOURSELF

1. As you practice the guitar, there is an increase in the area of motor cortex that becomes activated each time you press the string with your middle finger. Why might this occur (at the level of individual neurons)?
2. Describe changes that occur in the areas of the frontal cortex as a behavior becomes automatized.
3. Imagine that you suffer cerebellar damage. Describe the problems that might occur while lifting a cup of coffee to your mouth.

9.4 DIGGING DEEPER INTO THE NEUROBIOLOGY OF MEMORY

Finally, we turn to three forms of learning that neuroscientists have studied in great detail:

1. **Fear conditioning**. A warning stimulus predicts danger, and the subject (usually a rat) quickly learns to fear the warning stimulus.
2. **Eyeblink conditioning**. A warning stimulus predicts an irritating puff of air to the eyes, and the subject (usually a rabbit) learns to blink its eyes as soon as the warning stimulus is presented.
3. **Habituation learning in sea slugs**. Touch is repeatedly applied to the body of the sea slug (***Aplysia***). At first, the animal responds with a defensive movement, but it soon learns to ignore the harmless event. The animal has habituated to the touch.

The greatest advances in understanding the neurobiology of learning and memory have come from the study of simple forms of learning in animals such as the rat, rabbit, or sea slug. For with these simple organisms, investigators can precisely manipulate the brain in ways they could not in humans. Such studies have revealed key neurobiological processes that give rise to many forms of learning in both humans and other animals.

9.4.1 Fear Conditioning

While sitting in the waiting room before a dental appointment, a patient hears the sound of the dentist's drill and becomes anxious. This person probably associates the sound of the drill with the pain of the dental procedure she has experienced in the past. The pain is an **unconditioned stimulus** (**US**) that provoked an innate or **unconditioned response** (**UR**), in this case fear. Once the person has associated the sound of the drill with pain, the sound itself becomes a **conditioned stimulus** (**CS**) capable of evoking a fear response, which in this case is called a **conditioned response** (**CR**).

In a typical fear-learning paradigm in the laboratory, a rat hears a tone and then receives a mild shock. During the first presentation (trial) of tone and shock, the rat shows no particular reaction to the tone. It is still a **neutral stimulus**. However, after a few tone/shock pairings, the tone has become a conditioned stimulus that produces fear-related responses such as increased blood pressure and heart rate, vigilance to other sensory stimuli, and immobility (freezing). How does the tone come to elicit these conditioned fear responses?

The Amygdala

Conditioned fear responses depend upon activation of the amygdala. As Figure 9.18 illustrates, activity of neurons in the **central nucleus of the amygdala** leads to activation of other brain areas responsible for generating the fear response. Outputs from the central nucleus of the amygdala to the **periaqueductal gray** region generate freezing; activation of the **lateral hypothalamus** generates sympathetic nervous system activity such as elevated heart rate; and activation of norepinephrine neurons in the **locus coeruleus** leads to increased vigilance. These fear-related outputs together give rise to much of what we describe as fear.

But how does the tone come to generate activity in the central nucleus? The tone activates auditory neurons that project to auditory regions of the **thalamus**. Thalamic neurons in turn project to the **lateral amygdala**. Neurons in the lateral amygdala communicate with neurons in the

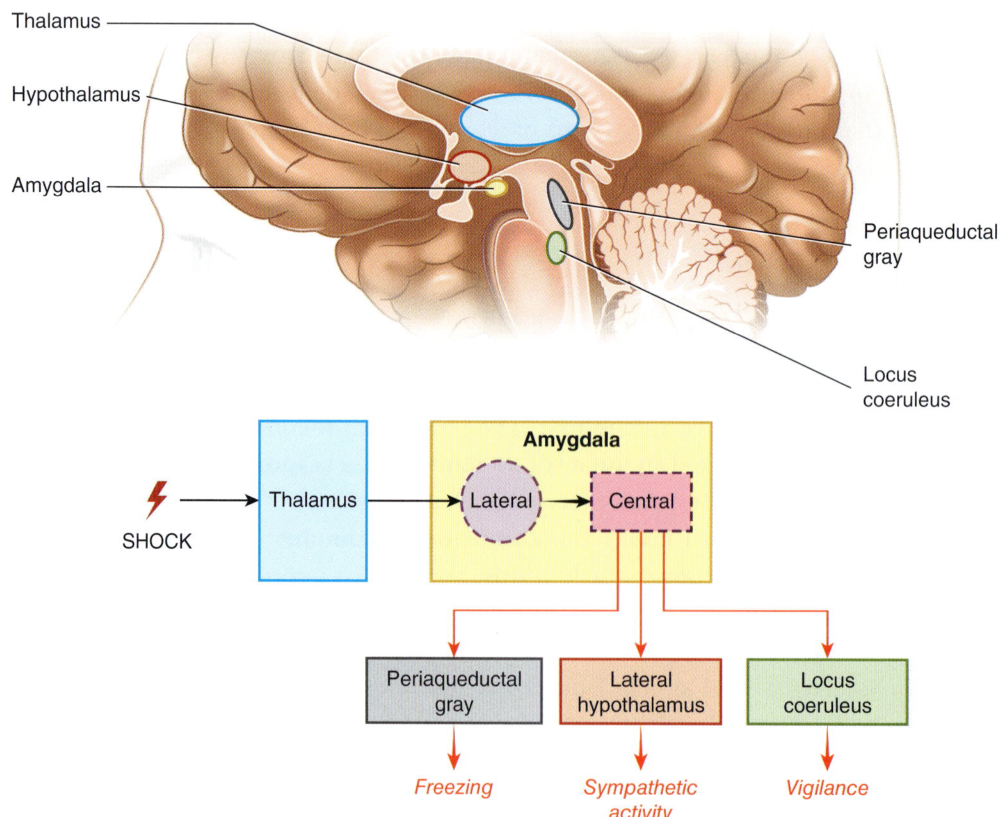

Figure 9.18 The anatomy of fear. The central nucleus of the amygdala sends outputs to brain regions that mediate different aspects of the conditioned fear response, such as freezing, sympathetic nervous system activation, and vigilance. (While the circuit is represented in a human brain here, most of the research that revealed the circuit came from studies in rats.)

central nucleus of the amygdala, and the central nucleus generates the fear response.

If it were not for the pairings of tone with shock, the rat would not fear the tone. The neutral tone does not activate neurons in the lateral amygdala sufficiently to cause activation of neurons in the central amygdala. However, over the course of repeated tone/shock pairings, the tone comes to elicit stronger responses in lateral amygdala neurons, activating the central nucleus and generating fear responses. A key question then is, "Why do lateral amygdala neurons respond more strongly to the tone after the tone has been followed by shock?"

As can be seen in Figure 9.19, shock information arrives at the lateral amygdala via somatosensory regions of the thalamus and strongly activates the lateral amygdala even prior to learning. One does not need to learn to be afraid of shock. Importantly, neurons that carry information

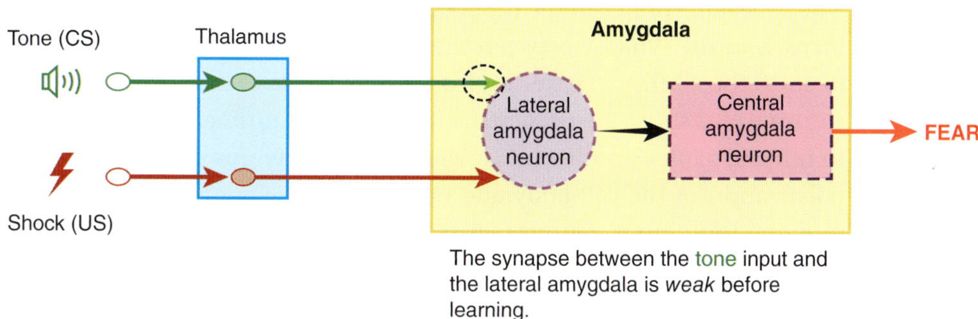

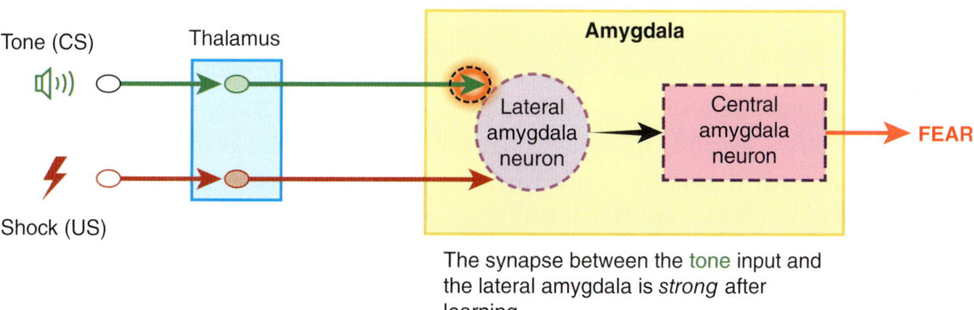

Figure 9.19 Lateral amygdala neurons receive synaptic inputs for both tone and shock. Thalamic neurons carrying information about the tone (CS) and the shock (US) synapse upon dendrites of the same individual neurons of the lateral amygdala. Top: The small arrowhead of the tone input represents a weak synapse, preventing the tone from strongly activating the amygdala before any learning has taken place. Bottom: After learning, the tone input has become strong.

about the tone (the CS) and those that carry information about the shock (the US) send axon terminals to the same individual neurons of the lateral amygdala. Before experiencing the tone and shock together, the synapse between the tone input and the lateral amygdala neuron is weak. The experience of the tone and shock together generates synaptic plasticity that strengthens this synapse.

Synaptic Plasticity Revisited

When tone- and shock-related inputs occur close together in time, the synapse between the tone input and the lateral amygdala neuron becomes stronger. This synaptic plasticity involves an increase in the number of glutamate AMPA receptors that appear on the postsynaptic membrane of the tone-to-lateral amygdala synapse, permitting the tone input to more strongly excite the amygdala neuron. How do the pairings of tone and shock cause more AMPA receptors to appear?

Plasticity in the amygdala follows rules similar to those discussed above when speaking of LTP in the hippocampus. In order for AMPA receptors to increase at the synapse between the tone input and the lateral amygdala neuron, the NMDA receptor at this synapse needs to be activated. When the tone and shock are presented close together in time, the shock input to other synapses on the same lateral amygdala neuron causes strong depolarization of the cell body and dendrites of the entire neuron. Therefore, the tone input neuron releases glutamate that binds to the NMDA receptor on the lateral amygdala neuron at a time when the amygdala neuron is in a depolarized state. As we have seen, NMDA receptors are activated (Ca^{++} flows through) when the postsynaptic neuron is sufficiently depolarized at the time that glutamate binds to it.

NMDA receptor activation at the tone synapse causes a chain of intracellular events that lead to DNA transcription and protein synthesis necessary for increased AMPA receptors at this synapse. Drugs that prevent activation of the NMDA receptor, gene transcription, or protein synthesis in the lateral amygdala prevent fear learning (Sigurdsson, Doyere, Cain, & LeDoux, 2007).

Fear learning in humans has not been examined at the level of neurobiological detail described here in the rat. However, to the extent that the neurobiology of fear and fear conditioning has been revealed through lesion and brain imaging studies in humans, a similar amygdala circuitry appears to be involved (LeDoux, 2012; Mendez-Bertolo et al., 2016).

Erasing Fear Memories

Bob was in front of his neighborhood grocery store when a man beat him up and robbed him. Now, when he sees the store he feels severe anxiety.

In fact, other grocery stores that resemble the one at the scene of his assault also trigger a conditioned fear response. Might Bob benefit from a drug, such as a protein synthesis inhibitor, that prevents the strengthening of synaptic connections in the lateral amygdala? There are two difficulties here. First, brain surgery would be needed in order to deliver the drug to his lateral amygdala, or to any specific brain region. But even if it were possible to develop a drug that would selectively block NMDA receptors or prevent protein synthesis to block the synaptic plasticity responsible for consolidation of fear memories, this would not help Bob. The fear memories regarding his assault have already been consolidated. Synapses carrying information about the grocery store to Bob's lateral amygdala neurons were probably strengthened within hours of his assault if we extrapolate from data on fear learning in rats.

But it may not be too late to "erase" the plasticity that has already occurred at amygdala synapses. There is evidence in rats to suggest that established fear memories can later be selectively erased (Nader & Hardt, 2009). A day after receiving tone/shock pairings, rats heard the tone again. Since the tone was presented without the shock, the fear responses they showed on this day reflected fear memory from the previous day's tone/shock experience. This is analogous to Bob seeing the grocery store the day after the assault and recalling the traumatic experience from yesterday. Immediately after hearing the tone on this day, one group of rats received a drug that inhibited protein synthesis to the lateral amygdala. This would be analogous to Bob receiving the drug after looking at the grocery store the day after his assault. Another group of rats (the control group) received an inactive solution. Twenty-four hours later, the control group continued to show strong fear responses when the tone was presented again (recalling the memory that was now 48 hours old). But rats that had received the protein synthesis inhibitor after the previous day's tone session showed no signs of fear to the tone. Blockade of protein synthesis just after animals had recalled the fear memory appears to have erased the established memory.

In order to erase the fear memory, was it necessary for the rats to hear the tone again before receiving the protein synthesis inhibitor? Apparently it was. Rats that received the protein synthesis inhibitor the day after the fear conditioning session, with no tone presented on that day, continued to fear the tone when tested the next day. Simply receiving the protein synthesis inhibitor was not enough to erase the fear memory. The drug had to be given while the rat recalled the fear memory.

These findings have been interpreted to suggest that, during recall, memories become fragile, and that recalled memories undergo **reconsolidation** via new protein synthesis each time they are retrieved. Blocking this reconsolidation erases the memory. The human implications of this research are intriguing (Silva & Soares, 2018). Might pharmacological treatments blocking reconsolidation of fear memories permit humans with **posttraumatic stress disorder** (**PTSD**) to "erase" the emotional content of their traumatic memories while leaving the episodic details of the memory intact? Is the fragile state of emotional memories each time we recall them a factor that may lead to memory distortion? Are episodic memories also reconsolidated and vulnerable to modification each time we recall them? We do not yet know.

9.4.2 Eyeblink Conditioning

If a puff of air lands on the cornea of your eye, you will reflexively blink. If a conditioned stimulus, such as a tone, regularly warns you that the air puff is coming, you will come to blink in response to the tone. Learning to blink in response to a conditioned stimulus is called eyeblink conditioning.

Research on eyeblink conditioning showed that learning can occur outside of the cerebral cortex. First, eyeblink conditioning was found to occur in rabbits even after the cerebral cortex was surgically removed (Oakley & Russell, 1972). Later studies demonstrated that eyeblink conditioning is lost following damage to the cerebellum (Thompson & Kim, 1996).

Why does this conditioning depend upon the cerebellum? As shown in Figure 9.20, air puffs have been observed to strongly activate a specific region of the cerebellum (called the **interpositus nucleus**). The same cerebellar region sends a signal to brainstem motor centers to generate eyeblinks. These cerebellar outputs therefore allow an air puff to produce an automatic eyeblink. No learning necessary. Before an animal has learned that a tone predicts the air puff, the tone does *not* produce an eyeblink. Why not?

Inputs carrying information about the tone arrive to the pons, where they excite neurons that transmit a signal to the cerebellum. However, the neurons carrying the tone signal from the pons have only weak connections with the cerebellar regions controlling the eyeblink. As we have seen in earlier sections, the key to learning is synaptic plasticity. In this case, the learning-related plasticity is within the cerebellum.

During learning trials of tone followed by air puff, the tone input to the cerebellum is weak, but then the air puff strongly excites the cerebellum. This causes the synapses carrying the tone input to the cerebellum to become stronger. As a result, the tone gains the ability to strongly activate neurons in the cerebellar nucleus which in turn triggers brainstem motor neurons to generate the blink response (Freeman & Steinmetz, 2011).

The important principle here is that synaptic plasticity during learning can strengthen (and sometimes weaken) connections between neurons,

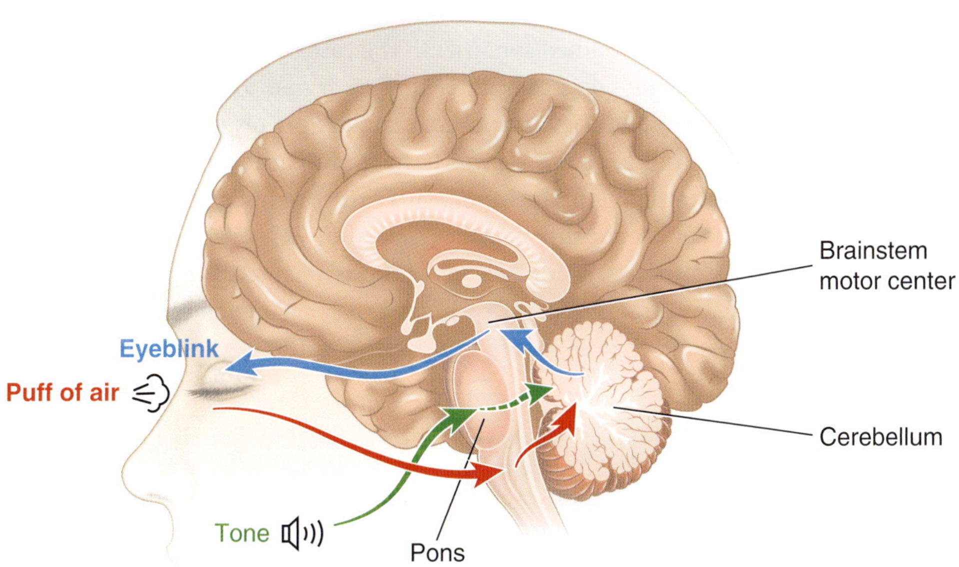

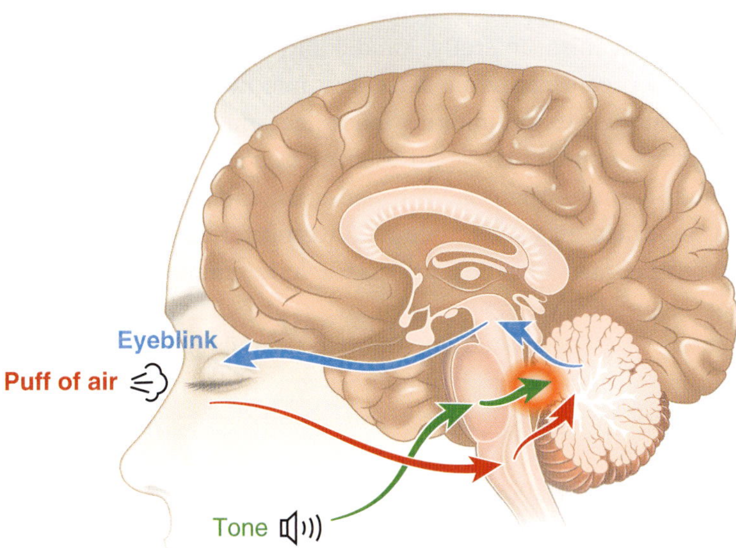

Figure 9.20 The cerebellar circuit necessary for eyeblink conditioning. Before conditioning (top), an air puff to the eye activates the cerebellum, generating an eyeblink response. However, the tone fails to activate this cerebellar region, and produces no eyeblink. After tone-air puff conditioning (bottom), the connection between the tone input and the cerebellum strengthens. This allows the tone to produce an eyeblink even without the air puff.

and these synaptic changes can produce learning. The type of learning depends upon the information carried by the input and output neurons on either side of the modified synapse. In the case of fear learning, the input neurons to the amygdala carried sensory information (e.g., representing a tone and shock) and the outputs generated a fear response. Modification of these synapses generated learning to fear a particular stimulus. In the cerebellar example here, the inputs also carried sensory information (e.g., tone and air puff), but the outputs generated by the cerebellum produced an eyeblink response. Modifications of these synapses give rise to eyeblink conditioning. Different forms of learning can be generated from similar mechanisms of synaptic plasticity.

9.4.3 Learning in *Aplysia*: Eric and the Snail

The human brain contains hundreds of billions of neurons. The rat brain contains millions. It is difficult to arrive at a detailed understanding of learning in a system containing so many elements. Some neuroscientists have turned to simpler organisms to understand the basic cellular mechanisms underlying learning and memory.

In the early 1960s, a young psychiatrist named Eric Kandel initiated a research program to understand learning in a simple organism. In choosing the organism to study, Kandel and his colleagues had several criteria. The organism should have a simple nervous system, with neurons large enough to be uniquely identified and manipulated. This would allow the researchers to learn each neuron's specific inputs and outputs. And, of course, the organism had to be capable of some form of learning, regardless of how simple. The winner of this learning-in-a-simple-organism contest was the California *Aplysia*, commonly known as the sea slug (Figure 9.21A).

The researchers began by studying **habituation**. Imagine that I stand behind you and drop a book on the floor. You initially have a strong **startle response**. However, if I repeat this action every 5 seconds, your startle response diminishes until it disappears completely. The startle response has habituated. Habituation is a decrease in the size of a simple evoked response that occurs as a result of that response being repeatedly triggered.

Aplysia also habituate to repeated stimuli. When at rest and relaxed, the *Aplysia*'s gills (the organs that take in oxygen) are exposed. When a nearby body part such as the siphon (used to expel waste from the body) is touched, the *Aplysia* rapidly withdraws its gills (Figure 9.21B). This gill-withdrawal response habituates with continued stimulation of the siphon. Years of painstaking research have identified the neural mechanisms responsible for this simple response.

A

B

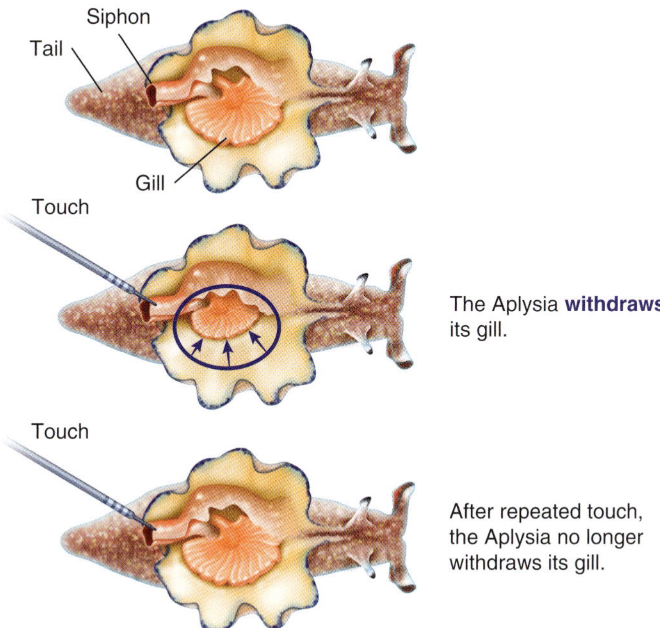

Figure 9.21 Habituation in *Aplysia*. In the photo (A) and drawings (B), the Aplysia is facing to the right, with its tail to the left. The Aplysia protects its gill by withdrawing it when a nearby body part (such as the siphon) is touched. However, with repeated touch, the Aplysia no longer withdraws its gill (the withdrawal response habituates). (A, © 2005, Wägele & Klussmann-Kolb; licensee BioMed Central Ltd.)

Stimulation of a sensory neuron from the siphon causes release of the excitatory neurotransmitter glutamate directly onto receptors on the motor neuron that controls gill-withdrawal. How is this withdrawal response reduced during habituation? First, the researchers showed that the sensory neuron in the siphon continues to fire with equal strength each time the siphon is stimulated. Therefore, habituation is not due to siphon touch producing only weak activation of the sensory neuron. Second, repeated direct stimulation of the motor neuron continues to elicit a neuronal response of equal strength each time. The change therefore occurred at the synaptic connection between these two neurons. After repeated touch to the siphon, the sensory neuron still fires normally; but when it fires, only a small amount of glutamate is released. Less glutamate released by the sensory neuron means a smaller activation of the motor neuron and little or no gill-withdrawal. Thus, a very simple form of learning can be mediated by a very simple change in neural plasticity. For this and other research on learning in *Aplysia*, Kandel received the 2000 Nobel Prize in Medicine.

KEY CONCEPTS

- **During fear conditioning, synaptic connections strengthen between neurons in the lateral amygdala, which receive sensory input, and neurons in the central amygdala, which generate fear responses. As a result, conditioned stimuli can activate the central amygdala to produce fear-related reactions such as elevated heart rate, freezing, and vigilance.**
- **During eyeblink conditioning, the cerebellum receives information about both the tone and the air puff to the eye. Outputs generate an eyeblink. Plasticity in the connection between the inputs and outputs permits the tone to generate an eyeblink even when presented alone (without the air puff).**
- **In *Aplysia*, habituation to a sensory event occurs because the sensory neuron releases less glutamate in response to repeated stimulation.**

TEST YOURSELF

1. **A neutral tone produces little activation of lateral amygdala neurons, while a tone paired with shock can strongly activate lateral amygdala neurons. How does this change in the lateral amygdala response to the conditioned tone occur?**
2. **You once got into a car accident in front of a gas station, and now you feel fear every time you pass that gas station. On the basis of research on the erasure of fear memories in rats, what would it mean to "erase" your fear memory? What (perhaps inconvenient) steps would be required?**
3. ***Aplysia* withdraw their gills in response to siphon touch. How do changes in synaptic transmission lead to habituation of the gill-withdrawal response?**

9.5 The Big Picture

Two key points emerge in this chapter. First, different types of memory and learning depend upon different brain circuits. For example, while the hippocampus plays a critical role in episodic memory, the amygdala plays a central role in fear conditioning. Second, all forms of memory and learning appear to share a common underlying neurobiological process: synaptic plasticity, a change in the strength of connections between neurons. Synaptic plasticity occurs in the brain constantly, from birth to death. It allows us to anticipate important events on the basis of earlier cues in the environment, to ignore unimportant events, to move through the world in a skillful manner. Memories that are explicit, or conscious, allow us to reflect upon the past events in our lives.

9.6 Creative Thinking

1. How might the activity of place cells and concept cells contribute to episodic memory?
2. Penfield's patients reported fragments of memory upon electrical stimulation of the temporal lobe. However, the patients were aware that they were recalling an event, rather than reexperiencing it. Do you think it is possible that a more sophisticated stimulation of neurons might someday provide the experience of truly reliving a past experience? Would you want to engage in such a simulation?
3. If you close your eyes and imagine a shiny red apple, what parts of your brain will be activated, and why?
4. In small animals, hippocampal place cells would obviously play a major role in scavenging the environment for food. In humans, how might the function of place cells have changed through evolution?

Key Terms

adult neurogenesis 377
AMPA receptor 372
anterograde amnesia 354
Aplysia 383
automatized behavior 380
basal ganglia 381
CA1 region of the hippocampus 360
CA3 region of the hippocampus 360
central nucleus of the amygdala 384
classical conditioning 351
concept neurons 366
conditioned response (CR) 383
conditioned stimulus (CS) 383
consolidation, memory 354
dentate gyrus of the hippocampus 360
distributed network 362
enriched environment 378
entorhinal cortex 361
episodic memory 350
explicit memory 350

References

Barnes, C. A., & McNaughton, B. L. (1980). Physiological compensation for loss of afferent synapses in rat hippocampal granule cells during senescence. *Journal of Physiology*, *309*, 473–485.

Bayley, P. J., Hopkins, R. O., & Squire, L. R. (2003). Successful recollection of remote autobiographical memories by amnesic patients with medial temporal lobe lesions. *Neuron*, *38*(1), 135–144.

Bowers, J. S. (2009). On the biological plausibility of grandmother cells: implications for neural network theories in psychology and neuroscience. *Psychological Review*, *116*(1), 220–251.

Caligiore, D., Pezzulo, G., Baldassarre, G., Bostan, A. C., Strick, P. L., Doya, K., ... Herreros, I. (2017). Consensus paper: towards a systems-level view of cerebellar function: the interplay between cerebellum, basal ganglia, and cortex. *Cerebellum*, *16*(1), 203–229.

Carr, M. F., Jadhav, S. P., & Frank, L. M. (2011). Hippocampal replay in the awake state: a potential substrate for memory consolidation and retrieval. *Nature Neuroscience*, *14*(2), 147–153.

Censor, N., Sagi, D., & Cohen, L. G. (2012). Common mechanisms of human perceptual and motor learning. *Nature Reviews Neuroscience*, *13*(9), 658–664.

Cerf, M., Thiruvengadam, N., Mormann, F., Kraskov, A., Quiroga, R. Q., Koch, C., & Fried, I. (2010). On-line, voluntary control of human temporal lobe neurons. *Nature, 467*(7319), 1104–U1115.

Dayan, E., & Cohen, L. G. (2011). Neuroplasticity subserving motor skill learning. *Neuron, 72*(3), 443–454.

Deng, W., Aimone, J. B., & Gage, F. H. (2010). New neurons and new memories: how does adult hippocampal neurogenesis affect learning and memory? *Nature Reviews Neuroscience, 11*(5), 339–350.

Diekelmann, S., & Born, J. (2010). The memory function of sleep. *Nature Reviews Neuroscience, 11*(2), 114–126.

Dijkstra, N., Bosch, S. E., & van Gerven, M. A. (2017). Vividness of visual imagery depends on the neural overlap with perception in visual areas. *Journal of Neuroscience, 37*(5), 1367–1373.

Drieu, C., & Zugaro, M. (2019). Hippocampal sequences during exploration: mechanisms and functions. *Frontiers in Cellular Neuroscience, 13*.

Ekstrom, A. D., Kahana, M. J., Caplan, J. B., Fields, T. A., Isham, E. A., Newman, E. L., & Fried, I. (2003). Cellular networks underlying human spatial navigation. *Nature, 425*(6954), 184–187.

Foster, D. J., & Wilson, M. A. (2006). Reverse replay of behavioural sequences in hippocampal place cells during the awake state. *Nature, 440*(7084), 680–683.

Freeman, J. H., & Steinmetz, A. B. (2011). Neural circuitry and plasticity mechanisms underlying delay eyeblink conditioning. *Learning & Memory, 18*(10), 666–677.

Fritsch, B., Reis, J., Martinowich, K., Schambra, H. M., Ji, Y. Y., Cohen, L. G., & Lu, B. (2010). Direct current stimulation promotes BDNF-dependent synaptic plasticity: potential implications for motor learning. *Neuron, 66*(2), 198–204.

Garrett, B. L. (2011). *Convicting the Innocent.* Cambridge, MA: Harvard University Press.

Gould, E., Beylin, A., Tanapat, P., Reeves, A., & Shors, T. J. (1999). Learning enhances adult neurogenesis in the hippocampal formation. *Nature Neuroscience, 2*(3), 260–265.

Hassabis, D., Kumaran, D., Vann, S. D., & Maguire, E. A. (2007). Patients with hippocampal amnesia cannot imagine new experiences. *Proceedings of the National Academy of Sciences of the United States of America, 104*(5), 1726–1731.

Ji, D. Y., & Wilson, M. A. (2007). Coordinated memory replay in the visual cortex and hippocampus during sleep. *Nature Neuroscience, 10*(1), 100–107.

Karni, A., Meyer, G., Jezzard, P., Adams, M. M., Turner, R., & Ungerleider, L. G. (1995). Functional MRI evidence for adult motor cortex plasticity during motor skill learning. *Nature, 377*(6545), 155–158.

Kempermann, G., Kuhn, H. G., & Gage, F. H. (1997). More hippocampal neurons in adult mice living in an enriched environment. *Nature, 386*(6624), 493–495.

LeDoux, J. (2012). Rethinking the emotional brain. *Neuron, 73*(4), 653–676.

Lever, C., Wills, T., Cacucci, F., Burgess, N., & O'Keefe, J. (2002). Long-term plasticity in hippocampal place-cell representation of environmental geometry. *Nature, 416*(6876), 90–94.

Lomo, T. (1966). Frequency potentiation of excitatory synaptic activity in the dentate area of the hippocampal formation. *Acta Physiologica Scandinavica,* Supplement *277,* 128.

Maguire, E. A., Gadian, D. G., Johnsrude, I. S., Good, C. D., Ashburner, J., Frackowiak, R. S., & Frith, C. D. (2000). Navigation-related structural change in the hippocampi of taxi drivers. *Proceedings of the National Academy of Sciences of the United States of America, 97*(8), 4398–4403.

Martin, S. J., Grimwood, P. D., & Morris, R. G. M. (2000). Synaptic plasticity and memory: an evaluation of the hypothesis. *Annual Review of Neuroscience, 23,* 649–711.

McClelland, J. L., Rumelhart, D.E., & Group, PDP Research. (1986). *Parallel Distributed Processing: Psychological and Biological Models.* Cambridge, MA: MIT Press.

Mendez-Bertolo, C., Moratti, S., Toledano, R., Lopez-Sosa, F., Martinez-Alvarez, R., Mah, Y. H., ... Strange, B. A. (2016). A fast pathway for fear in human amygdala. *Nature Neuroscience, 19*(8), 1041–1049.

Michon, F., Sun, J. J., Kim, C. Y., Ciliberti, D., & Kloosterman, F. (2019). Post-learning hippocampal replay selectively reinforces spatial memory for highly rewarded locations. *Current Biology, 29*(9), 1436–1444.

Milner, B. (1970). Memory and the medial temporal regions of the brain. In K. H. Pribram & D. E. Broadbent (Eds.), *Biology of Memory* (pp. 29–50). New York: Academic Press.

Minichiello, L. (2009). TrkB signalling pathways in LTP and learning. *Nature Reviews Neuroscience, 10*(12), 850–860.

Morris, R. G. M., Anderson, E., Lynch, G. S., & Baudry, M. (1986). Selective impairment of learning and blockade of long-term potentiation by an N-methyl-D-aspartate receptor antagonist, AP5. *Nature, 319*(6056), 774–776.

Moscovitch, M., Rosenbaum, R. S., Gilboa, A., Addis, D. R., Westmacott, R., Grady, C., ... Nadel, L. (2005). Functional neuroanatomy of remote episodic, semantic and spatial memory: a unified account based on multiple trace theory. *Journal of Anatomy, 207*(1), 35–66.

Muellbacher, W., Ziemann, U., Wissel, J., Dang, N., Kofler, M., Facchini, S., ... Hallett, M. (2002). Early consolidation in human primary motor cortex. *Nature, 415*(6872), 640–644.

Nadel, L., & Moscovitch, M. (1997). Memory consolidation, retrograde amnesia and the hippocampal complex. *Current Opinion in Neurobiology, 7*(2), 217–227.

Nader, K., & Hardt, O. (2009). A single standard for memory: the case for reconsolidation. *Nature Reviews Neuroscience, 10*(3), 224–234.

Oakley, D. A., & Russell, I. S. (1972). Neocortical lesions and Pavlovian conditioning. *Physiology & Behavior, 8*(5), 915–926.

Pascualleone, A., Dang, N., Cohen, L. G., Brasilneto, J. P., Cammarota, A., & Hallett, M. (1995). Modulation of muscle responses evoked by transcranial magnetic stimulation during the acquisition of new fine motor-skills. *Journal of Neurophysiology, 74*(3), 1037–1045.

Perrin, E., & Venance, L. (2019). Bridging the gap between striatal plasticity and learning. *Current Opinion in Neurobiology, 54*, 104–112.

Peters, A. J., Liu, H. X., & Komiyama, T. (2017). Learning in the rodent motor cortex. *Annual Review of Neuroscience, 40*, 77–97).

Polyn, S. M., Natu, V. S., Cohen, J. D., & Norman, K. A. (2005). Category-specific cortical activity precedes retrieval during memory search. *Science, 310*(5756), 1963–1966.

Quiroga, R. Q. (2012). Concept cells: the building blocks of declarative memory functions. *Nature Reviews Neuroscience, 13*(8), 587–597.

Rueda-Orozco, P. E., & Robbe, D. (2015). The striatum multiplexes contextual and kinematic information to constrain motor habits execution. *Nature Neuroscience, 18*(3), 453–460.

Rutishauser, U. (2019). Testing models of human declarative memory at the single-neuron level. *Trends in Cognitive Sciences, 23*(6), 510–524.

Sanes, J. N., & Donoghue, J. P. (2000). Plasticity and primary motor cortex. *Annual Review of Neuroscience, 23*, 393–415.

Schacter, D. L., & Loftus, E. F. (2013). Memory and law: what can cognitive neuroscience contribute? *Nature Neuroscience, 16*(2), 119–123.

Shadmehr, R., & Holcomb, H. H. (1997). Neural correlates of motor memory consolidation. *Science, 277*(5327), 821–825.

Shors, T. J., Miesegaes, G., Beylin, A., Zhao, M. R., Rydel, T., & Gould, E. (2001). Neurogenesis in the adult is involved in the formation of trace memories. *Nature, 410*(6826), 372–376.

Sigurdsson, T., Doyere, V., Cain, C. K., & LeDoux, J. E. (2007). Long-term potentiation in the amygdala: a cellular mechanism of fear learning and memory. *Neuropharmacology, 52*(1), 215–227.

Silva, M. B., & Soares, A. B. (2018). Reconsolidation of human motor memory: from boundary conditions to behavioral interventions –How far are we from clinical applications? *Behavioural Brain Research, 353*, 83–90.

Snyder, J. S. (2019). Recalibrating the relevance of adult neurogenesis. *Trends in Neurosciences, 42*(3), 164–178.

Squire, L. R., & Wixted, J. T. (2011). The cognitive neuroscience of human memory since H.M. *Annual Review of Neuroscience, 34*, 259–288.

Teyler, T. J., & DiScenna, P. (1986). The hippocampal memory indexing theory. *Behavioral Neuroscience, 100*(2), 147–154.

Thompson, R. F., & Kim, J. J. (1996). Memory systems in the brain and localization of a memory. *Proceedings of the National Academy of Sciences of the United States of America, 93*(24), 13438–13444.

Vargha-Khadem, F., Gadian, D. G., Watkins, K. E., Connelly, A., Van Paesschen, W., & Mishkin, M. (1997). Differential effects of early hippocampal pathology on episodic and semantic memory. *Science, 277*(5324), 376–380.

10

Attention and Working Memory

Kelvin Murray / Stone / Getty Images

Consider This …

Stanley and his wife had been married for over thirty years. Over the past month, his wife became concerned. Her husband loved to read books, but recently he'd complained of losing track of the storylines. One day, she noticed that Stanley would read normally from the right side of his book, but would skip pages on the left. He was also neglecting the food on the left side of his plate. The couple lived in Philadelphia, and made an appointment to see a neurologist at the nearby University of Pennsylvania.

Upon hearing of the symptoms, the doctor immediately suspected neurological damage that caused sensory neglect, or inattention, to one side. He showed Stanley a drawing of a house and asked him to copy it. Stanley copied the right side of the picture perfectly, but the left side of the house was mostly absent from his drawing. Tests confirmed that his vision was fine; his problem was with noticing objects to his left side.

After reviewing MRI images of Stanley's brain, the neurologist determined that he suffered from damage to the frontal lobe on the right side of his brain. This was causing **contralateral neglect**, inattention to the sensory world on the side opposite the brain damage. Like a person whom we take for granted because they are so often present, attentional processes are so much a part of our daily lives that we may fail to notice their importance. However, when these processes are impaired as they were in Stanley's case, it is clear that we normally depend upon them to select the objects of our attention at each moment.

Attention allows us to focus on particular stimuli from among the many that are surrounding us. Imagine you are at a crowded party. You scan the faces to see if you can find anyone you know. You're activating attention systems in order to scan for particular targets (familiar faces). It pays off. You recognize your friend Bob, with his freckles, curly hair, and characteristic smile. He now disappears from sight as he leaves the room. While he's no longer an object of your attention, you know he's nearby. You still have the image of his face in mind, in "working memory." **Working memory** keeps information about an object or event actively in mind after it is no longer present. This chapter will examine research on the neural underpinnings of attention and working memory. As we will see, these functions often work hand-in-hand to help us achieve our goals.

10.1 ATTENTION

Researchers studying attention distinguish between **alertness** and **selective attention**. Alertness refers to your current level of sensitivity or responsiveness to environmental stimuli. On the other hand, selective attention is your ability to select the specific objects in your environment to which you will devote your attentional resources. We begin this chapter by examining what it means to be "alert" from the point of view of the brain.

10.1.1 Norepinephrine Neurons Play a Key Role in Alertness

You're out for a walk with your friend, when suddenly he says, "Get ready. Something important is about to happen." This unusual statement is enough to put you into a state of high alertness without even knowing *what* is about to happen! When we say that you're alert, we mean that you are highly sensitive to sights, sounds, and other stimuli in the environment. You are "on the alert" for potentially important environmental events. Here, we will focus upon the actions of norepinephrine, a key neurochemical that heightens alertness.

Most norepinephrine neurons in the brain have their cell bodies in the locus coeruleus, a small area within the pons (Figure 10.1). When an animal is drowsy, locus coeruleus neurons fire at low rates. However, when the animal is aroused, these neurons fire rapidly and release norepinephrine throughout the cortex and other brain regions. Norepinephrine increases alertness by making the brain more responsive to environmental stimuli.

Take for example a neuron in an area of the cortex that is sensitive to the sight of faces. Before a face appears, the neuron might fire at some slow background rate, say one or two times per second. The neuron is not yet firing in response to anything in particular, and we say that the activity of the neuron simply represents "noise." We're not speaking of noise as in "sounds"; by noise, we mean a lack of specific information. When the face appears, the same neuron increases its rate of firing. The neuron's activity in the presence of the face is referred to as the "signal." If we were examining a neuron that responds to the color blue, then the neuron's response to the color blue would be its response to the signal, and the noise would again refer to the neuron's background activity level. If a neuron responds at a high rate in the presence of the signal, but an almost equally high rate in the absence of the signal, it has a poor **signal-to-noise ratio**, and is not very useful in detecting the face, color, or other stimulus attribute.

Figure 10.2 shows the activity of a somatosensory neuron in the brain of a rat, before and after a touch to its paw. The bottom left panel shows the neuronal response when the locus coeruleus releases only low levels of norepinephrine. As you can see, the neuron fires at a low background rate ("noise") before the experimenter touches the rat's paw. Touch to the

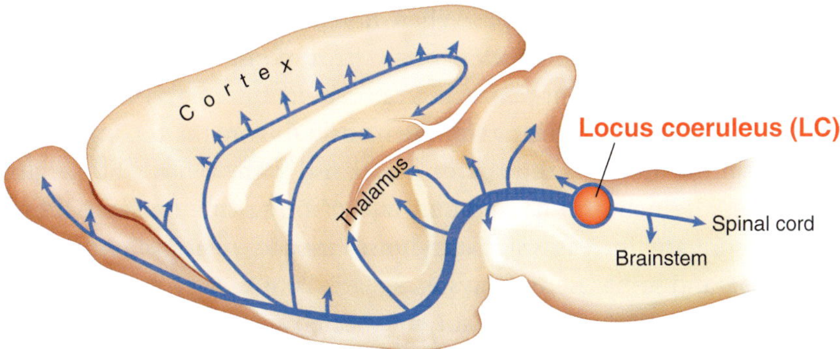

Figure 10.1 Norepinephrine neurons that originate in the locus coeruleus (LC) are important in alertness. While these neurons originate within a small area of the pons, they send widespread projections which release norepinephrine from their axon terminals (blue arrowheads). As a result, when arousing stimuli activate the LC, many brain areas are alerted at once.

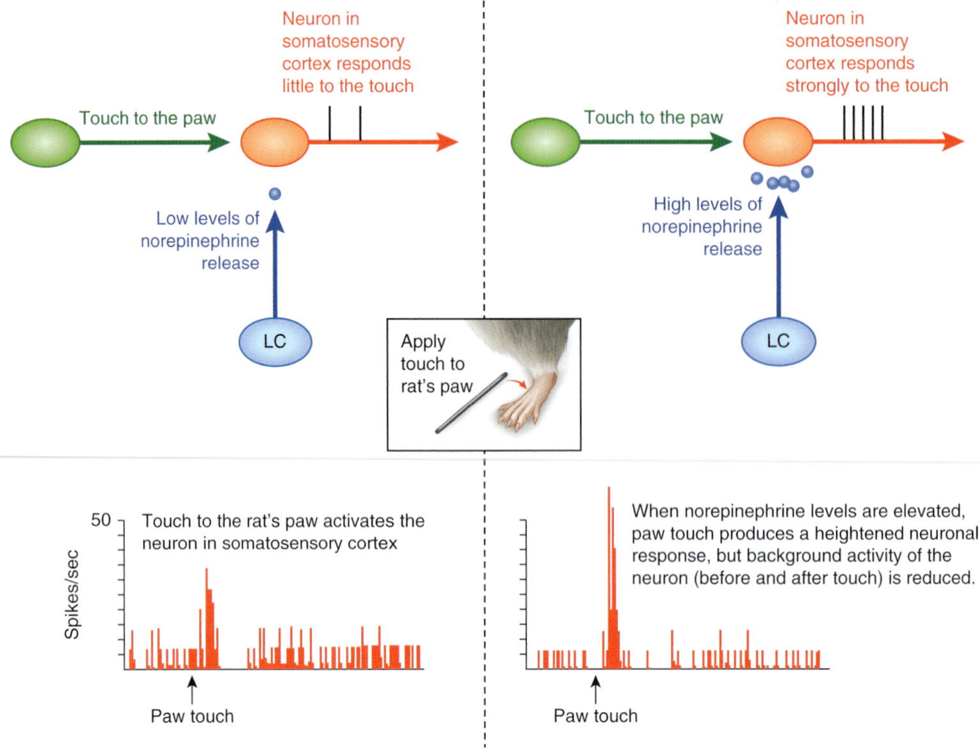

Figure 10.2 Norepinephrine enhances the response of neurons to sensory stimuli. Top: When the locus coeruleus (LC) releases more norepinephrine (blue, right panel), the somatosensory neuron responds strongly to paw touch. Bottom: Increased norepinephrine levels increase the neuronal response as soon as the paw is touched, but reduce the background rate of neuronal activity before, and a little while after, the touch. Bottom adapted from Waterhouse, Moises, & Woodward, 1998, fig. 1, © 1998 Elsevier Science B.V. All rights reserved.)

paw increases the rate of firing ("signal") and the neuron then returns to its background rate of firing. When norepinephrine levels are high, the somatosensory neuron fires strongly in response to the touch. But notice in the bottom right panel, high norepinephrine levels do not increase the background firing rate of the neuron (before the touch). While norepinephrine increases the neuron's response to the touch (the signal), it decreases the neuron's background rate of firing (the noise). Norepinephrine similarly increases signal-to-noise ratios for neurons in the auditory, visual, and somatosensory systems (Sara, 2009).

Arousing stimuli, for instance an unexpected sound or a sudden flash of light, cause norepinephrine neurons to fire at high rates. In turn, norepinephrine elevates neuronal signal-to-noise ratios, enhancing the ability of neurons to detect environmental change, that is, increasing alertness. This makes evolutionary sense because when a sudden change occurs in the environment, say the sound of a snake slithering in the grass, other unexpected and potentially important environmental changes may follow (the snake may suddenly raise its head near your leg!). It is advantageous for the nervous system to be on high alert as soon as the sound of the snake is detected.

Amphetamine and other psychostimulant drugs elevate synaptic levels of norepinephrine, and produce heightened states of alertness (Berridge & Arnsten, 2013). At certain drug doses, these stimulant drugs enhance the ability to detect stimuli. Soldiers during the Second World War were given amphetamine to increase their alertness during long periods on duty. By elevating norepinephrine levels, the drugs presumably enhanced signal-to-noise ratios in cortical neurons, facilitating detection of events relevant to combat.

10.1.2 Attention Can Be Stimulus-Driven or Goal-Directed

A key fact of mental experience is that we direct our attention selectively to *certain* stimuli and not to others. Can we identify brain systems responsible for selective attention?

Some stimuli grab our attention because they are **salient** – they possess highly noticeable physical properties. A sound grabs your attention because of its intensity (loudness) and sudden onset. A red rose in a garden filled with green grass stands out because of the contrast between its color and the background colors. The salience of a stimulus depends importantly upon the stimuli surrounding it. For instance, a flashing light that is highly salient when no other lights are present is much less salient when other flashing lights surround it.

The blue circle in the top panel of Figure 10.3 is salient because its color differs from the background stimuli in the display. The horizontal orange line in the lower display is salient for the same reason. Notice that the salient stimulus in the lower display is as easy to detect as the one above, even though the lower display contains more background or **distractor** stimuli. In each case, the salient stimulus pops out at you. This **pop-out effect** is a characteristic of the **stimulus-driven attention**, which responds automatically, involuntarily, to salient environment stimuli. Stimulus-driven attention is sometimes called **bottom-up attention**: "Bottom-up" because *low-level* circuits in the brain, which operate without awareness ("bottom") detect the salient physical characteristics of the stimulus and activate higher-order areas of the brain ("up"), which direct attention toward the stimulus.

In contrast, you might find your friend's face in a crowd even if her face is not very distinctive (assuming, she has not painted her face green or added some other feature that would produce a pop-out effect). You use

goal-directed attention to search through the faces in the crowd and identify hers. This attention system is also sometimes called **top-down attention** because high-order brain areas that represent a goal (top), such as finding your friend, influence lower-order brain areas (down) to detect relevant stimulus features, say her curved nose.

In Figure 10.4, you can only find the target stimuli by using goal-directed attention. You begin by determining the goal stimulus (an orange horizontal line in this case) and then scan through each item. This **serial search** strategy (going item-by-item) is necessary because the target does

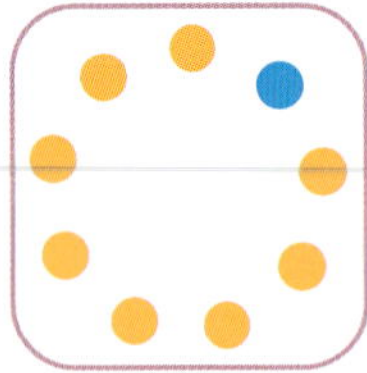

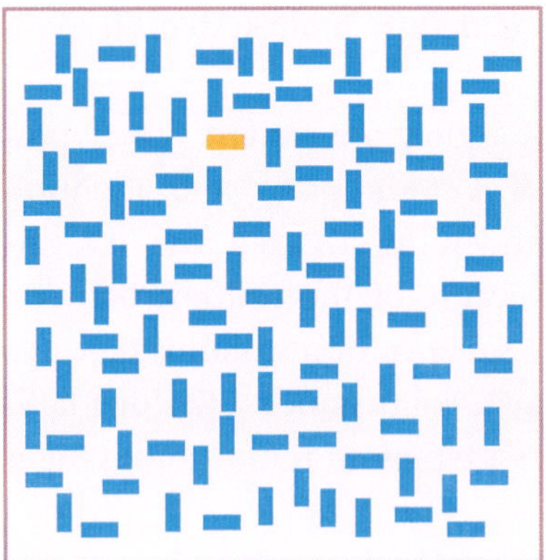

Figure 10.3 **Stimulus-driven attention and the pop-out effect**. Each display contains one item that pops out from the others due to its distinctive color. Stimuli that are physically salient engage an automatic and involuntary process known as stimulus-driven or bottom-up attention.

Figure 10.4 **Goal-directed attention searches item-by-item to find the target**. The target stimulus does not pop out from the background stimuli. The subject must search for it using goal-directed attention, which examines each item one at a time until a match is discovered between the item and goal (target) stimulus.

not produce an automatic pop-out effect. The target has one feature (color) in common with some distractors, and another (line orientation) in common with other distractors. The target is unique only in the *conjunction* of features – it is the only item that is both orange *and* horizontal. In the same way, your friend's nose may be similar to that of others in the crowd; her eyes may be similar to some of the other eyes, and so on. But her face is the only one with the exact conjunction (combination) of her kind of eyes, mouth, nose, and other features. Because stimuli do not pop out, they require goal-directed attention, which must search each stimulus one at a time.

Because goal-directed attention employs a serial search strategy, the more distractor items in the display, the longer it takes to find the target. On the other hand, when the target differs strongly from the background, stimulus-driven attention is engaged, and you do not need to search through each distractor item in order to locate the salient target. In this case, detection speed is unaffected by the number of distractors. In the display at the bottom of Figure 10.3 shown earlier, whether the screen contains 50 or 500 blue lines, the unique orange stimulus will pop out just as quickly. As we can see in Figure 10.5, as set size (number of distractors) increases, the reaction time increases during serial conjunction search (and goal-directed attention), but is unaffected by set size when the target has a distinct feature, and engages stimulus-driven attention (Treisman & Gelade, 1980).

Right now, as you read this book, your attention is guided by goal-directed, top-down, influences. The words on this page are no more salient than the other visual stimuli surrounding you, but you choose to attend to them in order to achieve your goal of reading the exciting chapter. On the other hand, the sound of a loud fire alarm could easily grab your attention by engaging bottom-up attentional processes. The interaction

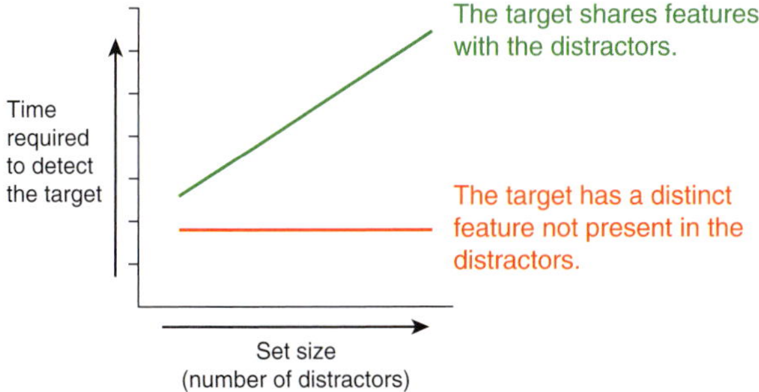

Figure 10.5 How long does it take to find a target among distractors? When a display contains a distinct target (see Figure 10.3), stimulus-driven attention detects the target quickly, regardless of the number of distractor stimuli. In contrast, when the target stimulus shares features with the distractors (see Figure 10.4), a serial search strategy is needed; so the more distractor stimuli, the more time needed to detect the target.

between the top-down and bottom-up attentional systems determines what we attend to at each moment in time.

Distinct Brain Regions Are Activated during Goal-Directed and Stimulus-Driven Attention

Stimulus-driven (bottom-up) attention and goal-directed (top-down) attention activate different **networks** (interconnected sets) of brain regions (Figure 10.6). Both attentional networks include areas of the frontal cortex and areas around the parietal cortex. However, stimulus-driven attention activates the **ventral frontal cortex** and an area between the temporal and parietal lobes called the **temporoparietal junction**. (To remember this, you might imagine salient and novel stimuli activating the ventral or "bottom" portion of the frontal cortex along with an area in between lobes.) The goal-directed network activates the **frontal eye fields** and an area of the parietal cortex called the **intraparietal sulcus**, i.e., near the sulcus or "groove" *within* the parietal cortex. (You might remember this by thinking of the frontal eye fields controlling eye movements as you scan the environment for your friend, your attentional "goal," with the help of neurons near a groove cutting through the parietal lobe.)

How do these two attentional networks respond when an individual is engaged in goal-directed attention, but is suddenly distracted by an unexpected stimulus that activates the stimulus-driven attentional

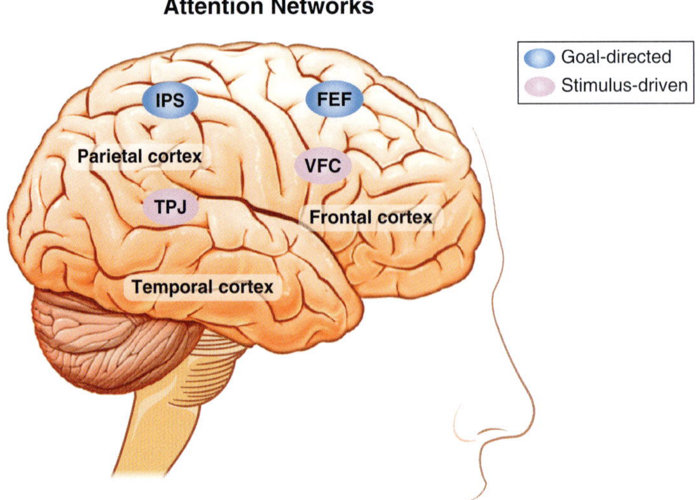

Figure 10.6 Visual attention networks. During stimulus-driven attention, visual information activates a network that includes the temporoparietal junction (TPJ) and ventral frontal cortex (VFC). During goal-directed attention, visual information is processed by a network that includes the intraparietal sulcus (IPS) and frontal eye fields (FEF).

network? In an interesting experiment, subjects were asked to view letters that appeared briefly on a screen. Each letter appeared for just one-tenth of a second, and was immediately followed by the next letter (Figure 10.7A). In order to engage the goal-directed attention system, subjects were asked to look for a *particular* target letter, for instance the letter X.

As the subject is viewing the rapid succession of letters on the screen (e.g., D, B, ...) and waiting for the letter X, a "surprise" stimulus

A

Figure 10.7 An unexpected stimulus disrupts goal-directed attention. (A) Letters appeared briefly on the screen, one after another. Goal-directed attention allowed subjects to detect the letter X (top panel). However, subjects often missed the X when a surprising stimulus (a face) appeared just before it (bottom panel). (B) The first few times the face is presented, it captures attention and prevents detection of the letter X. With repeated presentations, the face loses its ability to capture attention.
(Adapted from Asplund et al., 2010, fig. 1, © 2010, Nature Publishing Group.)

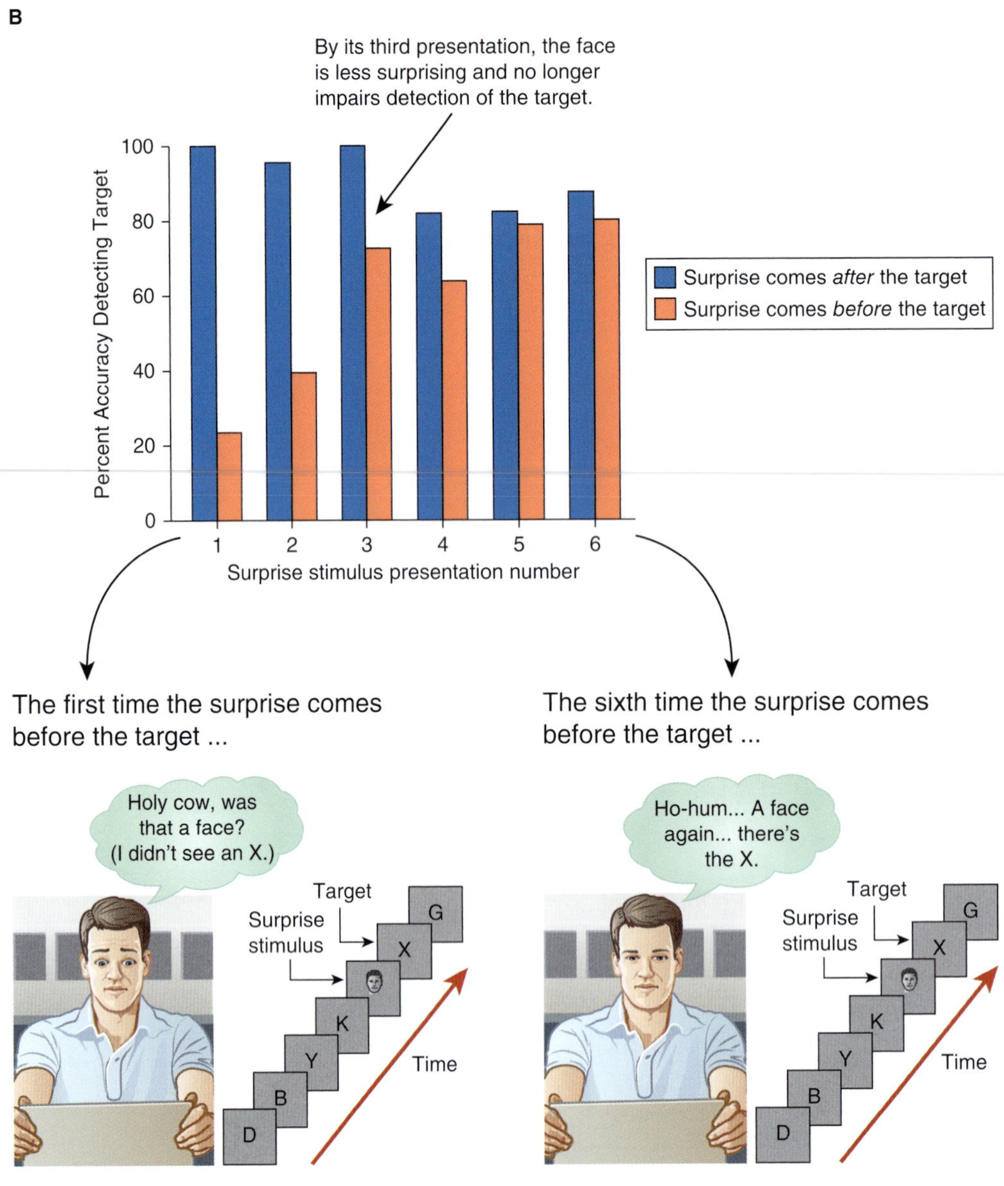

Figure 10.7 (cont.)

occasionally appears instead of a letter. In the experiment depicted in Figure 10.7A, the surprise stimulus was a face. The unexpected appearance of the face captured stimulus-driven attention. The face didn't grab attention because it was the target (or "goal") of the subject's attention; it grabbed attention because of its novelty. In fact, it captured attention so completely that, when the face appeared just before the X, subjects were often completely unaware that the X had been presented (Asplund, Todd, Snyder, & Marois, 2010). A salient stimulus that engaged stimulus-driven attention had disrupted goal-directed attention. As you might imagine, the unexpected face only maintained attention-grabbing power the first few times it was presented. With repeated presentations, it became less surprising, lost its ability to capture stimulus-driven attention, and no longer impaired detection of the target (Figure 10.7B).

We saw earlier that the frontal eye field and the intraparietal sulcus are key components of the goal-directed attention network. As predicted, fMRI showed activation of these brain regions while subjects directed their attention toward the goal (target) stimulus, the X (Figure 10.8, left panel). However, when subjects were distracted by the salient face stimulus, the stimulus-driven network became activated (Figure 10.8, right panel).

In the experiment described above, a surprising stimulus (face) activates the stimulus-driven network and interrupts goal-directed attention (searching for the X). Similarly, in everyday life, a surprising stimulus such as a fire alarm can activate the stimulus-driven attention network and interrupt goal-directed attention like reading the words of a textbook. In other cases, an individual might decide that the object of her goal-directed attention is so important that the distracting stimulus, which activates the stimulus-driven system, should be ignored.

How Do We Direct Attention to the Stimuli Most Relevant to Our Goals?

When you search for an object, say a particular face in a crowd or simply an object of a particular shape, the visual cortex responds to sensory information relevant to that goal object more strongly than to other stimuli (Reynolds, Pasternak, & Desimone, 2000). But how does attention

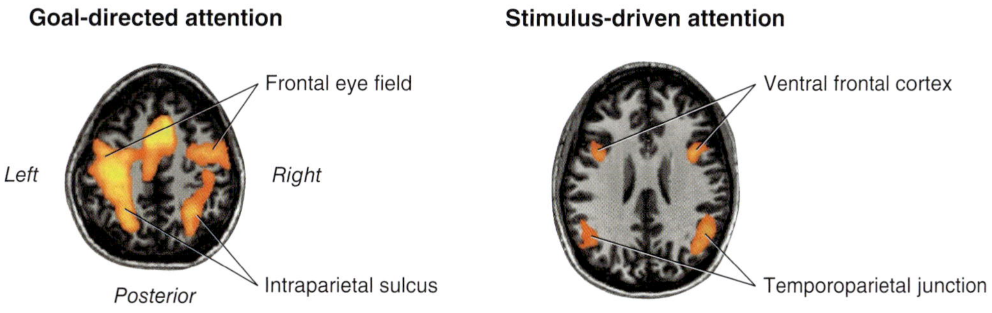

Goal-directed attention

Frontal eye field

Left

Right

Intraparietal sulcus

Posterior

Stimulus-driven attention

Ventral frontal cortex

Temporoparietal junction

Figure 10.8 **Brain activations associated with goal-directed versus stimulus-driven attention**. Goal-directed attention (look for the X) produced bilateral activation of the frontal eye field and intraparietal sulcus while stimulus-driven attention activated the ventral frontal cortex and temporoparietal junction (right).
(Adapted from Asplund et al., 2010, figs. 2 (right) and 3 (left), © 2010, Nature Publishing Group.)

increase neuronal responses to one object more than another? During goal-directed attention, higher-order brain areas influence the sensitivity of neurons in lower-order sensory regions. In order to understand this idea, it will be helpful to review what is meant by higher- and lower-order sensory regions of the brain.

Let's consider higher-order neurons in the visual system that identify particular visual objects, i.e., determining whether an object is a fork, a cup, or something else. Such neurons are part of the **ventral stream** of the visual system, sometimes called the **"what" pathway** (Figure 10.9). Neurons within higher-order areas of the ventral stream distinguish objects that differ in terms of their color, shape, and texture. However, these higher-order neurons of the ventral stream receive visual information from lower-order neurons that detect simpler visual details.

For instance, some neurons in V1 respond to line orientations, i.e., horizontal, vertical, and diagonal of various angles (Chapter 3). If you were recording the activity of a neuron only in V1, it would be impossible to know whether the neuron was firing in response to the image of a fork, a cup, or some other object. Neurons in V1 that respond to some combination of line orientations at particular areas of the retina communicate with neurons in higher-order areas of the ventral stream. Within the ventral stream, you will find individual neurons that respond selectively to objects of a particular shape, and some neurons that respond only to faces. The higher-order responses of these areas depend upon the more detailed information they receive from lower-order areas such as V1. The visual system is therefore described as hierarchically organized.

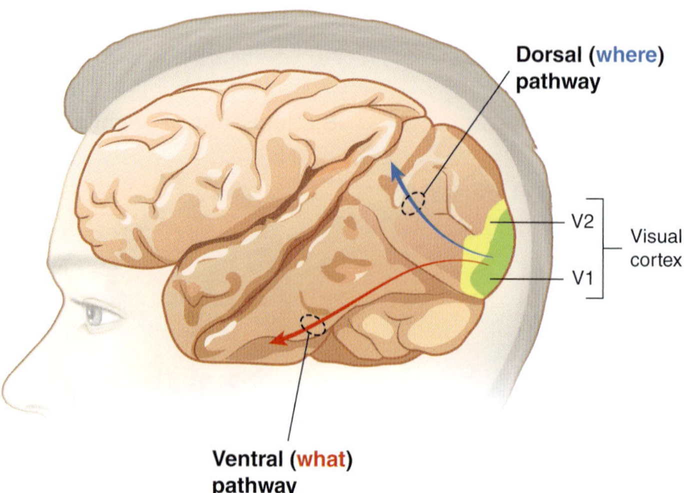

Figure 10.9 **The dorsal and ventral streams of the visual system**. The ventral visual pathway identifies an object, while the dorsal pathway locates its position in space.

In contrast to the ventral stream, the **dorsal stream** identifies object location and is called the **"where" pathway**. Neurons in the *where* pathway respond not to color, shape, or texture but to an object's position in space, direction of motion, speed and other characteristics that help us to locate an object in space (e.g., determining that your pencil is rolling toward the left edge of the table and is about to fall off). But these higher-order neurons of the dorsal stream also depend upon information they receive from lower-order visual processing areas (again, see Figure 10.9). When a soccer player prepares to receive the ball, his ventral stream neurons identify the round object of about 8.5 inches in diameter as the ball, while his dorsal stream neurons estimate the ball's current trajectory through the air. The two visual streams must work together in order for the player to be in the correct field location when the ball lands. (For further examination of the dorsal and ventral streams, see Chapter 3.)

Given that the ventral and dorsal streams use low-level information carried by V1 in order for higher-order areas to recognize the identity and location of objects, an interesting question arises: How do lower-order visual areas determine what information to respond most strongly to at a given moment in time? If a detective is searching for a man wearing a necktie with horizontal stripes, does his visual system become particularly sensitive to lines of horizontal orientation? Do certain brain regions choose the objects that are most important to detect and inform the V1 neurons to process information relevant to those objects?

Evidence suggests that when searching for a goal object, areas of the goal-directed attention network can communicate with higher-order visual areas of the ventral ("what") or dorsal ("where") streams (see Figure 10.10). These neurons, in turn, can bias lower-order visual areas like V2 and V1 to increase their sensitivity to stimuli relevant to current attentional goals (Hopfinger, Buonocore, & Mangun, 2000; Buffalo, Fries, Landman, Liang, & Desimone, 2010). Goal-directed attention can therefore influence stimulus processing in the ventral stream to select certain objects for heightened attention, and the dorsal stream to enhance sensitivity to particular spatial locations.

KEY CONCEPTS

- **Norepinephrine enhances alertness by increasing the sensitivity of sensory neurons. An increase in neuronal responses to sensory stimuli (signal) and reduction in background firing (noise) produces an increase in neuronal signal-to-noise ratios.**

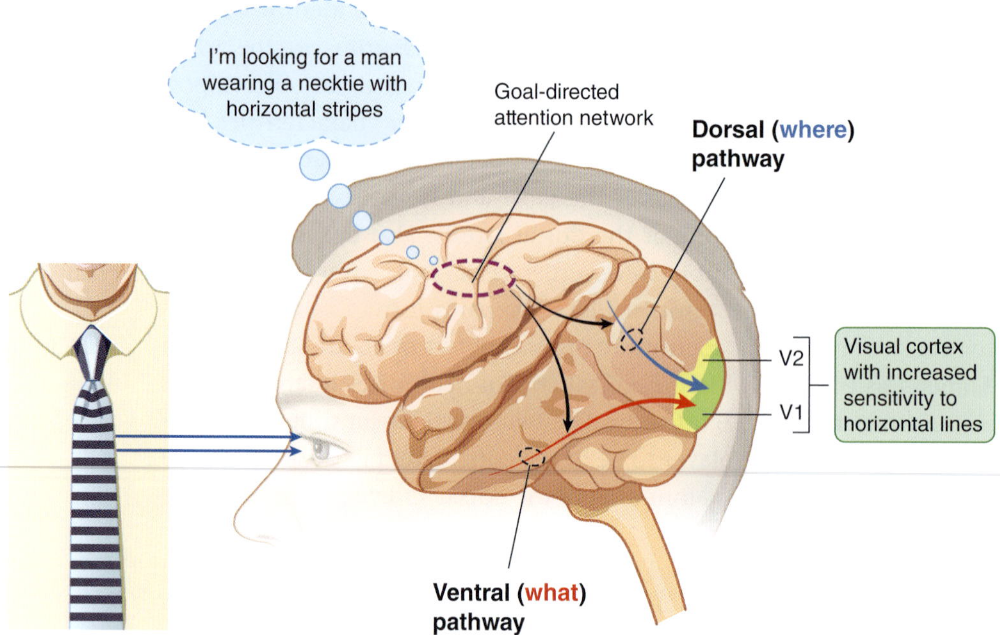

Figure 10.10 **The goal-directed attention network communicates with the visual system to heighten sensitivity to features relevant to the current goal.**

- The goal-directed attention system directs attention toward stimuli that are relevant to current goals. The network of brain areas activated during goal-directed attention includes the frontal eye fields and the intraparietal sulcus.
- Stimulus-driven attention responds to environmental stimuli with salient physical characteristics (like brightness or loudness) or novelty. Brain areas activated during stimulus-driven attention include the ventral frontal cortex and temporoparietal junction.
- During goal-directed visual attention, brain regions sensitive to the goals and needs of the moment communicate with high-order areas of the visual system. This in turn biases the sensitivity of low-order neurons that detect simple sensory features, allowing the sensory apparatus to select the most important stimuli at the moment.

TEST YOURSELF

1. What does it mean to say that norepinephrine increases a neuron's signal-to-noise ratio? For the graph in the bottom left of Figure 10.2, which activity is the "signal" and which is the "noise"? In the bottom right graph, which activity increased and which decreased?

2. What is the difference between stimulus-driven and goal-directed attention? Which is associated with the pop-out effect? Which is referred to as top-down attention?
3. You could find the target in Figure 10.4 more quickly if there were fewer distractor stimuli. Yet fewer distractors would not reduce the amount of time required to find the target in Figure 10.3. Why?
4. Stimulus-driven attention and goal-directed attention are associated with activation of two different attentional networks. What brain areas are associated with each?

10.1.3 Frontal and Parietal Damage Can Lead to Attentional Neglect

In a syndrome called **visuospatial neglect** or **contralateral neglect**, an individual like Stanley in the opening scenario completely ignores objects toward the side of space contralateral to his brain lesion. With a lesion on the right side of the brain, the individual may neglect to shave the left side of the face, miss food on the left side of the plate, and so on. Figure 10.11 shows that when patients with a lesion of the right parietal lobe are asked to copy a picture, they may ignore the contralateral half of each picture as if it did not exist.

In addition to neglecting objects contralateral to the lesion, attention may become "stuck" upon objects ipsilateral to (on the same side as) the brain lesion. Once the individual attends to the ipsilateral object, it may be difficult to disengage from that object in order to attend to something else. The patient can sometimes detect contralateral stimuli so long as there are no stimuli in the ipsilateral visual field to compete for attention. But as soon as an ipsilateral stimulus is presented, the subject becomes unaware of the contralateral stimulus. The results show that contralateral neglect is not sensory in nature (since it is *possible* for the patient to perceive contralateral stimuli) but attentional (they ignore those stimuli). The results also suggest the intriguing possibility that attentional circuits in the left and right sides of the brain may compete with one another.

It may not be surprising that damage to the frontal or parietal lobes often causes attentional neglect (Toba et al., 2018), for both goal-directed and stimulus-driven attention depend upon activity in these lobes. However, these patients most frequently show damage to brain regions associated with the stimulus-driven attention network such as the temporoparietal junction. Additional evidence that the impairment is principally one of stimulus-driven attention comes from the fact that patients frequently fail to detect salient objects that would "pop out" for a control subject.

Figure 10.11 **Drawings by individuals with visuospatial neglect**. The drawings of patients with damage to the right hemisphere often demonstrate a failure to attend to stimuli in the left visual field.

Yet when instructed to look for a particular object in the impaired field of vision (i.e., to use goal-directed attention) they are often able to do so. Taken together, these lines of data suggest that contralateral neglect may reflect a disruption of stimulus-driven rather than goal-directed attention (Corbetta & Shulman, 2002).

10.1.4 Frontal Lobe Executive Control Is Needed to Inhibit Attention to Distractors

We are often required to focus on something while faced with other sensory events that threaten to distract us. For instance, in the **cocktail party effect**, a person hears their own name spoken by someone in a crowded, noisy room. He is able to ignore the many loud voices surrounding him, in order to focus on the words being spoken about him.

Researchers often employ the **Stroop task** to examine resistance to distraction. In this task, a subject views the names of various colors. In some cases, the color word is printed in an ink of the corresponding color, for example the word "green" is printed in green ink. It is easy for subjects to quickly name the color in this **compatible** condition (see Figure 10.12). However, the task is more difficult when the word and ink color do not correspond, for example when the word "green" is printed in red ink. A subject instructed to name the word in this **incompatible condition** needs to ignore the color of the ink in order to attend to, and correctly name, the word. Subjects respond more slowly and less accurately in this case. In another version of the incompatible condition, the subject must ignore the word and name the color. This condition is particularly difficult because the subject must inhibit the strongly ingrained habit of reading words.

In the incompatible condition of the Stroop task, when subjects need to ignore one stream of information (say ink color) in order to attend to a target (word), fMRI studies consistently show frontal lobe activation in an area called the **anterior cingulate cortex** (see Figure 10.13). This activation is much lower in the compatible condition, when the word and color produce no conflict of attention. The **dorsolateral prefrontal cortex** (**dorsolateral PFC**) is another area activated during attentional conflict.

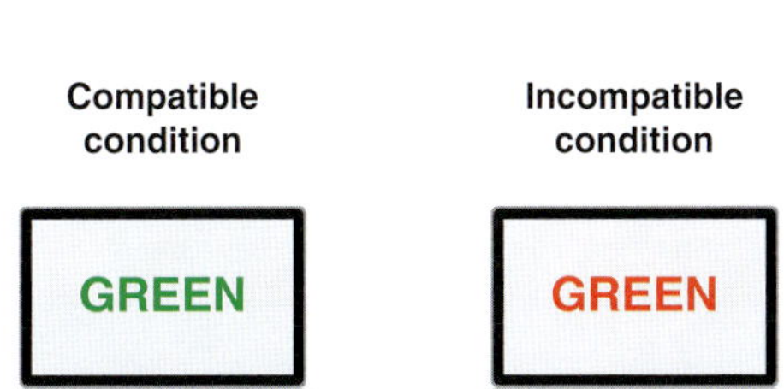

Figure 10.12 **Conditions of the Stroop task**. In the compatible condition, the word corresponds to its ink color. In the incompatible condition, the word is in a conflicting (incompatible) ink color.

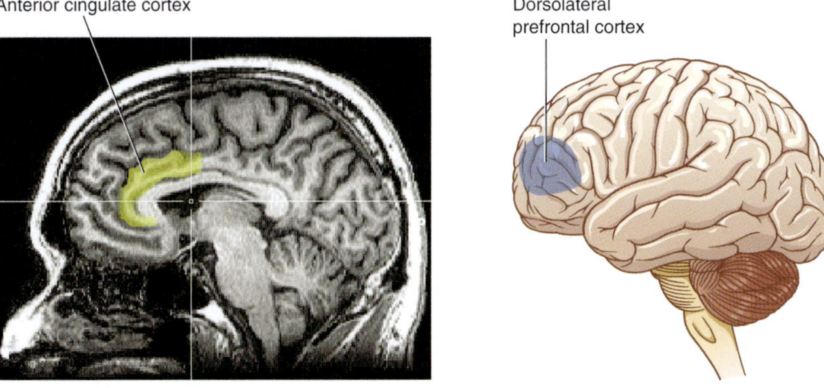

Figure 10.13 **The anterior cingulate cortex and dorsolateral prefrontal cortex**. These brain regions are activated during attentional conflict between two competing sources of information, for instance when a person tries to read the word "green" written in red ink as depicted in the preceding figure. Note that the anterior cingulate in located medially (within the interior of the brain), while the dorsolateral prefrontal cortex is on the surface of the cortex.
(Image on the left by Geoff B. Hall.)

Patients with damage to this area have great difficulty performing incompatible conditions of the Stroop task.

Say a person is viewing words printed in different ink colors, and is asked to name the color of the *ink*. On the current trial the word green appears in red ink (Figure 10.14, left). When viewing the word "green" in red ink, one part of the attention circuit detects the word green and prepares language areas to produce the spoken word "green"; another part of the attention circuit notices the red color of the ink and activates language areas to produce the spoken word "red" (Figure 10.14A). The brain is faced with a conflict: Should it increase attention to the color of the ink or to the meaning of the word? The brain may be faced with another conflict as well. If the subject is already preparing to say the words "red" and "green," one of these verbal responses must be inhibited.

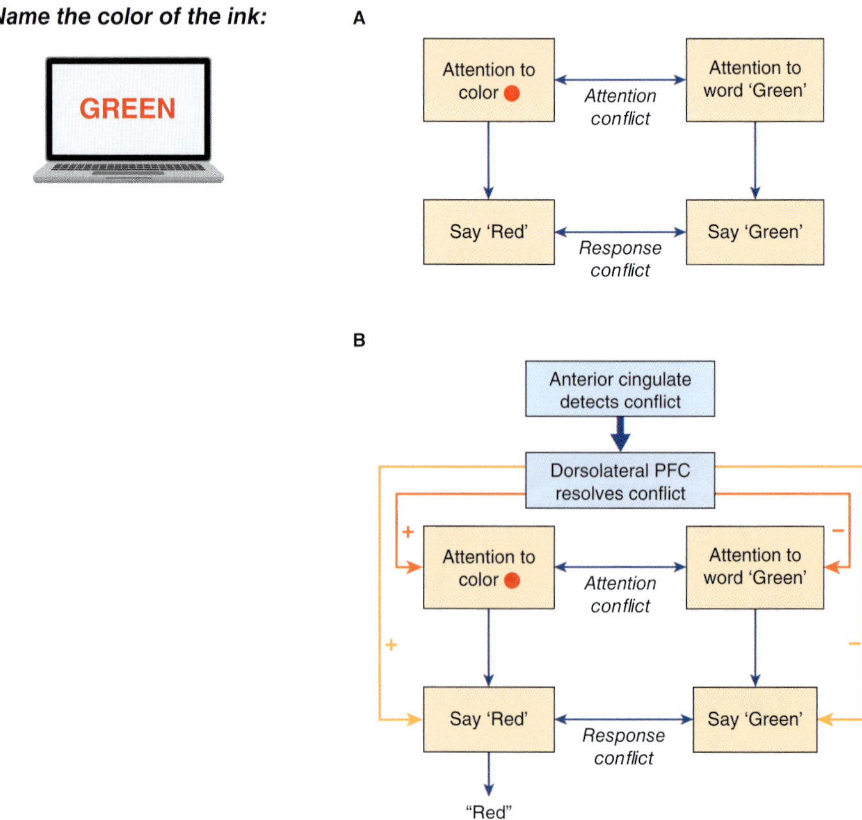

Figure 10.14 Models of attentional and behavioral inhibition. (A) Attention is divided between the color red and the word "green." This gives rise to two conflicting spoken responses. (B) According to a prominent model, the anterior cingulate detects the conflict. The dorsolateral prefrontal cortex (PFC) resolves the conflict by enhancing attention to one of the stimuli (red arrows) or by enhancing preparation of one of the spoken responses (orange arrows).

According to a prominent model depicted in Figure 10.14B, the anterior cingulate detects the conflict between two conflicting sources of information (here, the ink color and word meaning). The anterior cingulate instructs the dorsolateral PFC to resolve the conflict. The dorsolateral PFC responds by increasing attentional resources to either one or the other source of information (green word or red color), but not both (Cohen & Servanschreiber, 1992).

As illustrated in the figure, it is possible that the dorsolateral PFC resolves the conflict by enhancing attentional processing of one of the streams of information, and inhibiting the other. Alternatively, the dorsolateral PFC may resolve the conflict between the behavioral responses, by enhancing preparation of one response or another (Mansouri, Tanaka, & Buckley, 2009). It is also possible that the PFC resolves both kinds of conflict. While the precise roles of the anterior cingulate and dorsolateral PFC are still subject to debate, these areas play an important role in responding to one of multiple competing streams of information.

10.1.5 What Causes the Attentional Problems in Attention Deficit Hyperactivity Disorder?

Attention Deficit Hyperactivity Disorder (ADHD) occurs in about 5 percent of children, with relatively little variation across cultures and geographic regions (Faraone & Larsson, 2019). Symptoms include motor hyperactivity, inattention, and impulsiveness. Some children with ADHD become hyperactive when the environment does not provide much sensory stimulation. In one study, children with ADHD and a group of children without the disorder were videotaped while they waited in a room for 15 minutes. The children with ADHD showed higher levels of behavioral activity than children without ADHD. However, when both groups of children were shown a video during the waiting period, the activity levels of the two groups were more similar (Antrop, Roeyers, Van Oost, & Buysse, 2000). The results suggested that in unstimulating environments children with ADHD may be hyperactive because they require high levels of stimulation, and their own behavioral activity generates additional stimulation.

Remarkably, *attentional impairments in children with ADHD are greatest when they are engaged in attention tasks that are easiest.* When engaged in a difficult attention task involving, for instance, identification of a visual target stimulus surrounded by other similar stimuli as well as salient distractors, the children with ADHD were able to filter out the distractors and identify the target as well as children without ADHD (Friedman-Hill et al., 2010). However, when the task involved an easy discrimination, the children with ADHD were more likely than other children to become distracted. The results suggested that ADHD does not impair the capacity to filter out distracting stimuli, but under easy task conditions those with ADHD fail to engage their filtering mechanisms.

Compared to controls, children with ADHD also have trouble remaining engaged in tasks that do not lead to immediate rewards, but have no difficulty remaining engaged in tasks, such as video games, that provide a constant flow of reward. (In other words, they have no difficulty attending to activities that are fun!) According to some theories, ADHD involves an abnormality in dopamine reinforcement circuits (Chapter 11), leading to diminished motivation in the absence of immediate reinforcement (Sagvolden, Johansen, Aase, & Russell, 2005). The practical difficulty for those with ADHD is that important activities, such as attending class, often involve delayed reinforcement such as grades received at the end of a semester. A diminished effectiveness of delayed reinforcement makes it difficult to engage in behaviors that may be important but not intrinsically rewarding.

Consistent with a dopamine abnormality in ADHD, the symptoms can often be reduced by stimulants such as methylphenidate, which increase synaptic dopamine levels. Some studies have reported an association between ADHD and a form (allele) of a gene that codes for the dopamine D4 receptor, leading to a form of the receptor that is relatively insensitive to dopamine. This could explain the therapeutic efficacy of drugs that elevate dopamine levels. However, not all studies have reported a link between ADHD and the gene for a subsensitive dopamine receptor. Research suggests that any single genetic abnormality is unlikely to account for a large component of ADHD symptoms (Sagvolden et al., 2005; Faraone & Larsson, 2019).

10.1.6 Can Attentional Ability Be Improved with Neuroscience-Based Training?

If you wanted to help someone improve attentional focus, you might reward them when they are focusing well, and punish them (gently) when their attention begins to wane. A recent study used brain imaging during an attention task to identify when subjects' attention lapsed. Experimenters then gave subjects immediate feedback to help them stay focused (deBettencourt, Cohen, Lee, Norman, & Turk-Browne, 2015).

Subjects viewed images containing a merged combination of faces and scenes. During a block of trials, subjects were instructed to attend to either the face or the scene, to ignore the other, and to answer a question about the attended feature. For instance, when the instructed category was scenes, the subject would have to ignore the face (and other potential distractors) and press a button if the image was of an indoor rather than an outdoor scene. In another condition, the subject was required to ignore the scene stimuli and make a discrimination regarding the face component of the image.

The experimenters used fMRI to reveal areas of the brain where activation differed when the subject was instructed to attend to the faces versus the scenes. Experimenters could tell which of these kinds of stimuli the subjects were attending by examining patterns of activity within the attention-related areas of the frontal and parietal lobes described earlier. If a subject was instructed to attend to scenes on the screen for a particular group of trials, but at some point he accidentally shifted attention to something else (the face on the screen, or something else, like the TV series he is planning to watch this weekend), the experimenter could detect this because the distraction would disrupt the subject's pattern of brain activity associated with attention to the scene.

Whenever the subject's brain activity indicated poor attention to the instructed category, the experimenter changed the stimulus for the next trial to *reduce* the task-relevant (in this case, "scene") information in the display. So, the subject who failed to focus on the scene information on a given trial would see even less of that information in the display of the next trial. In effect, he was punished for his poor attention by a change in the stimulus that made it even more difficult on the next trial (see Figure 10.15).

On the other hand, when the brain scan revealed that the subject was attending to the correct dimension, the stimulus was changed on the next

Figure 10.15 Measuring attention and punishing inattention. The subject is instructed to focus upon the scene rather than the facial features of the image, and to press a button if the image depicts an indoor scene (left panel). If he becomes distracted (right panel), the experimenter detects a change in his pattern of brain activity and punishes him on the next trial by reducing the relevant scene information in the image, making the scene detection task more difficult.

(Adapted from Awh & Vogel, 2015, fig.1,)

trial to contain *more* task-relevant information. So, if the subject attended well to the instructed stimuli, the task became easier. In this way, the subject received clear feedback when his attention to the instructed features was strong or weak.

As a result of the feedback, subjects became better focused on the relevant stimulus dimension, as indicated both by patterns of brain activity and by correctly answering questions about the images. These results suggest that an individual's attentional failures are not a fixed property of their brain and cognitive ability. Attention can be trained. It is possible that, in the future, this kind of training may help individuals with ADHD and other problems of attention. In addition, training of this kind may be useful for individuals with jobs, such as baggage screeners, that demand long periods of sustained attention.

KEY CONCEPTS

- **Damage to frontal and/or parietal lobes on one side of the brain can produce contralateral neglect, a failure to attend to objects in the opposite side of space.**
- **The anterior cingulate and dorsolateral prefrontal cortex are important in choosing between more than one stream of information to attend to and/or respond to behaviorally.**
- **An individual with Attention Deficit Disorder typically possesses normal ability to selectively attend to stimuli but failure to engage these processes under conditions including low sensory stimulation, delayed reward, or easy task demands.**
- **New methods of training attention provide feedback to the individual regarding attentional lapses on the basis of changes in patterns of attention-related brain activity.**

TEST YOURSELF

1. **What are symptoms of attentional neglect? Give several real-life examples. What areas of the brain are most likely damaged in a patient with attention neglect for the left side of space?**
2. **What are some examples of situations in which a child with ADHD is likely to show normal attention?**

10.2 WORKING MEMORY

Earlier we considered a crowded party, where you were looking for someone you know. Your goal-directed attention systems enable you to locate an appropriate "target" object, your friend Bob. But when Bob leaves the room, and he's no longer an object of your *attention*, you may still keep Bob's face in mind, that is, in "working memory." Working memory allows us to maintain a mental representation of information about an object after it is no longer present. How does the brain represent an object that is not physically present?

10.2.1 How Much Information Can You Hold in Working Memory?

A famous paper by the cognitive psychologist George Miller in 1956 discussed evidence that the average person can hold "seven, plus or minus two" items in working memory at a time (Miller, 1956). You might hold in mind a combination of seven numerical digits, street names, ice cream flavors, etc. According to Miller, if a person tries to keep in mind another item beyond seven or so, one item currently in memory will have to be lost.

But if you are thinking of an ice cream made of chocolate with nuts, does that count as one item ("chocolate-with-nuts") or two ("chocolate" + "nuts")? What counts as a single remembered *item*? If you look at a chess board and close your eyes, you may remember the position of five or six chess pieces on the board. But if you become an experienced chess player, the relative positions of the rook and the queen become combined or **chunked** into a form that you easily hold in working memory as if it were one perceptual item. In the same way, you (as an ice cream expert) may combine chocolate and nuts together and remember "chocolate with nuts" as a single ice cream item. It is difficult to know how many "items" a person can hold in working memory unless we know when the person is chunking items together.

10.2.2 An Influential Model Described Three Key Components of Working Memory

In the 1970s, British psychologists Alan Baddeley and Graham Hitch proposed that working memory is divided into three key components (Figure 10.16). One component is for holding visual and spatial information. For instance, when you saw your friend Bob at the party, you may have kept in mind both the appearance of his face (visual stimuli) and also the location of the kitchen within the house (spatial information). According to Baddeley and Hitch, this visual and spatial information is held in working memory's "visuospatial sketch pad." Chess players presumably use the visuospatial sketch pad to keep chess positions in mind.

A second component of working memory is dedicated to verbal information such as phrases, words, and even the sounds of letters. At the party, you meet a woman named "Sarah," and you repeat her name to

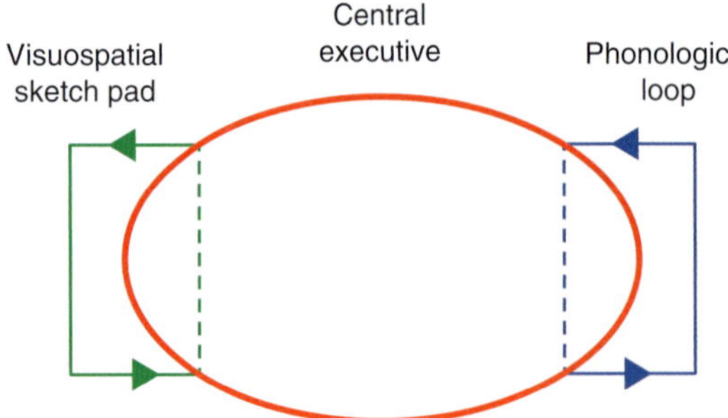

Figure 10.16 The Baddeley and Hitch three-component model of working memory. The visuospatial sketch pad temporarily stores visual and spatial information, the phonological loop stores speech-related information, and a central executive allocates cognitive resources between the two loops.

yourself several times in your head. This is called **rehearsal**. You ask her phone number, and she says 214–653-434X (last digit deleted for Sarah's privacy). You rehearse the number several times, keeping it in working memory until you find a pencil. You hold both her name and the digits of her phone number in working memory's "phonological loop." (The term phonological refers to the sound of a word.) When you keep a list of words in mind you use this phonological loop as well.

An important third component of the Baddeley and Hitch model of working memory is called the "central executive." Suppose you are trying to keep both Sarah's name and her phone number in working memory, and fear that by trying to remember both, you may forget one or the other or both. Maybe you should devote more processing resources to her name, even if you forget the number. At least then you could say, "Sarah, could you tell me your number again?" The central executive decides how to allocate working memory resources between various streams of information that you might want to keep in mind at the moment.

We begin our examination of the neural bases of working memory by asking perhaps the most fundamental question about it. How can the brain keep in mind information that is no longer present to the senses? Some of the most revealing data relevant to this question come from studies in monkeys that are shown a visual stimulus and are then required to hold it in working memory.

10.2.3 Neurons Become Active as Monkeys Hold Information in Working Memory

A monkey is seated in a chair and staring at a screen while the experimenter records its eye movements. A stimulus appears at the center of the screen. The trial has started. The monkey fixates its gaze on this central point. It has learned that it needs to do so in order to advance to the next stage of the task. Soon, another small shape, the *cue*, appears somewhere on the screen. It sometimes appears at the top of the screen, sometimes at the bottom, left, or right (Figure 10.17A). It quickly disappears.

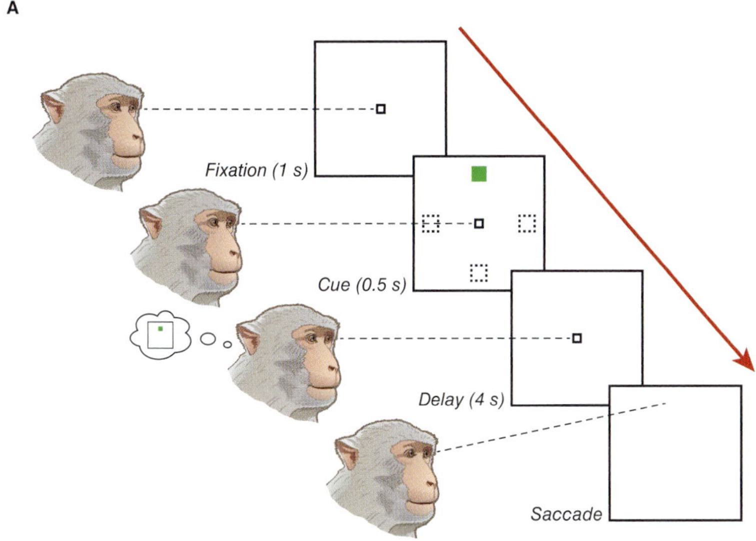

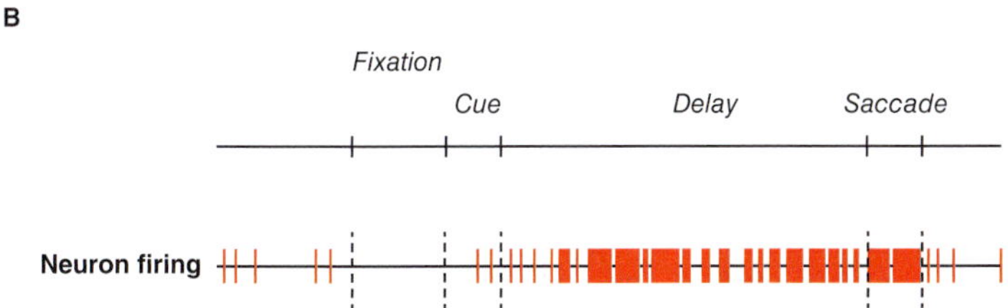

Figure 10.17 Neuronal activation during a memory delay period. (A) A monkey fixates its gaze upon a small centrally located square (Fixation). While still fixated at the center, a cue appears (green square; Cue). Then, during a delay period, the monkey maintains its fixation upon the central square (Delay). When the central square disappears, the monkey moves its eyes to the area where it remembers that the cue appeared (Saccade). (B) The four phases of the trial are depicted from left to right. The vertical marks represent the action potentials from a neuron in the prefrontal cortex that fires at a high rate during the delay period, as the monkey is required to keep the cue location in working memory.
(B, adapted from Funahashi, Bruce, & Goldman-Rakic, 1989, fig. 1.)

In order to earn a squirt of juice reward, the monkey must remember where the cue appeared. After a **delay period** of several seconds, the central stimulus appears again, signaling that the animal can now demonstrate that it remembers where the cue appeared by making a visual saccade to that remembered location. If the monkey moves its eyes to the location where the cue had appeared earlier, it receives the reward.

In addition to eye movements, the investigators record the firing of individual neurons during the task. In a number of brain regions, neurons show elevated firing rates while the animal holds information about the cue location in working memory (Fuster & Alexander, 1971; Funahashi, Bruce, & Goldman-Rakic, 1989). As shown in Figure 10.17B, a PFC neuron fires very little before the trial begins, while the animal gazes at the central fixation point, or when the cue appears on the screen. However, during the delay period while the animal is required to hold the cue location in working memory, the neuron fires at a very high rate. This rapid firing continues as the animal demonstrates its memory of the cue location with a saccade at the end of the trial. After the eye movement has been executed and the animal no longer has a reason to keep the cue information in working memory, the rate of neuronal firing slows down again.

Delay-period activity is frequently observed in neurons within the dorsolateral prefrontal cortex (DLPFC) and posterior parietal cortex (Figure 10.18). There are dense connections between these two areas, which are reciprocal (allowing communication in both directions). Recall that attention networks also involved the frontal and parietal lobes. Delay-period activity has also been observed in several other areas of the cortex, thalamus, basal ganglia, and hippocampus. Almost all of the areas showing delay-period neuronal activation have reciprocal connections with the prefrontal cortex. While the animal is holding information in working memory, delay-period neuronal activity may be present in many of these interconnected brain regions interacting with one another.

Suppose the cue appeared at the top of the screen, the animal kept that information in working memory during the delay period, and a set of neurons in the dorsolateral PFC were activated during the delay. On the next trial, the animal may be required to keep in mind a different cue location. Perhaps the next cue appears at the bottom of the screen. During the delay period, will the same neurons become active, or will a different set of dorsolateral PFC neurons fire? Does the delay-period activity of neurons represent *specific* information that is being held in working memory?

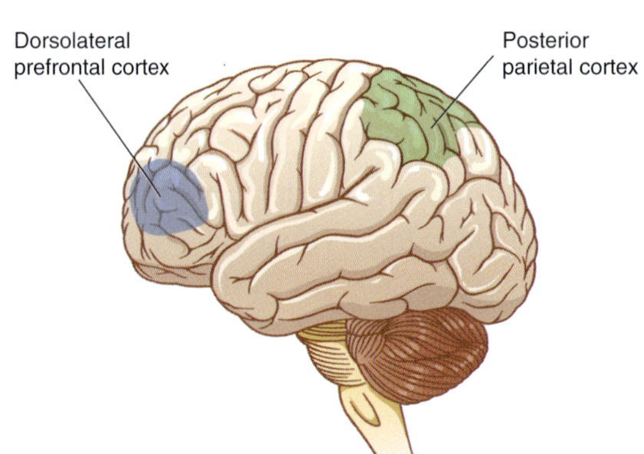

Figure 10.18 Delay-period activity is often observed in neurons of the dorsolateral prefrontal cortex and posterior parietal cortex.

To answer this question, experimenters recorded the activity of individual neurons in the DLPFC while monkeys were required to remember different cue locations (Figure 10.19, top). In Figure 10.19A, each vertical tick mark represents an action potential from an individual neuron.

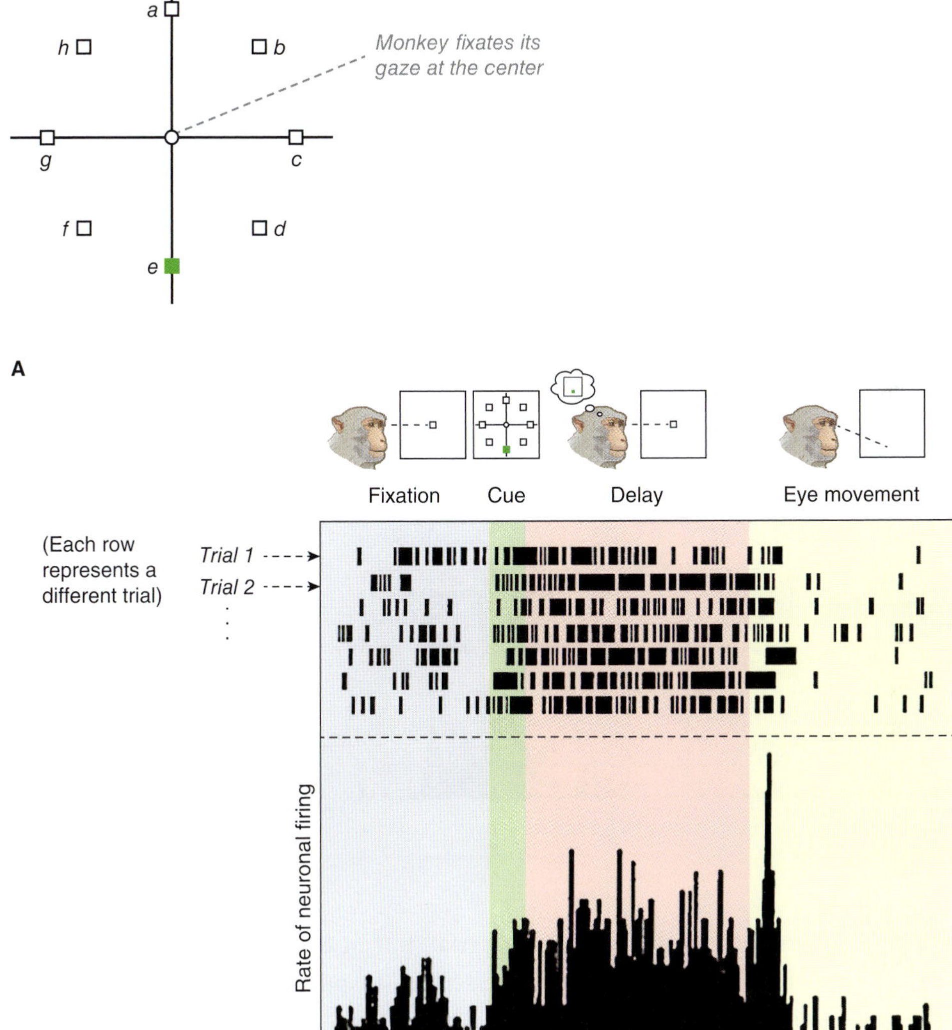

Figure 10.19 Delay-period activity represents memory of particular spatial positions. Top: The cue (e.g., green square) appeared in one of eight different positions (a through h). (A) The activity of a neuron in the dorsolateral prefrontal cortex on trials when the cue was presented in the bottom position (position "e"). (B) The neuron shows activity during the delay-period (pink) only on trials when the cue (green) was presented in the bottom position, but not when the cue was presented in other positions. (Adapted from Funahashi et al., 1989, fig. 3.)

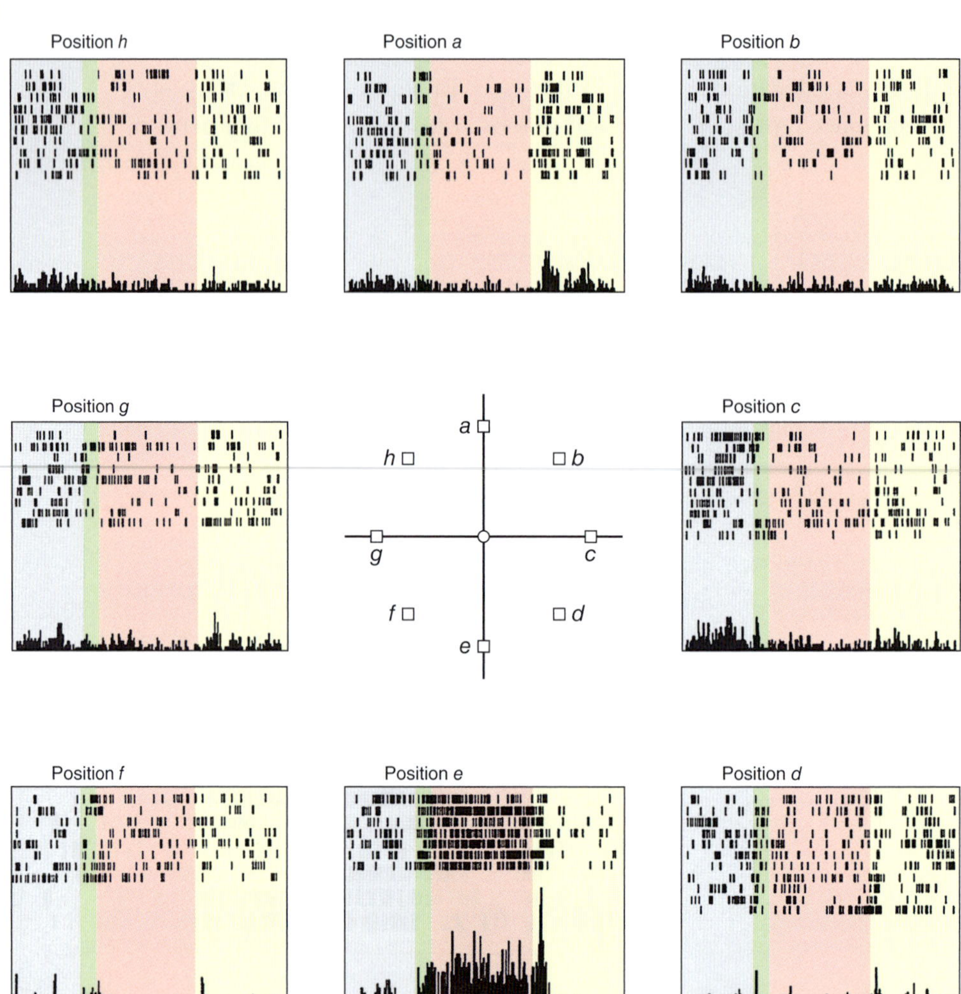

Figure 10.19 (cont.)

Each row represents a different trial, but in each of these trials, the cue appeared at the bottom of the screen (in position "e"). The bar graph in Figure 10.19A below the tick mark rows summarizes these data. It shows that the neuron fired at a high rate throughout the delay period, i.e., while the animal was presumably "remembering" the position of the cue. However, Figure 10.19B shows that the same neuron did not fire strongly when the animal needed to remember other cue locations (Funahashi et al., 1989). Activity of the neuron in this figure was specific for the working memory representation of the bottom location. While not shown in this figure, other neurons became active when the animal held other specific cue locations in working memory.

What is the relevance of the data in Figure 10.19 for our everyday experience of remembering locations? Imagine you went to see your friend in a play and she told you she would be on the far-left side of the stage as the curtain rises. Neurons in your dorsolateral prefrontal cortex are likely to be active while you wait for the play to begin, that is, during the delay period. Your friend also told you that after the intermission she would be on the right side of the stage. As the intermission comes to an end, a group of frontal cortical neurons become active. These neurons are distinct from those active when you expected her to appear to the left of the stage. But if such neurons failed to remain active during the delay period, would you fail to remember the location where your friend was to appear? As we will see in the next section, the answer appears to be "yes."

10.2.4 Why Does Working Memory Sometimes Fail?

It seems likely that neurons with working memory delay-period activity contribute to working memory. But is their activity *necessary* for working memory? Investigators noticed that when animals were engaged in a working memory task, neurons with strong delay-period activity occasionally failed to stay active throughout the entire delay period. On those trials when the neuron failed to remain active, the monkey often made an error. For instance, at the end of the delay period, the animal might saccade to the wrong location.

Figure 10.20 shows an example of how a monkey's working memory errors are related to a neuron's failure to maintain activity during the delay period of the task. The top three rows of the figure show the neuron's high level of firing during the delay period on three different trials of the task. For each trial, the monkey was required to remember a location to the left of the screen, and at the end of each of those three trials the monkey successfully shifted its eyes to the left. The bottom row shows a trial in which high rates of neuronal firing failed to last until the end of the delay period. At the end of that trial, the animal incorrectly shifted its eyes toward the top of the screen, indicating a failure to hold information about the cue location in working memory. When neuronal activation fails to last throughout the delay period, animals often fail to remember the correct location.

Worsening of working memory begins during middle age (Wang et al., 2011). A common complaint is not being able to remember "where I left my keys" or forgetting "a phone number someone just told me." Monkeys are a good model for examining age-related working memory decline. They have a well-developed prefrontal cortex, and they are not subject to

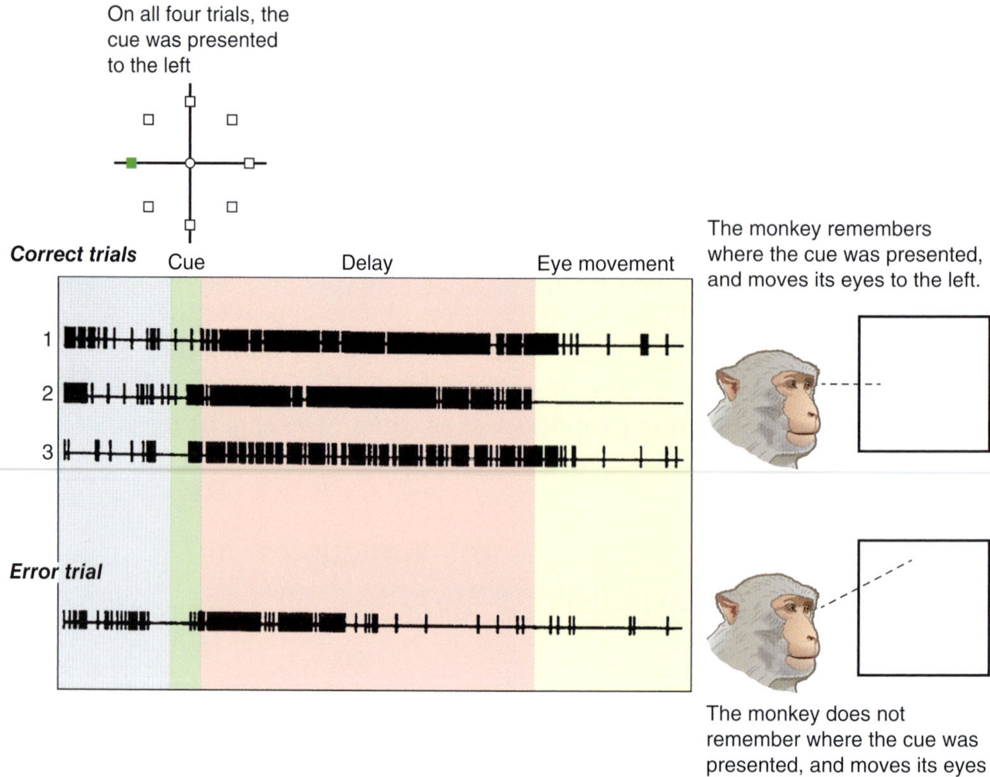

Figure 10.20 When delay-period activation fails, memory fails. The top three lines show trials where the neuron remained strongly active during the delay period, and the monkey remembered the cue location. The bottom row shows a trial where the neuron failed to maintain strong delay-period activity and the animal did not remember the cue location.
(Adapted from Funahashi et al., 1989, fig. 13.)

age-related dementias such as Alzheimer's. Therefore, when one observes a decline in their working memory capacity, it reflects normal aging rather than a disease affecting cognitive processes.

Figure 10.21 shows the activity of neurons in the prefrontal cortex of young, middle aged, and aged monkeys. The left panel shows neural activity in young monkeys. As we saw in the previous figures, some neurons respond to a particular cue location and stay active during the working memory delay period (the blue line in this figure). In aged monkeys, such neurons become only weakly activated in response to the cue, and the ability to maintain activity during the delay period is diminished.

If researchers can discover precisely *why* aged subjects lose the ability to maintain normal delay-period activity in prefrontal neurons, we may get closer to identifying effective treatments for age-related memory loss. A

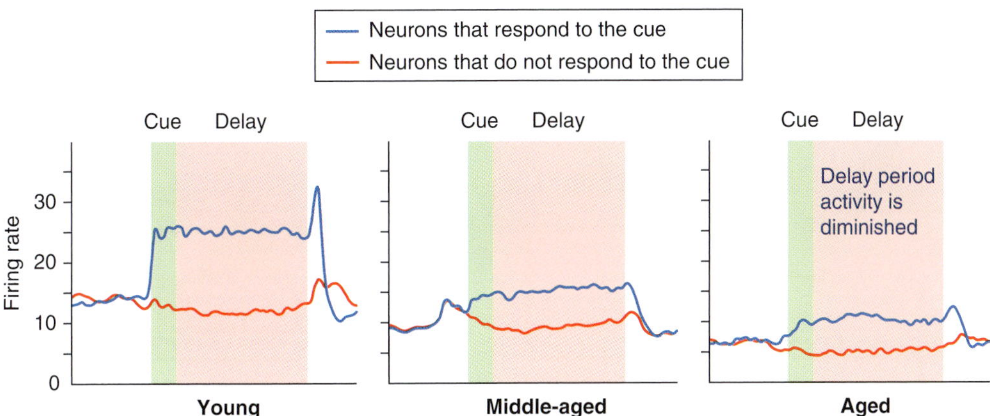

Figure 10.21 The effects of aging on working memory activity in the prefrontal cortex. In young monkeys, some prefrontal neurons are activated by a cue, and remain active during the working memory delay period. With age, such neurons show diminished activity in response to the cue, and they are only weakly activated during the working memory delay period.
(Adapted from Wang et al., 2011, fig. 1F, © 2011, Nature Publishing Group, a division of Macmillan Publishers Limited. All rights reserved.)

first step in understanding how neurons' delay-period activity is lost with age is to ask how the activity is normally maintained.

10.2.5 How Do Neurons Stay Active during the Delay Period of a Working Memory Task?

We saw that some neurons can remain active during the delay period of a working memory task, when the remembered cue location is no longer present on the screen. But how does a neuron stay active during a delay period when the cue is absent? One might answer that "memory" keeps the neuron active. But how? If you hear a man's voice in a cave for several seconds after he has stopped speaking, it may be that the sound waves from his voice are bouncing around the walls of the cave. How do memory-related neurons maintain their activity when the remembered stimulus is no longer present?

One possibility is that interconnected neurons excite one another to produce sustained delay-period activity. The interconnected neurons make up a **recurrent network**, in which each neuron helps to maintain the activity of the others. In the simplest case, imagine that when Neuron 1 fires, it releases excitatory transmitter onto Neuron 2; and when Neuron 2 fires it releases excitatory transmitter onto Neuron 1. This recurrent (turning back on itself) feedback allows neuronal activity to **reverberate** back and forth among the neurons of the network. Each time Neuron 1 fires, Neuron 2 fires; and each time Neuron 2 fires, Neuron 1

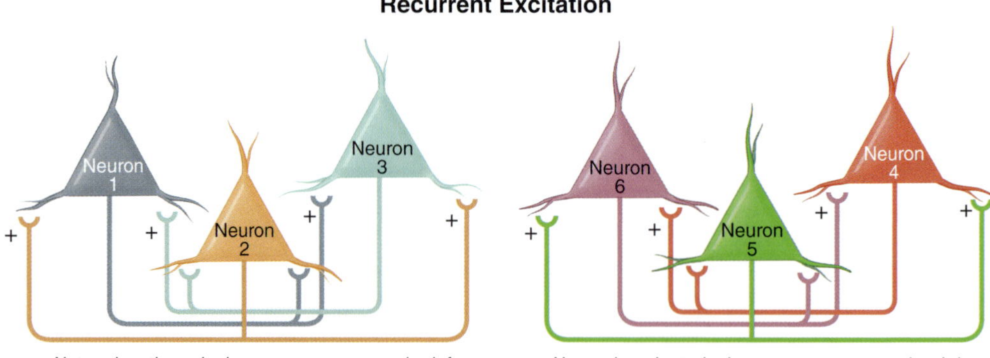

Figure 10.22 Neurons in a recurrent network excite one another. In both the left and right diagrams, three neurons each possess an axon (leaving the bottom center of the triangle-shaped cell body) that sends excitatory input (+) to the dendrites of other neurons in the network.

fires. Rather than a network of two neurons exciting one another, there may be networks comprising hundreds or thousands of neurons with dense excitatory interconnections capable of maintaining reverberatory activity. Figure 10.22 depicts a model in which some neurons become activated by a cue in a particular location, say the left side of the screen, and because the neurons send excitatory input to one another, they can maintain their activity even during a delay when the cue is no longer present.

10.2.6 Do Perception and Working Memory Activate Common Brain Areas?

When you represent your friend's face in working memory, does the brain reactivate some of the same visual areas that were active when you *viewed* her face? In a study by Lepsien and Nobre (2007), subjects saw a photograph of a particular face followed by a particular house (or the opposite order of presentation). The stimuli then disappeared from the screen, and while subjects held these images in working memory, they were instructed to focus upon their memory of the face or house they had just seen. When instructed to focus on their memory of the face, the fusiform gyrus became activated, an area activated when subjects view faces (Lepsien & Nobre, 2007). When they focused on the memory of the house, the parahippocampal gyrus was activated, the same area activated when they viewed a photo of the house (see Figure 10.23). While *remembering* the item, individuals activated the same brain region as when they *viewed* the item earlier.

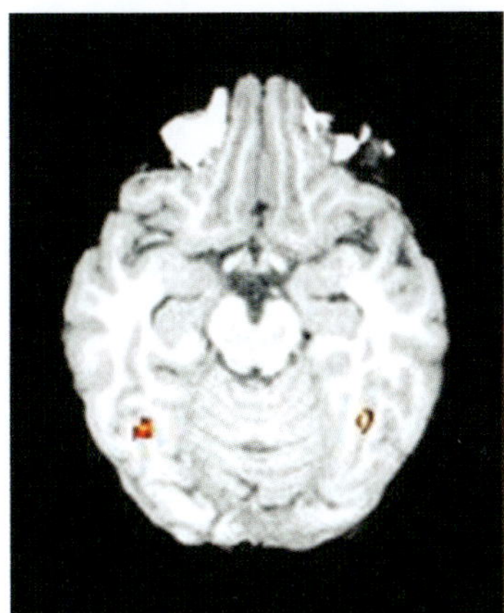

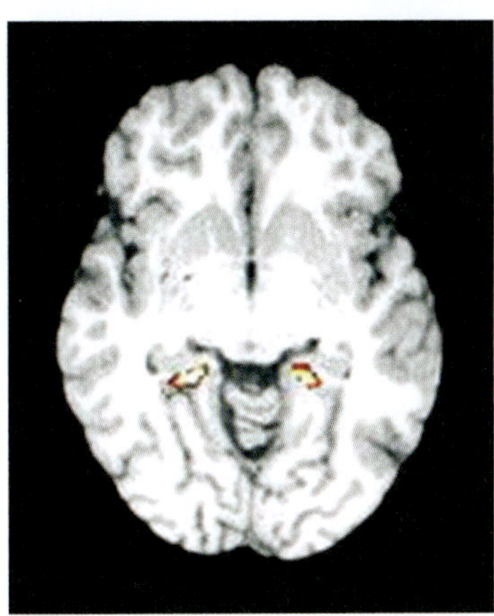

Figure 10.23 Brain areas active during both perception and memory of an item. The fusiform gyrus (left) is activated when subjects either perceive or remember faces. The parahippocampal gyrus (right) is activated when subjects either perceive or remember houses.
(Adapted from Lepsien & Nobre, 2007, fig. 3, © Oxford University Press.)

These results are consistent with a large body of evidence from brain imaging studies that sensory areas activated when an individual perceives a stimulus are reactivated when the same information (visual, auditory, tactile) is maintained in working memory (D'Esposito, 2007). Note, however, that human brain imaging techniques lack the spatial resolution to tell us whether or not the very same *neurons* are reactivated during perception and memory of the same object.

While examining the brain activations associated with working memory of face and house images, Lepsien and Nobre noticed something interesting. When they instructed subjects to switch their focus from their memory of the face to their memory of the house, attention-related brain areas of the frontal and parietal cortex became activated. You may recall that areas around the intraparietal sulcus and dorsal areas of the frontal cortex are activated when an individual focuses on a particular goal object (e.g., when searching for a friend's face). These areas that are active while selecting an external focus of attention are also activated when attention is directed inward to select an object to focus on in working memory.

Two interesting conclusions can be drawn from this study. First, the same brain regions activated when you perceive a stimulus may become activated when you remember it. Second, when we purposely shift attention from one item in working memory to another, we activate brain regions that are also activated when selecting objects of attention in the external environment.

10.2.7 Future Questions about Working Memory

We have seen that working memory is associated with activity in a number of brain regions, including areas of the frontal and parietal lobes, and in sensory areas that are involved in perception of the remembered event. Many investigators believe that the ability to hold information within working memory depends upon sustained activity of neurons when the item represented in working memory is no longer present in the environment. Animal models suggest that the ability to sustain working memory-related neuronal activity may diminish with age.

Many questions remain unanswered. For instance, what causes the age-related decline in the ability of neurons to sustain their activity? If we can identify the causal factors, can we slow or prevent age-related working memory deficits (Brem & Sensi, 2018)? Investigations in humans are currently examining possible benefits of guanfacine, a drug that may help to sustain the activity of working memory-related neurons in the prefrontal cortex (Arnsten & Jin, 2014; Duggins, Stewart, Choo, & Eliasmith, 2017). The drug appears to work by affecting molecular cascades related to the opening and closing of ion channels within the neurons.

Does working memory depend solely on the sustained activity of neurons? Some investigators are examining other possible mechanisms for working memory such as synaptic strengthening (see Chapter 9) that can last for about a minute (LaRocque, Lewis-Peacock, & Postle, 2014) and other molecular mechanisms that can allow neurons to hold information for brief periods of time without requiring them to fire continuously during working memory delay periods (Mongillo, Barak, & Tsodyks, 2008). The research is motivated largely by the hope that a more precise understanding of how neurons maintain information in working memory will lead to better treatments for individuals suffering deficits in working memory.

KEY CONCEPTS

- **Neurons in the prefrontal cortex and other brain regions fire in response to a given location in space, and remain active as the animal maintains that location in working memory.**
- **The set of neurons that stay active as the animal remembers a cue in the upper-left position are often different from the neurons activated while the animal remembers a cue located in another position. Therefore, neurons can show delay-period activity associated with specific working memory information.**

- **Failure to maintain delay-period activity is associated with failure to hold information in working memory. Both delay-period activity and working memory accuracy diminish in aged monkeys.**
- **Recurrent networks of neurons may respond to information such as a cue's position, causing mutual excitation, which allows neuronal activity to persist even when no external stimulus is present.**

TEST YOURSELF

1. **Some neurons remain active during the delay period of a working memory task. Describe the kind of working memory task typically used to examine this delay-period activity.**
2. **Some researchers believe that a neuron's delay-period activity during a working memory task is due to recurrent networks that sustain neuronal activation. What does this mean? Draw a diagram representing reverberation of activity in a recurrent network.**
3. **Do the brain areas involved in perceiving a sensory stimulus become reactivated when the stimulus is held in working memory?**

10.3 The Big Picture

Our state of alertness varies across the day. However, even in a state of high alertness, with norepinephrine neurons of the locus coeruleus firing rapidly, we cannot attend to all objects at once. Selective attention allows us to focus on particular objects. However, when we are seeking a particular object, say a friend in a crowded room, we must hold her face in working memory and look for a match. Assemblies of neurons in several areas of the cortex remain active as we keep our friend's face "in mind."

Some of the same brain regions involved in selective attention to external objects also allow us to focus upon particular items in working memory. For instance, particular prefrontal regions are involved both in attention and in working memory, and both functions may work together to direct our cognitive resources toward particular objects to the exclusion of others.

10.4 Creative Thinking

1. Recall five instances when you were engaged in goal-directed attention today. Similarly, note five instances of stimulus-driven attention. Are there any cases in which your attentional performance contained a mixture of goal-directed and stimulus-driven attention? Over the next

hour, note two more instances of goal-directed and stimulus-driven attention.

2. If you had a great deal of training finding a target of the type shown in Figure 10.4 (i.e., a target that shares features with the distractors), could you get faster at finding it? How about in the case of targets that "pop out," such as those in Figure 10.3? Explain.
3. Recall three instances from today in which you used both working memory and attention to achieve a goal.
4. In a working memory delay task, the monkey must keep its eyes fixated at the center of the screen throughout the delay period. If it moves its eyes away from the fixation point, the trial is cancelled. Why do the experimenters make this part of the task requirements?
5. We discussed enhancement in signal-to-noise ratio with respect to norepinephrine's influence on alertness or sensitivity to detecting a stimulus. Can you also use the concept of signal-to-noise ratio to describe the activity of working memory-related neurons shown in Figure 10.21? With age, does the signal-to-noise ratio of these neurons increase or decrease? Explain.

Key Terms

alertness 400
anterior cingulate cortex 415
bottom-up attention 403
chunked 421
cocktail party effect 414
compatible condition, Stroop 415
contralateral neglect 413
delay period 423
distractor 403
dorsal stream 411
dorsolateral prefrontal cortex (dorsolateral PFC) 415
frontal eye fields 406
goal-directed attention 404
incompatible condition, Stroop 415
intraparietal sulcus 406
networks, brain 406
pop-out effect 403
recurrent network 429
rehearsal 422
reverberation, neuronal activity 429
salient stimuli 403
selective attention 400
serial search 404
signal-to-noise ratio 401
stimulus-driven attention 403
Stroop task 414
temporoparietal junction 406
top-down attention 404
ventral frontal cortex 406
ventral stream 410
visuospatial neglect 413
"what" pathway 410
"where" pathway 411
working memory 400

References

Antrop, I., Roeyers, H., Van Oost, P., & Buysse, A. (2000). Stimulation seeking and hyperactivity in children with ADHD. *Journal of Child Psychology and Psychiatry, 41*(2), 225–231.

Arnsten, A. F. T., & Jin, L. E. (2014). Molecular influences on working memory circuits in dorsolateral prefrontal cortex. In Z. U. Khan & E. C. Muly (Eds.), *Molecular Basis of Memory* (Vol. 122, pp. 211–231). San Diego: Elsevier.

Asplund, C. L., Todd, J. J., Snyder, A. P., & Marois, R. (2010). A central role for the lateral prefrontal cortex in goal-directed and stimulus-driven attention. *Nature Neuroscience, 13*(4), 507–512.

Awh, E., & Vogel, E. (2015). Attention: feedback focuses a wandering mind. *Nature Neuroscience, 18*, 327–328.

Baddeley, A. D., & Hitch, G. J. (Eds.). (1974). *Working Memory* (Vol. 8). New York: Academic Press.

Berridge, C. W., & Arnsten, A. F. T. (2013). Psychostimulants and motivated behavior: arousal and cognition. *Neuroscience & Biobehavioral Reviews, 37*(9A), 1976–1984.

Brem, A. K., & Sensi, S. L. (2018). Towards combinatorial approaches for preserving cognitive fitness in aging. *Trends in Neurosciences, 41*(12), 885–897.

Buffalo, E. A., Fries, P., Landman, R., Liang, H. L., & Desimone, R. (2010). A backward progression of attentional effects in the ventral stream. *Proceedings of the National Academy of Sciences of the United States of America, 107*(1), 361–365.

Cohen, J. D., & Servanschreiber, D. (1992). Context, cortex, and dopamine – a connectionist approach to behavior and biology in schizophrenia. *Psychological Review, 99*(1), 45–77.

Corbetta, M., & Shulman, G. L. (2002). Control of goal-directed and stimulus-driven attention in the brain. *Nature Reviews Neuroscience, 3*(3), 201–215.

deBettencourt, M. T., Cohen, J. D., Lee, R. F., Norman, K. A., & Turk-Browne, N. B. (2015). Closed-loop training of attention with real-time brain imaging. *Nature Neuroscience, 18*(3), 470–475.

D'Esposito, M. (2007).From cognitive to neural models of working memory. *Philosophical Transactions of the Royal Society of London B: Biological Sciences, 362*(1481), 761–772.

Duggins, P., Stewart, T. C., Choo, X., & Eliasmith, C. (2017). The effects of guanfacine and phenylephrine on a spiking neuron model of working memory. *Topics in Cognitive Science, 9*(1), 117–134.

Faraone, S. V., & Larsson, H. (2019). Genetics of attention deficit hyperactivity disorder. *Molecular Psychiatry, 24*(4), 562–575.

Friedman-Hill, S. R., Wagman, M. R., Gex, S. E., Pine, D. S., Leibenluft, E., & Ungerleider, L. G. (2010). What does distractibility in ADHD reveal about mechanisms for top-down attentional control? *Cognition, 115*(1), 93–103.

Funahashi, S., Bruce, C. J., & Goldman-Rakic, P. S. (1989). Mnemonic coding of visual space in the monkey's dorsolateral prefrontal cortex. *Journal of Neurophysiology, 61*(2), 331–349.

Fuster, J. M., & Alexander, G. E. (1971). Neuron activity related to short-term memory. *Science, 173*(3997), 652–654.

Hopfinger, J. B., Buonocore, M. H., & Mangun, G. R. (2000). The neural mechanisms of top-down attentional control. *Nature Neuroscience, 3*(3), 284–291.

LaRocque, J. J., Lewis-Peacock, J. A., & Postle, B. R. (2014). Multiple neural states of representation in short-term memory? It's a matter of attention. *Frontiers in Human Neuroscience, 8*.

Lepsien, J., & Nobre, A. C. (2007). Attentional modulation of object representations in working memory. *Cerebral Cortex, 17*(9), 2072–2083.

Mansouri, F. A., Tanaka, K., & Buckley, M. J. (2009). Conflict-induced behavioural adjustment: a clue to the executive functions of the prefrontal cortex. *Nature Reviews Neuroscience, 10*(2), 141–152.

Miller, G. A. (1956). The magical number seven, plus or minus two: some limits on our capacity for processing information. *Psychological Review, 63*, 81–97.

Mongillo, G., Barak, O., & Tsodyks, M. (2008). Synaptic theory of working memory. *Science, 319*(5869), 1543–1546.

Repovs, G., & Baddeley, A. (2006). The multi-component model of working memory: explorations in experimental cognitive psychology. *Neuroscience, 139*(1), 5–21.

Reynolds, J. H., Pasternak, T., & Desimone, R. (2000). Attention increases sensitivity of V4 neurons. *Neuron, 26*(3), 703–714.

Sagvolden, T., Johansen, E. B., Aase, H., & Russell, V. A. (2005). A dynamic developmental theory of attention-deficit/hyperactivity disorder (ADHD) predominantly hyperactive/impulsive and combined subtypes. *Behavioral and Brain Sciences, 28*(3), 397–419; discussion 419–368.

Sara, S. J. (2009). The locus coeruleus and noradrenergic modulation of cognition. *Nature Reviews Neuroscience, 10*(3), 211–223.

Toba, M. N., Migliaccio, R., Batrancourt, B., Bourlon, C., Duret, C., Pradat-Diehl, P., ... Bartolomeo, P. (2018). Common brain networks for distinct deficits in visual neglect. A combined structural and tractography MRI approach. *Neuropsychologia, 115*, 167–178.

Treisman, A. M., & Gelade, G. (1980). A feature-integration theory of attention. *Cognitive Psychology, 12*(1), 97–136.

Wang, M., Gamo, N. J., Yang, Y., Jin, L. E., Wang, X. J., Laubach, M., ... Arnsten, A. F. T. (2011). Neuronal basis of age-related working memory decline. *Nature, 476*(7359), 210–213.

Waterhouse, B. D., Moises, H. C., & Woodward, D. J. (1998). Phasic activation of the locus coeruleus enhances responses of primary sensory cortical neurons to peripheral receptive field stimulation. *Brain Res, 790*(1–2), 33–44.

11
Reward, Reinforcement, and Addiction

Steven Puetzer / The Image Bank / Getty Images

Consider This ...

The woman, in her early twenties, had suffered from depression for years. Unresponsive to the available drugs, she agreed to undergo brain surgery. The surgeon implanted an electrode deep below her cerebral cortex to activate neurons within her brain. When he stimulated the electrode, the woman smiled and laughed for the first time in a long while. "What are you laughing about?" asked the surgeon. "I don't know," she said, still smiling. The experimenter then allowed her to press a button and deliver electrical stimulation to her own brain. Another button produced no stimulation. "I find this button best, most pleasurable," she said, as she selectively pressed the button that turned on the electrical brain stimulation. She pressed the button again and again.

This controversial surgery was performed in the early 1950s by a psychiatrist named Robert Heath. Based upon the woman's remarks, the electrode appears to have stimulated pleasure-related areas of the brain. The electrode was near the nucleus accumbens, a brain area that will figure importantly in the rest of this chapter.

The fact that this woman pressed the button repeatedly means that the stimulation was **reinforcing**. There is a difference between the terms pleasure and reinforcement. Unlike pleasure, reinforcement refers not to an inner state or feeling, but to the frequent repetition of a behavior (like pressing a button) that is followed by a reinforcer (such as rewarding brain stimulation). We can therefore tell whether or not electrical stimulation of a particular brain region is reinforcing even in a laboratory animal that cannot describe to us its inner experience.

Things that are pleasurable (that possess **hedonic** properties), such as chocolate cake or warm baths, are usually also reinforcing. You can tell that chocolate cake is capable of reinforcing my behavior simply by watching me return frequently to a bakery to purchase it again. The experience of pleasure and the behavioral effect of reinforcement may depend upon similar (perhaps identical) brain circuits. The precise relation between the two is unknown. In this chapter, we use the term "reward" circuits to refer either to those circuits associated with reports of pleasure in humans or to those associated with reinforcement in non-verbal animals.

Let's return now to the scenario between the neurosurgeon and the woman with the electrode in her brain. Did the surgeon electrically stimulate reward circuits of the brain? If so, where are they located? Does your favorite food or music activate these brain circuits? How about money? Do drugs of abuse, like cocaine and heroin, activate some of the same circuits activated by natural rewards? Is that why the drugs are rewarding?

11.1 REWARD-RELATED LEARNING

Imagine that your job is to teach a hungry rat to press a lever. You decide to reinforce its behavior with food. You begin the training session at a time when the rat is hungry in order to enhance food's value. If it presses the lever, it will receive food. But instead, it simply sniffs the floor and the corners of the cage. Sometimes it rears (stands) on its hind legs. Finally, it notices the lever, sniffs it, and goes back to sniffing the floor. How will you get the rat to press the lever?

Using a technique called **shaping by successive approximations**, you can train animals, human children and adults to quickly perform behaviors that would otherwise have been difficult to learn. The trick is to begin by reinforcing a simple version (an "approximation") of the

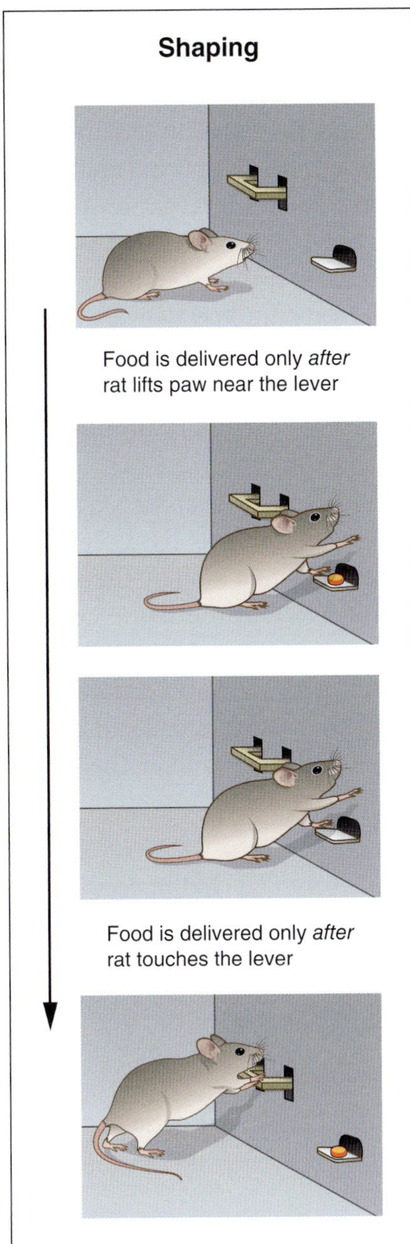

Figure 11.1 Shaping by successive approximations. A target behavior such as lever pressing is gradually molded by rewarding increasingly accurate approximations of the behavior such as standing near the lever, touching the lever, and so on, until the animal earns a reward for performing the complete behavior.

behavior that the subject already performs occasionally. Then, successively reward behaviors that more and more closely resemble the target behavior (Figure 11.1).

To train your rat to press the lever, you break the behavior into smaller, easier components, and begin with the easiest. For instance, whenever it stands near the lever, you might give it a pellet. The rat consumes the pellet, and goes back to that same location. You give it another pellet, and it is now spending nearly all its time standing near the lever. Now, you increase the behavioral requirement and reinforce the rat only when it is near the lever and rearing, with its forepaws (arms) touching the wall near the lever. The rat repeats this behavior frequently. Now, in order to earn a pellet, the rat must touch the lever, even if it doesn't press. Finally, you require the rat to lever press for each pellet. Soon it is lever pressing at a high rate and receiving food reward each time.

In this scenario, food is a **reinforcer** because it increases the rat's likelihood of repeating the behavior that preceded reinforcer delivery. Notice that the reinforcer didn't increase all the rat's behaviors. In fact, the rat ends up sniffing around the cage much less than it did at the start of the session. The food reinforcer only increased the behavior that occurred just before food was delivered – that was the lever press.

The left panel of Figure 11.2 shows the increase in lever pressing when it is followed by a reinforcer. Whether the reinforcer is food presented to a hungry rat or intravenous heroin presented to a human, the subject will **acquire** the behavior that leads to delivery of the reinforcer. The right side of the figure shows that the rate of performing a previously acquired behavior decreases when the reinforcer no longer follows. This reduction in the rate of behavior caused by reward omission is called **extinction**. When a lever press is no longer followed by food, the behavior "extinguishes."

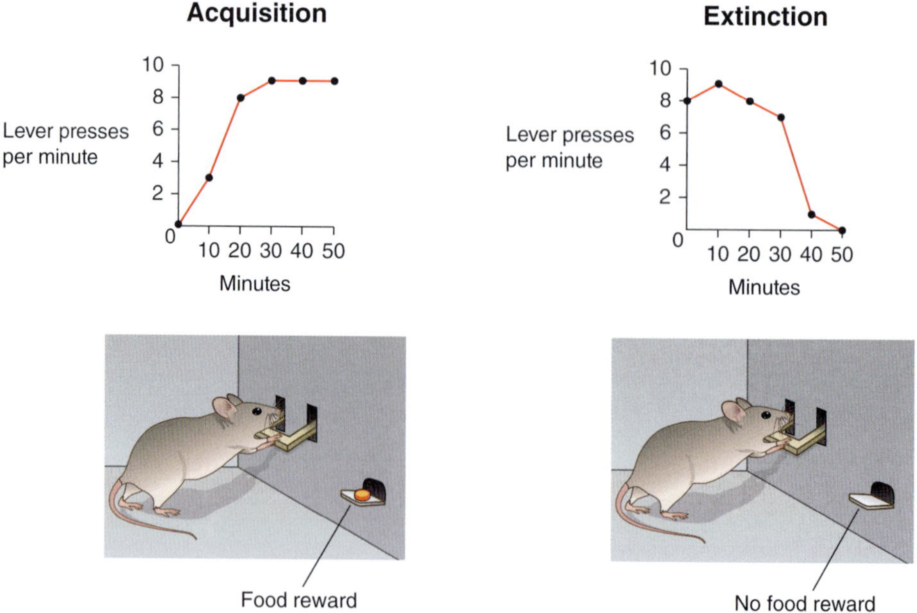

Figure 11.2 **Acquisition and extinction of lever pressing**. During acquisition (left), a behavior followed by a food pellet occurs at an increasing rate. During extinction (right), the reinforcer is omitted, and the rate of behavioral responding decreases.

Food when hungry, water when thirsty, and sex when aroused are all examples of **primary reinforcers**. They reinforce behavior by innate mechanisms. Other things, like money, are reinforcing because they are associated with primary reinforcers (e.g., the things that money can buy). Money is therefore a **conditioned reinforcer**. A drug like heroin is a primary reinforcer because its reinforcing properties do not require an association with another reinforcer. The heroin syringe may also act as a reinforcer, for the addict may acquire behaviors directed toward obtaining syringes. However, it is reinforcing only because of its association with heroin. Therefore, the syringe is a conditioned reinforcer.

In **operant** (also called **instrumental)** learning, an individual learns a relationship between a behavior (pressing a lever, injecting a drug) and a particular outcome (receiving food into the mouth or heroin into the bloodstream). In the case of **positive reinforcement**, the outcome is rewarding and the subject learns to perform a behavior that produces that outcome. In the case of **negative reinforcement**, the subject learns to perform a behavior in order to avoid an unpleasant outcome. Through negative reinforcement, a rat may learn to press a lever to avoid a shock; an addict may take a drug in order to avoid drug withdrawal symptoms such as anxiety. Notice that in these examples, the same behavior (take a drug) may be motivated by positive reinforcement (to experience drug-induced euphoria) or negative reinforcement (to avoid drug withdrawal symptoms).

Through **Pavlovian** (also called **classical**) conditioning, humans and other animals form connections between environmental stimuli (Figure 11.3). A drug user may form a Pavlovian association between

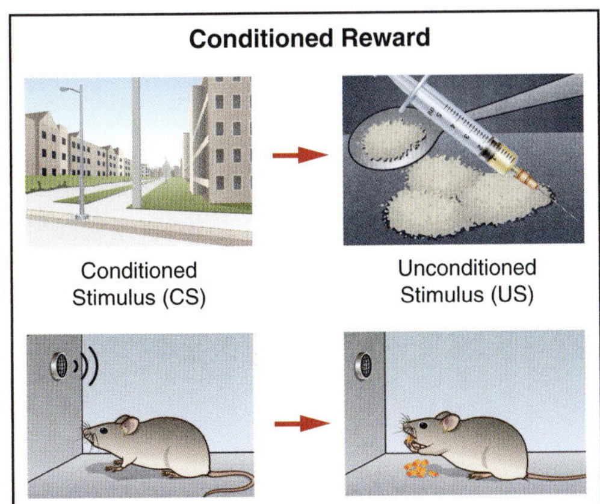

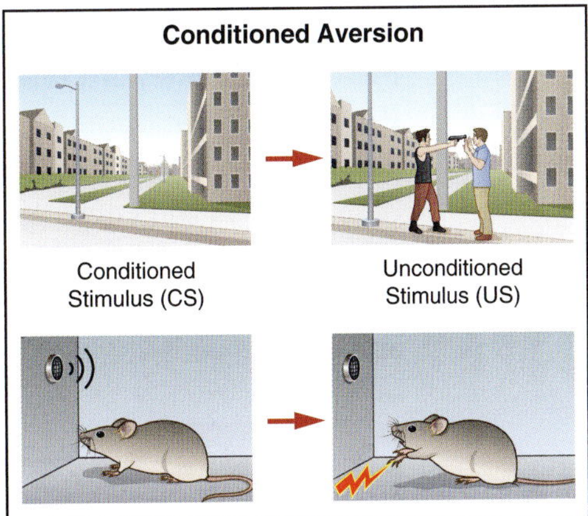

Figure 11.3 Pavlovian conditioning. Through Pavlovian conditioning, a conditioned stimulus or CS can become associated with an outcome (US) that is rewarding (left panel). For instance, a street corner may be associated with heroin, or a tone may be associated with food. Pavlovian conditioning can also lead to an association between a CS and an aversive outcome (US) such as a robbery or physical pain (right panel).

a particular street corner (**conditioned stimulus** or **CS**) and receipt of heroin (**unconditioned stimulus** or **US**). A rat may form an association between a tone (conditioned stimulus) and food (unconditioned stimulus). Notice that the value of the conditioned stimulus depends upon learning or "conditioning" (i.e., upon the association formed between the CS and US). The individual likes spending time on that street corner only because it has become associated with ("conditioned to") receiving heroin. However, the value of the unconditioned stimulus does *not* depend upon learning ("unconditioned" means unlearned). The person did not need to learn anything in order to enjoy heroin.

A subject can learn to associate a stimulus (e.g., a street corner) with a pleasant or an unpleasant (aversive) event (e.g., being physically harmed). An environmental stimulus that predicts the occurrence of a pleasant event is a **conditioned reward stimulus**; one signaling an unpleasant (aversive) event is a **conditioned aversive stimulus**. (Chapter 9 examined the neuroplasticity that occurs when a CS predicts an aversive event.)

Imagine that Tom is addicted to heroin, and goes to a hospital for a period of enforced abstinence. He leaves the hospital a few weeks later, after his withdrawal symptoms have subsided. For several days, he refrains from taking heroin. However, he soon passes the street corner where he used to take the drug, his cravings return, and he relapses. His relapse was caused by conditioned rewards previously associated with heroin because of Pavlovian conditioning. Over the subsequent weeks, through trial and error, he discovers a way of injecting the heroin that is particularly effective in generating a more intense "high." The more intense "high" may reinforce Tom's new drug injection method through operant learning.

In this section, we have emphasized terminology like *reinforcement*, *conditioned rewards*, and *extinction* because experiments on the brain mechanisms of reward often make use of these terms from operant and Pavlovian conditioning. Comfort with these terms makes it easier to understand the experiments we'll talk about later regarding the brain basis of reward and addiction. As we will see, natural and drug rewards activate many of the same reward circuits in the brain. What are the neurochemicals and brain regions that are critical to the reinforcing effects of natural and drug rewards?

KEY CONCEPTS

- **Operant learning involves an association between a behavior and an outcome.**
- **A behavior can be reinforced by a primary reinforcer (such as heroin) or a conditioned reinforcer (such as a syringe) that has been associated with the primary reinforcer.**

- **Subjects decrease their rate of performing a behavior (say, a lever press) when it is no longer followed by a reinforcer.**
- **In Pavlovian conditioning, two environmental stimuli are associated with one another (e.g., a street corner and heroin).**

TEST YOURSELF

1. **Give an example of acquisition and extinction of a reinforced behavior.**
2. **Give an example of both positive and negative reinforcement.**
3. **Come up with two real-life examples of operant conditioning.**
4. **Come up with two real-life examples of Pavlovian conditioning.**

11.2 DOPAMINE AND BRAIN STIMULATION REWARD

We begin our examination of the neurobiology of reward with the earliest discovery of brain reward circuits. In the 1950s, around the time that Robert Heath was delivering reinforcing brain stimulation to the young woman described in the opening of this chapter, investigators were delivering reinforcing brain stimulation to rats.

11.2.1 Electrical Brain Stimulation

Research on the brain's reward circuits began with a pair of Canadian researchers at McGill University, Olds and Milner. James Olds implanted electrodes into the brains of rats. The electrodes, which looked like thin sewing needles, could pass electrical current to the brain. In this way, Olds could activate neurons in particular brain areas and try to figure out how those neurons contribute to behavior. Olds' research advisor, Peter Milner, was interested in a key region within the brain's arousal system, the reticular activating system, and so Olds aimed the electrodes to that part of the rats' brains. While a rat was looking for food in a maze, Olds would deliver stimulation to the reticular activating system to determine whether the rat would suddenly pay more attention to the environment and learn to navigate the maze more quickly. Day after day, Olds stimulated the electrodes in the rats' brains, and tested their behavior in the maze. And then something odd happened.

One of the electrodes wasn't properly implanted, and instead of reaching the reticular activating system, it went to a neighboring brain area. The investigator stimulated the electrode, and noticed that the rat kept returning to the location where it was the last time it had received the brain stimulation. If the rat was in a particular corner of the maze when the brain stimulation was delivered, it would sniff vigorously in that corner, and look around. For the next several minutes, the rat wouldn't stray far from that particular corner. It was no longer interested in finding the exit to the maze where it would receive a food reward. It acted as if the reward was right there, wherever it was standing when the brain stimulation had been applied.

They implanted other rats with electrodes, this time purposely aimed at that same ("wrong") brain area near the reticular activating system, but some distance away from it.

Olds and Milner decided to put a lever in the box, and delivered brain stimulation whenever the rat pressed the lever. Soon, an entire group of rats were pressing levers in order to receive stimulation of the brain (Olds & Milner, 1954). The rats would press a lever, pull a chain, or anything else the experimenters required that they do in order to receive electrical stimulation of this brain area.

This discovery led to headlines in major newspapers about the newly discovered "pleasure centers" of the brain. Whether or not the investigators had stumbled upon the brain's pleasure center, the brain stimulation was certainly capable of reinforcing behavior. But the stimulation was activating many neurons in the brain. Which were responsible for the reinforcement effects?

While rats would press the lever for stimulation to a number of different brain areas, stimulation to certain regions caused the animals to press with particular vigor. They would even forgo food when hungry in favor of the electrical stimulation. These reinforcement "hotspots" were near the **medial forebrain bundle** (**MFB**) (see Figure 11.4). The MFB contains the axons of neurons connecting the midbrain (and brainstem) to various areas of the forebrain. These neurons release many different neurotransmitters. Humans with treatment-resistant depression who have opted for brain stimulation to the MFB report positive effects on mood (Schlaepfer, Bewernick, Kayser, Hurlemann, & Coenen, 2014), although additional studies are needed to determine whether MFB stimulation shows long-term safety and efficacy that would make it a viable treatment option (Coenen et al., 2019).

11.2.2 Anatomy of the Dopamine Pathways

Among the neurons bundled together in the MFB are dopamine neurons. If you point a finger toward the bridge of your nose, follow straight into the brain, and move your finger just a bit to each side, you will find the cell bodies of dopamine neurons in the **ventral tegmental area** (**VTA**). If you move the finger a bit more lateral, you would reach the cell bodies of dopamine neurons in the neighboring **substantia nigra** (**SN**) (Figure 11.5). These two small areas of the **midbrain** contain the large majority of dopamine neurons in the brain of the rat as well as the human.

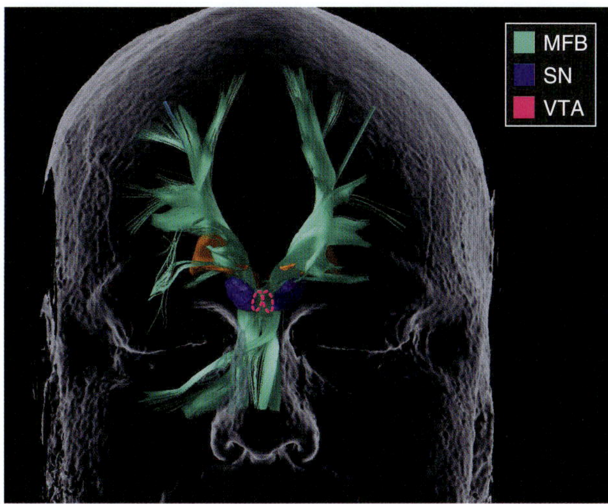

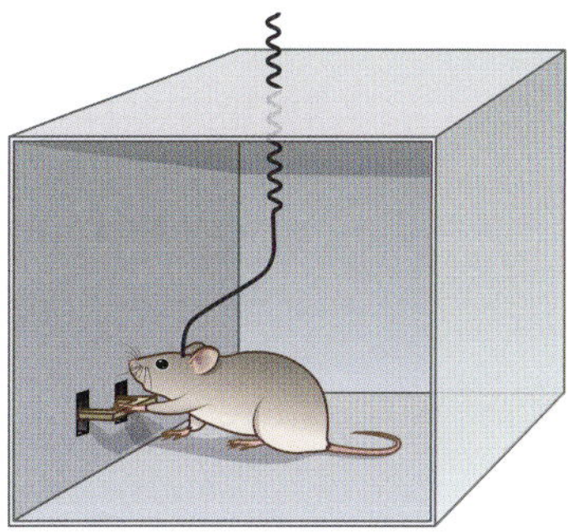

Figure 11.4 The medial forebrain bundle (MFB). Left: The MFB is a bundle of axons that includes dopamine neurons originating in the substantia nigra (SN) and ventral tegmental area (VTA). Stimulation of the MFB improves mood in depressed patients. The pathway shown here in humans is more precisely designated slMFB. Right: Rats will press a lever if each lever press is followed by MFB stimulation. (Image of slMFB courtesy of V. A. Coenen & T. E. Schläpfer, Freiburg University, Germany.)

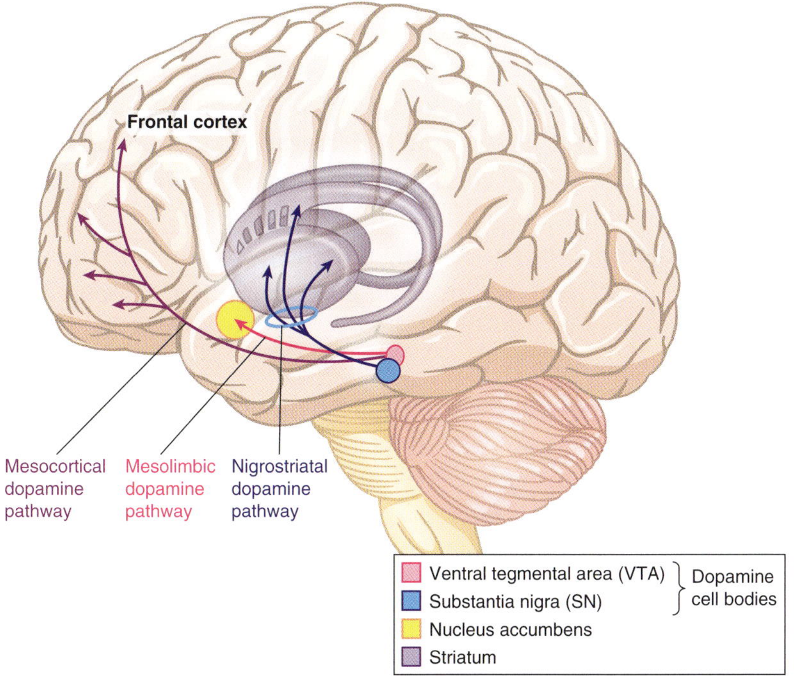

Figure 11.5 Mesolimbic, mesocortical, and nigrostriatal dopamine pathways. Most dopamine neurons originate in two neighboring areas of the midbrain, the VTA and SN. The VTA gives rise to two of the major dopamine pathways, one projecting to the frontal cortex (mesocortical pathway) and the other to the nucleus accumbens (mesolimbic pathway). Dopamine neurons in the SN project to the striatum, giving rise to the nigrostriatal pathway.

The midbrain dopamine neurons project to a number of target brain regions. The three regions receiving the most dopamine input are the **nucleus accumbens**, **prefrontal cortex**, and **striatum**. Many of the dopamine neurons in the VTA send axons to the nucleus accumbens, giving rise to the **mesolimbic dopamine pathway**. (*Meso-* refers to *mesencephalon*, meaning the midbrain.) Some VTA dopamine neurons project to the prefrontal cortex, making up the **mesocortical dopamine pathway**. SN dopamine neurons release their dopamine in the striatum. This **nigrostriatal dopamine pathway** degenerates in Parkinson's patients, who have great difficulty initiating movements as well as other motor abnormalities (Chapter 13). Normal activity of the nigrostriatal dopamine pathway is therefore critical in order to move normally.

11.2.3 Is Dopamine Responsible for the Reinforcing Effects of Brain Stimulation Reward?

Electrical stimulation of the MFB causes activation of all three major dopamine projections, as well as the release of other neurotransmitters in other brain regions. Which neurons were responsible for the reinforcing effects of the electrical brain stimulation?

Some researchers hypothesized that the rats were lever pressing for MFB stimulation in order to activate their dopamine neurons and increase the amount of dopamine released into the brain. To test this possibility, they trained rats to lever press for MFB electrical stimulation, and then asked whether the rats would continue to lever press for the stimulation while under the influence of a drug that blocked dopamine receptors (a **dopamine antagonist** drug). The drug prevented dopamine from binding to dopamine receptors and exerting effects on other neurons. Rats under the influence of the dopamine antagonist drastically reduced their rate of lever pressing (Fouriezos, Hansson, & Wise, 1978). Did the dopamine antagonist reduce rates of lever pressing because it reduced the reinforcing effects of the electrical stimulation?

Perhaps. However, reductions in nigrostriatal dopamine give rise to the motor impairments of Parkinson's disease. Did the rats press less because the dopamine antagonist drug reduced the rewarding effects of the electrical stimulation, or because it interfered with their ability to make the body movements necessary to press the lever at a normal rate?

A clue came from the animals' *pattern* of lever pressing. Rats under the influence of a dopamine antagonist made their first several lever presses quickly. (Recall that the rats had already learned to lever press for MFB stimulation.) During the early minutes of the session, the rats did not appear to have any difficulty pressing the lever, even though peak levels

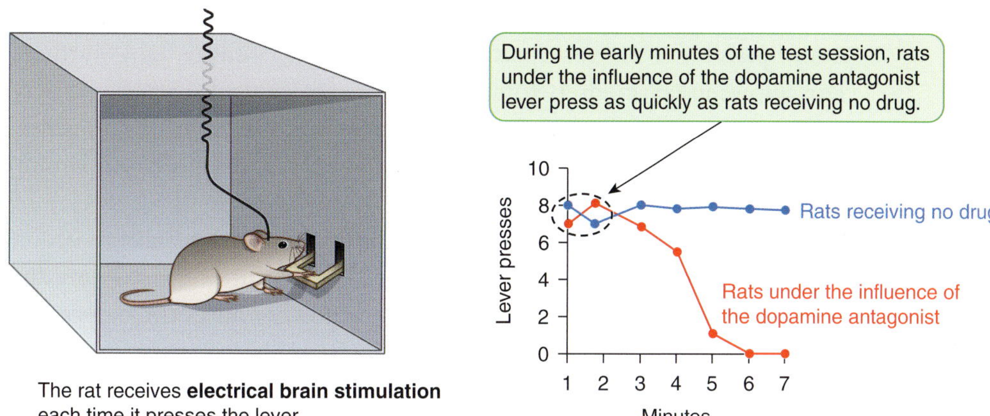

Figure 11.6 A dopamine antagonist produces an extinction-like pattern of lever pressing. Drug-free rats are trained to lever press for electrical brain stimulation reward. On the next day, rats under the influence of the dopamine antagonist drug begin to lever press at a normal rate, but soon give up, as if the drug had blocked the reward value of the electrical brain stimulation.

of the drug had already fully reached the brain. They did not start to press more slowly until later in the session (Figure 11.6). Their pattern of lever pressing resembled that of rats during extinction. They began pressing quickly, and then appeared to give up, as if the dopamine antagonist were blocking the reward value of the electrical brain stimulation.

Many of these studies were carried out by Roy Wise at Concordia University in Montreal from the late 1970s to the mid-1980s. Wise and his colleagues argued that the dopamine antagonist-treated rats' rapid lever presses early in the session show that they are capable of lever pressing at a high rate (Wise, 1982). According to Wise, the rats pressed more slowly later in the session only after they discovered that the brain stimulation was not rewarding under the influence of the drug.

Drugs that block norepinephrine also reduced the rats' rates of lever pressing, but only the dopamine antagonists produce the extinction-like pattern of responding characteristic of subjects that are no longer experiencing reward. Additional experiments showed that dopamine antagonists block the reinforcing effects of electrical brain stimulation even when the dopamine receptor blocking drugs are delivered directly to the nucleus accumbens (Duvauchelle, Levitin, MacConell, Lee, & Ettenberg, 1992). (Figure 11.5 shows the location of the nucleus accumbens).

Since stimulation of the MFB is reinforcing, and this is due to dopamine's actions within the nucleus accumbens, the following question arose: Will a rat press a lever solely to receive activation of the VTA dopamine neurons that project to the nucleus accumbens? Is it possible to deliver stimulation to a behaving animal that is so precise that it only stimulates those specific neurons? The technique of **optogenetics** makes it now possible to activate neurons in the brain by shining light on them. This allows experimenters to exert very precise control over the activity of neurons. Investigators have used the powerful technique of optogenetics to ask whether brain stimulation that only activates VTA dopamine neurons is reinforcing.

In order for light to activate neurons, animals receive a brain injection of a (harmless) virus that inserts a particular gene into neurons near the site of injection (Figure 11.7, first panel). That gene causes the neurons to synthesize many copies of a protein called **channelrhodopsin**, which becomes incorporated into the neuronal membrane. The channelrhodopsin protein forms a light-sensitive ion channel (Figure 11.7, second panel). Recall from Chapter 2 that ion channels are like tiny, gated tunnels in the neuronal membrane. They allow ions to pass from the outside to the inside of the neuron (or vice versa). You can imagine channelrhodopsin producing many tiny, gated tunnels all along the wall of the neuron, and each gate of the channel opens in response to light. When experimenters shine blue light onto the neurons, the channels open, sodium ions enter, and the neuron is activated.

Light-sensitive channels are incorporated into the entire membrane of the neuron. So, light delivered to the cell bodies of a neuron with light-sensitive channels will activate the neuron; but light delivered to the axon terminals will activate the neuron as well. In some studies, additional genetic manipulations allow the experimenter to introduce the light-sensitive protein not only to specific brain areas but also to specific *types* of neurons within that area, e.g., specifically to dopamine neurons.

In rats with these light-sensitive ion channels only in the dopamine neurons of the VTA, the experimenters positioned the light so it would shine into the nucleus accumbens and activate the axon terminals of the dopamine neurons. Rats will eagerly perform a lever press or other behavior in order to specifically activate their mesolimbic dopamine neurons (Steinberg et al., 2014; Wise & McDevitt, 2018).

As we have seen, early studies showed that animals would continuously perform behaviors that lead to electrical stimulation of certain brain regions. Later studies showed that this stimulation is reinforcing because it activates dopamine neurons. When dopamine receptors are blocked, the stimulation loses its reinforcing potency. Studies using optogenetics show that animals will work to receive stimulation specifically of dopamine neurons that project to the nucleus accumbens. The data suggest that activation of dopamine neurons is reinforcing.

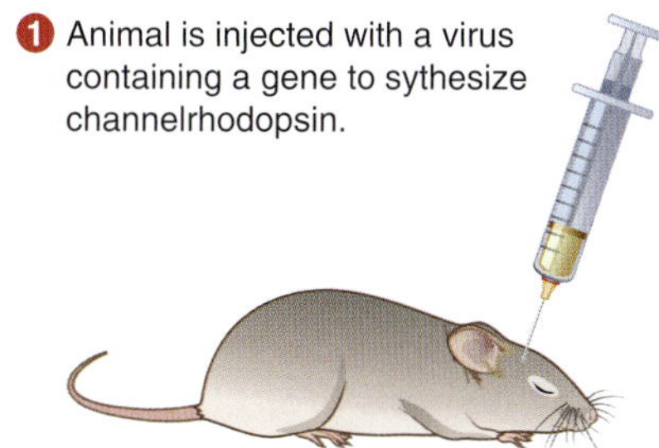

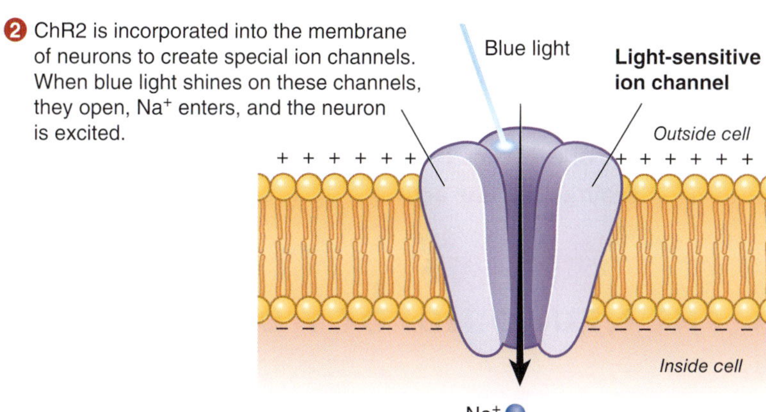

Figure 11.7 **Optogenetic stimulation of dopamine neurons**. Optogenetics allows experimenters to activate particular neurons in the brain by shining light on them. Rats will press a lever to receive light stimulation to dopamine cell bodies in the VTA. Similarly, rats will press the lever to receive light shined on the VTA dopamine terminals in the nucleus accumbens.

(Photo of rat, © John B. Carnett/Contributor/Getty Images.)

KEY CONCEPTS

- **Rats will lever press vigorously to receive electrical stimulation of the MFB.**
- **Dopamine antagonist drugs administered to the nucleus accumbens block the rewarding effect of MFB stimulation.**
- **Optogenetic stimulation of VTA dopamine neurons projecting to the nucleus accumbens is sufficient to reinforce behavior.**

TEST YOURSELF

1. **What are the two major areas of the midbrain containing dopamine neurons? Where do each of these areas release dopamine?**
2. **Describe two lines of evidence that electrical brain stimulation reward depends upon brain dopamine activity.**

11.3 THE NEUROBIOLOGY OF NATURAL REWARD

We have seen that animals will work to receive electrical or optogenetic stimulation of dopamine neurons. These artificial means of activating dopamine neurons are reinforcing. But do natural rewards like tasty food activate dopamine neurons? Is the activation of dopamine neurons what makes food and other natural rewards reinforcing?

11.3.1 Does Dopamine Play a Role in Food Reward?

Dopamine antagonist drugs reduce rats' rates of lever pressing for food. As we saw with brain stimulation, the drugs do not immediately cause lever pressing to slow, but produce an extinction-like pattern where the subjects begin pressing at high rates and then appear to "give up" as if the food has lost its value (Figures 11.2 and 11.6). The results suggest that dopamine is necessary for the reinforcing effects of both brain stimulation and naturally occurring rewards.

However, some research casts doubt on whether all of food's rewarding properties require dopamine activity. For instance, in one experiment rats were in a cage containing a lever they could press for their preferred food. The cage also contained a dish with a less palatable (less tasty) food they could eat "for free" (without having to press the lever). Most rats spent their time pressing for the tasty food, rather than consuming the less palatable pellets in the dish. However, under the influence of a dopamine antagonist drug, rats hardly pressed the lever at all.

This in itself is not surprising, for we know that dopamine antagonists reduce rates of lever pressing. The surprising fact was that the rats spent their time eating the free food instead (Salamone & Correa, 2012). Salamone and colleagues argued that if dopamine activity were necessary for all aspects of food reward, the rats should have consumed less food. The authors concluded that when dopamine activity is reduced, food retains its value; subjects are just less willing to expend energy to *work* for it.

Another experiment raised additional questions about dopamine's role in the hedonic (pleasure) properties of food. Like humans, animals react to hedonic (e.g., sweet) and aversive (e.g., bitter) foods with stereotypical **taste reactivity**, that is, facial expressions to certain tastes. They make one kind of facial expression when they taste foods that they like, and other expressions when they taste foods they dislike. After experimenters deplete nearly all the mesolimbic and nigrostriatal dopamine from a rat's brain, it will continue to show typical "liking" expressions when it consumes sweet foods and liquids (Berridge & Robinson, 1998).

This again suggests that, while dopamine may be necessary for food's reinforcing and/or behavior-energizing effects, it may not be the neurochemical responsible for its pleasurable qualities. Drugs that block opioid receptors within the nucleus accumbens do reduce the taste reactivity associated with normally "liked" foods. On the basis of such data, some investigators believe the hedonic properties of food (how much we *like* it) depend upon opioid activity within the nucleus accumbens, while the motivating effects of food (how much we *want* it) depend upon dopamine activity within the nucleus accumbens (Berridge & Kringelbach, 2013).

When a human subject sees, smells, or tastes highly palatable food, activations are seen in the VTA and SN, areas that contain the midbrain dopamine cell bodies, and also the nucleus accumbens, striatum, and prefrontal cortex, areas where dopamine is released (Small, Jones-Gotman, & Dagher, 2003; Wang et al., 2004; O'Doherty, Buchanan, Seymour, & Dolan, 2006). Pictures of high-calorie food produce stronger activation of the nucleus accumbens in obese compared to non-obese subjects (Stoeckel et al., 2008). Do these brain activations represent the amount that the subject wants and/or likes the food (Wiss, Avena, & Rada, 2018)? These questions remain the topic of investigations.

11.3.2 Dopamine Responses to Primary and Conditioned Food Reward

A major advance in understanding how dopamine neurons respond to reward stimuli came from studies in monkeys that examine changes in the firing of midbrain dopamine neurons at the very instant when the animal receives a reward or a conditioned stimulus predicting reward. Using brain imaging techniques, it is not possible to detect separate brain responses to two events occurring within less than a few seconds of one another, such as a conditioned stimulus followed a few seconds later by an unconditioned stimulus. The **time resolution** of brain imaging techniques is several seconds at best. In contrast, recordings of individual neurons (sometimes called "single unit" recording) can reveal changes in neuronal activity with millisecond time resolution.

The studies involving monkeys showed that dopamine neurons do not always respond to rewards. They only respond when a reward is better than expected. For instance, a small squirt of juice delivered at random times activates the dopamine neurons in both the SN and VTA (Figure 11.8, top). But when the animal learns that juice always arrives about a second after a conditioned stimulus (say a red circle), the juice no longer activates the dopamine neurons. When the juice arrives, it is not "better than expected," for the monkey has learned to expect that amount of juice 1 second after the conditioned stimulus (Figure 11.8, middle). As the conditioned stimulus becomes a predictor of the primary reward, the dopamine activation shifts to the time when the conditioned stimulus is presented (Mirenowicz & Schultz, 1994).

But what if a tone always comes on 1 second before the red circle, and the red circle continues to come on 1 second before the juice? Now the dopamine neuron does not fire to either the red circle or the juice, but only to the tone (Schultz, 1998). In this case, only the tone occurs at an unexpected time. Therefore, dopamine neurons are activated by primary and conditioned rewards, but only if they occur at unexpected times.

The bottom panel of Figure 11.8 shows what happens when a conditioned stimulus predicts the delivery of juice, but the juice isn't presented. Under this disappointing situation, the dopamine neurons become inhibited at around the time the animal expected the juice to arrive. As a general rule, dopamine neurons are activated when the subject receives a better-than-expected reward, and inhibited when she receives a worse-than-expected reward (or no reward at all).

If the monkey learns that a red circle is always followed by a *small* amount of food, but on a particular trial a *medium* amount is delivered instead, the dopamine neurons become activated by this better-than-expected amount of reward. On the other hand, if the animal had learned that the red circle signaled delivery of a *large* amount of food, and the medium amount was unexpectedly presented, the dopamine neuron would become inhibited at the time of the disappointingly small amount reward. The neuron would fire *below* its baseline rate of firing in response to this worse-than-expected reward. It is tempting to speculate on the relation between the dopamine response and the "spoiled" child who is disappointed by an expensive present when he was expecting

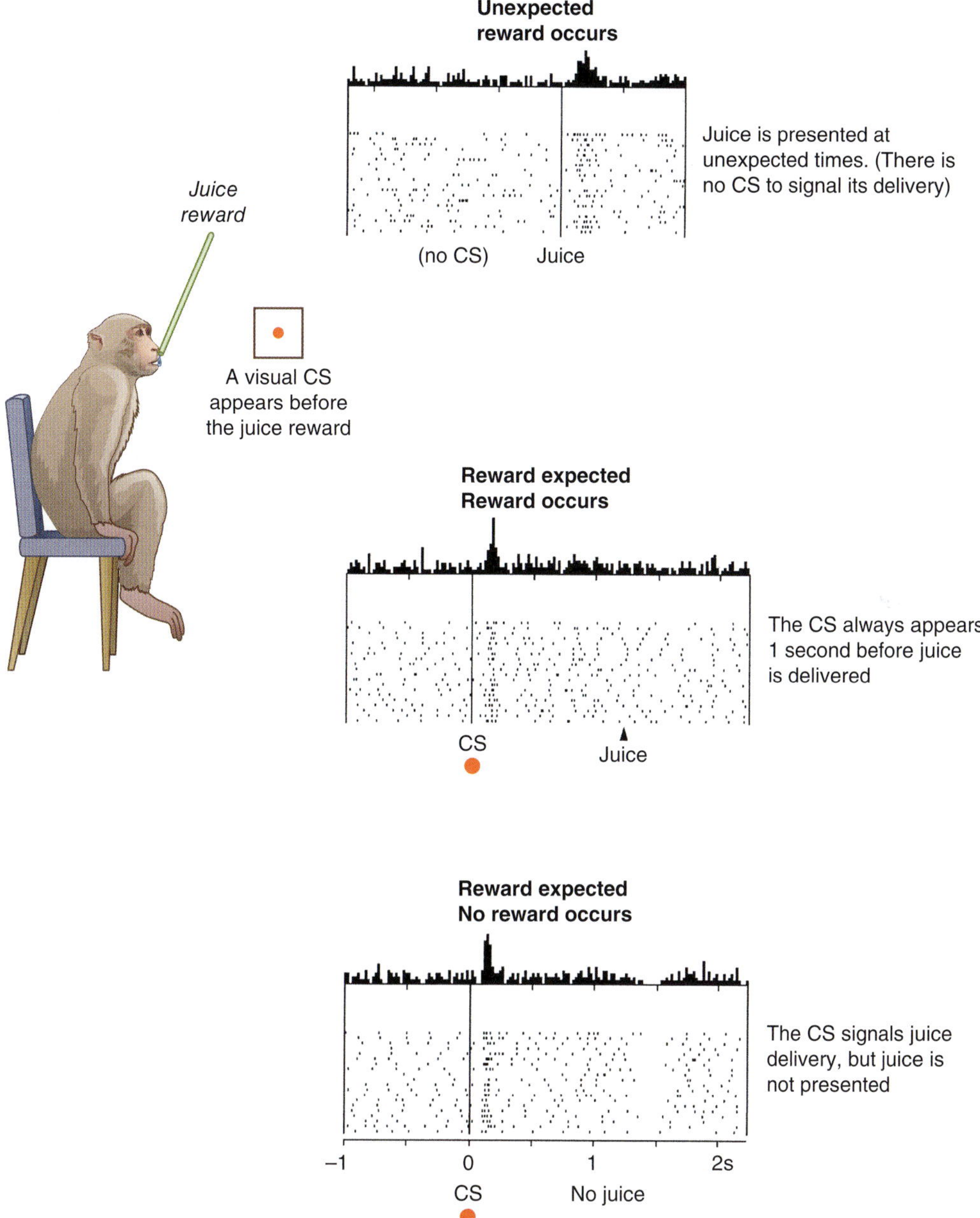

Figure 11.8 Dopamine neurons respond to unexpected primary and conditioned rewards. Each row of dots represents the firing of a dopamine neuron. The histograms show the likelihood of the dopamine neuron firing at particular moments in time. Dopamine neurons are likely to fire right after juice is delivered unexpectedly (top), and after a conditioned stimulus (CS) predicting juice delivery (middle). Dopamine is inhibited when juice is expected but not presented (bottom).
(Histograms adapted from Schultz, 1998, fig. 2.)

something even better. The spoiled child's disappointment is exactly what one might expect given the inhibition of dopamine neurons during worse-than-expected outcomes.

As you can see, dopamine neurons respond not to the absolute amount of reward received but to the *difference* between the reward delivered and the reward that was expected. This difference is called a **reward prediction error**. Dopamine neurons appear to transmit a reward prediction error.

11.3.3 Brain Responses to Financial, Social, and Sexual Reward

We have seen that dopamine neurons respond to food and to stimuli that predict it. Do they respond to other kinds of rewards as well? Investigators designed an experiment to examine the brain regions activated by stimuli related to another powerful reward – money. In the experiment, human subjects played a game where they could win or lose money. The game began when a circle appeared on the screen. The number of lines (1–3) within the circle indicated how much money the subject could win on the present trial (Figure 11.9). One line meant they could win 20 cents, two lines meant $1, and three lines meant $5. In order to win the money, the subject had to press a button as quickly as possible when an indicator appeared on the screen.

Individuals played the game while brain activity was monitored using fMRI. As the subject saw the circle indicating the opportunity to win $5, a large activation was seen in the nucleus accumbens (the destination site for mesolimbic dopamine neurons). The nucleus accumbens activation when subjects anticipated winning $5 was greater than that seen

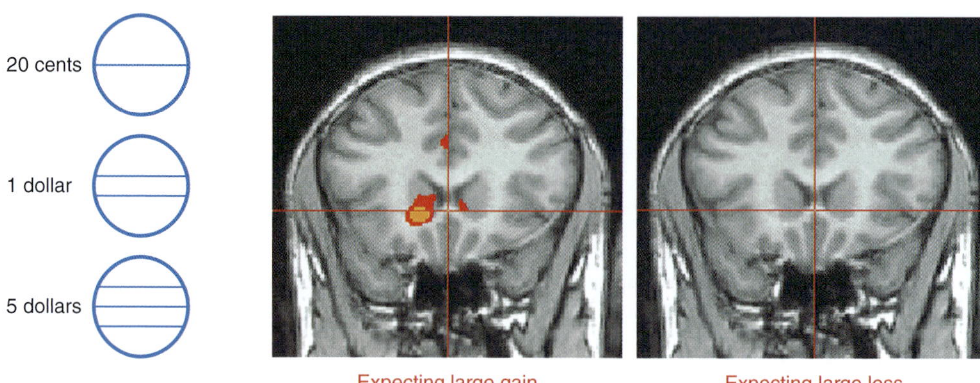

Figure 11.9 The nucleus accumbens is activated when subjects expect monetary gain. Subjects saw a circle containing one to three lines, signaling the opportunity for a small ($0.20), medium ($1), or large ($5) gain of money. The expectation of a large compared to small monetary gain increased nucleus accumbens activity (left); the expectation of a large versus small monetary loss did not affect nucleus accumbens activity (right).
(Brain images adapted from Knutson, Adams, Fong, & Hommer, 2001, fig. 3, © 2001, Society for Neuroscience.)

during anticipation of either the $1 or 20 cents (Knutson, Adams, Fong, & Hommer, 2001). In a variation of this game, subjects saw a square that also contained one to three lines, but in this case the lines indicated how much money would be *lost* if they performed poorly on the task. These symbols for loss did not affect brain activity within the nucleus accumbens. Nucleus accumbens activation appears to occur in anticipation of gains rather than losses.

Is the nucleus accumbens only activated when subjects *anticipate* winning money, or is it also activated when subjects *receive* the money? Receiving money activates both nucleus accumbens and striatum, but only when subjects *do not expect* to receive the money (Knutson et al., 2001; Abler, Walter, Erk, Kammerer, & Spitzer, 2006). These dopamine-receiving brain regions are the same ones activated when individuals receive an unexpected juice reward (Valentin & O'Doherty, 2009). Individuals with **gambling disorder** (an addiction-like compulsion to gamble) show abnormally high levels of dopamine release while gambling compared to levels seen in individuals without the disorder while engaged in the same gambling behavior (Clark, Boileau, & Zack, 2019).

Do we react to money differently when our dopamine levels are increased? Data suggest that approximately 22 percent of individuals receiving a dopamine agonist medication (to treat Parkinson's disease) show compulsive behaviors including pathological gambling and compulsive shopping (Hassan et al., 2011). The individuals also have a high incidence of binge eating and hypersexuality. Soon after doctors adjusted the patients' medication dose to decrease their dopamine levels, their behavioral compulsions were reduced or eliminated.

In addition to food and monetary reward, the nucleus accumbens responds to social rewards. For instance, the nucleus accumbens was activated when subjects saw a smiling face (Rademacher et al., 2010), especially when the face belonged to a member of the opposite sex (Spreckelmeyer, Rademacher, Paulus, & Grunder, 2013). Anticipation of a bigger smile (larger social reward) produced the largest activation of the nucleus accumbens (see Figure 11.10).

Sexually arousing stimuli also increase dopamine release and activate dopamine-receiving brain areas. In male rats, the sight or smell of a sexually receptive female rat behind a screen elevates nucleus accumbens dopamine levels (Damsma, Wenkstern, Pfaus, Phillips, & Fibiger, 1992). In humans, sexually arousing visual stimuli activate the nucleus accumbens. Sexually arousing stimuli also activate the **orbitofrontal cortex**, an area of the prefrontal cortex that receives a great deal of dopamine from the VTA (Hamann, Herman, Nolan, & Wallen, 2004).

We have seen that food, monetary, social, and sex rewards can all activate DA-receiving brain areas, such as the nucleus accumbens and

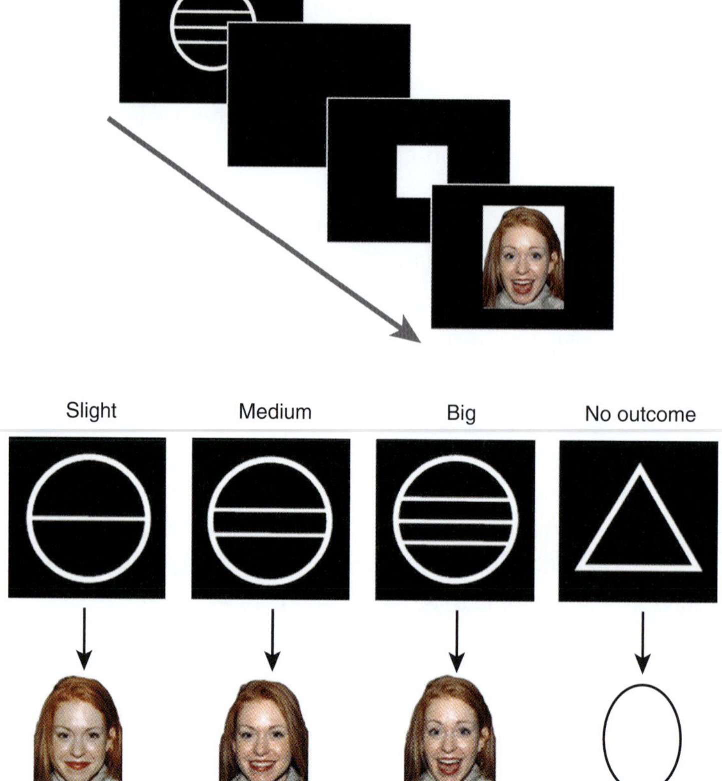

Figure 11.10 Social reward. Top: After seeing the circle, the subject must press a button as soon as a white square appears on the screen in order to receive a "smile" reward. Bottom: The circle with one, two, or three horizontal lines tells the subject whether the reward will be a slight, medium, or large smile. The triangle means that no reward is possible. The nucleus accumbens is most strongly activated when subjects see the circle signaling that a large smile is coming.
(Adapted from Rademacher et al., 2010, fig. 1, © Elsevier B.V. All rights reserved.)

orbitofrontal cortex. Listening to pleasurable music can activate many of these same brain regions. For instance, subjects listened to music that was so pleasurable they reported "chills" or "shivers down the spine." While listening to the music, they showed activations in several brain areas that receive strong dopamine inputs, such as the nucleus accumbens and orbitofrontal cortex (Blood & Zatorre, 2001).

KEY CONCEPTS

- **Dopamine antagonists appear to block food reinforcement.**
- **Some researchers believe that dopamine is necessary for the motivation or vigor with which animals work for rewards, rather than the pleasurable properties of the reinforcer.**

- **Unexpected rewards activate midbrain dopamine neurons.**
- **In the human brain, primary and conditioned stimuli associated with financial, social, and sexual rewards activate the nucleus accumbens and other brain regions that receive strong dopamine input.**

TEST YOURSELF

1. **Describe evidence that has led some investigators to believe that dopamine is not necessary for the hedonic properties of food.**
2. **Do dopamine neurons always respond to rewards, or only when the rewards are unexpected?**
3. **Describe a situation that is known to cause inhibition of dopamine firing.**
4. **Give two specific examples of stimuli that have been shown to activate the nucleus accumbens in human subjects.**

11.4 DRUG REWARD AND ADDICTION

Individuals can activate brain reward systems by using certain types of drugs. In addition to their reward value, these drugs have abuse potential. For instance, **stimulant drugs** such as cocaine and amphetamine produce arousal and alertness. Low doses of amphetamine have been used in the past to help soldiers to stay attentive and avoid fatigue while watching radar. Other stimulants, such as caffeine and nicotine, also increase attention and reduce mental fatigue. High stimulant doses can cause anxiety. In contrast, **alcohol** as well as **opioids** (such as heroin, morphine, and oxycodone) increase relaxation. Opioids, of course, also have analgesic properties, and are therefore used to control severe pain in medical settings.

While all of these drugs have reward properties, the nature of their subjective reward effects may differ. Cocaine users often report feelings of enhanced self-efficacy, powerfulness, and enjoyment of activities such as listening to music and engaging in conversation. Heroin users often describe feeling blissful and relaxed. Because of cocaine's anxiogenic (anxiety-producing) properties, some users combine cocaine with heroin for a drug combination called "speedball"; the opioid takes the "edge" off the anxiety that the stimulant can otherwise produce.

Individuals typically begin taking drugs because of social factors, such as peer pressure, positive portrayals of drug taking in film, or drug use in role models. Some take drugs as a kind of "self-medication." For instance, stimulants may temporarily reduce depression; alcohol can temporarily reduce anxiety.

When an individual takes a drug repeatedly despite adverse consequences to health and social life, we say that he or she is addicted. About 3 percent of adults in the USA become addicted to drugs. Like addictions to shopping, gambling, and other behaviors, drug addictions have a compulsive property; the individual has a diminished choice over whether or not to engage in the behavior. Some continue to take a drug even when it leads to problems in work or family, or even punishment by the legal system. The addicted individual devotes increasing amounts of time and resources to obtaining and consuming the drug, and less to the varied goals they pursued in the past.

However, the brain did not evolve reward circuits in order for drugs of abuse to reinforce behaviors! Reward circuits presumably evolved to reinforce those behaviors that lead to natural rewards such as food, water, and sex. In the view of many investigators, drugs of abuse take over or "hijack" the brain circuits that evolved to mediate natural reward. The drugs have the ability to activate these reward circuits more strongly than would occur naturally. The addict repeats those behaviors that lead to drug reward to the exclusion of other rewards in life.

We saw earlier, from animal studies, that natural rewards activate midbrain dopamine neurons, and that blockade of dopamine activity, particularly within the nucleus accumbens, reduces the reinforcing effects of reward stimuli. In human subjects, palatable food, sexual stimuli, and even a smile can drive activation of the nucleus accumbens and other dopamine target areas. Do drugs of abuse activate these same reward areas of the brain?

11.4.1 Cocaine and Amphetamine

Brad's coworkers noticed that he had recently been moving around restlessly, and talking rapidly, sometimes almost non-stop. Under the influence of cocaine, he could stay in the office and work while the others went out for lunch. He didn't feel hungry. He was using cocaine. It made him feel mentally alert, sometimes euphoric. Later in the day, he would often feel anxious or irritable. Cocaine, a stimulant drug, produces temporary increases in alertness and energy.

Cocaine elevates concentrations of synaptic dopamine and norepinephrine. It acts principally through its effects on neurotransmitter **reuptake**. After a neuron releases its neurotransmitter, neurotransmitter reuptake clears the molecules from the synapse (Chapter 2). Figure 11.11 illustrates dopamine release into the synapse, and its reuptake via a **dopamine transporter** that pulls the dopamine back into the releasing neuron. Reuptake is a kind of recycling mechanism that allows the neurotransmitter to be repackaged inside the axon terminal for future release.

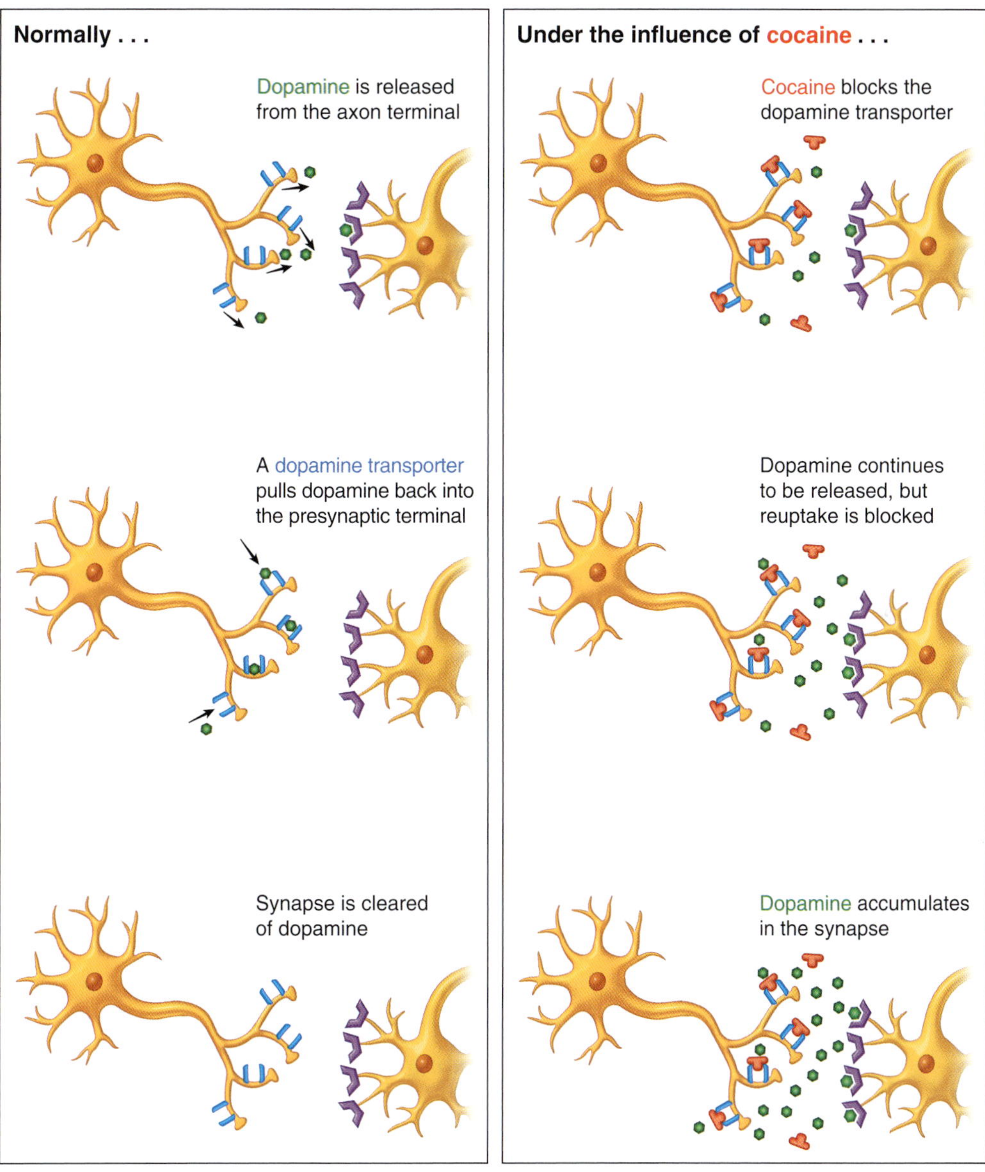

Figure 11.11 Cocaine blocks dopamine reuptake. Dopamine is released from a dopamine neuron, and eventually cleared from the synapse by the dopamine transporter (left panels). Cocaine disrupts the reuptake of dopamine, allowing dopamine to accumulate in the synapse (right panels).

Cocaine inhibits the dopamine transporter, preventing it from efficiently pulling dopamine from the synapse back into the presynaptic neuron. As a result, dopamine molecules accumulate in the synapse, and the dopamine receptors on the receiving neurons are surrounded by much higher levels of dopamine than normal. Dopamine, therefore, binds to the postsynaptic receptor more frequently than normal. Cocaine blocks not only the dopamine transporter, but also the norepinephrine transporter. Thus, cocaine elevates synaptic concentrations of dopamine and norepinephrine.

Amphetamine, like cocaine, increases synaptic catecholamine concentrations. However, it does so by enhancing the release of the neurotransmitters into the synapse rather than by blocking their reuptake into the presynaptic terminal. Consequently, while amphetamine increases the amount of catecholamine transmitters *released* into the synapse, cocaine reduces the speed at which these neurotransmitters are *cleared* from the synapse. The net result is similar: an increase in synaptic concentrations of dopamine and norepinephrine.

Because we have seen that dopamine plays a critical role in the reinforcing effects of brain stimulation and natural reward, it is logical to ask whether dopamine is necessary for the reinforcing effects of cocaine and amphetamine. We have seen that cocaine and amphetamine increase synaptic dopamine concentrations and also concentrations of norepinephrine (and to a lesser degree, serotonin). The reinforcing effects of cocaine and amphetamine might be due to any of these neurochemical changes produced by these stimulants. In addition, elevations in dopamine, norepinephrine, and serotonin cause changes in the activity of neurons throughout the brain that contain receptors for these transmitters. Which of these many effects of cocaine and amphetamine are responsible for their reinforcing properties?

A key piece of evidence that dopamine is important in the rewarding effects of stimulant drugs comes from studies of rats pressing a lever to receive intravenous cocaine. The rats generally press the lever a lot during the first several minutes of the session (as they "load up" on the drug), but then press at a relatively constant rate for the rest of the session, which in some cases lasts for several hours. For most of the session, the animal maintains a remarkably constant rate of lever pressing for cocaine.

For instance, if the animal presses the lever thirty times during 1 hour of the session, it is likely to press thirty times during each of the other hours as well. The pattern suggests that the animal desires a particular *amount* of cocaine in the bloodstream and is pressing the lever at a particular rate in order to maintain that amount in its system. (Human addicts often pace their drug taking in a similar manner.)

If the experimenter now gives the rat double the dose of cocaine (say from 0.25 mg to 0.50 mg) each time it presses the lever, the rat responds by reducing its rate of lever pressing (by about half). If the dose of the drug per lever press is cut in half (say from 0.25 to 0.125 mg), the rat doubles its rate of lever pressing (Figure 11.12). Again, the animal seems to sense the amount of cocaine in its bloodstream and to lever press at a rate that maintains its preferred level of the drug.

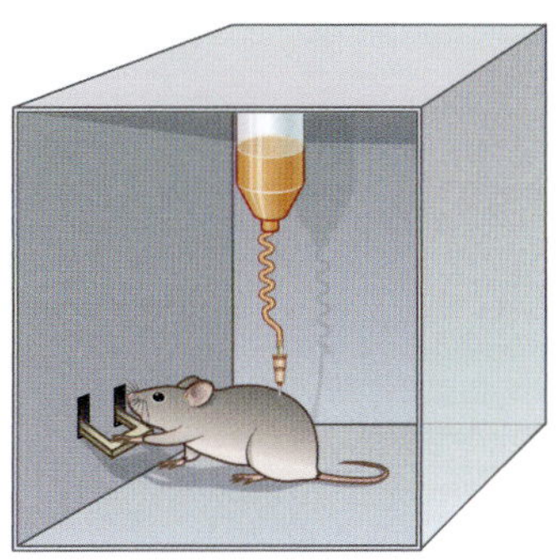

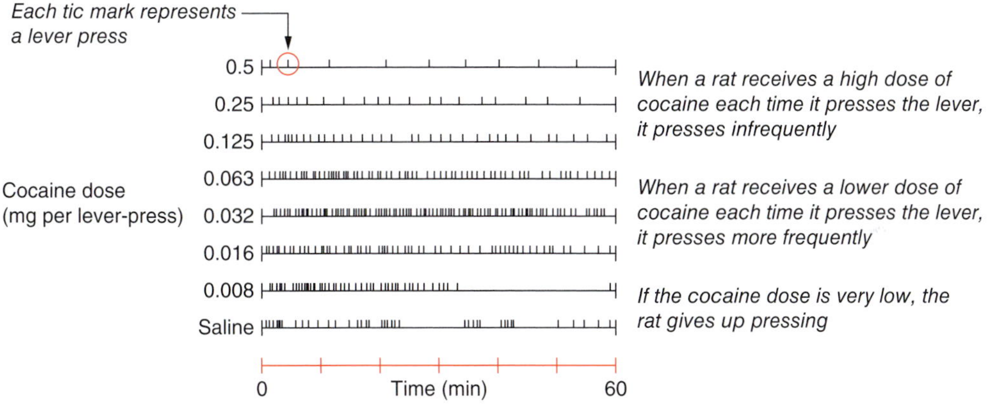

Figure 11.12 Lever pressing for cocaine. When a rat receives a low dose of cocaine each time it lever presses, it presses frequently in order to receive its desired amount of cocaine. However, when the dose is reduced to a very low level (or replaced by saline) the rat may give up pressing altogether.
(Data adapted from Weissenborn, Whitelaw, Robbins, & Everitt, 1998, fig. 6, © 1998, Springer-Verlag Berlin Heidelberg.)

Something remarkable happens when an animal trained to lever press for cocaine receives a drug that blocks dopamine receptors, i.e., a dopamine antagonist. The animal *increases* its rate of lever pressing for cocaine, at least temporarily. If the dose of the dopamine antagonist blocks some, but not all, of the dopamine receptors, the animal will press faster throughout the entire test session (Figure 11.13). This looks like the behavior of a rat that is receiving a reduced dose of cocaine. Whether cocaine dose is reduced or a dopamine antagonist is administered, the rat appears to lever press more in order to compensate for the reduced level of cocaine reward it experiences (Wise, 1982).

Let's consider this more carefully. The more often the rat presses the lever for cocaine, the more cocaine molecules travel through the bloodstream, reach the dopamine terminals, and block dopamine reuptake pumps. This causes more dopamine to accumulate in the synapses. While the dopamine antagonist causes blockade of some proportion of dopamine receptors (say half of them), the rat presses the lever for more

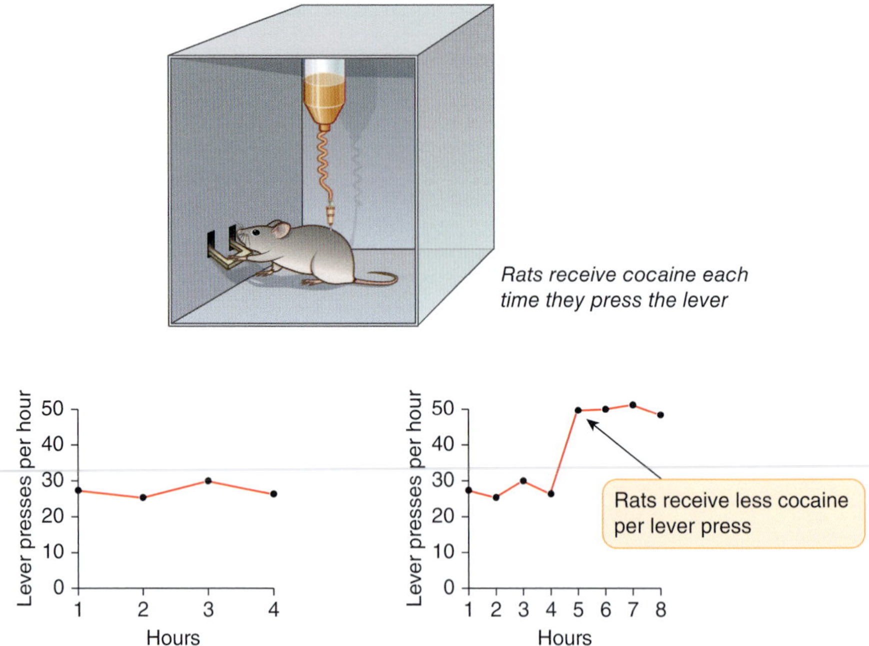

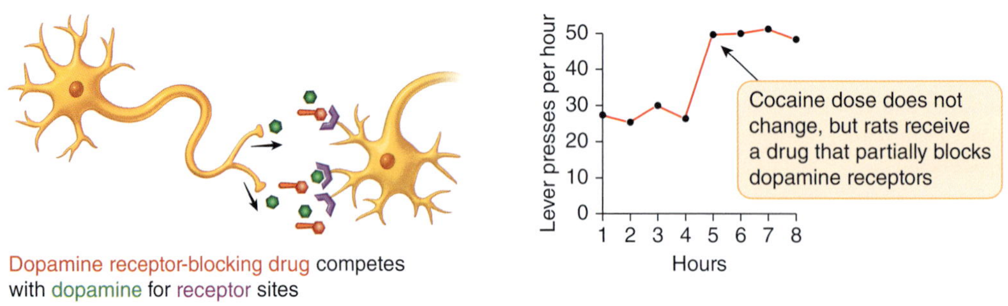

Figure 11.13 **Partially blocking dopamine receptors increases the rate of lever pressing for cocaine**. When the dose of cocaine per lever press is reduced, rats press at higher rates (top-right graph). If the dose of cocaine is held constant, but some of the dopamine receptors are blocked, rats also press for cocaine at higher rates (bottom graph). By pressing faster, rats increase dopamine levels, allowing dopamine to bind to more of the available dopamine receptors.

cocaine, and increases the number of dopamine molecules in the synapse. The increased dopamine can more successfully compete with the antagonist drug for receptor sites. In this way, the animal can lever press more in order to restore the level of dopamine receptor binding it prefers.

However, if the rat receives a very high dose of the dopamine antagonist, say a dose that blocks all of the dopamine receptors even when the rat is pressing for cocaine rapidly, the rat stops lever pressing. Rats lever pressing for either cocaine or amphetamine under the influence of a high dose of a dopamine antagonist show extinction-like patterns of lever pressing, patterns that suggest a reduction in the reward value of the drug. There are two families of dopamine receptors, D_1 and D_2. Cocaine self-administration depends in particular on dopamine binding to the D_1 receptor (Caine et al., 2007). While antagonists of other neurotransmitters, e.g., norepinephrine antagonists, reduce rates of lever pressing for cocaine, they do not produce the extinction-like pattern of behavior characteristic of reduced reinforcement.

Human brain imaging studies show that stimulant drugs similar to cocaine and amphetamine increase dopamine within the nucleus accumbens and striatum. (The subjects were not addicted to a drug; it was therefore important that the experimenters tested the effects of an amphetamine-like stimulant without addictive properties so that the subjects didn't leave the experiment with a drug addiction.) Individuals showing greater drug-induced dopamine elevations were most likely to report feeling "high" or euphoric (Volkow, Fowler, Wang, Baler, & Telang, 2009). When **chronic** cocaine users (those who use the drug regularly) received the same amphetamine-like stimulants, the drug produced only small increases in dopamine. This may be related to users' tolerance to the effects of repeated drug administration (discussed below).

It is curious that chronic cocaine users report strong drug cravings and continue to seek out cocaine even when it produces only small elevations in brain dopamine. It is possible that the rise in dopamine produced by early drug use plays a critical role in forming cocaine and amphetamine addiction; but once an addiction is formed, other brain mechanisms are responsible for continued drug use (Volkow et al., 2014). In addition, if the diminished dopamine response means that the chronic user experiences a diminished "high," he may be motivated to continue drug use in order to "chase the remembered high," a "high" that becomes increasingly difficult to reproduce (Volkow, Wise, & Baler, 2017).

Despite the large number of individuals addicted to stimulants, there are currently no FDA-approved medications to treat cocaine or amphetamine addiction. The development of medications to treat cocaine and amphetamine addiction is a top priority for the National Institute of Drug Abuse.

11.4.2 Nicotine

Carol has a meeting in a few minutes and doesn't want to be late. However, she runs outside to smoke a cigarette first. She feels that a little nicotine in her system will help her to stay awake during one of these sometimes-boring meetings. Besides, it has been about an hour since her last cigarette, and her craving for nicotine is becoming very hard to resist. Like cocaine and amphetamine, nicotine is a highly addictive stimulant that can produce strong cravings.

Nicotine binds to acetylcholine receptors. There are two types of acetylcholine receptors, muscarinic and nicotinic, and nicotine binds to the latter. Nicotinic receptors are found in many parts of the central and peripheral nervous system. For instance, it is the receptor located on muscle fibers responsible for muscle contraction (Chapter 4). In the brain, one of the many kinds of neurons containing nicotinic receptors is the VTA dopamine neuron.

When nicotine binds to VTA dopamine receptors, the dopamine neuron releases more dopamine in the nucleus accumbens and in the frontal cortex (review Figure 11.5). But is this increase in dopamine release responsible for the reinforcing effects of nicotine? To examine this question, experimenters trained mice to press a lever to receive nicotine into the bloodstream. As expected, mice learned to press for nicotine. However, mice genetically modified to lack nicotinic receptors (nicotinic **receptor knockout** mice) were unwilling to press for nicotine. So far, the results simply show us that nicotinic receptors are critical for the reinforcing effects of nicotine. However, the experimenters also observed that in the nicotinic knockout mice, nicotine produced no elevation in dopamine release within the nucleus accumbens. They wondered whether this lost DA response was the reason the mice were no longer willing to press the lever for nicotine.

In order to answer this question, they took some of the nicotinic receptor knockout mice (lacking nicotinic receptors) and, through an additional genetic manipulation, selectively restored nicotinic receptors *only on their VTA dopamine neurons*. This permitted their dopamine neurons to respond once again to nicotine. Like normal mice, these mice were now willing to lever press to receive nicotine (Maskos et al., 2005). Other evidence similarly suggests that the reinforcing effects of nicotine depend upon its binding to nicotinic receptors on dopamine neurons (Durand-de Cuttoli et al., 2018).

One treatment for nicotine addiction (smoking) is nicotine replacement therapies like the nicotine patch, gum, candy-flavored lozenges, or nasal spray. These are all effective in reducing cravings associated with abstinence from smoking. While users continue to receive nicotine through these methods, they are not taking in the many carcinogens associated with tobacco smoke such as formaldehyde and benzene. Some medications, such as Chantix (varenicline), reduce withdrawal symptoms of nicotine abstinence. Chantix is a nicotine partial agonist; this means that it stimulates the nicotine receptor, but does so with less efficacy than nicotine itself.

11.4.3 Heroin, Morphine, and Oxycodone

Jim sits on his bed, vaporizes heroin, and inhales it. He feels pleasure with the first hit. As he takes another hit, the pleasure grows. Soon, he's filled with a feeling of bliss. He lies down, looks up at the ceiling, and appreciates how perfect life is.

Heroin, morphine and oxycodone (sold as OxyContin) are **opioid drugs**, and the receptors they activate are called opioid receptors. Peptides naturally produced by the body called **endogenous opioids** activate these same receptors. The endogenous opioids include the enkephalins, which are natural analgesics (they reduce pain), and endorphins, which are released during intense physical activity and associated with runner's high. Opioid receptors are found throughout the brain, spinal cord, and digestive tract.

When heroin or other opioid drugs bind to opioid receptors on dopamine neurons, they elevate dopamine release in the nucleus accumbens. The precise brain mechanisms responsible for the reward properties of opioid drugs is controversial. However, several lines of research suggest that opioids exert reward effects both through VTA dopamine activation and through dopamine-independent actions within the nucleus accumbens (Koob & Volkow, 2010; Hearing, 2019).

Treatments for opioid drug addiction include methadone and buprenorphine, which are opioid replacement drugs. Like heroin, morphine, and oxycodone, the replacement drugs stimulate opioid receptors. Methadone reduces cravings for heroin, in part, by mimicking heroin's effects on the brain. But because methadone reaches the brain more slowly, it generates less of a "rush" or "high." Buprenorphine works in a similar manner.

Users of heroin that switch to one of the replacement drugs may remain dependent upon opioids. However, because the replacement drugs can be administered safely and legally, the user is not using needles and so there is less risk of HIV, hepatitis, and other diseases. Another drug widely used to treat opioid addiction is naltrexone, an opioid antagonist. It blocks the actions of opioid drugs, and is not addictive.

11.4.4 Alcohol

Sarah left the party feeling good. For an hour or so, her inhibitions left her, and she enjoyed dancing and talking to friends. But at a certain point, she noticed she was slurring her words as she spoke. As she walked home, she would sway from one side of the sidewalk to the other.

Nearly 15 million people in the USA suffered from alcohol dependence in 2019. About 88,000 people die from alcohol-related causes each year. Many of these deaths come from liver disease and automobile crashes.

Despite the dangers associated with alcohol dependence, the precise brain mechanisms by which alcohol produces its behavioral and reinforcing effects are unclear. A difficulty is that alcohol interacts with so many different neurotransmitter receptors in the brain (e.g., GABA, NMDA, acetylcholine, serotonin) it is difficult to know which are responsible for its effects on behavior.

Alcohol also binds to potassium ion channels located widely throughout the brain (Aryal, Dvir, Choe, & Slesinger, 2009). Recall from Chapter 2 that the flow of potassium (which has a positive charge) from the inside to the outside of a neuron inhibits neuronal activity. Alcohol enhances the outward flow of potassium through the potassium channels, and can exert widespread, often depressant, effects on neuronal activity

The opioid antagonist naltrexone has some efficacy for reducing alcohol consumption in people with alcohol dependency. In addition, the drug Disulfiram (Antabuse) reduces alcohol consumption by generating an unpleasant state (that includes nausea and vomiting) when the individual consumes alcohol.

11.4.5 Tolerance

Drug tolerance refers to a drug's reduced effectiveness in producing physiological and/or behavioral effects when used repeatedly. Because of tolerance, drug addicts need to elevate the amount of drug they consume in order to achieve the desired effect. It is common for experienced users to increase their dose of opioid drugs tenfold, and in some cases, by as much as hundredfold (Christie, 2008). One cause of tolerance is a reduced amount of drug reaching the target regions of the brain and periphery of the body because the body becomes better able to rid itself of the drug. This enhanced effectiveness at eliminating the drug is called **metabolic tolerance**. An example of metabolic tolerance would be a more efficient elimination (metabolism) of heroin before it reaches opioid receptors. In contrast, **functional tolerance** is the reduced sensitivity of target sites to the drug. For instance, a reduction in the number of opioid receptors present on neurons in the VTA or nucleus accumbens would give heroin fewer sites upon which to act, and would contribute to functional tolerance.

Conditioned drug tolerance is a peculiar phenomenon in which the individual becomes tolerant to a drug only in the environment in which he took the drug in the past. Imagine that Robert becomes tolerant to heroin, which he always takes in his bedroom. He takes progressively higher heroin doses in order to experience the original effects of the drug. If this is *conditioned* drug tolerance, then it may only occur in his bedroom or other environments that closely resemble his bedroom. While the drug produces only moderate effects when Robert is in his bedroom, the same drug dose may cause much stronger effects when he takes the drug in another environment, say on a street corner. Because heroin tolerance is partly conditioned to environmental stimuli, the chance of overdose (usually because of heroin's effects on the respiratory system) is elevated when the user takes the drug in a new environment (Gutierrez-Cebollada, de la Torre, Ortuno, Garces, & Cami, 1994), an environment in which the expected level of heroin tolerance does not occur.

Rats that receive heroin in a particular environment show a similar effect. They are more likely to die of overdose when later given the drug in an environment in which they had not previously received the drug. On the basis of the studies in rats, it has been theorized that environmental stimuli encountered under the influence of the drug become associated with the effects of the drug itself. When the animal receives the drug in a familiar environment, the conditioned stimuli exert physiological effects in a direction opposite to that of the drug, and effectively counteract the drug effects. While much of the research on conditioned tolerance has focused upon tolerance to heroin and other opioid drugs, conditioned tolerance has also been observed with alcohol and caffeine (Siegel, 2001).

11.4.6 Withdrawal and Craving

When an addict abstains from drug taking, withdrawal symptoms may last for days or even weeks. The symptoms may include mood changes such as fatigue, depression, irritability, and anxiety, as well as diarrhea, headache, nausea, and vomiting. Animal studies suggest that a common component of withdrawal is an increase in stress hormones such as corticotropin-releasing hormone (CRH) (Chapter 12). Drugs preventing this increase in CRH activity reverse the anxiety associated with alcohol and cocaine withdrawal. Withdrawal from all major addictive drugs also produces a decrease in dopamine and serotonin release to the nucleus accumbens (Koob & Volkow, 2010).

In humans, the state of withdrawal gives rise to a strong desire or craving for the drug. This is not surprising, for the individual has learned that the drug will quickly cause the aversive state of withdrawal to subside. To some extent, an addicted individual takes a drug in order to avoid unpleasant withdrawal effects. This is an example of negative reinforcement, that is the repetition of a behavior (e.g., drug taking) in order to avoid a negative consequence.

It is a common misconception, however, that drug addicts continue to take the abused drug solely to avoid withdrawal symptoms. If this were true, a stay in the hospital during a period of enforced abstinence and withdrawal would be sufficient for addicts to quit their habit. Unfortunately, even when the period of *physical dependence* has passed, the individual will often relapse when he encounters environmental stimuli associated with the abused drug. Passing by the street corner where he used to buy or inject the drug, meeting a friend with whom he took the drug frequently in the past, seeing a film depicting drug use – these types of drug-related environmental cues produce strong cravings, and are powerful triggers for relapse long after the period of physical dependence has passed. In fact, the incidence of relapse in heroin addicts within a year after they have stopped taking the drug is as high as 80 percent. Why do individuals relapse long after withdrawal symptoms have subsided?

These conditioned drug-related stimuli strongly elevate dopamine release and activate dopamine target regions including the nucleus accumbens, the striatum, and the prefrontal cortex (Volkow et al., 2009). Activation of the nucleus accumbens and prefrontal cortex is associated with cravings for cocaine (Garavan et al., 2000), nicotine (Wilson, Sayette, & Fiez, 2004), opioids (Sell et al., 2000), and alcohol (Tapert et al., 2003).

We have seen that conditioned drug-related cues can continue to produce cravings long after a person has stopped taking the drug. This is because the drugs can produce long-term changes in the connections between neurons, a form of neural plasticity (Chapters 8 and 9). Sensory areas of the cortex that respond to the environmental cues send signals to motivation-related brain regions such as the nucleus accumbens and striatum, allowing environmental stimuli to produce strong motivational states directed toward obtaining the drug. Natural rewards (food, sex, and so on) have the capacity to strengthen these connections (as described below), so that a sensory stimulus associated with a reward gains the ability to produce a strong motivational state directed toward seeking out the desired reward. Drugs of abuse produce especially strong and long-lasting connections between sensory and motivation-related brain regions such as the striatum and nucleus accumbens, allowing drug-related environmental stimuli to elicit craving long after the individual has stopped taking the drug. We will return to this idea in the final section of the chapter.

11.4.7 Impulse Control

If your goal is to practice the guitar, and you are confronted with the sound of the TV, the controls for a video game, and a pack of potato chips on the kitchen table, it requires **inhibitory control** to avoid watching TV, playing a video game, or eating the chips. Your ability to exert inhibitory control over attention and behavior keeps you from getting sidetracked, and allows you to remain directed in your behavior. In order to direct your behavior toward the goal of practicing the guitar, you need to prevent yourself from engaging with other stimuli (Feil et al., 2010).

For drug-addicted individuals, refraining from taking the drug requires enormous inhibitory control. This is true both during early stages of drug abstinence when withdrawal symptoms are present, and later when drug-related environmental stimuli may re-elicit the desire to take the drug. Inhibitory control depends importantly upon activity within the prefrontal cortex. Yet evidence suggests that the major drugs of abuse are associated with prefrontal cortical impairments – impairments that disrupt the very brain circuits necessary for inhibitory control (Ramey & Regier, 2019).

In order to investigate inhibitory control in the laboratory, investigators often use the **stop-signal task** (Figure 11.14A). In one version of this task, the subject sees a letter A, B, C, or D in the center of a screen for half a second, and is instructed to press a key when he sees particular letters. For instance, he may need to press key #1 when he sees the letter A or C, and key #2 if the letter is B or D. In this part of the task, regular cocaine users performed almost identically to (non-using) control subjects. Both groups responded to the letters with good accuracy. However, on a quarter of the trials, the letter on the screen (say B) was followed almost immediately (within less than a half a second) by a brief tone, which instructed the subject to *withhold* pressing either button during that trial. These were called "stop" trials. So, when the tone sounded, they needed to exert inhibitory control over their own behavior. While control subjects successfully inhibited their behavior on most of the trials, cocaine users did so less frequently (Fillmore & Rush, 2002).

These data suggest that cocaine users have difficulties inhibiting behavior, but they do not tell us whether chronic drug use causes inhibitory control problems, or whether inhibitory control problems place people at heightened risk for cocaine addiction. However, poor inhibitory control is seen both in chronic users of cocaine (and amphetamine) and also in their siblings who have no drug abuse history (Ersche et al., 2012). One would not expect to find this if cocaine were causing the inhibitory control problems. Instead, the data suggest that a deficit in inhibitory control is a "familial trait" (it runs in families) that places individuals at risk for drug use.

Is there something unusual about the brains of drug users and their siblings that might be associated with inhibitory control difficulties? Both groups of subjects (drug users and siblings) show abnormally low levels of white matter in a number of brain areas (Figure 11.14B). White matter comes from the myelin that helps speed neuronal communication across axons. Reduced white matter indicates a reduction in communication between neurons due to fewer axons connecting them and/or less myelination of the axons. Low levels of white matter in the frontal lobes of cocaine users and their siblings correlated with deficits in inhibitory control (Ersche et al., 2012). Brain imaging studies point to reduced brain

A

"Press the left key when you see 'A' or 'C', and right key when you see 'B' or 'D'"

Cocaine users are as accurate as control subjects

"But if you hear the stop signal, do NOT press either key"

Cocaine users were less able to inhibit their response

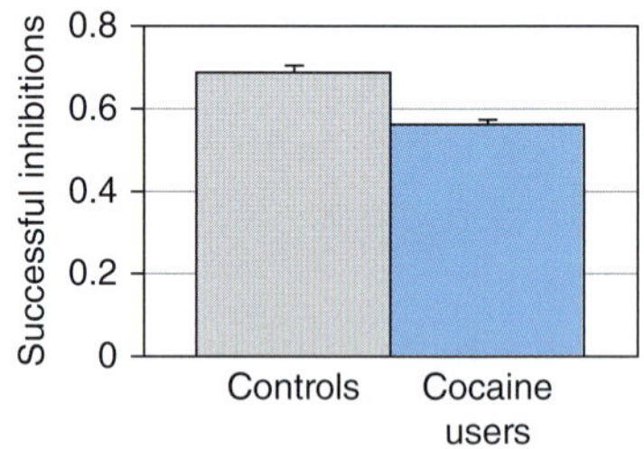

B

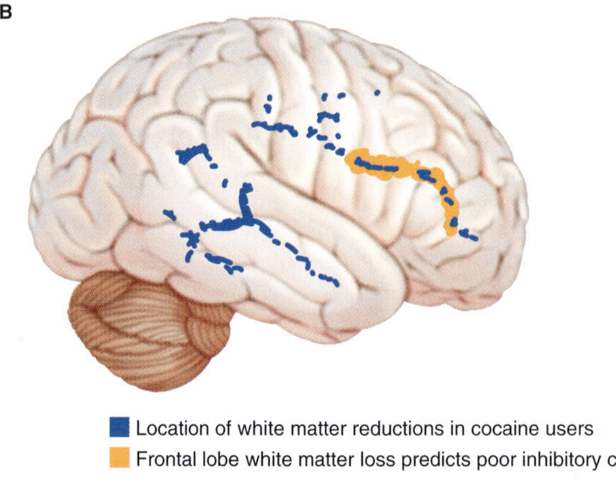

Figure 11.14 Cocaine use and inhibitory control. (A) Cocaine users were less likely than control subjects to successfully withold a button press when instructed to do so. (B) Cocaine users and their siblings showed reduced white matter compared to controls. Those individuals with the greatest reduction in white matter within the frontal lobes (in orange) showed the poorest inhibitory control.
(Data adapted from Ersche et al., 2012, fig. 1B.)

volume in several frontal cortical areas in stimulant-, opioid-, and alcohol-dependent subjects, but particularly in the **dorsolateral prefrontal cortex**, an area that is strongly tied to impulse control (Feil et al., 2010).

KEY CONCEPTS

- The major drugs of abuse differ with respect to their immediate effects on neurotransmitter activity. However, all appear capable of activating mesolimbic dopamine neurons.
- Drug tolerance refers to the reduced effectiveness of a drug in producing physiological and behavioral effects when used repeatedly. Various physiological and learning-related mechanisms can contribute to drug tolerance.
- When an addict abstains from drug taking, she is likely to experience withdrawal symptoms along with drug craving. However, environmental stimuli that remind the individual of the drug can produce cravings long after withdrawal symptoms have subsided.
- Drug addicts may have particular difficulties abstaining from drug use because the major drugs of abuse are associated with impaired impulse control. These impairments appear to stem from reduced communication of neurons in the frontal cortex with other neurons.

TEST YOURSELF

1. By what mechanisms does cocaine elevate synaptic dopamine concentration? How does this differ from the effects of amphetamine? Heroin? Alcohol?
2. On what receptors does nicotine bind? Describe evidence that nicotine reinforcement depends upon activation of VTA dopamine neurons.
3. Give an example of conditioned drug tolerance.

11.5 REWARD LEARNING AND PLASTICITY

We have seen that dopamine plays a key role in the reinforcing effects of natural and drug rewards. But how does it work? Researchers are still working to answer this question. However, one of the keys to dopamine's role in reinforcement and addiction appears to be its contribution to neural plasticity within motivation-related brain regions.

We saw above that neurons in the striatum receive dopamine input from the substantia nigra. However, striatal neurons also receive excitatory glutamate inputs from all areas of the cerebral cortex (auditory, visual, motor, etc. ...). In fact, the dendrites of striatal neurons are studded with both dopamine and glutamate receptors. From one moment to the next, as you notice particular sounds, sights, and other stimuli, neurons in the cortex respond to these stimuli and send inputs to the striatum. For instance, as a rat moves through a cage, visual areas of the cortex send information to the striatum about the lever it sees. Later, as the rat sees and smells food, another set of cortical neurons send visual and olfactory information to the striatum. At each moment, as the animal perceives new sets of stimuli, different groups of neurons in the cortex release glutamate to activate different sets of striatal neurons (Rueda-Orozco & Robbe, 2015). Similarly, as a person walks down the street looking for someone selling drugs, visual neurons in the person's cortex may release glutamate to excite particular neurons in the striatum. When the user looks at the powdered cocaine in a bag, another set of visual neurons in the cortex activate neurons in the striatum.

While the input to the striatal neurons represents sensory stimuli, the output of the striatal neurons relates to particular behaviors the subject may perform (Figure 11.15A). For instance, in the human taking drugs, a set of striatal neurons might fire as he places cocaine in a spoon before snorting it. A key part of reinforcement and the establishment of habits is to link together the current environmental stimuli with the behavior that leads to a reward. For instance, seeing cocaine in a bag becomes linked to putting the cocaine in a spoon and snorting it. In our rat example, seeing the lever becomes lined to pressing the lever. This means that a certain set of sensory neurons in the cortex (representing stimuli) become strongly connected to a certain set of neurons in the striatum (representing the behavior).

Imagine that activation of one set of striatal neurons leads to a rat's pressing the lever, and activation of another set is associated with its sniffing the corner of the cage (Figure 11.15B). Further, imagine that both of these neurons in the striatum receive input from the same neuron in the cortex, one which is activated when the animal sees the lever. If the animal sees the lever, and the cortical neuron releases glutamate that excites one set of neurons, the animal presses the lever; if the glutamate released from the cortical neuron activates the other set of striatal neurons, the rat sniffs the corner of the cage. The two actions will be equally probable if the synaptic connections between the cortical neuron and the different sets of striatal neurons are equally strong.

As we saw earlier in the chapter, both natural rewards like food and drug rewards like cocaine lead to large amounts of dopamine release in the striatum. A surge in dopamine strengthens the connection between cortical neurons and striatal neurons (Yagishita et al., 2014). A widely held view is that surges in dopamine specifically increase the strength of the

A

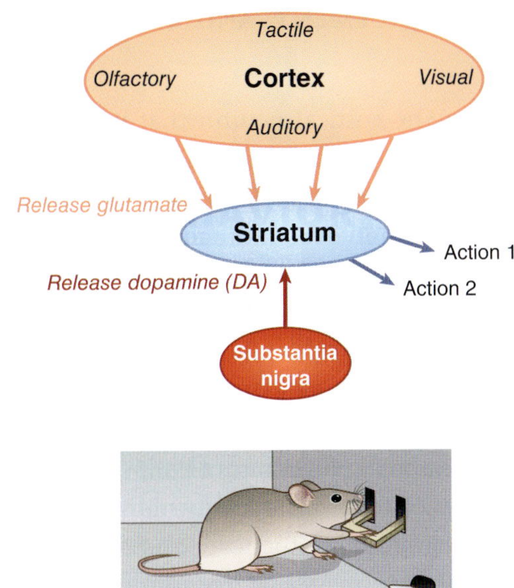

B

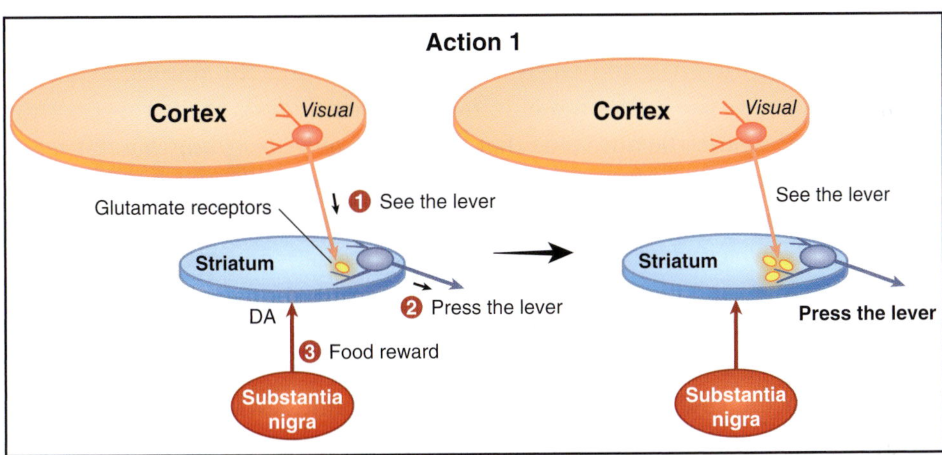

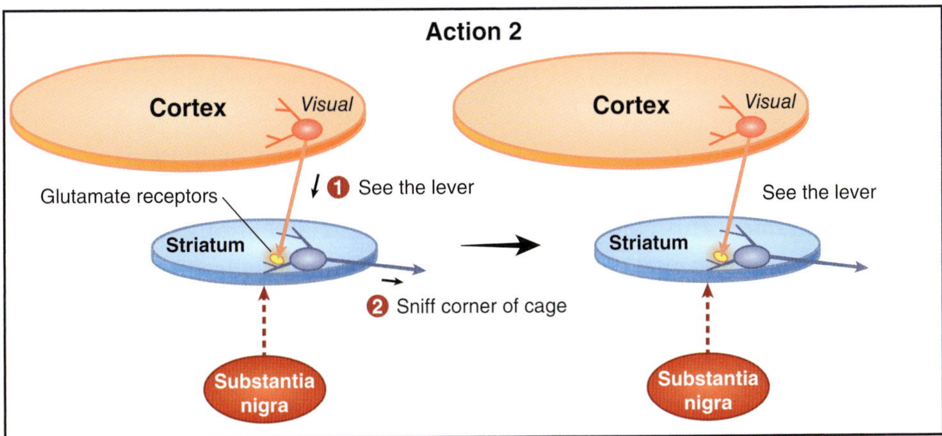

Figure 11.15 Behaviors performed just before a dopamine surge are reinforced. (A) Sensory inputs from the cortex release glutamate to activate striatal neurons that correspond to particular actions. Substantia nigra (SN) neurons release dopamine to the striatum in response to unexpected rewards. (B) Dopamine strengthens the connection between the most recently active cortical and striatal neurons, in this case between the cortical neurons activated when the rat sees the lever, and the striatal neurons activated as it presses the lever. An increase in glutamate receptors at that synapse makes the animal more likely to lever press in the future.

synapse between the cortical neuron that was just active (e.g., the one that responded to seeing the lever) and whichever striatal neurons were most recently active (Schultz, 1998). If the rat saw the lever and then pressed the lever to receive food, the most recently active striatal neurons were those associated with the lever press. The surge in dopamine produced by the food reward would therefore increase the strength of the synapse between the cortical input and these striatal neurons. As a result, the next time the animal sees the lever, the striatal neurons associated with pressing the lever are more likely to become active, and the animal is more likely to press the lever rather than sniff the corner of the cage.

When the rat receives a reward, why doesn't dopamine strengthen the connection between the see-the-lever and sniff-the-corner neurons? After all, food causes the release of dopamine widely throughout the striatum (and the nucleus accumbens), flooding the regions with dopamine molecules that can bind to receptors on many neurons. After the animal presses the lever and receives food, why doesn't the resulting surge in dopamine cause the animal to more frequently sniff at the corner of the cage? Again, the answer is that dopamine *only strengthens those synapses that are active at the time of the dopamine burst*. At the time when food is delivered and dopamine concentrations in the striatum surge, the most recently activated glutamate synapses were the synapses between the see-the-lever and press-the-lever neurons. After all, the rat must have seen the lever and pressed it in order for food to be delivered and dopamine levels to increase!

In the case of an action leading to cocaine reward, dopamine levels would rise as well. While food increases dopamine release by increasing the rate of firing of dopamine neurons, cocaine increases dopamine by reducing the rate of dopamine reuptake (as depicted earlier in Figure 11.11). In both cases, the connection between the most recently active cortical and striatal neurons is strengthened, and the behavior leading to the (natural or drug) reward is reinforced. However, drugs of abuse like cocaine can produce surges in dopamine that are greater than those that occur in nature. This can produce particularly fast and strong changes in the strength of neural connections in the striatum.

Researchers can visualize the dopamine-dependent strengthening of particular synapses in the striatum. Recall that the cortical neuron releases glutamate to the striatum, and glutamate binds to glutamate receptors on dendrites on a striatal neuron. In fact, the glutamate receptors are often located on extensions of the dendrite called **dendritic spines**. The dendritic spine includes a thin strand that leaves the dendrite, the **neck** of the spine, and ends in a doorknob-shaped enlargement called the **head** of the spine (Figure 11.16). On striatal neurons, the head of the dendritic spine contains glutamate receptors.

A

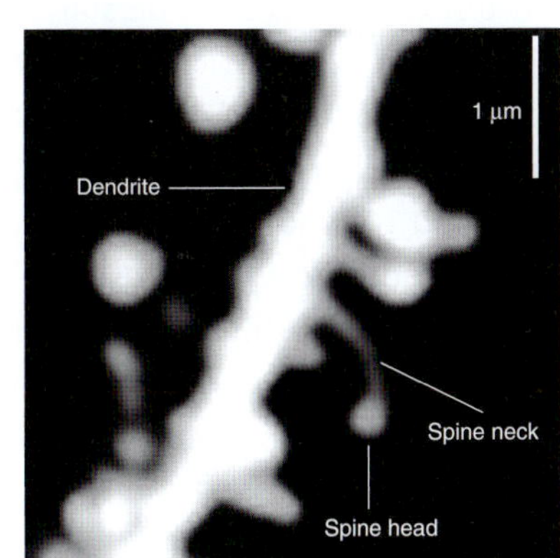

B

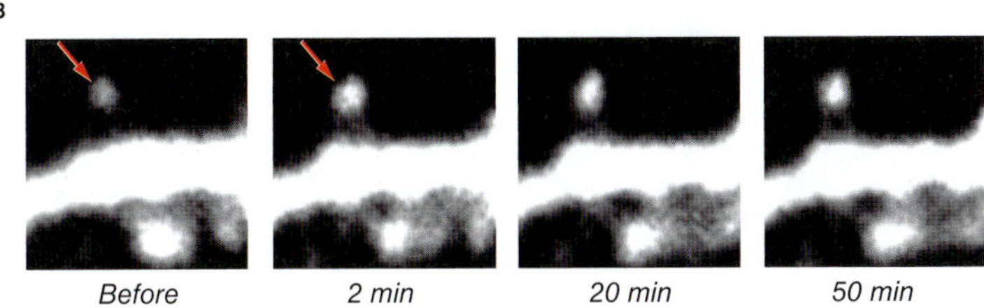

Figure 11.16 Dopamine enlarges dendritic spines. A small dendritic spine of a striatal neuron (red arrow) enlarges after glutamate and dopamine bind to receptors on an activated striatal neuron. The enlargement appears within 2 minutes and is long lasting. (A, public domain; B, adapted from Yagishita et al., 2014, fig. 1E.)

In a key experiment, investigators released glutamate onto individual dendritic spines of neurons in the striatum and activated the striatal neurons (Yagishita et al., 2014). This is what would normally occur when the cortex sends glutamate input to the striatum. About half a second later, they stimulated dopamine neurons of the ventral tegmental area. This is what would normally occur when a reward is presented. Within 2 minutes, the dendritic spine had grown! Increased dendritic spines contain more glutamate receptors. So, when dendritic spines enlarge, glutamate gains the ability to bind to more glutamate receptors and more strongly activate the receiving neuron in the future. In other words, the synapse becomes stronger. Under natural situations, this synaptic strengthening occurs when dopamine reward signals strengthen the cortical inputs to recently active striatal neurons.

We have focused here on dopamine's ability to strengthen connections between recently active neurons in the striatum. However, dopamine similarly strengthens connections between recently active neurons in the nucleus accumbens, and neural plasticity in the nucleus accumbens is involved in reinforcement as well (Wickens, 2009). The striatum and nucleus accumbens are part of a group of interconnected brain regions called the **basal ganglia** (Chapter 4), which are critically involved in habit formation. Current research seeks to understand how dopamine actions in the striatum and nucleus accumbens lead to changes in other parts of the basal ganglia circuits, and why changes in basal ganglia activity lead to habits that are so hard to reverse.

Earlier in this chapter, we said that addicted individuals are vulnerable to relapse even after their withdrawal symptoms have subsided. Years later, environmental cues associated with the drug may produce cravings that are hard to resist. We can now see that drugs of abuse, like natural rewards, can produce long-lasting changes in connections between neurons, and that these changes occur in motivation-related brain regions like the striatum and nucleus accumbens. Will neuroscience reveal ways to reverse these synaptic changes and help individuals regain the flexibility to choose other actions when confronted with drug-related environmental cues?

KEY CONCEPTS

- **Inputs to the striatum and nucleus accumbens carry information about environmental events, while the outputs contribute to performance of particular behaviors.**
- **Rewards activate dopamine, which in turn strengthens the connections between neurons representing stimuli and behaviors.**

TEST YOURSELF

1. **Describe conditions under which dopamine strengthens glutamate inputs to the striatum. What is the evidence for this?**

11.6 The Big Picture

Brain dopamine activity appears to be critical for natural rewards, like food, sex, and (for humans) even smiles. Conditioned rewards like money also stimulate dopamine activity, or at least activity in dopamine-receiving brain areas such as the nucleus accumbens. Drugs of abuse tap into these brain reward systems, producing abnormal elevations in dopamine activity, and strong reinforcement of behavior. Drug-dependent individuals not only have a strong desire to consume substances that drive brain reward systems, but they may also have diminished function of frontal cortical circuits that normally allow for inhibitory control over one's own behavior. Together, these factors make drugs of abuse particularly difficult to resist.

11.7 Creative Thinking

1. You are asked to train a cat to press keys on the piano. What steps of training might you carry out, using shaping by successive approximation?
2. In the opening scenario, a woman said that it was pleasurable to press the button for brain stimulation, and then she continued to press again and again. Must the brain activity responsible for her pleasure (the hedonic effects of the stimulation) be the same brain activity that causes her to repeat the pressing behavior (reinforcing effects)? Could different brain areas be responsible for the two different effects of reward?
3. Do you believe it is possible to build a robot that repeats behaviors (say moving to a particular location) that lead to particular outcomes (say receiving food, or a nice charge of electricity from a wall socket)? Do you believe it is possible to build a robot that experiences pleasure when it receives its reward?
4. Consider your behavior in a particular situation in the past, and describe the reinforcer(s) that motivated you to behave in the way that you did. Did positive reinforcement, negative reinforcement, or both influence you?
5. You discover a new drug that prevents rats from lever pressing for heroin. However, the drug also slows the animals' body movements, and this may account for the animals' reduced rate of lever pressing for heroin. Design two experiments to determine whether the drug has blocked heroin's reinforcing properties, or merely slowed the animals' movements.

Key Terms

acquisition of behavior 442
alcohol 459
basal ganglia 477
channelrhodopsin 450
chronic drug use 465
classical conditioning 443
conditioned aversive stimulus 444
conditioned drug tolerance 468
conditioned reinforcer 443
conditioned reward stimulus 444
conditioned stimulus (CS) 444
dendritic spine 476
dopamine antagonist 448
dopamine transporter 460
electrical brain stimulation 448
endogenous opioids 467
extinction of behavior 442
functional tolerance 468
gambling disorder 457
head of a dendritic spine 476
hedonic 440
inhibitory control 470
instrumental learning 443
medial forebrain bundle (MFB) 446

mesocortical dopamine pathway 448
mesolimbic dopamine pathway 448
metabolic tolerance 468
midbrain 446
neck of a dendritic spine 476
negative reinforcement 443
nigrostriatal dopamine pathway 448
nucleus accumbens 448
operant learning 443
opioid drugs 467
optogenetics 450
orbitofrontal cortex 457
Pavlovian conditioning 443
positive reinforcement 443
prefrontal cortex 448
primary reinforcer 443
receptor knockout 466
reinforcer 442
reinforcing 440
reuptake, neurotransmitter 460
reward prediction error 456
shaping by successive approximations 440
stimulant drugs 459
stop-signal task 471
striatum 448
substantia nigra (SN) 446
taste reactivity 453
time resolution 454
unconditioned stimulus (US) 444
ventral tegmental area (VTA) 446

References

Abler, B., Walter, H., Erk, S., Kammerer, H., & Spitzer, M. (2006). Prediction error as a linear function of reward probability is coded in human nucleus accumbens. *Neuroimage, 31*(2), 790–795.

Aryal, P., Dvir, H., Choe, S., & Slesinger, P. A. (2009). A discrete alcohol pocket involved in GIRK channel activation. *Nature Neuroscience, 12*(8), 988–U952.

Berridge, K. C., & Kringelbach, M. L. (2013). Neuroscience of affect: brain mechanisms of pleasure and displeasure. *Current Opinion in Neurobiology, 23*(3), 294–303.

Berridge, K. C., & Robinson, T. E. (1998). What is the role of dopamine in reward: hedonic impact, reward learning, or incentive salience? *Brain Research Reviews, 28*(3), 309–369.

Blood, A. J., & Zatorre, R. J. (2001). Intensely pleasurable responses to music correlate with activity in brain regions implicated in reward and emotion. *Proceedings of the National Academy of Sciences of the United States of America, 98*(20), 11818–11823.

Caine, S. B., Thomsen, M., Gabriel, K. I., Berkowitz, J. S., Gold, L. H., Koob, G. F., ... Xu, M. (2007). Lack of self-administration of cocaine in dopamine D_1receptor knock-out mice. *Journal of Neuroscience, 27*(48), 13140–13150.

Christie, M. J. (2008). Cellular neuroadaptations to chronic opioids: tolerance, withdrawal and addiction. *British Journal of Pharmacology, 154*(2), 384–396.

Clark, L., Boileau, I., & Zack, M. (2019). Neuroimaging of reward mechanisms in gambling disorder: an integrative review. *Molecular Psychiatry, 24*(5), 674–693.

Coenen, V. A., Bewernick, B. H., Kayser, S., Kilian, H., Bostrom, J., Greschus, S., ... Schlaepfer, T. E. (2019). Superolateral medial forebrain bundle deep brain stimulation in major depression: a gateway trial. *Neuropsychopharmacology, 44*(7), 1224–1232.

Damsma, G., Wenkstern, D., Pfaus, J. G., Phillips, A. G., & Fibiger, H. C. (1992). Sexual behavior increases dopamine transmission in the nucleus accumbens and striatum of male rats: comparison with novelty and locomotion. *Behavioral Neuroscience, 106*(1), 181–191.

Durand-de Cuttoli, R., Mondoloni, S., Marti, F., Lemoine, D., Nguyen, C., Naude, J., ... Mourot, A. (2018). Manipulating midbrain dopamine neurons and reward-related behaviors with light-controllable nicotinic acetylcholine receptors. *Elife, 7*.

Duvauchelle, C. L., Levitin, M., MacConell, L. A., Lee, L. K., & Ettenberg, A. (1992). Opposite effects of prefrontal cortex and nucleus accumbens infusions of flupenthixol on stimulant-induced locomotion and brain stimulation reward. *Brain Research, 576*(1), 104–110.

Ersche, K. D., Jones, P. S., Williams, G. B., Turton, A. J., Robbins, T. W., & Bullmore, E. T. (2012). Abnormal brain structure implicated in stimulant drug addiction. *Science, 335*(6068), 601–604.

Feil, J., Sheppard, D., Fitzgerald, P. B., Yucel, M., Lubman, D. I., & Bradshaw, J. L. (2010). Addiction, compulsive drug seeking, and the role of frontostriatal mechanisms in regulating inhibitory control. *Neuroscience & Biobehavioral Reviews*, *35*(2), 248–275.

Fillmore, M. T., & Rush, C. R. (2002). Impaired inhibitory control of behavior in chronic cocaine users. *Drug and Alcohol Dependence, 66*(3), 265–273.

Fouriezos, G., Hansson, P., & Wise, R. A. (1978). Neuroleptic-induced attenuation of brain stimulation reward in rats. *Journal of Comparative and Physiological Psychology, 92*(4), 661–671.

Garavan, H., Pankiewicz, J., Bloom, A., Cho, J. K., Sperry, L., Ross, T. J., ... Stein, E. A. (2000). Cue-induced cocaine craving: neuroanatomical specificity for drug users and drug stimuli. *American Journal of Psychiatry, 157*(11), 1789–1798.

Gutierrez-Cebollada, J., de la Torre, R., Ortuno, J., Garces, J. M., & Cami, J. (1994). Psychotropic drug consumption and other factors associated with heroin overdose. *Drug and Alcohol Dependence, 35*(2), 169–174.

Hamann, S., Herman, R. A., Nolan, C. L., & Wallen, K. (2004). Men and women differ in amygdala response to visual sexual stimuli. *Nature Neuroscience, 7*(4), 411–416.

Hassan, A., Bower, J. H., Kumar, N., Matsumoto, J. Y., Fealey, R. D., Josephs, K. A., & Ahlskog, J. E. (2011). Dopamine agonist-triggered pathological behaviors: surveillance in the PD clinic reveals high frequencies. *Parkinsonism & Related Disorders, 17*(4), 260–264.

Hearing, M. (2019). Prefrontal-accumbens opioid plasticity: implications for relapse and dependence. *Pharmacological Research, 139*, 158–165.

Knutson, B., Adams, C. M., Fong, G. W., & Hommer, D. (2001). Anticipation of increasing monetary reward selectively recruits nucleus accumbens. *Journal of Neuroscience, 21*(16), RC159.

Koob, G. F., & Volkow, N. D. (2010). Neurocircuitry of addiction. *Neuropsychopharmacology, 35*(1), 217–238.

Maskos, U., Molles, B. E., Pons, S., Besson, M., Guiard, B. P., Guilloux, J. P., ... Changeux, J. P. (2005). Nicotine reinforcement and cognition restored by targeted expression of nicotinic receptors. *Nature, 436*(7047), 103–107.

Mirenowicz, J., & Schultz, W. (1994). Importance of unpredictability for reward responses in primate dopamine neurons. *Journal of Neurophysiology, 72*(2), 1024–1027.

O'Doherty, J. P., Buchanan, T. W., Seymour, B., & Dolan, R. J. (2006). Predictive neural coding of reward preference involves dissociable responses in human ventral midbrain and ventral striatum. *Neuron, 49*(1), 157–166.

Olds, J., & Milner, P. (1954). Positive reinforcement produced by electrical stimulation of septal area and other regions of rat brain. *Journal of Comparative and Physiological Psychology, 47*, 419–427.

Rademacher, L., Krach, S., Kohls, G., Irmak, A., Grunder, G., & Spreckelmeyer, K. N. (2010). Dissociation of neural networks for anticipation and consumption of monetary and social rewards. *Neuroimage, 49*(4), 3276–3285.

Ramey, T., & Regier, P. (2019). Cognitive impairment in substance use disorders. *CNS Spectrums, 24*(1), 102–113.

Rueda-Orozco, P. E., & Robbe, D. (2015). The striatum multiplexes contextual and kinematic information to constrain motor habits execution. *Nature Neuroscience, 18*(3), 453–460.

Salamone, J. D., & Correa, M. (2012). The mysterious motivational functions of mesolimbic dopamine. *Neuron, 76*(3), 470–485.

Schlaepfer, T. E., Bewernick, B. H., Kayser, S., Hurlemann, R., & Coenen, V. A. (2014). Deep brain stimulation of the human reward system for major depression – rationale, outcomes and outlook. *Neuropsychopharmacology, 39*(6), 1303–1314.

Schleicher, A., Morosan, P., Amunts, K., & Zilles, K. (2009). Quantitative architectural analysis: a new approach to cortical mapping. *Journal of Autism and Developmental Disorders, 39*(11), 1568.

Schultz, W. (1998). Predictive reward signal of dopamine neurons. *Journal of Neurophysiology, 80*(1), 1–27.

Sell, L. A., Morris, J. S., Bearn, J., Frackowiak, R. S., Friston, K. J., & Dolan, R. J. (2000). Neural responses associated with cue evoked emotional states and heroin in opiate addicts. *Drug and Alcohol Dependence, 60*(2), 207–216.

Siegel, S. (2001). Pavlovian conditioning and drug overdose: when tolerance fails. *Addiction Research & Theory, 9*(5), 503–513.

Small, D. M., Jones-Gotman, M., & Dagher, A. (2003). Feeding-induced dopamine release in dorsal striatum correlates with meal pleasantness ratings in healthy human volunteers. *Neuroimage, 19*(4), 1709–1715.

Spreckelmeyer, K. N., Rademacher, L., Paulus, F. M., & Grunder, G. (2013). Neural activation during anticipation of opposite-sex and same-sex faces in heterosexual men and women. *Neuroimage, 66*, 223–231.

Steinberg, E. E., Boivin, J. R., Saunders, B. T., Witten, I. B., Deisseroth, K., & Janak, P. H. (2014). Positive reinforcement mediated by midbrain dopamine neurons requires $D_1$and D_2receptor activation in the nucleus accumbens. *PLOS ONE, 9*(4).

Stoeckel, L. E., Weller, R. E., Cook, E. W., 3rd, Twieg, D. B., Knowlton, R. C., & Cox, J. E. (2008). Widespread reward-system activation in obese women in response to pictures of high-calorie foods. *Neuroimage, 41*(2), 636–647.

Tapert, S. F., Cheung, E. H., Brown, G. G., Frank, L. R., Paulus, M. P., Schweinsburg, A. D., ... Brown, S. A. (2003). Neural response to alcohol stimuli in adolescents with alcohol use disorder. *Archives of General Psychiatry, 60*(7), 727–735.

Valentin, V. V., & O'Doherty, J. P. (2009). Overlapping prediction errors in dorsal striatum during instrumental learning with juice and money reward in the human brain. *Journal of Neurophysiology, 102*(6), 3384–3391.

Volkow, N. D., Fowler, J. S., Wang, G. J., Baler, R., & Telang, F. (2009). Imaging dopamine's role in drug abuse and addiction. *Neuropharmacology, 56*, 3–8.

Volkow, N. D., Tomasi, D., Wang, G. J., Logan, J., Alexoff, D. L., Jayne, M., ... Du, C. (2014). Stimulant-induced dopamine increases are markedly blunted in active cocaine abusers. *Molecular Psychiatry, 19*(9), 1037–1043.

Volkow, N. D., Wise, R. A., & Baler, R. (2017). The dopamine motive system: implications for drug and food addiction. *Nature Reviews Neuroscience, 18*(12), 741–752.

Wang, G. J., Volkow, N. D., Telang, F., Jayne, M., Ma, J., Rao, M. L., ... Fowler, J. S. (2004). Exposure to appetitive food stimuli markedly activates the human brain. *Neuroimage, 21*(4), 1790–1797.

Weissenborn, R., Whitelaw, R. B., Robbins, T. W., & Everitt, B. J. (1998). Excitotoxic lesions of the mediodorsal thalamic nucleus attenuate intravenous cocaine self-administration. *Psychopharmacology* (Berlin), *140*(2), 225–232.

Wickens, J. R. (2009). Synaptic plasticity in the basal ganglia. *Behavioural Brain Research, 199*(1), 119–128.

Wilson, S. J., Sayette, M. A., & Fiez, J. A. (2004). Prefrontal responses to drug cues: a neurocognitive analysis. *Nature Neuroscience, 7*(3), 211–214.

Wise, R. A. (1982). Neuroleptics and operant behavior: the anhedonia hypothesis. *Behavioral and Brain Sciences, 5*, 39–87.

Wise, R. A., & McDevitt, R. A. (2018). Drive and reinforcement circuitry in the brain: origins, neurotransmitters, and projection fields. *Neuropsychopharmacology, 43*(4), 680–689.

Wiss, D. A., Avena, N., & Rada, P. (2018). Sugar addiction: from evolution to revolution. *Frontiers in Psychiatry, 9*.

Yagishita, S., Hayashi-Takagi, A., Ellis-Davies, G. C. R., Urakubo, H., Ishii, S., & Kasai, H. (2014). A critical time window for dopamine actions on the structural plasticity of dendritic spines. *Science, 345*(6204), 1616–1620.

12 Stress, Fear, and Anxiety

Peter Dazeley / The Image Bank / Getty Images

Consider This …

Mr. and Mrs. Albert were a sociable couple and both had been free of medical problems throughout their lives. Mr. Albert was 48 and his wife was 55 when they got into a highway accident involving more than 100 vehicles and many deaths. While trapped in the car, they witnessed a child in a nearby car burn to death and feared their own fate. The Alberts escaped the car after Mr. Albert managed to break the windshield. The next day, he experienced flashbacks of the accident as if it were reoccurring. For many weeks after the accident, he would avoid talking or thinking about what had happened, for his memories of the event caused him severe anxiety. He found it difficult to sleep, and often woke to nightmares. His concentration was so impaired that he could no longer function at work. On the basis of interviews and a number of psychological tests a month after the accident, Mr. Albert was diagnosed with **posttraumatic stress disorder** (**PTSD**). He agreed to undergo an fMRI to monitor his brain activity while an experimenter read a description of the accident designed to evoke images and detailed memories of the event. As he listened to the description, Mr. Albert felt anxious and thought about how he might escape from the car, perhaps breaking the windshield again. (Lanius, Hopper, & Menon, 2003.)

As Mr. Albert recalled the traumatic event, fMRI showed high activation in the amygdala, visual cortex, and several other brain areas. The activation in the visual cortex was likely related to Mr. Albert's visual memories associated with the events (see Chapter 9), while the amygdala activation was likely related to his anxiety. After less than six months of exposure-based treatment (described later in this chapter), he no longer had PTSD.

Of course, not all individuals respond to traumatic stress in the same manner. Mr. Albert's wife was also diagnosed with PTSD and, like her husband, experienced difficulties sleeping and concentrating, and experienced flashbacks of the accident. But her flashbacks were without anxiety; instead, she felt emotionally numb. An fMRI of her brain while she recalled the accident showed activation of the occipital lobe along with a number of other brain regions, but no elevation in the amygdala. After six months of treatment, she still had PTSD.

The Alberts experienced a stressful event, or **stressor**, that was emotionally intense and life-threatening. Intense or long-lasting (**chronic**) stressors can lead to anxiety disorders such as PTSD or to depression. The relation between stress and depression is discussed in Chapter 13.

Why do some individuals undergo strong emotional responses to stressors, while others experience similar environmental events and quickly return to a balanced physiological and psychological state? Does our response to stress depend upon early childhood experiences? If so, how can such experiences produce long-lasting changes in our stress response systems? Why do individuals with PTSD and other anxiety disorders suffer from extreme fear and anxiety? Are they experiencing abnormally high levels of activation within brain regions responsible for normal fear experiences? Are there ways to reduce their excessive fear and anxiety with psychological therapy and/or drugs?

12.1 STRESS

Stressors may be intense, such as those associated with physical danger and/or violence. They may also be long lasting, such as when we lose a loved one, or care for a family member with a debilitating illness. Less intense stressors include pressure at work, taking an exam, or receiving a speeding ticket. Individuals under stress may report anxiety, nervousness, impatience, and irritability (Glaser & Kiecolt-Glaser, 2005). As we will see, stressors are associated with activation of the sympathetic nervous system and the hypothalamic–pituitary–adrenal (HPA) axis.

12.1.1 Stress Activates Fight or Flight Responses of the Sympathetic Nervous System

The **autonomic nervous system** is the part of the peripheral nervous system that influences the function of internal organs such as the heart, lungs, stomach, and adrenal glands. The autonomic nervous system has a **sympathetic** and **parasympathetic** division (see Figure 12.1). Stressors increase activity of the sympathetic nervous system. When a lion chases a zebra, the zebra's sympathetic nervous system generates a high arousal state that promotes "fight or flight" responses. After the zebra has escaped from danger, the parasympathetic nervous system is quickly activated, leading to reduced arousal.

The sympathetic and parasympathetic divisions of the autonomic nervous system are both described in Chapter 1. Here, our focus is on the sympathetic nervous system because of its key role in the body's response to stress. Let's look at the sympathetic response to danger in a bit more

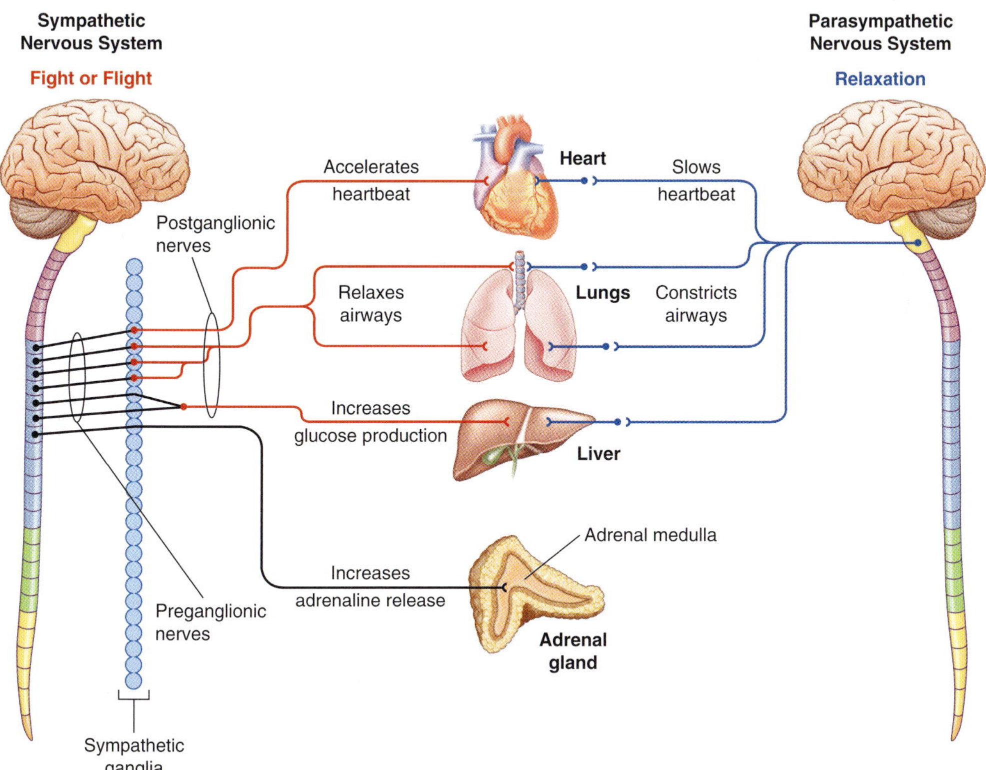

Figure 12.1 Sympathetic and parasympathetic divisions of the autonomic nervous system. Activation of the sympathetic nervous system promotes fight-or-flight responses, while parasympathetic activity reduces arousal. Here we are focusing on just a few of the key organs affected by activity of the autonomic nervous system.

detail. Within seconds after a threat appears, the sympathetic nervous system elevates the breathing rate, and widens airways in the lungs to allow more oxygen to enter with each breath. The heart pumps the oxygen-filled blood at an elevated rate, providing extra oxygen to the muscles. Elevated blood flow to the brain promotes enhanced alertness to sensory stimuli. Digestive organs such as the intestines are inhibited. After all, an emergency situation is no time to stop and digest a meal. Glucose released from the liver and other storage sites travels through the bloodstream to supply added energy to cells throughout the body. All of these reactions promote active behavioral and cognitive responses to a perceived threat.

Sympathetic **preganglionic** nerves (again, see Figure 12.1) leave the spinal cord and terminate in a nearby cluster of neural cell bodies called a **ganglion** (or **ganglia** in the plural). Here, the preganglionic neurons release acetylcholine and activate **postganglionic** nerves. This second set of sympathetic nerves have long axons that synapse, and release noradrenaline (also called norepinephrine), upon the heart, lungs, and other target organs. One of the target organs – the adrenal gland – receives direct input from a sympathetic nerve leaving the spinal cord (without involving a post-ganglionic nerve). Sympathetic activation causes the **adrenal medulla**, located at the center of the adrenal gland, to release adrenaline (also called epinephrine) and noradrenaline into the bloodstream. Adrenaline binds to receptors on the **vagus nerve**, which transmits information about the activity state of the body's organs to the brainstem (van Stegeren et al., 2007). In this way, the brain receives feedback regarding the state of autonomic arousal.

12.1.2 Stress Releases Hypothalamic–Pituitary–Adrenal Axis Hormones

After activation of the sympathetic nervous system, the hypothalamus initiates a second component of the body's stress response, activation of **glucocorticoid** stress hormones. Blood levels of glucocorticoids peak about 10 minutes after the onset of a stressor (Ulrich-Lai & Herman, 2009). Three regions are key to the control of glucocorticoid release: the hypothalamus, the pituitary, and the adrenal gland (Figure 12.2A). Together, these regions make up the **hypothalamic–pituitary–adrenal (HPA) axis** in humans, monkeys, rodents, birds, and other vertebrate species.

The HPA response to a stressor begins with the release of **corticotropin-releasing hormone (CRH)** from the **paraventricular nucleus (PVN)** of the hypothalamus (Figure 12.2B). CRH enters a group of blood vessels that connect the hypothalamus to the anterior pituitary, and triggers the release of **adrenocorticotropic hormone (ACTH)** from the anterior pituitary.

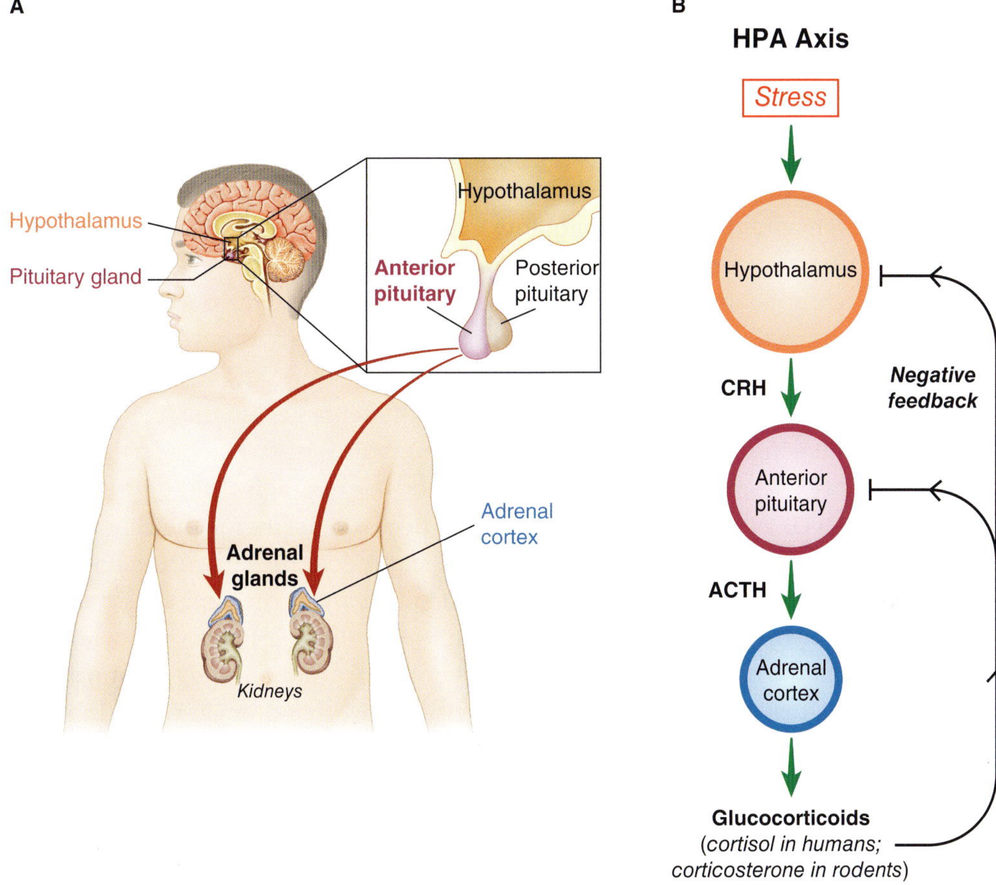

Figure 12.2 The hypothalamic–pituitary–adrenal (HPA) axis. (A) The hypothalamus, pituitary, and adrenal cortex make up the HPA axis. (B) Stress causes release of CRH from the hypothalamus, release of ACTH from the anterior pituitary, and finally release of glucocorticoids from the adrenal cortex. High glucocorticoid levels provide "negative feedback" to inhibit additional release of CRH and ACTH.

ACTH travels through the bloodstream to the adrenal cortex. The final step occurs when ACTH causes the **adrenal cortex** – the outer part of the adrenal gland – to release glucocorticoids into the bloodstream. The major glucocorticoid is **cortisol** in humans and **corticosterone** in rodents. In this chapter, we will often refer to these stress hormones released from the adrenal cortex by the general term, glucocorticoids.

Glucocorticoids easily pass the blood–brain barrier, and nearly all brain areas contain glucocorticoid receptors. High glucocorticoid levels cause the hypothalamus to release less CRH, and cause the pituitary to release less ACTH. This, of course, leads to reduced glucocorticoid release from the adrenal cortex. In this way, glucocorticoids produce **negative feedback**, reducing the activity of the HPA axis and limiting further glucocorticoid release.

Compared to the rapid onset and termination of the sympathetic nervous system response to stress, the HPA response is delayed (as noted above) and longer lasting. Hormones released by both the sympathetic nervous system and the HPA axis allow the animal to respond to stress quickly (via sympathetic arousal) and for a relatively long period of time (via release of HPA axis hormones). Both the sympathetic nervous system and the HPA axis promote increases in glucose availability, providing extra energy to cells of the brain and periphery, and enhance memory consolidation (McGaugh & Roozendaal, 2002). Remembering the environmental stimuli that accompanied the stressful event or threat in the past may help us to avoid the threat in the future.

Let's return to the earlier scene of the zebra fleeing the lion and experiencing high levels of sympathetic nervous system activity. The zebra is also experiencing strong activation of the HPA axis, leading to elevated levels of CRH, ACTH, and glucocorticoids. Luckily for the zebra, it will return to its baseline physiological state soon after its successful escape (Sapolsky, 1994). Unfortunately, humans activate the same stress response systems to less concrete, less identifiable threats. The person who fears the boss's criticism of his job performance may undergo sympathetic and HPA axis activation sustained by repetitive thoughts (**rumination**) about the work situation. The highly developed human forebrain gives us the ability to reflect upon previous events (Chapter 9) and to anticipate the future, a certain advantage in achieving many of our goals. But these cognitive systems allow us to experience stress responses long before the event has occurred, and, in some cases, even when the threat is unlikely to occur at all.

12.1.3 The Brain Responds to Threatening Situations and Controls Stress Responses

When the brain detects threatening stimuli, it activates the sympathetic nervous system and the HPA axis. Many brain regions contribute to these activations. A key control center for the sympathetic nervous system stress response is located within the medulla (Figure 12.3). Neurons in the medulla can, in turn, be activated by other brainstem neurons, including clusters of noradrenaline-releasing neurons in the **locus coeruleus** and serotonin-releasing neurons in the **dorsal raphe**. In addition, the **amygdala** and other emotion-related brain areas communicate with neurons in the brainstem and modulate sympathetic nervous system activity.

Many of the same brain areas that activate the sympathetic nervous system also activate the hypothalamic–pituitary–adrenal axis

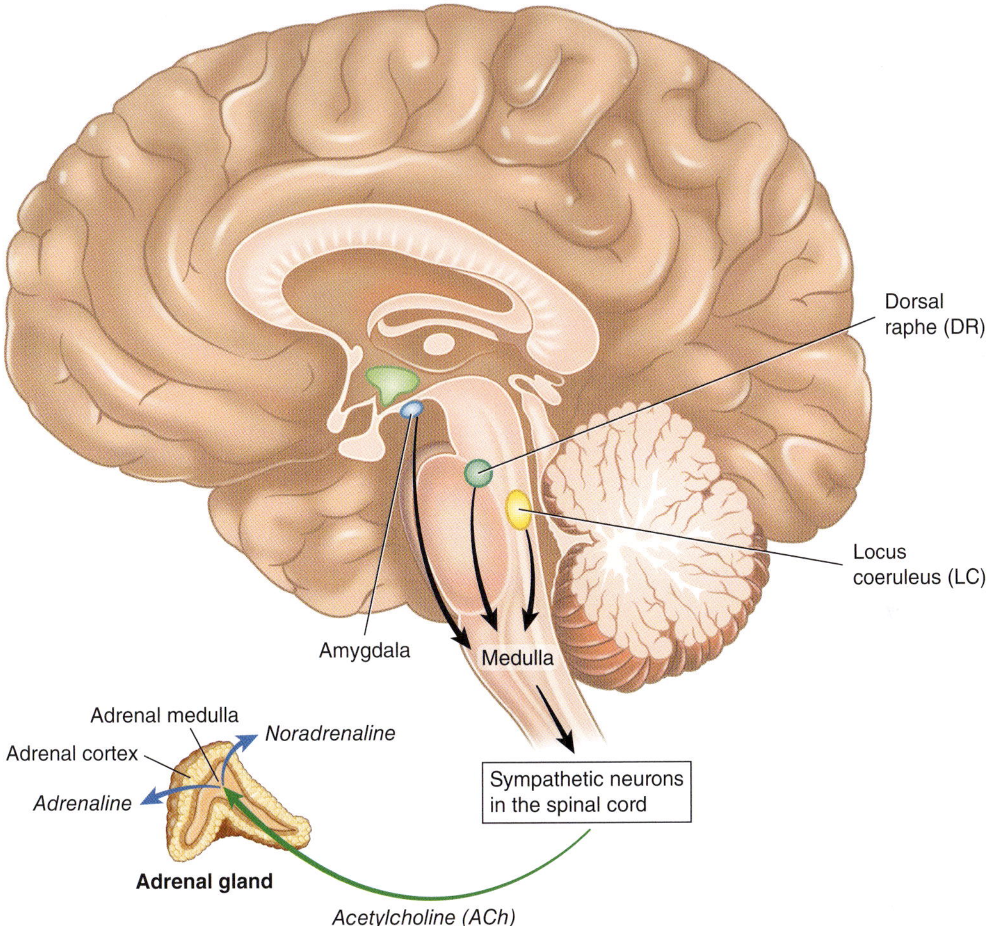

Figure 12.3 Neurons in the medulla control the sympathetic nervous system. Various brain areas send signals to the brainstem medulla in order to activate the sympathetic nervous system. Sympathetic neurons leave the spinal cord and terminate directly in the adrenal gland, triggering release of noradrenaline and adrenaline.

(Figure 12.4). The hypothalamus receives inputs from the locus coeruleus, dorsal raphe, and limbic areas including the amygdala. The PVN region of the hypothalamus integrates these inputs to determine the strength of the HPA axis stress response. While many brain regions work together to recognize threatening events, the amygdala is consistently activated by such events, and plays a key role in modulating the HPA axis stress response (Herman et al., 2003).

The fact that similar inputs control the sympathetic and HPA axis stress responses allows both response systems to become activated in response to threatening situations. On the other hand, both systems also receive a large number of distinct inputs, allowing activation levels of the two systems to vary with respect to one another.

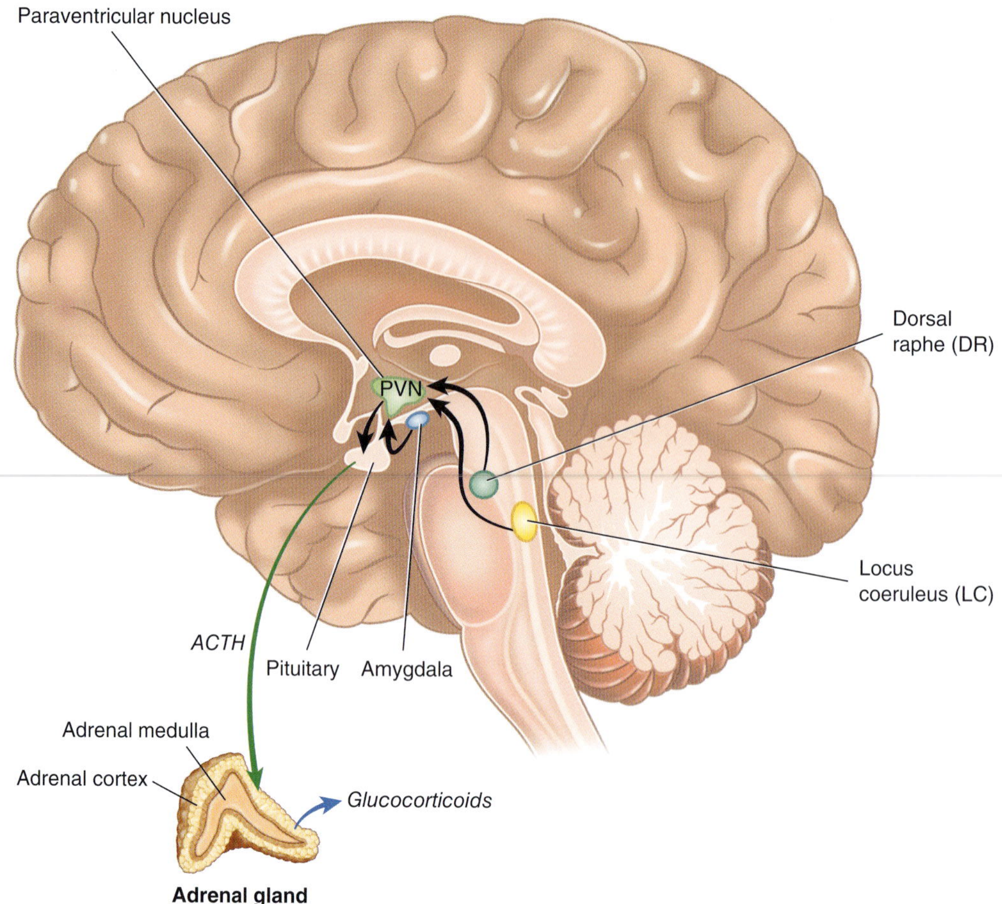

Figure 12.4 Brain areas that control the hypothalamic–pituitary–adrenal (HPA) stress response. Many of the same brain areas that control sympathetic nervous system activity (e.g., locus coeruleus) also control activation of the HPA axis.

KEY CONCEPTS

- **Stressors activate the sympathetic nervous system, leading to rapid physiological responses that include elevated heart rate and respiration, and release of adrenaline from the adrenal medulla.**
- **Stress causes a slower activation of the HPA axis, increasing release of glucocorticoids and other stress hormones.**
- **Under conditions of perceived threat, many of the same limbic and brainstem structures contribute to the activation of both the sympathetic nervous system and the HPA axis.**

TEST YOURSELF

1. **Draw a diagram illustrating a sympathetic nerve from the spinal cord to the heart. Include pre- and post-ganglionic neurons and the neurotransmitters released from each.**
2. **What neurotransmitters are released by the adrenal gland as a result of sympathetic nervous system activation?**
3. **What are the three brain regions and/or organs that comprise the HPA axis? What stress hormone does each release?**
4. **Name three brain regions that contribute to the control of both sympathetic and HPA axis activity.**

12.1.4 Stress Affects the Immune System

The immune system protects us from infection and illness caused by foreign microorganisms, or **pathogens**, such as bacteria, viruses, and fungi. Stress can increase susceptibility to infection and the duration of infectious illness (Glaser & Kiecolt-Glaser, 2005).

Stress impairs some aspects of immune function, but enhances others. In order to understand the effects of stress on the immune response, it is necessary to distinguish between two fundamental divisions of the immune system. One division is the **innate**, or **natural**, **immune system**, which responds to pathogens rapidly, sometimes within minutes. For instance, if a pathogen enters through a cut in the skin, the innate immune system's **macrophage** cells quickly congregate at the area of infection, where they surround the invader, kill it, and digest it. The macrophage also releases communication molecules, or **cytokines**, which can attract other macrophages to the area of infection to assist in the battle against the invading pathogens. Stress typically enhances the innate immune system response.

The other division of the immune system, the **adaptive**, or **specific**, **immune system,** kicks in more slowly, but mounts a more sophisticated defense. Unlike macrophage cells, each of which detects a range of pathogens (those that have been common in the evolutionary history of the organism), cells of your adaptive immune system *adapt* to the pathogens to which you have been exposed. These cells are tailor-made to *specifically* recognize those pathogens when they are encountered again in the future. It takes several days for the adaptive immune system to mount an army of immune cells that can fight the invading pathogen. Stress impairs the function of the adaptive immune system.

Why does stress enhance the innate immune system response and impair the adaptive immune system response? A compelling possibility is that, in general, stress promotes physiological responses that are of value to the immediate threats facing us. Physiological responses that might be beneficial over a longer time frame are put on hold. The innate immune system is immediately activated to fight an invading pathogen, while the specific immune system responds more slowly.

Consider the fleeing zebra again. It has a heightened risk of wounds, for instance from the lion's bite. Wounds allow pathogens to enter the bloodstream (Dhabhar, 2003). Activation of the innate immune system enhances the body's ability to deal with these immediate pathogenic invaders. On the other hand, the adaptive immune system takes days to mount a response. Stress-induced suppression of the adaptive immune system may reflect the body's decision to reduce resources that will not be immediately employed. When chased by a predator, the stress response is not focused on enhancing your survival next week or next month, but on maximizing the likelihood of living for another day.

When we say that stress enhances activation of the innate immune system and reduces activity of the adaptive immune system, we are speaking of acute stressors such as the sudden appearance of a predator. In humans, acute stressors such as jumping with a parachute, or public speaking, have been shown to increase the rapid innate immune response. However, chronic stressors such as the loss of a loved one can suppress both innate and adaptive immune system responses. The longer the duration of the chronic stress, the more the immune system is suppressed (Segerstrom & Miller, 2004). This does not necessarily mean that a chronic stressor will produce illness, for the immune system can undergo significant variations in function without compromising health. However, chronic stress is associated with a number of life-threatening diseases (Rohleder, 2019). The detrimental effects of stress may be greatest for those whose health is already compromised.

Figure 12.5 illustrates two important routes by which stress enhances the response of the innate immune system.

- First, activation of the sympathetic nervous system increases adrenaline release from the adrenal gland. Adrenaline then binds to receptors on immune system cells.
- Second, the HPA axis glucocorticoid stress hormones bind to receptors on cells of the immune system.

In animals, removal of the adrenal glands, which eliminates most adrenaline and glucocorticoids, prevents stress from enhancing the innate immune response (Dhabhar, 2003). This shows that the effects of stress on immune system function depend importantly upon elevations in stress hormone levels.

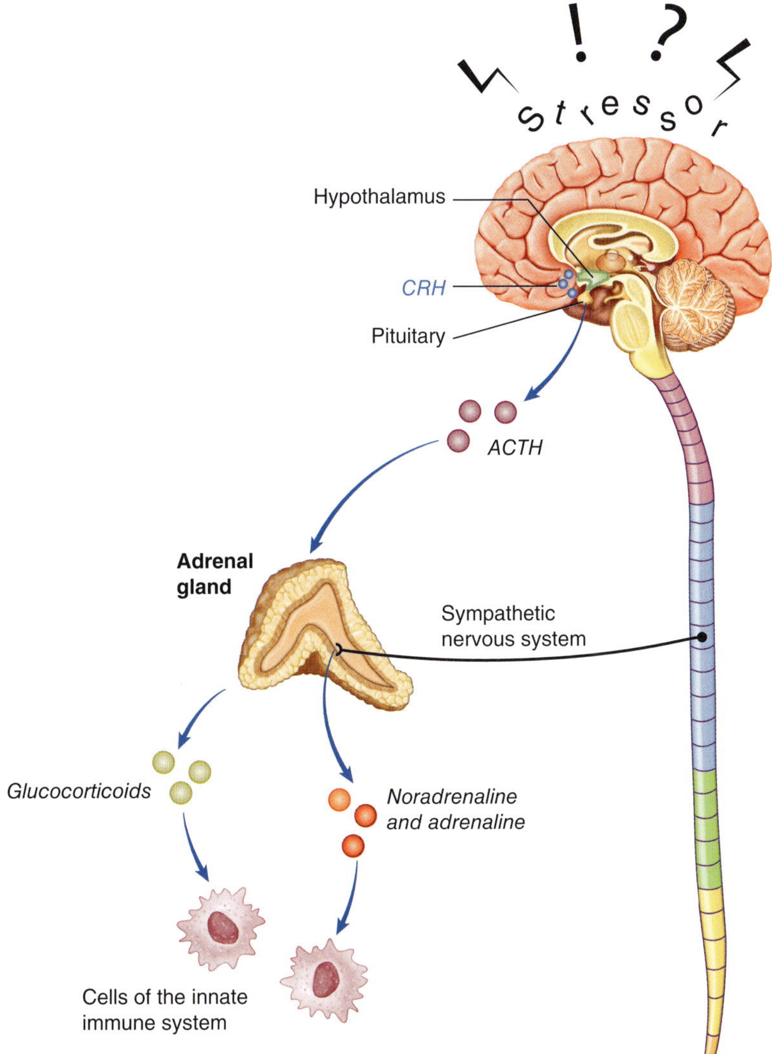

Figure 12.5 Stress chemicals communicate with innate immune system cells through two routes. Stress can affect immune function through the sympathetic nervous system (noradrenaline and adrenaline) and through the HPA axis (glucocorticoid hormones).

Similarly, human subjects subjected to mental stress (they had to respond quickly and continuously for 10 minutes on a memory task while competing with other subjects) show an elevation in activity of the innate immune system. A drug that blocks adrenaline receptors prevents this stress/immune interaction (Benschop et al., 1994). Such results suggest that elevated stress hormones are a key contributor to the effects of stress on the innate immune response. The precise mechanisms by which stress differentially affects cells of the innate versus the adaptive immune systems are a topic of many current investigations. Investigators are also examining other avenues of stress-immune interactions (Dudek, Kaufmann, Lavoie, & Menard 2021).

12.1.5 Why Do Some People Recover from Stress So Quickly?

Some individuals respond to mild stress with strong sympathetic and HPA axis activation. They easily become irritable, impatient, and/or anxious. **Stable** individuals may be exposed to the same potential stressors but deviate relatively little from their normal, or **baseline**, physiological state. Even after an environmental trigger produces a stress-related change in physiology, **resilient** individuals quickly return to their baseline state. Stability generally refers to one's ability to maintain physiological balance, or **homeostasis**, while resilience refers to the ability to return to the balanced state quickly, even if the individual has deviated from it substantially.

Extreme stressors such as physical violence or death of a close friend or family member can lead to disruption in physical functioning such as disrupted sleep, headaches, and/or digestive problems. They can also lead to psychological disturbances (depression, anxiety) and impairments in social functioning, such as withdrawal from others (Miller & Raison, 2016). For some, these reactions can last years (see Figure 12.6, "chronic" group). For others, disruptions in functioning may last months before

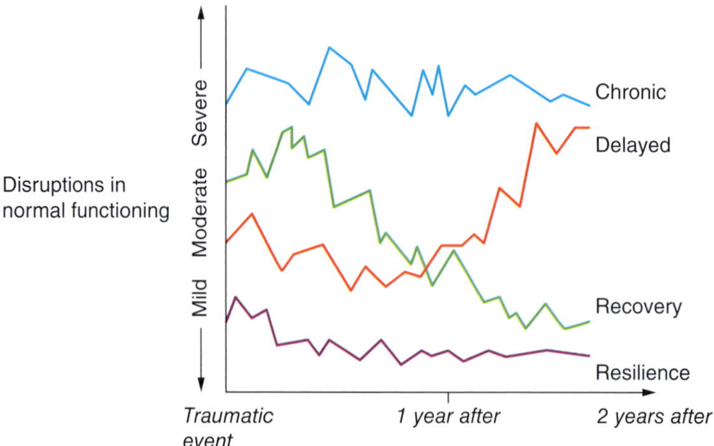

Figure 12.6 Individual differences in response to trauma. Individuals vary greatly in the duration and severity of their responses to trauma. Some show severe disruptions in physical, psychological, and social functions that last for years (chronic). Others show little or no disruption in functioning (resilience).
(Adapted from Bonanno, 2004, fig. 1.)

the person recovers ("recovery" in the figure), or may become severe only after a delay period ("delayed"). However, many individuals respond to these events with no disruption in functioning ("resilience").

In the past, theorists have viewed such resilience to severe stress to be highly unusual and/or a mask for symptoms that become apparent sometime in the future. Individuals who did not suffer prolonged distress or depression after the loss of a loved one were believed to be in denial of their grief. But evidence suggests that such resilient reactions to stress are not necessarily unhealthy and neither are they rare (Bonanno, 2004; Stainton et al., 2019). We saw in the opening case study that individuals who experience life-threatening or other highly stressful events can develop PTSD. We will examine this and other anxiety disorders later in the chapter. However, the majority of individuals who suffer physical assault, war combat, or other potentially threatening and violent events do not develop PTSD. Resilient individuals may maintain healthy functioning after potentially traumatic events, often with no apparent delay in symptoms (Bonanno, 2004).

What factors make a person more or less resilient to stress? One factor is social support, such as friends or family with whom one can communicate experiences and feelings (Oken, Chamine, & Wakeland, 2015; Stainton et al., 2019). In addition, resilient individuals often see themselves as capable of influencing important outcomes in their lives, and they tend to seek meaningful purpose in life. Resilience is also associated with the belief that both positive and negative life experiences can lead to personal growth (Bonanno, 2004).

Positive emotions such as feelings of gratitude for the positive things in one's life, interest in one's activities, love, and laughter are all associated with resilience. Of course, these positive emotions may themselves enhance social bonds, which as noted above, also promote resilience (Bonanno, 2004). Several kinds of meditation and yoga exercises reduce physiological stress responses as well as feelings of stress (Muehsam et al., 2017; Szabo, Nikhazy, Tihanyi, & Boros, 2017). These exercises may enhance stability and resilience (Oken et al., 2015).

12.1.6 Early Life Experiences Influence How an Individual Responds to Stress in Adulthood

Early life experiences can produce long-lasting changes in stress responses. For instance, rats whose mothers frequently licked and groomed their fur early in life became less likely to release glucocorticoids and other HPA axis stress hormones compared to rats whose mothers were less nurturing (Meaney, 2001).

How does a mother's contact with her pups influence their future stress reactivity? Changes that occur within the pups' hippocampus appear to be critical to this maternal influence. When glucocorticoids released from the adrenal cortex during stress reach the brain and activate hippocampal glucocorticoid receptors, the hippocampus reduces HPA-axis activity, suppressing additional glucocorticoid release (Figure 12.7). In other words, glucocorticoid receptors in the hippocampus (like those discussed earlier in the hypothalamus and pituitary) exert negative feedback upon the HPA-axis stress response. Pups exposed to maternal grooming grow more glucocorticoid receptors in their hippocampal neurons compared to those with less nurturing mothers. Therefore, the pups whose mothers groom them a lot have an enhanced negative feedback system that effectively limits the duration of the HPA axis response to stress.

But *how* does maternal grooming produce an increase in the number of the pups' hippocampal glucocorticoid receptors? When the mother

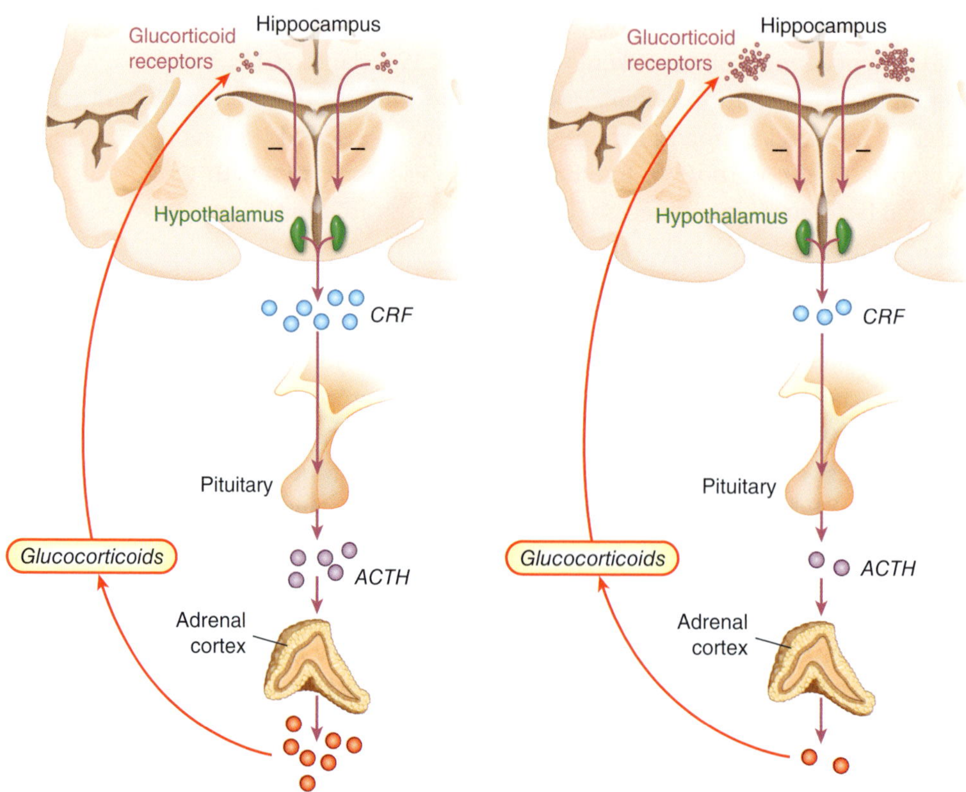

Figure 12.7 The hippocampus inhibits activity of the HPA axis. When glucocorticoids bind to hippocampal glucocorticoid receptors (left), the hippocampus inhibits activity of the HPA axis. As a result, an increase in glucocorticoid receptors (right) leads to reduced release of stress hormones. (Adapted from Hyman, 2009.)

grooms her pup, a gene (a segment of DNA) within the pup's hippocampal neurons is activated, or **expressed**. The gene codes for glucocorticoid receptors. That is to say, when the gene is expressed, additional glucocorticoid receptors are produced, or **synthesized** (Figure 12.8A).

Finally, let us examine more specifically how maternal grooming leads to expression of the glucocorticoid receptor gene. Normally, a **methyl** group is attached to a portion of DNA near the glucocorticoid receptor gene (Figure 12.8B). This methyl group prevents expression of the gene so that few glucocorticoid receptors are synthesized. Maternal grooming causes removal of this methyl group from the DNA (Figure 12.8C), allowing the gene to be expressed and large numbers of glucocorticoid receptors to be synthesized in the hippocampal neuron (Hyman, 2009). Researchers are attempting to figure out how maternal grooming leads to removal of the methyl group from the pup's DNA. When the pup matures to adulthood, the glucocorticoid receptor genes in its hippocampal neurons still lack the methyl group, so the neurons continue to produce high numbers of glucocorticoid receptors. These animals show low stress responses, and the females grow up to become nurturing mothers that groom their pups as well.

This can give rise to generations of rats with low stress reactivity due to a combination of environmental (grooming) and genetic (high expression of the glucocorticoid receptor gene) effects. Notice that in this case, the environmental influence exerted by the mother is what produces the "genetic effect" in the pups. The ability of environmental events to cause long-term changes in the state of the DNA that turn genes on or off is called **epigenetics**, and the ability of maternal care to activate the glucocorticoid receptor gene is a fascinating example of an epigenetic effect on behavior.

Early life experiences can also produce lasting effects on adult stress responses in humans. For instance, childhood abuse can lead to altered adult stress responses, including heightened release of HPA axis stress hormones (Heim & Nemeroff, 2001). Many researchers believe that epigenetic influences such as those described in rodents above may contribute to the effects of early life experience on human stress responses. Is it possible that childhood abuse produces long-lasting genetic changes in the hippocampus, perhaps in a direction opposite to that produced by maternal care in rodents? Might childhood abuse reduce the expression of hippocampal glucocorticoid receptors, and thereby reduce the hippocampus' ability to suppress stress hormone release?

Evidence, though indirect, suggests this may be the case. Researchers examined the brains of suicide victims with or without a history of childhood abuse. Those who had suffered abuse as children had fewer hippocampal glucocorticoid receptors. Further, the gene for glucocorticoid

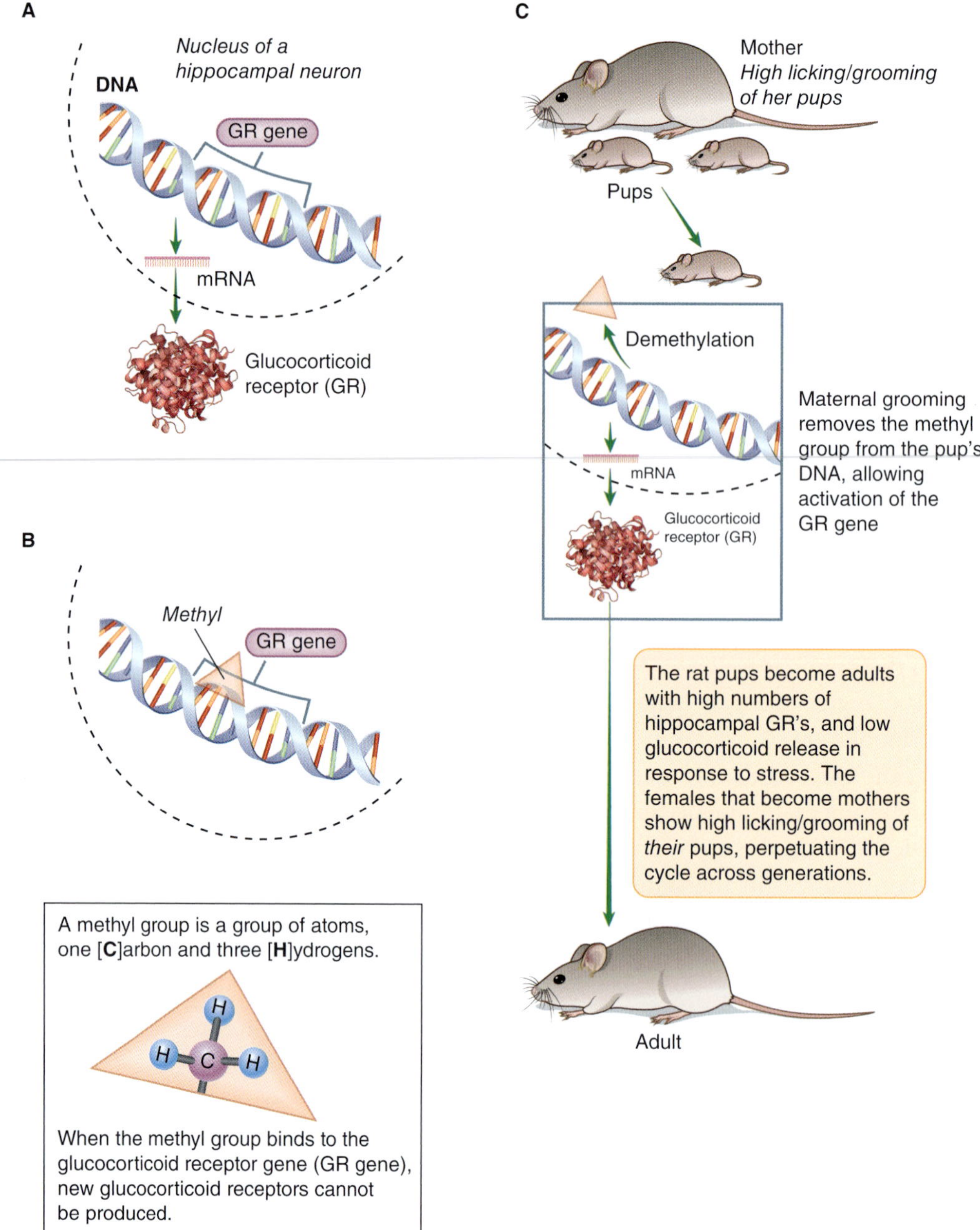

Figure 12.8 How does maternal grooming increase glucocorticoid receptors in the pup hippocampus? (A) Within hippocampal neurons, activation of the glucocorticoid receptor gene leads to synthesis of glucocorticoid receptors (GRs). (B) However, a methyl group blocks expression of the gene. (C) Maternal grooming leads to removal of the methyl group, increased expression of the gene, and an increased number of glucocorticoid receptors in the hippocampus.

receptors was methylated in a way that leads to reduced gene expression and glucocorticoid receptor synthesis (McGowan et al., 2009). The results of these studies in rats and humans, taken together, suggest the possibility that maternal care and child abuse may lead to opposite effects on expression of the glucocorticoid receptor in hippocampal neurons, and, as a result, opposite effects on vulnerability to stress in adulthood. These are examples of the more general discovery that positive or negative early-life experiences can produce epigenetic changes that influence behavior into adulthood (Hyman, 2009; Blaze & Roth, 2017; Keller, Doherty, & Roth, 2019; Perkeybile et al., 2019).

KEY CONCEPTS

- **The innate immune system responds rapidly to invading pathogens, while the adaptive immune system takes several days to mount its attack.**
- **Acute stress enhances activity of the innate immune system and inhibits activity of the adaptive immune system.**
- **Chronic stress suppresses both the innate and the adaptive immune systems.**
- **There is great variability in how individuals respond to potential stressors, even when these are severe or long lasting.**
- **Nurturing experiences early in life may enhance later resilience to stress while early trauma may have the opposite effect.**

TEST YOURSELF

1. **How does acute stress affect the function of the innate versus the adaptive immune system? How does chronic stress affect the functioning of these two divisions of the immune system?**
2. **What are three psychological attributes of resilient individuals?**
3. **How does nurturing maternal contact lead to reduced glucocorticoid release in rat pups?**

12.2 FEAR AND ANXIETY

The zebra running frantically from the lion has activated its HPA axis and sympathetic stress responses, and it is presumably in a state of great fear. As we will see in this section, the amygdala plays a critical role in generating fear. The amygdala also allows us to anticipate threatening events by recognizing the environmental stimuli that have preceded the threat in the past.

Activity of the amygdala allows the zebra to form an association between the sound of the lion rustling through leaves and the danger posed by its attack. By acquiring such associations, the zebra can predict the lion's presence even before it appears, allowing the zebra to begin its escape as the warning signs are detected.

In our wildlife example, fear and anxiety are likely to accompany the zebra's physiological stress responses of sympathetic and HPA axis activation. Often, these stress responses do occur as we are feeling anxious or afraid. But as we saw in the last section, stress responses can also be accompanied by irritability, impatience, frustration, or even depression. One might therefore think of fear and anxiety as a subset of the possible emotional responses that can be generated by environmental stressors, and which can accompany sympathetic and HPA axis responses to stress.

12.2.1 The Amygdala Responds to Threatening Stimuli

Threatening or **aversive** (unpleasant) **stimuli** activate neurons in the amygdala. In animals, these aversive stimuli include electric shock, unpleasant tastes, and unpleasant odors. In humans, loud unpleasant noises, unpleasant odors, and facial expressions of fear have all been shown to activate the amygdala (Figure 12.9A). The amygdala also responds to environmental stimuli that reliably precede, and therefore predict, the aversive event (Bishop, 2007).

When a rat receives a shock to its paw, the shock is an **unconditioned stimulus** (**US**). It produces an emotional response with no learning (no conditioning) necessary. Like humans, rats do not need to *learn* that shock is something to fear; they are innately wired to avoid shock and other aversive USs. However, imagine a rat learns that a tone always precedes the shock. The tone begins as a **neutral stimulus**; the rat neither likes nor fears it. As the rat comes to associate the tone with shock, the tone becomes a **conditioned stimulus** (**CS**), an environmental event that signals that the aversive US is coming.

The tone, once it has become a CS, can activate the sympathetic nervous system, increase HPA axis hormone levels, enhance vigilance, and in some cases cause the animal to freeze in position, unable to move. In other words, the rat responds to the conditioned tone with fear. Lesions of the amygdala prevent the acquisition of these conditioned fear responses (Johansen, Cain, Ostroff, & LeDoux, 2011).

As we saw in Chapter 9, the acquisition of conditioned responses to aversive stimuli involves neuronal plasticity, particularly a strengthening of excitatory synaptic connections between neurons in the thalamus and those in the lateral amygdala. Once the conditioned aversive stimulus

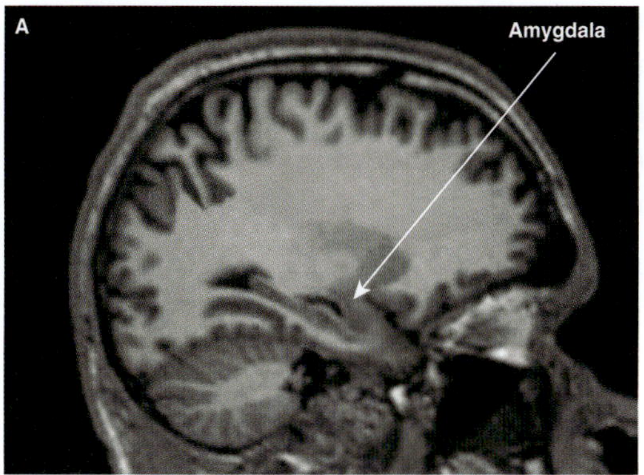

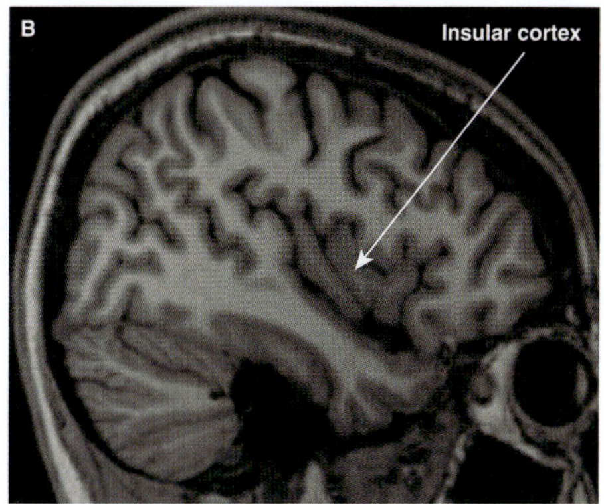

Figure 12.9 Two brain regions strongly linked to fear in humans. Activity of the amygdala (A) and insular cortex (B) are associated with fear in human subjects. Individuals suffering anxiety disorders show hyperactivity in both of these regions.
(Adapted from Shin & Liberzon, 2010, fig. 1, © 2009, American College of Neuropsychopharmacology.).

gains the ability to strongly activate the lateral amygdala, the lateral amygdala in turn activates the central nucleus of the amygdala. The central nucleus then activates brain regions that generate sympathetic arousal, freezing, vigilance, and other components of the fear response.

Activity of the amygdala and the **insular cortex** (Figure 12.9B) is strongly associated with the experience of fear in humans (Shin & Liberzon, 2010; Linsambarth, Moraga-Amaro, Quintana-Donoso, Rojas, & Stehberg, 2017). As we will see, individuals with excessive fear, or anxiety disorder, show hyperactivity of the amygdala and insular cortex.

12.2.2 The Woman without an Amygdala

Fortunately, few people have suffered damage that entirely destroys the amygdala, and even fewer have undergone complete amygdala loss on both sides of the brain (loss of both amygdalae), without damage to other nearby brain areas. However, a research paper in 1994 described a woman known as S.M. (abbreviated for confidentiality) with exclusive damage to her left and right amygdalae as a result of a rare genetic disease (Adolphs, Tranel, Damasio, & Damasio, 1994). In questionnaires about her daily experiences over a three-month period, she never reported more than very low levels of fear (Feinstein, Adolphs, Damasio, & Tranel, 2011). She recalled no experiences of fear in her entire life, despite having been the victim of several violent encounters. She was also unable to recognize facial expressions of fear when shown photos of frightened persons.

Investigators wished to directly observe her fear responses, or lack of them, under various situations that provoke fear in most individuals. When given the opportunity to hold a snake in a pet store (Figure 12.10A) she showed no signs of fear (Feinstein et al., 2011). She rubbed the snake's scales, touched its tongue, and watched as it slithered through her hands. "This is so cool!" she said, and she asked the store employee questions about the snakes (e.g., "When they look at you, what do they see?"). S.M. was asked to rate her fearfulness from 0 (no fear) to 10 (extreme fear) and her rating never exceeded a two. She would touch and poke the larger, more dangerous snakes in the store even though the employee warned her that the snakes could bite her. Before the pet store visit, she had told the investigators that she hated snakes. When asked why she wanted to touch something she claimed to hate, and which she knew was dangerous, she responded that she was overcome with "curiosity." Her comfort with snakes was not limited to the pet store environment, for her son recalled that she once picked up a large snake she had found outside. In the pet store, she also tried to touch the tarantula (Figure 12.10B) until an employee stopped her.

Researchers also observed S.M. as she went through the Waverly Hills Sanatorium's "haunted house" (Figure 12.10C). She went through the dark corridors with a group of five other people as "monsters," "murderers," and "ghosts" suddenly appeared, causing the others to scream in fright and to turn corners with great hesitancy. In contrast, S.M. would lead the way ("This way guys, follow me!"). She smiled and laughed at the monsters, and tried to talk to them and even touch them. At one point, she scared one of the "monsters" by poking its head because she was curious about what it felt like.

Without a functioning amygdala, one can experience at least one type of fear. Inhalation of carbon dioxide (CO2) causes people to gasp for air, to feel anxious and sometimes panicked, until they rip off the inhalation

Figure 12.10 Fear induction in Patient S.M. With bilateral damage to the amygdala, S.M. showed no signs of fear while handling a snake (left), touching a tarantula (middle), or walking through a "haunted house" (right).

(Adapted from Feinstein et al., 2011, fig. 1, © 2011 Elsevier Ltd. All rights reserved.)

mask. S.M. reported fear when she was exposed to CO2. So did several other patients with specific amygdala lesions. In fact, all three subjects experienced intense fear and anxiety, demonstrating that fear *can* be experienced in the absence of the amygdala (Feinstein et al., 2013). The subjects reported being surprised by their fear and said it was a novel experience. The results suggest that while the amygdala may be responsible for many, perhaps most, fear experiences, it is not the only brain substrate capable of generating fear.

12.2.3 Learning Not to Be Afraid

During several years of elementary school, Jimmy would bully Brad after school, sometimes with physical violence. The very sight of Jimmy's face, with its reddish complexion, was enough to make Brad's heart race with fear. By the time they'd reached high school, Jimmy had grown out of his bullying behavior, and wanted to befriend Brad. Even if Brad chooses to forgive Jimmy for his past behavior, will he continue to experience fear every time he sees Jimmy's face? Or, over time, will that automatic fear response subside? Will Brad experience less fear of Jimmy as he learns that Jimmy's face is no longer a conditioned stimulus that signals physical threat, that is to say, will Brad's conditioned fear response to Jimmy **extinguish**? After a tone CS has been paired with a shock US, fear of the CS can extinguish when it is presented repeatedly in the absence of the US. Perhaps the fear elicited by Jimmy's face will extinguish as well.

However, extinction learning is not simply a matter of weakening associations between the conditioned and unconditioned stimulus. The rat does not forget that the tone was paired with shock, and Brad will not likely forget Jimmy's past aggression. Instead, when the CS is now presented with no negative consequence, the subject stores a new association between the CS and *no* aversive outcome. For instance, tone-alone trials allow the rat to form new associations between the tone and the absence of shock. Friendly or neutral interactions with Jimmy allow Brad to learn new associations between Jimmy and the absence of violence. In summary, we can acquire the association that a CS predicts a US (CS → US) and also that a CS predicts the absence of the US (CS → no US). When we have stored both kinds of associations, our response to the CS in a given instance will depend upon which of these associations is most strongly activated.

How do we know that experiences of CS → no US do not erase the CS → US association from memory? Imagine that a rat receives CS → US (tone → shock) pairings until the CS reliably elicits conditioned fear responses. If you follow the tone/shock pairings with trials in which the tone is presented without shock, the rats show less fear to the tone. In fact, with enough tone-alone trials, the rat may show almost no fear at all to the tone. The conditioned fear response has extinguished. But a day, even a week, later when the tone is presented again, the rat once again shows signs of fear (Quirk, 2002). When a response to a CS has extinguished, and then reemerges after time has passed, we say that the response has undergone **spontaneous recovery**.

Spontaneous recovery of the conditioned fear response shows that even after many CS-alone trials and extinction of fear responses to the CS, the CS–US association remains in memory. The tone → no-shock association suppressed the rat's fear response to the tone. But when this extinction learning weakens with the passage of time, the tone/shock association once again generates fear to the tone. Extinction of a fear response to a CS does not mean that the brain has lost the association between the CS and the threatening US.

12.2.4 The Medial Prefrontal Cortex Inhibits Fear Responses

We saw earlier that the amygdala is necessary in order to learn an association between a tone CS and a threatening US such as shock. The investigator may measure the fear elicited by the tone by recording the amount of time an animal freezes, immobile, while the tone is on. During extinction trials where the tone is presented alone, what brain areas are involved in storing the CS → no US association?

The **medial prefrontal cortex** (**mPFC**) plays an important role in extinction learning and suppression of fear responses. In one experiment designed to study the role of the mPFC during extinction, rats received a number of tone → shock pairings on Day 1 (Milad & Quirk, 2002). During each trial, the tone came on for 30 seconds, and then the shock was briefly presented. Not surprisingly, rats spent more and more time freezing each time the tone came on (Figure 12.11, *Conditioning*). Later on the same day, rats received extinction trials, that is, repeated presentations of the tone by itself, with no shock. As shown in the figure, the rats froze less and less each time they heard the tone during extinction trials. Their fear of the tone was reduced (Figure 12.11, *Extinction*). On Day 2, the tone was presented by itself again. Did the rats show any signs of fear to the tone? Yes, as seen in the figure, they froze during the initial tone-alone trials. But notice that during the very first extinction trials on Day 2, the tone produced less freezing than it had during the first extinction trials on Day 1. On Day 2, the animals remembered some of the extinction experiences (tone → no-shock) they had during Day 1 extinction trials.

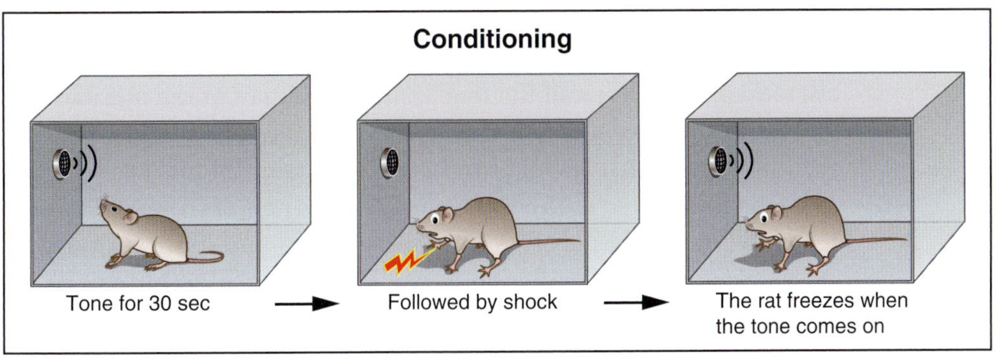

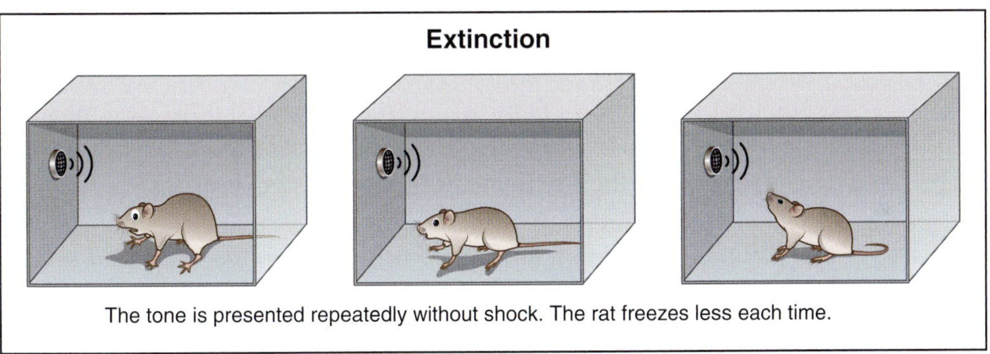

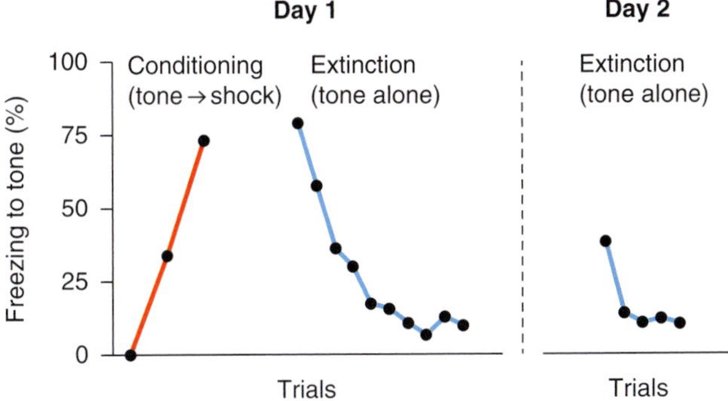

Figure 12.11 Extinction of conditioned fear over two days. By the end of tone/shock (Conditioning) trials on Day 1, rats froze about 75 percent of the time the tone was on. Later that day, tone-alone trials (Extinction) reduced their freezing to the tone. On the first extinction trial on Day 2, rats showed some freezing to the tone, but not very much. They seemed to recall the extinction trials from Day 1.

How did mPFC neurons respond during the fear conditioning and extinction trials? The mPFC neurons fired very little during the conditioning trials, when animals learned the tone → shock association. (Under the same conditions, amygdala neurons are strongly activated.) The mPFC neurons didn't fire much when the tone was presented by itself on Day 1 either. So, you don't need the mPFC in order to learn the tone → no-shock association either. What is it that activates these neurons? A hint came on Day 2, when the tone was presented by itself again (Day 2 extinction). During these trials, rats appeared to recall the tone → no-shock trials of the previous day, for they showed reduced fear of the tone from the very first trial. The rats that showed the least fear of the tone on Day 2 were the rats whose neurons in the mPFC fired at the highest rates. Activation of the mPFC appears to remind the rats of the previously learned tone → no-shock association.

What happens to extinction learning when the mPFC is destroyed? The rats are normal in associating the tone with shock; they become scared of the tone. When these rats with mPFC lesions receive tone-alone (extinction) trials later the same day, they show normal reductions in freezing to the tone. So, the lesions do not impair short-term extinction of the fear response. However, when the tone is presented alone for a second day of extinction trials, rats with mPFC lesions show strong fear responses. They do not seem to have stored (and/or are unable to retrieve) a long-term memory that the tone is no longer followed by shock (Quirk, Russo, Barron, & Lebron, 2000). This would be analogous to Brad showing reduced fear of Jimmy on Monday after several hours of friendly interactions, only to have his fear of Jimmy return full force on Tuesday. Without the mPFC, subjects are unable to recall extinction memories.

In humans and other primates, regions lining the medial walls of the PFC, including the ventromedial PFC (vmPFC), correspond anatomically to the part of the mPFC that is needed to recall extinction memories. The vmPFC (see Figure 12.12) is activated while humans undergo extinction trials in which a previously feared stimulus is no longer associated with a negative outcome (Andrewes & Jenkins, 2019; Gottfried & Dolan, 2004). The more the vmPFC is activated, the less fear the subject shows in response to the CS (Phelps, Delgado, Nearing, & LeDoux, 2004). The vmPFC, therefore, plays a role in extinction learning. In addition to the vmPFC, extinction of conditioned fear responses in humans is associated with hippocampal activation (Shin & Liberzon, 2010).

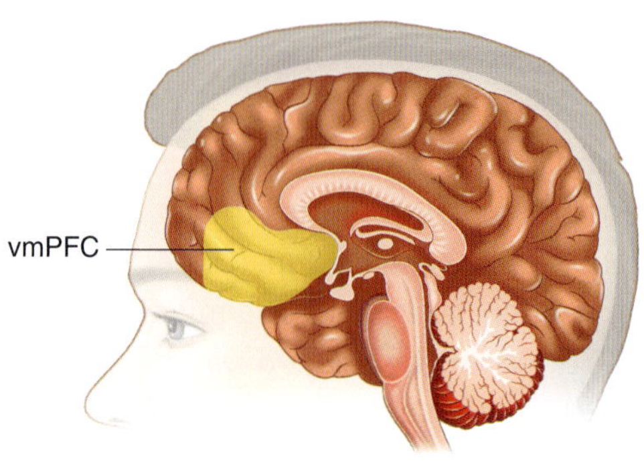

Figure 12.12 **Recalling that a cue is no longer followed by danger**. The ventromedial prefrontal cortex (vmPFC) is necessary for recall of extinction memories.

KEY CONCEPTS

- The amygdala plays an important role in associating a conditioned stimulus (CS) with a threatening unconditioned stimulus (US), and for generating fear responses to both the CS and the US.
- Humans with complete amygdala loss rarely experience fear.
- When an environmental stimulus (CS) previously associated with a threatening event is repeatedly presented alone, the fear responses to the CS extinguish. The ventromedial PFC is critical for reducing fear responses to a CS.

TEST YOURSELF

1. Describe three unusual behavioral and/or emotional characteristics seen in an individual without an amygdala.
2. Give an example of extinction and spontaneous recovery of an association between a conditioned stimulus and a threatening unconditioned stimulus. During extinction, are fear memories erased? Explain.
3. Give one line of evidence that activity of the ventromedial PFC is important in remembering that a conditioned stimulus no longer signals a threat.

12.2.5 Anxiety Disorders Are Associated with Abnormal Activation of Fear Circuitry

When someone says, "I am afraid that my boss will criticize me today" or "I feel anxious that she will criticize me today," they are using the concepts of "fear" and "anxiety" more or less interchangeably. However, researchers and clinicians typically refer to "fear" when describing a natural defensive response to an imminent threat. The fear response develops quickly and diminishes soon after the danger is gone.

"Anxiety" arises in anticipation of a more distant threat. Even a threat that is unlikely to occur can generate intense, long-lasting, and recurring anxiety. A person who is often anxious may focus upon possible dangers lurking in the future, physical harm due to injury or illness, job loss, and/or social disapproval. This focus on negative outcomes can produce a self-perpetuating state of anxiety. The more the person focuses on negative outcomes, the more anxious he becomes; and the more anxious he becomes, the more he focuses on negative outcomes, and on and on. Anxious individuals are highly attentive to potential threats in their environment (Bishop, 2007) and show high levels of amygdala activity and release of HPA axis stress hormones. One of these stress hormones, CRH, acts upon neurons in the bed nucleus of the stria terminalis to enhance anxiety (Davis, Walker, Miles, & Grillon, 2010).

Anxiety disorders are characterized by excessive fear and anxiety in the absence of true danger. There are several types of anxiety disorders, and approximately 30 percent of individuals will suffer from one of them over their lifetime. In posttraumatic stress disorder (PTSD), intense fear is triggered by reminders of a traumatic and highly stressful event, often one that involved threat of death or serious injury (Andrewes & Jenkins, 2019). As we saw in the story of Mr. Albert and his wife in the opening case study, an individual with PTSD may reexperience the traumatic event in great detail, including the remembered sights, sounds, and smells. In some cases, the person may reexperience the event in the form of nightmares. The intense anxiety associated with these traumatic memories leads him to avoid situations likely to generate fear. Individuals with PTSD often have difficulties concentrating and sleeping. In most cases, the PTSD symptoms disappear soon after the traumatic event (Breslau et al., 1998). However, for others the symptoms persist for years. The fact that patients may continue to show intense fear to stimuli that remind them of the trauma suggests a deficit in learning that the stimuli no longer predict a threatening event (Barrett & Armony, 2009) or a deficit in the ability of such extinction learning to influence behavior.

The most common anxiety disorder, **social anxiety disorder**, affects approximately 5 percent of the US population (Ruscio et al., 2008). Individuals with this disorder have an intense fear of social embarrassment or humiliation, and attempt to avoid social interactions. For other individuals, anxiety is triggered by specific objects (**specific phobia**). Specific phobias may involve fear of a particular type of animal such as spiders or cats, an aspect of the natural environment such as lightning or heights, fear of dark, small spaces such as closets (claustrophobia), and other specific environmental conditions. Individuals with **panic disorder** experience sudden and unexpected periods of intense fear and anxiety, accompanied by sweating, trembling, and chest pain. These individuals suffer great distress worrying about future panic attacks. For some individuals, a wide range of circumstances can trigger anxiety. Those with **generalized anxiety disorder** persistently and excessively worry about a number of different things. Even in situations where there is little cause for concern, those with generalized anxiety disorder expect the worst.

Individuals with anxiety disorder (social anxiety, specific phobias, panic disorder, and generalized anxiety disorder) show hyperactivity of the amygdala and insular cortex when presented with "negative emotional stimuli" such as photos of physical suffering, or facial expressions of fear or anger (Figure 12.13, top). These results are consistent with the fact that the disorders involve unusually high states of

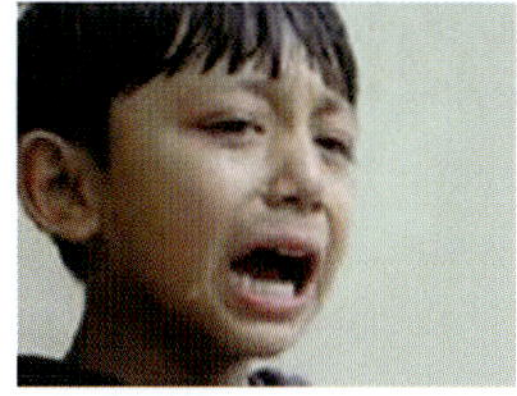

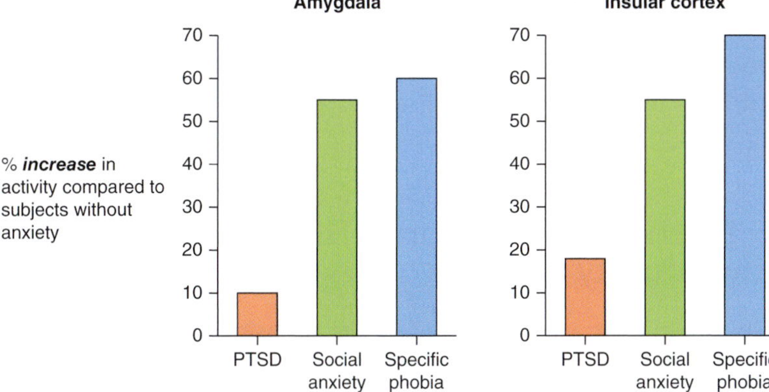

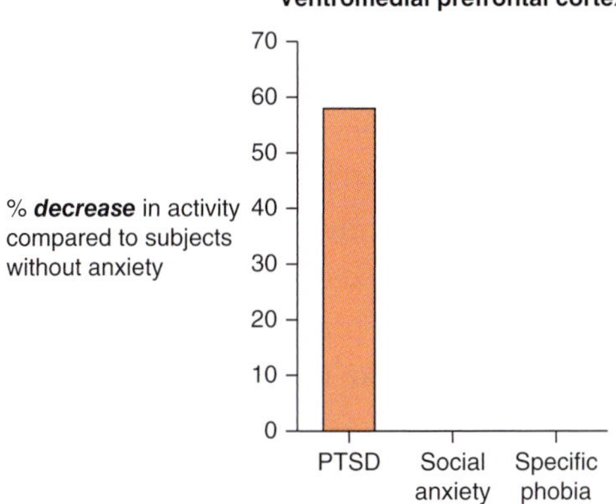

Figure 12.13 **The effect of negative emotional stimuli on the amygdala, insular cortex, and ventromedial PFC**. Top graphs: Negative emotional stimuli produced hyperactivation of the amygdala and insular cortex. The number 60 on the *y*-axis means that the brain region was on average 60 percent more activated in patients with the disorder compared to controls. Bottom graph: PTSD patients viewing the stimuli showed reduced activity in the vmPFC compared to controls.
(Photo, Schönfelder, Kanske, Heissler, & Wessa, 2013, © Oxford University Press.)

fear (Etkin & Wager, 2007; Gorka, Nelson, Phan, & Shankman, 2014). Hyperactivity of the amygdala in individuals with PTSD is more moderate compared to that seen in persons with other anxiety disorders.

PTSD also differs from other anxiety disorders in the vmPFC response to emotional stimuli. Activity of the vmPFC is *abnormally low* in PTSD patients compared to controls (Figure 12.13, bottom). We saw earlier that the vmPFC inhibits fear responses to threatening stimuli (Maren & Holmes, 2016). The data suggest that reduced vmPFC activity in PTSD may lead to excessive fear, particularly when the amygdala is driven by trauma-related stimuli (Shin & Liberzon, 2010; Andrewes & Jenkins, 2019). In some PTSD patients, such as those exposed to terrorism (Yamasue et al., 2003) or combat (Rauch, Shin, & Phelps, 2006), a reduction in the size of the vmPFC has been observed. While each of the anxiety disorders involves heightened amygdala activity and fear, the vmPFC abnormalities associated with PTSD suggest that individuals with this disorder may have particular difficulties diminishing fear triggered by memories of a traumatic event.

12.2.6 Psychological and Drug Therapies Can Reduce Excessive Anxiety

Therapists often treat anxiety disorders by exposing the individual to the feared event, or encouraging the individual to think about the feared event in the safety of the therapist's office (Rauch et al., 2006). Using one such exposure technique called **systematic desensitization**, a patient begins by identifying the stimulus that causes him anxiety. Say he fears snakes. The patient learns relaxation techniques, such as breathing exercises or tensing and relaxing different body parts until he feels relaxed. While in a relaxed state, the patient views snake-related stimuli, beginning with the least anxiety-provoking and ending with the most. The patient may practice entering a relaxed state after viewing a picture of a snake, and, once successful, he may practice relaxing in the presence of a small snake in a nearby room, a snake in a cage in front of him, touching the snake, and so on (Wolpe, 1968).

In this way, the therapist helps to extinguish the individual's fear responses associated with a particular stimulus (like snakes) or situation (such as a social event). But, as we saw, extinction does not necessarily involve a loss of fear-related associations. Spontaneous recovery and other related extinction phenomena show that even an apparently extinguished fear response may reemerge with time or when the feared stimulus is encountered in another context. Another challenge when employing exposure/extinction techniques to treat anxiety is that the individual typically avoids anxiety-provoking situations, and, outside of the therapist's office, may deprive himself of many opportunities for extinction learning under real-world conditions. For instance, a person with a fear of insects may learn, through desensitization, to relax in the presence of photos of insects. Later, he may learn to relax as he observes an insect crawling in a jar in the therapist's office. But it is important that he also expose himself to outdoor settings (say picnics) where he will encounter insects. If he avoids such natural settings, he will deprive himself of the opportunity to desensitize to insects outside of the controlled setting of the therapist's office.

Rational Emotive Behavioral Therapy and the closely related **Cognitive Behavioral Therapy** employ techniques designed to extinguish fear responses, but also encourage the patient (more often referred to as the client) to reevaluate anxiety-related thought processes as well (Beck & Clark, 1997; Ellis & Dryden, 2007). For instance, the therapist might help a client to examine specific thoughts and beliefs that come to her mind as she anticipates embarrassment in a particular social situation. Say she often thinks, "The people at this event may disapprove of the way I speak and act. I would be humiliated and I couldn't bear it. It would be awful." The therapist may help the client to more realistically assess the likelihood of social disapproval, and even to challenge their "worst case scenario." "If someone were to judge you in a negative manner, why exactly would it be awful?" the therapist might ask. "Even if so-and-so were to disapprove of the way you speak, could you not still have a happy life without their approval? Would it really be awful if they disapproved of you, or merely unfortunate?" Helping the client to reexamine or *challenge* anxiety-related cognitions (eventually on her own, without the therapist's help) can reduce anxiety to the point where she may more easily put herself into feared social situations. At that point, new potentially positive (or at least neutral) associations with the situation may be acquired. Such cognitive approaches have been shown to be effective in treating a wide range of anxiety disorders (Otte, 2011), and the reduction in symptoms is associated with reduced amygdala activation (Shin & Liberzon, 2010).

These findings suggest that changes in the way one thinks about or interprets a situation can influence the response of the brain's fear/anxiety circuitry. To examine the influence of cognitive interpretation on responses to potentially disturbing events, experimenters sometimes use a technique called **reappraisal**. For instance, in one experiment individuals were shown a photo of a person's face, and asked to imagine interacting with the person in a real-world situation. After a few seconds, they saw a video of the same face saying, "I hate you!" or some other negative statement (Figure 12.14). In another condition, the subject saw the face of a different person, followed by a video of that person making a neutral statement such as, "It's 4 o'clock." Needless to say, when the subject later rated the positive or negative emotion they felt upon seeing those faces, they gave a much more negative rating to the face associated with the negative comments. In a reappraisal condition, the subject saw a photo of a third person's face, again followed by a video of the person making very negative comments. However, in this case, the subject received instructions to interpret the video in such a way as to not feel upset, for instance

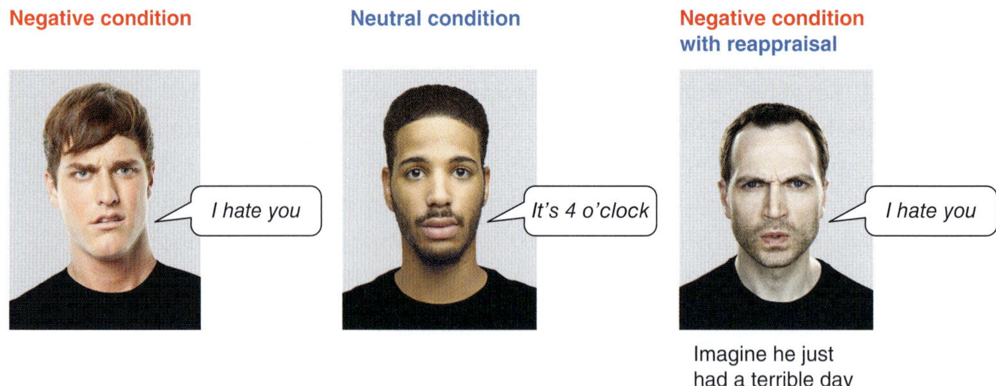

Figure 12.14 Reappraisal experiment methodology. Subjects see a brief video of a person making a negative (left) or neutral (middle) comment. In some cases, subjects are instructed to reappraise (reinterpret) the negative statements in a way that is not upsetting (right). (Left face, Verpaalen et al., 2019; middle and right faces, Jiang, Chen, & Wyer, 2014.)

by imagining that the speaker had a horrible day and was simply lashing out at people randomly, or that the person was practicing lines for a part in a drama. Reappraisal greatly reduced the negative ratings assigned to the person's face (Blechert et al., 2015).

When reappraising potentially negative stimuli, individuals reduce their amygdala activation (Ochsner, Bunge, Gross, & Gabrieli, 2002) and increase activity of the vmPFC (Urry et al., 2006). Those subjects with the largest increases in vmPFC activity show the greatest reductions in amygdala activation (Urry et al., 2006), consistent with a role of the vmPFC in suppressing amygdala activation, fear, and anxiety. It seems reasonable to speculate that cognitive therapies may similarly reduce activity of the amygdala and increase activity of the vmPFC.

Anxiety disorders are also treated with drug therapy (pharmacotherapy). **Selective serotonin reuptake inhibitors** (**SSRIs**) such as Prozac, which elevate synaptic serotonin levels (see Chapter 2), are effective in treating anxiety (Koen & Stein, 2011). Some patients benefit more from drugs such as Effexor that inhibit the reuptake of both serotonin and noradrenaline. **Benzodiazepines** such as Xanax reduce anxiety by increasing the effects of the inhibitory neurotransmitter gamma-aminobutyric acid (GABA). While GABA agonist drugs relieve anxiety, and were the treatment of choice for anxiety disorders for decades, they unfortunately cause drug tolerance and dependence (see Chapter 11). Further, by reducing attention and arousal, these GABA agonist drugs contribute to traffic accidents and other potential hazards. Benzodiazepines are now recommended only for short-term relief of symptoms. Unfortunately, existing pharmacologic treatments do not provide adequate long-term relief for many patients with anxiety disorders. Research suggests that there are benefits to combining psychological and drug therapy in the treatment of anxiety disorders (Bleakley, 2009; Maren & Holmes, 2016).

12.2.7 Glucocorticoid Stress Hormones Elevate Anxiety

Early in this chapter, we saw that emotion-related brain areas, including the amygdala, send signals to the hypothalamus, where they contribute to activation of the HPA axis stress response. If brain regions associated with fear and anxiety can drive stress hormone release, can stress hormones, in turn, promote fear and anxiety? Perhaps under conditions of threat, the brain's fear circuitry enhances release of hormones, which in turn promote activity of the brain's fear circuitry in a self-reinforcing cycle. While many details remain to be understood, there is evidence that glucocorticoid hormones contribute to promote anxiety by binding to glucocorticoid receptors in the brain.

In order to investigate the role of stress hormones on anxiety, a group of researchers in Germany created mutant mice lacking glucocorticoid receptors in the brain. These mice release normal amounts of glucocorticoids from the adrenal gland, but the glucocorticoids cannot influence brain activity because their brains do not possess glucocorticoid receptors. When these mice are placed in stressful conditions, they respond with very little anxiety (Tronche et al., 1999). For instance, when normal mice are placed on an elevated maze (Figure 12.15, left panel) they spend almost all their

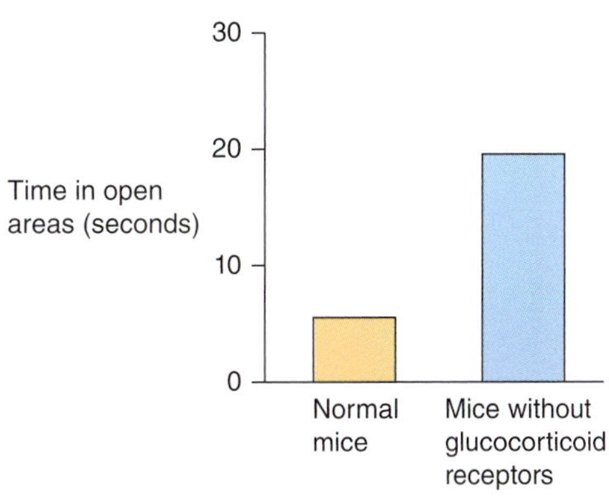

Figure 12.15 The elevated maze to test anxiety. The elevated maze contains enclosed areas surrounded by walls, and open areas without walls. Normal mice avoid the anxiety-provoking open areas. Mice without glucocorticoid receptors spend more time in the open areas compared to normal mice. (Data adapted from Tronche et al., 1999, fig. 5.)

time in enclosed parts of the maze, such as areas surrounded by high walls. They avoid open areas without walls. This is not surprising. If you were placed on a platform raised high above the ground (say ten times your own height or about 50 feet off the ground), you would also likely feel anxious and prefer to stay in an area enclosed within high walls rather than venturing out to the open platforms with no guardrail! Mice lacking the glucocorticoid receptor spend much more time in the open areas compared to control mice (Figure 12.15, right panel), suggesting that when glucocorticoids cannot influence the brain, anxiety is reduced.

Another test of anxiety is the dark–light crossing task, where the animal is placed in a dark compartment and allowed to choose between spending its time in the dark area or in an adjacent bright area (Figure 12.16, left). Mice prefer the dark. However, mice lacking brain glucocorticoid receptors quickly leave the dark area and explore the bright region (Figure 12.16, right). Again, the data suggest that when glucocorticoid transmission is reduced, mice respond to potentially stressful situations with reduced anxiety.

Conversely, elevations in glucocorticoid receptors increase anxiety levels. Mice genetically altered to produce an elevated number of glucocorticoid receptors in the forebrain spend less time in open areas of an elevated maze compared to normal mice, and they avoid the illuminated area in the dark–light crossing task even more than do controls (Wei et al., 2004). The precise manner in which glucocorticoid receptor binding elevates anxiety remains unclear. Given the central role of the amygdala in fear and anxiety, one might have assumed that glucocorticoids promote

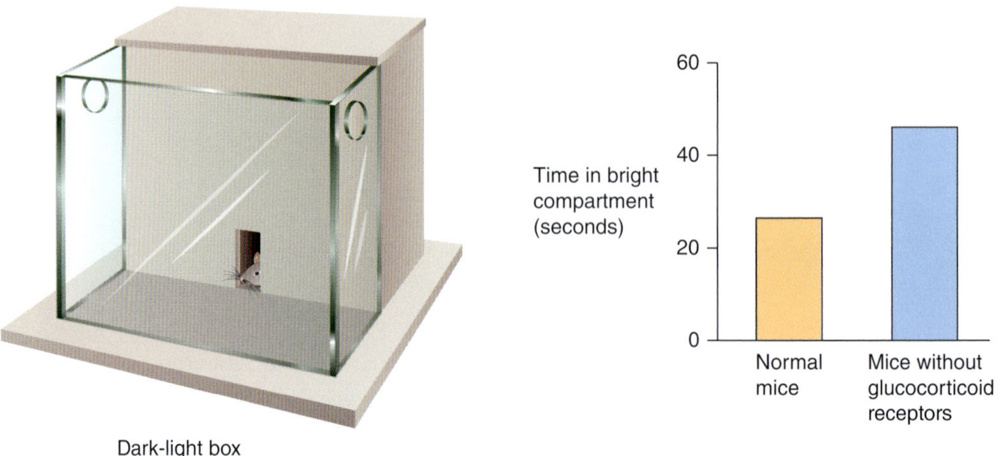

Figure 12.16 The dark–light crossing task to test anxiety. Normal mice spend most of their time in the dark compartment. Bright areas provoke anxiety. Mice without glucocorticoid receptors spend more time in the bright area compared to normal mice.
(Data adapted from Tronche et al., 1999, fig. 5.)

anxiety by binding to receptors in the amygdala. However, mice lacking glucocorticoid receptors only in the amygdala show normal levels of anxiety (Kolber et al., 2008). Glucocorticoids apparently promote anxiety through action in other brain regions.

Stress hormones can produce long-term changes in fear and anxiety by altering the architecture of the brain. For instance, glucocorticoids increase dendritic branching and neuronal excitability within the amygdala (Mitra & Sapolsky, 2008; Maren & Holmes, 2016). In contrast, stress hormones lead to reduced dendrites and neuron excitability within the prefrontal cortex and hippocampus (McEwen et al., 2015). Recall that while the amygdala plays a key role in fear, parts of the prefrontal cortex and hippocampus are associated with the inhibition of fear. Taken together, the research suggests that stress may lead to a long-term increase in excitability of brain areas associated with fear, while reducing the excitability of areas that normally inhibit fear responses (Figure 12.17).

Consistent with the ability of stress hormones to alter brain structures, individuals who have been exposed to extreme stress and suffer PTSD often show reductions in hippocampal size (Oken et al., 2015). In addition to potential effects of this hippocampal change on fear and anxiety, the reduction in hippocampal size may also lead to memory impairments. Chapter 9 examined the important role of the hippocampus in the

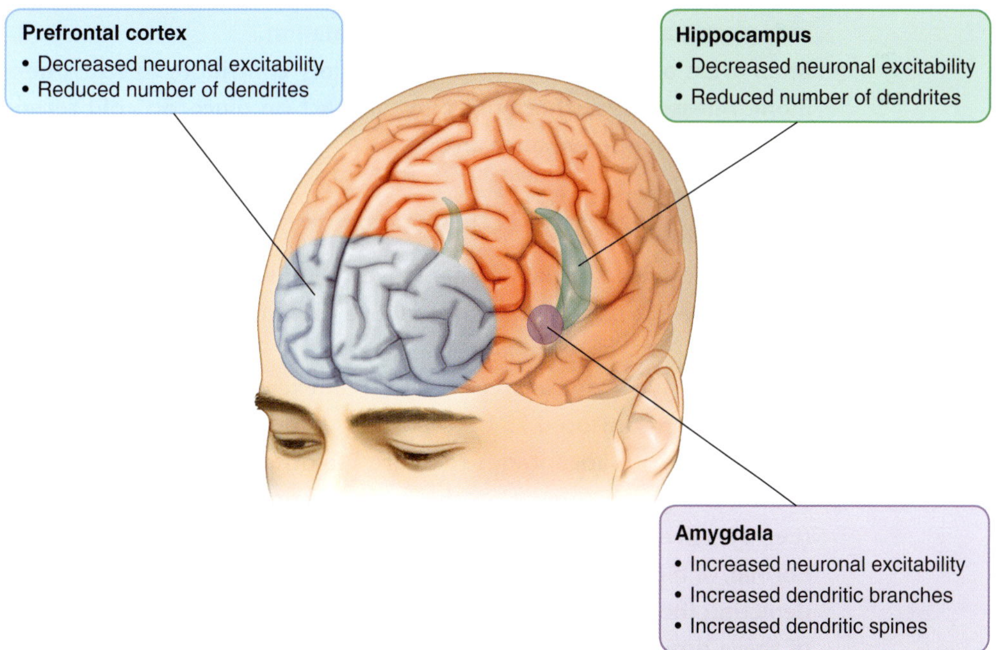

Figure 12.17 Structural changes following stress. Stress produces structural changes that increase amygdala activity while reducing prefrontal and hippocampal activity.

consolidation and retrieval of memories and in other aspects of cognition. Individuals with PTSD have a heightened risk for impairments in memory and cognition. Remarkably, PTSD patients treated with SSRI drugs undergo increases in hippocampal volume and improvements in memory (in addition to reduction in anxiety) (Vermetten, Vythilingam, Southwick, Charney, & Bremner, 2003). The drugs may be enlarging the hippocampus and improving memory by inducing neurogenesis, the birth of new neurons (see Chapter 9), for SSRIs have been shown to increase neurogenesis in the hippocampus (Anacker et al., 2011). By altering brain structure, stress can produce long-lasting effects on circuits underlying fear and anxiety, as well as cognitive functions. As researchers learn more about the mechanisms underlying long-term stress effects on the nervous system, they aim to provide more effective treatments for emotional and cognitive dysfunctions, and to thereby lessen cognitive difficulties and reduce emotional distress.

KEY CONCEPTS

- **Anxiety disorders are characterized by excessive fear and anxiety in the absence of true danger. High levels of amygdala activation and low activity in the ventromedial PFC are associated with excessive anxiety.**
- **Psychological and drug therapies are effective in treating anxiety disorders, and are often employed in combination.**
- **Brain areas associated with fear and anxiety contribute to stress hormone release. Stress hormones, in turn, act on glucocorticoid receptors in the brain to enhance anxiety.**

TEST YOURSELF

1. **What brain area is usually hyperactive in individuals with an anxiety disorder? What brain area is hypoactive in individuals suffering from PTSD?**
2. **Describe a psychological approach to treat excessive anxiety. What are some of the drugs used to treat anxiety? Do any of these drugs have advantages or disadvantages compared to other drugs?**
3. **Draw a bar graph comparing the mean latency to enter a brightly lit (i.e., aversive) area in the dark–light crossing task for mice with low, normal, or high anxiety. Draw another graph for the same three groups depicting the amount of time they spend in the brightly lit area. Which of these groups resembles animals lacking glucocorticoid receptors in the brain? Which resembles animals with an abnormally high number of glucocorticoid receptors?**

12.3 The Big Picture

The brain responds to threats by activating the sympathetic nervous system and HPA axis response systems. These systems likely evolved to promote physiological and behavioral responses to immediate danger. However, long-term activation of these systems can lead to adverse health consequences, including reductions in immune system function. While some individuals respond to severe stress with long-lasting disruptions in physical health and emotional well-being, others experience little or no disruption in their daily functioning.

Amygdala activity, which is strongly tied to fear and anxiety, is among the brain areas that control the body's stress responses. Much remains to be understood about how the brain and autonomic nervous system respond to threatening events, and how dysfunction in these systems can compromise physical and mental health.

12.4 Creative Thinking

1. Notice in Figure 12.2 that glucocorticoids inhibit release of CRH from the hypothalamus and ACTH from the anterior pituitary. This negative feedback prevents glucocorticoid levels from becoming excessively high. What would happen if an individual had an abnormality that caused glucocorticoids to elevate, rather than reduce, ACTH release?
2. As described in Chapter 9, the hippocampus is important for storing and retrieving memories of events that you have experienced, such as your memory of Thanksgiving dinner last year. In this chapter, we have seen that the amygdala plays a key role in associating stimuli with fear. Imagine an event from your past to which you have strong, negative emotional associations. If you lost the amygdala and not the hippocampus, might memories lose their emotional associations even though you can recall other details of the event? Can you think of memories for which this might be desirable?
3. Consider the chronic disturbances versus resilient responses to trauma depicted in Figure 12.6. Speculate on how these two groups of individuals might differ in terms of HPA axis responses and negative feedback produced by glucocorticoids. How might they differ in terms of amygdala and vmPFC responses to the trauma? Might they differ in terms of the number of glucocorticoid receptors in the hippocampus? How so?
4. This chapter discussed the unusual way a woman lacking an amygdala responded to normally fearful events. Suppose that, instead, a person had an abnormally hyperactive amygdala. How might their emotions and behaviors be unusual? What if the individual's amygdala became hyperactive at random times during the day, each time

for say 20 minutes? What if the person's amygdala was hyperactive only at night while dreaming (i.e., in REM sleep as described in Chapter 5)?

5. While anxiety disorders may be treated using pharmacotherapy or psychological therapy, the two approaches are often successfully combined together. Why might it be advantageous to combine the two approaches?

Key Terms

adaptive immune system 493
adrenal cortex 489
adrenal medulla 488
adrenocorticotropic hormone (ACTH) 488
amygdala 490
autonomic nervous system 487
aversive stimulus 502
baseline 496
benzodiazepines 514
chronic stressors 486
Cognitive Behavioral Therapy 513
conditioned stimulus (CS) 502
corticosterone 489
corticotropin-releasing hormone (CRH) 488
cortisol 489
cytokines 493
dorsal raphe nucleus 490
epigenetics 499
expression, gene 499
extinction 505
ganglion (pl. ganglia) 488
generalized anxiety disorder 510
glucocorticoid 488
homeostasis 496
hypothalamic-pituitary-adrenal (HPA) axis 488
innate immune system 493
insular cortex 503
locus coeruleus 490
macrophage 493
medial prefrontal cortex (mPFC) 506
methyl group 499
natural immune system 493
negative feedback 489
neutral stimulus 502
panic disorder 510
parasympathetic nervous system 487
paraventricular nucleus (PVN) 488
pathogens 493
postganglionic nerves 488
posttraumatic stress disorder (PTSD) 485
preganglionic nerves 488
Rational Emotive Behavioral Therapy 513
reappraisal 513
resilience 496
rumination 490
selective serotonin reuptake inhibitors (SSRIs) 514
social anxiety disorder 510
specific immune system 493
specific phobia 510
spontaneous recovery 506
stability 496
stressor 486
sympathetic nervous system 487
synthesis, receptor 499
systematic desensitization 512
unconditioned stimulus (US) 502
vagus nerve 488

References

Adolphs, R., Tranel, D., Damasio, H., & Damasio, A. (1994). Impaired recognition of emotion in facial expressions following bilateral damage to the human amygdala. *Nature, 372*(6507), 669–672.

Anacker, C., Zunszain, P. A., Cattaneo, A., Carvalho, L. A., Garabedian, M. J., Thuret, S., ... Pariante, C. M. (2011). Antidepressants increase human hippocampal neurogenesis by activating the glucocorticoid receptor. *Molecular Psychiatry, 16*(7), 738–750.

Andrewes, D. G., & Jenkins, L. M. (2019). The role of the amygdala and the ventromedial prefrontal cortex in emotional regulation: implications for post-traumatic stress disorder. *Neuropsychology Review, 29*(2), 220–243.

Barrett, J., & Armony, J. L. (2009). Influence of trait anxiety on brain activity during the acquisition and extinction of aversive conditioning. *Psychological Medicine, 39*(2), 255–265.

Beck, A. T., & Clark, D. A. (1997). An information processing model of anxiety: automatic and strategic processes. *Behaviour Research and Therapy, 35*(1), 49–58.

Benschop, R. J., Nieuwenhuis, E. E., Tromp, E. A., Godaert, G. L., Ballieux, R. E., & van Doornen, L. J. (1994). Effects of beta-adrenergic blockade on immunologic and cardiovascular changes induced by mental stress. *Circulation, 89*(2), 762–769.

Bishop, S. J. (2007). Neurocognitive mechanisms of anxiety: an integrative account. *Trends in Cognitive Sciences, 11*(7), 307–316.

Blaze, J., & Roth, T. L. (2017). Caregiver maltreatment causes altered neuronal DNA methylation in female rodents. *Development and Psychopathology, 29*(2), 477–489.

Bleakley, S. (2009). The pharmacological management of anxiety disorders. *Progress in Neurology and Psychiatry, 13*(6), 15–19.

Blechert, J., Wilhelm, F. H., Williams, H., Braams, B. R., Jou, J., & Gross, J. J. (2015). Reappraisal facilitates extinction in healthy and socially anxious individuals. *Journal of Behavior Therapy and Experimental Psychiatry, 46*, 141–150.

Bonanno, G. A. (2004). Loss, trauma, and human resilience: have we underestimated the human capacity to thrive after extremely aversive events? *American Psychologist, 59*(1), 20–28.

Breslau, N., Kessler, R. C., Chilcoat, H. D., Schultz, L. R., Davis, G. C., & Andreski, P. (1998). Trauma and posttraumatic stress disorder in the community: the 1996 Detroit Area Survey of Trauma. *Archives of General Psychiatry, 55*(7), 626–632.

Davis, M., Walker, D. L., Miles, L., & Grillon, C. (2010). Phasic vs sustained fear in rats and humans: role of the extended amygdala in fear vs anxiety. *Neuropsychopharmacology, 35*(1), 105–135.

Dhabhar, F. S. (2003). Stress, leukocyte trafficking, and the augmentation of skin immune function. *Annals of the New York Academy of Sciences, 992*, 205–217.

Dudek, K. A., Kaufmann, F. N., Lavoie, O., & Menard, C. (2021). Central and peripheral stress-induced epigenetic mechanisms of resilience. *Current Opinion in Psychiatry*, *34*(1), 1–9.

Ellis, A., & Dryden, W. (2007). *The Practice of Rational Emotive Behavior Therapy*: New York: Springer.

Etkin, A., & Wager, T. D. (2007). Functional neuroimaging of anxiety: a meta-analysis of emotional processing in PTSD, social anxiety disorder, and specific phobia. *American Journal of Psychiatry*, *164*(10), 1476–1488.

Feinstein, J. S., Adolphs, R., Damasio, A. R., & Tranel, D. (2011). The human amygdala and the induction and experience of fear. *Current Biology*, *21*(1), 34–38.

Feinstein, J. S., Buzza, C., Hurlemann, R., Follmer, R. L., Dahdaleh, N. S., Coryell, W. H., ... Wemmie, J. A. (2013). Fear and panic in humans with bilateral amygdala damage. *Nature Neuroscience*, *16*(3), 270–272.

Glaser, R., & Kiecolt-Glaser, J. K. (2005). Stress-induced immune dysfunction: implications for health. *Nature Reviews Immunology*, *5*(3), 243–251.

Gorka, S. M., Nelson, B. D., Phan, K. L., & Shankman, S. A. (2014). Insula response to unpredictable and predictable aversiveness in individuals with panic disorder and comorbid depression. *Biology of Mood & Anxiety Disorders*, *4*, 9–9.

Gottfried, J. A., & Dolan, R. J. (2004). Human orbitofrontal cortex mediates extinction learning while accessing conditioned representations of value. *Nature Neuroscience*, *7*(10), 1144–1152.

Heim, C., & Nemeroff, C. B. (2001). The role of childhood trauma in the neurobiology of mood and anxiety disorders: preclinical and clinical studies. *Biological Psychiatry*, *49*(12), 1023–1039.

Herman, J. P., Figueiredo, H., Mueller, N. K., Ulrich-Lai, Y., Ostrander, M. M., Choi, D. C., & Cullinan, W. E. (2003). Central mechanisms of stress integration: hierarchical circuitry controlling hypothalamo–pituitary–adrenocortical responsiveness. *Frontiers in Neuroendocrinology*, *24*(3), 151–180.

Hyman, S. E. (2009). How adversity gets under the skin. *Nature Neuroscience*, *12*(3), 241–243.

Jiang, Y., Chen, Z., & Wyer, R. S. (2014). Impact of money on emotional expression. *Journal of Experimental Social Psychology*, *55*, 228–233.

Johansen, J. P., Cain, C. K., Ostroff, L. E., & LeDoux, J. E. (2011). Molecular mechanisms of fear learning and memory. *Cell*, *147*(3), 509–524.

Keller, S. M., Doherty, T. S., & Roth, T. L. (2019). Pharmacological manipulation of DNA methylation normalizes maternal behavior, DNA methylation, and gene expression in dams with a history of maltreatment. *Scientific Reports*, *9*.

Koen, N., & Stein, D. J. (2011). Pharmacotherapy of anxiety disorders: a critical review. *Dialogues in Clinical Neuroscience*, *13*(4), 423–437.

Kolber, B. J., Roberts, M. S., Howell, M. P., Wozniak, D. F., Sands, M. S., & Muglia, L. J. (2008). Central amygdala glucocorticoid receptor action promotes fear-associated CRH activation and conditioning. *Proceedings of the National Academy of Sciences of the United States of America*, *105*(33), 12004–12009.

Lanius, R. A., Hopper, J. W., & Menon, R. S. (2003). Individual differences in a husband and wife who developed PTSD after a motor vehicle accident: a functional MRI case study. *American Journal of Psychiatry, 160*(4), 667–669.

Linsambarth, S., Moraga-Amaro, R., Quintana-Donoso, D., Rojas, S., & Stehberg, J. (2017). "The amygdala and anxiety," in B. Ferry (Ed.), *The Amygdala* (pp. 59–77). London: IntechOpen.

Maren, S., & Holmes, A. (2016). Stress and fear extinction. *Neuropsychopharmacology, 41*(1), 58–79.

McEwen, B. S., Bowles, N. P., Gray, J. D., Hill, M. N., Hunter, R. G., Karatsoreos, I. N., & Nasca, C. (2015). Mechanisms of stress in the brain. *Nature Neuroscience, 18*(10), 1353–1363.

McGaugh, J. L., & Roozendaal, B. (2002). Role of adrenal stress hormones in forming lasting memories in the brain. *Current Opinion in Neurobiology, 12*(2), 205–210.

McGowan, P. O., Sasaki, A., D'Alessio, A. C., Dymov, S., Labonte, B., Szyf, M., ... Meaney, M. J. (2009). Epigenetic regulation of the glucocorticoid receptor in human brain associates with childhood abuse. *Nature Neuroscience, 12*(3), 342–348.

Meaney, M. J. (2001). Maternal care, gene expression, and the transmission of individual differences in stress reactivity across generations. *Annual Review of Neuroscience, 24*, 1161–1192.

Milad, M. R., & Quirk, G. J. (2002). Neurons in medial prefrontal cortex signal memory for fear extinction. *Nature, 420*(6911), 70–74.

Miller, A. H., & Raison, C. L. (2016). The role of inflammation in depression: from evolutionary imperative to modern treatment target. *Nature Reviews Immunology, 16*(1), 22–34.

Mitra, R., & Sapolsky, R. M. (2008). Acute corticosterone treatment is sufficient to induce anxiety and amygdaloid dendritic hypertrophy. *Proceedings of the National Academy of Sciences of the United States of America, 105*(14), 5573–5578.

Muehsam, D., Lutgendorf, S., Mills, P. J., Rickhi, B., Chevalier, G., Bat, N., ... Gurfein, B. (2017). The embodied mind: a review on functional genomic and neurological correlates of mind–body therapies. *Neuroscience and Biobehavioral Reviews, 73*, 165–181.

Ochsner, K. N., Bunge, S. A., Gross, J. J., & Gabrieli, J. D. (2002). Rethinking feelings: an FMRI study of the cognitive regulation of emotion. *Journal of Cognitive Neuroscience, 14*(8), 1215–1229.

Oken, B. S., Chamine, I., & Wakeland, W. (2015). A systems approach to stress, stressors and resilience in humans. *Behavioural Brain Research, 282*, 144–154.

Otte, C. (2011). Cognitive behavioral therapy in anxiety disorders: current state of the evidence. *Dialogues in Clinical Neuroscience, 13*(4), 413–421.

Perkeybile, A. M., Carter, C. S., Wroblewski, K. L., Puglia, M. H., Kenkel, W. M., Lillard, T. S., ... Connelly, J. J. (2019). Early nurture epigenetically tunes the oxytocin receptor. *Psychoneuroendocrinology, 99*, 128–136.

Phelps, E. A., Delgado, M. R., Nearing, K. I., & LeDoux, J. E. (2004). Extinction learning in humans: role of the amygdala and vmPFC. *Neuron, 43*(6), 897–905.

Quirk, G. J. (2002). Memory for extinction of conditioned fear is long-lasting and persists following spontaneous recovery. *Learning & Memory, 9*(6), 402–407.

Quirk, G. J., Russo, G. K., Barron, J. L., & Lebron, K. (2000). The role of ventromedial prefrontal cortex in the recovery of extinguished fear. *Journal of Neuroscience, 20*(16), 6225–6231.

Rauch, S. L., Shin, L. M., & Phelps, E. A. (2006). Neurocircuitry models of posttraumatic stress disorder and extinction: human neuroimaging research – past, present, and future. *Biological Psychiatry, 60*(4), 376–382.

Rohleder, N. (2019). Stress and inflammation – The need to address the gap in the transition between acute and chronic stress effects. *Psychoneuroendocrinology, 105*, 164–171.

Ruscio, A. M., Brown, T. A., Chiu, W. T., Sareen, J., Stein, M. B., & Kessler, R. C. (2008). Social fears and social phobia in the USA: results from the National Comorbidity Survey Replication. *Psychological Medicine, 38*(1), 15–28.

Sapolsky R. (1994). *Why Zebras Don't Get Ulcers: A Guide to Stress, Stress-Related Diseases and Coping*. New York:W. H. Freeman.

Schönfelder, S., Kanske, P., Heissler, J., & Wessa, M. (2013). Time course of emotion-related responding during distraction and reappraisal. *Social Cognitive and Affective Neuroscience, 9*(9), 1310–1319.

Segerstrom, S. C., & Miller, G. E. (2004). Psychological stress and the human immune system: a meta-analytic study of 30 years of inquiry. *Psychological Bulletin, 130*(4), 601–630.

Shin, L. M., & Liberzon, I. (2010). The neurocircuitry of fear, stress, and anxiety disorders. *Neuropsychopharmacology, 35*(1), 169–191.

Stainton, A., Chisholm, K., Kaiser, N., Rosen, M., Upthegrove, R., Ruhrmann, S., & Wood, S. J. (2019). Resilience as a multimodal dynamic process. *Early Intervention in Psychiatry, 13*(4), 725–732.

Szabo, A., Nikhazy, L., Tihanyi, B., & Boros, S. (2017). An in-situ investigation of the acute effects of Bikram yoga on positive- and negative affect, and state-anxiety in context of perceived stress. *Journal of Mental Health, 26*(2), 156–160.

Tronche, F., Kellendonk, C., Kretz, O., Gass, P., Anlag, K., Orban, P. C., ... Schutz, G. (1999). Disruption of the glucocorticoid receptor gene in the nervous system results in reduced anxiety. *Nature Genetics, 23*(1), 99–103.

Ulrich-Lai, Y. M., & Herman, J. P. (2009). Neural regulation of endocrine and autonomic stress responses. *Nature Reviews Neuroscience, 10*(6), 397–409.

Urry, H. L., van Reekum, C. M., Johnstone, T., Kalin, N. H., Thurow, M. E., Schaefer, H. S., ... Davidson, R. J. (2006). Amygdala and ventromedial prefrontal cortex are inversely coupled during regulation of negative affect and predict the diurnal pattern of cortisol secretion among older adults. *Journal of Neuroscience, 26*(16), 4415–4425.

van Stegeren, A. H., Wolf, O. T., Everaerd, W., Scheltens, P., Barkhof, F., & Rombouts, S. A. R. B. (2007). Endogenous cortisol level interacts with noradrenergic activation in the human amygdala. *Neurobiology of Learning and Memory*, *87*(1), 57–66.

Vermetten, E., Vythilingam, M., Southwick, S. M., Charney, D. S., & Bremner, J. D. (2003). Long-term treatment with paroxetine increases verbal declarative memory and hippocampal volume in posttraumatic stress disorder. *Biological Psychiatry*, *54*(7), 693–702.

Verpaalen, I. A. M., Bijsterbosch, M., Mobach, L., Bijlsrtra, G., Rinck, M., & Klein, A. M. (2019). Validating the Radboud faces database from a child's perspective. *Cognition and Emotion*, *33*(8), 1531–1547.

Wei, Q., Lu, X. Y., Liu, L., Schafer, G., Shieh, K. R., Burke, S., ... Akil, H. (2004). Glucocorticoid receptor overexpression in forebrain: a mouse model of increased emotional lability. *Proceedings of the National Academy of Sciences of the United States of America*, *101*(32), 11851–11856.

Wolpe, J. (1968). Psychotherapy by reciprocal inhibition. *Conditional Reflex*, *3*(4), 234–240.

Yamasue, H., Kasai, K., Iwanami, A., Ohtani, T., Yamada, H., Abe, O., ... Kato, N. (2003). Voxel-based analysis of MRI reveals anterior cingulate gray-matter volume reduction in posttraumatic stress disorder due to terrorism. *Proceedings of the National Academy of Sciences of the United States of America*, *100*(15), 9039–9043.

13

Neuropathology in Neurology and Psychiatry

Fanatic Studio/Gary Waters / SCIENCE PHOTO LIBRARY / Getty Images

Consider This ...

Sister Mary O'Reilly gets lost when she leaves her home. As she walks down the street, she passes neighbors she's known for years and doesn't recognize any of them. She sometimes looks at relatives as if they were strangers. Like others with Alzheimer's disease, changes have occurred in her brain, changes that profoundly affect how she remembers, thinks, and interacts with others.

In the 1980s, Dr. David Snowdon received permission to study the brains of nearly 700 elderly nuns following their death. Some had Alzheimer's before they died. Was there something different about their brains? Were there any *non-biological* clues that might have foretold which nuns would get Alzheimer's and which would not?

Snowdon discovered that when the nuns had entered the convent fifty years earlier, each was asked to write a brief autobiographical essay. Those essays had been preserved over the intervening years. Might they contain clues about which nuns would later get Alzheimer's? Snowdon and his colleagues discovered that the nuns whose essays were rich in ideas and clarity of expression were less likely to later suffer the mental deterioration associated with Alzheimer's disease. The content of the essays written half a century earlier allowed the researchers to predict with 92 percent accuracy whether or not the brain of a particular nun would contain neurons with the clusters of abnormally folded protein (amyloid plaques and neurofibrillary tangles) characteristic of the disease (Snowdon et al., 1996).

What do these results mean? Why should cognitive capacity early in life influence the likelihood of a pathology in cognition toward the end of life? Researchers continue to debate the meaning and the reliability of such results. What are the factors that make an individual more or less vulnerable to Alzheimer's and other neurological diseases? Does Alzheimer's arise largely from genetic factors, environmental influences, or a combination of the two? What are the brain abnormalities that produce loss of memory in Alzheimer's, and disruptions in other aspects of cognition, emotion, and behavior in other neurological and psychiatric disorders, that is, in disorders that affect the brain?

This chapter will examine **neuropathologies** (abnormalities of the nervous system) associated with depression, schizophrenia, Parkinson's disease, and Alzheimer's. Depression and schizophrenia are usually treated by a psychologist and/or a psychiatrist, while Alzheimer's and Parkinson's disease are treated by a neurologist. As we learn more about the neuropathologies associated with psychiatric and neurological disorders, the dividing line between them becomes blurry. Each of these disorders emerges from changes in brain activity, even those for which social and environmental factors contribute as well.

Imagine, for instance, that Sally suffers from depression, and that the prolonged periods when she feels worthless and hopeless come from an interaction between genes and childhood trauma. Imagine that when she was 5 her parents died in a car accident, and this left a lasting emotional scar that she still struggles to overcome. There is an identifiable childhood experience that likely contributed to her depression in adulthood. But the fact that her traumatic experience exerted a lasting influence on her emotional state means that it must have produced long-lasting changes in the functioning of emotion- and motivation-related circuits of her brain. The most effective treatment for Sally may involve psychological therapy, antidepressant medication, or a combination of the two.

Even therapy alone derives its value from the changes it produces in the brain. Changes in thinking, feeling, and behaving require changes in the function of the brain. The four major disorders considered here have as their most obvious symptoms dysfunctions in emotion (major depressive disorder), cognition and perception (schizophrenia), behavior (Parkinson's), and memory (Alzheimer's). We begin our exploration by focusing on major depressive disorder.

13.1 MAJOR DEPRESSIVE DISORDER

After a deep disappointment, such as the end of an important personal relationship, we may feel deep sadness for many days. However, this temporary sadness is different from "clinical depression," also called major depressive disorder. In major depressive disorder, the person loses interest in daily activities and experiences a continuous drop in mood that lasts for several weeks or more. Another name for major depressive disorder is **unipolar depression** to distinguish it from the depressive phase of **bipolar disorder** (formerly called manic depression), where the individual alternates between high-energy states of elation (manic episodes), episodes of depression, and intervening periods of normal mood.

13.1.1 Major Depression Includes Feelings of Hopelessness, Worthlessness, and a Risk of Suicide

Depression is the leading cause of disability in the USA. Approximately 5–10 percent of those suffering from depressive disorder attempt suicide. Besides the suffering of the afflicted individual, depression also may devastate family and friends. Approximately 5–15 percent of the population of the industrialized nations will suffer major depression at some point in their life. Women are diagnosed as depressed twice as often as men.

There are two peak decades in life for onset of depression: the twenties and the sixties. This coincides with two periods of life accompanied by major social pressures: first, the processes of seeking employment and, for some, the beginning of marriage and family; second, the contemplation of retirement along with more frequent illness in self, family, and friends.

Common signs of depression include:

- feelings of hopelessness, guilt, worthlessness
- loss of interest in activities that were once pleasurable
- difficulty concentrating, remembering details, and making decisions
- fatigue
- insomnia, excessive sleeping, or other disruptions of the daily sleep–wake cycle
- irritability, restlessness

- changes in eating (overeating or appetite loss)
- suicidal thoughts, suicide attempts.

If several of these signs persist for longer than two weeks, a mental health professional may diagnose major depression. The initial assessment usually involves lengthy interviews with the patient, and sometimes the patient may be asked to answer a series of written questions on a depression scale designed to assess the individual's level of depression. No biological test exists for diagnosing depression.

13.1.2 Stress, Genes, and Their Interaction May Cause Depression

Researchers have identified several important factors that contribute to one's vulnerability to major depression. These include environmental stressors, genes, and an interaction between the two.

Stress

Stressful life events that contribute to depression are often long-lasting (such as a prolonged period of abuse) and/or intense (such as the death of a family member). As we saw in Chapter 12, life stressors activate two major physiological systems: the hypothalamic–pituitary–adrenal (HPA) axis and the sympathetic branch of the autonomic nervous system.

Depressed individuals often show physiological signs of stress such as elevated cortisol levels (Wieck, 1989), and abnormalities in cortisol release can affect the brain. For example, elevated levels of cortisol can reduce the size of the hippocampus, impair hippocampal-based memory storage, and decrease neurogenesis (the birth of new neurons) in the hippocampus (Gould & Tanapat, 1999). Stress-induced changes in the hippocampus are implicated in depression (Jacobs, van Praag, & Gage, 2000; Singhal & Baune, 2017). As we will see, major depression is linked to other neuroanatomical changes as well. For now, the key idea is that stress leads to physiological changes that may contribute to symptoms of depression.

Genes

The fact that depression runs in families suggests that depression is heritable (inherited). However, it is also possible that a depressed person with one or two depressed parents may have developed depression simply by being in close contact with them for years. Twin studies make it possible to disentangle the impact of one's social environment from genetic contributions to depression.

Monozygotic (identical) twins develop from a single fertilized egg and therefore have identical genetic makeup. In contrast, dizygotic (fraternal) twins develop from two fertilized eggs and are no more genetically similar than any two biological siblings. Identical and fraternal twins usually share the same (or a very similar) environment. The **concordance rate** for identical twins is 60–70 percent. That is to say, if one of the identical twins has the disorder, there is a 60–70 percent chance that the other will also have the disorder too. Is that due to shared genes or similar environments? The concordance for fraternal twins is only about 10–20 percent – not much higher than for siblings (Kendler & Prescott, 1999). Therefore, a similar environment (which is shared by both fraternal and identical twins) does not appear to be key to predicting depression. The strong predictor is that they share genes. In fact, the high concordance rate for identical twins is seen even when they are raised in separate homes (e.g., by different sets of adoptive parents). These data provide strong evidence for a genetic contribution to depression.

Depression seems to arise from a large number of diverse genes, each of which exerts a small effect, rather than a single "depression gene." A gene–environment interaction may result from a large set of genes that act together to make the individual vulnerable to depression when faced with intense or long-lasting environmental stressors.

Epigenetics

A key area of neuroscience investigation asks how genetic and environmental influences interact. In the last chapter, we saw a dramatic example of gene–environment interaction in a study of maternal influence on the DNA of their offspring. The mothers' caresses did not change their pups' genes; the DNA sequences remained the same. Instead, the caresses changed the way in which their genes were "expressed" (activated to produce proteins) (Meaney, 2001). Luckily for those pups with nurturing mothers, their alteration in gene expression led to changes in neuronal circuits related to stress, and the pups grew up to become "laid back" rats. The capacity of environmental events to turn genes on or off without altering the DNA sequence is called **epigenetics**. Unfortunately, extreme stressors early in life such as physical abuse can lead to epigenetic changes that make the individual more prone to experience stress and depression later in life (McGowan et al., 2009; Nestler, 2014).

13.1.3 Depression Is Associated with Changes in Brain Structure and Function

Major depression is associated with reduced gray matter (reduced neurons and/or dendrites of existing neurons) in a number of areas (Figure 13.1).

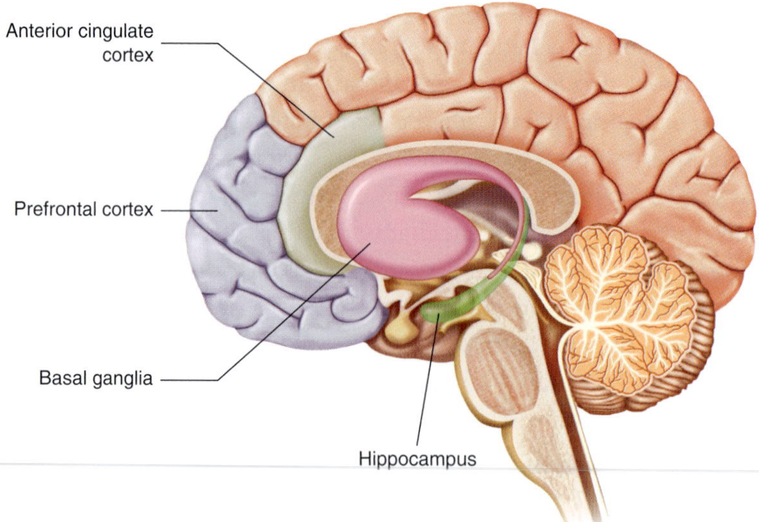

Figure 13.1 Major depression is associated with reduced gray matter within several brain regions. The most reliable reductions are seen in the prefrontal cortex, anterior cingulate cortex, hippocampus, and basal ganglia.

Areas that consistently show reductions include those involved in cognition (prefrontal cortex and hippocampus), emotion (cingulate cortex), and motivation (basal ganglia) (Bora, Harrison, Davey, Yuecel, & Pantelis, 2012; Grieve, Korgaonkar, Koslow, Gordon, & Williams, 2013; Hellewell et al., 2019).

Changes in brain volume associated with depression may be reduced or even reversed with antidepressant drugs. The **selective serotonin reuptake inhibitor** (**SSRI**) antidepressants increase synaptic concentrations of serotonin throughout the brain. SSRIs have been shown to increase brain volume in the hippocampus and other brain areas in depressed patients (Arnone et al., 2013; Kraus, Castren, Kasper, & Lanzenberger, 2017). The ability of these medications to preserve or increase the thickness of the cerebral cortex in individual patients predicts the drugs' efficacy in alleviating depressive symptoms (Dusi, Barlati, Vita, & Brambilla 2015; Aydogan et al., 2019).

In addition to changes in brain volume, fMRI has revealed abnormal levels of *activity* within various brain regions in individuals with major depression. While some areas are hypoactive, others are typically overactive (Hamilton, 2012). The hyperactivity of the amygdala often seen in depression is consistent with the role of this area in negative emotional reactivity, while a reduced activation in areas of the prefrontal cortex is consistent with the prefrontal role in cognitive functions and emotional inhibition.

13.1.4 Drugs and Psychotherapy Help Many People with Depression, and New Treatments Are Emerging

Here, we examine the use of pharmaceuticals, cognitive therapy, exercise, electroconvulsive therapy, transcranial magnetic stimulation, and deep brain stimulation treatments for depression. There is currently no single treatment that is effective in all cases.

Pharmaceuticals

Drugs remain by far the most commonly prescribed treatment for depression. The first class of antidepressants, the **monoamine oxidase inhibitors** (**MAOIs**) have been around since the 1950s. Monoamine oxidase (MAO) is an enzyme that breaks down the monoamine neurotransmitters serotonin, dopamine, norepinephrine, and epinephrine (adrenaline). Blocking (inhibiting) the action of MAO increases the levels of these neurotransmitters. Like most antidepressant drugs, MAOIs take several weeks to show therapeutic effects. While they relieve depression in some individuals, they can interact with certain foods and drugs to produce dangerous elevations of the monoamines throughout the body, potentially producing heart problems or other serious health issues.

Tricyclic antidepressants, introduced in the late 1950s, primarily block the reuptake of serotonin and norepinephrine, elevating the brain levels of these two neurotransmitters. While moderately effective, they also have some serious side effects. MAOIs and tricyclics are still used today, but because of their side effects they are usually prescribed only after a patient's mood fails to improve with one of the more recently discovered antidepressants.

Beginning in the mid-1980s, drugs with greater receptor specificity were introduced. SSRIs such as Prozac (fluoxetine) and Zoloft (sertraline) selectively elevate synaptic levels of serotonin. Normally, after serotonin is released into synapses, a **serotonin transporter protein** pulls it back into the terminal of the releasing neuron. This method of clearing serotonin from the synapse is called **reuptake** (Figure 13.2, left panel). This reuptake of serotonin normally ensures that only a limited amount of serotonin is in the synapse at a given moment. The SSRIs disrupt the action of the serotonin transporter (without affecting transporters for other neurotransmitters), and thereby selectively slow serotonin reuptake (hence the name selective serotonin reuptake inhibitors). The net result is that the SSRIs increase synaptic concentrations of serotonin (Figure 13.2, right panel).

Serotonin-norepinephrine reuptake inhibitors (**SNRIs**) such as Cymbalta (duloxetine) and Effexor (venlafaxine) block both the serotonin and

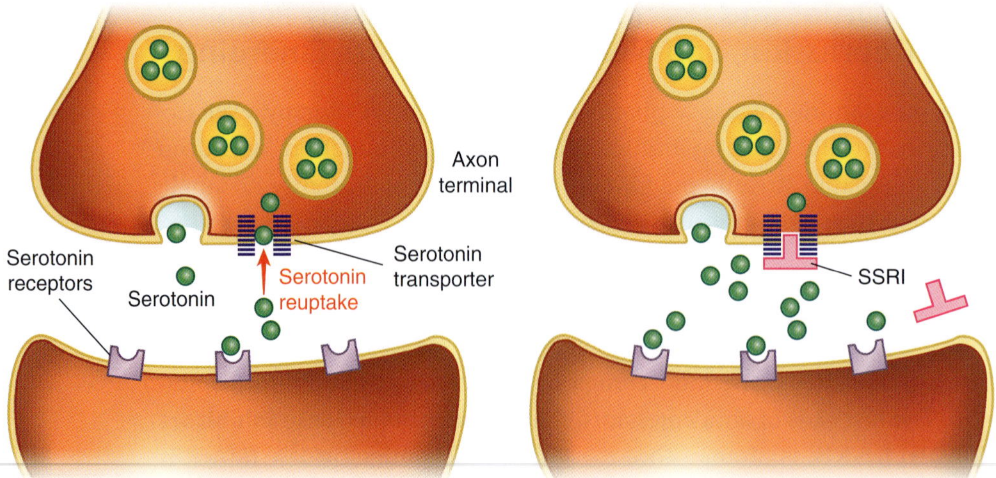

Figure 13.2 **Selective serotonin reuptake inhibitors (SSRIs)**. Under normal conditions, the serotonin transporter protein pulls serotonin back into the presynaptic terminal (left panel). The SSRI blocks this reuptake mechanism, allowing serotonin to accumulate in the synapse (right panel).

the norepinephrine transporters, prevent the reuptake of these transmitters, and thereby increase their synaptic concentrations. (We saw earlier that the tricyclics predominantly elevate levels of serotonin and norepinephrine, but SNRIs are more specific in targeting these two neurotransmitters.) It is not possible to predict which patient will respond to a particular class of antidepressant drug, so psychiatrists often prescribe one of the medications for several months and, if this is ineffective, prescribe another.

The selective reuptake inhibitors (SSRIs and SNRIs) are safer than the earlier antidepressants, but, like the MAOIs and tricyclics, they are slow to act. Therapeutic effects may appear during the first week of antidepressant treatment, but it can take weeks before peak effects are observed (Mitchell, 2006). The delayed action of antidepressants may represent a danger for a suicidal patient.

There are data to suggest that ketamine, an antagonist of the glutamate NMDA receptor, may provide fast-acting relief from depression (Newport et al., 2015; Hashimoto, 2019). It can quickly reduce life-threatening thoughts and behaviors, sometimes within hours. Despite its rapid short-term benefits, possible long-term side effects and potential for abuse remain the subject of investigations (Hashimoto, 2019; Na & Kim, 2021).

Cognitive Therapy

Both **Cognitive Behavioral Therapy** (**CBT**) and the closely related **Rational Emotive Behavioral Therapy** (**REBT**) are founded on the idea that emotional reactions do not emerge directly from one's circumstances, but from one's interpretation of those circumstances. Imagine, for instance, that Carol's friend failed to return her phone message. This perceived rejection might lead Carol to jump to the thoughts "Nobody likes me" or "I'm not a likable person," and to generate dysfunctional emotions (deep sadness) and behavior (avoiding human contact). The problem was not with the event (the absence of a phone call), but with Carol's interpretation of the event. Through therapy and practice, an individual may learn to challenge exaggerated and dysfunctional thoughts and behaviors, and to replace them with more realistic and useful ones ("It would be worth finding out if my friend is upset with me, or just very busy, or whether she didn't receive my message"; "*Even* if this particular person doesn't want to continue our relationship, it doesn't follow that I'm not likable"). For further discussion of these cognitive therapies, see Chapter 12.

CBT and REBT have been shown to be about as effective as treatment with antidepressant medication, and the consensus is that the combined use of therapy and drug treatment (e.g., an SSRI) is more effective than either treatment alone (Cuijpers et al., 2020).

Meditation

Over the past several decades, research on the neural correlates and therapeutic benefits of meditation has grown rapidly. **Mindfulness meditation** has attracted particular attention in the scientific community. During the meditation, the individual attends to present-moment experiences such as bodily sensations, sounds, and breathing, rather than permitting the mind to wander. To gain an idea of the experience of it, try the following:

> Close your eyes for about a minute and maintain an open awareness of the sensations of breathing at your nostrils. There is no need to do anything special, just continuously observe the sensations of breathing in and breathing out at the nostrils with curiosity and interest. You may notice that nearly as soon as you begin, your mind will wander. When it does, gently return it to the breath. (Creswell, 2017, p. 492)

When left alone to think, the mind often wanders between past experiences, future concerns, and other thoughts that catch hold of one's attention. By noticing thoughts that arise and returning attention to the breath (or other sensations), meditators become "mindful" of the experiences present at the moment.

Our minds are estimated to wander unintentionally about 47 percent of the time. The amount of time an individual spends lost in thought (as opposed to attending to what she's currently doing) predicts later unhappiness (Killingsworth & Gilbert, 2010). For individuals with a history of depression, studies show the benefits of mindfulness-based treatment (lasting eight weeks) on preventing depression relapse to be roughly equivalent to those of antidepressant medication or cognitive behavioral therapy, and possibly superior for those patients with the most severe depressive symptoms (Kuyken et. al., 2016; Creswell, 2017). Investigators are also examining neurobiological mechanisms that may underlie therapeutic effects of mindfulness-based treatments (Dutcher & Creswell, 2018). While the results so far appear promising, research on meditation is still relatively recent, and many of the studies involve a small number of subjects. Additional research will be needed to better understand the reliability and duration of these therapeutic effects.

Exercise

An aerobic exercise regimen, such as jogging, carried out for weeks or months, has an antidepressant effect (Schuch et al., 2016). As with CBT, patients who exercise in conjunction with other antidepressant treatments see better results than those patients who use only one treatment strategy. However, it can be difficult to convince clinically depressed patients to exercise since they commonly suffer from fatigue and lethargy.

Electroconvulsive Therapy (ECT)

Despite popular misconceptions, **electroconvulsive therapy** (**ECT**) is a relatively safe and highly effective treatment for depression. Patients who elect to undergo ECT are often those who have not responded to any other treatment. During ECT, the individual is lightly anesthetized, with electrodes on the scalp, often on both temples (Figure 13.3), permitting an electric current to pass through the brain in order to intentionally produce a series of seizures. The person wakes within minutes after the treatment and is allowed to leave the medical facility within a short time. The therapeutic regimen usually consists of three treatments per week for several weeks. Most patients see improvement in one or two weeks as compared to the longer delays associated with most antidepressant medications. Because of this relatively short time lag for therapeutic effect, ECT may be used for suicidal patients for whom rapid and effective treatment could be life-saving.

The most common and serious side effect of ECT is memory disruption, in the form of both forgetting previously known information (mostly things that occurred just before the procedure, but sometimes older memories as well) and having difficulty forming new memories following treatment. The inability to store new memories typically lasts for a few weeks to a few months. Most studies find that ECT is the most effective antidepres-

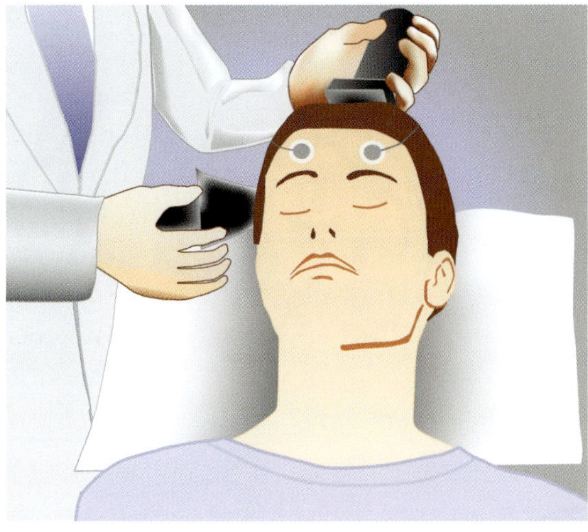

Figure 13.3 Electroconvulsive therapy (ECT). Electrodes on the head of a lightly anesthetized patient permit current to pass through the brain and to produce seizures. The rapid therapeutic effects of ECT can be life saving for a person who is suicidal. (Drawing from NIMH/NIH.)

sant treatment. Unfortunately, the positive effects appear to be no more long-lasting than those of other therapies. Even after seventy or more years of research, the mechanism by which ECT acts remains a mystery.

Transcranial Magnetic Stimulation (TMS)

Like ECT, **transcranial magnetic stimulation** (**TMS**) is a non-invasive treatment applied indirectly to the brain. A small coil placed against the scalp produces a rapidly changing magnetic field that induces an electrical current in the brain (Figure 13.4). Unlike ECT, which is designed to produce generalized seizures, TMS targets specific brain regions. Depending on the parameters, the current can either activate or inhibit neurons in the targeted brain region.

TMS can be carried out without anesthesia in a doctor's office or an outpatient facility. During the procedure, the patient is fully awake and can listen to music, watch a video, or converse with others. A typical treatment regimen is five 30-minute sessions per week, for six or seven weeks. Stimulation applied over the left frontal cortex appears to be most effective (Trevizol & Blumberger, 2019). TMS is not known to cause memory loss. Improvement in symptoms of depression usually take ten or more sessions.

Deep Brain Stimulation (DBS)

Brain imaging studies have shown that the **anterior cingulate cortex** (Figure 13.5) is overly active in depressed patients, particularly those who fail to derive benefits from antidepressant drugs, cognitive therapy, or ECT. In deeply depressed patients, electrical stimulation of axons leading into the anterior cingulate cortex produced immediate improvement that outlasted

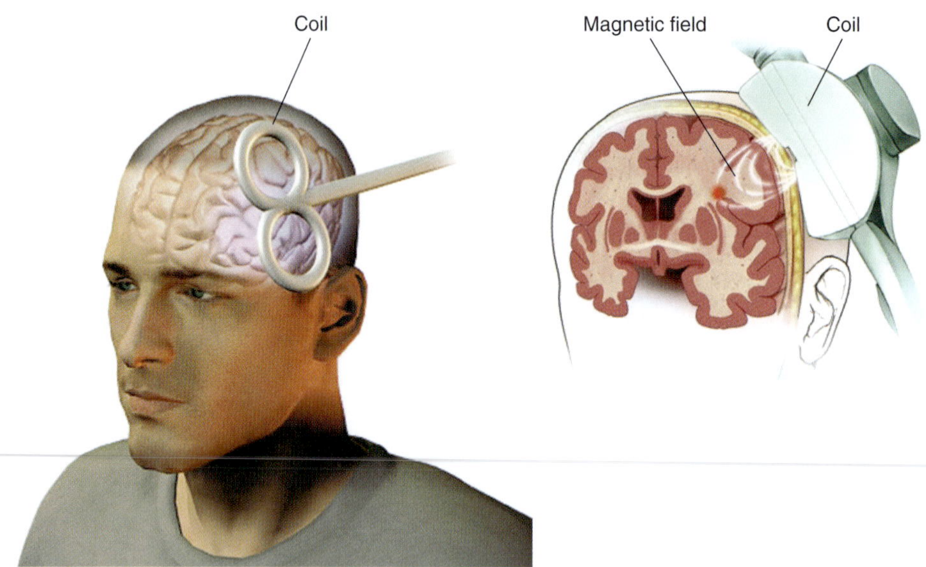

Figure 13.4 Transcranial magnetic stimulation (TMS). A coil placed against the scalp produces a magnetic field, which can target a specific brain region. The procedure can produce therapeutic effects without memory-related side effects.
(Images used with permission of Mayo Foundation for Medical Education and Research, all rights reserved.)

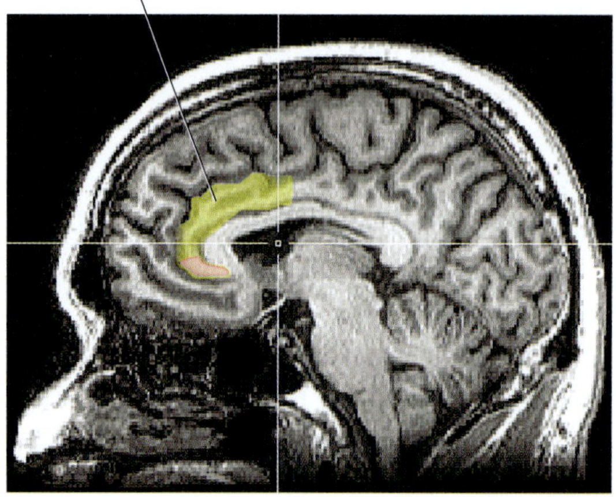

Figure 13.5 The subgenual cingulate cortex. The subgenual cingulate cortex is highly active in patients with treatment-resistant depression. Deep brain stimulation of the region reduces this activity and, for some patients, produces a long-lasting reduction in depression.
(Adapted from image by Geoff B. Hall.)

the stimulation period and remained for six months or more (Mayberg et al., 2005). Not only was there a decrease in neuronal activity in the cingulate cortex, but brain activity in many related brain regions involved in emotion regulation was normalized in the successfully treated patients. Subsequent investigations continue to point to successful outcomes with deep brain stimulation (Delaloye & Holtzheimer, 2014). It is currently one of the most promising research programs for treating depression.

KEY CONCEPTS

- Major depressive disorder is a debilitating condition, often accompanied by feelings of worthlessness and helplessness, insomnia, and fatigue.
- Multiple genes, each of which exerts a small effect, may interact to enhance vulnerability to depression. This genetic vulnerability may interact with intense or prolonged stress.
- Depression is associated with reduced gray matter in several brain regions, as well as abnormal activity of brain areas implicated in emotional regulation.
- For decades, the most common treatment strategy has been SSRIs, which elevate synaptic levels of serotonin. A number of other treatments are currently available, including brain stimulation, cognitive therapy, and meditation.

TEST YOURSELF

1. Describe at least four signs of major depressive disorder. How does major depression differ from the experience of everyday disappointment and sadness? How does it differ from bipolar disorder?
2. Describe evidence for a genetic contribution to major depression coming from twin studies.
3. How do SSRI antidepressants increase synaptic levels of serotonin?
4. When is electroconvulsive therapy most likely to be used? How does it differ from transcranial magnetic stimulation and deep brain stimulation?

13.2 SCHIZOPHRENIA

Schizophrenia is a major psychotic disorder with symptoms that include delusions, hallucination, cognitive impairments, and reductions in social engagement and motivation. About 20 percent of those diagnosed with schizophrenia show symptoms continuously throughout their lives, more than half suffering long-term psychiatric problems with periods of symptom remission (disappearance), while others show complete remission of symptoms and restoration of normal function. The bizarre behaviors that make up a psychotic episode first appear in early adulthood, usually between the ages of 18 and 35 and rarely before 16 (Mueser, Deavers, Penn, & Cassisi, 2013).

Approximately 1 percent of the world population will be diagnosed with schizophrenia, which is an astonishing 70 million people. The disease knows no geographic, racial, or religious boundaries. Life expectancy in schizophrenic patients is shortened by ten to fifteen years compared with healthy individuals. An estimated 5 percent with the disease commit suicide.

Descriptions of a syndrome similar to what we now call schizophrenia first appeared in the mid-1800s. Near the turn of the twentieth century, the German psychiatrist Eugen Bleuler provided a clear description of the disorder, characterized by a cluster of cognitive and emotional symptoms, that he named schizophrenia. The word, derived from the Greek, literally means "splitting of the mind." However, this does not mean that the patient has different personalities. Bleuler was referring to a split between cognitive and emotional processes that normally work together to produce a stable, functional personality.

13.2.1 Clinical Signs of Schizophrenia Include Positive, Negative, and Cognitive Symptoms

Symptoms of schizophrenia are typically divided into positive and negative symptoms. We begin with the positive symptoms. They characterize the psychotic episodes that usually first bring an individual with schizophrenia into the mental health system.

Positive Symptoms

Positive symptoms, also called **psychotic symptoms**, involve a loss of contact with reality. There are three major positive symptoms of schizophrenia:

1. ***Delusions*** are strong and unfounded beliefs that no amount of evidence can disprove. The details of a delusion vary with each individual; however, certain themes commonly occur. For instance:
   - Others are communicating with me in subtle ways. E.g., the gesture of a stranger or the words of a TV announcer are directed to me, and may have great significance (*delusions of reference*).

- Others can read my mind (*thought broadcasting*).
- I'm having thoughts that someone else has put into my head (*thought insertion*).
- External forces can control my behavior. E.g., passing trucks contain machines that can exert control over me (*delusions of control*).
- A person or organization (e.g., the government) is trying to harm me. E.g., I need to avoid signing any letter, even to a friend, because the government may find it and use it to track me down (*delusions of persecution*).
- I am a person of high rank or power (including supernatural power). The delusion is often mixed with thoughts about religion. E.g., I am the second coming of Jesus Christ (*delusions of grandeur*).

2. ***Hallucinations*** are illusory sensory experiences. In about 80 percent of cases, they are auditory (hearing voices), while in some cases they are tactile, for instance believing that snakes are crawling inside the stomach. Unlike the hallucinations produced by LSD and other psychedelic drugs, visual hallucinations rarely occur in schizophrenia. Often, a patient's delusions and hallucinations are associated with one another. For instance, an individual may have the delusion (of grandeur) that he is playing a key role in shaping the destiny of the world, and may hear a voice telling him that he must take a certain action immediately or all will be lost.
3. ***Thought disorders*** are abnormalities in thinking.
   - Patients with thought disorder often string ideas together in an illogical manner (*disorganized thinking*). Here is an example from a patient with disorganized thinking: "If you think you are being wise to send me a bill for money I have already paid, I am in nowise going to do so unless I get the whys and wherefores from you to me. But where the fours have been, then fives will be, and other numbers and calculations and accounts to your no-account … " (Maher, Manschreck, & Molino, 1983). Notice that some of the individual phrases are sensible, but the speech overall is not. Here is another example: "They're destroying too many cattle and oil just to make soap. If we need soap when you can jump into a pool of water, and then when you go to buy your gasoline, my folks always thought they should, get pop but the best thing to get, is motor oil, and, money" (Andreasen, 1986).
   - Some patients use made-up words (neologisms), e.g., "I got so angry I picked up a dish and threw it at the geshinker" (Andreasen, 1986).
   - Other patients may stop speaking in the middle of a thought (*thought blocking*). An individual with thought blocking may later describe feeling as if someone had taken the thought from his head and left his mind suddenly empty.

Delusions, hallucinations, and thought disorder are referred to as "positive symptoms" because they are *present* in those with schizophrenia and normally absent in healthy individuals. In some patients, these symptoms recede and recur intermittently; in others, they persist without interruption.

Negative Symptoms

Negative symptoms of schizophrenia represent the *absence* of particular behavioral and/or emotional functions:

- reduced motivation and pleasure from daily activities
- social withdrawal (isolating oneself)
- reduced speaking
- flat affect (reduced expression of emotions via the face or voice).

Cognitive Symptoms

In addition to the positive and negative symptoms, individuals with schizophrenia often show problems with attention (difficulty sustaining attention to a particular thing or event), working memory, and decision making. These difficulties are often described as **cognitive symptoms**. You may notice that positive symptoms of schizophrenia involve cognitive abnormalities as well (especially delusions and thought disorder). While delusions and thought disorders involve bizarre changes in cognition, the "cognitive symptoms" of schizophrenia are deficits in carrying out normal cognitive functions.

Negative and cognitive symptoms tend to be chronic, while positive symptoms tend to be intermittent. Compared to positive symptoms, the negative and cognitive symptoms can be difficult to detect, for they are also associated with other disorders, such as depression. Some individuals show negative symptoms years before their first psychotic break (positive symptoms) brings them into the mental health system. Those with predominantly negative symptoms and earlier symptom onset typically suffer a more severe illness and a poorer prognosis.

Unfortunately, there are no universally agreed upon biological measures that would be diagnostic for schizophrenia. Many clinicians and researchers believe that the disease we currently describe with the umbrella term "schizophrenia" may really be comprised of several different disorders with overlapping symptoms, but each with distinct neurobiological causes. As we learn more about the biology of schizophrenia, it may be possible to diagnose individuals in a more precise manner, i.e., one that allows treatments to be more specifically geared to the underlying disorder.

13.2.2 Genes and Environmental Influences Contribute to Schizophrenia

Schizophrenia runs in families, which suggests a strong genetic influence. This could mean that the disease is influenced by family dynamics, by genetics inherited from parents, or by some combination. As we saw with depression, investigators attempt to disentangle genetic from environmental contributions to the disease. Adoption studies give us some answers. If an adopted person develops schizophrenia, the likelihood that his or her biological relatives (shared genes, different family environment) will have signs of this disorder is about 15 percent. By comparison, the likelihood of schizophrenia in the family that adopted the individual (shared family environment, different genes) is less than 3 percent (Kety et al., 1994). Furthermore, the concordance rate for schizophrenia (likelihood that the relative of a person with schizophrenia will also have schizophrenia) is greatest for relatives with the closest genetic relationship (see Figure 13.6).

A large number of genes contribute to schizophrenia. In fact, most of the twenty-three chromosomes in the human genome include genes that may be related to the disorder. There may be multiple genetic pathways to schizophrenia, each resulting from different groups of genes. Genes associated with schizophrenia code for proteins with diverse nervous system functions. Many of these proteins play important roles in pre- and post-natal

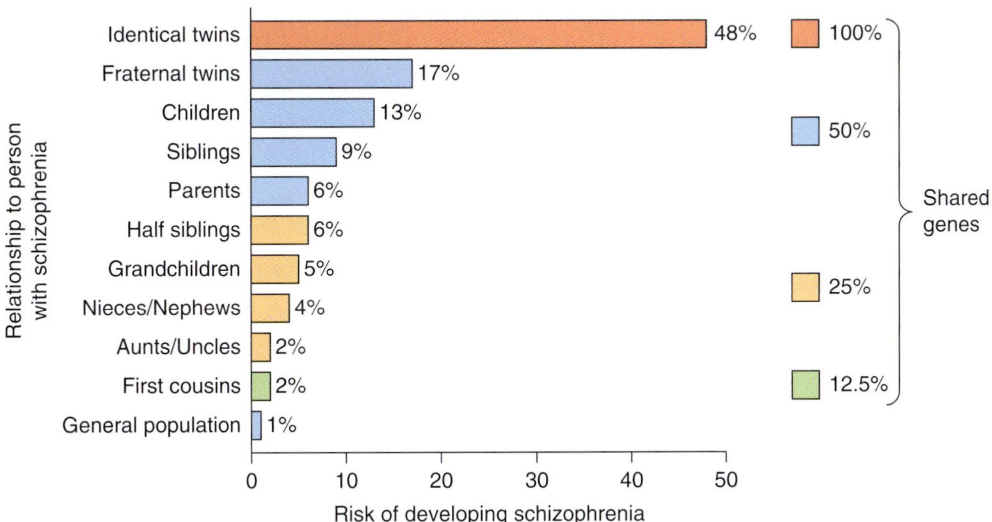

Figure 13.6 The risk of schizophrenia is elevated in family members of a person with schizophrenia. The more genes one shares with an individual with schizophrenia, the greater the risk of developing the disease.

development of the nervous system. Their roles include neuronal migration and differentiation, synapse formation, synaptic transmission, axonal guidance, and protein transcription. Therefore, at least some of the genetic abnormalities associated with schizophrenia are likely to lead to abnormalities in brain development. Some of these abnormalities may lead to changes in the size of particular brain areas, and in dysfunctions of neurotransmission at dopamine and glutamate synapses, as described in sections below.

In addition to genetics, a number of events or environmental conditions appear to contribute to the development of schizophrenia. These include:

- stress
- exposure to environmental toxins
- drug abuse
- traumatic brain injury
- unemployment and poverty
- maternal stress, malnutrition, and infection during pregnancy
- viral infection early in life.

The large number of environmental conditions associated with schizophrenia makes it difficult to ascertain precisely which factors are contributors to the disease. If any generalization can be made, it would be that events before or immediately after birth have the greatest impact. Furthermore, there is a consensus that none of these conditions, by themselves, can be considered a cause of schizophrenia. The environmental factors become significant only when they interact with a susceptibility factor, most likely a genetic predisposition. We also know that, whatever potentially pathological state is produced by this gene–environment interaction, the disease typically remains unexpressed until early adulthood (schizophrenia is rarely diagnosed in prepubescent children). Some neurobiological events presumably trigger the first psychotic episode, and the trigger may be the result of environmental conditions, biological processes, or a combination of the two.

Like depression, schizophrenia may be subject to epigenetic influences. That is to say, environmental factors may alter the ability of genes to produce proteins without altering the basic DNA sequence of the genetic code. For example, childhood sexual abuse may alter gene expression and produce increased vulnerability to factors triggering schizophrenia (Nestler, 2014; Popovic et al., 2019).

In summary, there is strong evidence for a genetic predisposition for schizophrenia. As we have seen, the concordance rate for identical twins is high. However, the fact that identical twins aren't always concordant for schizophrenia suggests that what is inherited is a genetic predisposition that interacts with environmental, social, and/or physiological stressors to produce the disease.

13.2.3 Schizophrenia Is Associated with Structural and Functional Abnormalities of the Brain

One of the most striking discoveries regarding brain abnormalities in schizophrenia was the doubling of the size of the lateral ventricles in patients with chronic schizophrenia due to the loss of brain cells surrounding them (Weinberger, Torrey, Neophytides, & Wyatt, 1979) (Figure 13.7). The loss of brain tissue is seen in regions normally involved in memory, cognition, and language (e.g., the hippocampus) and decision making (the prefrontal cortex). The reduced size of these brain regions and enlargement of the fluid-filled ventricles is sometimes seen even in young people with early warning signs of the disease.

fMRI allows visualization of activity in the brains of patients with schizophrenia while they are engaged in cognitive tasks. Those with schizophrenia show abnormalities in activity within a large number of brain regions (including the hippocampus, prefrontal cortex, amygdala, thalamus, and basal ganglia). Abnormalities in the activity of this large collection of structures should not be surprising, given the variety of symptoms observed in schizophrenia. In the brain regions showing abnormal activity, postmortem analyses frequently find unusual cell shape, changes

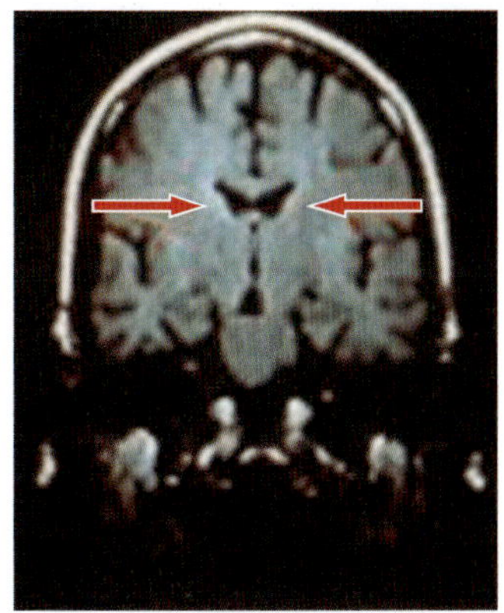

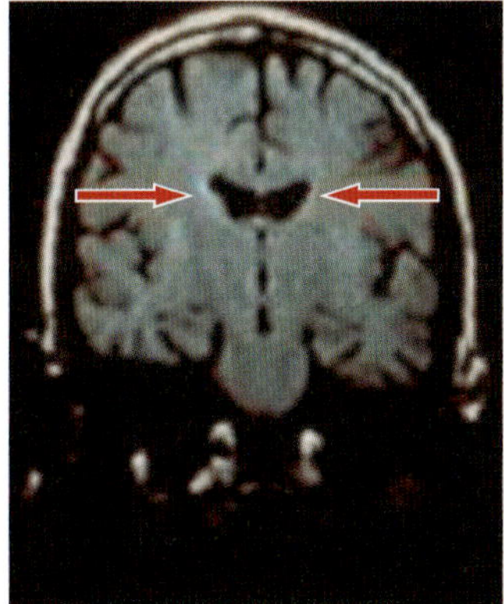

Figure 13.7 Enlarged ventricles in schizophrenia. The increased size of the lateral ventricles in persons with schizophrenia is associated with loss of surrounding brain tissue.
(Adapted from image by Dr. Daniel Weinberger, NIMH, Clinical Brain Disorders Branch.)

in dendritic spines, decreased density of cells, thinning of cortical areas, and a reduction in oligodendrocytes.

Let us come back to one of the important rules of brain and behavior. Changes in behavior and cognition as complex as what we find in schizophrenia must be due to alterations in functional circuits of the brain rather than to individual brain structures like those listed above. Diffusion MRI is a technique that measures the size of axon bundles and thereby allows us to assess the strength of *connections* between neurons in specific brain regions. Such analysis reveals that schizophrenia is associated with decreases in neural communication between some brain structures and increases between others.

13.2.4 Nearly All Antipsychotic Drugs Block Dopamine Receptors

Prior to the mid-twentieth century, patients with schizophrenia and those with other mental illnesses were often housed in institutions where they were neglected or mistreated (Figure 13.8). This treatment was sometimes interspersed by enlightened periods when patients were looked after and treated kindly. Today, we look back upon past treatments with astonishment: insulin-induced coma, ice bath, electroshock, drug-induced

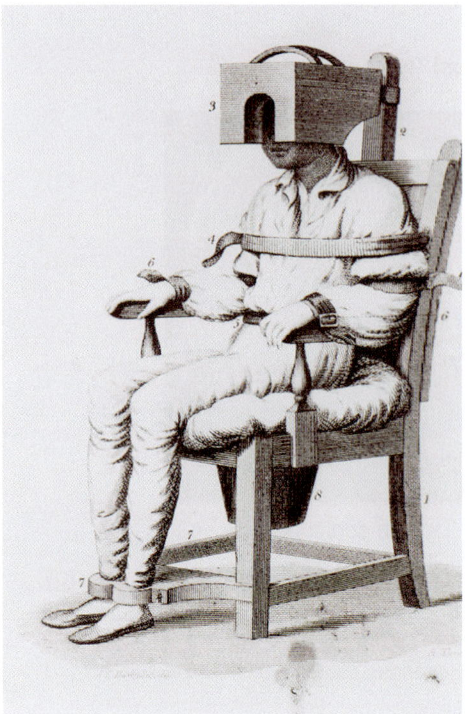

Figure 13.8 The tranquilizing chair. Designed by Dr. Benjamin Rush (a signer of the US constitution), the chair was in use at Pennsylvania Hospital during the early 1800s. "Madness" was believed to be caused by abnormal blood flow, and restraining a patient in the chair was thought to relieve "insanity" by reducing the flow of blood toward the brain.
(Source: US National Library of Medicine.)

seizures, and, most notoriously, prefrontal lobotomy (in which the prefrontal cortex was surgically disconnected from the rest of the brain).

Modern biological psychiatry began in the 1950s, when the drug chlorpromazine (Thorazine) was found to have a powerful and calming effect on schizophrenic patients, apparently reducing their delusions and hallucinations. The use of this and other **antipsychotic drugs** (or **neuroleptics**) to treat schizophrenia changed the course of psychiatry – treatment with a small pill! These drugs allowed millions of patients with chronic mental illnesses to be released from their institutions. From this point on, biological treatments came to dominate and revolutionize the field.

The early antipsychotics like chlorpromazine blocked the activity of many types of receptors (dopamine, serotonin, norepinephrine, acetylcholine, histamine, and others). These non-specific pharmacological actions are associated with non-specific and undesirable psychological and behavioral effects, including sedation and movement difficulties. As additional antipsychotic drugs became available, researchers found that the ones that were most effective in treating psychotic symptoms had strong blocking actions at the **dopamine D_2 receptor.** In fact, the ability of a particular drug to block the D_2 receptor in a laboratory test tube is an almost perfect predictor of its potency in treating psychotic symptoms (Figure 13.9) (Seeman, Lee, Chau-Wong, & Wong, 1976).

This finding led to the **dopamine hypothesis of schizophrenia**: the idea that overactivity of brain dopamine transmission at the D_2 dopamine receptor is an important factor in the cause of schizophrenia. Additional

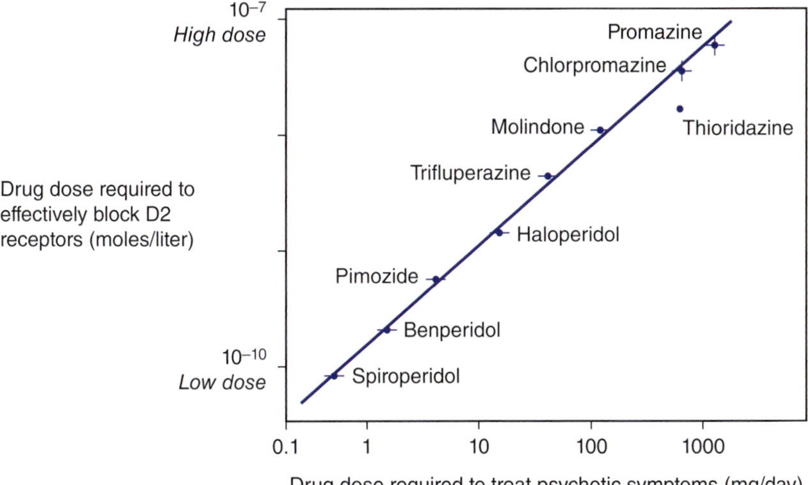

Figure 13.9 Correlation between antipsychotic potency and dopamine D_2 receptor affinity. The drugs that treat symptoms of schizophrenia at low doses are the same drugs that effectively block D_2 receptors at low doses.
(Adapted from Seeman, Lee, Chau-Wong, & Wong, 1976, fig. 1.)

evidence for this idea comes from the fact that amphetamine and cocaine both increase dopamine activity in the brain. When taken in high doses, users frequently end up in hospital emergency rooms with delusions and hallucinations resembling those of schizophrenia. In fact, trained psychiatrists are typically unable to distinguish the delusions of an individual who has overdosed on amphetamine from those of an individual with paranoid schizophrenia. Similarly, people with Parkinson's disease who overdose on drugs that increase synaptic DA concentrations in the brain may become delusional.

One explanation for the role of dopamine in schizophrenic psychosis relates to the kinds of stimuli that normally activate midbrain dopamine neurons. We saw in Chapter 11 that primary and conditioned reward stimuli (e.g., food, sex, and money) activate dopamine neurons and increase activity of the nucleus accumbens and other dopamine-receiving areas of the brain. However, some dopamine neurons respond to auditory, visual, and other stimuli that are novel, intense, unexpected, or otherwise **salient** (attention-grabbing) (Horvitz, 2000). Some investigators have proposed that because dopamine activation normally signals salient events, abnormal dopamine activation in schizophrenia may cause the individual to sense that an important event has occurred, even when no obvious external cause for this feeling is evident.

This may account for the fact that positive symptoms of schizophrenia are often accompanied by (or preceded by) a sense that normal events have a hidden meaning (Winton-Brown, Fusar-Poli, Ungless, & Howes, 2014). From this point of view, delusions may reflect the individual's way of making sense out of what would otherwise appear to be randomly occurring experiences of meaning. Dopamine antagonists, then, may reduce delusions by reducing the effects of abnormal dopamine activation, and the abnormal signals that cause events to appear strangely salient and important. Investigations in human subjects have shown that dopamine release and binding to D_2 receptors is indeed elevated in patients who exhibit psychotic symptoms (Fusar-Poli et al., 2013).

Dopamine antagonist drugs might seem like a perfect treatment for schizophrenia. However, many of these drugs produce serious motor effects, such as involuntary tics, grimacing, and tongue protrusion. These effects of dopamine antagonists on motor behavior are not surprising, given the important role of dopamine in the basal ganglia, one of the brain's key subcortical motor systems (Chapter 4).

Another problem with these dopamine antagonist drugs for treating schizophrenia is that, while they reduce hallucinations and delusions, they are often ineffective in reducing negative symptoms of schizophrenia, such as social withdrawal and in reducing cognitive deficits. In fact, some negative symptoms, such as reduced motivation, may even become more pronounced under the influence of the drugs. Given the role of frontal cortical dopamine in attention and working memory, dopamine antagonist drugs may exacerbate problems in these cognitive functions as well.

These drawbacks led to a newer series of drugs termed *atypical antipsychotics*. These drugs block the D_2 receptor, but also influence activity at other receptors, such as the serotonin 2 receptor. Atypical antipsychotics are less likely to produce motor symptoms, and may be somewhat more effective in treating negative symptoms than the traditional dopamine antagonists. Nevertheless, even with these newer antipsychotics, negative symptoms remain particularly resistant to treatment, and only about 30 percent of patients show long-term (>2 year) remission from symptoms (Novick, Haro, Suarez, Vieta, & Naber, 2009). The search continues for a treatment that has more manageable side effects and that effectively treats positive, negative, and cognitive symptoms. One line of current interest in drug development for schizophrenia involves drugs that act upon glutamate receptors (Nicoletti et. al., 2019).

13.2.5 Is Psychological Therapy Beneficial for Individuals with Schizophrenia?

Given the demonstrated efficacy of psychological therapy, particularly CBT, for treating anxiety and depression, it's natural to ask whether such therapy might help those with schizophrenia. Goals of CBT for patients with schizophrenia include helping the patient to recognize environmental situations that trigger their symptoms, and reducing the patient's embarrassment about the symptoms. Of course, a key question is whether or not the therapy reduces symptoms. Some studies report that CBT does reduce symptoms of schizophrenia (Wykes, Steel, Everitt, & Tarrier, 2008; Morrison et al., 2014), while others have failed to observe benefits (Garety et al., 2008; Klingberg et al., 2011). Meta-analyses of the results of a large number of studies show some positive effects of CBT on positive symptoms of schizophrenia, although the effects are small (Jauhar, Laws, & McKenna, 2019).

Remission of symptoms may not be the only valuable endpoint in the psychological treatment of schizophrenia. Mental health professionals can also help the individual to develop self-management skills that better meet their personal goals, help manage medications, and improve social skills (Mueser et al., 2013).

KEY CONCEPTS

- **Schizophrenia includes positive symptoms (hallucinations, delusions, and thought disorders) and negative symptoms (reduced motivation, social withdrawal, flat affect), as well as cognitive impairments.**
- **Schizophrenia is heritable and has a fairly strong genetic component.**
- **In chronic schizophrenia the lateral ventricles are enlarged due to loss of brain cells surrounding them.**
- **Many antipsychotic medications target the dopamine D_2 receptor. However, continued use of these drugs can produce motor abnormalities, and they do not treat the negative symptoms. Newer antipsychotics produce fewer motor symptoms.**
- **The benefits of psychological treatment of schizophrenia remain controversial. Evidence suggests that while Cognitive Behavioral Therapy may reduce symptoms, the reductions are small in magnitude.**

TEST YOURSELF

1. **What are the three major positive symptoms of schizophrenia? Give at least three examples of schizophrenic delusions.**
2. **Describe the major negative symptoms of schizophrenia.**
3. **Describe the major cognitive symptoms of schizophrenia.**
4. **What is the relation between the early appearance of negative symptoms and prognosis for recovery from the disease?**
5. **What is the evidence that dopamine receptors play an important role in schizophrenia? Is the relation between dopamine receptors more strongly linked to positive or negative symptoms? Explain the evidence for your answer.**

13.3 PARKINSON'S DISEASE

Parkinson's disease is a disabling movement disorder involving the death of dopamine neurons in the midbrain. The disease is **progressive** (it worsens over time); as more dopamine neurons are lost, the movement difficulties become more severe. Parkinson's is more or less evenly distributed across the globe. Its occurrence is two to three times higher in men than women.

13.3.1 Parkinsonian Motor Symptoms Result from the Loss of Nigrostriatal Dopamine Neurons

The three key signs of Parkinson's disease are **resting tremor**, **rigidity**, and **slowness of movement** (Figure 13.10). The severity of the illness can vary widely from one patient to another.

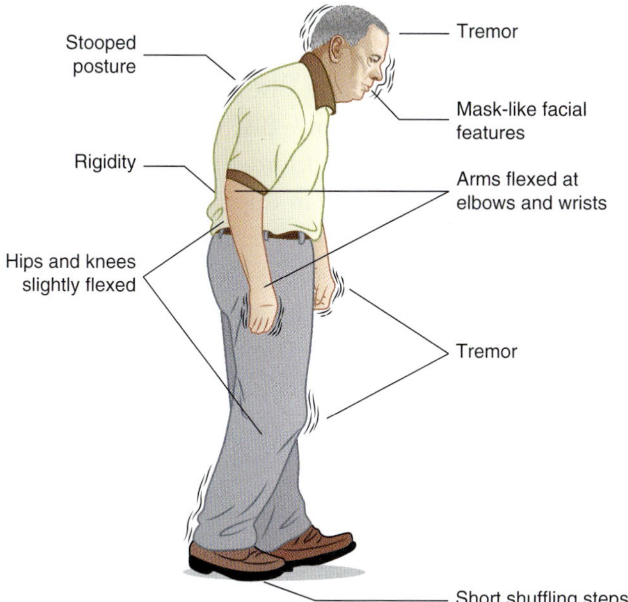

Figure 13.10 Outward signs of Parkinson's disease. The illustration shows two of the cardinal signs: rigidity and tremor. A third key sign, slow movement, can appear as lack of facial expressiveness or "mask-like face." Other signs shown in the illustration (stooped posture, shuffling steps, flexed joints) are related to rigidity.

- Resting tremor. The patient shakes, mostly in a hand or foot, but sometimes in the face as well. The symptom is called "resting tremor" because it occurs mostly when the person is relaxed, for instance when the person's hands are folded in their lap. When performing an action, like drinking a glass of water, the tremor decreases.
- Rigidity. The major muscles of the body controlling the limbs, torso, and neck are stiff due to increased muscle tension. Try simultaneously flexing your arm without moving the joint (as people do during isometric exercise). Parkinson's patients experience this kind of limb rigidity involuntarily, and it can be uncomfortable and even painful. Rigidity is easily seen in the stiff shuffling movements of the patient as he walks.
- Slowness or absence of movement. This is also called **bradykinesia**, and comes from the Greek *brady* (slow) and *kinesia* (movement). Some behaviors are difficult to carry out so slowly. For instance, getting up from a chair, buttoning a shirt, or cutting food with a knife, require certain movements to occur quickly. Patients with bradykinesia have great difficulty carrying out such movements. In later stages of the disease, there may be a virtually complete lack of movement, termed **akinesia**.

Other outward signs of Parkinson's include short stooped posture, shrinkage in the size of handwriting, difficulty in turning during walking, and instability of balance.

The time between initial diagnosis to death can be anywhere from five to twenty years, depending, in part, on the age of the patient at onset. While most cases emerge around age 50–60, the disease can emerge much earlier. The actor Michael J. Fox had Parkinson's disease onset at age 30, and the boxer Muhammad Ali developed the disorder around age 40.

Parkinson's disease is due to the loss of brain dopamine neurons that originate in the **substantia nigra** (**SN**). The dopamine neurons in this area release dopamine to the **striatum**, a region of the basal ganglia that plays a key role in movement (Chapter 4). This dopamine pathway is called the **nigrostriatal dopamine pathway** (Figure 13.11). The striatum (comprised of the **caudate** and **putamen**) allows us to choose and initiate everyday actions, like lifting a cup, standing up from a chair, typing on a computer, and even speaking. When the nigrostriatal dopamine neurons degenerate, the striatum is deprived of normal dopamine levels, and neurons in the striatum no longer send commands that permit individuals to perform normal movements. The severity of Parkinson's motor symptoms correlates with the amount of nigrostriatal dopamine loss. Individuals with Parkinson's have typically lost more than 50 percent of their SN dopamine neurons by the time they are diagnosed with the disease (Surmeier, Obeso, & Halliday, 2017). This suggests that some threshold number of dopamine neurons must be lost before clear signs of the disease are evident.

Before we end this section, it's worth mentioning a bizarre aspect of the Parkinson's motor problems. Despite severe impairment in moving the body, some patients can move surprisingly well under certain circumstances. For instance, Parkinson's patients with great difficulty

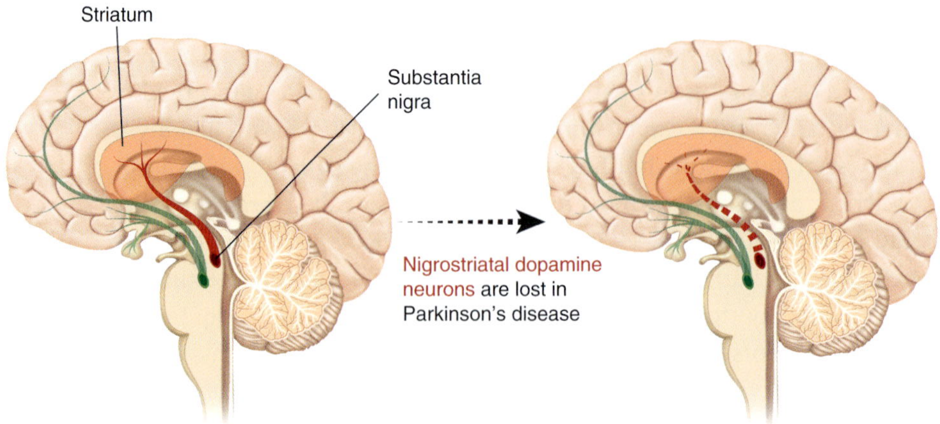

Figure 13.11 Parkinson's disease and the loss of nigrostriatal dopamine neurons. The figure depicts several major dopamine pathways (in green and red). The motor symptoms of Parkinson's disease arise specifically from the degeneration of the nigrostriatal dopamine pathway. Neurons in this pathway originate in the substantia nigra, and normally release dopamine to the striatum.

locomoting (walking) have been reported to walk quickly or even run out of a hospital room in response to a fire alarm. The normal behavior seen in a Parkinson's patient exposed to a salient external stimulus is called **paradoxical kinesia** (Martin 1967; Jahanshahi & Frith, 1998). Another example of paradoxical kinesia is the Parkinson's patient who freezes when he begins to walk, yet has no problem walking over clear (e.g., large bright) lines drawn on the ground. For some reason, the motor problems of Parkinson's patients are reduced in the presence of strong eliciting stimuli in the environment.

Paradoxical kinesia shows that the motor problems of Parkinson's patients are not due to a problem with the muscles that move the body or to the spinal cord neurons that access those muscles. The muscles are activated normally so long as there is a strong external stimulus to trigger the behavior. Neither are the patient's movement difficulties due to a lack of motivation. The patient *wants* to perform particular movements, but sometimes cannot. With a loss of nigrostriatal dopamine, the difficulty appears to be in translating the motivation to move into the correct motor commands for carrying out the movement. Parkinson's disease is sometimes called a "voluntary" motor disorder, one in which the person's volition or will to move no longer produces appropriate motor commands.

13.3.2 Clumps of Misfolded Proteins Are Often Found within Dying Dopamine Neurons

A German neurologist Frederic Lewy observed a roundish foreign substance in the brains of patients who had died of Parkinson's disease. This strange substance, which Lewy observed in 1912, is today referred to as **Lewy bodies** (Figure 13.12). One of the brain regions containing Lewy bodies is the substantia nigra, the midbrain region containing nigrostriatal dopamine neurons. What exactly are these Lewy bodies?

If you examine them carefully, you find that they are made up of proteins that clump together. Several kinds of proteins make up these clumps, but the main type is **alpha-synuclein** (Spillantini et al., 1997). Like other proteins, alpha-synuclein folds in a particular way that gives it its three-dimensional shape. Alpha-synuclein is found in normal, healthy brains. However, in Parkinson's patients the protein is *misfolded* and has an abnormal three-dimensional structure. When alpha-synuclein proteins are misfolded, they combine with other proteins to form large aggregates (Lewy bodies) both inside and outside of cells.

Could these Lewy bodies, with their clumps of alpha-synuclein, be responsible for the death of dopamine neurons seen in Parkinson's patients? It is unclear. While high levels of alpha-synuclein lead to cell death in some dopamine neurons, other dopamine neurons exposed to

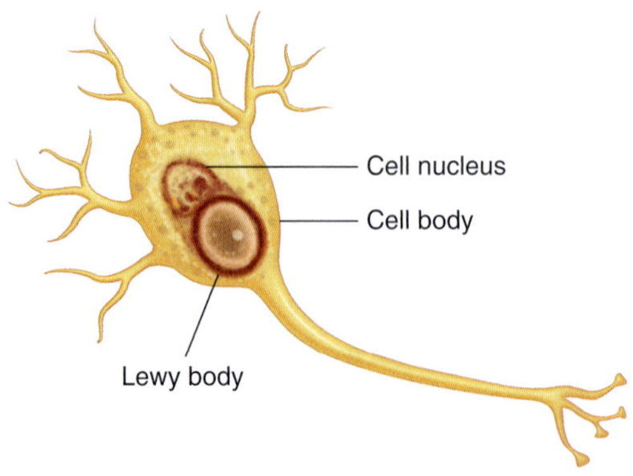

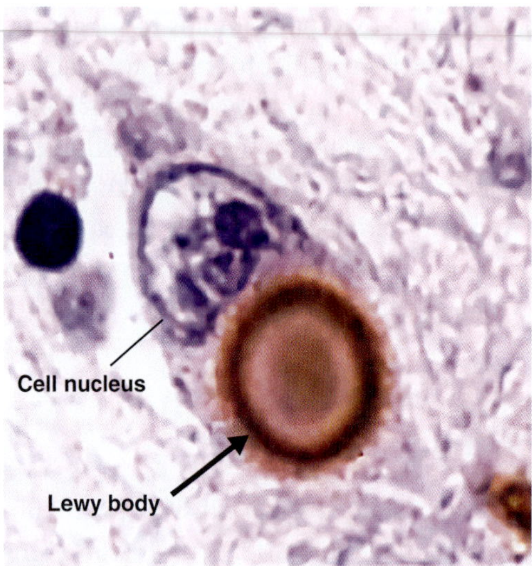

Figure 13.12 Lewy bodies. In Parkinson's patients, neurons in the substantia nigra and nearby regions often contain Lewy bodies. As seen in the drawing at the top, the Lewy body has a roundish shape within a neuron's cell body. In the photograph below, the halo-like dark brown circle surrounding the Lewy body is comprised of alpha-synuclein protein.
(Adapted from Hishikawa, Hashizuma, Yoshida, & Sobue, 2003, fig. 3A, © 2003, Springer-Verlag.)

the same alpha-synuclein levels survive for decades (Surmeier et al., 2017). It is possible that Lewy bodies combine with other abnormalities in the cell to create lethal conditions. One of the other factors that may contribute to dopamine cell death is an abnormality of the cell's mitochondria, the key organelle responsible for providing cellular energy. Cells with mitochondrial dysfunction have difficulty maintaining their own energy needs. When Lewy bodies are added to a dopamine neuron with mitochondrial dysfunction, the energy demands of the neuron may pass a tipping point where it can no longer survive.

Some Parkinson's patients possess a mutation in the gene for alpha-synuclein which causes the protein to fold incorrectly and aggregate. Many patients with this gene mutation begin to show signs of Parkinson's disease at an early age (about 46). Researchers are working to develop treatments that will prevent alpha-synuclein proteins from aggregating. Ultimately, the cure for Parkinson's will depend on coming up with ways to prevent the death of dopamine neurons in the SN, whether by treatments that prevent the accumulation of misfolded alpha-synuclein or by some other means.

13.3.3 Genetic and Environmental Factors Contribute to Parkinson's Disease

We next examine what is known about genetic contributions to Parkinson's disease, and evaluate evidence for environmental contributions, particular toxin exposure.

Genes

There is a link between genes and Parkinson's disease, but only for a relatively small proportion of cases. About 5–10 percent of Parkinson's patients have first-degree relatives with the disease, suggesting a genetic contribution at least for this subgroup of patients. However, keep in mind that family members typically share environmental conditions as well as genes.

A role of genes in the disease can be examined more clearly in twin studies where researchers compare the likelihood of having Parkinson's when one's identical (monozygotic) versus fraternal (dizygotic) twin has the disease. If genes play a key role in determining who gets the disease, the concordance rate should be higher in identical compared to fraternal twins. But the concordance rate is similar in identical and fraternal twins. These findings suggest that many cases of Parkinson's are not explained by genes alone.

Certain gene mutations (genes with unusual alterations in their DNA sequence) do increase one's risk for Parkinson's disease. Recall that some Parkinson's patients possess a mutation in the gene for alpha-synuclein, and their brains contain a form of alpha-synuclein that folds incorrectly and aggregates to form Lewy bodies. However, fewer than 40 percent of the people with the Parkinson's-related gene mutation will get the disease. Therefore, while genes are believed to play a role in some cases of Parkinson's disease, an individual's likelihood of getting the disease appears to depend upon interactions of various genetic and environmental factors.

Environment

Exposure to paraquat, the most common substance used to kill weeds, is associated with an increased risk of Parkinson's disease (Kamel, 2013). Farmers who have used paraquat for more than a week have a 3.6-fold increase in risk for Parkinson's, while farmers who have used it for less time have a smaller (2.4-fold) increase in the risk. Parkinson's disease is associated with exposure to other pesticides as well.

Studies of Parkinson's risk from pesticides usually examine individuals who use pesticides professionally, for instance pesticide sprayers (often farmers) and plantation workers. However, it is difficult to point to the risk associated with specific pesticides, and how much exposure is needed before the risk of Parkinson's disease increases. The difficulty comes first, because pesticides are often used in combination, and second, because non-professionals (those using pesticides in the home garden) are rarely aware of what pesticides they've been exposed to. Researchers believe that some individuals may have genes that make them more vulnerable to the effects of toxin exposure on risk of Parkinson's (Goldman, 2014).

In 1982, a small group of adults in California sought medical attention after taking a synthetic heroin-like drug. Two to six weeks after use, they all began to show rigid movements, shuffling gait, immobility, and other signs of Parkinson's disease. The symptoms were permanent (Langston, Ballard, Tetrud, & Irwin, 1983). The synthetic heroin turned out to be comprised almost completely of a chemical called MPTP, which is toxic to dopamine neurons. In a successful attempt to produce an animal model of Parkinson's disease for research purposes, scientists administered MPTP to monkeys. As it did in humans who had taken it, the drug produced clinical signs of Parkinson's. The clearly toxic effect of MPTP enables researchers to examine the death of dopamine neurons under controlled conditions, and to conduct experiments to attempt to reverse that dopamine loss.

In addition to toxin exposure, head injury increases the risk of Parkinson's about twofold (Kamel, 2013). Surprisingly, nicotine and caffeine *reduce* the risk of Parkinson's. (This is one of the few demonstrated benefits of nicotine, which, as you know, is associated with a large number of health risks.)

13.3.4 L-DOPA Is the Gold Standard for Treating Parkinson's Disease

As we have seen, Parkinsonian motor symptoms are known to be related to the death of nigrostriatal dopamine neurons. Treatments for Parkinson's disease typically involve drugs that aim to restore normal or near-normal dopamine levels in the brain. One of the challenges faced by researchers has been how to deliver dopamine to the brain when dopamine itself does not cross the blood–brain barrier.

L-DOPA, the immediate precursor in the synthesis of dopamine, does cross the blood–brain barrier. In 1962, a team of researchers in Vienna administered L-DOPA intravenously to patients with Parkinson's, and the results were phenomenal. Immobilized patients could suddenly move about freely, some even jumped. Those with previous speech problems could now clearly articulate (Birkmayer & Hornykiewicz, 1962). It is not an overstatement to describe this as a miracle of science.

However, the elevation of dopamine in Parkinson's patients is not without side effects. Dopamine is found not only in the nigrostriatal system, but also in other brain regions, and even in areas outside the brain. Aside from their nigrostriatal dopamine loss, Parkinson's patients often have normal levels of dopamine in these other areas. Administration of L-DOPA can therefore produce an oversupply of dopamine in some dopamine-containing areas of the brain and outside the brain. The side effects can include nausea and vomiting, gastrointestinal bleeding, and respiratory difficulty. Psychiatric side effects have included insomnia and disturbing dreams, and, as we saw in the previous section, high doses of L-DOPA can produce psychotic symptoms. Many of these problems are reduced or eliminated by co-administering L-DOPA with a drug that decreases the synthesis of dopamine from L-DOPA *outside* the brain.

Still, if the story ended there, L-DOPA treatment might be one of the triumphant success stories in medicine. However, continued use of L-DOPA and the unremitting progression of Parkinson's disease typically lead to decreased effectiveness of the treatment. L-DOPA allows existing dopamine neurons to release extra dopamine, but it does not prevent the dopamine neurons from dying. As the nigrostriatal dopamine neurons continue to degenerate, the effectiveness of L-DOPA tends to diminish. The beneficial action of the drug can unpredictably halt several years after the treatments begin. No existing treatment can halt the progression of Parkinson's, nor can any existing drug therapy restore normal motor function in the long term.

13.3.5 Modern Technologies Promise Better Ways to Overcome Parkinsonian Motor Impairments

In the 1980s and 1990s, several types of brain surgery were developed to treat Parkinson's motor symptoms. These surgeries involved lesions or stimulation of particular regions of the basal ganglia. As described in Chapter 4, the basal ganglia are a complex network of subcortical areas that include the striatum and globus pallidus, and which play a key role in initiation of movements. Regions of the globus pallidus are overactive in Parkinson's patients, and this overactivity contributes to the patient's movement difficulties. Surgery that destroys a small portion of the globus pallidus relieves motor symptoms in some patients.

Currently, a more common approach is **deep brain stimulation**. Recall that deep brain stimulation applied to particular regions of the brain has therapeutic effects for depression. For treatment of Parkinson's, the patient is implanted with a battery-operated neural stimulator (similar to a pacemaker for the heart) under the skin, and the stimulator sends low-intensity stimulation to thin electrodes within particular regions of the basal ganglia. Although the device is called a "stimulator," its therapeutic effect appears to involve blocking abnormal signals through the basal ganglia. The surgeons may implant the electrodes to different areas of the basal ganglia depending upon the patient. Often, the electrodes are placed in a region of the basal ganglia called the subthalamic nucleus (Figure 13.13).

Because the various parts of the basal ganglia interact with one another in complex ways, it is difficult to know precisely how deep brain stimulation of the subthalamic nucleus or any other part of the basal ganglia affects other parts of the circuit to normalize motor performance. While deep brain stimulation improves motor function in many Parkinson's patients, scientists are still working to understand precisely *how* this stimulation reduces motor symptoms.

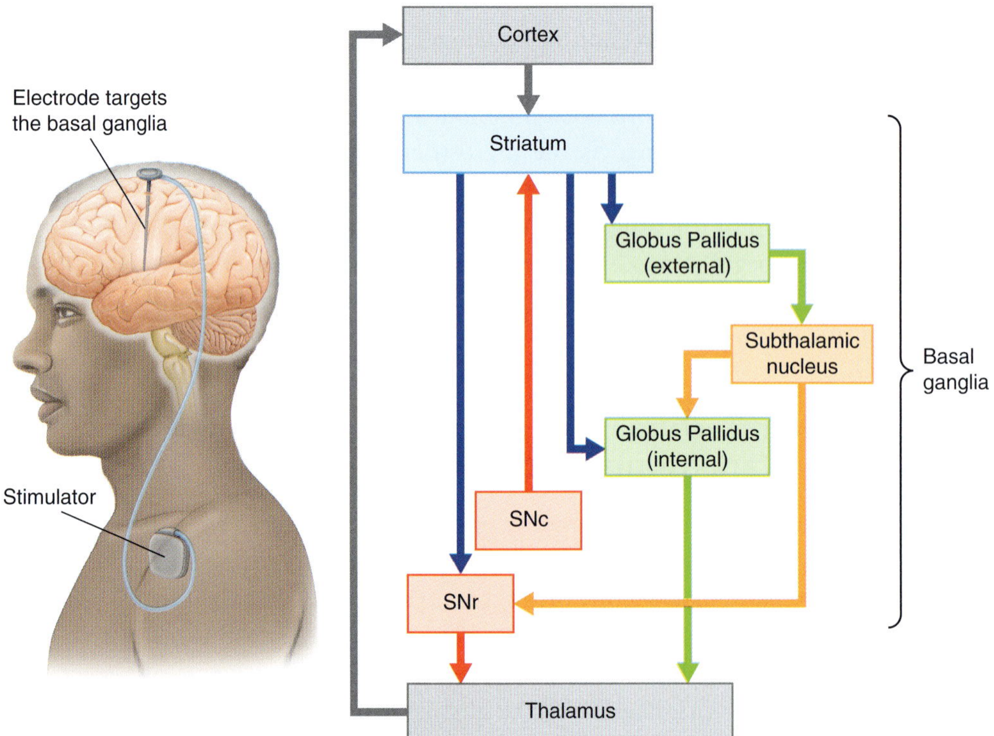

Figure 13.13 Deep brain stimulation to reduce Parkinson's motor symptoms. Left: A stimulator implanted under the skin sends low-intensity electrical stimulation to electrodes that target the subthalamic nucleus or other areas of the basal ganglia. This improves motor function in many patients. Right: The complex circuitry of the basal ganglia makes it difficult to precisely predict the effects of brain stimulation to any one region.

Finally, in what many see as a potential cure for many diseases, stem cells might be able to replace lost or damaged cells, including dopamine neurons. Stem cells are *pluripotent*; they are capable of differentiating into any one of many different cell types (Chapter 8). They can become cells of the heart, liver, brain, etc. In this case, stem cells can be harvested from bone marrow and then biochemically induced to develop into dopamine neurons. However, the problem would be not only to create dopamine neurons but then to promote their integration into the existing circuitry once they are implanted in the brain (Fiorenzano et al., 2021).

KEY CONCEPTS

- **Parkinson's disease is a progressive disorder with onset typically at 50–60 years. There is no cure, it cannot be prevented, and the effectiveness of treatments decreases over time.**
- **The primary signs of Parkinson's are tremor, rigidity, and slowness of movement.**
- **Motor symptoms of Parkinson's are strongly correlated with the death of dopamine-containing neurons in the nigrostriatal pathway.**
- **More recent research has suggested that the death of dopamine neurons is due, at least in part, to intracellular Lewy bodies containing misfolded alpha-synuclein protein.**
- **Key treatments for Parkinson's are drugs that increase brain dopamine concentrations, including L-DOPA, the biochemical precursor to dopamine.**
- **Researchers are examining a number of treatment approaches. These include trying to reverse the aggregation of alpha-synuclein, electrically stimulating regions of the basal ganglia, and using stem cells to replace lost dopamine neurons.**

TEST YOURSELF

1. **What are the primary signs of Parkinson's disease?**
2. **Motor dysfunctions in Parkinson's disease are strongly related to loss of which neurotransmitter pathway?**
3. **What is the name of the abnormal protein aggregates (clumps) found in the brains of Parkinson's patients? What is the primary component of these protein aggregates?**
4. **What evidence suggests that genes alone may be unable to account for Parkinson's disease?**
5. **What are two environmental factors that have been linked to the disease?**
6. **Describe the limitations of L-DOPA as a treatment for Parkinson's disease. What other newer treatments are being employed?**

13.4 ALZHEIMER'S DISEASE

In the opening story to this chapter, we described Sister Mary O'Reilly roaming her neighborhood lost and unable to recognize the faces most familiar to her. Every year, over the past several decades, more and more individuals suffer from the deteriorated memory and thought processes that characterize Alzheimer's. The increased numbers of cases are attributable primarily to increased life expectancy. Simply put, the longer you live, the greater the likelihood that you will develop the disease.

The disease is rarely seen before age 40. Beyond age 65, the likelihood of developing Alzheimer's doubles about every five years. For people in their seventies, approximately 5–10 percent will be diagnosed with the disease, while for people in their mid-eighties, the numbers skyrocket to 40 percent. President Ronald Reagan was diagnosed at age 83. Following diagnosis, the average survival time is six to seven years. Women are over 50 percent more likely than men to develop the disease.

In 1899, Alois Alzheimer, a German psychiatrist, described the case of a patient who was under his care. She was at times incoherent and delusional, and displayed severe memory loss. After her death, Alzheimer examined her brain and found two striking abnormalities: (1) masses of proteins in the extracellular space between neurons (**amyloid plaques**), and (2) proteins twisted around one another (**neurofibrillary tangles**) inside many of the neurons in her brain. Several years later, the condition was named Alzheimer's disease. What, if anything, did the strange amyloid plaques and neurofibrillary tangles have to do with the patient's disordered thought processes and memory loss? We'll return to these questions below. First, let's examine in more detail the mental deterioration associated with Alzheimer's disease.

13.4.1 Alzheimer's Includes Memory Loss and Other Signs of Cognitive Deterioration

The most obvious symptom of Alzheimer's is memory loss. However, because Alzheimer's is a progressive disease, the clinical signs depend on how far the disease has progressed. During early stages of Alzheimer's, patients show memory impairments severe enough to disrupt daily functioning. These early-stage symptoms include:

- Frequent difficulty remembering specific words.
- Frequently misplacing things. (Notice that these first two signs are commonly part of normal aging; in Alzheimer's, however, they occur with an exaggerated frequency.)

- Forgetting how to carry out tasks, such as putting on a tie or operating a microwave, that were not difficult in the past.
- Repeatedly asking the same question without remembering having asked it before.

As the disease progresses, symptoms become more severe. They include:

- Confusion, irritability, and inexplicable mood swings.
- Forgetting key events in one's own personal history (although very old memories such as those from childhood are often maintained to a surprising degree).
- Disorientation about dates, seasons, the passage of time.
- Disorientation about where one is at the moment, and an increased risk of wandering around and becoming lost.
- Speech becomes difficult, and reading and writing deteriorate.
- Delusions and paranoia may appear.

At this point, patients are often institutionalized because family and friends can no longer provide the necessary care.

In the final stages, language is severely diminished, and in some cases the patient may become mute. Some patients with late-stage Alzheimer's cannot leave their beds. They may require assistance in eating and maintaining personal hygiene, sometimes becoming incontinent. The disease itself is typically not fatal, but because of decreased mobility and being bedridden, patients may die due to a secondary illness, such as pneumonia.

Unfortunately, there are currently no established effective treatments for Alzheimer's. This raises the question of whether a diagnosis of the disease is even helpful. There are nevertheless some advantages to a diagnosis. For instance, something that looks like Alzheimer's might be discovered to be another form of dementia that has an effective treatment. Further, some diagnosed patients can enter a clinical trial aimed at a novel treatment which could have efficacy at some point in the near future. Finally, families of Alzheimer's patients may gain access to support and services.

13.4.2 Neuronal Loss, Amyloid Plaques, and Neurofibrillary Tangles Are Signs of Alzheimer's

Alzheimer's disease is associated with neuronal loss and damage within a number of brain areas. The hippocampal formation and other areas of the temporal lobe essential to memory abilities are among the first to show neuropathology (Hallbeck, Nath, & Marcusson, 2013). As Alzheimer's progresses, neuronal damage spreads to prefrontal cortical regions, which

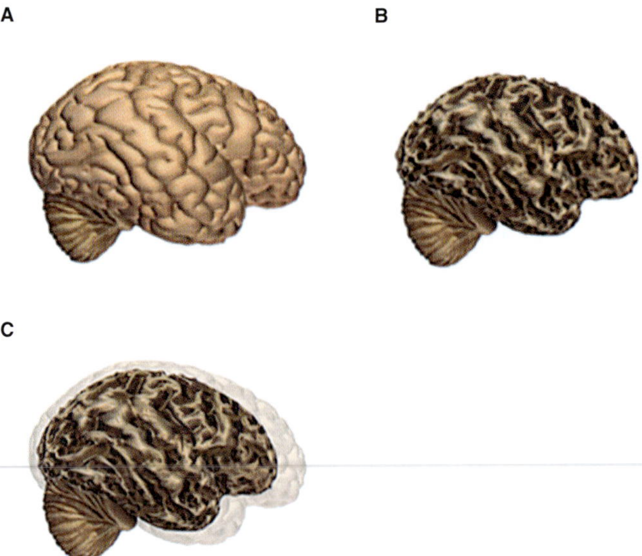

Figure 13.14 **Shrinkage of the brain in Alzheimer's disease**. (A) A normal brain. (B) A brain with advanced Alzheimer's. (C) A comparison of the two.
(Illustrations by Stacy Jannis, © 2020 Alzheimer's Association. www.alz.org. All rights reserved.)

also play a key role in working memory and attention. The disease is also associated with loss of acetylcholine-releasing neurons that normally project densely to the hippocampus and cortex. As the Alzheimer's pathology progresses, neurons within subcortical regions and the brainstem may die as well. With the death of neurons and loss of brain tissue, the brain shrinks (Figure 13.14).

What is responsible for the death of neurons in the brains of Alzheimer's patients? We saw earlier that over a hundred years ago Dr. Alzheimer noticed two strange features in the brain of his patient: *amyloid plaques* and *neurofibrillary tangles* (Figure 13.15). These two signs of brain pathology are still considered to be key brain characteristics of Alzheimer's disease.

Amyloid Plaques

The main constituent of amyloid plaques is a protein called beta amyloid. Beta amyloid is formed inside the neuron, but it may be released into synapses. In Alzheimer's patients, large amounts of beta amyloid accumulate outside the neuron. Extracellular clumps of beta amyloid form spherical patches of material – the amyloid plaques. They may be observed in extracellular spaces throughout the brain.

Some researchers believe that high levels of beta amyloid contribute to Alzheimer's patients' cognitive dysfunctions. For example, studies in mice and rats show that exposure to high levels of beta amyloid causes

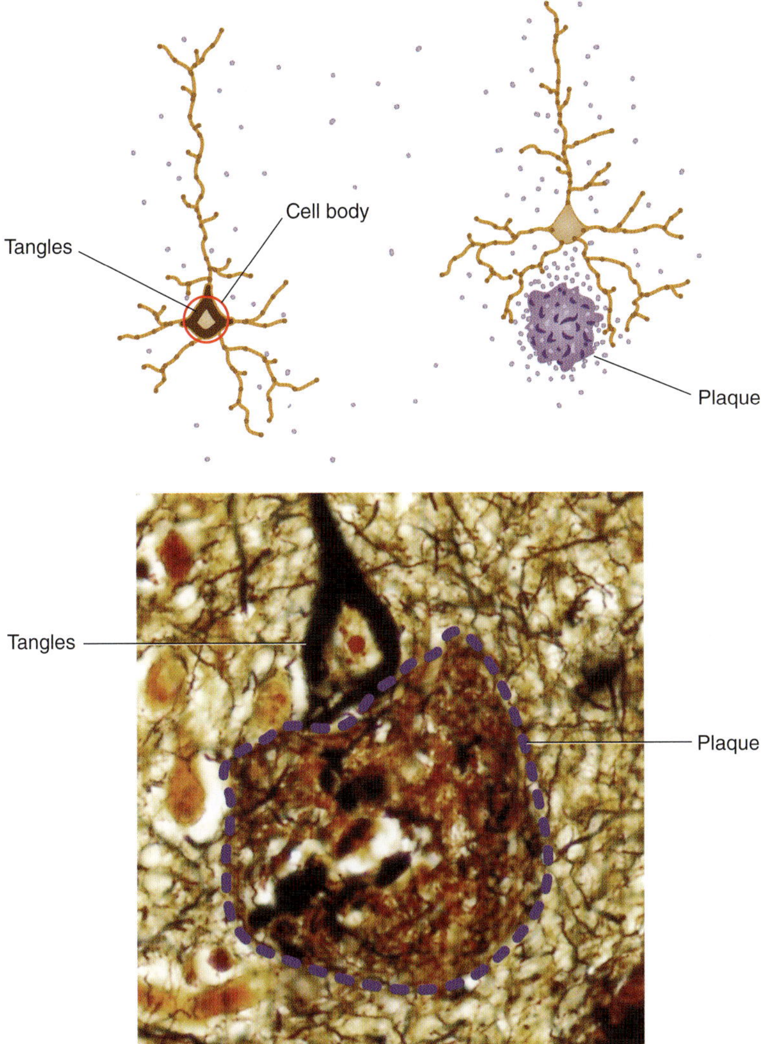

Figure 13.15 Plaques and tangles. The top panel depicts neurofibrillary tangles within neurons (dark brown), beta amyloid molecules (small purple dots), and amyloid plaques (large purple sphere). The bottom panel shows nervous tissue stained to reveal the tangles (the dark brown shadow filling much of the cell body of the neuron), and plaques (large circular mass outlined in purple).
(Bottom, adapted from a silver-stain image kindly provided by Dr. Dimitri P. Agamanolis.)

memory impairments (Westerman et al., 2002), and that neurons exposed to beta amyloid undergo a loss of dendritic spines and reductions in synaptic plasticity (Mucke & Selkoe, 2012). These data suggest that the beta amyloid protein that makes up the amyloid plaques may contribute to the loss of neural functions required for memory. Much current research on Alzheimer's disease is directed toward understanding why the patients accumulate so much beta amyloid in their brains (Yuksel & Tacal, 2019).

But not all evidence points to a link between beta amyloid and the disease. Beta amyloid levels are normally produced and released into synapses of highly active neurons (Jagust & Mormino, 2011), and many people without cognitive impairment nevertheless have large accumulations of amyloid plaques (Perez-Nievas et al., 2013). Even among those with Alzheimer's, the number of plaques does not correlate with the degree of dementia (Terry, 1996). According to an influential view, accumulation of beta amyloid only becomes dangerous when it leads to a more serious neural change, neurofibrillary tangles. As we will see below, neurofibrillary tangles are directly implicated in the cognitive decline seen in Alzheimer's patients.

Neurofibrillary Tangles

Neurofibrillary tangles are aggregates of misfolded protein located inside the cell body, dendrites, and axons of neurons. The protein clusters that make up the neurofibrillary tangles are mostly composed of a protein called **tau**. (As a mnemonic device, it may be worth remembering "**T**au-**T**angles," the terrible Ts.) Normally, the tau protein binds to microtubules, the tracks located inside the neuron that allow material to move from one part of the neuron to another (Figure 13.16). However, in the brains of Alzheimer's patients, the tau proteins undergo a chemical change (hyper-phosphorylation) that prevents them from binding properly to the microtubules, and instead causes them to twist around one another and bunch up to form tangles. In addition, without normal tau protein binding to them, the microtubules can become unstable and lose the ability to transport materials along the axon.

Unlike the amyloid plaques, which are found broadly throughout the brain, tangles are found exclusively in the hippocampus and cortex. Like beta amyloid, misfolded tau proteins may spread directly from neuron to neuron, in this case leaving trails of neurofibrillary tangles. The number of neurofibrillary tangles found in the brains of Alzheimer's patients is correlated both with neuronal loss and with the degree of the patient's cognitive decline (Gomez-Isla et al., 1997; Spires-Jones & Hyman, 2014).

As noted earlier, evidence suggests that the accumulation of beta amyloid can lead to the development of neurofibrillary tangles. For instance, a study using human neural cells maintained in culture (in small glass dishes) found that neurons exposed to high levels of beta amyloid develop both amyloid plaques and the form of tau protein that produces neurofibrillary tangles (Choi et al., 2014). By reducing exposure to beta amyloid, investigators were able to reduce the production of neurofibrillary tangles.

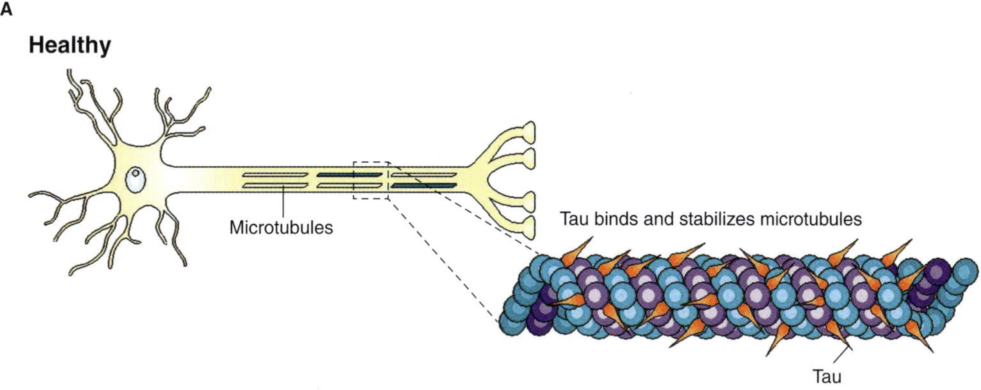

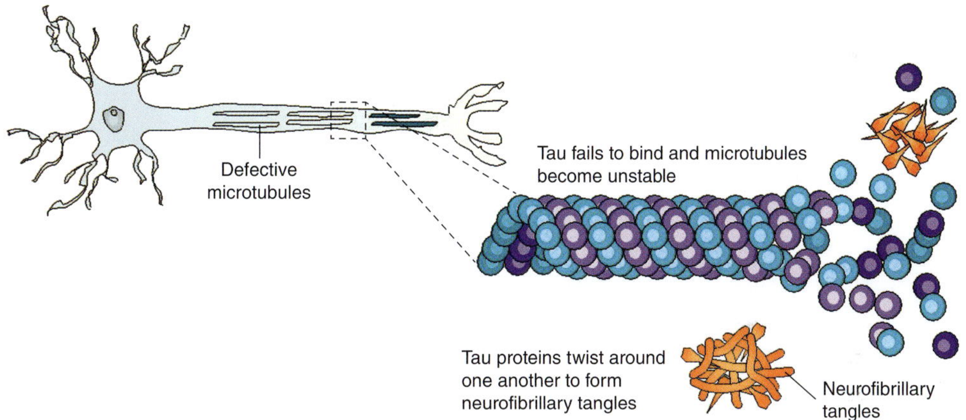

Figure 13.16 Abnormal tau produces neurofibrillary tangles and disrupts microtubules. (A) Normally, tau protein (orange) binds to microtubules to stabilize them. (B) In Alzheimer's disease, tau undergoes a chemical change that prevents it from binding to the microtubules. As a result, the microtubules lose stability. The abnormal tau proteins form neurofibrillary tangles.
(Adapted from Brunden, Trojanowski, & Lee 2009, © 2009, Nature Publishing Group.)

The data are consistent with the theory that beta amyloid drives the production of neurofibrillary tangles, and that it is neurofibrillary tangles that lead to neuronal death and cognitive decline.

13.4.3 Genetic Factors Contribute to Alzheimer's

There are two distinct forms of Alzheimer's: early and late onset. Early-onset Alzheimer's strikes individuals in their forties. It is rare and frequently runs in families. A patient with early-onset Alzheimer's often has a mutation in one of three genes, each of which produces a protein that can contribute to the formation of beta amyloid, and to the development of amyloid plaques.

- The first mutation is in the gene that produces **amyloid precursor protein** (**APP**), a large protein that is cleaved (cut) within the cell to produce amyloid protein. Whether or not this cleavage of APP produces the beta amyloid protein depends upon *where* in the molecule the cleavage occurs. Mutations of the APP gene can lead to a form of APP that is likely to generate beta amyloid when cleaved, and therefore to increase formation of amyloid plaques (Figure 13.17).
- Mutations in two other genes, **presenilin 1** (*PSEN1*) and **presenilin 2** (*PSEN2*), play a role in the cleavage process itself. They, too, enhance the likelihood that APP cleavage will produce plaque-forming beta amyloid. The chromosomes containing the genes for each of these proteins are known, and individuals can be screened for the presence of mutations in one of the genes related to early-onset Alzheimer's.

A number of genetic mutations have been implicated in patients with the more common, late-onset, form of Alzheimer's. In this case, there are ten or more gene suspects, and so there is not yet a clear biological

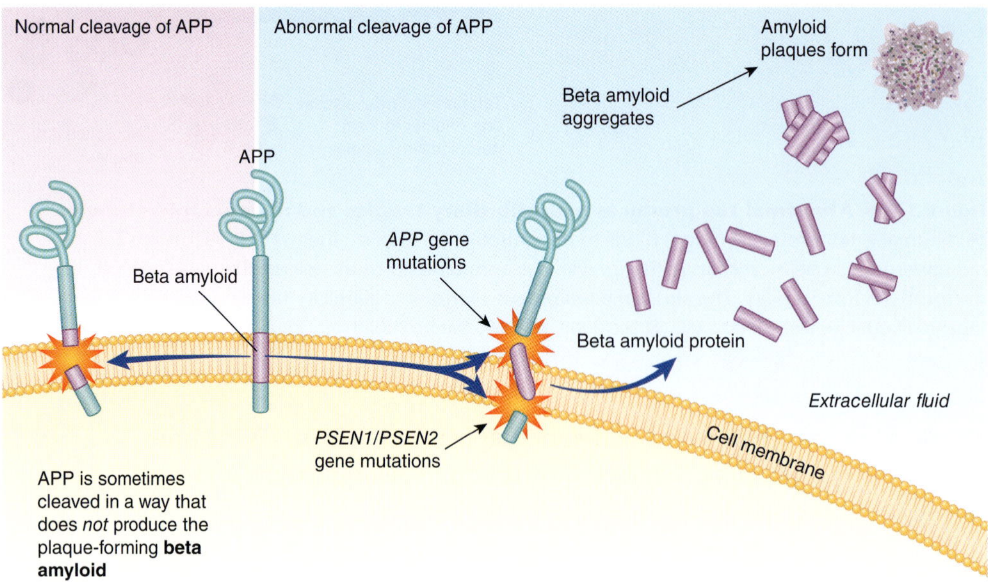

Figure 13.17 Amyloid precursor protein (APP), presenilin 1 (PSEN1), and presenilin 2 (PSEN2) gene mutations lead to excess formation of beta amyloid protein. Mutation of the APP, PSEN1, or PSEN 2 genes causes enzymes to cleave the APP protein at a site that liberates beta amyloid protein. Beta amyloid is then free to aggregate in the extracellular space and to form amyloid plaques.

marker for late-onset Alzheimer's. There may also be non-genetic forms of late-onset Alzheimer's that involve environmental factors, although the nature of these factors remains unclear.

13.4.4 It Remains Unclear Whether Environmental Factors Contribute to Alzheimer's

There are many hypotheses regarding environmental factors that might reduce the risk of Alzheimer's. Studies have looked at the effects of low-fat diets, dietary supplements, vitamins, anti-inflammatory drugs, and exercise. Despite some tantalizing positive results, the research remains inconclusive.

However, there is evidence that enriched environments and enhanced cognitive activity may be protective against Alzheimer's. In one study, mice were genetically bred to develop Alzheimer-like amyloid plaques and raised in either a standard laboratory cage or an "enriched environment." The mice raised in the enriched environment were able to interact with other mice, explore objects ("toys"), and exercise in running wheels. Compared to mice raised in the standard cage, they developed fewer amyloid plaques (Lazarov et al., 2005). These data suggest the possibility that cognitive abilities and environmental conditions that enhance cognitive function can reduce the risk of Alzheimer's and Alzheimer's-related brain pathology.

High levels of cognitive activity over an individual's life may also lower vulnerability to the detrimental effects of Alzheimer's-related neuropathologies (including beta amyloid accumulation). For instance, individuals with more years of education tend to show less cognitive deterioration than those with less education when both groups have suffered a similar amount of brain neuropathology. Evidence also suggests that bilingualism (which represents an enhanced level of verbal activity) may delay the age of onset of Alzheimer's (Xu, Yu, Tan, & Tan, 2015). In order to account for such findings, it has been proposed that high levels of cognitive activity over the lifetime enhance the number of neurons in the brain and the efficiency with which neural circuits solve problems. It has been argued that these enhancements provide the individual with **cognitive reserve**, the ability to maintain high levels of functioning even when challenged by neuropathology (Barulli & Stern, 2013). Not all studies find a link between cognitive activity and reduced Alzheimer's risk (Gidicsin et al., 2015). Researchers continue to ask whether environmental factors, including education and intellectual activity, might reduce the risk of both the cognitive deterioration and the neuropathology that come with Alzheimer's disease.

13.4.5 Current Research Is Focused on Preventing Plaques and Tangles

A major difficulty in the search for prevention or treatment of Alzheimer's is the fact that the disease is usually well underway, by years or even decades, by the time a clear diagnosis is made and medical help is sought.

Because Alzheimer's disease is associated with dramatic loss of acetylcholine neurons that project to the hippocampus and cortex, drug treatments for Alzheimer's have largely focused on those that increase brain acetylcholine (donepezil, rivastigmine, and galantamine). While these drugs may slow cognitive decline during the first year of treatment, there is unfortunately no evidence that they slow the long-term progression of the disease (Scheltens et al., 2016). Over the years, simple manipulation of acetylcholine and other brain chemicals (such as glutamate) has produced only small and short-term benefits.

Most current research on treatments for Alzheimer's aims instead to reduce amyloid plaques, neurofibrillary tangles, and other neuropathologies associated with the disease. These new therapeutic approaches to Alzheimer's hold the possibility of preventing or reversing cognitive impairment associated with this terrible disease.

KEY CONCEPTS

- **Alzheimer's disease typically begins with forgetfulness and progresses to confusion about time and place. Finally, patients may become bedridden and unable to independently eat and maintain personal hygiene.**
- **The typical age of onset is in the sixties and seventies. By the time people reach 85, their probability of having Alzheimer's is approximately 40 percent.**
- **As Alzheimer's progresses, much of the brain shrinks. Most heavily affected are areas involved in memory and cognition. Often the pathology begins in and around the hippocampus, which helps explain prominent memory dysfunction.**
- **The two key pathological signs of Alzheimer's in the brain are amyloid plaques and neurofibrillary tangles.**
- **A rare, early-onset form of Alzheimer's is heritable and involves mutations in one of three genes. However, most cases of Alzheimer's occur later in life. Several gene mutations have been associated with late-onset Alzheimer's.**
- **Traditional drugs for Alzheimer's have targeted acetylcholine and other neurotransmitter systems, but have not been effective in preventing the long-term progression of the disease. New approaches**

that investigate ways to slow or reverse underlying neuropathologies associated with Alzheimer's hold promise for the future.

TEST YOURSELF

1. **Describe the symptoms of Alzheimer's as the disease progresses.**
2. **What are the two major pathological signs in the brains of Alzheimer's patients?**
3. **What brain regions show early signs of neuropathology in Alzheimer's?**
4. **Describe evidence that beta amyloid protein contributes to the development of neurofibrillary tangles.**
5. **What are the current treatments for Alzheimer's disease? How effective are they, and how can we explain their effectiveness (or lack thereof)?**

13.5 The Big Picture

This chapter has covered both psychiatric and neurological disorders: from individuals burdened by feelings of hopelessness (depression) and delusional beliefs (schizophrenia) to those who have lost the ability to act (Parkinson's disease) and remember (Alzheimer's disease). In each case, genetic and environmental conditions appear to interact to produce emotional, cognitive, and/or behavioral symptoms. Some brain abnormalities, such as those in Alzheimer's disease, leave obvious visible marks that can be viewed in a microscope. Other brain abnormalities, such as those seen in major depressive disorder, may be less clearly visible, but even in these cases, changes in brain structure and function can often be detected. As we discover more about the biological roots of mental illness, the traditional distinctions between neurological and psychiatric conditions continue to blur.

13.6 Creative Thinking

1. Imagine you are a psychiatrist. One of your patients is suffering from major depressive disorder, without suicidal thoughts. You may design a treatment plan involving drugs, therapy, some kind of brain stimulation, or a combination. Describe your plan, including the order in which you would try possible treatments. Another patient has the same disorder but has already made several suicide attempts. Would this influence your treatment plan? In what ways?

2. Again, as a psychiatrist, one of your patients is a man with schizophrenia, 26 years old, with a combination of positive, negative, and cognitive symptoms. You devise a treatment plan for him. Describe your plan. Does it involve medications? If so, which kind would you try first? Why? Would you also include cognitive therapy? Explain your thinking.
3. Why is the concordance rate for schizophrenia in monozygotic (identical) twins not 100 percent? List as many possible reasons as you can.
4. Both depression and schizophrenia are associated with changes in structure and/or function in a number of brain areas. Is there any overlap in the affected brain areas? Might overlapping brain abnormalities explain any symptoms seen in both disorders? You might want to review earlier chapters that discuss these brain areas in order to answer this question.
5. A patient with Parkinson's disease has severe motor impairment, particularly in the initiation of movements. However, she gets up from her wheelchair when someone yells "Fire!" and she smells smoke. How do you explain this?
6. Which of the disorders described in this chapter (depression, schizophrenia, Parkinson's, and Alzheimer's) would be most difficult for you to live with? Which of them would be easiest to live with?

Key Terms

akinesia 551
alpha-synuclein 553
amyloid plaques 560
amyloid precursor protein (APP) 566
anterior cingulate cortex 537
antipsychotic drugs 547
bipolar disorder 529
bradykinesia 551
caudate 552
Cognitive Behavioral Therapy (CBT) 534
cognitive reserve 567
cognitive symptoms 542
concordance rate 531
deep brain stimulation 557
delusions 540
dopamine D_2 receptor 547
dopamine hypothesis of schizophrenia 547
electroconvulsive therapy (ECT) 536
epigenetics 531
hallucinations 541
Lewy bodies 553
mindfulness meditation 535
monoamine oxidase inhibitors (MAOIs) 533
negative symptoms of schizophrenia 542
neurofibrillary tangles 560
neuroleptics 547
neuropathology 528
nigrostriatal dopamine pathway 552
paradoxical kinesia 553

References

American Psychiatric Association. (2013). *Diagnostic and Statistical Manual of Mental Disorders* (5th ed.). Washington, DC: APA.

Andreasen, N. C. (1986). The scale for assessment of thought, language and communication (TLC). *Schizophrenia Bulletin, 12*, 473–482.

Arnone, D., McKie, S., Elliott, R., Juhasz, G., Thomas, E.J., Downey, D., ... Anderson, I. M. (2013). State-dependent changes in hippocampal grey matter in depression. *Molecular Psychiatry 18*, 1265–1272.

Aydogan, A. S., Oztekin, E., Esen, M. E., Dusmez, S., Gelal, F., Besiroglu, L., & Zorlu, N. (2019). Cortical thickening in remitters compared to non-remitters with major depressive disorder following 8-week antidepressant treatment. *Acta Psychiatrica Scandinavica, 140*.

Barulli, D., & Stern, Y. (2013). Efficiency, capacity, compensation, maintenance, plasticity: emerging concepts in cognitive reserve. *Trends in Cognitive Sciences, 17*(10), 502–509.

Birkmayer, W., & Hornykiewicz, O. (1962). [The L-dihydroxyphenylalanine (L-DOPA) effect in Parkinson's syndrome in man: on the pathogenesis and treatment of Parkinson akinesis]. *Archiv fur Psychiatrie und Nervenkrankheiten, Vereinigt mit Zeitschrift fur die Gesamte Neurologie und Psychiatrie, 203*, 560–574.

Bora, E., Harrison, B.J., Davey, C. G., Yuecel, M., & Pantelis, C. (2012). Meta-analysis of volumetric abnormalities in cortico-striatal-pallidal-thalamic circuits in major depressive disorder. *Psychological Medicine, 42*(4), 671–681.

Brunden, K. R., Trojanowski, J. Q. & Lee, V. M. (2009). Advances in tau-focused drug discovery for Alzheimer's disease and related tauopathies. *Nature Reviews Drug Discoveries, 8*(10), 783–793.

Choi, S. H., Kim, Y. H., Hebisch, M., Sliwinski, C., Lee, S., D'Avanzo, C., & Kim, D. Y. (2014). A three-dimensional human neural cell culture model of Alzheimer's disease. *Nature, 15*, 274–278.

Creswell, J. D. (2017). Mindfulness interventions. *Annual Review of Psychology, 68*, 491–516.

Cuijpers, P., Noma, H., Karyotaki, E., Vinkers, C. H., Cipriani, A., & Furukawa, T. A. (2020). A network meta-analysis of the effects of psychotherapies, pharmacotherapies and their combination in the treatment of adult depression. *World Psychiatry, 19*(1), 92–107.

Delaloye, S., & Holtzheimer, P. E. (2014). Deep brain stimulation in the treatment of depression. *Dialogues in Clinical Neuroscience, 16*(1), 83–91.

Desplats, P., Lee, H. J., Bae, E. J., Patrick, C., Rockenstein, E., Crews, L., ... Lee, S. J. (2009). Inclusion formation and neuronal cell death through neuron-to-neuron transmission of alpha-synuclein. *Proceedings of the National Academy of Sciences of the United States of America, 106*(31), 13010–13015.

Drysdale, A. T., Grosenick, L., Downar, J., Dunlop, K., Mansouri, F., Meng, Y., ... Liston, C. (2017). Resting-state connectivity biomarkers define neurophysiological subtypes of depression. *Nature Medicine, 23*(1), 28–38.

Dusi, N., Barlati, S., Vita, A., & Brambilla, P. (2015). Brain structural effects of antidepressant treatment in major depression. *Current Neuropharmacology, 13*(4), 458–465.

Dutcher, J. M., & Creswell, J. D. (2018). Behavioral interventions in health neuroscience. *Annals of the New York Academy of Sciences, 1428*(1), 51–70.

Fiorenzano, A., Sozzi, E., Parmar, M., & Storm, P. (2021). Dopamine neuron diversity: recent advances and current challenges in human stem cell models and single cell sequencing. *Cells, 10*(6).

Fusar-Poli, P., Borgwardt, S., Bechdolf, A., Addington, J., Riecher-Rössler, A., Schultze-Lutter, F., ... Yung, A. (2013). The psychosis high-risk state: a comprehensive state-of-the-art review. *JAMA Psychiatry 70*, 107–120.

Garety, P. A., Fowier, D. G., Freeman, D., Bebbington, P., Dunn, G., & Kuipers, E. (2008). Cognitive-behavioural therapy and family intervention for relapse prevention and symptom reduction in psychosis: randomised controlled trial. *British Journal of Psychiatry, 192*, 412–423.

Gidicsin, C. M., Maye, J. E., Locascio, J. J., Pepin, L. C., Philiossaint, M., Becker, J. A., ... Johnson, K. A. (2015). Cognitive activity relates to cognitive performance but not to Alzheimer disease biomarkers. *Neurology, 85*(1), 48–55.

Goldman, S. M. (2014). Environmental toxins and Parkinson's disease. *Annual Review of Pharmacology and Toxicology, 54*, 141–164.

Gomez-Isla, T., Hollister, R., West, H., Mui, S., Growdon, J. H., Petersen, R. C., ... Hyman, B. T. (1997). Neuronal loss correlates with but exceeds neurofibrillary tangles in Alzheimer's disease. *Annals of Neurology, 41*(1), 17–24.

Gottesman, I. I., & Wolfgram, D. L. (1991). *Schizophrenia Genesis: The Origins of Madness*. New York: Freeman.

Gould, E., & Tanapat, P. (1999). Stress and hippocampal neurogenesis. *Biological Psychiatry, 46*(11), 1472–1479.

Grieve, S. M., Korgaonkar, M. S., Koslow, S. H., Gordon, E., & Williams, L. M. (2013). Widespread reductions in gray matter volume in depression. *NeuroImage: Clinical, 3*, 332–339.

Hallbeck, M., Nath, S., & Marcusson, J. (2013). Neuron-to-neuron transmission of neurodegenerative pathology. *Neuroscientist, 19*(6), 560–566.

Hamilton, J. P. (2012). Functional neuroimaging of major depressive disorder: a meta-analysis and new integration of base line activation and neural response data. *American Journal of Psychiatry, 169*(7), 693–703.

Hashimoto, K. (2019). Rapid-acting antidepressant ketamine, its metabolites and other candidates: a historical overview and future perspective. *Psychiatry and Clinical Neurosciences, 73*(10), 613–627.

Hellewell, S. C., Welton, T., Maller, J. J., Lyon, M., Korgaonkar, M. S., Koslow, S. H., ... Grieve, S. M. (2019). Profound and reproducible patterns of reduced regional gray matter characterize major depressive disorder. *Translational Psychiatry, 9*.

Hishikawa, N., Hashizuma, Y., Yoshida, M., & Sobue, G. (2003). Clinical and neuropathological correlates of Lewy body disease. *Acta Neuropathologica, 105*, 341–350.

Horvitz, J. C. (2000). Mesolimbocortical and nigrostriatal dopamine responses to salient non-reward events. *Neuroscience, 96*(4), 651–656.

Jacobs, B. L., van Praag, H., & Gage, F. H. (2000). Adult brain neurogenesis and psychiatry: a novel theory of depression. *Molecular Psychiatry, 5*(3), 262–269.

Jagust, W. J., & Mormino, E. C. (2011). Lifespan brain activity, beta-amyloid, and Alzheimer's disease. *Trends in Cognitive Sciences, 15*(11), 520–526.

Jahanshahi, M., & Frith, C. D. (1998). Willed action and its impairments. *Cognitive Neuropsychology, 15*(6–8), 483–533.

Jauhar, S., Laws, K. R., & McKenna, P. J. (2019). CBT for schizophrenia: a critical viewpoint. *Psychological Medicine, 49*(8), 1233–1236.

Kamel, F. (2013). Paths from pesticides to Parkinson's. *Science, 341*(6147), 722–723.

Kendler, K. S., & Prescott, C. A. (1999). A population-based twin study of lifetime major depression in men and women. *Archives of General Psychiatry, 56*(1), 39–44.

Kety, S., Wender, P., Jacobsen, B., Ingraham, L., Jansson, L., Faber, B., & Kinney, D. (1994). Mental-illness in the biological and adoptive relatives of schizophrenic adoptees – Replication of the Copenhagen study in the rest of Denmark. *Archives of General Psychiatry, 51*(6), 442–455.

Killingsworth, M. A., & Gilbert, D. T. (2010). A wandering mind is an unhappy mind. *Science, 330*(6006), 932.

Klingberg, S., Wolwer, W., Engel, C., Wittorf, A., Herrlich, J., Meisner, C., ... Wiedemann, G. (2011). Negative symptoms of schizophrenia as primary target of cognitive behavioral therapy: results of the randomized clinical TONES study. *Schizophrenia Bulletin, 37*(suppl. 2), S98–11Q.

Kraus, C., Castren, E., Kasper, S., & Lanzenberger, R. (2017). Serotonin and neuroplasticity – Links between molecular, functional and structural pathophysiology in depression. *Neuroscience and Biobehavioral Reviews, 77*, 317–326.

Kuyken, W., Warren, F. C., Taylor, R. S., Whalley, B., Crane, C., Bondolfi, G., ... Dalgleish, T. (2016). Efficacy of mindfulness-based cognitive therapy in prevention of depressive relapse: an individual patient data meta-analysis from randomized trials. *JAMA Psychiatry, 73*(6), 565–574.

Langston, J. W., Ballard, P., Tetrud, J. W., & Irwin, I. (1983). Chronic Parkinsonism in humans due to a product of meperidine-analog synthesis. Science, *219*(4587), 979–980.

Lazarov, O., Robinson, J., Tang, Y. P., Hairston, I. S., Korade-Mirnics, Z., Lee, V. M., ... Sisodia, S. S. (2005). Environmental enrichment reduces Abeta levels and amyloid deposition in transgenic mice. *Cell, 120*(5), 701–713.

Maher, B. A., Manschreck, T. C., Molino, M. A. (1983). Redundancy, pause distributions and thought disorder in schizophrenia. *Language and Speech, 26*, 191–199.

Martin, J. P. (1967). *The Basal Ganglia and Posture*. London: Pitman Medical.

Mayberg, H. S., Lozano, A. M., Voon, V., McNeely, H. E., Seminowicz, D., Hamani, C., ... Kennedy, S. H. (2005). Deep brain stimulation for treatment-resistant depression. *Neuron, 45*(5), 651–660.

McGowan, P. O., Sasaki, A., D'Alessio, A. C., Dymov, S., Labonte, B., Szyf, M., ... Meaney, M. J. (2009). Epigenetic regulation of the glucocorticoid receptor in human brain associates with childhood abuse. *Nature Neuroscience, 12*(3), 342–348.

Meaney, M. J. (2001). Maternal care, gene expression, and the transmission of individual differences in stress reactivity across generations. *Annual Review of Neuroscience, 24*, 1161–1192.

Mitchell, A. J. (2006). Two-week delay in onset of action of antidepressants: new evidence. *British Journal of Psychiatry, 188*(2), 105–106.

Morrison, A. P., Turkington, D., Pyle, M., Spencer, H., Brabban, A., Dunn, G., ... Hutton, P. (2014). Cognitive therapy for people with schizophrenia spectrum disorders not taking antipsychotic drugs: a single-blind randomised controlled trial. *Lancet, 383*(9926), 1395–1403.

Mucke, L., & Selkoe, D. J. (2012). Neurotoxicity of amyloid beta-protein: synaptic and network dysfunction. *Cold Spring Harbor Perspectives in Medicine, 2*(7).

Mueser, K. T., Deavers, F., Penn, D. L., & Cassisi, J. E. (2013). Psychosocial treatments for schizophrenia. *Annual Review of Clinical Psychology, 9*, 465–497.

Murrough, J. W., Abdallah, C. G., & Mathew, S. J. (2017). Targeting glutamate signalling in depression: progress and prospects. *Nature Reviews Drug Discovery, 16*(7), 472–486.

Na, K. S., & Kim, Y. K. (2021). Increased use of ketamine for the treatment of depression: benefits and concerns. *Progress in Neuro-Psychopharmacology & Biological Psychiatry, 104*.

Nestler, E. J. (2014). Epigenetic mechanisms of depression. JAMA Psychiatry. http://archpsyc.jamanetwork.com/data/Journals/PSYCH/929925/ynp130009.pdf

Newport, D. J., Carpenter, L. L., McDonald, W. M., Potash, J. B., Tohen, M., Nemeroff, C. B., & Novel, APA Council Res Task Force. (2015). Ketamine and other NMDA antagonists: early clinical trials and possible mechanisms in depression. *American Journal of Psychiatry, 172*(10), 950–966.

Nicoletti, F., Orlando, R., Di Menna, L., Cannella, M., Notartomaso, S., Mascio, G., ... Bruno, V. (2019). Targeting mGlu receptors for optimization of antipsychotic activity and disease-modifying effect in schizophrenia. *Frontiers in Psychiatry, 10*.

Novak, P., Schmidt, R., Kontsekova, E., Zilka, N., Kovacech, B., Skrabana, R., ... Novak, M. (2017). Safety and immunogenicity of the tau vaccine AADvac1 in patients with Alzheimer's disease: a randomised, double-blind, placebo-controlled, phase 1 trial. *Lancet Neurology, 16*(2), 123–134.

Novick, D., Haro, J. M., Suarez, D., Vieta, E., & Naber, D. (2009). Recovery in the outpatient setting: 36-month results from the Schizophrenia Outpatients Health Outcomes (SOHO) study. *Schizophrenia Research, 108*(1–3), 223–230.

Perez-Nievas, B. G., Stein, T. D., Tai, H. C., Dols-Icardo, O., Scotton, T. C., Barroeta-Espar, I., ... Gomez-Isla, T. (2013). Dissecting phenotypic traits linked to human resilience to Alzheimer's pathology. *Brain, 136*(8), 2510–2526.

Popovic, D., Schmitt, A., Kaurani, L., Senner, F., Papiol, S., Malchow, B., ... Falkai, P. (2019). Childhood trauma in schizophrenia: current findings and research perspectives. *Frontiers in Neuroscience, 13*.

Scheltens, P., Blennow, K., Breteler, M. M. B., de Strooper, B., Frisoni, G. B., Salloway, S., & Van der Flier, W. M. (2016). Alzheimer's disease. *Lancet, 388*(10043), 505–517.

Schuch, F. B., Vancampfort, D., Richards, J., Rosenbaum, S., Ward, P. B., & Stubbs, B. (2016). Exercise as a treatment for depression: a meta-analysis adjusting for publication bias. *Journal of Psychiatric Research, 77*, 42–51.

Seeman, P., Lee, T., Chau-Wong, M., & Wong, K. (1976). Antipsychotic drug doses and neuroleptic/dopamine receptors. *Nature, 261*(5562), 717–719.

Singhal, G., & Baune, B. T. (2017). Microglia: an interface between the loss of neuroplasticity and depression. *Frontiers in Cellular Neuroscience, 11*.

Snowdon, D. A., Kemper, S. J., Mortimer, J. A., Greiner, L. H., Wekstein, D. R., & Markesbery, W. R. (1996). Linguistic ability in early life and cognitive function and Alzheimer's disease in late life. Findings from the Nun Study. *JAMA, 275*, 528–532.

Spillantini, M., Schmidt, M., Lee, V. Y., Trojanowski, J. Q., Jakes, R., & Goedert, M. (1997). α-Synuclein in Lewy bodies. *Nature 388*, 839–840.

Spires-Jones, T. L., & Hyman, B. T. (2014). The intersection of amyloid beta and tau at synapses in Alzheimer's disease. *Neuron, 82*(4), 756–771.

Surmeier, D. J., Obeso, J. A., & Halliday, G. M. (2017). Selective neuronal vulnerability in Parkinson disease. *Nature Reviews Neuroscience, 18*(2), 101–113.

Terry, R. D. (1996). The pathogenesis of Alzheimer disease: an alternative to the amyloid hypothesis. *Journal of Neuropathology & Experimental Neurology 55*, 1023–1025.

Trevizol, A. P., & Blumberger, D. M. (2019). An update on repetitive transcranial magnetic stimulation for the treatment of major depressive disorder. *Clinical Pharmacology & Therapeutics, 106*(4), 747–762.

Weinberger, D., Torrey, E., Neophytides, A., & Wyatt, R. (1979). Lateral cerebral ventricular enlargement in chronic schizophrenia. *Archives of General Psychiatry, 36*(7), 735–739.

Westerman, M. A., Cooper-Blacketer, D., Mariash, A., Kotilinek, L., Kawarabayashi, T., Younkin, L. H., … Ashe, K. H. (2002). The relationship between A beta and memory in the Tg2576 mouse model of Alzheimer's disease. *Journal of Neuroscience, 22*(5), 1858–1867.

Wieck, A. (1989). Endocrine aspects of postnatal mental disorders. *Baillieres Clinical Obstetrics and Gynaecology, 3*(4), 857–877.

Winton-Brown, T. T., Fusar-Poli, P., Ungless, M. A., & Howes, O. D. (2014). Dopaminergic basis of salience dysregulation in psychosis. *Trends in Neurosciences, 37*(2), 85–94.

Wykes, T., Steel, C., Everitt, B., & Tarrier, N. (2008). Cognitive behavior therapy for schizophrenia: effect sizes, clinical models and methodological rigor. *Schizophrenia Bulletin, 34*, 523–537.

Xu, W., Yu, J. T., Tan, M. S., & Tan, L. (2015). Cognitive reserve and Alzheimer's disease. *Molecular Neurobiology, 51*(1), 187–208.

Yanamandra, K., Kfoury, N., Jiang, H., Mahan, T. E., Ma, S. M., Maloney, S. E., … Holtzman, D. M. (2013). Anti-tau antibodies that block tau aggregate seeding in vitro markedly decrease pathology and improve cognition in vivo. *Neuron, 80*(2), 402–414.

Yuksel, M., & Tacal, O. (2019). Trafficking and proteolytic processing of amyloid precursor protein and secretases in Alzheimer's disease development: an up-to-date review. *European Journal of Pharmacology, 856*.

14
Higher Cognitive Function

Miguel Navarro / DigitalVision / Getty Images

Consider This ...

Linda was 19 when she underwent a **split-brain operation** for her uncontrollable epileptic seizures, when neural activity would spread like a storm through her brain. The key to the operation was a surgical cutting of the **corpus callosum**, the pathway of neurons that connects the left and right hemispheres of the brain. Cutting the corpus callosum prevented the storm from spreading from one hemisphere to the other, and made the seizures much less severe. Split-brain surgery is rare. It's a last resort for those with debilitating epilepsy and who do not respond to anti-seizure medication.

A colleague and I visited Linda in the hospital shortly after her operation to see how she was doing. The nurse explained that Linda had been stealing milk from the food tray of the woman sharing her hospital room. My colleague said: "Linda, I heard that you are stealing your neighbor's milk. Is that true?" She nodded her head affirmatively and said: "Yeah, Lefty's been up to his old tricks again." She was referring to her left hand. Each side of the brain controls the opposite side of the body. Therefore, Linda's left hand (or "Lefty," as she called it) was controlled by the right hemisphere of her brain. But Linda didn't seem to take ownership for the actions of this hand.

The left side of Linda's brain, the side that contains most of her language functions, was speaking to us about an action carried out by the other hemisphere. With the corpus callosum severed, the two hemispheres are no longer integrated. Because the verbal left hemisphere was now largely isolated from the right, conversing with Linda essentially meant conversing with the left side of her brain. Later, when Linda returned home from the hospital, her mother noticed other unusual behaviors. For instance, she would sometimes button her jacket with one hand while unbuttoning it with the other.

These types of behaviors reflect the inability of the two disconnected hemispheres to come up with integrated goals. Instead, each side of the brain seems to impose its will upon the contralateral side of the body. After a few months, Linda no longer showed these odd behaviors. This may reflect some degree of neuroplasticity that enhances communication between the two hemispheres. However, as we will see, individuals who have had a split-brain operation eventually learn clever strategies that help them hide some of the behavioral effects of hemispheric disconnection.

Since the early research studies with split-brain patients in the 1960s, researchers have been fascinated by the question of how the left and right hemispheres interact. Beyond the left hemisphere specialization for language, do the functions of the two hemispheres differ in other ways? Do all language functions occur within a particular region of the left hemisphere, or are some language functions distributed widely throughout the brain? How about the brains of bilinguals, individuals who speak more than one language? Do they process language differently than those who speak a single language?

This chapter explores cognitive specializations of the left and right hemispheres, and focuses particularly upon anatomical substrates of language processing (which are mostly, but not exclusively, in the left hemisphere). We will also examine some of the more recent and growing areas of cognitive neuroscience that ask how our minds can reflect, not only upon the external world, but upon our own thoughts and those of others.

14.1 THE TWO-SIDED BRAIN

The left and right sides of the brain are highly symmetrical; they are approximate mirror images. But close examination shows that there are asymmetries in the structure of the two hemispheres. For instance, the frontal lobe is larger on the right side, while the occipital lobe is larger on the left (Figure 14.1). The largest asymmetries are seen in brain areas involved in speech perception (Toga & Thompson, 2003). The two hemispheres are also asymmetrical in terms of their functions. While both sides of the brain are always active during cognitive activity, each side nevertheless has a number of distinct specializations.

14.1.1 The Left and Right Hemispheres Have Distinct Specializations

For instance, for almost all right-handed individuals, language depends more strongly upon the left hemisphere than the right. As a result,

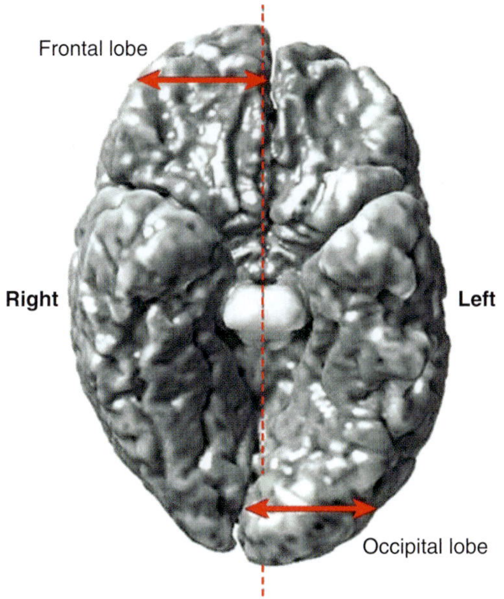

Figure 14.1 The left and right hemispheres are asymmetrical. This 3-D depiction of an MRI scan of the inferior (bottom) surface of the brain illustrates left and right hemisphere asymmetries. Double-sided arrows indicate regions that are larger in one hemisphere than the other. This image is exaggerated in order to highlight the left/right asymmetries, which are actually subtler than those depicted here.
(From Toga & Thompson, 2003, fig. 2, © 2003, Nature Publishing Group.)

right-handers are much more likely to suffer **aphasia** (language disorder) following damage to the left hemisphere than the right. In fact, this relation between left hemisphere damage and aphasia is also seen in most left-handers, suggesting that the left hemisphere plays the dominant role in language for left-handers as well. However, for about 30 percent of left-handers, language functions are distributed across the two hemispheres, and for these individuals damage to the left hemisphere is less disruptive, since their intact right hemisphere can carry out most language functions following left hemisphere damage.

The right hemisphere, on the other hand, is specialized for some aspects of language, such as sensitivity to the way that voice intonation and stress upon certain words can change the meaning of a sentence. In some cases, right hemisphere damage leads to speech lacking intonation and without stress upon words. Other right hemisphere specializations include musical ability, which is more often lost following damage to the right than the left hemisphere. Right hemisphere damage can also disrupt an individual's ability to recognize faces, i.e., it causes prosopagnosia (see Chapter 3). Another right hemisphere specialization is the ability to imagine the shape of an object as it is rotated in space, or folded from three dimensions into a flat, two-dimensional form. While conducting mental rotation tasks, blood flow to the right hemisphere increases, and right hemisphere lesions of the parietal lobe frequently disrupt the ability to carry out tasks of this sort.

According to some theories, the right hemisphere specialization for perceiving faces and melodies is an example of a more general right hemisphere mode of processing stimuli in a holistic manner, that is, by combining elements to perceive their configuration as a whole rather than as a collection of parts (Springer & Deutsch, 1997). From this point of view, the left hemisphere perceives faces as a nose, mouth, eyes, and other features, and a melody as collections of individual notes, while the right hemisphere perceives faces and melodies in a manner that is whole and indivisible.

It is a popular misconception that creativity resides within the right hemisphere. While much remains to be understood about brain processes involved in creativity, research suggests that it involves activity distributed across both sides of the brain, and in many anatomical areas (Lindell & Kidd, 2011). In one study, for example, researchers found the greatest levels of creativity (defined as an ability to come up with many solutions to a problem) in individuals who strongly activated the frontal lobe of *both* sides of the brain, not just the right hemisphere (Gibson, Folley, & Park, 2009).

14.1.2 Split-Brain Surgery Interrupts Communication between the Two Hemispheres

Contralateral control of movement means that the left hemisphere predominantly controls movements of the right side of the body, and the right hemisphere predominantly controls the left (Figure 14.2). Normally, the two hemispheres work together to produce coordinated movements (see Chapter 4).

We saw that split-brain surgery involves a surgical cut of the corpus callosum, a bundle of nerve fibers that transfers information between the left and right hemispheres. The procedure is sometimes called a **corpus callosotomy**, or simply a callosotomy. Even after the surgery, each side of the brain controls, and receives information from, the contralateral side of the body. But severing the corpus callosum greatly reduces communication between the two hemispheres (Figure 14.3).

After the surgery, many patients show strange behavior. For instance, as we saw in the case of Linda in the opening scenario, a split-brain patient may button her jacket with one hand while unbuttoning it with the other. Why does this occur? Recall that each hand is controlled by the contralateral side of the brain, and without the corpus callosum connecting the two sides the left and right hemispheres have little ability to coordinate behaviors to achieve a unified goal (Gazzaniga, Bogen, & Sperry, 1967). The independent and conflicting actions of the two hands appear to reflect the fact that the left hand is carrying out commands from the right hemisphere, and the right hand is carrying out commands from the left.

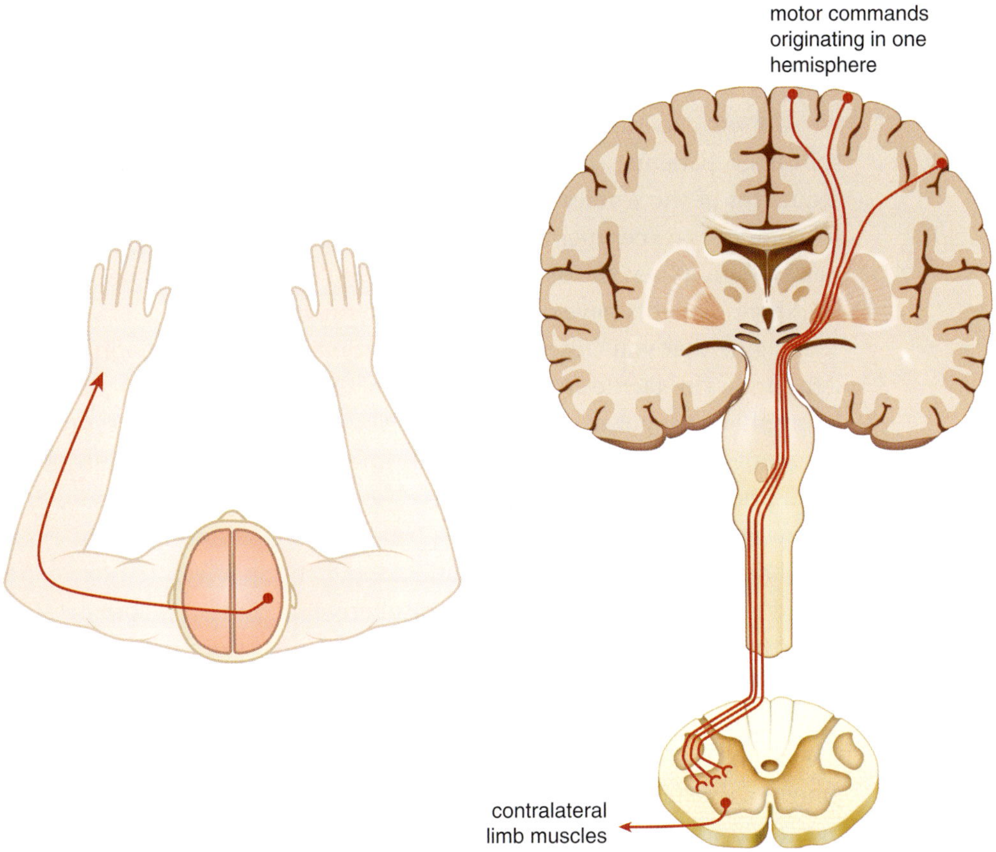

motor commands originating in one hemisphere

contralateral limb muscles

Figure 14.2 Contralateral control of movement. Motor commands from the cortex mostly cross from one side of the brain to control limbs on the contralateral (opposite) side of the body.

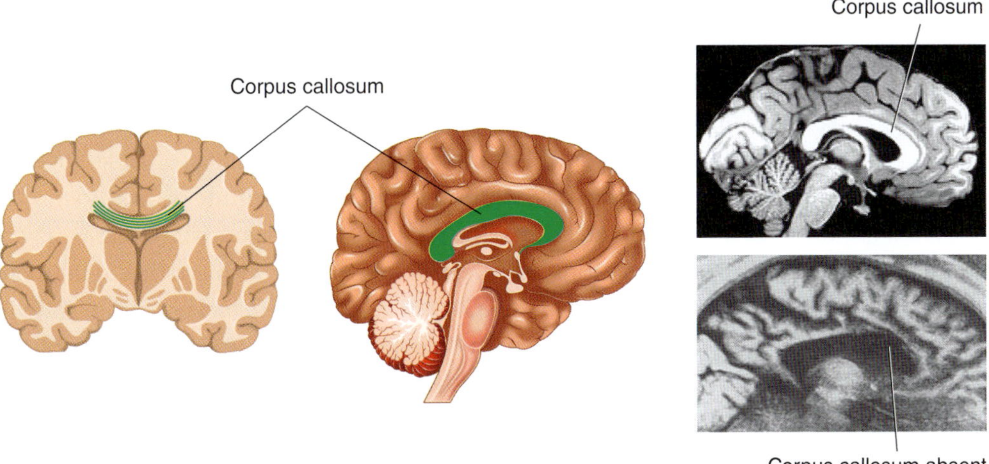

Figure 14.3 Corpus callosum. The corpus callosum connects the left and right hemispheres of the brain. The images to the right show MRIs of a normal brain with the corpus callosum intact (bright white region in top image), and after a split-brain operation that removed the patient's corpus callosum (bottom image).

Fortunately, the signs of the split-brain surgery diminish with time. If you were to meet an individual who had undergone the procedure, chances are you'd detect nothing unusual in his behavior. However, as we will see, experimenters have devised ways of testing the behavior of split-brain patients, and these tests reveal striking and often lasting consequences of the severed connections between hemispheres. In these behavioral tests, experimenters present a tactile or visual object to just one hemisphere. When the object is presented to the right hemisphere alone, split-brain patients have difficulty identifying it verbally.

Imagine that you close your eyes and someone places a spoon in your left hand. The tactile information about the spoon arrives to the right hemisphere. Language depends mostly upon the left hemisphere, but you can name the object because the tactile information crosses from the right hemisphere to the left via the corpus callosum. Once information reaches language regions of the left hemisphere, you are able to name it. For a split-brain patient, tactile information about the spoon in the left hand would also be sent to the right hemisphere. But without a corpus callosum, there is no route for the information to cross from the right hemisphere to the left, and the patient is unable to name the object.

Is there any way for the patient to communicate his knowledge about the spoon? Do we even know that the right hemisphere perceived it? If the patient uses the left hand to feel an object (say a spoon), the information in the right hemisphere cannot be described verbally. However, the right hemisphere controls the left hand, allowing him to pick out the spoon from among a group of objects when feeling the objects, one by one, with his left hand. The information in the right hemisphere does not, however, allow the patient to identify the spoon using the right hand. The right hand is controlled by the *left* hemisphere, which has no knowledge of the spoon. Similarly, if the object is presented to the right hand (left hemisphere), only the right hand can later pick it out (Sperry, 1984).

Michael Gazzaniga and Roger Sperry carried out many of these investigations with split-brain patients at the California Institute of Technology in the 1960s. Even after decades of working with these patients, Gazzaniga was startled by an observation he made while working with another split-brain patient about thirty years later (Gazzaniga, 2013). He had asked the patient to make a hitchhiker gesture with the right hand. The verbal left hemisphere should have understood the verbal instruction, and the patient should therefore be able to make the gesture with the right hand. Sure enough, the patient extended the thumb of his right hand (Figure 14.4). But when Gazzaniga asked the patient to make the gesture with the left hand, the patient was able to do that as well. Gazzaniga wondered how that could occur. The left hand is under control of the right hemisphere. But without a corpus callosum the verbal instructions should not have traveled from the verbal left

Figure 14.4 **Experimenter instructs a split-brain patient to make hand gestures**. The split-brain patient was expected to be able to make the hand gesture with the right hand. Experimenters were surprised when he could do it with the left hand as well.

hemisphere to the right. Perhaps the patient's right hemisphere contained enough language to understand the request. Or perhaps there was another explanation for the results.

The experimenter next asked the patient to make the "A-Okay" sign with the right hand. No problem. Left hand? Again, no problem. Then it dawned on Gazzaniga: The patient was watching himself make the right-handed movement! Visual information about the hand gesture reached the patient's right hemisphere, and the right hemisphere was therefore able to instruct the left hand to carry out the gesture as well. So he asked the patient to close his eyes. "Make the hitchhiker sign with the right hand." No problem. "Now make the hitchhiker sign with the left hand." The patient could not do it. The right hemisphere only understood the command if it had a non-verbal way of deciphering it. Otherwise, the right hemisphere had no way of knowing what commands to send to the left hand.

If the visual system were like the tactile system, one might imagine that the left eye sends information to the right hemisphere of the brain and vice versa. However, this is incorrect. Each eye sends information to both hemispheres. Instead, visual information *in the left or right visual field* (not the eye) is sent to the contralateral hemisphere. So the left hemisphere sees objects present in your right visual field and the right hemisphere sees things in the left visual field. Imagine watching a movie and staring at the center of the screen. A bird that suddenly appears to the right of the screen (your right), will be perceived by your left hemisphere even though the image of the bird falls upon the retina of both left and right eyes (Figure 14.5). This would only be true if the bird appears quickly and then disappears. If it stays on the screen longer, you will automatically center your gaze upon it, and it will no longer be in your left or right visual field. Remember, the left and right visual field refers to the part of space to the left and right of wherever you center your gaze, that is, your "fixation point" (see Chapter 10).

In light of this connection between the right visual field and the left hemisphere of the brain, you would be correct in guessing that if you flash the image of an object to a split-brain patient's right visual field, the patient has no trouble naming it. In contrast, when flashed to the left visual field/right hemisphere, the patient is usually unable to name

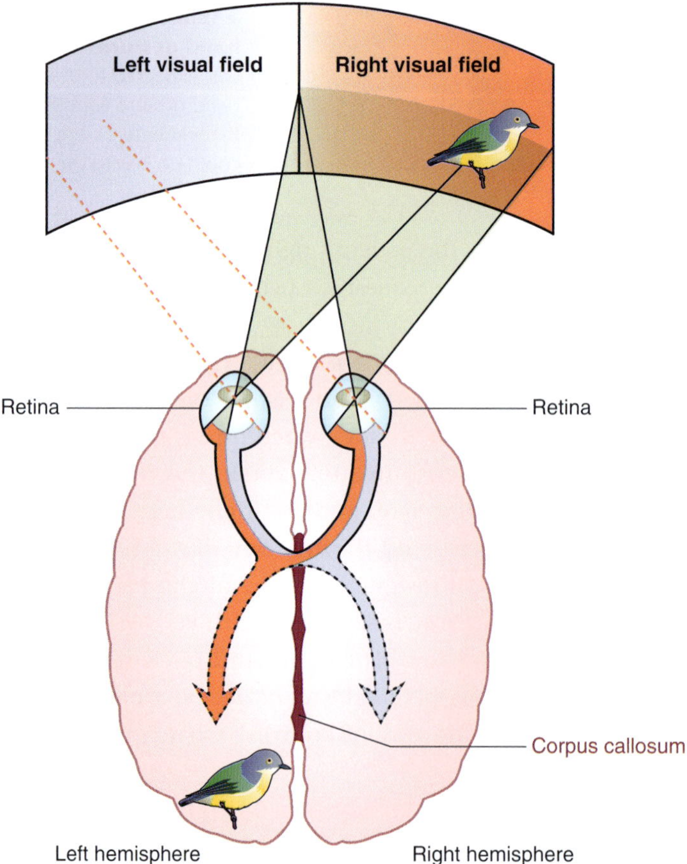

Figure 14.5 Which hemisphere perceives objects in your right visual field? Objects in the right visual field are perceived in the left hemisphere, and vice versa. The corpus callosum normally permits information about the perceived object to transfer to the other hemisphere.

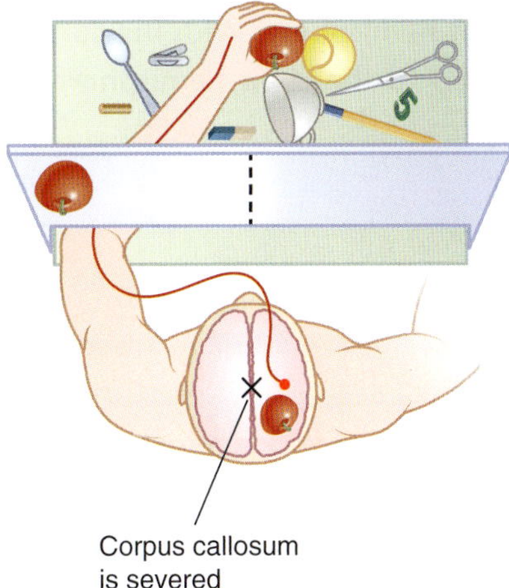

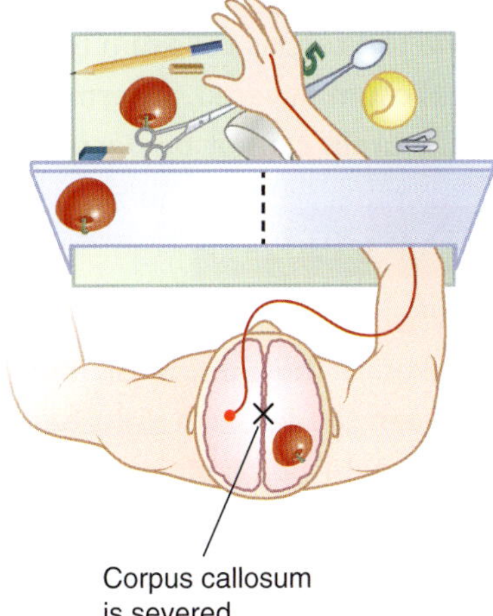

Figure 14.6 In a split-brain patient, the object perceived by the right hemisphere can only be identified using the left hand.

it, often simply saying that he did not see it (Gazzaniga et al., 1967). In this case, the patient can identify it by touch, using the left hand (Sperry, 1984) (Figure 14.6).

In order to describe something verbally, left hemisphere language areas must gain access to the information. With the corpus callosum intact, this information transfer occurs rapidly, seamlessly, and outside of our awareness. It is only when the corpus callosum is severed that a division becomes evident between a mostly non-verbal right hemisphere and a verbal left hemisphere. In 1981, a Nobel Prize was awarded to Roger Sperry for decades of work, much of it with Gazzaniga, showing that when the left and right hemispheres are disconnected, each can independently control behavior. Philosophers and neuroscientists have been intrigued by the implication that the two hemispheres may each possess its own independent realm of consciousness, and by the question of how interhemispheric communication somehow gives rise to unified consciousness and integrated behavior.

KEY CONCEPTS

- **Movements of one side of the body are predominantly controlled by the contralateral side of the brain.**
- **Tactile information on one side of the body is sent mostly to the contralateral half of the brain, and visual information to the left or right visual field is sent to the contralateral side of the brain.**

- **Split-brain surgery severs the corpus callosum, disconnecting the left and right hemispheres.**
- **Because language is usually in the left side of the brain, information presented to the right hemisphere can only be verbalized by crossing via the corpus callosum to the verbal left hemisphere. With the corpus callosum severed, information presented to the right hemisphere of the brain cannot be described verbally.**

TEST YOURSELF

1. **What are some of the specializations of the right hemisphere?**
2. **What is the bundle of fibers that permits information to travel between the left and right hemispheres?**
3. **The right hemisphere receives most of its tactile information from the ____ hand. The right hemisphere predominantly controls movement of the ____ arm.**
4. **You pick up a pencil with your left hand. Tactile information about the pencil goes primarily to somatosensory areas of the _____ hemisphere. Someone asks you, "What is in your hand?" In order to answer that it is a pencil, the information must be transferred to language areas of the ____ hemisphere via the ________.**

14.2 LANGUAGE AND THE BRAIN

Quietly listen to your thoughts, the inner voice speaking silently in words. Do the thoughts exist before they have been turned into words? Many cognitive scientists believe so, and refer to these pre-word ideas as **conceptual representations**. According to some theories, the tip-of-the-tongue experience occurs when a conceptual representation fails to generate a word. You know the word you want to retrieve, but cannot quite get to it (Hickok, 2012).

Words can be represented in various ways. When you read or imagine the written form of a word, word representations are visual. When you listen to someone speak, words are represented in an auditory, or **phonological**, form. Usually, when we think in words, the words are represented phonologically.

In order to communicate your thoughts to another person, your (phonological) word representations somehow lead to movements of your mouth, tongue, and other parts of your vocal apparatus. You create a stream of word sounds, or **phonemes**. (The words "cat" and "kit" begin with different letters, but with the same phoneme.) To say a word, you must articulate each of its phonemes by moving the vocal apparatus in particular ways (Figure 14.7). Scientists believe that this conversion of

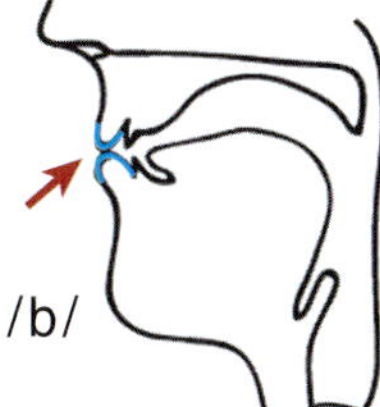

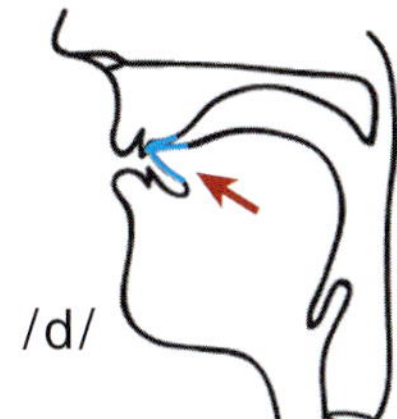

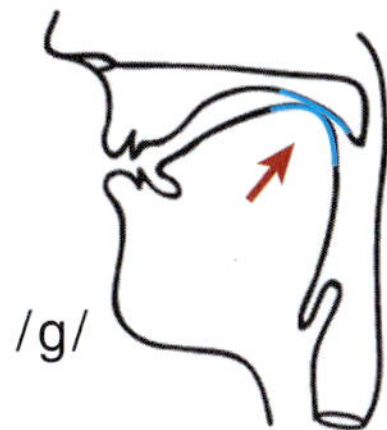

Figure 14.7 **Different phonemes are produced by different contact points in the vocal apparatus**. When you produce the phoneme /b/ (as in the word "bat"), your lips come together, and a burst of sound is released as they part. Notice that to say /d/, the contact occurs further back, with the tongue touching the roof of the mouth behind the teeth. A burst of sound occurs as the tongue is lowered. With /g/ the contact point is even further back. With each word you speak, the brain must control the sequence of word sounds, each involving muscle activation to move particular parts of the vocal apparatus.

words to vocal movements requires activity within language and motor areas of the left frontal cortex.

Perhaps you wish to tell your friend that you walked to the park today. You use your **mental lexicon**, a kind of dictionary stored in memory, to find the words that correspond to the ideas you want to express. Your mental lexicon is filled with all the words you know, 50,000–100,000 words for most adults, each linked to meanings, pronunciations, and other word features (Levelt, 1999; Ullman, 2001). After you find the words that correspond to the idea of walking to the park today, you need to determine the ending to add to the verb: "I walk," "I walks," "I walking," or perhaps "I walked"? The last one is right because it communicates the fact that you're speaking of the past. How do you pronounce it? Does the word "walked" need two syllables as the word "rested" does? No, just one syllable for "walked." Your brain has now determined the phonological form of the word – how it should sound. While we say that this word information is contained in the mental lexicon, associated with the verb "to walk," neuroscientists do not yet understand how the brain stores this information, and retrieves it correctly before every utterance.

You must also determine the correct order of your words. For example, "I park walked to the today" will not be understood because it does not follow the rules of word order, or **syntax**, of English. (Japanese and various other languages operate according to different rules of syntax, but they all have rules about the order of words.) To appreciate the information we gain from syntax, consider this sentence: "He slorked the mago." Even with these made-up words, your knowledge of syntax tells you that he did something to a "mago" (whatever a "mago" is). We'd have problems understanding phrases if we lost our ability to use word order appropriately.

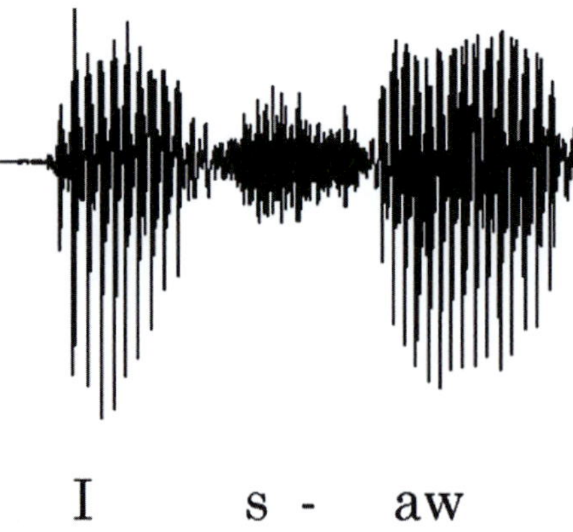

Figure 14.8 **As we speak, we create oscillating soundwaves.** The auditory system converts these soundwaves into the phonemes that comprise words.
(Adapted from Lee, van Santen, Möbius, & Olive, 2005, fig. 6.)

In short, your brain finds words, determines the verb tense and pronunciation, comes up with word order that makes sense, and sends instructions that the motor cortex can use to control the musculature of your vocal apparatus – all in less than half a second (Sahin, Pinker, Cash, Schomer, & Halgren, 2009). Thank goodness you didn't have to consciously work out those kinds of details, or it might take you all day to say one sentence.

Your friend hears you say, "I walked to the park today." Each of the phonemes making up these words creates sound waves (Figure 14.8) that reach her auditory system and activate areas of her temporal lobe. As we will see below, the temporal lobe in the left hemisphere analyzes these sounds, and detects the component phonemes, and ultimately the words they comprise. She uses her mental lexicon to match the phonological representations of words to their meaning, or **semantic content**.

14.2.1 Speech Production and Comprehension Depend upon Different Brain Areas

Researchers have learned a great deal about the brain areas involved in language by studying individuals with aphasias (language disorders) resulting from **stroke** (a loss of oxygen to a brain area due to blocked or broken blood vessels) or other brain injuries. The two main types of aphasia primarily affect either speech production or comprehension.

14.2.2 Broca's Aphasia Disrupts Speech Production

A nineteenth-century French anatomist and physician, Paul Broca, examined the brains of stroke patients who had lost the ability to speak. Nearly all had damage within the **left inferior frontal gyrus**, in a region now known as **Broca's area** (Figure 14.9). Broca noticed that despite their

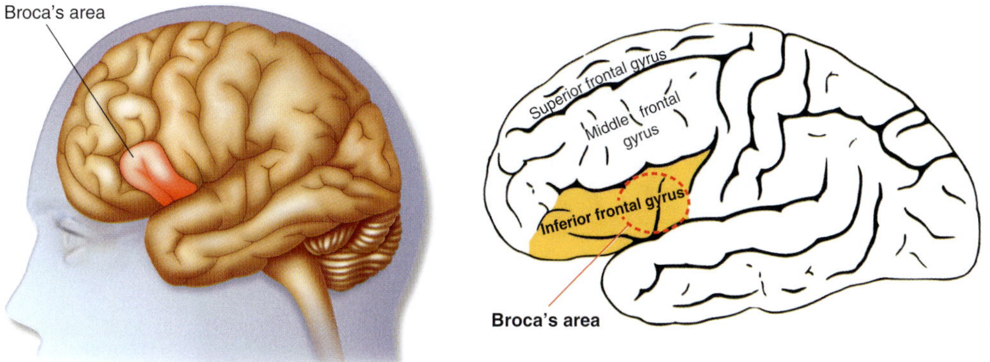

Figure 14.9 **Broca's area**. Broca's area is located in the left inferior frontal gyrus.

difficulties speaking, they had retained the ability to move the musculature of the mouth, tongue, or other parts of the vocal apparatus. Their difficulty was specifically with the **expression** (production) of speech. Disorders in speech expression are known as **Broca's aphasia,** or **expressive aphasia**.

Individuals with Broca's aphasia speak very slowly, pausing as they struggle to find the words they wish to express. Usually, their utterances are less than four words long. For instance, "Boy ... .fall" may be said to express the idea that a boy has fallen down. Asked about the weather, a patient may say, "Weather ... overcast" or simply "overcast." The content words are present but omission of pronouns, conjunctions, and other small grammatical words makes their speech sound telegraphic. Their writing is similarly disrupted (Geschwind, 1970), and deaf patients have similar problems using sign language (Cicone, Wapner, Foldi, Zurif, & Gardner, 1979).

Although individuals with Broca's aphasia have problems with speech production, their comprehension is relatively good. They typically have no difficulty understanding simple sentences such as, "Mary gave balloons to Bob." However, comprehension of complex sentences is often impaired. For instance, hearing the sentence, "The balloons were given to John by Mary," the patient may be confused about who gave balloons to whom. The problem isn't with understanding the meaning of the individual words (such as "balloons"), but in extracting meaning from the articles of speech and the order of words, that is, in decoding the syntax of the sentence.

Brain damage that disrupts speech expression is said to produce Broca's aphasia regardless of the area of brain damage. As seen in red areas in Figure 14.10, Broca's aphasia may arise from damage to frontal lobe areas of the left hemisphere that extend well beyond Broca's area

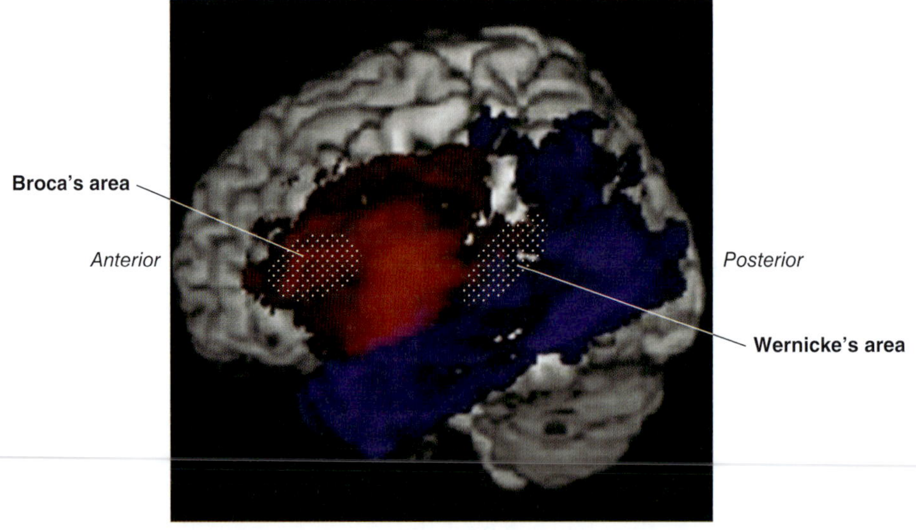

Figure 14.10 **Wide areas of cortical damage can produce Broca's and Wernicke's aphasia.** Lesions that produce Broca's aphasia are seen in areas of the left frontal lobe (solid red) that extend beyond the boundaries of Broca's area (stippled). Similarly, Wernicke's aphasia may result from damage to regions of the left temporal and parietal lobes (solid blue) that extend beyond Wernicke's area (stippled).
(Adapted from Henseler, Regenbrecht, & Obrig, 2014, fig. 2, © 2014, Oxford University Press.)

(Henseler, Regenbrecht, & Obrig, 2014). Broca's area appears to be part of a larger network of brain regions involved in speech expression.

14.2.3 What Does Broca's Area Do?

According to the classic model that originated over a hundred years ago, Broca's area holds representations or "memories" of the way that each word is spoken (Poeppel & Hickok, 2004), and instructs the motor cortex to activate the vocal apparatus in a way that corresponds to each word. Modern neuroscience studies have suggested a number of functions for Broca's region, but at least one of these functions is to contribute to speech articulation.

For instance, in one study, normal subjects heard words such as "dog" or "house" and were instructed to repeat them. Investigators placed electrodes in three brain regions: the auditory cortex, Broca's area, and the motor cortex (Flinker et al., 2015). As subjects listened to each word, the auditory cortex became active (see Figure 14.11). Before the subject spoke the word, Broca's area was activated. Finally, the motor cortex became active just before the subject spoke the word and during speech itself. It is clear from the figure that Broca's area largely ends its activation (the peak of the green line has fallen) before speech (indicated

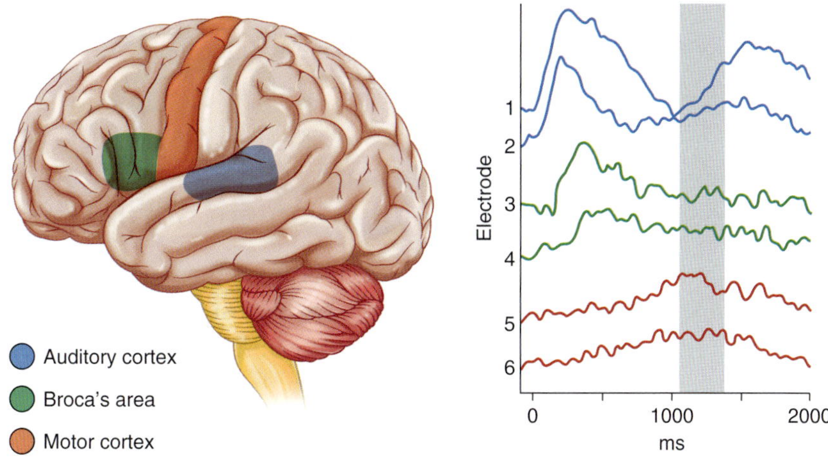

Figure 14.11 Relative timing of brain activation in subjects repeating a word. The graph shows brain activity in a subject who is presented with a spoken word (at time 0 on the *x*-axis) and repeats it (at the time indicated by the shaded region). Activation is seen first in the auditory cortex, followed by Broca's area, and finally in the motor cortex. Notice that activation of Broca's area has largely ended before the word is spoken. (Adapted from Flinker et al., 2015, fig. 1B.).

by the shaded region in the figure) has begun. This pattern of activity is consistent with the view that Broca's area receives information from the auditory cortex about the sound of the word to be spoken, and sends instructions to the motor cortex, which in turn sends motor commands to move the muscles of the vocal apparatus.

In the experiment above, Broca's area was activated before subjects repeated a word they just heard. However, our speech does not normally involve repeating words that we hear. Presumably, Broca's area also receives information about the words we *intend* to say, and produces instructions that allow the motor cortex to generate these words (Sahin et al., 2009). Deaf subjects who communicate through sign language activate Broca's area under similar conditions, suggesting that the area's involvement in language production is independent of the kind of motor behavior used for communication (Campbell, MacSweeney, & Waters, 2008).

Recent research also suggests that Broca's area plays a role in using syntax (Friederici, 2018). When normal subjects listen either to simple phrases such as "The boy kicked the girl," or to phrases with more complex syntax such as "The boy is kicked by the girl," phrases with complex syntax more strongly activate (subregions within) Broca's area.

We saw in the previous section that patients with Broca's aphasia often suffer difficulties in (a) language expression and (b) using syntax. We have also seen that Broca's patients usually suffer damage that extends beyond Broca's area to surrounding areas of the left frontal lobe. It therefore seems likely that brain regions in or near Broca's area contain neural circuits necessary for both normal language expression and the use of syntax. Individuals with disruptions to these circuits show abnormalities in either language articulation, sensitivity to syntax, or both.

14.2.4 Wernicke's Aphasia Disrupts the Comprehension and Meaningful Content of Speech

In contrast to the slow and labored speech in Broca's aphasia, the patient with **Wernicke's aphasia** (also called **receptive aphasia**) speaks fluently, sometimes faster than normal. However, the meanings of the utterances are difficult to decipher. Wernicke's patients also show poor comprehension for both spoken and written language. Deaf individuals with Wernicke's aphasia show similar deficits comprehending sign language, and blind Wernicke's patients are impaired in reading Braille (Birchmeier, 1985; Petitto et al., 2000).

Here is an example of the speech of a Wernicke's patient: "I was over in the other one, and then after they had been in the department, I was in this one" (Geschwind, 1970). Notice that the sentence includes words like "in," "the," "and," the very parts of speech usually absent in individuals with Broca's aphasia. The sentence is also much longer than that of a Broca's aphasiac, although it lacks meaningful content.

Wernicke's aphasiacs sometimes use non-existent words, or **neologisms**. For instance, when asked about his speech problem, a Wernicke's aphasiac replied: "Because no one gotta scotta gowan thwa, thirst, gell, gerst, derund, gystrol, that's all" (Brown, 1972). Unlike the Broca's aphasiac who grows frustrated by his difficulty communicating, the Wernicke's aphasiac seems unaware that his sentences are incomprehensible. He continues to speak quickly, maintaining the rhythm and intonation of normal speech.

Wernicke's aphasia is named after Carl Wernicke, the physician who first described the condition in the 1870s. The disorder was originally believed to result from specific damage to an area of the posterior left temporal cortex or **Wernicke's area** (again, see Figure 14.10). However, like Broca's aphasia, Wernicke's aphasia results from damage that extends far beyond the boundaries originally associated with the disorder. Brain damage in Wernicke's aphasiacs often includes regions throughout much of the left temporal and parietal cortices.

14.2.5 Perceiving Words Activates Different Brain Regions than Understanding Their Meanings

The widespread brain damage associated with Wernicke's aphasia makes it difficult to pinpoint those regions that specifically contribute to speech comprehension. Furthermore, speech comprehension likely involves many different processes, which may take place in different brain regions. In the case of spoken language, during early stages of speech perception the brain recognizes particular sounds as phonemes, combinations of phonemes are recognized as words, and words and phrases give rise to associated meanings.

Early stages of speech perception involve activity within the temporal cortex, which contains three large **gyri** (bulges): the superior, middle, and **inferior temporal gyrus** (Figure 14.12). Wernicke's area is located in the posterior part of the superior temporal gyrus.

A key region necessary for speech perception is the superior temporal gyrus (STG) of the left temporal cortex. As subjects listen to words and phrases, the STG becomes activated. The activations produced by speech are much greater than those produced by other kinds of sounds (DeWitt & Rauschecker, 2012; Yi, Leonard, & Chang, 2019).

Different areas of the left STG are activated by these different units of speech (Figure 14.13). For instance, a posterior region of the left STG becomes most active when listening to individual phonemes; words (which are combinations of phonemes) activate a more anterior part of the STG; phrases (comprised of individual words) activate an even more anterior STG region. Therefore, the larger units of speech activate the more anterior STG regions.

How would disruptions of the STG affect language perception? Experimental disruptions of the STG impair the ability to recognize spoken words. This was demonstrated in a fascinating study. An experimenter read sentences to subjects while a neurosurgeon applied electrical stimulation

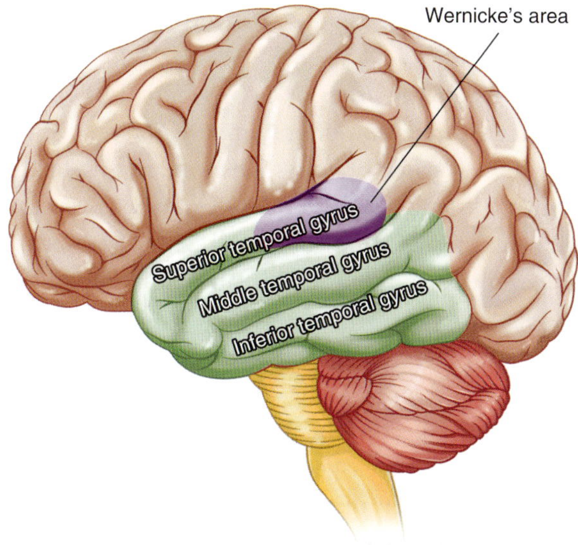

Figure 14.12 The three gyri of the temporal cortex. The temporal cortex includes the superior, middle, and inferior temporal gyri. Wernicke's area is in the posterior part of the superior temporal gyrus.

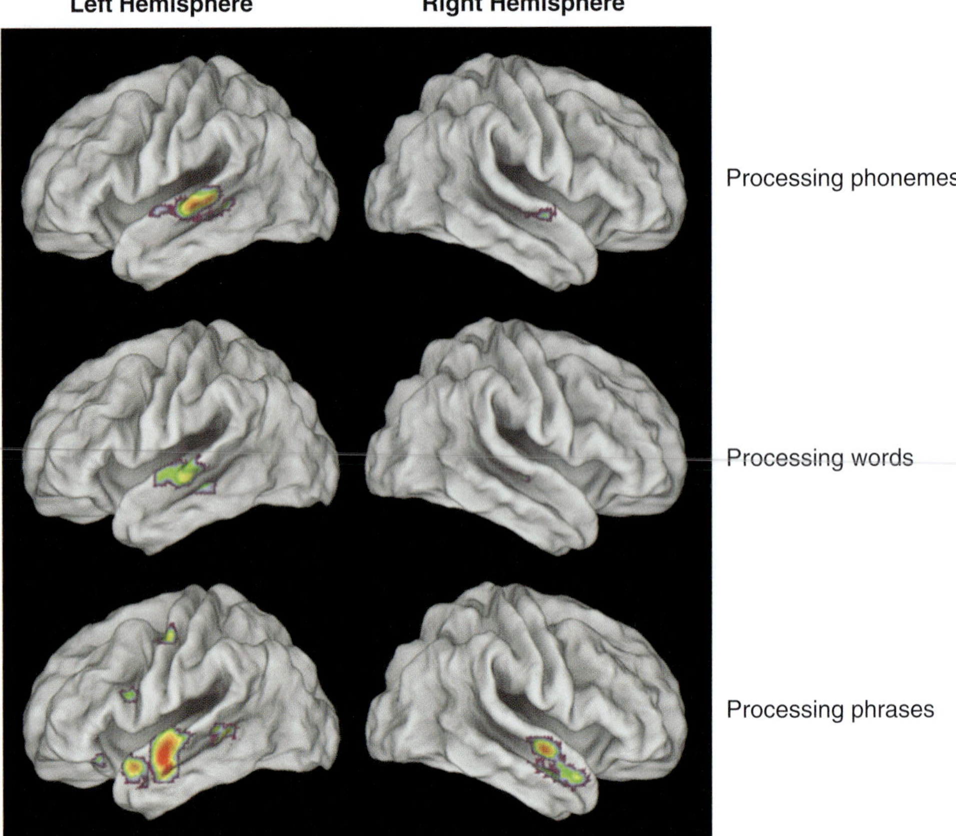

Figure 14.13 **Different units of speech activate different areas of the left superior temporal gyrus.** The results of many different fMRI studies were combined in order to identify cortical areas activated during perception of phonemes, words, or phrases. Notice that the smallest units of speech (phonemes) activate posterior areas of the superior temporal gyrus while larger units of speech (phrases) activate more anterior areas.
(From DeWitt & Rauschecker, 2012, fig. 1.)

that interfered with the activity of the anterior STG (Figure 14.14). (As with many other cases of direct stimulation of brain tissue, the procedure took place prior to epilepsy surgery when brain regions were stimulated to ensure that no critical tissue was removed.) One subject who received the stimulation reported that he could tell that the experimenter was speaking, but the sentences themselves sounded like meaningless utterances (Matsumoto et al., 2011).

While the subject could not understand the spoken sentences, the stimulation did not prevent him from reading and understanding the same sentences. The stimulation specifically impaired comprehension of spoken words. The problem was not a general impairment in hearing, since it did not prevent recognition of music, the sound of a bell, a waterfall, or other non-linguistic sounds. Instead, subjects were unable

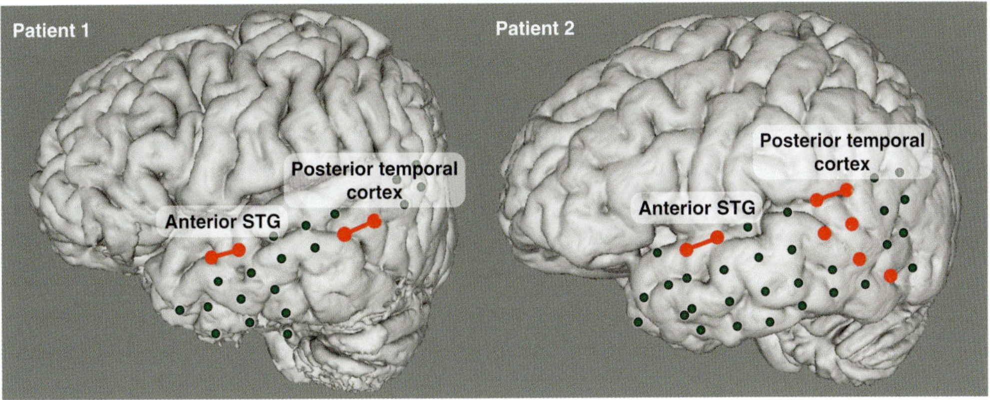

Figure 14.14 Disrupting activity in the superior temporal gyrus impairs language. A neurosurgeon applied disruptive stimulation to many areas of the left temporal cortex, shown as small green dots and large red circles and lines. Only disruptive stimulation to the areas marked in red produced language impairment. Disruptions to the anterior superior temporal gyrus specifically impaired recognition of spoken words.
(Adapted from Matsumoto et al., 2011, © 2011, Elsevier Ltd.)

to recognize that they were listening to phrases in a language they knew. When experimenters disrupted posterior regions of the temporal cortex near Wernicke's area, subjects lost the ability to understand either spoken or written language.

Individuals with **pure word deafness** have relatively normal hearing but have severe impairments in detecting words. The widespread brain damage often seen in these patients makes it difficult to pinpoint the precise areas of damage associated with the problems in word perception. However, as one might expect given the apparent role of the STG in word recognition, the damage often includes the STG (Buchman, Garron, Trost-Cardamone, Wichter, & Schwartz, 1986).

While the STG is important in perceiving spoken words, we have seen that Wernicke's aphasiacs usually have difficulties in language comprehension regardless of whether the words are spoken or written (or signed or written in Braille). Their primary problem therefore cannot solely be the result of damage to brain circuits needed for perception of spoken words. Instead, they are likely to suffer damage to brain regions important for word comprehension regardless of the sensory modality in which words are perceived.

Large areas of the brain are involved in deriving meaning from words and sentences (Friederici, 2012; Skeide & Friederici, 2016). Subjects who listened to more than 2 hours of recorded stories containing over 10,000 different words revealed brain activations associated with word comprehension in widespread areas of the temporal, frontal, and parietal cortices in both the left and right sides of the brain (Figure 14.15). Different areas

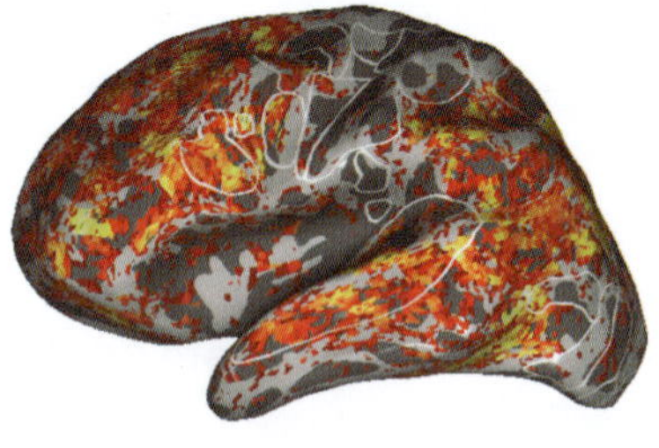

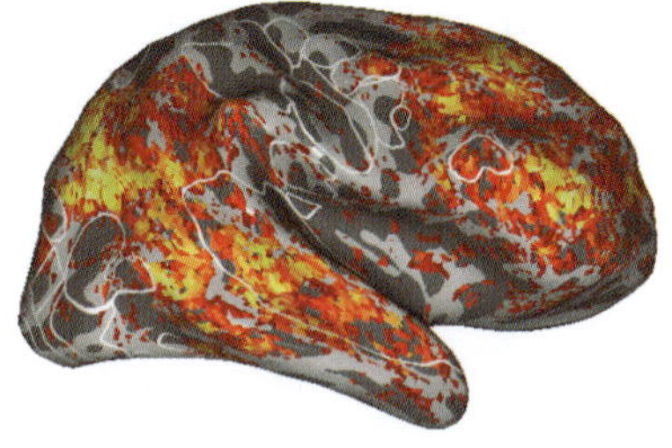

Figure 14.15 Brain activations associated with word comprehension. Regions with activity related to semantic content (the meaning) of words were seen over widespread areas of the left and right sides of the brain. Red coloring represents areas that were most strongly activated.
(From Huth et al., 2016, fig. 1,)

of the cortex were activated by particular categories of words (Huth, de Heer, Griffiths, Theunissen, & Gallant, 2016). For instance, brain responses to *visual* words like "yellow," "red," and "bright," were clustered together, *numeric* words like "four," "ten," and "double" activated their own clusters of brain regions, and brain responses to *emotional* words like "despised," "angry," and "joyful" were clustered in yet other areas.

As Figure 14.15 shows, wide areas of the cortex contribute to the comprehension of words. It is possible that Wernicke's patients suffer damage to areas of the left hemisphere (again, see Figure 14.10) that are needed in order for words to gain access to the various areas of the cortex that give the words their meanings. Because the tools of modern neuroscience have only recently been applied to understand language comprehension, the neurobiological mechanisms that allow us to derive meaning from words (whether spoken, written, or signed) remain largely a mystery.

14.2.6 Beyond Broca's or Wernicke's Aphasia

We have seen that one can divide language operations into those associated with speech production and those associated with comprehension. Broca's aphasia primarily impairs speech production and Wernicke's primarily disrupts comprehension. However, some patients show deficits in both the production and the comprehension of speech. These patients with **global aphasia** often show damage to widespread language areas of the left hemisphere. On the other hand, patients with the rare disorder called **conduction aphasia** are unable to repeat sentences, even though their language comprehension is good and speech production is fluent. These patients sometimes make odd errors in spontaneous speech, by omitting syllables and phonemes, or replacing them with incorrect ones. For instance, a patient may say "snowall" instead of "snowball" or "velitision" instead of television.

Not all cases of aphasia fit into an easy diagnostic category. For instance, the Wernicke's patient with his fluent but largely meaningless phrases usually has poor comprehension. But some individuals with the fluent and jumbled words of the Wernicke's patient have good comprehension. As neuroscience learns more about how brain circuits contribute to specific language functions, we are likely to gain a clearer understanding of the relation between brain damage and aphasiac symptoms.

KEY CONCEPTS

- **We choose our words from a mental lexicon, a mental dictionary storing word meanings, pronunciations, and other word features.**
- **Broca's aphasia is characterized by slow and effortful speech. It is caused by damage to left frontal lobe regions within and surrounding Broca's area.**
- **Wernicke's aphasia involves deficits in speech comprehension, with fluent but often meaningless utterances. It can be caused by damage to Wernicke's area, but also to other areas of the left temporal and parietal cortices.**
- **Phonemes are processed by posterior areas of the left superior temporal gyrus, while words and phrases are processed by more anterior parts of the region.**
- **Language comprehension is associated with activation, not only of Wernicke's area, but of widespread cortical regions on both sides of the brain.**

TEST YOURSELF

1. **Neurons in left frontal lobe language areas, including Broca's area, appear to send instructions to the _____ _____ to produce the necessary vocal movements for articulating words.**
2. **Contrast the language abnormalities in Broca's compared to Wernicke's aphasia.**
3. **On the basis of brain imaging and other neuroscience techniques, what brain area(s) are most important in word perception? Language comprehension?**

14.2.7 Dyslexia Is Associated with Reduced Activity in the Visual Word Form Area

Individuals with **dyslexia** (approximately 5 percent of the population) have trouble reading despite normal eyesight, intelligence, and motivation. They are often slow or inaccurate in recognizing words, and have difficulties pronouncing them. They often misspell words, for instance "rog" instead of "rug." As a result of their difficulties in word recognition, they sometimes have problems with reading comprehension.

Reading requires perception of written letters, which are combined and then converted into word sounds. Word sounds are, in turn, associated with meanings. Those with dyslexia have problems with the visual-to-auditory conversion, or **phonological processing**, of written material. When reading, most individuals without dyslexia show strong activation of the **visual word form area** (Figure 14.16). This area is relatively inactive in those with dyslexia (Eden & Moats, 2002). It is possible that dysfunction within this region, located in the occipitotemporal junction of the left hemisphere, prevents visual word stimuli from activating the superior temporal gyrus or other areas needed for generating word sounds. Lesions of the visual word form area following a stroke or traumatic brain injury can produce **pure word blindness** in which written words cannot be recognized at all.

Individuals with dyslexia show great variability in the nature of their reading challenges. Some have difficulty sounding out words letter by letter, but can recognize a whole written word if they have already memorized its sound. Others have difficulties recognizing whole words. Dyslexia has a strong genetic component (Thambirajah, 2010). Dyslexics

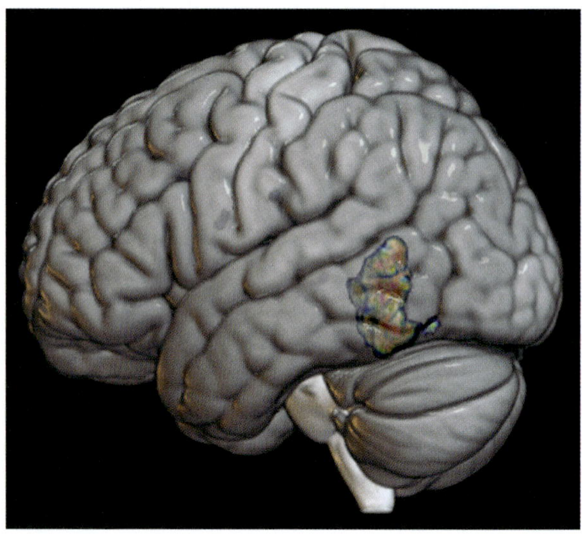

Figure 14.16 The visual word form area. The red coloring indicates high activity in the visual word form area during reading in normal readers. (Left, John Beal, LSU Health Sciences Center; right, from Paulesu et al., 2001, fig. 3.)

often have a family member with a history of reading or spelling problems, even if they were not diagnosed as dyslexic. The concordance rate (the likelihood of two individuals both suffering the same disorder) for dyslexia is higher for identical compared to fraternal twins.

14.2.8 Bilinguals Show Increased Density of Connections between Brain Areas

In recent years, fascinating research has examined brain representation of language in bilinguals (Calabria, Costa, Green, & Abutalebi, 2018; Luo et al., 2019). Most of this research has been carried out on **successive bilinguals**, individuals who learn a second language later in life through formal instruction or immersion in an environment where the second language is spoken. (In contrast, **simultaneous bilinguals** are exposed to both languages from birth.) Research suggests that many of the same brain areas are engaged regardless of whether the individual is using her first or second language. While both the first and the second language activate language areas of the left frontal and left temporal lobes, the second language often produces more widespread brain activation, including more extensive regions surrounding Broca's area and wider regions of the left superior temporal gyrus. Many researchers believe that these differences are related to the extra effort required to speak the second, less fluent language. Consistent with this view, differences in brain activation by the two languages diminishes as bilinguals become more proficient in the second language (Abutalebi, 2008).

Nevertheless, even when bilinguals are speaking their first language, activation of language areas is stronger than that seen when **monolinguals** speak their only language. Some researchers interpret these observations to suggest that bilinguals need to more strongly recruit language circuits, even in their first language, in order to inhibit retrieval of word meanings in the other language (Parker Jones et al., 2012). That is, bilinguals may always need to engage language processing areas more strongly because they are juggling two languages. Consistent with this hypothesis, these same language areas show increased activity when monolinguals read complex reading material requiring high mental effort.

Some studies report the fascinating observation that bilinguals have denser axonal connections between brain areas compared to monolinguals. These enhanced neuronal connections are seen both in language-related areas and in brain regions associated with other cognitive functions. For instance, bilinguals show increased volume of the anterior cingulate, a region involved in "top-down" control of attention (Chapter 10) (Costa & Sebastian-Galles, 2014). Bilinguals have also been reported to perform better than monolinguals on various cognitive tasks, and show a smaller decline in cognitive performance with age. Some evidence suggests that bilingualism may delay the onset of Alzheimer's disease (Perani & Abutalebi, 2015; Woumans et al., 2015).

One explanation for this effect is that increased neuronal growth in bilinguals provides them with **cognitive reserve**. From this point of view, neuronal pathology or loss does not produce Alzheimer's symptoms until the number of healthy neurons falls below a certain threshold number. The enhanced number of neurons associated with bilingualism provides a reserve that keeps the number of functioning neurons above the threshold for normal cognitive function even as neurons are lost. On the other hand, studies have not all observed a relation between bilingualism and delayed onset of Alzheimer's disease, or only find a weak relationship (Costa & Sebastian-Galles, 2014; Antoniou, 2019). Investigators continue to probe the relation between bilingualism and possible protection against age-related cognitive loss.

KEY CONCEPTS

- **Dyslexia often includes problems recognizing and spelling words.**
- **Some individuals with dyslexia show under-activity in the left hemisphere visual word form area.**
- **Compared to monolinguals, bilinguals appear to show reduced or slowed age-related decline in cognitive function.**

TEST YOURSELF

1. **Persons with dyslexia have problems with the visual-to-auditory conversion, or ______ processing, of written material.**
2. **When reading, most individuals without dyslexia show strong activation of the ____ ____ area. Dyslexia is associated with decreased activity in this brain area.**
3. **How does the activation of left hemisphere brain regions differ in bilinguals compared to monolinguals? How might you explain the observed differences?**

14.3 THE THINKING SELF

While some cognitive neuroscience laboratories examine how the brain processes language, others examine neuronal processes associated with attention or working memory (Chapter 10). Still others monitor brain activity as we retrieve previously studied lists of words (Chapter 9), or plan actions (Chapter 4). However, when we are not listening to someone else's words or formulating a verbal response, or attending to an object, or planning a particular action, the mind is still processing information.

We dedicate the last section of this chapter to examine three related, and rapidly growing, areas of cognitive neuroscience that investigate the human mind as it is turned inward to reflect upon its own contents. The first area of investigation examines the **default network**, brain areas activated while we engage in spontaneous thought, rather than attending to external events. The second pertains to a particular kind of thought process – **metacognition** – in which we reflect upon our own thoughts. The third – **mentalizing** – pertains to our cognitions about the thoughts and emotions we imagine to be occurring in the minds of those around us. Research on the default network, metacognition, and mentalizing reveals considerable overlap in the brain areas that subserve these cognitive activities.

In earlier chapters, we examined neural underpinnings of our sensory experience, behavioral responses, attention to external stimuli, emotional responses to stressors, and other topics related to the mind and behavior. We end this chapter, and this book, by considering the kinds of thinking that we engage in when no external stimulus demands our attention and no particular action is called for.

14.3.1 The Default Network: The Wandering Mind

In an attention task, certain brain areas are activated while the subject attends to an item, and become less active during rest periods while the subject waits for the next trial to begin. Other brain areas are activated when subjects are asked to retrieve memories of things that happened to them in the past (**autobiographical memories**); however, in this case, researchers found that during the rest periods before the next trial began, several brain areas remained active, including the memory-related areas (Shulman et al., 1997; Raichle et al., 2001). When asked what they were doing between trials, subjects reported that their minds had wandered between memories of the past, thoughts about the future, and other personal thoughts (Andreasen et al., 1995; Buckner, Andrews-Hanna, & Schacter, 2008). Between trials, the subjects were engaged in spontaneous thought.

A group of about five brain areas communicate with one another during spontaneous thought and comprise what is called the default network. The network is not active when subjects attend to external stimuli, or when they work on effortful cognitive tasks like solving a math problem. Instead, the default network becomes active when awareness turns inward. Individuals who practice meditation to reduce such spontaneous

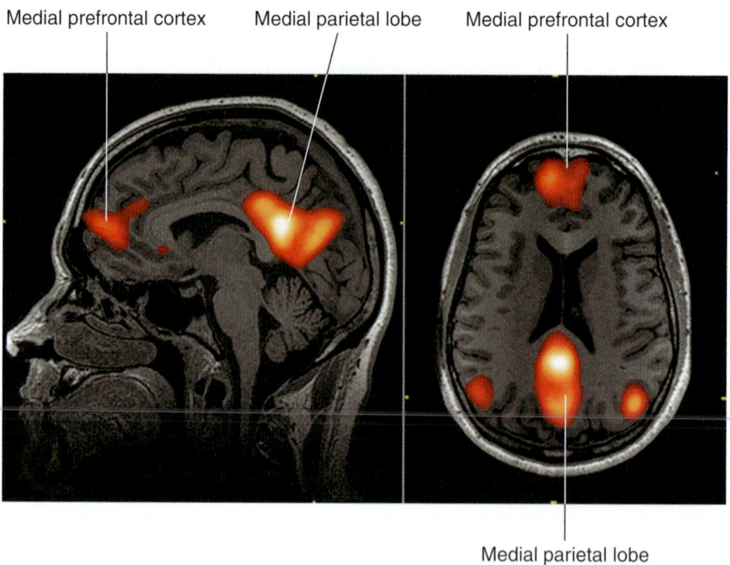

Figure 14.17 **Default mode network brain activity**. These fMRI images show that two key areas of the default mode network are the medial prefrontal cortex and the medial parietal lobes.
(From Graner et al., 2013, fig. 2.)

thoughts and quiet the mind show a marked reduction in default network activity (Brewer et al., 2011; Tang, Holzel, & Posner, 2015).

The two largest regions of the network are the medial prefrontal cortex and medial parietal lobes (Figure 14.17). In both areas, the activation is seen toward the midline of the brain. (Recall from Chapter 2 that a line from the center of your forehead straight to the back of the head would fall on the midline.) While several areas of the medial prefrontal and medial parietal lobes are normally active during spontaneous thought, individuals with schizophrenia, autism, and Alzheimer's disease show abnormalities within these midline regions and other parts of the default network (Buckner et al., 2008).

The hippocampus is another region within the default network, perhaps not surprising given its role in memory (see Chapter 9). While the hippocampus does not comprise a large part of the network in terms of the volume it occupies, its activity is strongly correlated with other parts of the network. In other words, when the medial prefrontal cortex, posterior cingulate, and other areas of the default network become active, the hippocampus usually becomes active as well (Vincent et al., 2006; Buckner et al., 2008). During moments when the brain turns away from the external world, it engages a default network, and daydreams.

14.3.2 Metacognition: Thinking about Thinking

Metacognition refers to cognition about one's own cognitions, thinking about one's own thinking. It is the ability to reflect upon one's own mental processes. Say you ask a child, "What's the name of your aunt who wears the funny hats?" "Aunt Molly," she answers. The child is not using metacognition because she is not thinking about her own thinking. She's thinking about funny hats and whether or not Aunt Molly wears them.

Next, you ask the child how *sure* she is that Aunt Molly is the one who wears the funny hats. What does the child need to think about now? She needs to reflect upon her own level of certainty about Aunt Molly and the hats. She needs to make a judgment about one of her own beliefs. Regardless of whether she answers, "I'm not very sure" or "I'm almost positive," she is using metacognition. She is thinking (in this case, making a certainty judgment) about her own thoughts.

Do other animals engage in metacognition, or is it unique to humans? Experimenters presented sounds of either short or long duration to rats, and taught them to press a left lever when they heard the short duration sound, and a lever on the right when they heard the long duration sound. When they pressed the correct lever, they received a reward of six food pellets. When they pressed the incorrect lever, they received no reward and had to wait a while before the next trial began. The rats quickly got good at this: short duration (any noise between 2 and 3½ seconds), press left; long duration (any noise between 4½ and 8 seconds), press right. When the sounds were very short (say 2 seconds) or very long (8 seconds), the rats accurately chose the correct lever. However, when the durations were close to the middle, say 5 seconds long, the rats often pressed the wrong lever and got no reward. These were the difficult trials. None of this involves metacognition.

But the rats also learned that if they were not sure whether the sound was long or short, they could poke their nose in an illuminated hole in the wall and decline the test. This led to an immediate end of the trial along with a small reward of three pellets (instead of the six they would have received for the correct response). In other words, the rats could choose, "I'm not sure," and receive a consolation prize. When they heard the intermediate duration sounds, they frequently nose-poked to pass on the trial (Foote & Crystal, 2007). This behavior is what one might expect if rats *know when they don't know* and, combined with other evidence (Kwok, Cai, & Buckley, 2019), suggests that animals besides humans may be capable of metacognition.

In the examples above, the child and the rat both demonstrated metacognition by forming a judgment regarding how certain they were about a particular cognition (whether Aunt Molly wears the funny hats;

whether the sound was long or short duration). At least in humans, metacognition also allows us to exert *control* over our own thought processes. Say you are trying to work out a difficult interpersonal issue. You come to a solution, and then think to yourself, "I don't think I'm thinking clearly about this. I'd better re-evaluate it." In that case, your metacognition involves not only a reflection upon your thinking, but, as a result, a change in your thinking. Metacognition is associated with activation of the anterior prefrontal cortex (Gallo, Kensinger, & Schacter, 2006; Paul et al., 2015), and prefrontal damage produces impairments in metacognition both in human (Schnyer et al., 2004; Fleming & Dolan, 2012) and in monkey subjects (Kwok et al., 2019).

14.3.3 Mentalizing: Reflecting on the Thoughts of Others

We all know that we are not the only ones with thoughts, emotions, desires, and beliefs. Other people have mental states, too. We all possess what cognitive scientists call a **theory of mind**, the awareness that other people experience mental states.

Theory of mind is believed to be largely absent in infants less than a year old (Slaughter, 2015). The baby may feel joy when his mother approaches, but without a theory of mind he does not think about what his mother feels or wants. He is apparently unaware of the existence of emotions and desires aside from his own. Theory of mind develops gradually over the first five years of childhood, and helps us to navigate the complex world of social relations (Mar, 2011).

While we interact with others, we imagine their mental states and how they may be changing from one moment to the next. Say you tell your friend an amusing story that makes her laugh. You infer that she found it funny. Later, she looks off into space with what you believe to be a sad look in her eyes, and you imagine that she is reminiscing about a happy time shared with a family member who has passed away. You might infer that she desires time alone, or perhaps you think she'd like to talk. When you make such inferences, you are **mentalizing**, thinking about another person's mental states. Your mentalizations may be right or wrong, perhaps depending upon your knowledge and insight regarding the other person.

Some use the term *mentalizing* and *theory of mind* interchangeably, but there is a distinction. Mentalizing is something you do when you imagine what another person is thinking or feeling. The fact that you are mentalizing demonstrates that you understand that others have mental states, just like you do; it demonstrates that you have a theory of mind.

The ability to mentalize about the thought and feelings of others is a key feature of what researchers call **social cognition**. The area of research that asks about the brain bases of social cognition is called **social cognitive neuroscience**. Here is an example of the kind of story that experimenters in social cognitive neuroscience might present to a subject while examining brain areas activated as they mentalize:

> A soldier is captured by the enemy and interrogated about the location of his country's troops. The soldier assumes that the interrogators will interpret anything he says as a lie, so he tells them the true location of the troops in the hope that they will look in another location instead.

In order to understand this story, the listener must consider the soldier's belief. In fact, while listening to this story, we consider the soldier's beliefs about the interrogator's beliefs! Brain activity under this condition is compared to that observed in subjects listening to a story with similar content and difficulty but one that does not require mentalization:

> One army has air superiority over another. However, fog descends upon the battlefield, neutralizing air power and allowing the other army to win the battle.

By comparing brain activity observed during the two stories, researchers observe that mentalizing is associated with high levels of activity in three key brain areas: the medial prefrontal cortex, the temporoparietal junction, and the precuneus (Figure 14.18). These areas are consistently activated during experimental manipulations that encourage subjects to consider another person's point of view.

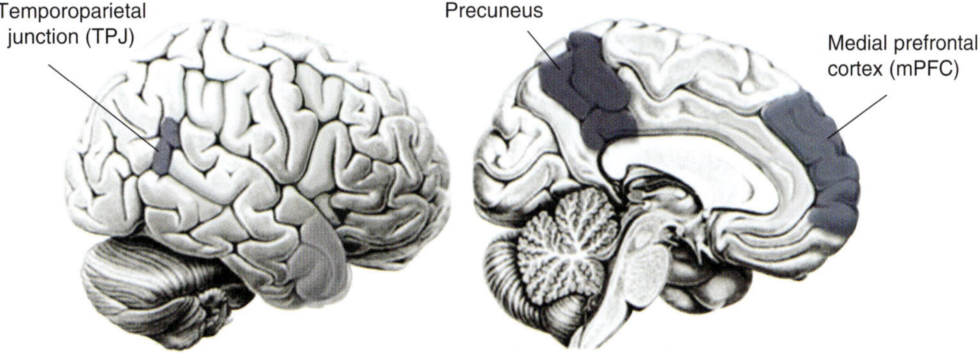

Figure 14.18 Brain areas often active while mentalizing. The temporoparietal junction (TPJ), medial prefrontal cortex (mPFC), and precuneus consistently show strong activation when subjects are imagining the thoughts, beliefs, or emotions of others. The TPJ can be seen on the exterior surface of the brain (left image), while the mPFC and precuneus can be seen along the medial portion of the brain (right image).

(From Zaki & Ochsner, 2012, fig. 2,)

Figure 14.19 Social and non-social scenes used in studies of mentalizing. Subjects with a strong tendency to mentalize show strong medial prefrontal cortical activation when looking at social scenes (top photo) but not when looking at photos of flowers and other kinds of non-social scenes (bottom photo). (From Wagner, Kelley, & Heatherton, 2011, fig. 1, © 2011, Oxford University Press.)

When shown a photo of people interacting with one another (see Figure 14.19), subjects who most often thought about the thoughts and feelings of others showed the highest activation in the medial portion of the prefrontal cortex. These subjects did not show high levels of prefrontal activity while looking at non-social photos, such as scenes containing flowers or animals; the medial prefrontal cortex only kicked in strongly while they viewed social scenes and mentalized (Wagner, Kelley, & Heatherton, 2011).

KEY CONCEPTS

- **While subjects quietly think on their own, with no particular goal, the mind wanders from past memories to future plans. This spontaneous thinking engages the default network including midline areas of the prefrontal cortex and parietal lobes as well as the hippocampus.**
- **Metacognition, the ability to think about our own thoughts, also depends upon activity of the anterior prefrontal cortex. Research suggests that, like humans, some animals (perhaps even rats) may also be able to reflect upon their own thought processes.**

- **A key aspect of social cognition is our ability to mentalize, that is, to think about the mental states of others. Subjects who engage in mentalizing more than others show greater activation of the medial prefrontal cortex.**

TEST YOURSELF

1. **What are some of the key brain regions in the default network? When is the default network activated?**
2. **Give an example of metacognition in humans. What evidence points to its existence in animals?**
3. **What is theory of mind? What brain areas are implicated in mentalizing?**

14.4 The Big Picture

In this chapter, we saw that the left and right hemispheres normally function in an integrated manner, but that in split-brain patients one hemisphere may carry out an action that is not integrated with the goals of the other. With the corpus callosum severed, the verbal left hemisphere can no longer communicate mental processes occurring in the disconnected right hemisphere.

We also examined research on the brain basis of language which shows that "verbal" expression and comprehension is comprised of many separate processes, most occurring in the left hemisphere, but some in the right. Over 150 years after investigators originally discovered that left hemisphere damage causes speech abnormalities, neuroscience is probing more specific relations between language functions and brain activity.

Finally, this chapter revisited a topic introduced in Chapter 1 of this book: the relation between mental activity and the activity of the brain. Descartes saw our thoughts and decisions as immaterial processes, part of the soul. In order to reflect upon our memories and other contents of the mind, Descartes invoked a non-material spirit. Yet, not only do thoughts depend upon neuronal activity, but our ability to reflect upon these thoughts is a brain function as well. Descartes would surely have been surprised to know that activation of particular brain regions is reliably seen during metacognition, or when individuals mentalize about the minds of others, or when they simply allow their minds to roam freely and daydream.

14.5 Creative Thinking

1. The corpus callosum allows the left and right hemispheres of the brain to communicate with one another. This allows the verbal left

hemisphere to speak about things that are sensed in the right hemisphere. But why do we have two hemispheres to begin with, and why should they have different specializations?

2. Computer programs within many mobile phones can detect and transcribe spoken words. If a computer program could detect all spoken words, would it understand language? What would be missing? How would you know whether a computer was able to understand you?
3. How much of your time awake is spent listening to your internal voice? Are there times during the day when you are most aware of it? Does it ever stop? Can you think without words?
4. Contrast the functions served by social cognition to those served by metacognition. If social cognition helps us to interact successfully with others, what benefits do we gain from metacognition?

Key Terms

aphasia 581
autobiographical memory 603
Broca's aphasia 591
Broca's area 590
cognitive reserve 602
conceptual representation 588
conduction aphasia 598
contralateral control 582
corpus callosotomy 582
corpus callosum 579
default network 603
dyslexia 600
expression, speech 591
expressive aphasia 591
global aphasia 598
gyrus (pl. gyri) 595
inferior temporal gyrus 595
left inferior frontal gyrus 590
mental lexicon 589
mentalizing 606
metacognition 603
monolinguals 601
neologisms 594
phonemes 588
phonological 588
phonological processing 600
pure word blindness 600
pure word deafness 597
receptive aphasia 594
semantic content 590
simultaneous bilinguals 601
social cognition 606
social cognitive neuroscience 607
split-brain operation 579
stroke 590
successive bilinguals 601
syntax 589
theory of mind 606
visual word form area 600
Wernicke's aphasia 594
Wernicke's area 594

References

Abutalebi, J. (2008). Neural aspects of second language representation and language control. *Acta Psychologica (Amsterdam), 128*(3), 466–478.

Andreasen, N. C., O'Leary, D. S., Cizadlo, T., Arndt, S., Rezai, K., Watkins, G. L., ... Hichwa, R. D. (1995). Remembering the past: two facets of episodic memory explored with positron emission tomography. *American Journal of Psychiatry, 152*(11), 1576–1585.

Antoniou, M. (2019). The advantages of bilingualism debate. *Annual Review of Linguistics, 5*, 395–415.

Birchmeier, A. K. (1985). Aphasic dyslexia of Braille in a congenitally blind man. *Neuropsychologia, 23*(2), 177–193.

Brewer, J. A., Worhunsky, P. D., Gray, J. R., Tang, Y.-Y., Weber, J., & Kober, H. (2011). Meditation experience is associated with differences in default mode network activity and connectivity. *Proceedings of the National Academy of Sciences of the United States of America, 108*(50), 20254–20259.

Brown, J. W. (1972). *Aphasia, Apraxia, and Agnosia: Clinical and Theoretical Aspects*. Springfield, IL: C. C. Thomas.

Buchman, A. S., Garron, D. C., Trost-Cardamone, J. E., Wichter, M. D., & Schwartz, M. (1986). Word deafness: one hundred years later. *Journal of Neurology, Neurosurgery & Psychiatry, 49*(5), 489–499.

Buckner, R. L., Andrews-Hanna, J. R., & Schacter, D. L. (2008). The brain's default network. *Annals of the New York Academy of Sciences, 1124*(1), 1–38.

Calabria, M., Costa, A., Green, D. W., & Abutalebi, J. (2018). Neural basis of bilingual language control. *Annals of the New York Academy of Sciences, 1426*(1), 221–235.

Campbell, R., MacSweeney, M., & Waters, D. (2008). Sign language and the brain: a review. *Journal of Deaf Studies and Deaf Education, 13*(1), 3–20.

Cicone, M., Wapner, W., Foldi, N., Zurif, E., & Gardner, H. (1979). The relation between gesture and language in aphasic communication. *Brain and Language, 8*(3), 324–349.

Costa, A., & Sebastian-Galles, N. (2014). How does the bilingual experience sculpt the brain? *Nature Reviews Neuroscience, 15*(5), 336–345.

DeWitt, I., & Rauschecker, J. P. (2012). Phoneme and word recognition in the auditory ventral stream. *Proceedings of the National Academy of Sciences of the United States of America, 109*(8), E505–E514.

Eden, G. F., & Moats, L. (2002). The role of neuroscience in the remediation of students with dyslexia. *Nature Neuroscience, 5* (Suppl.), 1080–1084.

Fleming, S. M., & Dolan, R. J. (2012). The neural basis of metacognitive ability. *Philosophical Transactions of the Royal Society of London B: Biological Sciences, 367*(1594), 1338–1349.

Flinker, A., Korzeniewska, A., Shestyuk, A. Y., Franaszczuk, P. J., Dronkers, N. F., Knight, R. T., & Crone, N. E. (2015). Redefining the role of Broca's area in speech. *Proceedings of the National Academy of Sciences of the United States of America, 112*(9), 2871–2875.

Foote, A. L., & Crystal, J. D. (2007). Metacognition in the rat. *Current Biology, 17*(6), 551–555.

Friederici, A. D. (2012). The cortical language circuit: from auditory perception to sentence comprehension. *Trends in Cognitive Sciences, 16*(5), 262–268.

(2018). The neural basis for human syntax: Broca's area and beyond. *Current Opinion in Behavioral Sciences, 21*, 88–92.

Gallo, D. A., Kensinger, E. A., & Schacter, D. L. (2006). Prefrontal activity and diagnostic monitoring of memory retrieval: FMRI of the criterial recollection task. *Journal of Cognitive Neuroscience, 18*(1), 135–148.

Gazzaniga, M. S. (2013). Shifting gears: seeking new approaches for mind/brain mechanisms. *Annual Review of Psychology, 64*(1), 1–20.

Gazzaniga, M. S., Bogen, J. E., & Sperry, R. W. (1967). Dyspraxia following division of the cerebral commissures. *Archives of Neurology, 16*(6), 606–612.

Geschwind, N. (1970). The organization of language and the brain. *Science, 170*(3961), 940–944.

Gibson, C., Folley, B. S., & Park, S. (2009). Enhanced divergent thinking and creativity in musicians: a behavioral and near-infrared spectroscopy study. *Brain and Cognition, 69*(1), 162–169.

Graner, J., Oakes, T. R., French, L. M., & Riedy, G. (2013). Functional MRI in the investigation of blast-related traumatic brain injury. *Frontiers in Neurology*, 4 March.

Henseler, I., Regenbrecht, F., & Obrig, H. (2014). Lesion correlates of patholinguistic profiles in chronic aphasia: comparisons of syndrome-, modality- and symptom-level assessment. *Brain, 137*(3), 918–930.

Hickok, G. (2012). Computational neuroanatomy of speech production. *Nature Reviews Neuroscience, 13*(2), 135–145.

Huth, A. G., de Heer, W. A., Griffiths, T. L., Theunissen, F. E., & Gallant, J. L. (2016). Natural speech reveals the semantic maps that tile human cerebral cortex. *Nature, 532*(7600), 453–458.

Kwok, S. C., Cai, Y. D., & Buckley, M. J. (2019). Mnemonic introspection in macaques is dependent on superior dorsolateral prefrontal cortex but not orbitofrontal cortex. *Journal of Neuroscience, 39*(30), 5922–5934.

Lee, M., van Santen, J. P. H., Möbius, B., & Olive, J. P. (2005). Formant tracking using context-dependent phonemic information. *IEEE Transactions on Speech and Audio Processing, 13*, 741–750.

Levelt, W. J. M. (1999). Models of word production. *Trends in Cognitive Sciences, 3*(6), 223–232.

Lindell, A. K., & Kidd, E. (2011). Why right-brain teaching is half-witted: a critique of the misapplication of neuroscience to education. *Mind, Brain, and Education, 5*(3), 121–127.

Luo, D. Y., Kwok, V. P. Y., Liu, Q., Li, W. L., Yang, Y., Zhou, K., ... Tan, L. H. (2019). Microstructural plasticity in the bilingual brain. *Brain and Language*, 196.

Mar, R. A. (2011). The neural bases of social cognition and story comprehension. *Annual Review of Psychology, 62*, 103–134.

Matsumoto, R., Imamura, H., Inouchi, M., Nakagawa, T., Yokoyama, Y., Matsuhashi, M., ... Ikeda, A. (2011). Left anterior temporal cortex actively engages in speech perception: a direct cortical stimulation study. *Neuropsychologia, 49*(5), 1350–1354.

Parker Jones, O., Green, D. W., Grogan, A., Pliatsikas, C., Filippopolitis, K., Ali, N., ... Price, C. J. (2012). Where, when and why brain activation differs for bilinguals and monolinguals during picture naming and reading aloud. *Cerebral Cortex*, *22*(4), 892–902.

Paul, E. J., Smith, J. D., Valentin, V. V., Turner, B. O., Barbey, A. K., & Ashby, F. G. (2015). Neural networks underlying the metacognitive uncertainty response. *Cortex*, *71*, 306–322.

Paulesu, E., Démonet, J. F., Fazio, F., McCrory, E., Chanoine, V., ... Frith, U. (2001). Dyslexia: cultural diversity and biological unity. *Science 291*, 2165.

Perani, D., & Abutalebi, J. (2015). Bilingualism, dementia, cognitive and neural reserve. *Current Opinion in Neurology*, *28*(6), 618–625.

Petitto, L. A., Zatorre, R. J., Gauna, K., Nikelski, E. J., Dostie, D., & Evans, A. C. (2000). Speech-like cerebral activity in profoundly deaf people processing signed languages: implications for the neural basis of human language. *Proceedings of the National Academy of Sciences of the United States of America*, *97*(25), 13961–13966.

Poeppel, D., & Hickok, G. (2004). Towards a new functional anatomy of language. *Cognition*, *92*(1–2), 1–12.

Raichle, M. E., MacLeod, A. M., Snyder, A. Z., Powers, W. J., Gusnard, D. A., & Shulman, G. L. (2001). A default mode of brain function. *Proceedings of the National Academy of Sciences of the United States of America*, *98*(2), 676–682.

Sahin, N. T., Pinker, S., Cash, S. S., Schomer, D., & Halgren, E. (2009). Sequential processing of lexical, grammatical, and phonological information within Broca's area. *Science*, *326*(5951), 445–449.

Samson, S., Ehrle, N., & Baulac, M. (2001). Cerebral substrates for musical temporal processes. *Annals of the New York Academy of Sciences*, *930*, 166–178.

Schnyer, D. M., Verfaellie, M., Alexander, M. P., LaFleche, G., Nicholls, L., & Kaszniak, A. W. (2004). A role for right medial prefontal cortex in accurate feeling-of-knowing judgements: evidence from patients with lesions to frontal cortex. *Neuropsychologia*, *42*(7), 957–966.

Shulman, G. L., Fiez, J. A., Corbetta, M., Buckner, R. L., Miezin, F. M., Raichle, M. E., & Petersen, S. E. (1997). Common blood flow changes across visual tasks: II. Decreases in cerebral cortex. *Journal of Cognitive Neuroscience*, *9*(5), 648–663.

Skeide, M. A., & Friederici, A. D. (2016). The ontogeny of the cortical language network. *Nature Reviews Neuroscience*, *17*, 323–332.

Slaughter, V. (2015). Theory of mind in infants and young children: a review. *Australian Psychologist*, *50*(3), 169–172.

Sperry, R. (1984). Consciousness, personal identity and the divided brain. *Neuropsychologia*, *22*(6), 661–673.

Springer, S. P., & Deutsch, G. (1997). *Left brain, right brain*. New York: Freeman.

Tang, Y. Y., Holzel, B. K., & Posner, M. I. (2015). The neuroscience of mindfulness meditation. *Nature Reviews Neuroscience*, *16*(4), 213–U280.

Thambirajah, M. S. (2010). Developmental dyslexia: an overview. *Advances in Psychiatric Treatment*, *16*(4), 299–307.

Toga, A. W., & Thompson, P. M. (2003). Mapping brain asymmetry. *Nature Reviews Neuroscience, 4*(1), 37–48.

Ullman, M. T. (2001). A neurocognitive perspective on language: the declarative/procedural model. *Nature Neuroscience, 2*(10), 717–726.

Vincent, J. L., Snyder, A. Z., Fox, M. D., Shannon, B. J., Andrews, J. R., Raichle, M. E., & Buckner, R. L. (2006). Coherent spontaneous activity identifies a hippocampal-parietal memory network. *Journal of Neurophysiology, 96*(6), 3517–3531.

Wagner, D. D., Kelley, W. M., & Heatherton, T. F. (2011). Individual differences in the spontaneous recruitment of brain regions supporting mental state understanding when viewing natural social scenes. *Cerebral Cortex, 21*(12), 2788–2796.

Woumans, E., Santens, P., Sieben, A., Versijpt, J., Stevens, M., & Duyck, W. (2015). Bilingualism delays clinical manifestation of Alzheimer's disease. *Bilingualism: Language and Cognition, 18*(3), 568–574.

Yi, H. G., Leonard, M. K., & Chang, E. F. (2019). The encoding of speech sounds in the superior temporal gyrus. *Neuron, 102*(6), 1096–1110.

Zaki, J., & Ochsner, K. (2012). The neuroscience of empathy: progress, pitfalls and promise. *Nature Neuroscience, 15*(5), 675–680.

Index

Page numbers in italics refer to content in figures; page numbers in bold refer to content in tables and boxes.